DEVIANCE

THE INTERACTIONIST PERSPECTIVE

SIXTH EDITION

EARL RUBINGTON
Northeastern University

MARTIN S. WEINBERG
Indiana University

ALLYN AND BACON
Boston   London   Toronto   Sydney   Tokyo   Singapore

To
Sara and Alex,
Barbara, Ellana, and Marion

Executive Editor: Karen Hanson
Editorial Assistant: Jennifer Jacobson
Marketing Manager: Joyce Nilsen
Production Administrator: Deborah Brown
Editorial-Production Service: P. M. Gordon Associates
Cover Administrator: Suzanne Harbison
Cover Designer: Susan Paradise
Composition Buyer: Linda Cox
Manufacturing Buyer: Megan Cochran

Library of Congress Cataloging-in-Publication Data

Deviance, the interactionist perspective.

    1. Deviant behavior.   2. Social interaction.
I. Rubington, Earl.   II. Weinberg, Martin S.
HM291.D4836 1987   302.5′42   86-2917
0–02-404412–1 U-5972-7

Printed in the United States of America
10 9 8 7 6 5 4 3 2 1   00 99 98 97 96

CONTENTS

PREFACE

The purpose of this book has been to present students with recent and important work in the sociology of deviance. We have, however, limited ourselves to one particular approach to this study. We call this approach the interactionist perspective.

The interactionist approach to the study of deviance is by no means new. But until the appearance of the first edition of *Deviance: The Interactionist Perspective,* students had to search for statements of the approach as well as for studies that exemplified it. The purpose of the first edition, then, was to present the interactionist approach to the study of deviance and to make readily available the excellent studies that set forth or illustrate it. In the succeeding editions, we have updated the readings and made special efforts to make our own text more readable.

We see this book as having two major uses. As a statement on the interactionist perspective on deviance and a collection of readings employing that approach, the book can be used in deviance courses that are taught from the interactionist point of view. The second use is that of adjunct to deviance courses that are organized around other points of view. Most of the papers presented in this book can very easily stand on their own merits, and even if the book does nothing more than familiarize readers with these works, it will have served its purpose.

In this edition we have incorporated fourteen new readings. In this way, we have tried to continue to update *Deviance: The Interactionist Perspective.*

E. R.
M. S. W.

GENERAL INTRODUCTION

This book examines deviance as a social phenomenon. Central to this approach is the notion that deviance is, above all, a matter of social definition. That is, an alleged behavior or condition is "deviant" if people say it is. The social aspect of deviance becomes clear when someone perceives another person as departing from accepted norms, interprets the person to be some kind of deviant, and influences others also to regard the person as deviant and to act on the basis of that interpretation. As a *social* phenomenon, then, deviance consists of a set of interpretations and social reactions.

When people are interpreted as being deviant, they are usually regarded as being a particular *type* of deviant. These types may be general (e.g., ex-convict, mentally ill, sexually "loose," retarded), or they may be more specific (e.g., car thief, paranoid schizophrenic, call girl, Mongoloid). Whether these labels are general or specific, they usually suggest what one can expect of the so-called deviant and how one should act toward the deviant (e.g., with suspicion, avoidance, vigilance, vengeance). And in coming to terms with such labeling the "deviants" may revise their self-concepts and their actions in accordance with the way they have been labeled. For example, a child who has been typed by school authorities as having a speech problem may become self-conscious and shy, with a concomitant loss of self-esteem, because s/he has been told s/he doesn't talk properly.

At the same time, social typing does allow people to relate to one another in an organized manner. Imagine how much more complicated it would be for policemen, for example, to do their jobs if they did not have a set of categories in which to place people ("she's a hooker"; "he's a junkie"; "he looks like he might be casing that store"; "she's a teenaged runaway"; "he's a derelict with no place to go").

The interactionist perspective focuses on just such issues as these—how people typify one another; how they relate to one another on the basis of these typifications; and the consequences of these social processes. As such, the interactionist perspective helps immensely in our understanding not only of the sociology of deviance but also of social process in general.

THE PLAN OF THE BOOK

The selections that follow spell out the interactionist perspective in greater detail. The first half of the book, which consists of Parts I and II, deals with how people define some persons as deviant and act on the basis of these definitions. Part I shows how deviance is dealt with in primary groups and informal relations and how a person is singled out and assigned a deviant status by intimates such as family members. Part II deals with these processes in the formal regulation of deviance. For example, it considers how agents of social control, such as the police, define persons as deviants, how they act on these definitions, and what some of the consequences of formal sanctions are.

The second half of the book (Parts III and IV) discusses the deviants themselves: how they respond to being typed by others, how they type themselves, and how they form deviant groups. Part III examines how deviants develop and sustain their own subcultures and how people become involved in them. Part IV shows how persons may take on deviant identities through self-typing, how they manage deviant identities, and how they may eventually regain "respectability."

This book, then, focuses not on people's motivations for doing things that are regarded as deviant but rather on the *sociology* of deviance—the processes that divide society into different types of people and the social effects of these processes.

PART ONE

THE SOCIAL DEVIANT

Sociology is the study of social relations. Sociologists study how people arrive at common definitions of their situation; how they form groups based on such definitions; how they go on to set down rules of conduct, assign social roles to each other, and enforce their rules. Sociologists examine these questions as part of the larger question: How is social order produced and sustained?

Deviance refers to an alleged breach of a social norm. By looking at deviance we can come to a better understanding of the dominant social order. At the same time, the study of deviance also sheds light on the way "deviant" patterns and lifestyles are themselves organized.

There are at least two ways of studying deviance as a social phenomenon. The first is to approach deviance as objectively given; the second, as subjectively problematic.

Deviance as objectively given. Sociologists who treat deviance as objectively given delineate the norms of the society under study and regard any deviation from these norms as "deviant." These sociologists generally make three assumptions. First, they assume that there is widespread consensus in the society in the realm of norms; this widespread agreement, they believe, makes it relatively easy to identify deviance. Second, they assume that deviance typically evokes negative sanctions such as gossip or legal action. Third, they assume that the punishment meted out to the deviant reaffirms for the group that is it bound by a set of common norms. The major questions raised by this approach are the following: What sociocultural conditions are most likely to produce deviance? Why do people continue to deviate despite the negative sanctions that are brought to bear on them? and How can deviance best be minimized or controlled?

From these assumptions and questions, certain procedures have evolved for studying deviants. First list the "do's" and "don'ts" of the society or group. Then study the official records kept on persons who violate these rules. Interview persons appearing in these records and consult agents of social control such as police and judges. Try to discover the ways in which deviants differ from nondeviants (e.g., are deviants more likely than nondeviants to come from broken homes?) in order to discern the kinds of social and cultural conditions that seem to make deviant behavior more likely. Try to derive a theory to "explain" deviance, and then apply the theory for the correction and prevention of deviance.

The strength of this approach is the sharpness and simplicity with which it phrases questions. The weak points of this approach follow from its key assumptions. In the United States there are so many different groups and ways of thinking that people often do not agree on norms. Because of this lack of agreement, and also because of the fact that some people get caught whereas others avoid discovery, it is often very difficult and complex to identify who is deviant and who is not. Also, most social control agencies operate with selective enforcement, so that certain categories of people are more likely than others to be punished for their deviance. Thus the nature, causes, and consequences of deviance are neither simple nor uniform.

Deviance as subjectively problematic. Sociologists who focus on the social differentiation of deviants generally make another set of assumptions. First, they assume that when people and groups interact they communicate with one another by means of shared symbols (verbal and body language, style of dress, etc.). Through such symbolic communication, it is assumed, people are able to type one another and formulate their actions accordingly. Second, they assume that deviance can best be understood in terms of this process, that deviant labels are symbols that differentiate and stigmatize the people to whom they are applied. Finally, sociologists using this approach assume that people act on the basis of such definitions. Thus people treat the alleged deviant differently from other people. The alleged deviant, in turn, may also react to this definition. On the basis of these assumptions, sociologists using this perspective focus on social definitions and on how these influence social interaction. On the one hand, they focus on the perspective and actions of those who define a person as being deviant. They look at the circumstances under which a person is most likely to get set apart as deviant, how a person is cast into a deviant role, what actions others take on the basis of that definition of a person, and the consequences of these actions. On the other hand, these sociologists also focus on the perspective and reactions of the person adjudged to be deviant. They consider how a person reacts to being so adjudged, how a person adopts a deviant role, what changes in group memberships result, and what changes occur in the alleged deviant's self-concept.

Whereas the objectively given approach focuses primarily on the characteristics of the deviant or the conditions that give rise to deviant acts, the subjectively problematic approach focuses on the definitions and actions both of the deviants themselves and of the people who label them deviant, and on the social interaction between the two. Thus we call the latter approach the interactionist perspective.

This book adopts the interactionist perspective, approaching deviance as subjectively problematic rather than as objectively given. In this book, then, deviants are considered simply as people who are socially typed in a certain way. Such typing usually involves an attempt to make sense of seemingly aberrant acts. As people seek to make sense of such acts, they generally employ stereotypical interpretations that define the actor as a particular kind of person (a kook, a drunk, a psychopath, etc.), that include a judgment about the moral quality of the deviant or his or her motives, and that suggest how a person should act toward the deviant. The social definitions of deviance, then, consist of a *description,* an *evaluation,* and a *prescription.* For example, a "kook" is a person who is mildly eccentric (description). The term connotes that "kooks" are odd but not particularly evil or dangerous (evaluation). Thus one may display dislike or friendly disrespect toward them (prescription). A person who comes to be defined as a "psychopath," on the other hand, is considered to be both odd and severely unpredictable (description). The psychopath is often regarded as self-centered, evil, and dangerous (evaluation). And the psychopath is to be taken seriously at all times; a person who shows dislike or disrespect toward a "psychopath" does so at great personal risk (prescription). Thus the definition of a person as a particular type of deviant organizes people's responses to that person. And the more people who share the definition that a person is a particular type of deviant, the greater the consequences.

Taking the subjective approach to deviance, Part I of this book examines such phenomena more specifically. The topics treated in this part of the book include how people type, or label, others as deviants; the accommodations people make to the so-called deviance; the cultural context of typing; and how people may collaborate to exclude deviants from their midst.

THE PROCESS OF SOCIAL TYPING

Sociologically, deviance is approached here in terms of social differentiation. This differentiation arises from the perception that something is amiss. If a potential typer, or labeler, ignores or excuses the alleged aberrant quality of a person or event, it goes unlabeled as deviant. For instance, a person who works hard is expected sometimes to be tired and cranky, and in such situations people may not attach any particular importance to this behavior. Once an act or a person is typed as "deviant," however, a variety of social phenomena may come into play. These phenomena include who types whom, on what grounds, in what ways, before or after what acts (real or imputed), in front of what audience, and with what effects.

Let us for a moment consider the conditions that seem to make typing more effective. First, typing generally has the most effect when the typer, the person typed as deviant, and other people all share and understand the deviant definition in their social relationships. The typer and others act toward the "deviant" in accord with their shared understanding of the situation. Aware of having been so typed, the deviant, in turn, takes that shared understanding into account in relating to people. Thus, willingly or otherwise, all parties may subscribe to the definition. When this happens, the definition of the person as a particular type of deviant is most socially effective, or confirmed. As an example, Frank Tannenbaum, one of the fathers of the interactionist perspective on deviance, has said: "The process of making the criminal...is a process of tagging, defining, identifying, segregating, describing, emphasizing, and evoking the very traits that are complained of.... The person becomes the thing he is described as being." Tannenbaum says that "the community cannot deal with people whom it cannot define" and that "the young delinquent becomes bad because he is defined as bad and because he is not believed if he is good."[1]

Second, social types are generally more apt to be accepted by other people if a high-ranking person does the typing. Effective social typing usually flows down rather than up the social structure. For example, an honor bestowed by the President of the United States is more likely to be consequential than an honor bestowed by a low-ranking official. Conversely, a denunciation by a very high-ranking person such as the president of a company will usually carry more weight, and be confirmed by more people, than a denunciation by a low-ranking person such as one of the company's janitors.

Third, deviant typing is also more apt to be effective if there is a sense that the alleged deviant is violating important norms and that the violations are extreme. For instance, if factory workers are tacitly expected to turn out only a limited amount of work, a worker who produces much more than the norm may be singled out and ostracized as a "rate-buster." On the other hand, a person who jaywalks is unlikely to be typed and treated as a deviant.

Fourth, it also seems that negative social typing is more readily accepted than positive typing. For one thing, "misery loves company"; people find comfort in learning about the frailties of others. In addition, norms seem to be highlighted more by infraction than by conformity. Also, negative typing is seen as a valuable safeguard if the type indicates an aberrant pattern that will probably continue and that has major consequences. Some police officers, for instance, expect upper-class adolescents to misbehave in their youth but later to become influential and respected citizens, while they expect slum adolescents who are vandals, troublemakers, or delinquents to become hardened criminals in adulthood; thus such police officers are more likely to negatively type slum youths than upper-class youths who break the same laws.

Fifth, typing will be accepted more readily if the audience stands to gain from the labeling. Endorsing attention to another person's deviant behavior, for example, may divert attention from one's own. It may also sustain a status difference between oneself and the so-called deviant.

When social typing is effective, there are three kinds of consequences that most often follow: self-fulfilling prophecy, typecasting, and recasting. In the self-fulfilling prophecy, typing is based on false beliefs about the alleged deviant, but the actions other people take on the basis of these false beliefs eventually make them become a reality. For example, both black and white police officers believe that it is more difficult to arrest blacks than whites. As a result, they tend to use more force in arresting blacks, and in turn they experience more resistance from blacks. In typecasting, the deviant stereotype is so widely accepted that confirmation of the typing proceeds rapidly, and typer, audience, and the person typed relate to each other in an automatic manner. For instance, if one person types another as a thief, any audience can generally predict and understand the typer's attitudes and actions. In recasting, the most complex of the three consequences, the deviant is expected to behave conventionally and is encouraged to disprove the deviant typing (e.g., to reform). Probation officers, for example, may encourage conventionality by restricting the opportunities of their probationers to continue their deviant ways. In the first two consequences of typing, the typer and audience restrict the deviant's opportunities to disprove the deviant typing. In recasting, the typer and the audience restrict the deviant's opportunities to confirm the deviant typing.

ACCOMMODATION TO DEVIANCE

As noted previously, sociologically, deviants are persons who have been effectively labeled as deviant, and *effectively* means simply that the label does in fact affect social relations. The person who has been typed as a deviant, for example, acquires a special status that carries a set of new rights and duties or changes in old ones, and a new set of expectations about future conduct. Thus when people type a certain person as deviant, they imply, "We now expect you to engage in deviant actions." In some cases, this expectation amounts to a license to deviate, as when a group may not only tolerate but actually shelter a deviant in its midst. More often, however, the expectation of deviant conduct gives other people license to treat the deviant in a demeaning way.

The pace of events in the labeling process is one of the critical factors in this entire process. If aberrant conduct occurs only gradually and irregularly within a small, intimate group, deviant typing may not take place at all. Even if the events place some immediate strain on relationships, members of the group may adjust to the strain without perceiving the person any differently. Eventually, though, some critical point may be reached at which the group becomes aware that things are not what they used to be. Sometimes the members of the group have long entertained suspicions of deviance, and their accommodation represents an acknowledgement that the deviation is here to stay. In other instances, though, even as they type the person as deviant, group members may be optimistic that the deviance is only temporary. In any case, the group's accommodation to the so-called deviance has usually been going on for some time before labeling actually occurs.

THE CULTURAL CONTEXT

The process of social typing occurs within a cultural context. Each culture, for example, has its own assortment and corresponding vocabulary of types. Thus in our own culture we no longer talk about "witches"; consequently, no one is so typed. Similarly, if we had no word for or concept of "psychopath," no one would be so typed. The culture's repertoire of deviant types and stereotypes is ordinarily created, defined, sustained, and controlled by highly valued realms of the culture (e.g., psychiatry, law, religion). In addition, it should also be noted, different categories are used in different subcultures. "Sinners," for example, are typed only in the religious sector.

Because different groups and cultures have different ideas about deviance, however, typing often has an ethnocentric bias. People in one culture or subculture may be quick to type an outsider as deviant, for instance, simply because the outsider's lifestyle is so different from their own. Among persons within the same culture or subculture, on the other hand, the risks of being typed deviant are usually smaller.

Once a person has been labeled, the question of how to relate to the deviant is more easily resolved when cultural prescriptions exist. These include the prescriptions, for example, that sick people should be treated and evil people punished. In sum, typing is easier to act on when cultural guidelines exist.

THE ROLE OF THIRD PARTIES

As already noted, in intimate, primary groups, people are usually slower to type one of their members as deviant than are outsiders. Such in-group labeling does happen at times, however, particularly if the deviant's aberrant behavior has begun to cause considerable strain for the rest of the group. When this happens, the typing of the person as deviant is often facilitated or precipitated by some outsider or outside agency—in short, by some third party.

In some cases the third party may act without solicitation. A wife, for example, may fail to recognize that her husband is involved with another woman until the community gossip (the third party) so informs her; she may then type her husband as a "son of a bitch" and may, through separation or divorce, exclude him from the family.

In other cases a member of the primary group may seek out the third party in order to validate such typing or to exclude the deviant from the group. If a man's wife is emotionally disturbed, for example, he may turn to third parties outside the family (a psychiatrist, the courts, the sheriff, etc.) in order to remove his wife from the home, officially labeling her as mentally disturbed and seeking treatment for her.

Thus we have seen some of the ways in which the social definition of deviants proceeds. A real or imputed violation of norms can activate the process of social typing, and a variety of social factors affect its success. The nature and likelihood of this typing are influenced by the cultural context. People may at first attempt to accommodate these alleged violations. Over the course of time, however, the deviant may no longer be protected. Third parties may intervene, and at that point exclusion of the deviant may take place.

NOTE

1. Frank Tannenbaum, *Crime and the Community,* New York: Columbia University Press, 1938; pp. 19–20.

CHAPTER 1

THE PROCESS OF SOCIAL TYPING

Alleged deviance implies that some norm has been violated. Yet not all such violations are noticed and labeled as deviant. Also, different groups are quicker to label certain types of violations as deviant, and the same group may be quicker to label at one time than another.

In the first reading Becker describes a number of conditions that are involved when a person is labeled deviant; he also discusses the consequences of such labeling. In the next selection Kitsuse uses homosexuality to illustrate how people type a person as deviant and how they then act on this social definition. In the final selection Erikson discusses the basis on which communities single out certain types of conduct to be defined as deviant.

Outsiders

HOWARD S. BECKER

DEVIANCE AND THE RESPONSES
OF OTHERS

[One sociological view]. . . defines deviance as the infraction of some agreed-upon rule. It then goes on to ask who breaks rules, and to search for the factors in their personalities and life situations that might account for the infractions. This assumes that those who have broken a rule constitute a homogeneous category, because they have committed the same deviant act.

Such an assumption seems to me to ignore the central fact about deviance: it is created by society. I do not mean this in the way it is ordinarily understood, in which the causes of deviance are located in the social situation of the deviant or in "social factors" which prompt his action. I mean, rather, that *social groups create deviance by making the rules whose infraction constitutes deviance,* and by applying those rules to particular people and labeling them as outsiders. From this point of view, deviance is *not* a quality of the act the person commits, but rather a consequence of the application by others of rules and sanctions to an "offender." The deviant is one to whom that label has successfully been applied; deviant behavior is behavior that people so label.[1]

Since deviance is, among other things, a consequence of the responses of others to a person's act, students of deviance cannot assume that they are dealing with a homogeneous category when they study people who have been labeled deviant. That is, they cannot assume that those people have actually committed a deviant act or broken some

rule, because the process of labeling may not be infallible; some people may be labeled deviant who in fact have not broken a rule. Furthermore, they cannot assume that the category of those labeled deviant will contain all those who actually have broken a rule, for many offenders may escape apprehension and thus fail to be included in the population of "deviants" they study. Insofar as the category lacks homogeneity and fails to include all the cases that belong in it, one cannot reasonably expect to find common factors of personality or life situation that will account for the supposed deviance.

What, then, do people who have been labeled deviant have in common? At the least, they share the label and the experience of being labeled as outsiders. I will begin my analysis with this basic similarity and view deviance as the product of a transaction that takes place between some social group and one who is viewed by that group as a rule-breaker. I will be less concerned with the personal and social characteristics of deviants than with the process by which they come to be thought of as outsiders and their reactions to that judgment. . . .

The point is that the response of other people has to be regarded as problematic. Just because one has committed an infraction of a rule does not mean that others will respond as though this had happened. (Conversely, just because one has not violated a rule does not mean that he may not be treated, in some circumstances, as though he had.)

The degree to which other people will respond to a given act as deviant varies greatly. Several kinds of variation seem worth noting. First of all, there is variation over time. A person believed to have committed a given "deviant" act may at one time be responded to much more leniently than he would be at some other time. The occurrence of "drives" against various kinds of deviance illustrates this clearly. At various times, enforcement officials may decide to make an all-out attack on some particular kind of deviance, such as gambling, drug addiction, or homosexuality. It is obviously much more dangerous to engage in one of these activities when a drive is on than at any other time. (In a very interesting study of crime news in Colorado newspapers, Davis found that the amount of crime reported in Colorado newspapers showed very little association with actual changes in the amount of crime taking place in Colorado. And, further, that people's estimate of how much increase there had been in crime in Colorado was associated with the increase in the amount of crime news but not with any increase in the amount of crime.)[2]

The degree to which an act will be treated as deviant depends also on who commits the act and who feels he has been harmed by it. Rules tend to be applied more to some persons than others. Studies of juvenile delinquency make the point clearly. Boys from middle-class areas do not get as far in the legal process when they are apprehended as do boys from slum areas. The middle-class boy is less likely, when picked up by the police, to be taken to the station; less likely when taken to the station to be booked; and it is extremely unlikely that he will be convicted and sentenced.[3] This variation occurs even though the original infraction of the rule is the same in the two cases. Similarly, the law is differentially applied to Negroes and whites. It is well known that a Negro believed to have attacked a white woman is much more likely to be punished than a white man who commits the same offense; it is only slightly less well known that a Negro who murders another Negro is much less likely to be punished than a white man who commits murder.[4] This, of course, is one of the main points of Sutherland's analysis of white-collar crime: crimes committed by corporations are almost always prosecuted as civil cases, but the same crime committed by an individual is ordinarily treated as a criminal offense.[5]

Some rules are enforced only when they result in certain consequences. The unmarried mother furnishes a clear example. Vincent[6] points out that illicit sexual relations seldom result in severe punishment or social censure for the offenders. If, however, a girl becomes pregnant as a result of such activities the reaction of others is likely to be severe. (The illicit pregnancy is also an interesting example of the differential enforcement of rules on different categories of people. Vincent notes that unmarried fathers escape the severe censure visited on the mother.)

Why repeat these commonplace observations? Because, taken together, they support the proposition that deviance is not a simple quality, present in some kinds of behavior and absent in others. Rather, it is the product of a process which involves responses of other people to the behavior. The same behavior may be an infraction of the rules at one time and not at another; may be an infraction when committed by one person, but not when committed by another; some rules are broken with impunity, others are not. In short, whether a given act is deviant or not depends in part on the nature of the act (that is, whether or not it violates some rule) and in part on what other people do about it.

Some people may object that this is merely a terminological quibble, that one can, after all, define terms any way he wants to and that if some people want to speak of rule-breaking behavior as deviant without reference to the reactions of others they are free to do so. This, of course, is true. Yet it might be worthwhile to refer to such behavior as *rule-breaking behavior* and reserve the term *deviant* for those labeled as deviant by some segment of society. I do not insist that this usage be followed. But it should be clear that insofar as a scientist uses "deviant" to refer to any rule-breaking behavior and takes as his subject of study only those who have been *labeled* deviant, he will be hampered by the disparities between the two categories.

If we take as the object of our attention behavior which comes to be labeled as deviant, we must recognize that we cannot know whether a given act will be categorized as deviant until the response of others has occurred. Deviance is not a quality that lies in behavior itself, but in the interaction between the person who commits an act and those who respond to it. . . .

In any case, being branded as deviant has important consequences for one's further social participation and self-image. The most important consequence is a drastic change in the individual's public identity. Committing the improper act and being publicly caught at it places him in a new status. He has been revealed as a different kind of person from the kind he was supposed to be. He is labeled a "fairy," "dope fiend," "nut" or "lunatic," and treated accordingly.

In analyzing the consequences of assuming a deviant identity let us make use of Hughes' distinction between master and auxiliary status traits.[7] Hughes notes that most statuses have one key trait which serves to distinguish those who belong from those who do not. Thus the doctor, whatever else he may be, is a person who has a certificate stating that he has fulfilled certain requirements and is licensed to practice medicine; this is the master trait. As Hughes points out, in our society a doctor is also informally expected to have a number of auxiliary traits: most people expect him to be upper middle class, white, male, and Protestant. When he is not there is a sense that he has in some way failed to fill the bill. Similarly, though skin color is the master status trait determining who is Negro and who is white, Negroes are informally expected to have certain status traits and not to have others; people are surprised and find it anomalous if a Negro turns out to be a doctor or a college professor. People often have the master status trait but lack some of the auxiliary, informally expected characteristics; for example, one may be a doctor but be female or Negro.

Hughes deals with this phenomenon in regard to statuses that are well thought of, desired and desirable (noting that one may have the formal qualifications for entry into a status but be denied full entry because of lack of the proper auxiliary traits), but the same process occurs in the case of deviant statuses. Possession of one deviant trait may have a generalized symbolic value, so that people automatically assume that its bearer possesses other undesirable traits allegedly associated with it.

To be labeled a criminal one need only commit a single criminal offense, and this is all the term formally refers to. Yet the word carries a number of connotations specifying auxiliary traits characteristic of anyone bearing the label. A man who has been convicted of housebreaking and thereby labeled criminal is presumed to be a person likely to break into other houses; the police, in rounding up known offenders for investigation after a crime has been committed, operate on this premise. Further, he is considered likely to commit other kinds of crimes as well, because he has shown himself to be a person without "respect for the law." Thus, apprehension for one deviant act exposes a person to the likelihood that he will be regarded as deviant or undesirable in other respects.

There is one other element in Hughes' analysis we can borrow with profit: the distinction between master and subordinate statuses.[8] Some statuses, in our society as in others, override all other statuses and have a certain priority. Race is one of these. Membership in the Negro race, as socially defined, will override most other status considerations in most other situations; the fact that one is a physician or middle-class or female will not protect one from being treated as a Negro first and any of these other things second. The status of deviant (depending on the kind of deviance) is this kind of master status. One receives the status as a result of breaking a rule, and the identification proves to be more important than most others. One will be identified as a deviant first, before other identifications are made. . . .

NOTES

1. The most important earlier statements of this view can be found in Frank Tannenbaum, *Crime and the Commu-*

nity (New York: Columbia University Press, 1938), and E. M. Lemert, *Social Pathology* (New York: McGraw-Hill Book Co., Inc., 1951). A recent article stating a position very similar to mine is John Kitsuse, "Societal Reaction to Deviance: Problems of Theory and Method," *Social Problems,* 9 (Winter, 1962), 247–256.

2. F. James Davis, "Crime News in Colorado Newspapers," *American Journal of Sociology,* LVII (January, 1952), 325–330.

3. See Albert K. Cohen and James F. Short, Jr., "Juvenile Delinquency," in Robert K. Merton and Robert A. Nisbet, eds., *Contemporary Social Problems* (New York: Harcourt, Brace, and World, 1961), p. 87.

4. See Harold Garfinkel, "Research Notes on Inter- and Intra-Racial Homicides," *Social Forces,* 27 (May, 1949), 369–381.

5. Edwin H. Sutherland, "White Collar Criminality," *American Sociological Review,* V (February, 1940), 1–12.

6. Clark Vincent, *Unmarried Mothers* (New York: The Free Press of Glencoe, 1961), pp. 3–5.

7. Everett C. Hughes, "Dilemmas and Contradictions of Status," *American Journal of Sociology,* L (March, 1945), 353–359.

8. *Ibid.*

Societal Reaction to Deviant Behavior

JOHN I. KITSUSE

Sociological theory and research in the area traditionally known as "social pathology" have been concerned primarily with the classification and analysis of *deviant forms of behavior* and relatively little attention has been given to societal reactions to deviance.[1] In a recent paper, Merton has noted this lack of a "systematic *classification* of the responses of the conventional or conforming members of a group to deviant behavior."[2] Similarly, Cohen has observed that "a sociology of deviant behavior-conformity will have to devise ways of conceptualizing responses to deviant behavior from the standpoint of their relevance to the production or extinction of deviant behavior."[3] In this paper, I shall discuss some of the theoretical and methodological issues posed by the problem of societal reactions to deviant behavior and report on a preliminary attempt to formulate a research design which specifically takes them into account.

I propose to shift the focus of theory and research from the forms of deviant behavior to the *processes by which persons come to be defined as deviant by others.* Such a shift requires that the sociologist view as problematic what he generally assumes as given—namely, that certain forms of behavior are *per se* deviant and are so defined by the "conventional or conforming members of a group." This assumption is frequently called into question on empirical grounds when the societal reaction to behaviors defined as deviant by the sociologist is nonexistent, indifferent, or at most mildly disapproving. For example, in his discussion of "ritualism" as a form of deviant behavior, Merton states that it is not that such behavior is treated by others as deviant which identifies it as deviant "since the overt behavior is institutionally permitted, though not culturally prescribed."[4] Rather, the behavior is deviant because it "clearly represents a departure from the cultural model in which men are obliged to move onward and up-

Reprinted from "Societal Reaction to Deviant Behavior: Problems of Theory and Method," *Social Problems,* Vol. 9, No. 3 (Winter 1962), pp. 247–256, by permission of the Society for the Study of Social Problems and the author.

ward in the social hierarchy."[5] The discrepancy between the theoretically hypothesized and empirically observable societal reaction is also noted by Lemert: "It is fairly easy to think of situations in which serious offenses against laws commanding public respect have only mild penalty or have gone entirely unpunished. Conversely, cases are easily discovered in which a somewhat minor violation of legal rules has provoked surprisingly stringent penalties."[6]

Clearly, the forms of behavior *per se* do not activate the processes of societal reaction which sociologically differentiate deviants from nondeviants. Thus, a central problem for theory and research in the sociology of deviance may be stated as follows: What are the behaviors which are defined by members of the group, community, or society as deviant, and how do those definitions organize and activate the societal reactions by which persons come to be differentiated and treated as deviants? In formulating the problem in this way, the point of view of those who interpret and define behavior as deviant must explicitly be incorporated into a sociological definition of deviance. Accordingly, deviance may be conceived as a process by which the members of a group, community, or society (1) interpret behavior as deviant, (2) define persons who so behave as a certain kind of deviant, and (3) accord them the treatment considered appropriate to such deviants. In the following pages, this conception of deviance and societal reaction will be applied to the processes by which persons come to be defined and treated as homosexuals.

SOCIETAL REACTIONS TO "HOMOSEXUAL BEHAVIOR"

As a form of deviant behavior, homosexuality presents a strategically important theoretical and empirical problem for the study of deviance. In the sociological and anthropological literature[7] homosexual behavior and the societal reactions to it are conceptualized within the framework of ascribed sex statuses and the socialization of individuals to

those statuses. The ascription of sex statuses is presumed to provide a complex of culturally prescribed roles and behaviors which individuals are expected to learn and perform. Homosexual roles and behaviors are conceived to be "inappropriate" to the individual's ascribed sex status, and thus theoretically they are defined as deviant.

With reference to American society, Allison Davis states: "Sex-typing of behavior and privileges is even more rigid and lasting in our society than is age-typing. Indeed, sexual status and color-caste status are the only life-long forms of rank. In our society, one can escape them in approved fashion only by death. Whereas sexual mobility is somewhat less rare today than formerly, sex-inappropriate behavior, social or physical, is still one of the most severely punished infractions of our social code."[8] In Lemert's terminology, norms concerning sex-appropriate behavior have a high degree of "compulsiveness" and social disapproval of violations is stringent and effective.[9] Homosexuals themselves appear to share this conception of the societal reaction to their behavior, activities, and subculture.[10]

Such a view of homosexuality would lead one to hypothesize that "sex-appropriate" (and conversely "sex-inappropriate") behaviors are unambiguously prescribed, deviations from those prescriptions are invariably interpreted as immoral, and the reactions of the conventional and conforming members of the society to such deviations are uniformly severe and effective. The evidence which apparently supports this hypothesis is not difficult to find, particularly with reference to the definition and treatment of male homosexuals. Individuals who are publicly identified as homosexuals are frequently denied the social, economic, and legal rights of "normal" males. Socially they may be treated as objects of amusement, ridicule, scorn, and often fear; economically they may be summarily dismissed from employment; legally they are frequently subject to interrogation and harassment by police.

In citing such evidence, however, it is important to note that the societal reaction to and the differentiation of homosexuals from the "normal" population is a consequence of the fact that the former are "known" to be homosexuals by some individuals, groups or agencies. Thus, within the framework of the present formulation of homosexuality as a form of deviant behavior, the processes by which individuals come to be "known" and treated as sexually deviant will be viewed as problematic and a problem for empirical investigation. I shall not be concerned here with the so-called "latent homosexual" unless he is so defined by others and differentially treated as a consequence of that definition. Nor will I be concerned with the variety of "internal" conflicts which may form the "clinical" picture of the homosexual except insofar as such conflicts are manifested in behavior leading others to conceive of him as a homosexual. In short, I shall proceed on the principle that it is only when individuals are defined and identified by others as homosexuals and accorded the treatment considered "appropriate" for individuals so defined that a homosexual "population" is produced for sociological investigation.[11] With reference to homosexuality, then, the empirical questions are: What forms of behavior do persons in the social system consider to be "sex-inappropriate," how do they interpret such behaviors, and what are the consequences of those interpretations for their reactions to individuals who are perceived to manifest such behaviors?

In a preliminary attempt to investigate these questions, an interview schedule was constructed[12] and administered to approximately seven hundred individuals, most of whom were college undergraduates. The sample was neither random nor representative of any specified population, and the generalizability of the interview materials is limited except insofar as they are relevant to the previously noted hypothesis that homosexual behavior is uniformly defined, interpreted, and negatively sanctioned. The interview materials will therefore be used for the purpose of illustrating the theory and method of the present conception of deviance and societal reaction.

The objectives of the interview were threefold: It attempted to document (1) the behavior forms which are interpreted as deviant, (2) the processes by which persons who manifest such behaviors are defined and (3) treated as deviant. Thus, in the construction of the interview schedule, what the interviewees considered to be "deviant" behavior, the interpretations of such behavior, and the actions of subjects toward those perceived as deviant were addressed as empirical questions. Labels such as alcoholic, illiterate, illegitimate child, and ex-convict were assumed to be categories employed by persons in everyday life to classify deviants, but the behavior forms by which they identify individuals as deviants were treated as problematic. "Sexual deviant" was one of ten categories of deviants about which subjects were questioned in the interview. Among the more than seven hundred subjects interviewed, seventy-five stated they had "known" a homosexual and responded to questions concerning their experiences with such individuals. The data presented below are drawn from the protocols of interviews with this group of subjects.

The interview proceeded as follows:

The subject was asked "Have you ever known anyone who was a sexual deviant?" If he questioned the meaning of "deviant," the subject was asked to consider the question using his own meaning of "sexual deviant."

When the subject stated he had known a sexual deviant—a homosexual in this case—as he defined the term, he was asked to think about the most recent incident involving him in an encounter with such a person. He was then asked "When was the first time you noticed (found out) that this person was a homosexual?" followed by "What was the situation? What did you notice about him? How did he behave?" This line of questioning was focused on the interaction between the subject and the alleged deviant to obtain a detailed description of the situation which led the subject to define the person as homosexual. The subject's description of the person's behavior was systematically probed to clarify the terms of his description, particularly those which were interpretive rather than descriptive.

EVIDENCE OF HOMOSEXUALITY

Responses to the question "When was the first time you noticed (found out) that this person was homosexual?" and the related probes suggest that an individual's sexual "normality" may be called into question with reference to two broad categories of evidence. (*a*) *Indirect evidence* in the form of a rumor, an acquaintance's experience with the individual in question subsequently communicated to the subject, or general reputational information concerning the individual's behavior, associates, and sexual predilections may be the occasion for suspecting him to be "different." Many subjects reported that they first "found out" or "knew" that the individuals in question were homosexuals through the reports of others or by "reputation." Such information was generally accepted by the subjects without independent verification. Indeed, the information provided a new perspective for their retrospective as well as prospective observations and interpretations of the individuals' behaviors. An example of how hearsay organizes observation and interpretation is the following statement by a 35-year-old male (a draftsman):

I: Then this lieutenant was a homosexual?

S: Yes.

I: How did you find out about it?

S: The guy he approached told me. After that, I watched him. Our company was small and we had a bar for both enlisted men and officers. He would come in and try to be friendly with one or two of the guys.

I: Weren't the other officers friendly?

S: Sure, they would come in for an occasional drink; some of them had been with the company for three years and they would sometimes slap you on the back, but he tried to get over friendly.

I: What do you mean "over friendly"?

S: He had only been there a week. He would try to push himself on a couple of guys—he spent more time with the enlisted personnel than is expected from an officer.

(*b*) *Direct observation* by the subject of the individual's behavior may be the basis for calling the latter's sexual "normality" into question. The descriptions of behavior which subjects took to be indicative of homosexuality varied widely and were often vague. Most frequently the behaviors cited were those *"which everyone knows"* are indications of homosexuality. For example, a 20-year-old male subject reports an encounter with a stranger at a bar:

I: What happened during your conversation?

S: He asked me if I went to college and I said I did. Then he asked me what I was studying. When I told him psychology he appeared very interested.

I: What do you mean "interested"?

S: Well, you know queers really go for this psychology stuff.

I: Then what happened?

S: Ah, let's see. I'm not exactly sure, but somehow we got into an argument about psychology and to prove my point I told him to pick an area of study. Well, he appeared to be very pensive and after a great thought he said, "Okay, let's take homosexuality."

I: What did you make of that?

S: Well, by now I figured the guy was queer so I got the hell outta there.

The responses of other subjects suggest that an individual is particularly suspect when he is observed to behave in a manner which deviates from the *behaviors-held-in-common* among members of the group to which he belongs. For example, a behavior which is presumed to be held-in-common among sailors in the U.S. Navy is intense and active sexual activity. When a sailor does not affirm, at least verbally, his interest in such activity, his competence as a "male" may be called into question. A 22-year-old engineer, recently discharged from the Navy, responds to the "how did you first know" question as follows:

> All of a sudden you just get suspicious of something. I began to wonder about him. He didn't go in for leave activities that most sailors go for. You know, girls and high times. He just never was interested and when you have been out at sea for a month or two you're interested. That just wasn't Navy, and he was a career man.

Although the responses of our subjects indicate there are many behavioral gestures which "everyone knows" are indicators of homosexuality in males, there are relatively few such gestures that lead persons to suspect females of homosexuality. Following is an excerpt from a 21-year-old college co-ed whose remarks illustrate this lack of definite indicators *prior* to her labeling of an acquaintance as a homosexual:

I: When was the first time you noticed she was a deviant?

S: I didn't notice it. I thought she had a masculine appearance when I first saw her anyway.

I: What do you mean?

S: Oh, her haircut, her heavy eyebrows. She had a rather husky build.

I: Exactly when did you think she had a masculine appearance?

S: It was long after [the first meeting] that I found out that she was "one."

I: How do you define it?

S: Well, a lesbian. I don't know too much about them. It was _____ who told me about her.

I: Did you notice anything else about her [at the first meeting]?

S: No, because you really don't know unless you're looking for those things.

Unlike "effeminate" appearance and gestures in males, "masculine" appearance in females is apparently less likely to be immediately linked to the suspicion or imputation of homosexuality. The statements of the subject quoted above indicate that although "masculine appearance" is an important element in her conception of a lesbian, its

significance did not become apparent to her until a third person told her the girl was a homosexual. The remarks of other subjects in our sample who state they have "known" female homosexuals reveal a similar ambiguity in their interpretations of what they describe as indicators of sexual deviance.

A third form of evidence by direct observation is behaviors which the subjects interpreted to be *overt sexual propositions*. Descriptions of such propositions ranged from what the subjects considered to be unmistakable evidence of the person's sexual deviance to ambiguous gestures which they did not attempt to question in the situation. The following is an excerpt from an interview with a 24-year-old male school teacher who recounts an experience in a Korean Army barrack:

I: What questions did he [the alleged homosexual] ask?

S: "How long have you been in Korea?" I told him. "What do you think of these Korean girls?" which I answered, "Not too much because they are dirty." I thought he was probably homesick and wanted someone to talk to. I do not remember what he said then until he said, "How much do you have?" I answered him by saying, "I don't know, about average I guess." Then he said, "Can I feel it just once?" To this I responded with, "Get the hell out of here," and I gave him a shove when he reached for me as he asked the question.

In a number of interviews, the subjects' statements indicate that they interpreted the sequence of the alleged deviants' behavior as progressively inappropriate or peculiar in the course of their interaction with them. The link between such behavior and their judgment that a sexual proposition was being made was frequently established by the subjects' growing realization of its deviant character. A 21-year-old male subject recalls the following experience involving his high school tennis coach who had invited him to dinner:

S: Anyway, when I get there he served dinner, and as I think back on it—I didn't notice it at the time—but I remember that he did act sort of effeminate. Finally he got up to change a record and picked up some of my English themes. Then he brought them over and sat down beside me. He began to explain some of my mistakes in my themes, and in the meantime he slipped his arms around me.

I: Would you say that this was done in a friendly manner or with an intent of hugging you or something?

S: Well, no, it was just a friendly gesture of putting his arm around my shoulder. At that time, I didn't think anything of it, but as he continued to explain my mistakes, he started to rub my back. Then he asked me if I wanted a back rub. So I said, "No! I don't need one." At this time, I began thinking something was funny anyway. So I said that I had to go. . . .

THE IMPUTATION OF HOMOSEXUALITY

When a detailed description of the subject's evidence concerning the alleged homosexual was obtained, he was asked, "What did you make of that?" to elicit information about how he interpreted the persons observed or reported behavior. This line of questioning yielded data on the inferential process by which the subject linked his information about the individual to the deviant category "homosexual."

A general pattern revealed by the subjects' responses to this section of the interview schedule is that when an individual's sexual "normality" is called into question, by whatever form of evidence, the imputation of homosexuality is documented by *retrospective interpretations* of the deviant's behavior, a process by which the subject re-interprets the individual's past behavior in the light of the new information concerning his sexual deviance. This process is particularly evident in cases where the prior relationship between the subject and the alleged homosexual was more than a chance encounter or casual acquaintanceship. The subjects indicate that they reviewed

their past interactions with the individuals in question, searching for subtle cues and nuances of behavior which might give further evidence of the alleged deviance. This retrospective reading generally provided the subjects with just such evidence to support the conclusion that "this is what was going on all the time."

Some of the subjects who were interviewed were themselves aware of their retrospective interpretations in defining individuals as sexually deviant. For example, a 23-year-old female graduate student states:

I: Will you tell me more about the situation?

S: Well, their relationship was a continuous one, although I think that it is a friendship now as I don't see them together as I used to; I don't think it is still homosexual. When I see them together, they don't seem to be displaying the affection openly as they did when I first realized the situation.

I: How do you mean "openly"?

S: Well, they would hold each other's hand in public places.

I: And what did you make of this?

S: Well, I really don't know, because I like to hold people's hands, too! I guess I actually didn't see this as directly connected with the situation. What I mean is that, if I hadn't seen the other incident [she had observed the two girls in bed together] I probably wouldn't have thought of it [i.e., hand-holding] very much. . . . Well, actually, there were a few things that I questioned later on that I hadn't thought really very much about. . . . I can remember her being quite affectionate towards me several times when we were in our room together, like putting her arm around my shoulder. Or I remember one time specifically when she asked me for a kiss. I was shocked at the time, but I laughed it off jokingly.

**THE INTERACTIONAL CONTEXTS
OF SOCIETAL REACTIONS**

When the description of the alleged deviant's behavior and the subject's interpretations of that behavior were recorded, the subject was asked "What did you do then?" This question was directed toward documenting societal reactions to deviant behavior. Forms of behavior *per se* do not differentiate deviants from non-deviants; it is the responses of the conventional and conforming members of the society who identify and interpret behavior as deviant which sociologically transform persons into deviants. Thus, in the formulation of deviance proposed here, if the subject observes an individual's behavior and defines it as deviant but does not accord him differential treatment as a consequence of that definition, the individual is not sociologically deviant.

The reactions of the subjects to individuals they defined as homosexuals ranged from immediate withdrawal from the scene of interaction and avoidance of further encounters with the alleged deviants to the maintenance of the prior relationship virtually unaltered by the imputation of deviance. The following responses to the question "What did you do then?" illustrate the variation in sanctions directed toward persons defined as homosexuals.

Explicit disapproval and immediate withdrawal: The most negatively toned and clearly articulated reaction reported by our subjects is that of the previously quoted Korean War veteran. It is interesting to note that extreme physical punishment as a reaction to persons defined as homosexuals, a reaction which is commonly verbalized by "normal" males as proper treatment of "queers," is not reported by any of the subjects. When physical force is used, it is invariably in response to the deviant's direct physical overtures, and even then it is relatively mild, e.g., "I gave him a shove when he reached for me."

Explicit disapproval and subsequent withdrawal: In the following excerpt, a 20-year-old male college student describes an encounter with a man whom he met in a coffee shop. In the course of their conversation, the man admitted his homosexuality to the subject. The two left the coffee shop and walked together to the subway station.

I: What happened then?

S: We got to the subway whereupon he suggested that he hail a cab and take me up to Times Square—a distance of almost 40 blocks.

I: Did you agree, and what did you think?

S: Yes, I thought he was just being very nice and I had no qualms about getting in a cab with a homosexual since I was quite sure I could protect myself against any advances in a cab.

I: What happened then?

S: When we had ridden a little distance, he put his hand on my knee, and I promptly removed it saying that it just wasn't right and that I wanted nothing of it. However, after a while, he put his hand back. This time I didn't take it away for a while because I was interested in what he would do. It was the funniest thing— he rubbed and caressed my knee the same way in which I would have done this to a girl. This time I took his hand and hit him across the chest with it, telling him to "cut it out." Finally, we got to Times Square, and I got out.

This example and that provided by the Korean War veteran's reaction to behavior interpreted as overt sexual propositions suggest the possibility that responses to persons suspected of homosexuality or defined as homosexuals on the basis of more indirect evidence of appearance, "confessions," hearsay, reputation, or association will vary within an even wider range of applied sanctions. Indeed, the statements of subjects concerning their responses to persons alleged to be deviant on such evidence indicate that the modal reaction is disapproval, implicitly rather than explicitly communicated, and a restriction of interaction through partial withdrawal and avoidance. It should be noted further that although the subject's silent withdrawal from an established relationship with an alleged deviant may represent a stronger disapproval than an explicitly communicated, physically enforced sanction against a stranger, moral indignation or revulsion is not necessarily communicated to the deviant. The subject's prior relationship with the alleged deviant and the demands of propriety in subsequent interactions with him qualify the form and intensity of the sanctions which are applied. Thus, when the organization of the subject's day-to-day activities "forces" him into interaction with the deviant, expressions of disapproval are frequently constrained and diffused by the rules of deference and demeanor.[13] The following excerpts provide illustrations:

Implicit disapproval and partial withdrawal: A 20-year-old co-ed's reaction to a girl she concluded was a homosexual was expressed as follows:

> *Well, I didn't want to be alone with X [the homosexual] because the four of us had two connecting rooms and I was in the room with X. As much as I liked the girl and felt sorry for her, I knew she could really wring me through the wringer. So the rest decided that I should tell her that if she and Y wanted to be homos, to do it somewhere else and not in the room.*

No disapproval and relationship sustained: The "live and let live" response to homosexuals, which is implied in the preceding reaction, was not uncommon among the subjects. Some subjects not only affirmed the right of the homosexual to "live his own life" but also reported that their knowledge of the deviance has had little or no effect upon their subsequent relationships with the deviants. In this regard, the mildest reaction, so mild that it might be considered no reaction at all, was that of a 19-year-old male college student:

I: What was your reaction to him?

S: My reactions to him have always been friendly because he seems like a very friendly person. Uh, and he has a very nice sense of humor and I've never been repelled by anything he's said. For one thing, I think he's tremendously interesting because he seems to have such a wide range for background. . . .

I: When was the last time you saw this person?

S: Last night. . . . I was sitting in a restaurant and he walked in with some friends. . . . He just stopped in and said hello, and was his usual friendly self.

I: What in particular happened after that?

S: Actually, nothing. He sat down with his friends, and we exchanged a few words about the records that were playing on the juke box. But nothing, actually. . . .

The theoretical significance of these data for the conception of deviance and societal reaction presented here is not that the subjects' information is of dubious accuracy or questionable relevance as evidence of homosexuality. Nor is it that the subjects' interpretations of them are unreasonable, unjustifiable, or spurious. They suggest rather that the conceptions of persons in everyday life concerning "sex-appropriate" or "sex-inappropriate" behavior may lead them to interpret a variety of behavioral forms as indications of the same deviation, and the "same" behavioral forms as indications of a variety of deviant as well as "normal" behavior. An individual's sexual "normality" may be made problematic by his interpretations and reinterpretations of his behavior by others, and the interpretive process may be activated by a wide range of situational behaviors which lend new significance to the individual's past and present behavior. His behavior with respect to speech, interests, dress, dating, or relations with other males are not *per se* significant in the deviant defining process. The data suggest that the critical feature of the deviant-defining process is not the behavior of individuals who are defined as deviant, but rather the interpretations others make of their behaviors, whatever those behaviors may be.

With specific reference to homosexuality as a form of deviant behavior, the interview materials suggest that while reactions toward persons defined as homosexuals tend to be negatively toned, they are far from homogeneous as to the forms or intensity of the sanctions invoked and applied. Indeed, reactions which may appear to the sociological observer or to the deviant himself as negative sanctions, such as withdrawal or avoidance, may be expressions of embarrassment, a reluctance to share the burden of the deviant's problems, fear of the deviant, etc., as well as moral indignation or revulsion. In none of the interviews does the subject react with extreme violence, explicitly define or directly accuse the deviant of being a "queer," "fairy," or other terms of opprobrium, nor did any of them initiate legal actions against the deviant. In view of the extreme negative sanctions against homosexuality which are posited on theoretical grounds, the generally mild reactions of our subjects are striking.

The relative absence of extreme and overtly expressed negative sanctions against homosexuals among our subjects may, of course, reflect the higher than average educational level of the sample. A sample of subjects less biased toward the highly educated, middle-class segment of the population than was interviewed in this preliminary study may be expected to reflect a more definite pattern with reference to such negative reactions. We must, therefore, be cautious in generalizing the range of reactions among our subjects to the general population. It is equally important to note, however, that these data do indicate that reactions to homosexuals in American society are not *societal* in the sense of being uniform within a narrow range; rather, they are significantly conditioned by sub-cultural as well as situational factors. Thus, not only are the processes by which persons come to be defined as homosexuals contingent upon the interpretations of their behavior by others, but also the sanctions imposed and the treatment they are accorded as a consequence of that definition vary widely among conventional members of various sub-cultural groups.

The larger implications of these data are that a sociological theory of deviance must explicitly take into account the variety and range of conceptions held by persons, groups, and agencies within the society concerning any form of behavior. The increasing differentiation of groups, institutions, and sub-cultures in modern society generates a continually changing range of alternatives and tolerance for the expression of sexual as well as other forms of behavior. Consequently, it is difficult if not impossible to theoretically derive a set of *specific behavioral prescriptions* which will in

fact be normatively supported, uniformly practiced, and socially enforced by more than a segment of the total population. Under such conditions, it is not the fact that individuals engage in behaviors which diverge from some theoretically posited "institutionalized expectations" or even that such behaviors are defined as deviant by the conventional and conforming members of the society which is of primary significance for the study of deviance. A sociological theory of deviance must focus specifically upon the interactions which not only define behaviors as deviant but also organize and activate the application of sanctions by individuals, groups, or agencies. For in modern society, the socially significant differentiation of deviants from the non-deviant population is increasingly contingent upon circumstances of situation, place, social and personal biography, and the bureaucratically organized activities of agencies of control.[14]

NOTES

1. A notable exception is the work of Edwin M. Lemert who systematically incorporates the concept of societal reaction in his theory of sociopathic behavior. See *Social Pathology,* McGraw-Hill: New York, 1951.
2. Robert K. Merton, "Social Conformity, Deviation, and Opportunity-Structures: A Comment on the Contributions of Dubin and Cloward," *American Sociological Review,* 24 (1959), pp. 177–189.
3. Albert K. Cohen, "The Study of Social Disorganization and Deviant Behavior," in *Sociology Today,* R. Merton, L. Broom, and L. Cottrell, eds., Basic Books: New York, 1959, pp. 465–466.
4. Robert K. Merton, *Social Theory and Social Structure,* revised, Free Press: New York, 1957, p. 150.
5. *Ibid.,* p. 150.
6. *Op. Cit.,* p. 55.
7. For examples, see Talcott Parsons and Robert F. Bales, *Family Socialization and Interaction Process,* Free Press: New York, 1955, pp. 101–105; Ruth Benedict, "Continuities and Discontinuities in Cultural Conditioning," *Psychiatry,* 1 (1938), pp. 161–167; Abram Kardiner and Associates, *Psychological Frontiers of Society,* Columbia University Press: New York, 1945, pp. 57, 88, etc.; Clifford Kirkpatrick, *The Family,* Ronald

Press: New York, 1955, pp. 57–58; Margaret Mead, *Sex and Temperament,* William Morrow: New York, 1955.

8. Allison Davis, "American Status Systems and the Socialization of the Child," *American Sociological Review,* 6 (1941), p. 350.

9. *Op. cit.,* Chapter 4.

10. Evelyn Hooker, "Sequences in Homosexual Identification," read at the meetings of the American Sociological Association, 1960; Donald Webster Cory, *The Homosexual in America,* Greenburg: New York, 1951, esp. Part I.

11. This principle has been suggested by Harold Garfinkel. See "Some Sociological Concepts and Methods for Psychiatrists," *Psychiatric Research Reports,* 6 (1956), pp. 181–195.

12. The interview schedule and methods were conceived and constructed in consultation with Aaron V. Cicourel.

13. Erving Goffman, "The Nature of Deference and Demeanor," *American Anthropologist,* 58 (1956), pp. 473–502.

14. For a discussion of such contingencies, see Edwin M. Lemert, *op. cit.,* Chapter 4, and Erving Goffman, "The Moral Career of the Mental Patient," *Psychiatry,* 22 (1959), pp. 121–142.

Notes on the Sociology of Deviance

KAI T. ERIKSON

From a sociological standpoint, deviance can be defined as conduct which is generally thought to require the attention of social control agencies— that is, conduct about which "something should be done." Deviance is not a property *inherent in* certain forms of behavior; it is a property *conferred upon* these forms by the audiences which directly or indirectly witness them. The critical variable in the study of deviance, then, is the social audience rather than the individual actor, since it is the audience which eventually determines whether or not any episode of behavior or any class of episodes is labeled deviant.

This definition may seem a little indirect, but it has the advantage of bringing a neglected sociological issue into proper focus. When a community acts to control the behavior of one of its members, it is engaged in a very intricate process of selection. After all, even the worst miscreant in society conforms most of the time, if only in the sense that he uses the correct spoon at mealtime, takes good care of his mother, or in a thousand other ways respects the ordinary conventions of his group; and if the community elects to bring sanctions against him for the occasions when he does misbehave, it is responding to a few deviant details set within a vast array of entirely acceptable conduct. Thus it happens that a moment of deviation may become the measure of a person's position in society. He may be jailed or hospitalized, certified as a full-time deviant, despite the fact that only a fraction of his behavior was in any way unusual or dangerous. The community has taken note of a few scattered particles of behavior and has decided that they reflect what kind of person he "really" is.

The screening device which sifts these telling details out of the person's over-all performance, then, is a very important instrument of social control. We know very little about the properties of this screen, but we do know that it takes many factors into account which are not directly related to the deviant act itself: it is sensitive to the suspect's

This is a slightly revised version of a paper that appeared in *Social Problems,* Vol. 9, No. 4 (Spring 1962), pp. 307–314; reprinted by permission of the Society for the Study of Social Problems and the author.

social class, his past record as an offender, the amount of remorse he manages to convey, and many similar concerns which take hold in the shifting moods of the community. This may not be so obvious when the screen is dealing with extreme forms of deviance like serious crimes, but in the day-by-day filtering processes which take place through the community this feature is easily observable. Some men who drink too much are called alcoholics and others are not, some men who act oddly are committed to hospitals and others are not, some men who have no visible means of support are hauled into court and others are not—and the difference between those who earn a deviant label and those who go their own way in peace depends almost entirely on the way in which the community sifts out and codes the many details of behavior to which it is a witness. In this respect, the community screen may be a more relevant subject for sociological research than the actual behavior which is filtered through it.

Once the problem is phrased in this way we can ask: How does a community decide what forms of conduct should be singled out for this kind of attention? The conventional answer to this question, of course, is that society sets up the machinery of control in order to protect itself against the "harmful" effects of deviation, in much the same way that an organism mobilizes its resources to combat an invasion of germs. Yet this simple view of the matter has not always proven to be a very productive one. In the first place, as Durkheim and Mead pointed out some years ago, it is by no means clear that all acts considered deviant in a culture are in fact (or even in principle) harmful to group life.[1] In the second place, it is gradually becoming more evident to sociologists engaged in this area of research that deviant behavior can play an important part in keeping the social order intact.

This raises a number of interesting questions for sociology.

In recent years, sociological theory has become more and more concerned with the concept "social system"—an organization of society's component parts into a form which sustains internal equilibrium, resists change, and is boundary maintaining. In its most abstract form, the "system" concept describes a highly complex network of relations, but the scheme is generally used by sociologists to draw attention to those forces in the social order which promote a high level of uniformity among human actors and a high degree of symmetry within human institutions. The main organizational drift of a system, then, is seen as centripetal: it acts to draw the behavior of actors toward those centers in social space where the core values of the group are figuratively located, bringing them within range of basic norms. Any conduct which is neither attracted toward this nerve center by the rewards of conformity nor compelled toward it by other social pressures is considered "out of control," which is to say, deviant.

This basic model has provided the theme for most contemporary thinking about deviation, and as a result little attention has been given to the notion that systems operate to maintain boundaries. To say that a system maintains boundaries is to say that it controls the fluctuation of its constituent parts so that the whole retains a defined range of activity, a unique pattern of constancy and stability, within the larger environment.[2] Because the range of human behavior is potentially so wide, social groups maintain boundaries in the sense that they try to limit the flow of behavior within their domain so that it circulates within a defined cultural territory. Boundaries, then, are an important point of reference for persons participating in any system. A people may define its boundaries by referring to a geographical location, a set of honored traditions, a particular religious or political viewpoint, an occupational specialty, a common language, or just some local way of doing things; but in any case, members of the group have some idea about the contours of the niche they occupy in social space. They know where the group begins and ends as a special entity; they know what kinds of experience "belong" within these precincts and what kinds do not.

For all its apparent abstractness, a social system is organized around the movements of persons joined together in regular social relations. The only material found in a system for marking boundaries, then, is the behavior of its participants; and the kinds of behavior which best perform this function are often deviant, since they represent the most extreme variety of conduct to be found within the experience of the group. In this sense, transactions taking place between deviant persons on the one side and agencies of control on the other are boundary maintaining mechanisms. They mark the outside limits of the area within which the norm has jurisdiction, and in this way assert how much diversity and variability can be contained within the system before it begins to lose its distinct structure, its cultural integrity.

A social norm is rarely expressed as a firm rule or official code. It is an abstract synthesis of the many separate times a community has stated its sentiments on a given kind of issue. Thus the norm has a history much like that of an article of common law: it is an accumulation of decisions made by the community over a long period of time which gradually gathers enough moral eminence to serve as a precedent for future decisions. And like an article of common law, the norm retains its validity only if it is regularly used as a basis for judgment. Each time the group censures some act of deviation, then, it sharpens the authority of the violated norm and declares again where the boundaries of the group are located.

It is important to notice that these transactions between deviant persons and agents of control have always attracted a good deal of attention in this and other cultures. In our own past, both the trial and punishment of deviant offenders took place in the public market and gave the crowd a chance to participate in a direct, active way. Today we no longer parade deviants in the town square or expose them to the carnival atmosphere of Tyburn, but it is interesting to note that the "reform" which brought about this change in penal policy coincided almost precisely with the development of newspapers as media of public information. Perhaps this is no more than an accident of history, but it is nevertheless true that newspapers (and now radio and television) offer their readers the same kind of entertainment once supplied by public hangings or the use of stocks and pillories. An enormous amount of modern "news" is devoted to reports about deviant behavior and its punishment: indeed the largest circulation newspaper in the United States prints very little else. Yet how do we explain what makes these items "newsworthy" or why they command the great attention they do? Perhaps they satisfy a number of psychological perversities among the mass audience, as commentators sometimes point out, but at the same time they constitute our main source of information about the normative contours of society. In a figurative sense, at least, morality and immorality meet at the public scaffold, and it is during this meeting that the community declares where the line between them should be drawn.

People who gather together into communities need to be able to describe and anticipate those areas of experience which lie outside the immediate compass of the group—the unseen dangers which in any culture and in any age seem to threaten its security. Traditional folklore depicting demons, devils, witches and evil spirits, may be one way to give form to these otherwise formless dangers, but the visible deviant is another kind of reminder. As a trespasser against the group norms, he represents those forces which lie outside the group's boundaries: he informs us, as it were, what evil looks like, what shapes the devil can assume. And in doing so, he shows us the difference between the inside of the group and the outside. It may well be that without this ongoing drama at the outer edges of group space, the community would have no inner sense of identity and cohesion, no sense of the contrasts which set it off as a special place in the larger world.

Thus deviance cannot be dismissed simply as behavior which *disrupts* stability in society, but may itself be, in controlled quantities, an important condition for *preserving* stability. . . .

NOTES

1. Emile Durkheim, *The Division of Labor in Society* (translated by George Simpson), New York: The Free Press of Glencoe, 1952; and George Herbert Mead, "The Psychology of Punitive Justice," *American Journal of Sociology,* 23 (1918), 577–602.

2. Cf. Talcott Parsons, *The Social System,* New York: The Free Press of Glencoe, 1951.

CHAPTER 2

ACCOMMODATION TO DEVIANCE

When an alleged violation of norms has occurred, people may respond in a variety of ways. At first they may fail to notice the alleged deviation. When they do notice it, they may respond in several different ways: they may optimize, neutralize, normalize, or pessimize. To optimize is simply to see the assumed deviance as only temporary. To neutralize is to disregard it as not really significant. To normalize is to regard it as but a variation of normal behavior. To pessimize is to regard the deviance as permanent. These can be considered accommodations when they enable people to live with the deviance.

In the first reading in this chapter Marian Yarrow, Charlotte Schwartz, Harriet Murphy, and Leila Deasy describe the ways in which wives manage, for a time, to normalize their husbands' mental illness. Michael Lynch then shows how family members and close associates accommodate persons who are a source of trouble for others. In the final reading Joan Jackson describes the various stages wives go through in trying to deal with their husbands' alcoholism.

The Psychological Meaning of Mental Illness in the Family

MARIAN RADKE YARROW, CHARLOTTE GREEN SCHWARTZ, HARRIET S. MURPHY, and LEILA CALHOUN DEASY

The manifestations of mental illness are almost as varied as the spectrum of human behavior. Moreover, they are expressed not only in disturbance and functional impairment for the sick person but also in disruptive interactions with others. The mentally ill person is often, in his illness, a markedly deviant person, though certainly less so than the popular stereotype of the "insane." One wonders what were the initial phases of the impact of mental illness upon those within the ill person's social environment. How were the disorders of illness interpreted and tolerated? What did the patients, prior to hospitalization, communicate of their needs, and how did others—those closest to the ill persons—attempt, psychologically and behaviorally, to cope with the behavior? How did these persons come to be recognized by other family members as needing psychiatric help?

This paper presents an analysis of cognitive and emotional problems encountered by the wife in coping with the mental illness of the husband. It is concerned with the factors which lead to the reorganization of the wife's perceptions of her husband from a *well* man to a man who is mentally sick or in need of hospitalization in a mental hospital. The process whereby the wife attempts to understand and interpret her husband's manifestations of mental illness is best communicated by considering first the concrete details of a single wife's experiences. The findings and interpretations based on the total sample are presented following the case analysis.

Reprinted from the *Journal of Social Issues*, Vol. 11, No. 4 (1955), pp. 12–24.

ILLUSTRATIVE CASE

Robert F., a 35-year-old cab driver, was admitted to Saint Elizabeth's Hospital with a diagnosis of schizophrenia. How did Mr. F. get to the mental hospital? Here is a very condensed version of what his wife told an interviewer a few weeks later.

Mrs. F. related certain events, swift and dramatic, which led directly to the hospitalization. The day before admission, Mr. F. went shopping with his wife, which he had never done before, and expressed worry lest he lose her. This was in her words, "rather strange." (*His behavior is not in keeping with her expectations for him.*) Later that day, Mr. F. thought a TV program was about him and that the set was "after him." "Then I was getting worried." (*She recognizes the bizarre nature of his reactions. She becomes concerned.*)

That night, Mr. F. kept talking. He reproached himself for not working enough to give his wife surprises. Suddenly, he exclaimed he did have a surprise for her—he was going to kill her. "I was petrified and said to him, 'What do you mean?' Then, he began to cry and told me not to let him hurt me and to do for him what I would want him to do for me. I asked him what was wrong. He said he had cancer.... He began talking about his grandfather's mustache and said there was a worm growing out of it." She remembered his watching little worms in the fish bowl and thought his idea came from that. Mr. F. said he had killed his grandfather. He asked Mrs. F. to forgive him and wondered if she were his mother or God. She denied this. He vowed he was being punished for killing people during the war. "I thought maybe...worrying about the war so much...had gotten the best of him. (*She tries to understand his behavior. She stretches the range of normality to include it.*) I thought he should see a psychiatrist...I don't know how to explain it. He was shaking. I knew it was beyond what I could do...I was afraid of him...I thought he was losing his normal mental attitude and mentality, but I wouldn't say that he was insane or crazy, because he had always bossed me around before..." (*She shifts back and forth in thinking his problem is psychiatric and in feeling it is normal behavior that could be accounted for in terms of their own experience.*) Mr. F. talked on through the night. Sometime in the morning, he "seemed to straighten out" and drove his wife to work. (*This behavior tends to balance out the preceding disturbed activities. She quickly returns to a normal referent.*)

At noon, Mr. F. walked into a store where his wife worked as a clerk. "I couldn't make any sense of what he was saying. He kept getting angry because I wouldn't talk to him.... Finally, the boss's wife told me to go home." En route, Mr. F. said his male organs were blown up and little seeds covered him. Mrs. F. denied seeing them and announced she planned to call his mother. "He began crying and I had to promise not to. I said,...'Don't you think you should go to a psychiatrist?' and he said, 'No, there is nothing wrong with me.'...Then we came home, and I went to pay a bill..." (*Again she considers, but is not fully committed to, the idea that psychiatric help is needed.*)

Back at their apartment, Mr. F. talked of repairing his cab while Mrs. F. thought of returning to work and getting someone to call a doctor. Suddenly, he started chasing her around the apartment and growling like a lion. Mrs. F. screamed, Mr. F. ran out of the apartment, and Mrs. F. slammed and locked the door. "When he started roaring and growling, then I thought he was crazy. That wasn't a human sound. You couldn't say a thing to him..." Later, Mrs. F. learned that her husband

went to a nearby church, created a scene, and was taken to the hospital by the police. (*Thoroughly threatened, she defines problem as psychiatric.*)

What occurred before these events which precipitated the hospitalization? Going back to their early married life, approximately three years before hospitalization, Mrs. F. told of her husband's irregular work habits and long-standing complaints of severe headaches. "When we were first married, he didn't work much and I didn't worry as long as we could pay the bills." Mrs. F. figured they were just married and wanted to be together a lot. (*Personal norms and expectations are built up.*)

At Thanksgiving, six months after marriage, Mr. F. "got sick and stopped working." During the war he contracted malaria, he explained, which always recurred at that time of year. "He wouldn't get out of bed or eat.... He thought he was constipated and he had nightmares.... What I noticed most was his perspiring so much. He was crabby. You couldn't get him to go to a doctor.... I noticed he was nervous. He's always been a nervous person.... Any little thing that would go wrong would upset him—if I didn't get a drawer closed right.... His friends are nervous, too.... I came to the conclusion that maybe I was happy-go-lucky and everyone else was a bundle of nerves.... For a cab driver, he worked hard—most cab drivers loaf. When he felt good, he worked hard. He didn't work so hard when he didn't." (*She adapts to his behavior. The atypical is normalized as his type of personality and appropriate to his subculture.*)

As the months and years went by, Mrs. F. changed jobs frequently, but she worked more regularly than did her husband. He continued to work sporadically, get sick intermittently, appear "nervous and tense" and refrain from seeking medical care. Mrs. F. "couldn't say what was wrong." She had first one idea, then another, about his behavior. "I knew it wasn't right for him to be acting sick like he did." Then, "I was beginning to think he was getting lazy because there wasn't anything I could see." During one period, Mrs. F. surmised he was carrying on with another woman. "I was right on the verge of going, until he explained it wasn't anyone else." (*There is a building up of deviant behavior to a point near her tolerance limits. Her interpretations shift repeatedly.*)

About two and a half years before admission, Mrs. F. began talking to friends about her husband's actions and her lack of success in getting him to a doctor. "I got disgusted and said if he didn't go to a doctor, I would leave him. I got Bill (the owner of Mr. F.'s cab) to talk to him. . . . I begged, threatened, fussed . . ." After that, Mr. F. went to a VA doctor for one visit, overslept for his second appointment and never returned. He said the doctor told him nothing was wrong.

When Mr. F. was well and working, Mrs. F. "never stopped to think about it." "You live from day to day . . . When something isn't nice, I don't think about it. If you stop to think about things, you can worry yourself sick . . . He said he wished he could live in my world. He'd never seem to be able to put his thinking off the way I do . . ." (*Her mode of operating permits her to tolerate his behavior.*)

Concurrently, other situations confronted Mrs. F. Off and on, Mr. F. talked of a coming revolution as a result of which Negroes and Jews would take over the world. If Mrs. F. argued that she didn't believe it, Mr. F. called her "dumb" and "stupid." "The best thing to do was to change the subject." Eighteen months before admission, Mr. F. began awakening his wife to tell of nightmares about wartime experiences, but she "didn't think about it." Three months later, he decided he wanted to do something besides drive a cab. He worked on an invention but discovered it was patented. Then, he began to write a book about his wartime experiences and science. "If you saw what he wrote, you couldn't see anything wrong with it. . . . He just wasn't making any money." Mrs. F. did think it was "silly" when Mr. F. went to talk to Einstein about his ideas and couldn't understand why he didn't talk to someone in town. Nevertheless, she accompanied him on the trip. (*With the further accumulation of deviant behavior, she becomes less and less able to tolerate it. The perceived seriousness of his condition is attenuated so long as she is able to find something acceptable or understandable in his behavior.*)

Three days before admission, Mr. F. stopped taking baths and changing clothes. Two nights before admission, he awakened his wife to tell her he had just figured out that the book he was writing had nothing to do with science or the world, only with himself. "He said he had been worrying about things for ten years and that writing a book solved what had been worrying him for ten years." Mrs. F. told him to burn his writings if they had nothing to do with science. It was the following morning that Mrs. F. first noticed her husband's behavior as "rather strange."

In the long prelude to Mr. F.'s hospitalization, one can see many of the difficulties which arise for the wife as the husband's behavior no longer conforms and as it strains the limits of the wife's expectations for him. At some stage the wife defines the situation as one requiring help, eventually psychiatric help. Our analysis is concerned primarily with the process of the wife's getting to this stage in interpreting and responding to the husband's behavior. In the preceding case are many reactions which appear as general trends in the data group. These trends can be systematized in terms of the following focal aspects of the process:

1. The wife's threshold for initially discerning a problem depends on the accumulation of various kinds of behavior which are not readily understandable or acceptable to her.
2. This accumulation forces upon the wife the necessity for examining and adjusting expectations for herself and her husband which permit her to account for his behavior.
3. The wife is in an "overlapping" situation, of problem—not problem or of normal—not

normal. Her interpretations shift back and forth.

4. Adaptations to the atypical behavior of the husband occur. There is testing and waiting for additional cues in coming to any given interpretation, as in most problem solving. The wife mobilizes strong defenses against the husband's deviant behavior. These defenses take form in such reactions as denying, attenuating, balancing and normalizing the husband's problems.

5. Eventually there is a threshold point at which the perception breaks, when the wife comes to the relatively stable conclusion that the problem is a psychiatric one and/or that she cannot alone cope with the husband's behavior.

These processes are elaborated in the following analysis of the wives' responses.

METHOD OF DATA COLLECTION

Ideally, to study this problem one might like to interview the wives as they struggled with the developing illness. This is precluded, however, by the fact that the problem is not "visible" until psychiatric help is sought. The data, therefore, are the wives' reconstructions of their earlier experiences and accounts of their current reactions during the husband's hospitalization.

It is recognized that recollections of the pre-hospital period may well include systematic biases, such as distortions, omissions and increased organization and clarity. As a reliability check, a number of wives, just before the husband's discharge from the hospital, were asked again to describe the events and feelings of the prehospital period. In general, the two reports are markedly similar; often details are added and others are elaborated, but events tend to be substantially the same. While this check attests to the consistency of the wives' reporting, it has, of course, the contamination of overlearning which comes from many retellings of these events.

THE BEGINNINGS OF THE WIFE'S CONCERN

In the early interviews, the wife was asked to describe the beginnings of the problem which led to her husband's hospitalization. ("Could you tell me when you first noticed that your husband was different?") This question was intended to provide an orientation for the wife to reconstruct the sequence and details of events and feelings which characterized the period preceding hospitalization. The interviewer provided a minimum of structuring in order that the wife's emphases and organization could be obtained.

In retrospect, the wives usually cannot pinpoint the time the husband's problem emerged. Neither can they clearly carve it out from the contexts of the husband's personality and family expectations. The subjective beginnings are seldom localized in a single strange or disturbing reaction on the husband's part but rather in the piling up of behavior and feelings. We have seen this process for Mrs. F. There is a similar accumulation for the majority of wives, although the time periods and kinds of reported behavior vary. Thus, Mrs. Q. verbalizes the impact of a concentration of changes which occur within a period of a few weeks. Her explicit recognition of a problem comes when she adds up this array: her husband stays out late, doesn't eat or sleep, has obscene thoughts, argues with her, hits her, talks continuously, "cannot appreciate the beautiful scene" and "cannot appreciate me or the baby."

The problem behaviors reported by the wives are given in Table 1. They are ordered roughly; the behaviors listed first occurred primarily, but not exclusively, within the family; those later occurred in the more public domain. Whether the behavior is public or private does not seem to be a very significant factor in determining the wife's threshold for perceiving a problem.

There are many indications that these behaviors, now organized as a problem, have occurred many times before. This is especially true where alcoholism, physical complaints or personality

TABLE 1   Reported Problem Behavior at Time of the Wife's Initial Concern and at Time of the Husband's Admission to Hospital

	INITIALLY		AT HOSPITAL ADMISSION	
Problem Behavior	Psychotics N	Psycho-neurotics N	Psychotics N	Psycho-neurotics N
Physical problems, complaints, worries	12	5	7	5
Deviations from routines of behavior	17	9	13	9
Expression of inadequacy or hopelessness	4	1	5	2
Nervous, irritable, worried	19	10	18	9
Withdrawal (verbal, physical)	5	1	6	1
Changes or accentuations in personality "traits" (slovenly, deceptive, forgetful)	5	6	7	6
Aggressive or assaultive and suicidal behavior	6	3	10	6
Strange or bizarre thoughts, delusions, hallucinations and strange behavior	11	1	15	2
Excessive drinking	4	7	3	4
Violation of codes of "decency"	3	1	3	2
Number of Respondents	23	10	23	10

"weaknesses" enter the picture. The wives indicate how, earlier, they had assimilated these characteristics into their own expectations in a variety of ways: the characteristics were congruent with their image of their husbands, they fitted their differential standards for men and women (men being less able to stand up to troubles), they had social or environmental justifications, etc.

When and how behavior becomes defined as problematic appears to be a highly individual matter. In some instances, it is when the wife can no longer manage her husband (he will no longer respond to her usual prods); in others, when his behavior destroys the status quo (when her goals and living routines are disorganized); and, in still others, when she cannot explain his behavior. One can speculate that her level of tolerance for his behavior is a function of her specific personality needs and vulnerabilities, her personal and family value systems and the social supports and prohibitions regarding the husbands' symptomatic behavior.

INITIAL INTERPRETATIONS OF HUSBAND'S PROBLEM

Once the behavior is organized as a problem, it tends also to be interpreted as some particular kind of problem. More often than not, however, the husband's difficulties are not seen initially as manifestations of mental illness or even as emotional problems (Table 2).

Early interpretations often tend to be organized around physical difficulties (18% of cases) or "character" problems (27%). To a very marked degree, these orientations grow out of the wives' long-standing appraisals of their husbands as weak and ineffective or physically sick men.

TABLE 2   Initial Interpretations of the Husbands's Behavior

INTERPRETATION	PSYCHOTICS N	PSYCHONEUROTICS N
Nothing really wrong	3	0
"Character" weakness and "controllable" behavior (lazy, mean, etc.)	6	3
Physical problem	6	0
Normal response to crisis	3	1
Mildly emotionally disturbed	1	2
"Something" seriously wrong	2	2
Serious emotional or mental problem	2	2
Number of Respondents	23	10

These wives describe their husbands as spoiled, lacking will-power, exaggerating little complaints and acting like babies. This is especially marked where alcoholism complicates the husband's symptomatology. For example, Mrs. Y., whose husband was chronically alcoholic, aggressive and threatening to her, "raving," and who "chewed his nails until they almost bled," interprets his difficulty thus: "He was just spoiled rotten. He never outgrew it. He told me when he was a child he could get his own way if he insisted, and he is still that way." This quotation is the prototype of many of its kind.

Some wives, on the other hand, locate the problem in the environment. They expect the husband to change as the environmental crisis subsides. Several wives, while enumerating difficulties and concluding that there is a problem, in the same breath say it is really nothing to be concerned about.

Where the wives interpret the husband's difficulty as emotional in nature, they tend to be inconsistently "judgmental" and "understanding." The psychoneurotics are more often perceived initially by their wives as having emotional problems or as being mentally ill than are the psychotics. This is true even though many more clinical signs (bizarre, confused, delusional, aggressive and disoriented behavior) are reported by

the wives of the psychotics than of the psychoneurotics.

Initial interpretations, whatever their content, are seldom held with great confidence by the wives. Many recall their early reactions to their husbands' behaviors as full of puzzling confusion and uncertainty. Something is wrong, they know, but, in general, they stop short of a firm explanation. Thus, Mrs. M. reports, "He was kind of worried. He was kind of worried before, not exactly worried..." She thought of his many physical complaints; she "racked" her "brain" and told her husband, "Of course, he didn't feel good." Finally, he stayed home from work with "no special complaints, just blah," and she "began to realize it was more deeply seated."

CHANGING PERCEPTIONS OF THE HUSBAND'S PROBLEM

The fog and uneasiness in the wife's early attempts to understand and cope with the husband's difficulties are followed, typically, by painful psychological struggles to resolve the uncertainties and to change the current situation. Usually, the wife's perceptions of the husband's problems undergo a series of changes before hospitalization is sought or effected, irrespective of the length of time elapsing between the beginnings of concern and hospitalization.

Viewing these changes macroscopically, three relatively distinct patterns of successive redefinitions of the husband's problems are apparent. One sequence (slightly less than half the cases) is characterized by a progressive intensification; interpretations are altered in a definite direction—toward seeing the problem as mental illness. Mrs. O. illustrates this progression. Initially, she thought her husband was "unsure of himself." "He was worried, too, about getting old." These ideas moved to: "He'd drink to forget.... He just didn't have the confidence.... He'd forget little things.... He'd wear a suit weeks on end if I didn't take it away from him.... He'd say nasty things." Then, when Mr. O. seemed "so confused," "to forget all kinds of things...where he'd come from...to go to work," and made "nasty, cutting remarks all the time," she began to think in terms of a serious personality disturbance. "I did think he knew that something was wrong...that he was sick. He was never any different this last while and I couldn't stand it any more.... You don't know what a relief it was..." (when he was hospitalized). The husband's drinking, his failure to be tidy, his nastiness, etc., lose significance in their own right. They move from emphasis to relief and are recast as signs of "something deeper," something that brought "it" on.

Some wives whose interpretations move in the direction of seeing their husbands as mentally ill hold conceptions of mental illness and of personality that do not permit assigning the husband all aspects of the sick role. Frequently, they use the interpretation of mental illness as an angry epithet or as a threatening prediction for the husband. This is exemplified in such references as: "I told him he should have his head examined," "I called him a half-wit," "I told him if he's not careful, he'll be a mental case." To many of these wives, the hospital is regarded as the "end of the road."

Other wives showing this pattern of change hold conceptions of emotional disturbance which more easily permit them to assign to their husbands the role of patient as the signs of illness become more apparent. They do not as often regard hospitalization in a mental hospital as the "last step." Nevertheless, their feelings toward their husbands may contain components equally as angry and rejecting as those of the wives with the less sophisticated ideas regarding mental illness.

A somewhat different pattern of sequential changes in interpreting the husband's difficulties (about one-fifth of the cases) is to be found among wives who appear to cast around for situationally and momentarily adequate explanations. As the situation changes or as the husband's behavior changes, these wives find reasons or excuses but lack an underlying or synthesizing theory. Successive interpretations tend to bear little relation to one another. Situational factors tend to lead them to seeing their husbands as mentally ill. Immediate, serious and direct physical threats or the influence of others may be the deciding factor. For example, a friend or employer may insist that the husband see a psychiatrist, and the wife goes along with the decision.

A third pattern of successive redefinitions (slightly less than one-third of the cases) revolves around an orientation outside the framework of emotional problems or mental illness. In these cases, the wife's specific explanations change but pivot around a denial that the husband is mentally ill.

A few wives seem not to change their interpretations about their husband's difficulties. They maintain the same explanation throughout the development of his illness, some within the psychiatric framework, others rigidly outside that framework.

Despite the characteristic shiftings in interpretations, in the group as a whole, there tend to be persisting underlying themes in the individual wife's perceptions that remain essentially unaltered. These themes are a function of her systems of thinking about normality and abnormality and about valued and devalued behavior.

THE PROCESS OF RECOGNIZING THE HUSBAND'S PROBLEM AS MENTAL ILLNESS

In the total situation confronting the wife, there are a number of factors, apparent in our data, which make it difficult for the wife to recognize and accept the husband's behavior in a mental-emotional-psychiatric framework. Many cross-currents seem to influence the process.

The husband's behavior itself is a fluctuating stimulus. He is not worried and complaining all of the time. His delusions and hallucinations may not persist. His hostility toward the wife may be followed by warm attentiveness. She has, then, the problem of deciding whether his "strange" behavior is significant. The greater saliency of one or the other of his responses at any moment of time depends in some degree upon the behavior sequence which has occurred most recently.

The relationship between husband and wife also supplies a variety of images and contexts which can justify varied conclusions about the husband's current behavior. The wife is likely to adapt to behavior which occurs in their day to day relationships. Therefore, symptomatic reactions which are intensifications of long-standing response patterns become part of the fabric of life and are not easily disentangled as "symptomatic."

Communications between husband and wife regarding the husband's difficulties act sometimes to impede and sometimes to further the process of seeing the difficulties within a psychiatric framework. We have seen both kinds of influences in our data. Mr. and Mrs. F. were quite unable to communicate effectively about Mr. F.'s problems. On the one hand, he counters his wife's urging that he see a doctor with denials that anything is wrong. On the other hand, in his own way through his symptoms, he tries to communicate his prob-

lems, but she responds only to his verbalized statements, taking them at face value.

Mr. and Mrs. K. participate together quite differently, examining Mr. K.'s fears that he is being followed by the F.B.I., that their house has been wired and that he is going to be fired. His wife tentatively shares his suspicions. At the same time, they discuss the possibility of paranoid reactions.

The larger social context contributes, too, in the wife's perceptual tug of war. Others with whom she can compare her husband provide contrasts to his deviance, but others (Mr. F.'s nervous friends) also provide parallels to his problems. The "outsiders," seeing less of her husband, often discount the wife's alarm when she presses them for opinions. In other instances, the friend or employer, less adapted to or defended against the husband's symptoms, helps her to define his problem as psychiatric.

This task before the wife, of defining her husband's difficulties, can be conceptualized as an "overlapping" situation (in Lewin's terms), in which the relative potencies of the several effective influences fluctuate. The wife is responding to the various sets of forces simultaneously. Thus, several conclusions or interpretations of the problem are simultaneously "suspended in balance," and they shift back and forth in emphasis and relief. Seldom, however, does she seem to be balancing off clear-cut alternatives, such as physical versus mental. Her complex perceptions (even those of Mrs. F. who is extreme in misperceiving cues) are more "sophisticated" than the casual questioner might be led to conclude.

Thus far, we have ignored the personally threatening aspects of recognizing mental illness in one's spouse, and the defenses which are mobilized to meet this threat. It is assumed that it is threatening to the wife not only to realize that the husband is mentally ill but further to consider her own possible role in the development of the disorder, to give up modes of relating to her husband that may have had satisfactions for her and to see a future as the wife of a mental patient. Our data provide systematic information only on the first aspect of this problem, on the forms of defense against the recognition of the illness. One or more of the following defenses are manifested in three-fourths of our cases.

The most obvious form of defense in the wife's response is the tendency to *normalize* the husband's neurotic and psychotic symptoms. His behavior is explained, justified or made acceptable by seeing it also in herself or by assuring herself that the particular behavior occurs again and again among persons who are not ill. Illustrative of this reaction is the wife who reports her husband's hallucinations and assures herself that this is normal because she herself heard voices when she was in the menopause. Another wife responds to her husband's physical complaints, fears, worries, nightmares, and delusions with "A lot of normal people think there's something wrong when there isn't. I think men are that way; his father is that way."

When behavior cannot be normalized, it can be made to seem less severe or less important in a total picture than an outsider might see it. By finding some grounds for the behavior or something explainable about it, the wife achieves at least momentary *attenuation* of the seriousness of it. Thus, Mrs. F. is able to discount partly the strangeness of her husband's descriptions of the worms growing out of his grandfather's mustache when she recalls his watching the worms in the fish bowl. There may be attenuation, too, by seeing the behavior as "momentary." ("You could talk him out of his ideas.") or by rethinking the problem and seeing it in a different light.

By *balancing* acceptable with unacceptable behavior or "strange" with "normal" behavior, some wives can conclude that the husband is not seriously disturbed. Thus, it is very important to Mrs. R. that her husband kissed her goodbye before he left for the hospital. This response cancels out his hostile feelings toward her and the possibility that he is mentally ill. Similarly, Mrs. V. rea-

sons that her husband cannot be "out of his mind" for he had reminded her of things she must not forget to do when he went to the hospital.

Defense sometimes amounts to a thorough-going *denial*. This takes the form of denying that the behavior perceived can be interpreted in an emotional or psychiatric framework. In some instances, the wife reports vividly on such behavior as repeated thoughts of suicide, efforts to harm her and the like and sums it up with "I thought it was just a whim." Other wives bend their efforts toward proving the implausibility of mental illness.

After the husband is hospitalized, it might be expected that these denials would decrease to a negligible level. This is not wholly the case, however. A breakdown of the wives' interpretations just following the husband's admission to the hospital shows that roughly a fifth still interpret their husband's behavior in another framework than that of a serious emotional problem or mental illness. Another fifth ambivalently and sporadically interpret the behavior as an emotional or mental problem. The remainder hold relatively stable interpretations within this framework.

After the husband has been hospitalized for some time, many wives reflect on their earlier tendencies to avoid a definition of mental illness. Such reactions are almost identically described by these wives: "I put it out of my mind—I didn't want to face it—anything but a mental illness." "Maybe I was aware of it. But you know you push things away from you and keep hoping." "Now you think maybe you should have known about it. Maybe you should have done more than you did and that worries me."

DISCUSSION

The findings on the perceptions of mental illness by the wives of patients are in line with general findings in studies of perception. Behavior which is unfamiliar and incongruent and unlikely in terms of current expectations and needs will not be readily recognized, and stressful or threatening stimuli will tend to be misperceived or perceived with difficulty or delay.

We have attempted to describe the factors which help the wife maintain a picture of her husband as normal and those which push her in the direction of accepting a psychiatric definition of his problem. The kind and intensity of the symptomatic behavior, its persistence over time, the husband's interpretation of his problem, interpre-

tations and defining actions of others, including professionals, all play a role. In addition, the wives come to this experience with different concepts of psychological processes and of the nature of emotional illness, itself, as well as with different tolerances for emotional disturbance. As we have seen, there are also many supports in society for maintaining a picture of normality concerning the husband's behavior. Social pressures and expectations not only keep *behavior* in line but to a great extent *perceptions* of behavior as well....

Accommodation to Madness

MICHAEL LYNCH

People are committed to mental hospitals after informal efforts to accommodate them in society fail. Studies report that spouses of prospective mental patients (Cumming and Cumming, 1957; Mayo *et al.,* 1971; Sampson *et al.,* 1962; Spitzer *et al.,* 1971; Yarrow *et al.,* 1955), co-workers (Lemert, 1962), and police officers (Bittner, 1967) claim that they contact psychiatric authorities only as a last resort, when informal methods of "care" are unavailable or are overwhelmed by the extremity of the person's disorder. There is widespread reluctance, especially in lower-class fami-

Reprinted from "Accommodation Practices: Vernacular Treatments of Madness," *Social Problems*, Vol. 31, No. 2 (December, 1983), pp. 152–164, by permission of the Society for the Study of Social Problems and the author.

The author thanks Renee Anspach, David Davis, Robert Emerson, Harold Garfinkel, Richard Hilbert, James Holstein, Melvin Pollner, and Steven Vandewater for their comments. The exercise on accommodation practices which I used in this research was adapted from a similar exercise used by Robert Emerson and Melvin Pollner in their courses on the Sociology of Mental Illness at the University of California, Los Angeles. During part of this research I was supported by a fellowship from the National Institute's of Mental Health Postdoctoral Training Program in Mental Health Evaluation Research, (# MH 14583). Correspondence to: School of Social Sciences, University of California, Irvine, CA.

lies (Hollingshead and Redlich, 1958:172–79; Myers and Roberts, 1959:213–20), to take a perspective on relational disorders which supports professional intervention and hospitalization. As a result, the population of potential mental patients is said to vastly outnumber the population of professionally treated patients (Srole *et al.,* 1962). Accommodating families can hide potential patients from official scrutiny by placing few demands upon them and allowing them to "exist as if in a one-person chronic ward, insulated from all but those in a highly tolerant household" (Freeman and Simmons, 1958:148).

Such observations suggest that a massive program of community care exists independently of formally established programs of inpatient and outpatient treatment. Countless numbers of undiagnosed, but troublesome, individuals, as well as an increasing number of diagnosed outpatients, are consigned by default to the informal care of family and community. Although the social characteristics of professionally administered mental health care institutions have been exhaustively analyzed, the practices that make up ordinary lay-operated "institutions" of care remain largely unexamined. In this study I call attention to such accommodation practices, elaborate upon previous descriptions of the practices, and present some conjectures on the social construction of the individual.

Accommodation practices are interactional techniques that people use to manage persons they view as persistent sources of trouble. Accommodation implies attempts to "live with" persistent and ineradicable troubles.[1] Previous studies mention a number of accommodation practices. Lemert (1962) describes how people exclude distrusted individuals from their organization's covert activities by employing methods of "spurious interaction." Such forms of interaction are:

> ...distinguished by patronizing, evasion, "humoring," guiding conversation onto selected topics, underreaction, and silence, all calculated either to prevent intense interaction or to protect individual and group values by restricting access to them. When the interaction is between two or more persons in the individual's presence it is cued by a whole repertoire of subtle expressive signs which are meaningful only to them (1962:8).

Other methods for managing perceived "troublemakers" include: isolation and avoidance (Lemert, 1962; Sampson et al., 1962), relieving an individual of ordinary responsibilities associated with their roles (Sampson et al., 1962); hiding liquor bottles from a heavily drinking spouse (Jackson, 1954); and "babying" (Jackson, 1954).

Some studies (Yarrow et al., 1955) treat accommodation practices as sources of delay in the recognition and treatment of mental illness; others (Goffman, 1961, 1969; Lemert, 1962) portray them as primary constituents of "illness." Whether the studies assume a realist or a societal reaction perspective on the nature of mental illness, they attempt to explain how persons become mental patients by reconstructing the social backgrounds of hospitalized patients. As Emerson and Messinger (1977:131) point out, retrospective analyses of the "careers" of diagnosed mental patients presuppose a specific pathological outcome to the "prepatient's" biography. To avoid this problem, social

scientists need to abandon retrospective methods and analyze contemporary situations where troublesome individuals are accommodated. Such people are not yet patients, and may never attain that status. Therefore, institutional records cannot be used to locate cases for study. An appropriate way to find them is to use vernacular accounts of madness or mental illness, and to document the patterns of accommodation that others use to control such troublesome people.

THE STUDY

This study is an analysis of the results of an assignment which I gave to students in classes on the sociology of mental illness in 1981 and 1982. I instructed students to locate someone in a familiar social environment who was identified by others (and perhaps by themselves) as "crazy"; the subject need not appear "mentally ill," but need only be a *personal* and *persistent* source of trouble for others. The vast majority of the students had little trouble finding such subjects. I instructed them to interview persons who consistently dealt with the troublemaker in a living or work situation. The interviews were to focus on the practices used by others to "live with" the troublemaker from day to day. Students who were personally acquainted with the troublemaker were encouraged to refer to their own recollections and observations in addition to their interviews. They were instructed not to interview or otherwise disturb the troublemakers. Each student wrote a 5–7 page paper on accommodation practices with an appendix of notes from their interviews.

THE SUBJECTS

The persons the students interviewed described subjects who had already developed to an intermediate stage in the "natural history of trouble" (Emerson and Messinger, 1977). Few troublemakers carried formal designations of mental illness, but each was associated with recurrent organizational troubles. The troubles were defined non-re-lationally (Goffman, 1969); they were attributed to the personal agency of a troublemaker, and any possible mitigating factors were no longer considered pertinent. Although the students and their interviewees claimed a consensus on the fact that *something* was wrong with the troublemaker, just what was wrong was often a matter of speculation. Troublemakers' friends and acquaintances sometimes resorted to amateur psychologizing to account for the subjects' "problem," but often they expressed moral exasperation and disgust, without any mention of a possible "illness."

Students and those they interviewed used a rich variety of vernacular epithets for personal character types to identify their subjects. These included common insults, "crazy" terms used as insults, and a few straightforward "illness" designators. The following expressions illustrate different shadings in the ambiguity of the troublemakers' statuses as moral offenders and/or "sick" persons:

1. Commonplace vernacular terms for faults and faulted persons, without reference to insanity: "bullshitter," "bird" (as in "turkey"), "off the wall," "spiteful, nasty girl," "rude and argumentative," "an obnoxious pest," "catty," "space cadet," "chronic complainer," "frivolous and ridiculous," and nicknames such as "Ozone" and "The Deviant."
2. Vernacular cognates of madness which do not necessarily compel the serious connotation of illness: "crazy," "nuts," "bananas," "weird," "strange," "unpredictable," "highly emotional," "attention seeking and manipulative," "explosive, angry," and "sick."
3. Amateur uses of accounts associated with the helping professions: "paranoid," "developmentally disabled," "chemically imbalanced in the brain," "low self-esteem," "obsessed with food," and "alcoholic."

Except in a few cases when students reported a specific medical diagnosis, their accounts did not provide unique labels corresponding to stable categories of disorder. They did, however, point to a history of incidents supporting the conclusion that *something* was wrong with the person in question.

Some accounts emphasized that it was impossible to describe just what was wrong with the person. There was far more to the trouble than could be described by a few episodes: "disgusting eating habits," "he smells terrible," "he stands too close to people," "she asks you to repeat things over and over again," "she is so promiscuous that one of the fraternities has a song about fucking her!" Not all accounts were wholly negative or rejecting. At least some acquaintances whom students interviewed expressed some affection or attachment to troublemakers, or an obligation to maintain a minimal level of civility toward the person.

In the few cases where the troublemaker had a history of mental or neurological disorder, students reported that their informants used the illness to excuse incidents believed to be symptomatic of the disorder. Such special understandings did not entirely replace more hostile reactions, for many of the "symptoms" were also personal offenses:

> Margaret explained that she always attempts to start off calm when dealing with Joan and thinking of her as being a "lonely and sick woman," but that Joan "gets you so angry that it is difficult to stay level-headed and then I start screaming and have to leave." (Student report of an interview concerning a "senile" woman.)

The students investigated a number of different organizational environments. Fraternities and sororities were most popular, followed by families (both nuclear and extended), dormitory residents, work groups, friendship cliques, athletic teams, and residents of apartment suites and local neighborhoods. One case dealt with a board and care home; another described a group of students on a retreat. Among the work groups observed were employees of a book store, a clothing store, a pharmacy, and a fast food restaurant. One noteworthy case involved a rock and roll band and its crew on a national tour. In each of these cases, membership in the group or organization provided the local basis of the troublemaker's existence. Membership furnished the context for day-to-day interactions with the troublemaker, and for accumulating an oral history of the troublemaker's antics. In the following discussion, I will use the term *members* to refer to all those who knew or related to the troublesome person through common membership in some organized group, network of relationship, acquaintance, or friendship.[2]

Because of the highly sensitive nature of the interactional circumstances which the students were investigating, I repeatedly asked them to respect the privacy of their subjects. They proved to be highly skilled at doing so, perhaps because they relied upon their own skills at performing accommodation practices to hide their inquiries from the troublemaker's attention.

I did not initially design the assignment in order to gather data for my own analysis. However, after reading the students' reports on their observations and interviews I found that despite their variability in descriptive and analytic quality and their obvious shortcomings as data, they described a diversity of accommodation practices, and suggested recurrent features of those practices which were not comprehensively treated in the literature. The information seemed worth reporting and students gave me permission to quote from their papers. I analyzed material from 32 of the student reports, each of which discussed a different case. In the remainder of this paper, all quotes not attributed to sources come from the students' papers.

I have organized accommodation practices under three thematic headings: (1) practices which *isolate* the troublemaker within the group; (2) practices which *manipulate* the troublemaker's behavior, perception, and understanding; and (3) practices which members use to influence how others react to the troublemaker. The first set of practices defines and limits the troublemaker's chances for interaction, expression, and feedback within the group. The second set directs the de-

tails of the troublemaker's actions and establishes the discrepant meanings of those actions for "self" and "other." The third set includes attempts to make the troublemaker's public identity into a covert communal project.

MINIMIZING CONTACT WITH THE TROUBLEMAKER

Avoiding and *ignoring* were the two accommodation practices mentioned most often by students. Both were methods for minimizing contact with the troublemaker, and had the effect of isolating the troublemaker within the organizational network. While both were negative methods of behavior control, attenuating the troublemaker's actual and possible occasions of interaction, they worked quite differently. Avoiding limited the gross *possibility* of interaction, while ignoring worked *within* ongoing occasions of interaction to limit the interactional *reality* of the encounter. Where avoiding created an absence of encounter, ignoring created a dim semblance to ordinary interaction.

AVOIDING

In virtually every student's account, one or more of the members they interviewed mentioned that they actively avoided the troublemaker. Avoidance created an interactional vacuum around the troublemaker. Members managed to stay out of the way of the troublemaker without actually requesting or commanding the troublemaker to stay away from them. Methods of avoidance included individual and joint tactics such as "ducking into restrooms," "keeping a lookout for her at all times," and "hiding behind a newspaper or book."

Some members were better placed than others within the structure of the organization to avoid the troublemaker. In larger organizations like fraternities and sororities, persons could stake out positions which minimized contact with the troublemaker. In more intimate circles avoidance ran more of a risk of calling attention to the *ab-*

sence of usual interactional involvement. Avoidance *did* occur in such intimate groups as families (Sampson *et al.,* 1962), but only at the cost of threatening the very integrity of the group.

IGNORING/NOT TAKING SERIOUSLY

Ignoring differed from avoiding because it entailed at least some interaction, though of an attenuated and inauthentic kind. One account described conversations with the troublemaker as being "reduced to superficial 'hellos,' most of which are directed at her feet; there is an obvious lack of eye contact." Many accounts mentioned the superficiality of interactions with troublemakers. In some cases this was accomplished by what one student called "rehearsed and phony responses" to limit the openness of their conversations to a few stock sequences.[3]

Although ignoring entailed interaction, it was like avoidance in that it circumscribed the troublemaker's interactional possibilities. Where avoidance operated to limit, in a gross way, the intersection of pathways between troublemaker and other members, ignoring operated intensively to trivialize the troublemaker's apparent involvements in group activities.[4] Bids for positive notice were ignored, and had little effect on the troublemaker's position within the group.

DIRECTLY MANAGING THE TROUBLEMAKER'S ACTIONS

Members used a number of more direct interventions to control and limit the troublemaker's behavior, including humoring, screening, taking over, orienting to local prospects of normality, and practical jokes and retaliations. While such methods had little hope of permanently modifying the behavior, they were used to curtail episodic disruptions by the troublemaker.

HUMORING

Members often used the term humoring to describe attempts to manage the troublemaker by maintaining a veneer of agreement and geniality in the face of actions which would ordinarily evoke protest or disgust. For example, in the case of "an obnoxiously argumentative person," members offered superficial tokens of agreement in response to even the most outlandish pronouncements for the sake of avoiding more extreme disruptions.

Humoring was often made possible through insight into recurrent features of the troublemaker's behavior. Members recognized recurrent situations in ordinary interactions which triggered peculiar reactions by the troublemaker. They developed a heightened awareness of ordinary and seemingly innocuous details of interaction which could touch off an explosive reaction. One student described how her parents managed a "crazy aunt," who she said was prone to sudden and violent verbal assaults:

> *My parents avoided discussing specific topics and persons that they knew distressed her. Whenever she began talking about an arousable [sic] event or person, my parents and her husband attempted to change the subject.*[5]

Although members rationalized humoring as a way "to make it easy for everybody," they did not always find it easy to withhold their reactions to interactional offenses. A student wrote about her efforts to prepare her fiance for a first encounter with her grandmother, said to be suffering from senile dementia, Alzheimer type;

> *I attempted to explain to him that he should not say anything controversial, agree with whatever she says, and generally stay quiet as much as possible. [He assured her that everything would be okay, but when he was confronted with the actual grandmother, the assurance proved quite fragile.] That encounter proved to be quite an experience for Charles—we left Grandma's house with Charles screaming back at her for his self-worth.*

Other accounts mentioned the strain and difficulty of trying to humor troublemakers. They described an exceedingly fragile interactional situation which was prone to break down at any moment:

You don't want to set him off, so you're very careful about what you do and say. You become tense trying to keep everything calm, and then something happens to screw it up anyway: The car won't start, or a light bulb blows. It's all my fault because I'm a rotten wife and mother.

Humoring often entailed obedience or deference to what members claimed (when not within earshot of the troublemaker) were outrageous or absurd demands:

Everyone did what she asked in order to please her and not cause any bad scenes.

In some cases, members exerted special efforts or underwent severe inconvenience for the sake of a person they secretly despised. Not surprisingly, such efforts often, though not always, were exerted by persons over whom the troublemaker had formal authority. In one case the members of a crew traveling with a rock and roll band would set up the troublesome member's equipment before that of the others and set up daily meetings with him to discuss his "technical needs," while at the same time they believed it was foolish of him to demand such special attention. They described the special meetings and favors as a "bogus accommodation." In every case, whether correlated with formal divisions of authority or not, humoring contributed to the troublemaker's sense of interactional power over others.

Humoring always included a degree of duplicity in which members "kept a straight face" when interacting with the troublemaker or acted in complicity with the troublemaker's premises— premises which members otherwise discounted as delusional or absurd:

We played along with her fantasy of a boyfriend, "John." We never said what a complete fool she was for waiting for him.

Commonly, members practiced *serial* duplicity by waiting until the troublemaker was out of earshot to display for one another's appreciation the "real" understanding they had previously suppressed:

They pretend to know what she is talking about, they act as if they are interested...they make remarks when she is gone.

At other times they practiced *simultaneous* duplicity by showing interest and serious engagement to the troublemaker's face while expressing detachment and sarcasm to one another through furtive glances, gestures, and double entendres (Lemert, 1962:8).

Those employees who she is not facing will make distorted faces and roll their eyes around to reaffirm the fact that she is a little slow. All the time this occurs Susan is totally oblivious to it, or at least she pretends to be.

In one fraternity, members devised a specific hand gesture (described as "wing flapping") which they displayed for one another when interacting with a troublemaker they called "the bird."

Members occasionally rationalized their duplicity by describing the troublemaker as a self-absorbed and "dense" person, whose lack of orientation to others provided ample opportunity for their play:

People speak sarcastically to him, and Joe, so wrapped up in himself, believes what they are saying and hears only what he wants to hear.

SCREENING

Jackson (1954:572) reported that alcoholics' wives attempted to manage their husbands' heavy drinking by hiding or emptying liquor bottles in the house and curtailing their husbands' funds. One student described a similar practice used by friends of a person who they feared had suicidal tendencies. They systematically removed from the person's environment any objects that could be used to commit suicide.

Screening and monitoring of troublemakers' surroundings also occurred in the interactional realm. A few accounts mentioned attempts to monitor the moods of a troublemaker, and to screen the person's potential interactions on the basis of attributed mood. When one sorority's

troublemaker was perceived to be especially vola-
tile, members acted as her covert receptionists by
turning away her visitors, explaining that she was
not in or was ill. In this case members were concerned not only to control the potential actions of
the individual, but also to conceal those actions
from others, and by doing so to protect the collective "image" of their sorority from contamination.

TAKING OVER

A number of accounts mentioned efforts by members to do activities which ordinarily would be
done by someone in the troublemaker's social position. Like published accounts of cases in which
husbands or mothers take over the household duties of a wife (Sampson *et al.,* 1962), the apartment mates of a troublemaker washed dishes and
paid bills for her "as if she wasn't there." A circle
of friends insisted on driving the automobile of a
man they considered dangerously impulsive. Fraternity members gradually and unofficially took
over the duties of their social chairman in fear of
the consequences of his erratic actions and inappropriate attire. Taking over sometimes included
such intimate personal functions as grooming and
dressing, as when the spouse of a drunk diligently
prepared her husband for necessary public appearances.

ORIENTING TO LOCAL PROSPECTS OF NORMALITY

Yarrow *et al.* (1955) mention that wives of mental
patients sustained efforts to live with their husbands by treating interludes between episodes as
the beginnings of "recovery" rather than as periods of calm before the inevitable storms. By keeping tabs on the latest developments in the
troublemaker's behavior, members were often
able to determine when it was "safe" to treat the
troublemaker as a "normal" person. This method
was not always as unrealistic as one would be led
to believe from Yarrow *et al.* (1955). Since most
troublemakers were viewed as persons whose difficulties, though inherent, were intermittent, liv-

ing with them required knowing what to expect in
the immediate interactional future:

> *I have observed the occasion when a friend at the
> fraternity house entered the television room and
> remained in the rear of the room, totally quiet,
> watching Danny, waiting for a signal telling him
> how to act. When Danny turned and spoke to him
> in a friendly, jovial manner, the young man enthu-
> siastically pulled his chair up to sit next to Danny
> and began speaking freely.*

Members described many troublemakers as
persons with likeable and even admirable qualities, whose friendship was valued during their
"good times." When a member anticipated an encounter with a troublemaker, he or she wanted
most of all to avoid touching off a "bad scene."
The local culture of gossip surrounding a troublemaker tended to facilitate such an aim by providing a running file on the current state of his or her
moods. By using the latest news members could
decide when to avoid encounters and when they
could approach the troublemaker without undue
wariness.

PRACTICAL JOKES AND RETALIATIONS

Although direct expressions of hostility toward
troublemakers were rarely mentioned, it is possible that they occurred more frequently than was
admitted. Practical jokes and other forms of retaliation were designed not to reveal their authors.
The troublemaker would be "clued in" that *somebody* despised him or was otherwise "out to get"
him, but he would be left to imagine just who it
was. Some jokes were particularly cruel, and were
aimed at the troublemaker's particular vulnerabilities. A member of a touring rock and roll band
was known to have difficulty forming relationships with women:

> *They would get girls to call his room and make
> dates they would never keep. Apparently, the spot-
> light operator was the author of a series of hot
> love letters of a mythical girl who was following
> Moog [a pseudonym for the troublemaker] from*

town to town and would soon appear in his bedroom. The crew must have been laughing their heads off for days. Moog was reading the letters out loud in the dressing room.

INFLUENCING THE REACTION TO THE TROUBLEMAKER

A group of practices, instead of focusing solely on the troublemaker's interactional behavior, attempted to control others' *reactions to* and *interpretations of* that behavior. These accommodations recognized that there could be serious consequences in the reactions of outsiders—nonmembers—to the troublemaker. Such practices included efforts by members to control the reactions of persons outside the group; and to control assessments not only of the individual troublemaker, but of the group as well. The responsibilities for, and social consequences of, the individual's behavior were thus adopted by members as a collective project.

TURNING THE TROUBLEMAKER INTO A NOTORIOUS CHARACTER

In stories to outsiders as well as others in the group, members were sometimes able to turn the troublemaker into a fascinating and almost admirable character. A classic case was the fraternity "animal." Although litanies of crude, offensive, and assaultive actions were recounted, the character's antics were also portrayed with evident delight. Such descriptions incorporated elements of heroism, the prowess of the brawler, or the fearlessness and outrageousness of a prankster. In one case a student reported that the fraternity troublemaker, nicknamed "the deviant," was supported and encouraged by a minority faction who claimed to an outsider that he was merely "a little wild," and that nothing was wrong with him. This faction seemed unembarrassed by, and perhaps a bit proud of, the troublemaker's "animal" qualities that others might ascribe to the fraternity as well. The quasi-heroic or comical repute of the troublemaker did not overshadow many members' distaste for the disruptions, but it did constitute a supportive moral counterpoint.

SHADOWING

In one instance a group of students living in a dorm arranged covertly to escort their troublemaker on his frequent trips to local bars. He had a reputation for drinking more than his capacity and then challenging all comers to fights. To inhibit such adventures members of the group volunteered to accompany him under various pretexts, and to quell any disputes he precipitated during the drinking sessions. In the case of the member of the rock and roll band, other members chaperoned him during interviews with media critics. When he said something potentially offensive, his chaperon attempted to turn his statement into a joke. Another account described efforts by a group to spy on a member who they believed was likely to do something rash or violent.

ADVANCE NOTICES

As Lemert (1962) points out, members often build a legacy of apocryphal stories about their troublemaker. Stories told by one member to another about the troublemaker's latest antics provided a common source of entertainment, and perhaps solidarity. Some members admitted that they could not imagine what they would talk about with one another if not the troublemaker's behavior:

> *The highlight of the day is hearing the latest story about Joanie.*

Such gleeful renditions helped to prepare nonmembers for first encounters with the troublemaker.

A few students mentioned that the troublemakers they studied appeared normal or even charming during initial encounters, but that members soon warned them to be careful about getting involved with the person. Subsequent experience confirmed the warnings, although it was difficult to discern whether this was a result of their accuracy or of the wariness they engendered.

Members of a group that included a persistently troublesome character "apologized for him beforehand" to persons who shortly would be doing business with him. They also warned women he approached that he was "a jerk." In addition to preparing such persons for upcoming encounters, the apologies and warnings carried the tacit claim that "we're not like him." This mitigated any potential contamination of the group's moral reputation.

HIDING AND DILUTING THE TROUBLEMAKER

Some fraternities and sororities institutionalized a "station" for hiding troublemakers during parties and teas where new members were recruited. Troublemakers were assigned out-of-the-way positions in social gatherings and, in some cases, were accompanied at all times by other members whose job it was to cut off the troublemaker's interaction with prospective members.

The methods used for hiding and diluting were especially artful when they included pretexts to conceal from the troublemakers that their role had been diminished. The troublemaker in the rock and roll band was said to embarrass other members with "distasteful ego tripping" on stage during public concerts. Such "ego trips" were characterized by loud and "awful" playing on his instrument and extravagant posturing in attempts to draw the audience's attention to himself. These displays were countered by the sound and light men in the crew.

> On those nights the sound man would turn up the monitors on stage so Moog sounded loud to himself and would turn down Moog in the [concert] hall and on the radio.

Simultaneously, the lighting director would "bathe him in darkness" by dimming the spotlights on him. These practices, in effect, technically created a delusional experience for the troublemaker. They produced a systematic distortion of his perception of the world and simultaneously diminished his public place in that world.

COVERING FOR/COVERING UP

Friends and intimates sometimes went to great lengths to smooth over the damages and insults done to others by the troublemaker. The husband of a "crazy woman" monitored his wife's offenses during her "episodes" and followed in the wake of the destruction with apologies and sometimes monetary reparations to offended neighbors. Similar efforts at restoring normality also occurred in immediate interactional contexts:

> Before she will even tell you her name, she is telling you how one day she was hitchhiking and was gang raped by the five men who picked her up. This caused so many problems for her that she ended up in a mental hospital and is now a lesbian. The look on people's faces is complete shock.... Those hearing this story for the first time will sit in shock as if in a catatonic stupor, with wide eyes and their mouths dropped open, absolutely speechless. Someone who has already heard this story will break the silence by continuing with the previous conversation,...putting it on extinction by ignoring it as if she never said anything.

Members sometimes conspired, ostensibly on behalf of the troublemaker, to prevent the relevant authorities from detecting the existence and extent of the troubles. One group of girls in a freshman dorm deliberately lied to hide the fact that one of their members was having great difficulty and, in their estimation, was potentially suicidal. When her parents asked how she was doing the students responded that she was doing "fine." Members tried to contain her problems and to create a "blockade" around any appearances of her problems that might attract the attentions of university authorities. Once underway, such coverups gained momentum, since the prospect of exposure increasingly threatened to make members culpable for not bringing the matter to the attention of remedial agents.

DISCUSSION

A prevailing theme in the students' accounts of accommodation practices was the avoidance of confrontation. They described confrontation as potentially "unpleasant," to be avoided even when considerable damage and hardship had been suffered:

> When students' money began disappearing from their rooms, we had a group meeting to discuss our mode of intervention. Although we all believed Chris was responsible, we did not confront her. Instead, we simply decided to make sure we locked our bedroom doors when not in our rooms.

In general, a number of reasons for avoiding confrontation were given, including the anticipation of denial by the troublemaker, fear that the troublemaker would create a "bad scene," and the belief that confrontation would make no difference in the long run.

Less direct methods were used to communicate the group's opinions to the troublemaker. Instead of telling the troublemaker in so many words, members employed a peculiar sort of gamesmanship. Systematic "leaks" were used to *barely* and *ambiguously* expose the duplicity and conspiracy, so that the troublemaker would realize something was going on, but would be unable or unwilling to accuse specific offenders. Duplicitous gestures or comments which operated *just* on the fringes of the troublemaker's awareness produced maximum impact.

The successful operation of these practices relied, in part, on the troublemaker's complicity in the conspiracy of silence.

> Once I was in the room next door to her and the girls were imitating her. Two minutes later she walked in asking [us] to be quiet because she was trying to sleep. I thought I was going to die. Obviously Tammy realized what was going on as the walls are extremely thin; however, Tammy seems to be conspiring on the side of her "friends" to prevent any confrontation of the actual situation.

Hostilities were therefore expressed, and retaliations achieved, often with rather specific reference to the particular offenses and their presumed source. At the same time, they remained "submerged" in a peculiar way. They were not submerged in a psychological "unconscious," since both members and troublemakers were aware of what was going on. Instead, both members and troublemakers made every effort to assure that the trouble did not disturb the overtly normal interaction. "Business as usual" was preserved at the cost of keeping secret deep hostilities within the organization.

A few accounts did mention instances of explicit confrontation. However, members claimed that such confrontations did not alter troublemakers' subsequent behaviors; instead they resulted in misunderstandings or were received by troublemakers in a defensive or unresponsive way.

Efforts to remove troublemakers from organizations were rarely described, though members of the rock band eventually expelled their troublemaker after he hired a lawyer to redress his grievances against the group. In another case a fraternity "de-pledged" a new recruit who had not yet been fully initiated. In no other case was an established member removed, although numerous dramatic offenses were recounted and widespread dislike for troublemakers was commonly reported.

Taken as a whole, accommodation practices reveal *the organizational construction of the normal individual*. The individual is relied upon both in commonsense reasoning and social theory as a source of compliance with the standards of the larger society. The normal individual successfully adapts to the constraints imposed by social structure. Troublemakers were viewed as persons who, for various reasons, could not be given full *responsibility* for maintaining normality. Instead, the burden of maintaining the individual's normal behavior and appearance was taken up by others. Troublemakers were not overtly sanctioned; instead, they were shaped and guided through the superficial performances of ordinary action. Their integration into society was not a cumulative mastery learned "from inside"; it was a constant project executed by others from the "outside."

Accommodation practices allow us to glimpse the project of the self as a practical struggle. A semblance of normal individuality for troublemakers was a carefully constructed artifact produced by members. When the responsibility for normality is assumed as an individual birthright, it appears inevitable that conformity or defiance proceeds "from inside" the individual, just as it appears in commonsense that gender is a natural inheritance. In the latter instance, a transsexual's unusual experience indicates the extent to which the ordinary behavior and appearance of being female is detachable from the individual's birthright, and can be explicated as a practical accomplishment (Garfinkel, 1967). Similarly, for the organizational colleagues of a troublemaker, the elements of normal individuality cannot be relied upon, but must be achieved through deliberate practice. Members together performed the work of minding the troublemaker's business, of guiding the troublemaker through normal interactional pathways, and of filling the responsibilities and appearances associated with the troublemaker's presence for others.[6]

Of course, such projects were less than successful; members complained of the undue burden, disruptions occurred despite their efforts, and the troublemaker was provided with a diminished self and a distorted reality. Perhaps all would have been better off had they "left the self inside where it belongs." Nevertheless, accommodation practices enable us to see the extent to which the division between self and other is permeable, and subject to negotiation and manipulation. We can see that individual responsibility for the conduct of affairs is separable from the actual performance of those affairs. Troublemakers were manipulated into a tenuous conformity by members who relied upon the fact that such conformity would be attributed to the individual's responsibility. The individual was thus reduced to the subject of an informal code of responsibility, separable from any substantive source of action (Goffman, 1969:357).

IMPLICATIONS

Previous research on accommodation practices in the societal reaction tradition has suggested that the individual symptoms of disorder can be explained in reference to social organization (Goffman, 1969; Lemert, 1962). I have not been concerned with how individual *disorder* is generated by social reaction. My interest instead has been to investigate how individual *normality* is socially constructed. This issue has both practical and theoretical consequences.

On a practical level, given the current institutional emphasis on the "community care" of mental disorders, it should be useful to know as much as possible about ordinary "institutions" of accommodation. The descriptive inventory provided in this study goes a small distance in that direction. Based on this study, it appears that accommodation practices are analogous, on a social level, to individual "defense mechanisms" (Henry, 1972:49). What remains to be determined is whether some of the practices are more effective than others; whether, like Freudian defense mechanisms, some can be viewed as pathological whereas others are relatively effective. It also remains to be seen whether accommodation practices can be improved by instruction, and operated in a humane and insightful fashion.

On a theoretical level, the analysis of accommodation practices enables us to consider the self as a social and normative construct as much as an internal province of operations. This is more than to say that the self is an *attribution* by others, since accommodation includes concrete actions to manipulate and maintain a semblance of normal selfhood on behalf of a troublemaker. In psychology and social-psychology, an inscrutable ego is normally required as a locus of operations for directing behavior and impression management (the latter by reacting to the reactions of others). Here we see both behavior and impression management being directed by overt and covert operations external to the individual. By implication, the individual's domain of action and responsibility is only provisionally established if it can be taken over by others.

Accommodation practices integrate the troublemaker into society, while requiring minimal initiative from the troublemaker. At the extreme, the troublemaker can be turned into a puppet whose behavior (especially in its more public consequences) is divorced from internal control. The individual is never altogether out of the picture, since at every turn individual responsibility is attributed. The puppet is given life (a life not of its making) through the conventional appearance of its overt actions. Instead of an ego projecting significant symbols outward, we find the surface of an individual being managed and shaped by communal activity, with or without the individual's knowledge and compliance. Whether this applies more generally than to the pathological circumstances described here remains to be established, but my research suggests that the individual self is a moral and attributional construct not to be confused with the theoretical requirements of social action.

NOTES

1. The equally interesting topic of how patients accommodate to their own disorders (Critchley, 1971:290; O. Sacks, 1974:227) is not included in this discussion of interactional practices.
2. Here the term *member* does not bear the more radical implication of "a mastery of natural language," defined in Garfinkel and Sacks (1970:350).
3. A topic needing further study is how members use greetings and other conversational "adjacency pairs" (Sacks *et al.,* 1974) to foreclose conversation with troublemakers at the earliest convenient point, but in such a way as not to call attention to their action as a snub.
4. See Wulbert (n.d.) for a poignant discussion of trivializing practices.

5. Jefferson and Lee (1980) characterize some of the detailed ways in which participants in ordinary conversations head off "troubles talk" and transform it to "business as usual." Such procedures are much more varied and intricate than can adequately be described by such phrases as "changing the subject."
6. My discussion of the social production of the individual is heavily indebted to Pollner and Wikler's (1981) treatment of that theme. Pollner and Wikler (1981) discuss a family's efforts to construct the appearance of normality for their (officially diagnosed) profoundly retarded daughter. Not only does *normality* become a communal project in these cases, *abnormality* becomes shared as well. One student in my research described an alcoholic's family as "three characters revolving around a central theme—alcoholism." The preoccupation with alcohol was shared along with the *denial* that the man's drinking was an official problem.

REFERENCES

Bittner, Egon. 1967. "Police Discretion in Emergency Apprehension of Mentally Ill Persons." *Social Problems,* 14(3):278–292.

Critchley, MacDonald. 1971. *The Parietal Lobes.* New York: Hafner Publishing Co.

Cumming, Elaine and John Cumming. 1957. *Closed Ranks.* Cambridge, MA: Harvard University Press.

Emerson, Robert and Sheldon Messinger. 1977. "The Micro-politics of Trouble." *Social Problems,* 25(2):121–134.

Freeman, Howard and Ozzie Simmons. 1958. "Mental Patients in the Community: Family Settings and Performance Levels." *American Sociological Review,* 23(2):147–154.

Garfinkel, Harold. 1967. *Studies in Ethnomethodology.* Englewood Cliffs, NJ: Prentice-Hall.

Garfinkel, Harold and Harvey Sacks. 1970. "Formal Structures of Practical Actions." In John McKinney and Edward Tiryakian (eds.), Theoretical Sociology: Perspectives and Development. New York: Appleton-Century Crofts, pp. 337–366.

Goffman, Erving. 1961. *Asylums.* Garden City, NY: Doubleday.

———. 1969. "The Insanity of Place." *Psychiatry,* 32(4):352–388.

Henry, Jules. 1972. *Pathways to Madness.* New York: Random House.

Hollingshead, August and Frederick Redlich. 1958. *Social Class and Mental Illness.* New York: Wiley.

Jackson, Joan. 1954. "The Adjustment of the Family to the Crisis of Alcoholism." *Quarterly Journal of Studies on Alcohol,* 15(4):562–586.

Jefferson, Gail and John Lee. 1980. "The Analysis of Conversations in Which Anxieties and Troubles Are Expressed." Unpublished report for the Social Science Research Counsel, University of Manchester, England.

Lemert, Edwin. 1962. "Paranoia and the Dynamics of Exclusion." *Sociometry,* 25(1):2–20.

Mayo, Clara, Ronald Havelock, and Diane Lear Simpson. 1971. "Attitudes Towards Mental Illness among Psychiatric Patients and Their Wives." *Journal of Clinical Psychology,* 27(1):128–132.

Myers, Jerome and Bertram Roberts. 1959. *Family and Class Dynamics.* New York: Wiley.

Pollner, Melvin and Lynn Wikler. 1981. "The Social Construction of Unreality: A Case Study of the Practices of Family Sham and Delusion." Unpublished paper, Department of Sociology, University of California, Los Angeles.

Sacks, Harvey, Emanuel Schegloff, and Gail Jefferson. 1974. "A Simplest Systematics for the Organization of Turn Taking in Conversation." *Language,* 50(4):696–735.

Sacks, Oliver. 1974. *Awakenings.* New York: Doubleday.

Sampson, Harold, Sheldon Messinger, and Robert Towne. 1962. "Family Processes and Becoming a Mental Patient." *American Journal of Sociology,* 68(1):88–98.

Spitzer, Stephan, Patricia Morgan, and Robert Swanson. 1971. "Determinants of the Psychiatric Patient Career: Family Reaction Patterns and Social Work Intervention." *Social Service Review,* 45(1):74–85.

Srole, Leo, Thomas Langer, Stanley Michael, Marvin Opler, and Thomas Rennie. 1962. *Mental Health in the Metropolis: The Midtown Manhattan Study.* New York: McGraw-Hill.

Wulbert, Roland. n.d. "Second Thoughts about Commonplaces." Unpublished paper, Department of Sociology, Columbia University (circa, 1974).

Yarrow, Marian, Charlotte Schwartz, Harriet Murphy, and Leila Deasy. 1955. "The Psychological Meaning of Mental Illness in the Family." *Journal of Social Issues,* 11(4):12–24.

The Adjustment of the Family to the Crisis of Alcoholism

JOAN K. JACKSON

...Over a 3-year period, the present investigator has been an active participant in the Alcoholics Anonymous Auxiliary in Seattle. This group is composed partly of women whose husbands are or were members of Alcoholics Anonymous, and partly of women whose husbands are excessive drinkers but have never contacted Alcoholics Anonymous. At a typical meeting one fifth would be the wives of Alcoholics Anonymous members who have been sober for some time; the husbands of another fifth would have recently joined the fellowship; the remainder would be equally divided between those whose husbands were "on and off" the Alcoholics Anonymous program and those whose husbands had as yet not had any contact with Alcoholics Anonymous.

At least an hour and a half of each formal meeting of this group is taken up with a frank discussion of the current family problems of the members. As in other meetings of Alcoholics Anonymous the questions are posed by describing the situation which gives rise to the problem and the answers are a narration of the personal experi-

Reprinted from *Quarterly Journal of Studies on Alcohol,* Vol. 15 (December, 1954), pp. 564–586.

From the Department of Psychiatry, University of Washington School of Medicine, Seattle, Washington. This report is part of an alcoholism project at the University of Washington which has been supported by the State of Washington Research Fund under Initiative 171.

ences of other wives who have had a similar problem, rather than direct advice. Verbatim shorthand notes have been taken of all discussions, at the request of the group, who also make use of the notes for the group's purposes. Informal contact has been maintained with past and present members. In the past three years 50 women have been members of this group.

The families represented by these women are at present in many different stages of adjustment and have passed through several stages during the past few years. The continuous contact over a prolonged period permits generalizations about processes and changes in family adjustments.

In addition, in connection with research on hospitalized alcoholics, many of their wives have been interviewed. The interviews with the hospitalized alcoholics, as with male members of Alcoholics Anonymous, have also provided information on family interactions. Further information has been derived from another group of wives, not connected with Alcoholics Anonymous, and from probation officers, social workers and court officials.

The following presentation is limited insofar as it deals only with families seeking help for the alcoholism of the husband. Other families are known to have solved the problem through divorce, often without having attempted to help the alcoholic member first. Others never seek help and never separate. There were no marked differences between the two groups seeking help, one through the hospital and one through the A.A. Auxiliary. The wives of hospitalized alcoholics gave a history of the family crisis similar to that given by women in the Auxiliary.

A second limitation is that only the families of male alcoholics are dealt with. It is recognized that the findings cannot be generalized to the families of alcoholic women without further research. Due to differences between men and women in their roles in the family as well as in the pattern of drinking, it would be expected that male and female alcoholics would in some ways have a different effect on family structure and function.

A third limitation is imposed for the sake of clarity and brevity: only the accounts of the wives of their attempts to stabilize their family adjustments will be dealt with. For any complete picture, the view of the alcoholic husband would also have to be included.

It must be emphasized that this paper deals with the definitions of the family situations by the wives, rather than with the actual situation. It has been noted that frequently wife and husband do not agree on what has occurred. The degree to which the definition of the situation by the wife or husband correlates with actual behavior is a question which must be left for further research.

The families represented in this study are from the middle and lower classes. The occupations of the husbands prior to excessive drinking include small business owners, salesmen, business executives, skilled and semiskilled workers. Prior to marriage the wives have been nurses, secretaries, teachers, saleswomen, cooks or waitresses. The economic status of the childhood families of these husbands and wives ranged from very wealthy to very poor.

METHOD

From the records of discussions of the Alcoholics Anonymous Auxiliary, the statements of each wife were extracted and arranged in a time sequence. Notes on informal contacts were added at the point in the sequence where they occurred. The interviews with the wives of hospitalized alcoholics were similarly treated. These working records on individual families were then examined for uniformities of behavior and for regularities in changes over time.

The similarities in the process of adjustment to an alcoholic family member are presented here as stages of variable duration. It should be stressed that only the similarities are dealt with. Although the wives have shared the patterns dealt with here, there have been marked differences in the length of time between stages, in the number of stages passed through up to the present time, and in the relative importance to the family constellation of any one type of behavior. For example, all admitted nagging but the amount of nagging was variable.

When the report of this analysis was completed it was read before a meeting of the Auxiliary with a request for correction of any errors in fact or interpretation. Corrections could be presented either anonymously or publicly from the floor. Only one correction was suggested and has been incorporated. The investigator is convinced that her relationship with the group is such that there would be no reticence about offering corrections. Throughout her contact with this group her role has been that of one who is being taught, very similar to the role of the new member. The overall response of the group to the presentation indicated that the members individually felt that they had been portrayed accurately.

The sense of having similar problems and similar experiences is indicated also in the reactions of new members to the Auxiliary's summarization of the notes of their discussions. Copies of these summaries are given to new members, who commonly state that they find it a relief to see that their problems are far from unique and that there are methods which successfully overcome them.

STATEMENT OF THE PROBLEM

For purposes of this presentation, the family is seen as involved in a cumulative crisis. All family members behave in a manner which they hope will resolve the crisis and permit a return to stability. Each member's action is influenced by his previous personality structure, by his previous role and status in the family group, and by the history of the crisis and its effects on his personality, roles and status up to that point. Action is also influenced by the past effectiveness of that particular action as a means of social control before and during the crisis. The behavior of family members in each phase of the crisis contributes to the form which the crisis takes in the following stages and

sets limits on possible behavior in subsequent stages.

Family members are influenced, in addition, by the cultural definitions of alcoholism as evidence of weakness, inadequacy or sinfulness; by the cultural prescriptions for the roles of family members; and by the cultural values of family solidarity, sanctity and self-sufficiency. Alcoholism in the family poses a situation defined by the culture as shameful but for the handling of which there are no prescriptions which are effective or which permit direct action not in conflict with other cultural prescriptions. While in crises such as illness or death the family members can draw on cultural definitions of appropriate behavior for procedures which will terminate the crisis, this is not the case with alcoholism in the family. The cultural view has been that alcoholism is shameful and should not occur. Only recently has any information been offered to guide families in their behavior toward their alcoholic member and, as yet, this information resides more in technical journals than in the media of mass communication. Thus, in facing alcoholism, the family is in an unstructured situation and must find the techniques for handling it through trial and error.

STAGES IN FAMILY ADJUSTMENT TO AN ALCOHOLIC MEMBER

The Beginning of the Marriage. At the time marriage was considered, the drinking of most of the men was within socially acceptable limits. In a few cases the men were already alcoholics but managed to hide this from their fiancées. They drank only moderately or not at all when on dates and often avoided friends and relatives who might expose their excessive drinking. The relatives and friends who were introduced to the fiancée were those who had hopes that "marriage would straighten him out" and thus said nothing about the drinking. In a small number of cases the men spoke with their fiancées of their alcoholism. The women had no conception of what alcoholism meant, other than that it involved more than the usual frequency of drinking, and they entered the marriage with little more preparation than if they had known nothing about it.

Stage 1. Incidents of excessive drinking begin and, although they are sporadic, place strains on the husband–wife interaction. In attempts to minimize drinking, problems in marital adjustment not related to the drinking are avoided.

Stage 2. Social isolation of the family begins as incidents of excessive drinking multiply. The increasing isolation magnifies the importance of family interactions and events. Behavior and thought become drinking-centered. Husband–wife adjustment deteriorates and tension rises. The wife begins to feel self-pity and to lose her self-confidence as her behavior fails to stabilize her husband's drinking. There is an attempt still to maintain the original family structure, which is disrupted anew with each episode of drinking, and as a result the children begin to show emotional disturbance.

Stage 3. The family gives up attempts to control the drinking and begins to behave in a manner geared to relieve tension rather than achieve long-term ends. The disturbance of the children becomes more marked. There is no longer an attempt to support the alcoholic in his roles as husband and father. The wife begins to worry about her own sanity and about her inability to make decisions or act to change the situation.

Stage 4. The wife takes over control of the family and the husband is seen as a recalcitrant child. Pity and strong protective feelings largely replace the earlier resentment and hostility. The family becomes more stable and organized in a manner to minimize the disruptive behavior of the husband. The self-confidence of the wife begins to be rebuilt.

Stage 5. The wife separates from her husband if she can resolve the problems and conflicts surrounding this action.

Stage 6. The wife and children reorganize as a family without the husband.

Stage 7. The husband achieves sobriety and the family, which had become organized around an alcoholic husband, reorganizes to include a sober father and experiences problems in reinstating him in his former roles.

STAGE 1. ATTEMPTS TO DENY THE PROBLEM

Usually the first experience with drinking as a problem arises in a social situation. The husband drinks in a manner which is inappropriate to the social setting and the expectations of others present. The wife feels embarrassed on the first occasion and humiliated as it occurs more frequently. After several such incidents she and her husband talk over his behavior. The husband either formulates an explanation for the episode and assures her that such behavior will not occur again; or he refuses to discuss it at all. For a time afterward he drinks appropriately and drinking seems to be a problem no longer. The wife looks back on the incidents and feels that she has exaggerated them, feels ashamed of herself for her disloyalty and for her behavior. The husband, in evaluating the incident, feels shame also and vows such episodes will not recur. As a result, both husband and wife attempt to make it up to the other and, for a time, try to play their conceptions of the ideal husband and wife roles, minimizing or avoiding other difficulties which arise in the marriage. They thus create the illusion of a "perfect" marriage.

Eventually another inappropriate drinking episode occurs and the pattern is repeated. The wife worries but takes action only in the situations in which inappropriate drinking occurs, as each long intervening period of acceptable drinking behavior convinces her that a recurrence is unlikely. As time goes on, in attempting to cope with individual episodes, she runs the gamut of possible trial and error behaviors, learning that none is permanently effective.

If she speaks to other people about her husband's drinking, she is usually assured that there is no need for concern, that her husband can control his drinking and that her fears are exaggerated. Some friends possibly admit that his drinking is too heavy and give advice on how they handled similar situations with their husbands. These friends convince her that her problem will be solved as soon as she hits upon the right formula for dealing with her husband's drinking.

During this stage the husband–wife interaction is in no way "abnormal." In a society in which a large proportion of the men drink, most wives have at some time had occasion to be concerned, even though only briefly, with an episode of drinking which they considered inappropriate (1). In a society in which the status of the family depends on that of the husband, the wife feels threatened by any behavior on his part which might lower it. Inappropriate drinking is regarded by her as a threat to the family's reputation and standing in the community. The wife attempts to exert control and often finds herself blocked by the sacredness of drinking behavior to men in America. Drinking is a private matter and not any business of the wife's. On the whole, a man reacts to his wife's suggestion that he has not adequately controlled his drinking with resentment, rebelliousness and a display of emotion which makes rational discussion difficult. The type of husband–wife interaction outlined in this stage has occurred in many American families in which the husband never became an excessive drinker.

STAGE 2. ATTEMPTS TO ELIMINATE THE PROBLEM

Stage 2 begins when the family experiences social isolation because of the husband's drinking. Invitations to the homes of friends become less frequent. When the couple does visit friends, drinks are not served or are limited, thus emphasizing the reason for exclusion from other social activities of the friendship group. Discussions of drinking begin to be side-stepped awkwardly by friends, the wife and the husband.

By this time the periods of socially acceptable drinking are becoming shorter. The wife, fearing that the full extent of her husband's drinking will become known, begins to withdraw from social participation, hoping to reduce the visibility of his behavior, and thus the threat to family status.

Isolation is further intensified because the family usually acts in accordance with the cultural dictate that it should be self-sufficient and manage to resolve its own problems without recourse to outside aid. Any experiences which they have had with well-meaning outsiders, usually relatives, have tended to strengthen this conviction. The husband has defined such relatives as interfering and the situation has deteriorated rather than improved.

With increasing isolation, the family members begin to lose perspective on their interaction and on their problems. Thrown into closer contact with one another as outside contacts diminish, the behavior of each member assumes exaggerated importance. The drinking behavior becomes the focus of anxiety. Gradually all family difficulties become attributed to it. (For example, the mother who is cross with her children will feel that, if her husband had not been drinking, she would not have been so tense and would not have been angry.) The fear that the full extent of drinking may be discovered mounts steadily; the conceptualization of the consequences of such a discovery becomes increasingly vague and, as a result, more anxiety-provoking. The family feels different from others and alone with its shameful secret.

Attempts to cover up increase. The employer who calls to inquire about the husband's absence from work is given excuses. The wife is afraid to face the consequences of loss of the husband's pay check in addition to her other concerns. Questions from the children are evaded or they are told that their father is ill. The wife lives in terror of the day when the children will be told by others of the nature of the "illness." She is also afraid that the children may describe their father's symptoms to teachers or neighbors. Still feeling that the family must solve its own problems, she keeps her troubles to herself and hesitates to seek outside help. If her husband beats her, she will bear it rather than call in the police. (Indeed, often she has no idea that this is even a possibility.) Her increased isolation has left her without the advice of others as to sources of help in the community. If she knows of them, an agency contact means to her an admission of the complete failure of her family as an independent unit. For the middle-class woman particularly, recourse to social agencies and law-enforcement agencies means a terrifying admission of loss of status.

During this stage, husband and wife are drawing further apart. Each feels resentful of the behavior of the other. When this resentment is expressed, further drinking occurs. When it is not, tension mounts and the next drinking episode is that much more destructive of family relationships. The reasons for drinking are explored frantically. Both husband and wife feel that if only they could discover the reason, all members of the family could gear their behavior to making drinking unnecessary. The discussions become increasingly unproductive, as it is the husband's growing conviction that his wife does not and cannot understand him.

On her part, the wife begins to feel that she is a failure, that she has been unable to fulfill the major cultural obligations of a wife to meet her husband's needs. With her increasing isolation, her sense of worth derives almost entirely from her roles as wife and mother. Each failure to help her husband gnaws away at her sense of adequacy as a person.

Periods of sobriety or socially acceptable drinking still occur. These periods keep the wife from making a permanent or stable adjustment. During them her husband, in his guilt, treats her like a queen. His behavior renews her hope and rekindles positive feelings toward him. Her sense of worth is bolstered temporarily and she grasps desperately at her husband's reassurance that she is really a fine person and not a failure and an unlovable shrew. The periods of sobriety also keep her family from facing the inability of the husband to control his drinking. The inaccuracies of the cultural stereotype of the alcoholic—particularly that he is in a constant state of inebriation—also contribute to the family's rejection of the idea

of alcoholism, as the husband seems to demonstrate from time to time that he can control his drinking.

Family efforts to control the husband become desperate. There are no culturally prescribed behavior patterns for handling such a situation and the family is forced to evolve its own techniques. Many different types of behavior are tried but none brings consistent results; there seems to be no way of predicting the consequences of any action that may be taken. All attempts to stabilize or structure the situation to permit consistent behavior fail. Threats of leaving, hiding his liquor away, emptying the bottles down the drain, curtailing his money, are tried in rapid succession, but none is effective. Less punitive methods, as discussing the situation when he is sober, babying him during hangovers, and trying to drink with him to keep him in the home, are attempted and fail. All behavior becomes oriented around the drinking, and the thought of family members becomes obsessive on this subject. As no action seems to be successful in achieving its goal, the wife persists in trial-and-error behavior with mounting frustration. Long-term goals recede into the background and become secondary to just keeping the husband from drinking today.

There is still an attempt to maintain the illusion of husband–wife–children roles. When father is sober, the children are expected to give him respect and obedience. The wife also defers to him in his role as head of the household. Each drinking event thus disrupts family functioning anew. The children begin to show emotional disturbances as a result of the inconsistencies of parental behavior. During periods when the husband is drinking the wife tries to shield them from the knowledge and effects of his behavior, at the same time drawing them closer to herself and deriving emotional support from them. In sober periods, the father tries to regain their favor. Due to experiencing directly only pleasant interactions with their father, considerable affection is often felt for him by the children. This affection becomes increasingly difficult for the isolated wife to tolerate, and an additional source of conflict. She feels that she needs and deserves the love and support of her children and, at the same time, she feels it important to maintain the children's picture of their father. She counts on the husband's affection for the children to motivate a cessation of drinking as he comes to realize the effects of his behavior on them.

In this stage, self-pity begins to be felt by the wife, if it has not entered previously. It continues in various degrees throughout the succeeding stages. In an attempt to handle her deepening sense of inadequacy, the wife often tries to convince herself that she is right and her husband wrong, and this also continues through the following stages. At this point the wife often resembles what Whalen (2) describes as "The Sufferer."

STAGE 3. DISORGANIZATION

The wife begins to adopt a "What's the use?" attitude and to accept her husband's drinking as a problem likely to be permanent. Attempts to understand one another become less frequent. Sober periods still engender hope, but hope qualified by skepticism; they bring about a lessening of anxiety and this is defined as happiness.

By this time some customary patterns of husband–wife–children interaction have evolved. Techniques which have had some effectiveness in controlling the husband in the past or in relieving pent-up frustration are used by the wife. She nags, berates or retreats into silence. Husband and wife are both on the alert, the wife watching for increasing irritability and restlessness which mean a recurrence of drinking, and the husband for veiled aspersions on his behavior or character.

The children are increasingly torn in their loyalties as they become tools in the struggle between mother and father. If the children are at an age of comprehension, they have usually learned the true nature of their family situation, either from outsiders or from their mother, who has given up attempts to bolster her husband's position as father. The children are often bewildered, but questioning their parents brings no satisfactory

answers as the parents themselves do not understand what is happening. Some children become terrified; some have increasing behavior problems within and outside the home; others seem on the surface to accept the situation calmly.[1]

During periods of the husband's drinking, the hostility, resentment and frustrations felt by the couple are allowed expression. Both may resort to violence—the wife in self-defense or because she can find no other outlet for her feelings. In those cases in which the wife retaliates to violence in kind, she feels a mixture of relief and intense shame at having deviated so far from what she conceives to be "the behavior of a normal woman."

When the wife looks at her present behavior, she worries about her "normality." In comparing the person she was in the early years of her marriage with the person she has become, she is frightened. She finds herself nagging and unable to control herself. She resolves to stand up to her husband when he is belligerent but instead finds herself cringing in terror and then despises herself for her lack of courage. If she retaliates with violence, she is filled with self-loathing at behaving in an "unwomanly" manner. She finds herself compulsively searching for bottles, knowing full well that finding them will change nothing, and is worried because she engages in such senseless behavior. She worries about her inability to take constructive action of any kind. She is confused about where her loyalty lies, whether with her husband or her children. She feels she is a failure as a wife, mother and person. She believes she should be strong in the face of adversity and instead feels herself weak.

The wife begins to find herself avoiding sexual contact with her husband when he has been drinking. Sex under these circumstances, she feels, is sex for its own sake rather than an indication of affection for her. Her husband's lack of consideration of her needs to be satisfied leaves her feeling frustrated. The lack of sexual responsiveness reflects her emotional withdrawal from him in other areas of family life. Her husband, on his part, feels frustrated and rejected; he accuses her of frigidity and this adds to her concern about her adequacy as a woman.[2]

By this time the opening wedge has been inserted into the self-sufficiency of the family. The husband has often been in difficulty with the police and the wife has learned that police protection is available. An emergency has occurred in which the seeking of outside help was the only possible action to take; subsequent calls for aid from outsiders do not require the same degree of urgency before they can be undertaken. However, guilt and a lessening of self-respect and self-confidence accompany this method of resolving emergencies. The husband intensifies these feelings by speaking of the interference of outsiders, or of his night in jail.

In Stage 3 all is chaos. Few problems are met constructively. The husband and wife both feel trapped in an intolerable, unstructured situation which offers no way out. The wife's self-assurance is almost completely gone. She is afraid to take action and afraid to let things remain as they are. Fear is one of the major characteristics of this stage: fear of violence, fear of personality damage to the children, fear for her own sanity, fear that relatives will interfere, and fear that they will not help in an emergency. Added to this, the family feels alone in the world and helpless. The problems, and the behavior of family members in attempting to cope with them, seem so shameful that help from others is unthinkable. They feel that attempts to get help would meet only with rebuff, and that communication of the situation will engender disgust.

At this point the clinical picture which the wife presents is very similar to what Whalen (2) has described as "The Waverer."

STAGE 4. ATTEMPTS TO REORGANIZE IN SPITE OF THE PROBLEM

Stage 4 begins when a crisis occurs which necessitates that action be taken. There may be no money or food in the house; the husband may

have been violent to the children; or life on the level of Stage 3 may have become intolerable. At this point some wives leave, thus entering directly into Stage 5.

The wife who passes through Stage 4 usually begins to ease her husband out of his family roles. She assumes husband and father roles. This involves strengthening her role as mother and putting aside her role as wife. She becomes the manager of the home, the discipliner of the children, the decision-maker; she becomes somewhat like Whalen's (2) "Controller." She either ignores her husband as much as possible or treats him as her most recalcitrant child. Techniques are worked out for getting control of his pay check, if there still is one, and money is doled out to her husband on the condition of his good behavior. When he drinks, she threatens to leave him, locks him out of the house, refuses to pay his taxi bills, leaves him in jail overnight rather than pay his bail. Where her obligations to her husband conflict with those to her children, she decides in favor of the latter. As she views her husband increasingly as a child, pity and a sense of being desperately needed by him enter. Her inconsistent behavior toward him deriving from the lack of predictability inherent in the situation up to now, becomes reinforced by her mixed feelings toward him.

In this stage the husband often tries to set his will against hers in decisions about the children. If the children have been permitted to stay with a friend overnight, he may threaten to create a scene unless they return immediately. He may make almost desperate efforts to gain their affection and respect, his behavior ranging from getting them up in the middle of the night to fondle them, to giving them stiff lectures on children's obligations to fathers. Sometimes he will attempt to align the males of the family with him against the females. He may openly express resentment of the children and become belligerent toward them physically or verbally.

Much of the husband's behavior can be conceptualized as resulting from an increasing awareness of his isolation from the other members of the family and their steady withdrawal of respect and affection. It seems to be a desperate effort to regain what he has lost, but without any clear idea of how this can be accomplished—an effort to change a situation in which everyone is seen as against him; and, in reality, this is becoming more and more true. As the wife has taken over control of the family with some degree of success, he feels, and becomes, less and less necessary to the ongoing activity of the family. There are fewer and fewer roles left for him to play. He becomes aware that members of the family enjoy each other's company without him. When he is home he tries to enter this circle of warmth or to smash it. Either way he isolates himself further. He finds that the children discuss with the mother how to manage him and he sees the children acting on the basis of their mother's idea of him. The children refuse to pay attention to his demands: they talk back to him in the same way that they talk back to one another, adding pressure on him to assume the role of just another child. All this leaves him frustrated and, as a result, often aggressive or increasingly absent from home.

The children, on the whole, become more settled in their behavior as the wife takes over the family responsibilities. Decisions are made by her and upheld in the face of their father's attempts to interfere. Participation in activities outside the home is encouraged. Their patterns of interaction with their father are supported by the mother. Whereas in earlier stages the children often felt that there were causal connections between their actions and their father's drinking, they now accept his unpredictability. "Well," says a 6-year-old, "I'll just have to get used to it. I have a drunken father."

The family is more stabilized in one way but in other ways insecurities are multiplied. Pay checks are received less and less regularly. The violence or withdrawal of the father increases. When he is away the wife worries about automobile accidents or injury in fights, which become more and more probable as time passes. The hus-

band may begin to be seriously ill from time to time; his behavior may become quite bizarre. Both of these signs of increasing illness arouse anxiety in the family.

During this stage hopes may rise high for father's "reform" when he begins to verbalize wishes to stop drinking, admits off and on his inability to stop, and sounds desperate for doing something about his drinking. Now may begin the trek to sanitariums for the middle-class alcoholic, to doctors, or to Alcoholics Anonymous. Where just the promise to stop drinking has failed to revive hope, sobriety through outside agencies has the ability to rekindle it brightly. There is the feeling that at last he is "taking really constructive action." In failure the discouragement is deeper. Here another wedge has been inserted into the self-sufficiency of the family.

By this time the wedges are many. The wife, finding she has managed to bring some semblance of order and stability to her family, while not exactly becoming a self-assured person, has regained some sense of worth which grows a little with each crisis she meets successfully. In addition, the very fact of taking action to stabilize the situation brings relief. On some occasion she may be able to approach social agencies for financial help, often during a period when the husband has temporarily deserted or is incarcerated. She may have gone to the family court; she may have consulted a lawyer about getting a restraining order when the husband was in a particularly belligerent state. She has begun to learn her way around among the many agencies which offer help.

Often she has had a talk with an Alcoholics Anonymous member and has begun to look into what is known about alcoholism. If she has attended a few Alcoholics Anonymous meetings, her sense of shame has been greatly alleviated as she finds so many others in the same boat. Her hopes rise as she meets alcoholics who have stopped drinking, and she feels relieved at being able to discuss her problems openly for the first time with an audience which understands fully. She begins to gain perspective on her problem and learns that she herself is involved in what happens to her husband, and that she must change. She exchanges techniques of management with other wives and receives their support in her decisions.

She learns that her husband is ill rather than merely "ornery," and this often serves to quell for the time being thoughts about leaving him which have begun to germinate as she has gained more self-confidence. She learns that help is available but also that her efforts to push him into help are unavailing. She is not only supported in her recently evolved behavior of thinking first of her family, but now this course also emerges from the realm of the unconceptualized and is set in an accepted rationale. She feels more secure in having a reason and a certainty that the group accepts her as "doing the right thing." When she reports deviations from what the group thinks is the "right way," her reasons are understood; she receives solid support but there is also pressure on her to alter her behavior again toward the acceptable. Blaming and self-pity are actively discouraged. In group discussions she still admits to such feelings but learns to recognize them as they arise and to go beyond them to more productive thinking.

How much her altered behavior changes the family situation is uncertain, but it helps her and gives her security from which to venture forth to further actions of a consistent and constructive type, constructive at least from the point of view of keeping her family on as even a keel as possible in the face of the disruptive influence of the husband. With new friends whom she can use as a sounding board for plans, and with her growing acquaintance with the alternatives and possible patterns of behavior, her thinking ceases to be circular and unproductive. Her anxiety about her own sanity is alleviated as she is reassured by others that they have experienced the same concern and that the remedy is to get her own life and her family under better control. As she accomplishes this, the difference in her feelings about herself convinces her that this is so.

Whether or not she has had a contact with wives of Alcoholics Anonymous members or other wives who have been through a similar experience and have emerged successfully, the very fact of taking hold of her situation and gradually making it more manageable adds to her self-confidence. As her husband is less and less able to care for himself or his family, she begins to feel that he needs her and that without her he would be destroyed. Such a feeling makes it difficult for her to think of leaving him. His almost complete social isolation at this point and his cries for help reinforce this conviction of being needed.

The drinking behavior is no longer hidden. Others obviously know about it, and this becomes accepted by the wife and children. Already isolated and insulated against possible rejection, the wife is often surprised to find that she has exaggerated her fears of what would happen were the situation known. However, the unpredictability of her husband's behavior makes her reluctant to form social relationships which could be violently disrupted or to involve others in the possible consequences of his behavior.

STAGE 5. EFFORTS TO ESCAPE THE PROBLEM

Stage 5 may be the terminal one for the marriage. In this stage the wife separates from her husband. Sometimes the marriage is reestablished after a period of sobriety, when it appears certain that the husband will not drink again. If he does revert to drinking, the marriage is sometimes finally terminated but with less emotional stress than the first time. If the husband deserts, being no longer able to tolerate his lack of status in his family, Stage 6 may be entered abruptly.

The events precipitating the decision to terminate the marriage may be near-catastrophic, as when there is an attempt by the husband to kill the wife or children, or they may appear trivial to outsiders, being only the last straw to an accumulation of years.

The problems in coming to the decision to terminate the marriage cannot be underestimated. Some of these problems derive from emotional conflicts; some are related to very practical circumstances in the situation; some are precipitated by the conflicting advice of outsiders. With several children dependent on her, the wife must decide whether the present situation is more detrimental to them than future situations she can see arising if she should leave her husband. The question of where the money to live on will come from must be thought out. If she can get a job, will there be enough to provide for child care also while she is away from home? Should the children, who have already experienced such an unsettled life, be separated from her to be cared for by others? If the family still owns its own home, how can she retain control of it? If she leaves, where can she go? What can be done to tide the family over until her first earnings come in? How can she ensure her husband's continued absence from the home and thus be certain of the safety of individuals and property in her absence? These are only a small sample of the practical issues that must be dealt with in trying to think her way through to a decision to terminate the marriage.

Other pressures act on her to impede the decision-making process. "If he would only stay drunk till I carry out what I intend to do," is a frequent statement. When the husband realizes that his wife really means to leave, he frequently sobers up, watches his behavior in the home, plays on her latent and sometimes conscious feelings of her responsibility for the situation, stresses his need for her and that without her he is lost, tears away at any confidence she has that she will be able to manage by herself, and threatens her and the children with injury or with his own suicide if she carries out her intention.

The children, in the meantime, are pulling and pushing on her emotions. They think she is "spineless" to stay but unfair to father's chances for ultimate recovery if she leaves. Relatives, who were earlier alienated in her attempts to shield her family but now know of the situation, do not believe in its full ramifications. They often feel she is exaggerating and persuade her to stay with him, Especially is this true in the case of a "solitary drinker." His drinking has been so well concealed

that the relatives have no way of knowing the true nature of the situation. Other relatives, afraid that they will be called on for support, exert pressure to keep the marriage intact and the husband thereby responsible for debts. Relatives who feel she should leave him overplay their hands by berating the husband in such a manner as to evoke her defense of him. This makes conscious the positive aspects of her relationship with him, causing her to waver in her decision. If she consults organized agencies, she often gets conflicting advice. The agencies concerned with the well-being of the family may counsel leaving; those concerned with rehabilitating the husband may press her to stay. In addition, help from public organizations almost always involves delay and is frequently not forthcoming at the point where she needs it most.

The wife must come to terms with her own mixed feelings about her husband, her marriage and herself before she can decide on such a step as breaking up the marriage. She must give up hope that she can be of any help to her husband. She must command enough self-confidence, after years of having it eroded, to be able to face an unknown future and leave the security of an unpalatable but familiar past and present. She must accept that she has failed in her marriage, not an easy thing to do after having devoted years to stopping up the cracks in the family structure as they appeared. Breaking up the marriage involves a complete alteration in the life goals toward which all her behavior has been oriented. It is hard for her to rid herself of the feeling that she married him and he is her responsibility. Having thought and planned for so long on a day-to-day basis, it is difficult to plan for a long-term future.

Her taking over of the family raises her self-confidence, but failure to carry through on decisions undermines the new gains that she has made. Vacillation in her decisions tends to exasperate the agencies trying to help her, and she begins to feel that help from them may not be forthcoming if she finally decides to leave.

Some events, however, help her to arrive at a decision. During the absences of her husband she has seen how manageable life can be and how smoothly her family can run. She finds that life goes on without him. The wife who is working comes to feel that "my husband is a luxury I can no longer afford." After a few short-term separations in which she tries out her wings successfully, leaving comes to look more possible. Another step on the path to leaving is the acceptance of the idea that, although she cannot help her husband, she can help her family. She often reaches a state of such emotional isolation from her husband that his behavior no longer disturbs her emotionally but is only something annoying which upsets daily routines and plans.

STAGE 6. REORGANIZATION OF PART OF THE FAMILY

The wife is without her husband and must reorganize her family on this basis. Substantially the process is similar to that in other divorced families, but with some additions. The divorce rarely cuts her relationship to her husband. Unless she and her family disappear, her husband may make attempts to come back. When drunk, he may endanger her job by calls at her place of work. He may attempt violence against members of the family, or he may contact the children and work to gain their loyalty so that pressure is put on the mother to accept him again. Looking back on her marriage, she forgets the full impact of the problem situation on her and on the children and feels more warmly toward her husband, and these feelings can still be manipulated by him. The wide circulation of information on alcoholism as an illness engenders guilt about having deserted a sick man. Gradually, however, the family becomes reorganized.

STAGE 7. RECOVERY AND REORGANIZATION OF THE WHOLE FAMILY

Stage 7 is entered if the husband achieves sobriety, whether or not separation has preceded. It was pointed out that in earlier stages most of the problems in the marriage were attributed to the alcoholism of the husband, and thus problems in adjustment not related directly to the drinking were unrecognized and unmet. Also, the "sober personality" of the husband was thought of as the "real" personality, with a resulting lack of recognition of other factors involved in his sober behavior, such as remorse and guilt over his actions, leading him to act to the best of his ability like "the ideal husband" when sober. Irritation or other signs of growing tension were viewed as indicators of further drinking, and hence the problems giving rise to them were walked around gingerly rather than faced and resolved. Lack of conflict and lack of drinking were defined as indicating a perfect adjustment. For the wife and husband facing a sober marriage after many years of an alcoholic marriage, the expectations of what marriage without alcoholism will be are unrealistically idealistic, and the reality of marriage almost inevitably brings disillusionments. The expectation that all would go well and that all problems be resolved with the cessation of the husband's drinking cannot be met and this threatens the marriage from time to time.

The beginning of sobriety for the husband does not bring too great hope to the family at first. They have been through this before but are willing to help him along and stand by him in the new attempt. As the length of sobriety increases, so do the hopes for its permanence and efforts to be of help. The wife at first finds it difficult to think more than in terms of today, waking each morning with fear of what the day will bring and sighing with relief at the end of each sober day.

With the continuation of sobriety, many problems begin to crop up. Mother has for years managed the family, and now father again wishes to be reinstated in his former roles. Usually the first role reestablished is that of breadwinner, and the economic problems of the family begin to be alleviated as debts are gradually paid and there is enough left over for current needs. With the resumption of this role, the husband feels that the family should also accept him at least as a partner in the management of the family. Even if the wife is willing to hand over some of the control of the children, for example, the children often are not able to accept this change easily. Their mother has been both parents for so long that it takes time to get used to the idea of consulting their father on problems and asking for his decisions. Often the father tries too hard to manage this change overnight, and the very pressure put on the children toward this end defeats him. In addition, he is unable to meet many of the demands the children make on him because he has never really become acquainted with them or learned to understand them and is lacking in much necessary background knowledge of their lives.

The wife, who finds it difficult to conceive of her husband as permanently sober, feels an unwillingness to let control slip from her hands. At the same time she realizes that reinstatement of her husband in his family roles is necessary to his sobriety. She also realizes that the closer his involvement in the family the greater the probability of his remaining sober. Yet she remembers events in the past in which his failure to handle his responsibilities was catastrophic to the family. Used to avoiding anything which might upset him, the wife often hesitates to discuss problems openly. At times, if she is successful in helping him to regain his roles as father, she feels resentful of his intrusion into territory she has come to regard as hers. If he makes errors in judgment which affect the family adversely, her former feelings of being his superior may come to the fore and affect her interaction with him. If the children begin to turn to him, she may feel a resurgence of self-pity at being left out and find herself attempting to swing the children back toward herself. Above all, however, she finds herself feeling resentful that some other agency achieved what she and the children could not.

Often the husband makes demands for obedience, for consideration and for pampering which members of the family feel unable to meet. He may become rather euphoric as his sobriety continues and feel superior for a time.

Gradually, however, the drinking problem sinks into the past and marital adjustment at some level is achieved. Even when this has occurred, the drinking problem crops up occasionally, as when the time comes for a decision about whether the children should be permitted to drink. The mother at such times becomes anxious, sees in the child traits which remind her of her husband, worries whether these are the traits which mean future alcoholism. At parties, at first, she is watchful and concerned about whether her husband will take a drink or not. Relatives and friends may, in a party mood, make the husband the center of attention by emphasizing his nondrinking. They may unwittingly cast aspersions on his character by trying to convince him that he can now "drink like a man." Some relatives and friends have gone so far as secretly to "spike" a non-alcoholic drink and then cry "bottoms up!" without realizing the risk of reactivating patterns from the past.

If sobriety has come through Alcoholics Anonymous, the husband frequently throws himself so wholeheartedly into A.A. activities that his wife sees little of him and feels neglected. As she worries less about his drinking, she may press him to cut down on these activities. That this is dangerous, since A.A. activity is correlated with success in Alcoholics Anonymous, has been shown by Lahey (4). Also, the wife discovers that, though she has a sober husband, she is by no means free of alcoholics. In his Twelfth Step work, he may keep the house filled with men he is helping. In the past her husband has avoided self-searching; and now he may become excessively introspective, and it may be difficult for her to deal with this.

If the husband becomes sober through Alcoholics Anonymous and the wife participates actively in groups open to her, the thoughts of what is happening to her, to her husband and to her family will be verbalized and interpreted within the framework of the Alcoholics Anonymous philosophy and the situation will probably be more tolerable and more easily worked out....

SUMMARY

The onset of alcoholism in a family member has been viewed as precipitating a cumulative crisis for the family. Seven critical stages have been delineated. Each stage affects the form which the following one will take. The family finds itself in an unstructured situation which is undefined by the culture. Thus it is forced to evolve techniques of adjustment by trial and error. The unpredictability of the situation, added to its lack of structure, engenders anxiety in family members which gives rise to personality difficulties. Factors in the culture, in the environment and within the family situation prolong the crisis and deter the working out of permanent adjustment patterns. With the arrest of the alcoholism, the crisis enters its final stage. The family attempts to reorganize to include the ex-alcoholic and makes adjustments to the changes which have occurred in him.

It has been suggested that the clinical picture presented by the wife to helping agencies is not only indicative of a type of basic personality structure but also of the stage in family adjustment to an alcoholic. That the wives of alcoholics represent a rather limited number of personality types can be interpreted in two ways, which are not mutually exclusive.

(*a*) That women with certain personality attributes tend to select alcoholics or potential alcoholics as husbands in order to satisfy unconscious personality needs;

(*b*) That women undergoing similar experiences of stress, within similarly unstructured situations, defined by the culture and reacted to by members of the society in such a manner as to place limits on the range of possible behavior, will emerge from this experience showing many similar neurotic personality traits. As the situation evolves some of these personality traits will also change. Changes have been observed in the women studied which correlate with altered family interaction patterns. This hypothesis is supported also by observations on the behavior of individuals in other unstructured situations, in situations in which they were isolated from supporting group interaction. It is congruent also with the theory of reactions to increased and decreased stress.

NOTES

1. Some effects of alcoholism of the father on children have been discussed by Newell (3).
2. It is of interest here that marriage counselors and students of marital adjustment are of the opinion that unhappy marriage results in poor sexual adjustment more often than poor sexual adjustment leads to unhappy marriage. If this proves to be true, it would be expected that most wives of alcoholics would find sex distasteful while their husbands are drinking. The wives of the inactive alcoholics report that their sexual adjustments with their husbands are currently satisfactory; many of those whose husbands are still drinking state that they enjoyed sexual relationships before the alcoholism was established.

REFERENCES

1. Club and Educational Bureaus of Newsweek. 1950. "Is Alcoholism Everyone's Problem?" Platform, N.Y., p. 3 (January).
2. Whalen, T. 1953. "Wives of Alcoholics: Four Types Observed in a Family Service Agency." *Quarterly Journal of Studies on Alcohol,* 14:632–641.
3. Newell, N. 1950. "Alcoholism and the Father-image." *Quarterly Journal of Studies on Alcohol,* 11:92–96.
4. Lahey, W. W. 1950. *A Comparison of Social and Personal Factors Identified with Selected Members of Alcoholics Anonymous.* Master's Thesis: University of Southern California.

CHAPTER 3

THE CULTURAL CONTEXT

Cultures include ideas about different types of people. While most of these ideas deal with conventional types, many deal with deviant types. In analyzing these ideas about deviance, a number of questions can be posed. What categories of deviance are found in a particular culture? Who formulates these categories? Who has the right to apply these labels, and what norms affect the application and consequence of these labels? Finally, whose interests are served by these definitions of deviance?

In the first selection Jane Mercer claims that because higher-class people have a clearer definition of mental retardation than do lower-class people, higher-class parents are more likely to label one of their children retarded and to institutionalize the child. Peter Conrad discusses the medicalization of deviance and the implications of the creation of the "hyperkinetic syndrome" label by doctors. Finally, Craig Reinarman argues that media, entrepreneurs, and interest groups combined at different stages in U.S. history to define users of drugs as members of the "dangerous classes."

Labeling the Mentally Retarded

JANE R. MERCER

The clinical perspective is the frame of reference most commonly adopted in studies of mental deficiency, mental illness, drug addiction, and other areas which the students of deviance choose to investigate.[1,2] This viewpoint is readily identified by several distinguishing characteristics.

First, the investigator accepts as the focus for study those individuals who have been labeled deviant. In so doing, he adopts the values of whatever social system has defined the person as deviant and assumes that its judgements are the valid measure of deviance.... Groups in the social structure sharing the values of the core culture tend to accept the labels attached as a consequence of the application of these values without serious questioning....

A second distinguishing characteristic of the clinical perspective is the tendency to perceive deviance as an attribute of the person, as a meaning inherent in his behavior, appearance, or performance. Mental retardation, for example, is viewed as a characteristic of the person, a lack to be explained. This viewpoint results in a quest for etiology. Thus, the clinical perspective is essentially a medical frame of reference, for it sees deviance as individual pathology requiring diagnostic classification and etiological analysis for

Reprinted from "Social System Perspective and Clinical Perspective: Frames of Reference for Understanding Career Patterns of People Labeled as Mentally Retarded," *Social Problems,* 13:1 (Summer 1965), pp. 21–30, 33–34, by permission of the Society for the Study of Social Problems and the author.

Supported in part by the National Institute of Mental Health, Grant No. 3M-9130: Population Movement of Mental Defectives and Related Physical, Behavioral, Social, and Cultural Factors; and Grant No. MH-5687: Mental Retardation in a Community, Pacific State Hospital, Pomona, California. Appreciation for assistance is expressed to the Western Data Processing Center, Division of the Graduate School of Business Administration, University of California, Los Angeles.

the purpose of determining proper treatment procedures and probable prognosis.

Three additional characteristics of the clinical perspective are the development of a diagnostic nomenclature, the creation of diagnostic instruments, and the professionalization of the diagnostic function.

When the investigator begins his research with the diagnostic designations assigned by official defining agents, he tends to assume that all individuals placed in a given category are essentially equivalent in respect to their deviance.... Individuals assigned to different categories of deviance are compared with each other or with a "normal" population consisting of persons who, for whatever reason, have escaped being labeled. The focus is on the individual.

Another characteristic of the clinical perspective is its assumption that the official definition is somehow the "right" definition....

Finally, when deviance is perceived as individual pathology, social action tends to center upon changing the individual or, that failing, removing him from participation in society. Prevention and cure become the primary social goals....

The social system [labeling] perspective, on the other hand, attempts to see the definition of an individual's behavior as a function of the values of the social system within which he is being evaluated. The professional definers are studied as one of the most important of the evaluating social systems but within the context of other social systems which may or may not concur with official definitions.

Defining an individual as mentally ill, delinquent, or mentally retarded is viewed as an interpersonal process in which the definer makes a value judgement about the behavior of the persons being defined.... Deviation is not seen as a characteristic of the individual or as a meaning inherent in his behavior, but as a socially derived label which may be attached to his behavior by some social systems and not by others.[3]

... Thus, it follows that a person may be mentally retarded in one system and not mentally retarded in another. He may change his label by changing his social group. This viewpoint frees us from the necessity of seeing the person as permanently stigmatized by a deviant label and makes it possible to understand otherwise obscure patterns in the life careers of individuals.... The research reported in this paper attempts to answer these questions about a group of persons who shared the common experience of having been labeled retarded by official defining agencies and placed in a public institution for the retarded....

The specific question which this study seeks to investigate within the above framework is: "Why do the families of some individuals take them back home after a period of institutionalization in a hospital for the retarded while other families do not, when, according to official evaluations, these individuals show similar degrees of deviance, that is, have comparable intelligence test scores, and are of equivalent age, sex, ethnic status, and length of hospitalization?"...

METHOD

Two groups of labeled retardates were studied. One group consisted of patients who had been released to their families from a state hospital for the retarded and the other group consisted of a matched group of patients still resident in the hospital at the time of the study.[4]

Specifically, the released group was made up of all patients released to their families during a three year period (1957–59), who had not been readmitted to another institution for the retarded at the time of the study, and who were reported to be living within a one hundred mile radius of the hospital. Only those cases in which the family had

assumed responsibility for the patient were included. Of the 76 patients who met these qualifications, it was possible to complete interviews with 63 of the families. Six families refused to be interviewed and seven could not be located.

The resident group was selected to match the released group in intelligence quotient, age, sex, ethnic status, and year of admission, other studies having demonstrated that these factors are related to the probability of release.[5]

The matched group of resident patients was selected in the following manner: all patients on the hospital rolls were sorted into two groups by sex, two groups by age, three groups by ethnic status, three groups by intelligence quotient, and two groups by year of admission. All released patients were likewise assigned to the proper category. Resident patients were than chosen at random from within each cell in sufficient numbers to correspond to the number of discharged patients also falling in that cell. Each resident case was required to have a family living within a one hundred mile radius of the hospital. If a case did not meet this requirement, another case was drawn randomly from the appropriate cell until there was an equal number of discharged and resident cases in each cell. Sex distribution in each group was 53 males and 23 females; ethnic distribution, 47 Caucasians, 20 Mexicans, and 9 [African Americans].

... Of the 76 resident cases selected to match the released cases, interviews were completed with 70 families. Two refused to be interviewed and four families could not be located. Using a Kolmogorov-Smirnov Test of two independent samples, we found that all differences between the interviewed groups could be accounted for by chance.

When the 19 non-interviewed cases were compared with the 133 interviewed cases, no significant differences were found in the sex, age, I.Q., or ethnic status of the patients, or the socioeconomic level of the families....

The hospital file for each patient selected for the study was searched for relevant data and an interview was held with a family member. In 75% of the cases the mother was interviewed; in 8% the father was interviewed; and in the remaining cases some other relative served as informant....

To clarify the circumstances under which members of the released group returned to their families, the respondent was asked two questions: "Who was the most important person in getting you to take——out of the hospital?" and "What were the main reasons you decided to have——discharged from the hospital?"

In 12 cases the parents reported that someone in the hospital, i.e., a social worker, family care mother, or a ward technician, had first suggested that the patient could be released to the family. In the 51 remaining cases the families were the active agents in release....

It is clear... that most of the patients who returned to their families returned because the family made an effort to secure their release....

FINDINGS

SOCIAL STATUS OF RELEASED PATIENTS

Several indices were used to measure the socioeconomic level of the family of each retardate. A socioeconomic index score based on the occupation and education of the head of the household, weighted according to Hollingshead's system, was used as the basic measure. In addition, the interviewer rated the economic status of the street on which the patient's home was located, rated the physical condition of the housing unit, and completed a checklist of equipment present in the household.... [T]he families of the released patients rated significantly lower than the families of the resident patients on every measure. The heads of the households in the families of released patients had less education and lower level jobs, the family residence was located among less affluent dwellings, the housing unit was in a poorer state of repair, and the dwelling was less elaborately furnished and equipped. Contrary to the pattern

found in studies of those placed as mentally ill,[6] it is the "retardate" from lower socioeconomic background who is most likely to be released to his family while higher status "retardates" are more likely to remain in the hospital.

From the clinical perspective, several explanations may be proposed for these differences. It has been found in hospital populations that patients with an I.Q. below 50 are more likely to come from families which represent a cross-section of social levels, while those with an I.Q. between 50 and 70 are more likely to come from low status families.[7] Since persons with higher I.Q.'s have a higher probability of release, this could account for higher rates of release for low status persons. However, in the present study, the tested level of intelligence was equal for both groups, and this hypothesis cannot be used as an explanation.

A second possible explanation from a clinical perspective might be based on the fact that persons who have more physical handicaps tend to be institutionalized for longer periods of time than persons with few handicaps.[8] Should it be found that high status patients have more physical handicaps than low status patients, then this could account for the latter's shorter hospitalization. Data from the present sample were analyzed to determine whether there was a significant relationship between physical handicap and social status. Although released patients tended to have fewer physical handicaps than resident patients, this was irrespective of social status. When high status patients were compared with low status patients, 50% of the high status and 56% of the low status patients had no physical handicaps....

A third explanation from the clinical perspective may hinge on differences in the diagnostic categories to which retardates of different social status were assigned.... A diagnostic label of "familial" or "undifferentiated" ordinarily indicates that the individual has few or no physical stigmata and is essentially normal in body structure. All other categories ordinarily indicate that he has some type of physical symptomatology. Although released patients were more likely to be diagnosed as familial or undifferentiated than resident patients...this, like physical handicap, was irrespective of social status. Fifty-seven per cent of the high status retardates, and 69% of the low status retardates were classified as either undifferentiated or familial, a difference which could be accounted for by chance....

DIVERGENT DEFINITIONS

In analyzing social status, four types of situations were identified. The modal category for resident patients was high social status with a smaller number of resident patients coming from low status families. The modal category for released patients was low status with a smaller number of released patients coming from higher status families. If we are correct in our hypothesis (that higher release rates for low status patients are related to the fact that the family social system [labeling] is structurally more distant from the core culture and that its style of life, values, and definitions of the patient are more divergent from official definitions than that of high status families), we could expect the largest differences to occur when high status resident families are compared to low status released families....

[T]hree questions [were] asked to determine the extent to which family members concurred in the official label of "retardation," the extent to which they believed the patient's condition amenable to change, and the extent to which they anticipated that the individual could live outside the hospital and, perhaps, fill adult roles. The patterns of the divergent definitions of the situation which emerged for each group are illuminating.

When asked whether *he* believed the patient to be retarded, the high status parent more frequently concurred with the definitions of the official defining agencies while the low status parent was more prone to disagree outright or to be uncertain. This tendency is especially marked when the two modal categories are compared. While 33.3% of the parents of the low status released patients stated that they did not think the patient was retarded and 25.6% were uncertain whether he was retarded, only 4.6% of the parents of high status resident patients felt he was not retarded and 20.9% were uncertain.

When parents were asked whether they believed anything could change the patient's condition, the differences between all groups were significant at the .02 level or beyond. The high status parent was most likely to believe that nothing could change his child's condition, and this was significantly more characteristic of parents whose children were still in the hospital than those who had taken their child from the hospital on both status levels.

When asked what they saw in the future for their child, all groups again differed significantly in the expected direction. The modal, high status group was least optimistic and the modal, low status group, most optimistic about the future. Fully 46% of the parents of the latter group expressed the expectation that their child would get a job, marry, and fulfill the usual adult roles while only 6.9% of the modal, high status group responded in this fashion. High status parents, as a group, more frequently see their child playing dependent roles. It is interesting to note that, although a large percentage of parents of released patients believe the patient will be dependent, they demonstrate their willingness to accept responsibility for the retarded child themselves by their responding that they foresee him having a future in which he is dependent at home. Only 9.3% of the high status and 22.2% of the low status parents of the resident patients see this as a future prospect. Release to the family clearly appears to be contingent upon the willingness of the family to accept the patient's dependency, if they do not foresee him assuming independent adult roles.

FACTORS IN THE LABELING PROCESS

From the social system [labeling] perspective, retardation is viewed as a label placed upon an individual after someone has evaluated his behavior within a specific set of norms. Retardation is not a meaning necessarily inherent in the behavior of the individual. We have seen that the parents of low status, released patients tend to reject the label of retardation and to be optimistic about the future. We surmised that this divergent definition could well be related to factors in the process by which the child was first categorized as subnormal, such as his age at the time, the type of behavior which was used as a basis for making the evaluation, and the persons doing the labeling. Consequently, parents were asked specifically about these factors....

Children from lower status families were labeled as mentally subnormal at a significantly later age than children from high status families. Seventy-nine per cent of the patients in the high status, modal group were classified as retarded by the age of six while only 36.1% of those in the low status, modal group were identified at such an early age. The largest percentage of low status retardates were first classified after they reached public school age. This indicates that relatives and friends, who are the individuals most likely to observe and evaluate the behavior of young children, seldom saw anything deviant in the early development of lower status children later labeled retarded, but that the primary groups of higher status children did perceive early deviation.

This is related to the responses made when parents were asked what first prompted someone to believe the patient retarded. The modal, high status group reported slow development in 48.8% of the cases and various types of physical symptoms in an additional 20.9%, while only 14.7% and 11.8% of the modal, low status parents gave these responses. On the other hand, 55.9% of the modal, low status group were first labeled because they had problems learning in school, while this was true of only 9.3% of the modal high status group.

When parents were asked who was the most important person influencing them in placing the child in the hospital, a parallel pattern emerged. Medical persons are the most important single group for the modal, high status persons while the police and welfare agencies loom very significant in 64.1% of the cases in the modal, low status group. These findings are similar to those of Hollingshead and Redlich in their study of paths of the hospital for the mentally ill.[9] Of additional interest is the fact that the person important in placement differentiates the low status released from the low status resident patient at the .01 level. The resident low status patient's path to the hospital is similar to that of the high status patient and markedly different from released low status persons. When authoritative figures such as police and welfare are primary forces in placement, the patient is more likely to return home.

We interpret these findings to mean that when the family—or persons whose advice is solicited by the family, i.e., medical persons—is "most important" in placing a person in a hospital for the retarded, the primary groups have themselves first defined the individual as a deviant and sought professional counsel. When their own suspicions are supported by official definitions, they are most likely to leave the patient in an institution.

Conversely, when a person is labeled retarded by an authoritative, government agency whose advice is not solicited and who, in the case of the police, may be perceived as a punishing agent, the family frequently rejects the official definition of the child as retarded and withdraws him from the institution at the first opportunity. This attitude was clearly exemplified by one mother who, when asked why the family had taken the child from the hospital, replied, "Why not? He had served his time."

The police [are more of] a factor in labeling the low status person as retarded.... Fifty per cent of the low status retardates had some type of police record while only 23% of the high status subnormals were known to the police....

DISCUSSION AND CONCLUSIONS

The life space of the individual may be viewed as a vast network of interlocking social systems [labeling] through which the person moves during the course of his lifetime. Those systems which exist close to one another in the social structure tend, because of overlapping memberships and frequent communication, to evolve similar patterns of norms. Most individuals are born and live out their lives in a relatively limited segment of this social network and tend to contact mainly social systems which share common norms. When an individual's contacts are restricted to a circumscribed segment of the structure, this gives some stability to the evaluations which are made of his behavior and to the labels which are attached to him.

However, when the person's life career takes him into segments of the social network which are located at a distance from his point of origin, as when a Mexican-American child enters the public school or a black child gets picked up by police, he is then judged by a new and different set of norms. Behavior which was perfectly acceptable in his primary social systems [labeling] may now be judged as evidence of "mental retardation." At this point, he is caught up in the web of official definitions. However, because he has primary social systems [labeling] which may not agree with these official labels, he may be able to return to that segment of the social structure which does not label him as deviant after he has fulfilled the minimal requirements of the official system. That is, he can drop out of school or he can "serve his time" in the state hospital and then go home. By changing his location in social space, he can change his label from "retarded" to "not much different from the rest of us." For example, the mother of a Mexican-American, male, adult patient who had been released from the hospital after being committed following an incident in which he allegedly made sexual advances to a young girl, told the author, "There is nothing wrong with Benny. He just can't read or write." Since the mother spoke only broken English, had no formal schooling, and could not read or write, Benny did not appear deviant to her. From her perspective, he didn't have anything wrong with him.

The child from a high status family has no such recourse. His primary social systems [labeling] lie structurally close to the official social systems and tend to concur on what is acceptable. Definitions of his subnormality appear early in his life and are more universal in all his social groups. He cannot escape the retarded label because all his associates agree that he is a deviant.[10]

In conclusion, tentative answers may be given to the three questions raised earlier in this discussion. "Who sees whom as retarded?" Within the social system perspective, it becomes clear that persons who are clinically similar may be defined quite differently by their primary social systems. The person from lower status social systems is less likely to be perceived as mentally subnormal.

"What impact does this differential definition have on the life career of the person?" Apparently, these differential definitions do make a difference because the group which diverges most widely from official definitions is the group in which the most individuals are released from the institution to their families.

Finally, "What are the characteristics of the social systems [labeling] which diverge most widely from official definitions?" These social systems [labeling] seem to be characterized by low educational achievement, high levels of dependency, and high concentrations of ethnic minorities.

A social system [labeling] perspective adds a useful dimension to the label "mental retardation" by its focus on the varied definitions which may be applied to behavior by different groups in society. For those interested in the care and treatment of persons officially labelled as mentally subnormal, it may be beneficial in some cases to seek systematically to relocate such individuals in the social structure in groups which will not define them as deviant. Rather than insisting that family members adopt official definitions of abnormality, we may frequently find it advisable to permit them to continue to view the patient within their own frame of reference and thus make it easier for them to accept him.

NOTES

1. August B. Hollingshead and Frederick C. Redlich, *Social Class and Mental Illness,* New York: John Wiley and Sons, 1958, Chapter 11.
2. H. E. Freeman and O. G. Simmons, "Social Class and Posthospital Performance Levels," *American Sociological Review,* 2 (June, 1959), p. 348.
3. Howard S. Becker, editor, *The Other Side: Perspectives on Deviance,* New York: The Free Press, 1964.
4. Pacific State Hospital, Pomona, California, is a state supported hospital for the mentally retarded with a population of approximately 3,000 patients.
5. G. Tarjan, S. W. Wright, M. Kramer, P. H. Person, Jr., and R. Morgan, "The Natural History of Mental Deficiency in a State Hospital. I: Probabilities of Release and Death by Age, Intelligence Quotients, and Diagnosis," *AMA J. Dis. Childr.,* 96 (1958), pp. 64–70.

6. August B. Hollingshead and Frederick C. Redlich, 1958, *op. cit.,* Chapter 11.
7. Georges Sabagh, Harvey F. Dingman, George Tarjan, and Stanley W. Wright, "Social Class and Ethnic Status of Patients Admitted to a State Hospital for the Retarded," *Pacific Sociological Review,* 2 (Fall, 1959), pp. 76–80.
8. G. Tarjan, S. W. Wright, M. Kramer, R. H. Person, Jr., and R. Morgan, 96, 1958, *op. cit.,* pp. 64–70.
9. August B. Hollingshead and Frederick C. Redlich, 1958, *op. cit.,* Chapter 11.
10. Lewis Anthony Dexter, "On the Politics and Sociology of Stupidity in Our Society" in *The Other Side: Perspectives on Deviance,* edited by Howard S. Becker, New York: The Free Press, 1964, pp. 37–49.

The Medicalization of Deviance in American Culture

PETER CONRAD

INTRODUCTION

The increasing medicalization of deviant behavior and the medical institution's role as an agent of social control has gained considerable notice (Freidson, 1970; Pitts, 1971; Kittrie, 1971; Zola, 1972). By medicalization we mean defining behavior as a medical problem or illness and mandating or licensing the medical profession to provide some type of treatment for it. Examples include alcoholism, drug addiction and treating violence as a genetic or brain disorder. This redefinition is not a new function of the medical institution: psychiatry and public health have always been concerned with social behavior and have traditionally functioned as agents of social control (Foucault, 1965; Szasz, 1970; Rosen, 1972)....

Reprinted from "The Discovery of Hyperkinesis: Notes on the Medicalization of Deviant Behavior," *Social Problems,* Vol. 23, No. 1 (October 1975), pp. 12–21, by permission of the Society for the Study of Social Problems and the author.

This paper describes how certain forms of behavior in children have become defined as a medical problem and how medicine has become a major agent for their social control since the discovery of hyperkinesis. By discovery we mean both origin of the diagnosis and treatment for this disorder; and discovery of children who exhibit this behavior. The first section analyzes the discovery of hyperkinesis and why it suddenly became popular in the 1960's. The second section will discuss the medicalization of deviant behavior and its ramifications.

THE MEDICAL DIAGNOSIS
OF HYPERKINESIS

Hyperkinesis is a relatively recent phenomenon as a medical diagnostic category. Only in the past two decades has it been available as a recognized diagnostic category and only in the last decade has it received widespread notice and medical popularity. However, the roots of the diagnosis and treatment of this clinical entity are found earlier.

Hyperkinesis is also known as Minimal Brain Dysfunction, Hyperactive Syndrome, Hyperkinetic Disorder of Childhood, and by several other diagnostic categories. Although the symptoms and the presumed etiology vary, in general the behaviors are quite similar and greatly overlap. [1] Typical symptom patterns for diagnosing the disorder include: extreme excess of motor activity (hyperactivity); very short attention span (the child flits from activity to activity); restlessness; fidgetiness; often wildly oscillating mood swings (he's fine one day, a terror the next); clumsiness; aggressive-like behavior; impulsivity; in school he cannot sit still, cannot comply with rules, has low frustration level; frequently there may be sleeping problems and acquisition of speech may be delayed (Stewart, 1966, 1970; Wender, 1971). Most of the symptoms for the disorder are deviant behaviors.[2] It is six times as prevalent among boys as among girls. We use the term hyperkinesis to represent all the diagnostic categories of this disorder.

THE DISCOVERY OF HYPERKINESIS

It is useful to divide the analysis into what might be considered *clinical factors* directly related to the diagnosis and treatment of hyperkinesis and *social factors* that set the context for the emergence of the new diagnostic category.

CLINICAL FACTORS

Bradley (1937) observed that amphetamine drugs had a spectacular effect in altering the behavior of school children who exhibited behavior disorders or learning disabilities. Fifteen of the thirty children he treated actually became more subdued in their behavior. Bradley termed the effect of this medication paradoxical, since he expected that amphetamines would stimulate children as they stimulated adults. After the medication was discontinued the children's behavior returned to premedication level.

A scattering of reports in the medical literature on the utility of stimulant medications for "childhood behavior disorders" appeared in the next two decades. The next significant contribution was the work of Strauss and his associates (Strauss and Lehtinen, 1947) who found certain behavior (including hyperkinesis behaviors) in postencephaletic children suffering from what they called minimal brain injury (damage). This was the first time these behaviors were attributed to the new organic distinction of minimal brain damage.

This disorder still remained unnamed or else it was called a variety of names (usually just "childhood behavior disorder"). It did not appear as a specific diagnostic category until Laufer, et al. (1957) described it as the "hyperkinetic impulse disorder" in 1957. Upon finding "the salient characteristics of the behavior pattern . . . are strikingly similar to those with clear cut organic causation" these researchers described a disorder with no clear-cut history or evidence for organicity (Laufer, et al., 1957).

In 1966 a task force sponsored by the U.S. Public Health Service and the National Association for Crippled Children and Adults attempted to clarify the ambiguity and confusion in terminology and symptomology in diagnosing children's behavior and learning disorders. From over three dozen diagnoses, they agreed on the term "minimal brain dysfunction" as an overriding diagnosis that would include hyperkinesis and other disorders (Clements, 1966). Since this time M.B.D. has been the primary formal diagnosis or label.

In the middle 1950's a new drug, Ritalin, was synthesized, that has many qualities of amphetamines without some of their more undesirable side effects. In 1961 this drug was approved by the F.D.A. for use with children. Since this time there has been much research published on the use of Ritalin in the treatment of childhood behavior disorders. This medication became the "treatment of choice" for treating children with hyperkinesis.

Since the early sixties, more research appeared on the etiology, diagnosis and treatment of hyperkinesis (cf. DeLong, 1972; Grinspoon and Singer, 1973; Cole, 1975)—as much as three-quarters concerned with drug treatment of the disorder. There had been increasing publicity of the disorder in the mass media as well. The *Reader's Guide to Periodical Literature* had no articles on hyperkinesis before 1967, one each in 1968 and 1969 and a total of forty for 1970 through 1974 (a mean of eight per year).

Now hyperkinesis has become the most common child psychiatric problem (Gross and Wilson, 1974: 142); special pediatric clinics have been established to treat hyperkinetic children, and substantial federal funds have been invested in etiological and treatment research. Outside the medical profession, teachers have developed a working clinical knowledge of hyperkinesis' symptoms and treatment (cf. Robin and Bosco, 1973); articles appear regularly in mass circulation magazines and newspapers so that parents often come to clinics with knowledge of this diagnosis. Hyperkinesis is no longer the relatively esoteric diagnostic category it may have been twenty years ago, it is now a well-known clinical disorder.

SOCIAL FACTORS

The social factors affecting the discovery of hyperkinesis can be divided into two areas: (1) The Pharmaceutical Revolution; (2) Government Action.

(1) *The Pharmaceutical Revolution.* Since the 1930's the pharmaceutical industry has been synthesizing and manufacturing a large number of psychoactive drugs, contributing to a virtual revolution in drug making and drug taking in America (Silverman and Lee, 1974).

Psychoactive drugs are agents that affect the central nervous system. Benzedrine, Ritalin, and Dexedrine are all synthesized psychoactive stimulants which were indicated for narcolepsy, appetite control (as "diet pills"), mild depression, fatigue, and more recently hyperkinetic children.

Until the early sixties there was little or no promotion and advertisement of any of these medications for use with childhood disorders.[3] Then two major pharmaceutical firms (Smith, Kline and French, manufacturer of Dexedrine, and CIBA, manufacturer of Ritalin) began to advertise in medical journals and through direct mailing and efforts of the "detail men." Most of this advertising of the pharmaceutical treatment of hyperkinesis was directed to the medical sphere; but some of the promotion was targeted for the educational sector also (Hentoff, 1972). This promotion was probably significant in disseminating information concerning the diagnosis and treatment of this newly discovered disorder.[4] Since 1955 the use of psychoactive medications (especially phenothiazines) for the treatment of persons who are mentally ill, along with the concurrent dramatic decline in inpatient populations, has made psychopharmacology an integral part of treatment for mental disorders. It has also undoubtedly increased the confidence in the medical profession for the pharmaceutical approach to mental and behavioral problems.

(2) *Government Action.* Since the publication of the U.S.P.H.S. report on M.B.D. there have been at least two significant governmental reports on treating school children with stimulant medications for behavior disorders. Both of these came as a response to the national publicity created by the *Washington Post* report (1970) that five to ten percent of the 62,000 grammar school children in Omaha, Nebraska were being treated with "behavior modification drugs to improve deportment and increase learning potential" (quoted in Grinspoon and Singer, 1973). Although the figures were later found to be a little exaggerated, it nevertheless spurred a Congressional investigation (U.S. Government Printing Office, 1970) and a conference sponsored by the Office of Child Development (1971) on the use of stimulant drugs in the treatment of behaviorally disturbed school children.

The Congressional Subcommittee on Privacy chaired by Congressman Cornelius E. Gallagher held hearings on the issue of prescribing drugs for hyperactive school children. In general, the committee showed great concern over the facility in which the medication was prescribed; more specifically that some children at least were receiving drugs from general practitioners whose primary diagnosis was based on teachers' and parents' reports that the child was doing poorly in school. There was also a concern with the absence of follow-up studies on the long-term effects of treatment.

The H.E.W. committee was a rather hastily convened group of professionals (a majority were M.D.'s) many of whom already had commitments to drug treatment for children's behavior problems. They recommended that only M.D.'s make the diagnosis and prescribe treatment, that the pharmaceutical companies promote the treatment of the disorder only through medical channels, that parents should not be coerced to accept any particular treatment and that long-term follow-up research should be done. This report served as blue ribbon approval for treating hyperkinesis with psychoactive medications.

DISCUSSION

We will focus discussion on three issues: How children's deviant behavior became conceptualized as a medical problem; why this occurred when it did; and what are some of the implications of the medicalization of deviant behavior.

How does deviant behavior become conceptualized as a medical problem? We assume that before the discovery of hyperkinesis this type of deviance was seen as disruptive, disobedient, rebellious, anti-social or deviant behavior. Perhaps the label "emotionally disturbed" was sometimes used, when it was in vogue in the early sixties, and the child was usually managed in the context of the family or the school or in extreme cases, the child guidance clinic. How then did this constellation of deviant behaviors become a medical disorder?

The treatment was available long before the disorder treated was clearly conceptualized. It was

twenty years after Bradley's discovery of the "paradoxical effect" of stimulants on certain deviant children that Laufer named the disorder and described its characteristic symptoms. Only in the late fifties were both the diagnostic label and the pharmaceutical treatment available. The pharmaceutical revolution in mental health and the increased interest in child psychiatry provided a favorable background for the dissemination of knowledge about this new disorder. The latter probably made the medical profession more likely to consider behavior problems in children as within their clinical jurisdiction.

There were agents outside the medical profession itself that were significant in "promoting" hyperkinesis as a disorder within the medical framework. These agents might be conceptualized in Becker's terms as "moral entrepreneurs," those who crusade for creation and enforcement of the rules (Becker, 1963).[5] In this case the moral entrepreneurs were the pharmaceutical companies and the Association for Children with Learning Disabilities.

The pharmaceutical companies spent considerable time and money promoting stimulant medications for this new disorder. From the middle 1960's on, medical journals and the free "throwaway" magazines contained elaborate advertising for Ritalin and Dexedrine. These ads explained the utility of treating hyperkinesis and urged the physician to diagnose and treat hyperkinetic children. The ads run from one to six pages. For example, a two-page ad in 1971 stated:

MBD ... MEDICAL MYTH OR DIAGNOSABLE DISEASE ENTITY What medical practitioner has not, at one time or another, been called upon to examine an impulsive, excitable hyperkinetic child? A child with difficulty in concentrating. Easily frustrated. Unusually aggressive. A classroom rebel. In the absence of any organic pathology, the conduct of such children was, until a few short years ago, usually dismissed as ... spunkiness, or evidence of youthful vitality. But it is now evident that in many of these children the hyperkinetic syndrome exists as a distinct medical entity. This syndrome is readily diagnosed through patient histories, neurologic signs, and psychometric testing—has been classified by an expert panel convened by the United States Department of Health, Education and Welfare as Minimal Brain Dysfunction, MBD.

The pharmaceutical firms also supplied sophisticated packets of "diagnostic and treatment" information on hyperkinesis to physicians, paid for professional conferences on the subject, and supported research in the identification and treatment of the disorder. Clearly these corporations had a vested interest in the labeling and treatment of hyperkinesis; CIBA had $13 million profit from Ritalin alone in 1971, which was 15 percent of the total gross profits (Charles, 1971; Hentoff, 1972).

The other moral entrepreneur, less powerful than the pharmaceutical companies, but nevertheless influential, is the Association for Children with Learning Disabilities. Although their focus is not specifically on hyperkinetic children, they do include it in their conception of Learning Disabilities along with aphasia, reading problems like dyslexia and perceptual motor problems. Founded in the early 1950's by parents and professionals, it has functioned much as the National Association for Mental Health does for mental illness: promoting conferences, sponsoring legislation, providing social support. One of the main functions has been to disseminate information concerning this relatively new area in education, Learning Disabilities. While the organization does have a more educational than medical perspective, most of the literature indicates that for hyperkinesis members have adopted the medical model and the medical approach to the problem. They have sensitized teachers and schools to the conception of hyperkinesis as a medical problem.

The medical model of hyperactive behavior has become very well accepted in our society. Physicians find treatment relatively simple and the results sometimes spectacular. Hyperkinesis minimizes parents' guilt by emphasizing "it's not their fault, it's an organic problem" and allows for nonpunitive management or control of deviance. Medication often makes a child less disruptive in the classroom and sometimes aids a child in learning. Children often like their "magic pills" which make their behavior more socially acceptable and they probably benefit from a reduced stigma also.

THE MEDICALIZATION OF DEVIANT BEHAVIOR

Pitts has commented that "medicalization is one of the most effective means of social control and that it is destined to become the main mode of *formal* social control" (1971:391). Kittrie (1971) has termed it "the coming of the therapeutic state."

Medicalization of mental illness dates at least from the seventeenth century (Foucault, 1965; Szasz, 1970). Even slaves who ran away were once considered to be suffering from the disease *drapedomania* (Chorover, 1973). In recent years alcoholism, violence, and drug addiction as well as hyperactive behavior in children have all become defined as medical problems, both in etiology or explanation of the behavior and the means of social control or treatment.

There are many reasons why this medicalization has occurred. Much scientific research, especially in pharmacology and genetics, has become technologically more sophisticated, and found more subtle correlates with human behavior. Sometimes these findings (as in the case of XYY chromosomes and violence) become etiological explanations for deviance. Pharmacological technology that makes new discoveries affecting behavior (e.g., antabuse, methadone and stimulants) are used as treatment for deviance. In part this application is encouraged by the prestige of the medical profession and its attachment to science. As Freidson notes, the medical profession has first claim to jurisdiction over anything that deals with the functioning of the body and especially anything that can be labeled illness (1970:251). Advances in genetics, pharmacology and "psychosurgery" also may advance medicine's jurisdiction over deviant behavior.

Second, the application of pharmacological technology is related to the humanitarian trend in the conception and control of deviant behavior. Alcoholism is no longer sin or even moral weakness, it is now a disease. Alcoholics are no longer arrested in many places for "public drunkenness," they are now somehow "treated," even if it is only to be dried out. Hyperactive children are now considered to have an illness rather than to be disruptive, disobedient, overactive problem children. They are not as likely to be the "bad boy" of the classroom; they are children with a medical disorder. Clearly there are some real humanitarian benefits to be gained by such a medical conceptualization of deviant behavior. There is less condemnation of the deviants (they have an illness, it is not their fault) and perhaps less social stigma. In some cases, even the medical treatment itself is more humanitarian social control than the criminal justice system.

There is, however, another side to the medicalization of deviant behavior. The four aspects of this side of the issue include (1) the problem of expert control; (2) medical social control; (3) the individualization of social problems; and (4) the "depoliticization" of deviant behavior.

1. *The problem of expert control.* The medical profession is a profession of experts; they have a monopoly on anything that can be conceptualized as illness. Because of the way the medical profession is organized and the mandate it has from society, decisions related to medical diagnoses and treatment are virtually controlled by medical professionals.

Some conditions that enter the medical domain are not *ipso facto* medical problems, especially deviant behavior, whether alcoholism, hyperactivity or drug addiction. By defining a problem as medical it is removed from the public realm where there can be discussion by ordinary people and put on a plane where only medical people can discuss it. As Reynolds states,

The increasing acceptance, especially among the more educated segments of our populace, of tech-nical solutions—solutions administered by disinterested politically and morally neutral experts—results in the withdrawal of more and more areas of human experience from the realm of public discussion. For when drunkenness, juvenile delinquency, sub par performance and extreme political beliefs are seen as symptoms of an underlying illness or biological defect the merits and drawbacks of such behavior or beliefs need not be evaluated (1973:200–221).

The public may have their own conceptions of deviant behavior but that of the experts is usually dominant.

2. *Medical social control.* Defining deviant behavior as a medical problem allows certain things to be done that could not otherwise be considered; for example, the body may be cut open or psychoactive medications may be given. This treatment can be a form of social control.

In regard to drug treatment Lennard points out: "Psychoactive drugs, especially those legally prescribed, tend to restrain individuals from behavior and experience that are not complementary to the requirements of the dominant value system" (1971:57). These forms of medical social control presume a prior definition of deviance as a medical problem. Psychosurgery on an individual prone to violent outbursts requires a diagnosis that there was something wrong with his brain or nervous system. Similarly, prescribing drugs to restless, overactive and disruptive school children requires a diagnosis of hyperkinesis. These forms of social control, what Chorover (1973) has called "psychotechnology," are very powerful and often very efficient means of controlling deviance. These relatively new and increasingly popular forms of social control could not be utilized without the medicalization of deviant behavior. As is suggested from the discovery of hyperkinesis, if a mechanism of medical social control seems useful, then the deviant behavior it modifies will develop a medical label or diagnosis. No overt malevolence on the part of the medical profession is implied: rather it is part of a complex process, of which the medical profession is only a part.

The larger process might be called the individualization of social problems.

3. *The individualization of social problems.* The medicalization of deviant behavior is part of a larger phenomenon that is prevalent in our society, the individualization of social problems. We tend to look for causes and solutions to complex social problems in the individual rather than in the social system. This view resembles Ryan's (1971) notion of "blaming the victim"; seeing the causes of the problem in individuals rather than in the society where they live. We then seek to change the "victim" rather than the society. The medical perspective of diagnosing an illness in an individual lends itself to the individualization of social problems. Rather than seeing certain deviant behaviors as symptomatic of problems in the social system, the medical perspective focuses on the individual diagnosing and treating the illness, generally ignoring the social situation.

Hyperkinesis serves as a good example. Both the school and the parents are concerned with the child's behavior; the child is very difficult at home and disruptive in school. No punishments or rewards seem consistently to work in modifying the behavior; and both parents and school are at their wits' end. A medical evaluation is suggested. The diagnoses of hyperkinetic behavior leads to prescribing stimulant medications. The child's behavior seems to become more socially acceptable, reducing problems in school and at home.

But there is an alternate perspective. By focusing on the symptoms and defining them as hyperkinesis we ignore the possibility that behavior is not an illness but an adaptation to a social situation. It diverts our attention from the family or school and from seriously entertaining the idea that the "problem" could be in the structure of the social system. And by giving medications we are essentially supporting the existing systems and do not allow this behavior to be a factor of change in the system.

4. *The depoliticization of deviant behavior.* Depoliticization of deviant behavior is a result of both the process of medicalization and individualization of social problems. To our western world, probably one of the clearest examples of such a depoliticization of deviant behavior occurred when political dissenters in the Soviet Union were declared mentally ill and confined in mental hospitals (cf. Conrad, 1972). This strategy served to neutralize the meaning of political protest and dissent, rendering it the ravings of mad persons.

The medicalization of deviant behavior depoliticizes deviance in the same manner. By defining the overactive, restless and disruptive child as hyperkinetic we ignore the meaning of behavior in the context of the social system. If we focused our analysis on the school system we might see the child's behavior as symptomatic of some "disorder" in the school or classroom situation, rather than symptomatic of an individual neurological disorder.

CONCLUSION

I have discussed the social ramifications of the medicalization of deviant behavior, using hyperkinesis as the example. A number of consequences of this medicalization have been outlined, including the depoliticization of deviant behavior, decision-making power of experts, and the role of medicine as an agent of social control. In the last analysis medical social control may be the central issue, as in this role medicine becomes a *de facto* agent of the *status quo*. The medical profession may not have entirely sought this role, but its members have been, in general, disturbingly unconcerned and unquestioning in their acceptance of it. With the increasing medical knowledge and technology it is likely that more deviant behavior will be medicalized and medicine's social control function will expand.

NOTES

1. The U.S.P.H.S. report (Clements, 1966) included 38 terms that were used to describe or distinguish the condi-

tions that it labeled Minimal Brain Dysfunction. Although the literature attempts to differentiate M.B.D., hyperkinesis, hyperactive syndrome, and several other diagnostic labels, it is our belief that in practice they are almost interchangeable.

2. For a fuller discussion of the construction of the diagnosis of hyperkinesis, see Conrad (1976), especially Chapter 6.

3. The American Medical Association's change in policy in accepting more pharmaceutical advertising in the late fifties may have been important. Probably the F.D.A. approval of the use of Ritalin for children in 1961 was more significant. Until 1970, Ritalin was advertised for treatment of "functional behavior problems in children." Since then, because of an F.D.A. order, it has only been promoted for treatment of M.B.D.

4. The drug industry spends fully 25 percent of its budget on promotion and advertising. See Coleman et al. (1966) for the role of the detail men and how physicians rely upon them for information.

5. Freidson also notes the medical professional role as moral entrepreneur in this process also:

> The profession does treat the illnesses laymen take to it, but it also seeks to discover illness of which the laymen may not even be aware. One of the greatest ambitions of the physician is to discover and describe a "new" disease or syndrome . . . (1970:252).

REFERENCES

Becker, Howard S. 1963. *Outsiders: Studies in the Sociology of deviance.* New York: Free Press.

Bradley, Charles. 1937. "The Behavior of Children Receiving Benzedrine." *American Journal of Psychiatry,* 94 (March): 577–585.

Charles, Alan. 1971. "The Case of Ritalin." *New Republic,* 23 (October): 17–19.

Chorover, Stephen L. 1973. "Big Brother and Psychotechnology." *Psychology Today* (October): 43–54.

Clements, Samuel D. 1966. "Task Force I: Minimal Brain Dysfunction in Children." National Institute of Neurological Diseases and Blindness, Monograph no. 3. Washington, D.C.: U.S. Department of Health, Education, and Welfare.

Cole, Sherwood. 1975. "Hyperactive Children: The Use of Stimulant Drugs Evaluated." *American Journal of Orthopsychiatry,* 45 (January): 28–37.

Coleman, James, Elihu Katz, and Herbert Menzel. 1966. *Medical Innovation.* Indianapolis: Bobbs-Merrill.

Conrad, Peter. 1972. "Ideological Deviance: An Analysis of the Soviet Use of Mental Hospitals for Political Dissenters." Unpublished manuscript.

Conrad, Peter. 1976. *Identifying Hyperactive Children: A Study in the Medicalization of Deviant Behavior.* Lexington, Mass.: D. C. Heath and Co.

DeLong, Arthur R. (1972). "What Have We Learned from Psychoactive Drugs Research with Hyperactives?" *American Journal of Diseases in Children,* 123 (February): 177–180.

Foucault, Michel. 1965. *Madness and Civilization.* New York: Pantheon.

Freidson, Eliot. 1970. *Profession of Medicine: A Study of the Sociology of Applied Knowledge.* New York: Dodd, Mead.

Grinspoon, Lester and Susan Singer. 1973. "Amphetamines in the Treatment of Hyperactive Children." *Harvard Educational Review,* 43 (November): 515–555.

Gross, Mortimer B. and William E. Wilson. 1974. *Minimal Brain Dysfunction.* New York: Brunner Mazel.

Hentoff, Nat (1972). "Drug Pushing in the Schools: The Professionals." *The Village Voice,* 22 (May): 21–23.

Kittrie, Nicholas. 1971. *The Right to Be Different.* Baltimore: Johns Hopkins Press.

Laufer, M. W., Denhoff, E., and Solomons, G. 1975. "Hyperkinetic Impulse Disorder in Children's Behavior Problems." *Psychosomatic Medicine,* 19 (January): 38–49.

Lennard, Henry L. and Associates. 1971. *Mystification and Drug Misuse.* New York: Harper and Row.

Office of Child Development. 1971. "Report of the Conference on the Use of Stimulant Drugs in Treatment of Behaviorally Disturbed Children." Washington, D.C.: Office of Child Development, Department of Health, Education and Welfare, January 11–12.

Pitts, Jesse. 1968. "Social Control: The Concept." In David Sills (ed.), *International Encyclopedia of the Social Sciences.* Vol. 14. New York: Macmillan.

Reynolds, Janice M. 1973. "The Medical Institution." In Larry T. Reynolds and James M. Henslin, *American Society: A Critical Analysis.* New York: David McKay.

Robin, Stanley S. and James J. Bosco. 1973. "Ritalin for School Children: The Teacher's Perspective." *Journal of School Health,* 47 (December): 624–628.

Rosen, George. 1972. "The Evolution of Social Medicine." In Howard E. Freeman, Sol Levine, and Leo

Reeder, *Handbook of Medical Sociology*. Englewood Cliffs, N.J.: Prentice-Hall.

Ryan, William. 1970. *Blaming the Victim*. New York: Vintage.

Silverman, Milton and Philip R. Lee. 1974. *Pills, Profits and Politics*. Berkeley: University of California Press.

Sroufe, L. Alan and Mark Stewart. 1973. "Treating Problem Children with Stimulant Drugs." *New England Journal of Medicine* 289 (August 23): 407–421.

Stewart, Mark A. 1970. "Hyperactive Children." *Scientific American*, 222 (April): 794–798.

Stewart, Mark A., A. Ferris, N. P. Pitts, and A. G. Craig. 1966. "The Hyperactive Child Syndrome." *American Journal of Orthopsychiatry*, 36 (October): 861–867.

Strauss, A. A. and L. E. Lehtinen. 1947. *Psychopathology and Education of the Brain-Injured Child*. Vol. 1. New York: Grune and Stratton.

U.S. Government Printing Office. 1970. "Federal Involvement in the Use of Behavior Modification Drugs on Grammar School Children of the Right to Privacy Inquiry: Hearing Before a Subcommittee of the Committee on Government Operations." Washington, D.C.: 91st Congress, 2nd session (September 29).

Wender, Paul. 1971. *Minimal Brain Dysfunction in Children*. New York: John Wiley and Sons.

Zola, Irving. 1972. "Medicine as an Institution of Social Control." *Sociological Review,* 20 (November): 487–504.

The Social Construction of Drug Scares

CRAIG REINARMAN

Drug "wars," anti-drug crusades, and other periods of marked public concern about drugs are never merely reactions to the various troubles people can have with drugs. These drug scares are recurring cultural and political phenomena *in their own right* and must, therefore, be understood sociologically on their own terms. It is important to understand why people ingest drugs and why some of them develop problems that have something to do with having ingested them. But the premise of this [paper] is that it is equally important to understand patterns of acute societal concern about drug use and drug problems. This seems especially so for U.S. society, which has had *recurring* anti-drug crusades and a *history* of repressive anti-drug laws.

Many well-intentioned drug policy reform efforts in the U.S. have come face to face with staid

and stubborn sentiments against consciousness-altering substances. The repeated failures of such reform efforts cannot be explained solely in terms of ill-informed or manipulative leaders. Something deeper is involved, something woven into the very fabric of American culture, something which explains why claims that some drug is the cause of much of what is wrong with the world are *believed* so often by so many. The origins and nature of the *appeal* of anti-drug claims must be confronted if we are ever to understand how "drug problems" are constructed in the U.S. such that more enlightened and effective drug policies have been so difficult to achieve.

In this [paper] I take a step in this direction. First, I summarize briefly some of the major periods of anti-drug sentiment in the U.S. Second, I draw from them the basic ingredients of which drug scares and drug laws are made. Third, I offer a beginning interpretation of these scares and laws based on those broad features of American

Reprinted by permission of Craig Reinarman.

culture that make *self-control* continuously problematic.

DRUG SCARES AND DRUG LAWS

What I have called drug scares (Reinarman and Levine, 1989a) have been a recurring feature of U.S. society for 200 years. They are relatively autonomous from whatever drug-related problems exist or are said to exist.[1] I call them "scares" because, like Red Scares, they are a form of moral panic ideologically constructed so as to construe one or another chemical bogeyman, à la "communists," as the core cause of a wide array of pre-existing public problems.

The first and most significant drug scare was over drink. Temperance movement leaders constructed this scare beginning in the late 18th and early 19th century. It reached its formal end with the passage of Prohibition in 1919.[2] As Gusfield showed in his classic book *Symbolic Crusade* (1963), there was far more to the battle against booze than long-standing drinking problems. Temperance crusaders tended to be native born, middle-class, non-urban Protestants who felt threatened by the working-class, Catholic immigrants who were filling up America's cities during industrialization.[3] The latter were what Gusfield termed "unrepentant deviants" in that they continued their long-standing drinking practices despite middle-class W.A.S.P. norms against them. The battle over booze was the terrain on which was fought a cornucopia of cultural conflicts, particularly over whose morality would be the dominant morality in America.

In the course of this century-long struggle, the often wild claims of Temperance leaders appealed to millions of middle-class people seeking explanations for the pressing social and economic problems of industrializing America. Many corporate supporters of Prohibition threw their financial and ideological weight behind the Anti-Saloon League and other Temperance and Prohibitionist groups because they felt that traditional working-class drinking practices interfered with the new rhythms of the factory, and thus with productivity and profits (Rumbarger, 1989). To the Temperance crusaders' fear of the bar room as the breeding ground of all sorts of tragic immorality, Prohibitionists added the idea of the saloon as an alien, subversive place where unionists organized and where leftists and anarchists found recruits (Levine, 1984).

This convergence of claims and interests rendered alcohol a scapegoat for most of the nation's poverty, crime, moral degeneracy, "broken" families, illegitimacy, unemployment, and personal and business failure—problems whose sources lay in broader economic and political forces. This scare climaxed in the first two decades of this century, a tumultuous period rife with class, racial, cultural, and political conflict brought on by the wrenching changes of industrialization, immigration, and urbanization (Levine, 1984; Levine and Reinarman, 1991).

America's first real drug law was San Francisco's anti-opium den ordinance of 1875. The context of the campaign for this law shared many features with the context of the Temperance movement. Opiates had long been widely and legally available without a prescription in hundreds of medicines (Brecher, 1972; Musto, 1973; Courtwright, 1982; cf. Baumohl, 1992), so neither opiate use nor addiction was really the issue. This campaign focused almost exclusively on what was called the "Mongolian vice" of opium *smoking* by Chinese immigrants (and white "fellow travelers") in dens (Baumohl, 1992). Chinese immigrants came to California as "coolie" labor to build the railroad and dig the gold mines. A small minority of them brought along the practice of smoking opium—a practice originally brought to China by British and American traders in the 19th century. When the railroad was completed and the gold dried up, a decade-long depression ensued. In a tight labor market, Chinese immigrants were a target. The white Workingman's Party fomented racial hatred of the low-wage "coolies" with whom they now had to compete for work. The first law against opium smoking was only one of many laws enacted to harass and control Chinese workers (Morgan, 1978).

By calling attention to this broader political-economic context I do not wish to slight the specifics of the local political-economic context. In addition to the Workingman's Party, downtown businessmen formed merchant associations and urban families formed improvement associations, both of which fought for more than two decades to reduce the impact of San Francisco's vice districts on the order and health of the central business district and on family neighborhoods (Baumohl, 1992).

In this sense, the anti-opium den ordinance was not the clear and direct result of a sudden drug scare alone. The law was passed against a specific form of drug use engaged in by a disreputable group that had come to be seen as threatening in lean economic times. But it passed easily because this new threat was understood against the broader historical backdrop of long-standing local concerns about various vices as threats to public health, public morals, and public order. Moreover, the focus of attention were dens where it was suspected that whites came into intimate contact with "filthy, idolatrous" Chinese (see Baumohl, 1992). Some local law enforcement leaders, for example, complained that Chinese men were using this vice to seduce white women into sexual slavery (Morgan, 1978). Whatever the hazards of opium smoking, its initial criminalization in San Francisco had to do with both a general context of recession, class conflict, and racism, and with specific local interests in the control of vice and the prevention of miscegenation.

A nationwide scare focusing on opiates and cocaine began in the early 20th century. These drugs had been widely used for years, but were first criminalized when the addict population began to shift from predominantly white, middle-class, middle-aged women to young, working-class males, African-Americans in particular. This scare led to the Harrison Narcotics Act of 1914, the first federal anti-drug law (see Duster, 1970).

Many different moral entrepreneurs guided its passage over a six-year campaign: State Department diplomats seeking a drug treaty as a means of expanding trade with China, trade which they felt was crucial for pulling the economy out of recession; the medical and pharmaceutical professions whose interests were threatened by self-medication with unregulated proprietary tonics, many of which contained cocaine or opiates; reformers seeking to control what they saw as the deviance of immigrants and Southern Blacks who were migrating off the farms; and a pliant press which routinely linked drug use with prostitutes, criminals, transient workers (e.g., the Wobblies), and African-Americans (Musto, 1973). In order to gain the support of Southern Congressmen for a new federal law that might infringe on "states' rights," State Department officials and other crusaders repeatedly spread unsubstantiated suspicions, repeated in the press, that, e.g., cocaine induced African-American men to rape white women (Musto, 1973:6–10, 67). In short, there was more to this drug scare, too, than mere drug problems.

In the Great Depression, Harry Anslinger of the Federal Narcotics Bureau pushed Congress for a federal law against marijuana. He claimed it was a "killer weed" and he spread stories to the press suggesting that it induced violence—especially among Mexican-Americans. Although there was no evidence that marijuana was widely used, much less that it had any untoward effects, his crusade resulted in its criminalization in 1937—and not incidentally a turnaround in his Bureau's fiscal fortunes (Dickson, 1968). In this case, a new drug law was put in place by a militant moral-bureaucratic entrepreneur who played on racial fears and manipulated a press willing to repeat even his most absurd claims in a context of class conflict during the Depression (Becker, 1963). While there was not a marked scare at the time, Anslinger's claims were never contested in Congress because they played upon racial fears and widely held Victorian values against taking drugs solely for pleasure.

In the drug scare of the 1960s, political and moral leaders somehow reconceptualized this same "killer weed" as the "drop out drug" that was leading America's youth to rebellion and ruin (Himmelstein, 1983). Bio-medical scientists also published uncontrolled, retrospective studies of very small numbers of cases suggesting that, in addition to poisoning the minds and morals of youth, LSD produced broken chromosomes and thus genetic damage (Cohen et al., 1967). These studies were soon shown to be seriously misleading if not meaningless (Tijo et al., 1969), but not before the press, politicians, the medical profession, and the National Institute of Mental Health used them to promote a scare (Weil, 1972:44–46).

I suggest that the reason even supposedly hard-headed scientists were drawn into such propaganda was that dominant groups felt the country was at war—and not merely with Vietnam. In this scare, there was not so much a "dangerous class" or threatening racial group as multi-faceted political and cultural conflict, particularly between generations, which gave rise to the perception that middle-class youth who rejected conventional values were a dangerous threat.[4] This scare resulted in the Comprehensive Drug Abuse Control Act of 1970, which criminalized more forms of drug use and subjected users to harsher penalties.

Most recently we have seen the crack scare, which began in earnest *not* when the prevalence of cocaine use quadrupled in the late 1970s, nor even when thousands of users began to smoke it in the more potent and dangerous form of freebase. Indeed, when this scare was launched, crack was unknown outside of a few neighborhoods in a handful of major cities (Reinarman and Levine, 1989a) and the prevalence of illicit drug use had been dropping for several years (National Institute on Drug Abuse, 1990). Rather, this most recent scare began in 1986 when freebase cocaine was renamed crack (or "rock") and sold in pre-cooked, inexpensive units on ghetto streetcorners (Reinarman and Levine, 1989b). Once politicians and the media linked this new form of cocaine use to the

inner-city, minority poor, a new drug scare was underway and the solution became more prison cells rather than more treatment slots.

The same sorts of wild claims and Draconian policy proposals of Temperance and Prohibition leaders re-surfaced in the crack scare. Politicians have so outdone each other in getting "tough on drugs" that each year since crack came on the scene in 1986 they have passed more repressive laws providing billions more for law enforcement, longer sentences, and more drug offenses punishable by death. One result is the U.S. now has more people in prison than any industrialized nation in the world—about half of them for drug offenses, the majority of whom are racial minorities.

In each of these periods more repressive drug laws were passed on the grounds that they would reduce drug use and drug problems. I have found no evidence that any scare actually accomplished those ends, but they did greatly expand the quantity and quality of social control, particularly over subordinate groups perceived as dangerous or threatening. Reading across these historical episodes one can abstract a recipe for drug scares and repressive drug laws that contains the following *seven ingredients:*

1. *A Kernel of Truth.* Humans have ingested fermented beverages at least since human civilization moved from hunting and gathering into primitive agriculture thousands of years ago (Levine, forthcoming). The pharmacopia has expanded exponentially since then. So, in virtually all cultures and historical epochs, there has been sufficient ingestion of consciousness-altering chemicals to provide some basis for some people to claim that it is a problem.

2. *Media Magnification.* In each of the episodes I have summarized and many others, the mass media has engaged in what I call the *routinization of caricature*—rhetorically re-crafting worst cases into typical cases and the episodic into the epidemic. The media dramatize drug problems, as they do other problems, in the course of their routine news-generating and sales-promoting proce-

dures (see Brecher, 1972:321–34; Reinarman and Duskin, 1992; and Molotch and Lester, 1974).

3. *Politico-Moral Entrepreneurs.* I have added the prefix "politico" to Becker's (1963) seminal concept of moral entrepreneur in order to emphasize the fact that the most prominent and powerful moral entrepreneurs in drug scares are often political elites. Otherwise, I employ the term just as he intended: to denote the *enterprise,* the work, of those who create (or enforce) a rule against what they see as a social evil.[5]

In the history of drug problems in the U.S., these entrepreneurs call attention to drug using behavior and define it as a threat about which "something must be done." They also serve as the media's primary source of sound bites on the dangers of this or that drug. In all the scares I have noted, these entrepreneurs had interests of their own (often financial) which had little to do with drugs. Political elites typically find drugs a functional demon in that (like "outside agitators") drugs allow them to deflect attention from other, more systemic sources of public problems for which they would otherwise have to take some responsibility. Unlike almost every other political issue, however, to be "tough on drugs" in American political culture allows a leader to take a firm stand without risking votes or campaign contributions.

4. *Professional Interest Groups.* In each drug scare and during the passage of each drug law, various professional interests contended over what Gusfield (1981:10–15) calls the "ownership" of drug problems—"the ability to create and influence the public definition of a problem" (1981:10), and thus to define what should be done about it. These groups have included industrialists, churches, the American Medical Association, the American Pharmaceutical Association, various law enforcement agencies, scientists, and most recently the treatment industry and groups of those former addicts converted to disease ideology.[6] These groups claim for themselves, by virtue of their specialized forms of knowledge, the

legitimacy and authority to name what is wrong and to prescribe the solution, usually garnering resources as a result.

5. *Historical Context of Conflict.* This trinity of the media, moral entrepreneurs, and professional interests typically interact in such a way as to inflate the extant "kernel of truth" about drug use. But this interaction does not by itself give rise to drug scares or drug laws without underlying conflicts which make drugs into functional villains. Although Temperance crusaders persuaded millions to pledge abstinence, they campaigned for years without achieving alcohol control laws. However, in the tumultuous period leading up to Prohibition, there were revolutions in Russia and Mexico, World War I, massive immigration and impoverishment, and socialist, anarchist, and labor movements, to say nothing of increases in routine problems such as crime. I submit that all this conflict made for a level of cultural anxiety that provided fertile ideological soil for Prohibition. In each of the other scares, similar conflicts—economic, political, cultural, class, racial, or a combination—provided a context in which claims makers could viably construe certain classes of drug users as a threat.

6. *Linking a Form of Drug Use to a "Dangerous Class."* Drug scares are never about drugs per se, because drugs are inanimate objects without social consequence until they are ingested by humans. Rather, drug scares are about the use of a drug by particular groups of people who are, typically, *already* perceived by powerful groups as some kind of threat (see Duster, 1970; Himmelstein, 1978). It was not so much alcohol problems *per se* that most animated the drive for Prohibition but the behavior and morality of what dominant groups saw as the "dangerous class" of urban, immigrant, Catholic, working-class drinkers (Gusfield, 1963; Rumbarger, 1989). It was *Chinese* opium smoking dens, not the more widespread use of other opiates, that prompted California's first drug law in the 1870's. It was only when smokable cocaine found its way to the African-

American and Latino underclass that it made headlines and prompted calls for a drug war. In each case, politico-moral entrepreneurs were able to construct a "drug problem" by linking a substance to a group of users perceived by the powerful as disreputable, dangerous, or otherwise threatening.

7. *Scapegoating a Drug for a Wide Array of Public Problems.* The final ingredient is scapegoating, i.e., blaming a drug or its alleged effects on a group of its users for a variety of pre-existing social ills that are typically only indirectly associated with it. Scapegoating may be the most crucial element because it gives great explanatory power and thus broader resonance to claims about the horrors of drugs (particularly in the conflictual historical contexts in which drug scares tend to occur).

Scapegoating was abundant in each of the cases noted above. To listen to Temperance crusaders, for example, one might have believed that without alcohol use, America would be a land of infinite economic progress with no poverty, crime, mental illness, or even sex outside marriage. To listen to leaders of organized medicine and the government in the 1960s, one might have surmised that without marijuana and LSD there would have been neither conflict between youth and their parents nor opposition to the Vietnam War. And to believe politicians and the media in the past 6 years is to believe that without the scourge of crack the inner cities and the so-called underclass would, if not disappear, at least be far less scarred by poverty, violence, and crime. There is no historical evidence supporting any of this.

In short, drugs are richly functional scapegoats. They provide elites with fig leaves to place over unsightly social ills that are endemic to the social system over which they preside. And they provide the public with a restricted aperture of attribution in which only a chemical bogeyman or the lone deviants who ingest it are seen as the cause of a cornucopia of complex problems.

TOWARD A CULTURALLY-SPECIFIC THEORY OF DRUG SCARES

Various forms of drug use have been and are widespread in almost all societies comparable to ours. A few of them have experienced limited drug scares, usually around alcohol decades ago. However, drug scares have been *far* less common in other societies, and never as virulent as they have been in the U.S. (Brecher, 1972; Levine, 1992; MacAndrew and Edgerton, 1969). There has never been a time or place in human history without drunkenness, for example, but in *most* times and places drunkenness has not been nearly as problematic as it has been in the U.S. since the late 18th century (Levine, forthcoming). Moreover, in comparable industrial democracies, drug laws are generally less repressive. Why then do claims about the horrors of this or that consciousness-altering chemical have such unusual power in American culture?

Drug scares and other periods of acute public concern about drug use are not just discrete, unrelated episodes. There is a historical pattern in the U.S. that cannot be understood in terms of the moral values and perceptions of individual anti-drug crusaders alone. I have suggested that these crusaders have benefitted in various ways from their crusades. For example, making claims about how a drug is damaging society can help elites increase the social control of groups perceived as threatening (Duster, 1970), establish one class's moral code as dominant (Gusfield, 1963), bolster a bureaucracy's sagging fiscal fortunes (Dickson, 1968), or mobilize voter support (Reinarman and Levine, 1989a,b). However, the recurring character of pharmaco-phobia in U.S. history suggests that there is something about our *culture* which makes citizens more vulnerable to anti-drug crusaders' attempts to demonize drugs. Thus, an answer to the question of America's unusual vulnerability to drug scares must address why the scapegoating of consciousness-altering substances regularly *resonates* with or appeals to substantial portions of the population.

There are three basic parts to my answer. The first is that claims about the evils of drugs are especially viable in American culture in part because they provide a welcome *vocabulary of attribution* (cf. Mills, 1940). Armed with "DRUGS" as a generic scapegoat, citizens gain the cognitive satisfaction of having a folk devil on which to blame a range of bizarre behaviors or other conditions they find troubling but difficult to explain in other terms. This much may be true of a number of other societies, but I hypothesize that this is particularly so in the U.S. because in our political culture individualistic explanations for problems are so much more common than social explanations.

Second, claims about the evils of drugs provide an especially serviceable vocabulary of attribution in the U.S. in part because our society developed from a *temperance culture* (Levine, 1992). American society was forged in the fires of ascetic Protestantism and industrial capitalism, both of which demand *self-control*. U.S. society has long been characterized as the land of the individual "self-made man." In such a land, self-control has had extraordinary importance. For the middle-class Protestants who settled, defined, and still dominate the U.S., self-control was both central to religious world views and a characterological necessity for economic survival and success in the capitalist market (Weber, 1930 [1985]). With Levine (1992), I hypothesize that in a culture in which self-control is inordinately important, drug-induced altered states of consciousness are especially likely to be experienced as "loss of control," and thus to be inordinately feared.[7]

Drunkenness and other forms of drug use have, of course, been present everywhere in the industrialized world. But temperance cultures tend to arise only when industrial capitalism unfolds upon a cultural terrain deeply imbued with the Protestant ethic.[8] This means that only the U.S., England, Canada, and parts of Scandinavia have Temperance cultures, the U.S. being the most extreme case.

It may be objected that the influence of such a Temperance culture was strongest in the 19th and early 20th century and that its grip on the American *zeitgeist* has been loosened by the forces of modernity and now, many say, postmodernity. The third part of my answer, however, is that on the foundation of a Temperance culture, advanced capitalism has built a *postmodern, mass consumption culture* that exacerbates the problem of self-control in new ways.

Early in the 20th century, Henry Ford pioneered the idea that by raising wages he could simultaneously quell worker protests and increase market demand for mass-produced goods. This mass consumption strategy became central to modern American society and one of the reasons for our economic success (Marcuse, 1964; Aronowitz, 1973; Ewen, 1976; Bell, 1978). Our economy is now so fundamentally predicated upon mass consumption that theorists as diverse as Daniel Bell and Herbert Marcuse have observed that we live in a mass consumption culture. Bell (1978), for example, notes that while the Protestant work ethic and deferred gratification may still hold sway in the workplace, Madison Avenue, the media, and malls have inculcated a new indulgence ethic in the leisure sphere in which pleasure-seeking and immediate gratification reign.

Thus, our economy and society have come to depend upon the constant cultivation of new "needs," the production of new desires. Not only the hardware of social life such as food, clothing, and shelter but also the software of the self—excitement, entertainment, even eroticism—have become mass consumption commodities. This means that our society offers an increasing number of incentives for indulgence—more ways to lose self-control—and a decreasing number of countervailing reasons for retaining it.

In short, drug scares continue to occur in American society in part because people must constantly manage the contradiction between a Temperance culture that insists on self-control and a mass consumption culture which renders self-control continuously problematic. In addition to helping explain the recurrence of drug scares, I think this contradiction helps account for why in the last dozen years millions of Americans have joined 12-Step groups, more than 100 of which have nothing whatsoever to do with ingesting a drug (Reinarman, forthcoming). "Addiction," or the generalized loss of self-control, has become the meta-metaphor for a staggering array of human troubles. And, of course, we also seem to have a staggering array of politicians and other moral entrepreneurs who take advantage of such cultural contradictions to blame new chemical bogeymen for our society's ills.

NOTES

1. In this regard, for example, Robin Room wisely observes "that we are living at a historic moment when the rate of (alcohol) dependence as a cognitive and existential experience is rising, although the rate of alcohol consumption and of heavy drinking is falling." He draws from this a more general hypothesis about "long waves" of drinking and societal reactions to them: "[I]n periods of increased questioning of drinking and heavy drinking, the trends in the two forms of dependence, psychological and physical, will tend to run in opposite directions. Conversely, in periods of a "wettening" of sentiments, with the curve of alcohol consumption beginning to rise, we may expect the rate of physical dependence...to rise while the rate of dependence as a cognitive experience falls" (1991:154).

2. I say "formal end" because Temperance ideology is not merely alive and well in the War on Drugs but is being applied to all manner of human troubles in the burgeoning 12-Step Movement (Reinarman, forthcoming).

3. From Jim Baumohl I have learned that while the Temperance movement attracted most of its supporters from these groups, it also found supporters among many others (e.g., labor, the Irish, Catholics, former drunkards, women), each of which had its own reading of and folded its own agenda into the movement.

4. This historical sketch of drug scares is obviously not exhaustive. Readers interested in other scares should see, e.g., Brecher's encyclopedic work *Licit and Illicit Drugs* (1972), especially the chapter on glue sniffing, which illustrates how the media actually created a new drug

problem by writing hysterical stories about it. There was also a PCP scare in the 1970s in which law enforcement officials claimed that the growing use of this horse tranquilizer was a severe threat because it made users so violent and gave them such super-human strength that stun guns were necessary. This, too, turned out to be unfounded and the "angel dust" scare was short-lived (see Feldman et al., 1979). The best analysis of how new drugs themselves can lead to panic reactions among users is Becker (1967).

5. Becker wisely warns against the "one-sided view" that sees such crusaders as merely imposing their morality on others. Moral entrepreneurs, he notes, do operate "with an absolute ethic," are "fervent and righteous," and will use "any means" necessary to "do away with" what they see as "totally evil." However, they also "typically believe that their mission is a holy one," that if people do what they want it "will be good for them." Thus, as in the case of abolitionists, the crusades of moral entrepreneurs often "have strong humanitarian overtones" (1963:147–8). This is no less true for those whose moral enterprise promotes drug scares. My analysis, however, concerns the character and consequences of their efforts, not their motives.

6. As Gusfield notes, such ownership sometimes shifts over time, e.g., with alcohol problems, from religion to criminal law to medical science. With other drug problems, the shift in ownership has been away from medical science toward criminal law. The most insightful treatment of the medicalization of alcohol/drug problems is Peele (1989).

7. See Baumohl's (1990) important and erudite analysis of how the human will was valorized in the therapeutic temperance thought of 19th-century inebriate homes.

8. The third central feature of Temperance cultures identified by Levine (1992), which I will not dwell on, is predominance of spirits drinking, i.e., more concentrated alcohol than wine or beer and thus greater likelihood of drunkenness.

REFERENCES

Aronowitz, Stanley, *False Promises: The Shaping of American Working Class Consciousness* (New York: McGraw-Hill, 1973).

Baumohl, Jim, "Inebriate Institutions in North America, 1840–1920," *British Journal of Addiction* 85:1187–1204 (1990).

Baumohl, Jim, "The 'Dope Fiend's Paradise' Revisited: Notes from Research in Progress on Drug Law Enforcement in San Francisco, 1875–1915," *Drinking and Drug Practices Surveyor* 24:3–12 (1992).

Becker, Howard S., *Outsiders: Studies in the Sociology of Deviance* (Glencoe, IL: Free Press, 1963).

Becker, Howard S., "History, Culture, and Subjective Experience: An Exploration of the Social Bases of Drug-Induced Experiences," *Journal of Health and Social Behavior* 8:162–176 (1967).

Bell, Daniel, *The Cultural Contradictions of Capitalism* (New York: Basic Books, 1978).

Brecher, Edward M., *Licit and Illicit Drugs* (Boston: Little Brown, 1972).

Cohen, M. M., K. Hirshorn, and W. A. Frosch, "In Vivo and in Vitro Chromosomal Damage Induced by LSD-25," *New England Journal of Medicine* 227:1043 (1967).

Courtwright, David, *Dark Paradise: Opiate Addiction in America Before 1940* (Cambridge, MA: Harvard University Press, 1982).

Dickson, Donald, "Bureaucracy and Morality," *Social Problems* 16:143–156 (1968).

Duster, Troy, *The Legislation of Morality: Law, Drugs, and Moral Judgement* (New York: Free Press, 1970).

Ewen, Stuart, *Captains of Consciousness: Advertising and the Social Roots of Consumer Culture* (New York: McGraw-Hill, 1976).

Feldman, Harvey W., Michael H. Agar, and George M. Beschner, *Angel Dust* (Lexington, MA: Lexington Books, 1979).

Gusfield, Joseph R., *Symbolic Crusade: Status Politics and the American Temperance Movement* (Urbana: University of Illinois Press, 1963).

Gusfield, Joseph R., *The Culture of Public Problems: ·Drinking-Driving and the Symbolic Order* (Chicago: University of Chicago Press, 1981).

Himmelstein, Jerome, "Drug Politics Theory," *Journal of Drug Issues* 8 (1978).

Himmelstein, Jerome, *The Strange Career of Marihuana* (Westport, CT: Greenwood Press, 1983).

Levine, Harry Gene, "The Alcohol Problem in America: From Temperance to Alcoholism," *British Journal of Addiction* 84:109–119 (1984).

Levine, Harry Gene, "Temperance Cultures: Concern About Alcohol Problems in Nordic and English-Speaking Cultures," in G. Edwards et al., Eds., *The Nature of Alcohol and Drug Related Problems* (New York: Oxford University Press, 1992).

Levine, Harry Gene, *Drunkenness and Civilization* (New York: Basic Books, forthcoming).

Levine, Harry Gene, and Craig Reinarman, "From Prohibition to Regulation: Lessons from Alcohol Policy for Drug Policy," *Milbank Quarterly* 69:461–494 (1991).

MacAndrew, Craig, and Robert Edgerton, *Drunken Comportment* (Chicago: Aldine, 1969).

Marcuse, Herbert, *One-Dimensional Man: Studies in the Ideology of Advanced Industrial Society* (Boston: Beacon Press, 1964).

Mills, C. Wright, "Situated Actions and Vocabularies of Motive," *American Sociological Review* 5:904–913 (1940).

Molotch, Harvey, and Marilyn Lester, "News as Purposive Behavior: On the Strategic Uses of Routine Events, Accidents, and Scandals," *American Sociological Review* 39:101–112 (1974).

Morgan, Patricia, "The Legislation of Drug Law: Economic Crisis and Social Control," *Journal of Drug Issues* 8:53–62 (1978).

Musto, David, *The American Disease: Origins of Narcotic Control* (New Haven, CT: Yale University Press, 1973).

National Institute on Drug Abuse, *National Household Survey on Drug Abuse: Main Findings 1990* (Washington, DC: U.S. Department of Health and Human Services, 1990).

Peele, Stanton, *The Diseasing of America: Addiction Treatment Out of Control* (Lexington, MA: Lexington Books, 1989).

Reinarman, Craig, "The 12-Step Movement and Advanced Capitalist Culture: Notes on the Politics of Self-Control in Postmodernity," in B. Epstein, R. Flacks, and M. Darnovsky, Eds., *Contemporary Social Movements and Cultural Politics* (New York: Oxford University Press, forthcoming).

Reinarman, Craig, and Ceres Duskin, "Dominant Ideology and Drugs in the Media," *International Journal on Drug Policy* 3:6–15 (1992).

Reinarman, Craig, and Harry Gene Levine, "Crack in Context: Politics and Media in the Making of a Drug Scare," *Contemporary Drug Problems* 16:535–577 (1989a).

Reinarman, Craig, and Harry Gene Levine, "The Crack Attack: Politics and Media in America's Latest Drug Scare," pp. 115–137 in Joel Best, Ed., *Images of Is-*

sues: Typifying Contemporary Social Problems (New York: Aldine de Gruyter, 1989b).

Room, Robin G. W., "Cultural Changes in Drinking and Trends in Alcohol Problems Indicators: Recent U.S. Experience," pp. 149–162 in Walter B. Clark and Michael E. Hilton, Eds., *Alcohol in America: Drinking Practices and Problems* (Albany: State University of New York Press, 1991).

Rumbarger, John J., *Profits, Power, and Prohibition: Alcohol Reform and the Industrializing of America.* *1800–1930* (Albany: State University of New York Press, 1989).

Tijo, J. H., W. N. Pahnke, and A. A. Kurland, "LSD and Chromosomes: A Controlled Experiment," *Journal of the American Medical Association* 210:849 (1969).

Weber, Max, *The Protestant Ethic and the Spirit of Capitalism* (London: Unwin, 1985 [1930]).

Weil, Andrew, *The Natural Mind* (Boston: Houghton Mifflin, 1972).

CHAPTER 4

THE ROLE OF THIRD PARTIES

As we noted in Chapter 1, deviance reflects a process of social definition. Such definition is often affected or facilitated by third parties. Family members, for example, may enlist an outside defining agent to help them define deviance. How successful the labeling will be depends on how much consensus the defining agent can muster, and consensus is much easier to attain when significant outsiders cooperate in the labeling. When an important person in the community, for example, speaks for the community in labeling someone as deviant, they generally succeed in altering that person's "total identity"; in doing so, they accomplish what Harold Garfinkel has aptly titled a "status degradation ceremony."[1]

In the first reading Philip Davis points out that strangers are loath to act when they see parents mistreating their children in public and that even when they do intervene as third parties their action rarely brings the parents to the attention of the police. Next, Edwin Lemert shows how people actually do conspire to exclude so-called paranoids. And, in the final reading, Erving Goffman points out how family members and outside defining agents collaborate in a process that culminates in a person's being committed to a mental hospital.

NOTE

1. Harold Garfinkel, "Conditions of Successful Degradation Ceremonies," *American Journal of Sociology* (March, 1956) 61:421.

Stranger Intervention into Child Punishment in Public Places

PHILIP W. DAVIS

When they think the punishment of a child in public has gone too far, some people employ "hate stares" (Goffman 1963:83–83), a few others search for help from someone in charge, but only a minority initiate a face-to-face encounter (Gelles and Straus 1988:127). According to the National Committee for Prevention of Child Abuse (NCPCA 1990), for example, only 17 percent of its sample said they had "stopped someone they did not know from hitting a child," and this figure may be inflated by the vague wording of the question and a desire to report socially desirable actions. Given what we know about the prescription of noninvolvement among strangers in public (Edgerton 1979; Emerson 1970; Goffman 1963; Lofland 1989) and the low probability of involvement in all sorts of emergency and helping situations (Dovidio 1984; Latane and Darley 1970), it is not surprising that most people do not step in to voice their complaints and control other peoples' caretaking.

There are several indications from popular culture sources that public intervention by strangers is, however, becoming more normative. In his 1988 movie *Do The Right Thing,* for example, director Spike Lee includes a scene in which a child is nearly hit by a car. The angry mother starts hitting the child, a man intervenes, and the mother attacks the man. In April, 1989, an "Oprah" television show was devoted to the topic, "What should YOU do if you see someone abusing a child in public?" A month later, a *Parents* magazine article (Simms 1989) discussed why people do not intervene. The caption to a photo reads in

Reprinted from "Stranger Intervention into Child Punishment in Public Places," *Social Problems,* Vol. 38, No. 2 (May 1991), pp. 227–246, by permission of the Society for the Study of Social Problems and the author.

part, "There's a moral obligation to intervene...," and a boxed insert describes "THE RIGHT WAY TO INTERVENE." Ann Landers published two letters on the topic in November, 1989, and April, 1990. By the end of the year, Pulitzer Prize winner Richard Rhodes (1990) described in *Parade* how strangers freed him and his brother from abuse at the hands of their stepmother in an article titled, "Don't Be a Bystander." And Robbins (1990) in *New York* magazine wrote an elaborate article on "How to intervene when you suspect abuse."

Consistent with what Best (1990) calls the expanding domain of the child maltreatment problem culture, then, the public has been called upon to act as informal agents of social control, with this charge receiving some reinforcement in scholarly writing (e.g., Gelles and Straus 1988:191). Yet, no research exists on the kinds of experiences people have when they intervene, how the encounters are socially organized, or how social order is maintained. These gaps in research are addressed in the present study.

CHILD PUNISHMENT AND PUBLIC INTERVENTION

Within the family system, where the traditional parent role includes the right to exercise control over children (Goode 1971; Shehan and Lee 1990), parental force is legally protected so long as it is noninjurious and "reasonable" (NCCAN 1980). Physical punishment is practiced by the vast majority of parents (see, for example, Wauchope and Straus 1990), with the prevailing attitude being that slapping and spanking children is natural, normal, and necessary (Straus, Gelles, and Steinmetz 1980). In fact, parents who do not physically punish their children feel deviant and tend to keep their nonviolent proclivities to themselves (Carson 1986), while parents identified as abusive typically claim their actions originated in a disciplinary context (Fontana 1976; Kadushin and Martin 1981).

While no one is in favor of "too much punishment" (Harding and Ireland 1989), there is no clear cutting point between acceptable and excessive levels. It is widely recognized that cultural standards of abuse are varied, legal criteria are ambiguous, professional definitions are problematic, and labeling is selective (Gelles 1975; Gil 1970; Giovanonni and Becerra 1979; Johnson 1986; Korbin 1980). These uncertainties pose a vast array of emotional, relational, medical, and legal issues for parents, children, agencies, communities, institutions, and strangers—issues made more complex as more phenomena are regarded as maltreatment. . . .

The close, descriptive study of naturally occurring intervention in public "punishment" situations allows us to examine the processual nature of intervention, and the importance of social context and strategic interaction in shaping its course and outcomes.[1] These are what Emerson and Messinger (1977) call micro-political issues. They note that people who intervene face-to-face in relational troubles expand the initial conflict into a triadic arrangement, thus raising the issue of how rights and responsibilities are to be distributed. Moreover, there is a complex relationship between remedial action and deviant meanings. Ironically, concrete definitions of a person or event may follow, rather than precede efforts to remedy the matter. Remedial interchange can proceed along ritual lines (Goffman 1971) or flow from emergent claims and counter-claims about the nature of the problem and what should be done about it (Emerson and Messinger 1977). There is an array of *third party roles* (Black and Baumgartner 1981), *all of them capable of radically transforming the nature of a private trouble and establishing its deviant import.* [Italics added.] In this light, outcomes are simply the way things stand as negotiations end for the time being

(Gulliver 1979). An important factor in the social transformation of private troubles is whether the third party approaches interpersonal troubles as conflict or deviance, symmetrically with respect to culpability in the former and asymmetrically in the latter (Aubert 1965; also see Felstiner, Abel, and Sarat 1981).

Historically, the privatization of the family is associated with lower parent accountability, decreased community access, and less social control (Laslett 1973). In that sense Gelles (1987:14) notes, "Where privacy is high, the degree of social control will be low." As settings in which virtually anyone has the right to be present (Goffman 1963; Lofland 1973), public places frequently function as the testing grounds for challenges to authority (Lyman and Scott 1970). Thus, the potential for child maltreatment disputes among strangers in public places would seem great. But encounters between strangers are typically fleeting and segmented, and relations are shaped by the principles of civil inattention, audience role prominence, and civility towards diversity (Lofland 1989). As Milgram (1970) puts it, "don't meddle." Add to this the fact that child advocacy conflicts with the traditional family privacy construct (Feshbach and Feshbach 1978), and we can appreciate the symbolic, relational, and normative obstacles interveners face when they enter the fray. Given the normative structure of public places and the presence of heterogeneous populations, how is social order maintained and deviant import negotiated when people challenge the traditional authority of parents and other caretakers by asserting wrongdoing in their relations with children?

METHODS AND DATA

The data for analysis are from semi-structured interviews with 37 people who directly intervened in child punishment situations on at least one occasion. Another seven were with people who witnessed the intervention of others, six of whom also participated in some way. Six interveners could recount the details of two interventions each. Counting only those instances in which the intervener reported initiating the encounter, the interviews resulted in detailed, retrospective descriptions of 50 face-to-face interventions.[2] No two people were interviewed about the same instance. Interveners ranged in age from 19 to 45 and tended to have some college education. Of the interveners, 29 (78 percent) were women.

Because of the difficulty of locating study subjects, a convenience sample was obtained through several channels. I announced the project in several graduate and undergraduate sociology classes, spread word among friends and acquaintances, posted flyers on several church and preschool bulletin boards, and placed an announcement in two preschool newsletters. Finally, I placed a small display ad in a weekly entertainment newspaper and a classified ad in a local daily. The ads ran for three weeks. The headline in the display ad read: "HAVE YOU INTERVENED WHEN AN ADULT WAS PUNISHING A CHILD IN PUBLIC?"[3] This was followed by a promise of confidentiality, the author's name, affiliation, and office phone number. Twenty interviews were obtained by word of mouth, 18 from newspapers ads, and six from posted announcements. The interviews, which were tape recorded, ranged from 25 minutes to two hours, with the average at about forty-five minutes.

Witness-participants included a man observing in a mall for a psychology project who witnessed intervention and followed the parent, sure the parent knew he was doing so; a store manager who witnessed the intervention and was approached for help by the intervener; a mall security officer who saw a child hit with a belt, watched the intervention of a shopper, and was then hailed over to "do his job"; a woman at a rest room sink who witnessed an intervention occur through a closed stall door, only to be mistaken by the mother for the intervener when she left the stall to confront her accuser; and one person who saw the intervention take place as a member of the public audience in a department store, but did not participate in any other way.

Interviewees were asked when the event occurred, as best they could recall. The interval between the interview and the time of the event ranged from the same day to 12 years. Seven interventions occurred between four and twelve years prior to the interview; 11 between two and three years. It should be stressed that more than half the interventions occurred within a year of the interview, and several within weeks.

As a source of information on the dynamics of face-to-face intervention, these interview data are limited to the standpoints of interveners and witness-participants. Given the retrospective nature of the data, we cannot treat interveners' recollections as valid measures of the sequence of events, of the punitive adults' familial status, or of the exact things people said. This sample of intervention experiences probably overrepresents highly dramatic encounters with especially high levels of violence and hostility. With respect to retrospection and desirability, some people, no doubt, recast their experiences in light of any number of themes within the current child protection movement. It is also possible that respondents believed intervention *per se,* or their own technique, was being called into question. Despite these limitations, the interviews provide important information about how the encounter developed, the subtleties of interveners' interpretations of the punishment scene and their own actions, and the general patterns of meanings and arrangements pertaining to control outcomes.

CONTEXT AND CIRCUMSTANCES OF INTERVENTION

Unlike official control agents, when bystanders intervene in a stranger's punishment of a child, they do not possess formal protocols, mandated authority, or institutional resources. If police, doctors, and ministers constitute intervention "generalists" (Emerson and Messinger 1977) in the course of evolving remedial actions, the interveners in this study constitute an extremely general subgroup. They are people off the streets and from the market aisles that have only a circumstantial relationship to the situation. They do not know the people involved, no one has requested their help, and intervention is not required by their occupation. They are actively engaged in some everyday activity when they chance across the punishment scene and witness the trouble firsthand. Perhaps most importantly, they have immediate access to the wrongdoer *in situ*. Before examining the development of the encounter, we must discuss the immediate contexts in which intervention occurred in order to understand the interpretive backdrop to the experience.

LOCATION AND ACTIVITIES

According to the given wisdom, this kind of thing—public punishment of a child—happens in grocery stores. Markets are, in fact, the most common location cited by interviewees, but department stores and shopping malls were also common. Less often, people intervened in parks, in parking lots, on city sidewalks, in waiting rooms, in restaurants, at a zoo, by a highway roadside, at a beach, on a rapid transit platform, on a bus, on a train, and in a church cry room. In a little over half of the instances, interveners were already standing or walking very close to the family when the adult hit, dragged, shook, or kicked the child. Several interventions, quite literally, occurred "in passing." One couple jogging toward a crowded bus-stop watched a mother pull a boy from the bus, yell at him, and spank him hard as she dragged him up the sidewalk. The joggers stopped for a moment to argue and then resumed jogging. Other interveners were shopping near the adult and child in the same market aisle. Many said they "went over" to the pair, but usually just a short distance. One woman got up from her blanket at a crowded outdoor concert and went over to a mother a couple of blankets away. Another said he pulled over, stopped, and shouted profanities from his car to a father hitting a boy on the sidewalk.

According to interviewees, the encounter does not usually involve anyone but the intervener and punitive parent. Both were without adult companions in three out of five instances. Several interveners had their own children with them at the time. Interveners *never* asked another shopper or bystander for help at any point, even though others were usually in view.

SCENES AND REACTIONS

Two observational studies (Brown 1979; Davis 1990) indicate public punishment situations are short lived, with most hitting episodes involving a single hit in the absence of crying or complaining by the child, or yelling or explaining by the adult (Davis 1990). Even with multiple hits and the use of objects, the application of force lasts only a couple of seconds. As Goffman (1971) puts it, justice in public is summary. From an audience standpoint, the low visibility of the scene could easily make intervention seem "unnecessary."

When interveners chance across punishment situations, what do they see that leads them to step in and speak up? Most interveners say they witnessed something more than a mild spanking. I mention this because the negative intervener stereotype is of busybodies that "butt-in" at the slightest tap. In fact, only two interviewees described scenes in which the only force was a simple spank on the bottom. A few children were slapped on the hands, but repeatedly. In rough behavioral terms, half the interviewees say they saw adults hitting children hard or repeatedly with their hands. In one out of five interventions the parent used a belt or switch. In over a fourth of the instances, interviewees said the child was hit on the face or head. One child was bloodied at the time of the intervention, although the witness-participant (a friend of the mother's) said the bleeding was not from the blow. In six instances, the child was knocked to the ground.

Most interveners say they did not think much about whether to intervene, but instead, they found themselves "stepping over" and "stepping in," the words "just coming out" of their mouths. Several described the actions as having been "instinctive" or "a matter of reflexes." One man, for example, said he saw a mother on a bus take a belt from her bag and start hitting her boy for kneeling instead of sitting on the seat. The bus lurched forward and the boy fell across her. He said he stepped across the aisle, took the belt from her hand, and told her he would give it back when he got off. He said,

> *My reflex. I wish I could tell you I sat down and pondered it and decided to be heroic, but that's not the way it works. I watched it and I just did it, and then later—you think about it later that it might have had consequences. I don't know what else she could have had in the bag. (26)*

Others said:

> *I don't sit there and think I know I'm going to help this child. It bothers me and I react. I don't think that I think about it and say now, look at this child in trouble, what can I do here. I don't plan what I'm gonna do. It just happens. (41)*

> *I just wanted that woman to stop. It was like the breaking point of my emotions. I just had to make her stop. I had no choice like, "Do I or don't I?" I just had to, there was no choice about it. (49)*

Several watched as the adult continued to hit the child repeatedly, sometimes rapid-fire and sometimes spread out over a period of time. For these people, their comments suggest the building of *intervention momentum* (see Adler 1981) in which they tolerated the initial hitting, hoping it would stop. After seconds or minutes or heightening tension, they reach a point where, as they put it, they just had to say something. In one instance, the intervener felt momentum build over a long wait in a crowded pediatrician's office as a mother struggled with her child.

> *You could just tell by the look on her face that it was just embarrassing her.... So, she started slapping him on his hand. The frequency of this was just more and more and more.... So finally she took him outside and I don't know what happened*

> *out there. She came back inside and she finally started hitting him with the strap on her purse...you could feel the rest of the room jump every time she hit him, and I finally thought now I can't watch this any longer. (31)*

She volunteered her impression that before she said anything, the child was hit perhaps 25 times during the half hour they sat together.

Most interveners were bothered more by the manner, style, and context of what the adult did than by the fact the child was being physically punished, even though nearly half the interveners believed that no physical punishment is acceptable. They cited the facts that the adult used an object, hit the child in the face, did not stop after the first hit, or scowled and yelled angrily while hitting. Others felt the punishment did not fit the infraction or were dismayed that the parent would hit the child for failing to stop crying after a preceding hit. One woman in a warehouse toy store check-out line watched as a father repeatedly slapped a little girl's hand when she kept reaching up to tug on his beard:

> *Because that was more than just poor parenting skills. I really feared for that little girl's life. I mean, if she could be spanked for just touching his face! You could see the expression on his face was almost psychopathic, it was so detached. (10)*

One woman who intervened in a market reflected:

> *I felt like she should know if she's hit in the face like that she'd cry too. And she was hitting this baby in its face!...And she hit him hard, and that's so ridiculous,...and I felt like I should say something. (50)*

Another said:

> *What I objected to was the barrage all the way down the sidewalk, hitting and yelling, and then sitting on the bench and continuing to do it. It was just totally excessive. (43)*

Interveners chance across the punishment scene, step from the public audience role, and then typically enter into unsubtle debates, disputes, and arguments over the deviant import of the situation. I will now discuss their experience of these exchanges in some detail.

NEGOTIATION OF DEVIANT IMPORT

The deviant nature of the punishment scene, the allocation of wrongdoer and victim roles, the moral character of participants, and the rights of parents and strangers soon become the stuff of claims and counter-claims about what is taking place. Although the initial dyadic conflict expands to a triadic arrangement with the involvement of strangers, on an interactive level the child is typically the forgotten party. Of the 50 interventions, there were only two instances in which interveners said they briefly addressed the child. The negotiation of the situation's deviant import occurs between adults, while children bear silent witness to strangers complaining about what their parents and other caretakers have done. This is consistent with Cahill's (1987, 1990) observations that adults interact with children in public in ways that ritually instill and reaffirm their subordinate status.

Before discussing the key themes within actors' claims and counter-claims, it is important to note that in about one in three instances, the putative parent did not say anything at all in response to the intervener. In two instances the interveners also said nothing. In one of these silent interventions, a woman and her husband pulled to the side of the road, got out of their car, and started to walk back towards a man beating a child with his fists in the back seat of a parked car. Another car ahead of them had also pulled over. The man saw them coming, got into his car, and drove away. In the other instance, a woman and her mother heard screams coming from inside a department store women's rest room. They went inside and saw a woman holding a little girl off the floor, hitting her legs with a belt. She said:

We just walked in and just stood next to the little girl. We didn't say a word. I went and stood next to the little girl, and my mother went and stood di-

rectly in front of the mother. We just stood there and just looked at her. . . . We kind of sandwiched them: I was on one side and my mother was on the other. (37)

The mother led the girl from the rest room, handed the belt to a man waiting outside, he put it on, and the group left. The intervener said:

I was furious because I was looking at the mother and I was furious. . . . She looked at both of us, and then just acted like we weren't there, but she stopped. (37)

Even these silent transactions involve negotiations using body language and nonverbal gestures with which interveners convey disapproval and effect control.

There are several themes within parents' and interveners' claims and counter-claims as they negotiate the deviant import of the punishment situation, on the one hand, and the stranger's intervention on the other. I will discuss the four most common assertions: (1) the wrongful nature of child treatment, (2) the undue interest of the intervener, (3) the protection of parental pluralism, and (4) the fit of the abuse label. These ideas and assertions overlap considerably, and there is no necessary or typical sequence apart from the fact that all begin with interveners' assertions that something untoward between parent and child is taking place.

WRONGFUL CHILD TREATMENT

From their accounts, all but a few interveners entered the exchange clearly allocating wrongdoer and victim roles to parents and children, respectively. The most common approach consisted of terse, bold, accusatory complaints, requests, and demands to cease the wrongful action.[4] Interveners say they told parents the actions were reprehensible, excessive, harmful, or out of place, and that they were unworthy as caretakers. Several shouted at the parent to "STOP!" Others recalled saying "Please don't hit your child, you need to stop doing that!"; "You shouldn't hit your child, how dare you start beating on this little child!"; "Please don't do that anymore, please stop!"; and "You ought to be ashamed!" In what appears to be the most fleeting encounter of all, a woman shopper walked up to a mother who had just slapped a little girl across her face in a department store. The witness I interviewed said the intervener snapped angrily, "You ought to be horsewhipped!" and turned and walked away.

Other interveners say they mixed their accusations, and even threats to call the authorities, with commiseration and polite requests. One woman saw a mother and child in a rapid transit station:

> The child continues to whine and she backhands the child across the face and the child just drops to the floor with the force of this. And I immediately jumped up. I don't know what I thought I was gonna do. The violence of it just shocked me, and she went to hit the child again. I went up to her and I spoke in a very low voice and I said, "You must be really frustrated to do that to your child, but if you do it again I'll call the police." I guess I was serious. (28)

Only a few interveners described extremely gentle interventions in which their statements of wrongdoing were veiled or left implicit. In one instance the woman went over to a mother struggling with a crying child in a church cry room. The mother spanked the girl, told her she was a "bad girl," and spanked her again. The intervener put her arm around the mother and whispered in her ear, suggesting there were better ways to handle the situation.[5] She said the mother looked frightened and said, "I'm doing the best I can." In another instance a woman saw a mother slapping a boy's legs as he sat in a market shopping cart. On the floor was a large spill of Coke and a broken bottle. The intervener walked up and asked calmly, "Have you got a problem? Can I do anything?" When the mother complained the boy had tossed the bottle on the floor, the intervener said her boy had done the same thing when he was young.

UNDUE INTERVENER INTEREST

Without formal authority in the setting or an invitation by anyone to become involved, interveners often run up against a counter-claim that they have violated the norm of noninvolvement by taking an undue interest in the personal affairs of strangers: they are deviant for having meddled. This represents a shift in interactive focus from the wrongful punishment and suspect character of the parent to the deviant involvement and aberrant nosiness of the intervener. A few interviewees said:

> He was very belligerent [saying], "Who are you! Is this any of your business? Did I ask you anything!" (5)

> The mother said, "You need to get out of the way, too, or I'll beat your ass. Who do you think you are?" (12)

The assertion implies interveners lacked the social standing with respect to the child and the parent that would make their complaints reasonable and legitimate. In their responses, many interveners cited their relationship to the deed, victim, or wrongdoer that makes intervention seem reasonable. Most claim their involvement is justified in the name of child protection, criminal law, public civility, individual sensibilities, and personal inconvenience. One intervener said she heard screams from somewhere in a discount department store but did not try to track them down. She rounded the corner of an aisle and saw a woman "ramming" her shopping cart repeatedly into the crying child. She put her hands on the basket and held it in place. She said:

> I can't remember my exact words, but it was something to the effect if there's something I can do, there seems to be a problem here. She told me I could mind my own business. And I just looked at her and said, "My business is this child not getting hurt." And she just got real huffy and kind of walked off. (8)

Another woman was with a friend in a steak restaurant when a family in a nearby booth caught her eye:

The father reaches over the table and slaps that older kid in the face. I stood up and I went over to the table. I said, "You can't do that," or I said, "What are you doing?" or "You can't do that," or something like that. And the wife said, "Mind your own business." ...I said, "Well, you ruined my dinner. That is my business!" (29)

Interveners say they were typically angered by these assertions of undue interest, and only one did not recall having said anything in response.

Assertions of deviant involvement take on new meaning when it comes to physical contact between interveners and the children, with interveners more open to the complaint that they are the ones maltreating the child. Some people say they wanted to take up the child but resisted since, as one woman put it, that "was asking for trouble." In a few instances interveners touched or took the child without asking. One woman watched a mother struggle with her child's "tantrum" at a mall. As the boy lay on the floor crying and screaming, the mother tried talking to him. When that didn't work, she slapped his leg, and then his bottom. When she slapped his face, the intervener said she was furious and went over, picked up the screaming boy, and carried him to a pay phone to call the police. The mother stormed alongside threatening to have the intervener's own child (who trailed the group to the phone) taken away. When the mother spit in her face and threatened to beat her, the intervener said:

And I said, "Fine, let me make a phone call and I'll go outside with you." Meaning, if you want to fight, I'll fight. And I told her, "If it comes down to me and you, count on it, I will survive! I'll screw you to the wall, and you're not mean enough to beat me!" (48)

In another instance, a woman picked up a boy crying alone in a crowded warehouse supermarket and carried him towards customer service.[6] The father saw her coming, rushed up, grabbed the crying boy from her arms, shook him roughly, and snapped, "Where have you been!" Alarmed at his roughness, the woman said she reached out and

put her hands around the boy to take him back. She said:

Well this man just whirled the child around the other way and yelled, "DON'T YOU TOUCH HIM!" ...I backed off faster than you've ever seen anybody move. All I wanted to do was get in that crowd and get away from him. At the same time, I realized that I scared him. He probably thought that I was stealing his kid. (41)

She said she left feeling embarrassed at being thought a child-snatcher and unappreciated for trying to help.

PROTECTION OF PARENTAL DIFFERENCES

Within the family institution, the cultural value of individualism often translates into the idea that parents have a right to exercise autonomy of style. In intervention encounters, the value of parental pluralism translates into pithy assertions like, "It's MY child!" and "I can raise my child the way I want!" The rhetoric connotes the idea that interveners have mistaken acceptable variations of normal childrearing for deviant actions of public concern. Interveners say they generally acknowledged the privileged relationship between parent and child but still challenged the legitimacy of the action. Interveners said, for example:

She gave me a dirty look and she said, "That you know this is none of your business, and I raise my child the way I want to and you raise your child the way you want to." And I said, "That's fine, and I don't mean to interfere, it's just too painful for me to watch this." (31)

So I ran out there and I said, "Please don't do that anymore! Please stop!" The mother said, "She's my child." I said, "I know, but please don't do that anymore." (4)

In only one instance did an intervener say the adult pointed to the seriousness of the child's misbehavior to explain the severity of the "punishment." As the intervener neared the top of a mall escalator, she saw a man take off his belt and start hitting a boy on the legs.

I just started yelling in front of him and I said, "Don't do that in front of me!" I couldn't handle it, it was obvious he was just trying to humiliate this child. And he looked at me, and he said, "If he's old enough to mouth off at me, he's old enough for this." (53)

It was also the only instance in which another bystander joined the encounter. A man eating at a nearby patio table walked up and, according to the intervener, said, "I have to agree, I think this is the wrong place for you to be doing that."

FIT OF THE ABUSE LABEL

Over the past thirty years, the stigmatizing power of the child-abuse label has increased to the point where its use probably constitutes fighting words for most people. The designation and its effects have been examined in *official control contexts,* of course, but we know very little about its use in disputes in everyday settings among strangers. Not surprisingly, some interveners say they invoked the label and linked it to what was happening at the time. One intervener watched from her car as a woman tried hurrying her boy into a school office from a parking lot during a rain storm. The boy lagged and the woman shook him roughly. The intervener said she cried as she told the woman, "You can't do that." She said:

She just turned around full square, and said, "Who the hell are you and what business is it of yours?" And I said it's not really any business of mine unless you abuse that child, and if you abuse that child it becomes my business." (48)

The abuse label may be a last resort in intervention politics among strangers, used primarily to defend against claims of deviant involvement (on last resorts, see Emerson 1981).

Unable to obtain external corroboration or disconfirmation of one another's identities, strangers in public are free to defend and challenge their actions on the basis of *claims of child-abuse expertise,* of having the authority to determine the technical appropriateness of the label to the present situation. An art professor, for example, said he heard a girl's screams in a discount department store. Entering an aisle, he was angered when he saw a woman plant a little girl in the seat of a shopping cart and slap her face. In the next aisle, after the mother took the girl from the cart and nagged her to hurry along, she knocked the girl to the floor.

And I just sort of lost my cool, and I went up to the lady and I says, "LOOK! You stop that!"...She just says, "You just don't—" She looked at me like, "Who the hell are you?" And I says, "Look, I know about child abuse." I was sort of bluffing her. "I'm an authority on this sort of thing and, believe me, I KNOW you need help. (5)

In another instance an intervener at an amusement park saw a man kick a boy on his bottom, sending him to the ground. When the boy just lay there the father told him, "Get up!" She described the scene this way:

I said, "What do you expect when he was kicked like that." The first thing the mother said was, "Mind your own business." And I said, "No child should be treated like that."...She said something really disturbing. She said that there wasn't anything wrong with it and that she should know because she's a social worker. That kind of took me back because I mean it's definitely abuse that you shouldn't kick a child that way, definitely not in public. (30)

She said she wished she had come up with a retort, perhaps asking the woman the name of her supervisor so she could call and verify the story and report her.

CONTROL OUTCOMES AND INTERVENTION EFFECTS

What are the social control consequences and intervention effects in these situations? There were three categories of outcome: (1) situations that, as far as the intervener knew, ended with only informal understandings of the trouble; (2) experiences that involved official agents of control; and (3) interveners' lasting subjective concerns about the experience.

INFORMAL UNDERSTANDINGS

Despite interveners' clear-cut disapproval of how the children were treated and the anger they commonly felt when parents refused to acknowledge the wrongful nature of the punishment, their efforts did not usually lead to formal control. Most of these problematic situations were not transformed into official cases for formal agency processing. Usually, having made their assertions and defended their actions, interveners and parents brought the transaction to an abrupt and typically uncivil conclusion without apologies, explanations, farewells, or agreements about the meaning of the exchange or the consequences of the experience. As one intervener put it:

> She just pushed me several times, in the grass, off the sidewalk. I don't remember saying anything to her, I just knew there wasn't anything I could say. So I just took my daughter and we walked in the opposite direction, and then they left, and we left. (49A)

Although frequently angry and shaken, interveners go about their business shopping for groceries, strolling the mall, driving down the road, and so on. People parted company with no further action in about four out of five instances.

A few interveners said they were literally pulled from the encounter by their husbands, and were unhappy that their spouses were embarrassed or did not share their views. One, for example, said she shouted "STOP THAT!" at a man slapping a boy for touching clothes in a store. The father looked angry and about to say something to her when her husband took her arm and pulled her away:

> But what really stands in my mind was my husband was there and this really embarrasses him . . . that's hard because I was upset he was hitting his child.

> That bothers me that my husband would feel that way, but he does. (41)

In another instance, an intervener watched with her husband on a plaza outside a zoo entrance as a man lifted a boy by the arm and slapped him in the face. She went over to the man and said, "Quit it! You're hitting him!"

> My husband did come up and literally pulled me away. . . . He said, "You're lucky that he didn't smack you, you shouldn't have done that." And that it wasn't any of my business, and I really could have been hurt! Disappointed. I felt like he should be—feel the way I felt. (50)

Others say they actively monitored the actions of the parent to make sure they did not hit the child again. One kept listening while finishing up his shopping in the store. Another sat in her car in the parking lot watching the mother disappear down the street. A few saw the person again later in the setting, in another market aisle for example, or on the other side of the department store (one woman waved at the child from a distance), but only one said anything. The initial encounter ended when the intervener entered a shop, the mother still yelling at her from the sidewalk. After running some errands, and the intervener entered another store in the mall and saw the same woman and child. They met at the counter.

> I had avoided her in the store, and I said something to her like . . . "I finally found what I needed, did you find what you needed?" Or something like that. Cause she was standing right around with me, and she said, "Yes I finally did." (43)

While browsing in separate aisles, the intervener said she kept her distance for fear of being "jumped."

For some, the encounter has an interactive aftermath in which the meaning of the experience is shaped by the reactions of others who witnessed the intervention or were told the story. A few interveners are lauded as having accomplished something almost heroic, while others meet with more general approval. After leaving her store to intervene in the mall's main aisle, a clerk returned and heard from shoppers who witnessed the event:

> One woman asked me if I was O.K., and I said yes. She said, "I'm glad you did that, that was a double leather strap!" She said she couldn't believe it. And then another woman said, "I'm so glad you said something." (4)

She went for a walk around the mall to unwind and, later, another clerk heard the story and told her she was brave, making her feel good. Another intervener said:

> My 10-year-old daughter told me that she really admired me for doing what a lot of people [wouldn't]—there were so many people at the park that wouldn't do anything. They just stood there. (22)

Several interveners, however, say they met with discouraging reactions from significant others:

> I went home and told my husband, and he made the comment, "If you keep that up one of these days you may get your head blown off." (8)

> My husband came up to me a few minutes later, and I told him what I'd did and he said, "Don't ever do that. That guy could have jumped on me." That guy could have come after my husband. You know my husband, I was really ashamed in a way. I thought I would get a pat on the back from my husband but instead he discouraged me from doing things like that. (27)

In the instance when the mother said her dinner had been ruined in the restaurant, her friend encouraged her to go for a drive. In the car, she cried as her friend talked her out of going back to provoke the father into hitting her so she could call the police. She was disappointed her friend was so "shy."

OFFICIAL THIRD PARTIES

While most public child maltreatment confrontations between strangers are managed informally, some lead to the involvement of formal control agencies and institutions. Of the 50 face-to-face interventions described by interviewees, the police were involved in eight. In a few of those, the intervener called the police after the encounter, never knowing what, if anything, came of it. In a few others, the police arrived and spoke with both the intervener and the adult. One intervener demanded the fast food clerk telephone while he and a friend restrained a father who knocked a girl to the floor with a blow across her face with a leather belt. In another instance, an intervener saw a woman jerk a girl by her hair and slap a boy on the face on a park playground. She first shouted at the woman and then chased her down the sidewalk:

> She was ignoring me, and it really made me mad. So I went off, taking after her. Well, on the way I picked up this big rock, and I thought, "Well if this lady—I was so mad, all I could think of, I was just gonna knock her in the head myself.

She put the rock down and angrily asked the mother why she hit the child in the face.

> She said, "My baby no respect me." So I said, "Well, respect your baby before it will respect you."...I got real mad with her, and I told her there are other ways, and she really didn't speak that good English. I told her that was abuse, and she could be locked up for that, that how would she like for me to knock her in the face like that, and then, when I told her that, she just turned around with her kid and took off....And I thought, well I might go to jail for intervening in this, so I just went to the police myself. (22)

The intervener noted the house the mother entered, drove to the police station, reported the incident, and insisted the police drive to the address. She secretly waited outside the station, followed the squad car to make sure they responded to her complaint, and watched from her car across the street to make sure they knocked on the door and talked to the woman. Then she drove away. As far as the interviewees in this study knew, there were no arrests in any situation.

In only one instance was an intervener aware that a child abuse investigation was initiated. That was when the intervener picked up the child and carried him to a mall telephone. The police arrived and questioned the mother:

> They asked her, "Where did you strike the child?" and she said, "I didn't strike the child, I spanked him." And they said, "OK, where did your hand land on the child?" She said, "On the fanny and on the hand."...I turned the little boy's face and there was a hand print on his face.... He said, "Did you hit him in the face?" And she said, "Well, I may have." (48)

She said the officer told her the police could not take action, but he took identifying information from the mother and gave it to the intervener. She reported the incident to Child Protective Services and received a letter saying the child was temporarily out of the home pending further investigation.

In another instance the intervener did not know who called the police. He and some friends were in a market getting beer and snacks for their evening poker game when a woman behind them in check-out angrily shook her child. He told her to stop, and she argued back, saying they must be drunks since they had so much beer in their cart. She called him a "nigger lover" because one of his friends was black. When he told her, "Maybe you should be slung around on *your* arm like that," she left and returned with the father. The father silently took the screaming child out the door and the man followed. After the father "slung" the child onto the seat of a pick-up cab, the man said during the interview, "He turned around on me in a menacing manner, and I responded the best way I knew how." Punches were thrown, the intervener bloodying the father's nose. The mother came running from the store, shouting, "They called the police!" and the family drove off. The intervener speculated they fled because of drugs in the truck or to avoid a child abuse investigation. The police arrived and the intervener and his friends resented the fact an officer ran them for "wants and warrants" before taking information about the family. About the whole experience he said:

> It was just reflex. I mean I didn't hurt him, I mean, there was a little bit of blood comin' from his nose, but not enough as far as I was concerned. And then when I found out the police were there and I found it was going my way I was even more pleased, cause I wanted 'em to see this kid. I mean we weren't doing anything wrong. I mean, he might of got me for assault, I don't know. I was willing to take my chances with it. (24)

He said about the experience, "I wish I could have done more."

LASTING SUBJECTIVE CONCERNS

When interveners speak of the satisfactions of their efforts they refer to the preventive or therapeutic value of what they did. A few cite catharsis. Some believe their brief message planted a seed of doubt in the parent's mind about the illegitimacy of the present action, which interveners assumed was characteristic of the parent's approach to child control at home. One man, for example, passed a woman in a mall promenade after she slapped a girl twice in the face. He said:

> I might have told her she didn't have the right to do that. And she didn't say anything either. She just grabbed the kid and walked on...You could tell they stopped and were thinking about it. (46)

Even the few who believe their actions did not help the child or the parent, feel they at least expressed their own views and did the right thing.

> It didn't do any good, which was the most distressing thing. I don't know what you're supposed to do in that situation. Do you not act when you feel that disgusted? I feel that walking away from it, in retrospect, looking back on it, walking away I would have felt worse than doing something and having nothing come of it. (3)

Although satisfied they said something, most interveners feel a degree of ambivalence about the experience. I will discuss two related subjective concerns that emerge from their comments: the ideal intervener and amplification.

The Ideal Intervener

Only a few interveners regret having said something, but most express at least some regret about how they acted, what they said, or how they said it. They describe and evaluate their actions as though there is a scientifically proven, procedurally correct, and psychologically effective style of public intervention, one they did not employ. Their comments suggest they compare themselves to a noninstitutionalized construct of the *ideal intervener.* The growing popular literature on child maltreatment intervention I discussed earlier has certainly done nothing to dispel this idea, although no one I interviewed remembered having read or seen anything on the topic. Most commonly, people feel their technique was too accusatory and expressive, or insufficiently empathic and helpful:

> *I just felt like that I didn't handle the situation well because I got emotional. And that if I could calm down and go back in there I could say something to them. (29)*

> *Maybe what I should have done is walked up to the lady, and said, "Is there some way I can help you?" I regretted afterwards, but I was angry...I guess the truth is I didn't want to help her cause I was mad at her for acting that way. (43)*

> *I wish I said something better, but...what would that have been? I know you love your child. Please don't hit her. Think about what you're doing when you hit her. But I didn't. (4)*

Despite the fact they took action when other witnesses did not, many are ambivalent about not having "done more." A few regret not detaining the parents, following them into the parking lot to get a license plate number, or somehow getting a name and phone number:

> *I was glad I had done it. I guess I'm sorry I didn't do more. I don't know what you can do in a situation like that. Take her name and report her to the*

> *Child Welfare Bureau or whatever it is up in New York. I guess that was a possibility." (26)*

> *I would have to come in with a little more smart stuff this [next] time. I would say give me your name, and your phone number. I would be much more aggressive in making sure that something happened. (34)*

> *At any rate, I was so shaken and so upset...what I wish I had done, I wish I had followed them. I wish I hadn't said anything, and just quietly followed them out into the parking lot and got [their] license number. (10)*

In general, respondents' image of an ideal intervener is someone who calms the adult, protects the child, supports the family, considers a report, displays equanimity under attack, and, in less serious instances, provides situational resources in the form of a kind word, "magic" phone number, or childrearing tip. Most believe their own anger or lack of planning precluded doing it just right.

Amplification

Doing it just right might not matter so much if interveners did not believe children's safety was at stake. There is a widespread belief that intervention can make things worse for the child. Many are somewhat fearful that by angering parents, undermining their authority, or embarrassing them in front of strangers, they might have amplified the deviance:

> *I mean it's frustrating because you know that once she leaves it's gonna start again and maybe worse because of what I said. (31)*

> *Later I thought maybe that wasn't the right thing to do. Maybe I shouldn't have intervened at that point. What if the father is even angrier and goes home and does something to the child. (11)*

In a few instances interveners saw the parent hit the child again after they intervened, and tended to view the subsequent punishment as evidence they amplified the deviance. One saw a mother in a grocery store slapping her little girl:

And I said to her, "You know when someone's hitting you it's really hard not to cry and maybe you can talk to them about it or try something else." And she just reacted to me and said, "Mind your own business, you fucking bitch!" And I think it made her angrier at the child and what she did was want to prove that she was in control. I felt like I added to the child's punishment because she kept it up and kept it up . . . the moment after I did it she got more severe. (35)

She said the experience convinced her not to intervene again because it was "not a time parents are receptive" to well-intended messages about the way they treat their children. Another felt she had caused both the initial and subsequent spankings. She was 56, had no bottom teeth, and was bent from a back injury. She recalled casually passing a mother and daughter in a market aisle:

She (the little girl) said, "Look, mommy, a witch!" And her mother started whipping her for it. And I said, "Honey, she doesn't know any better. She couldn't help it." And I said it doesn't bother me for her talking that way. I begged her not to do it, but it looked like it made her mad, because I said something . . . and she just left, and I could hear her spanking her on the other side of the counter after she got her around in the next aisle. (45)

One man even feared that he might pick up the newspaper one day and see a picture of the child he had helped, and maybe hurt, in an article about an abused or slain child:

And, I felt like, maybe, I may have caused the child—I sort of read the papers, I sort of remember how she looks, but I never heard anything about it again. (5)

Most interveners, however, feel any repercussions to the child or to themselves were offset by having deterred the parent from administering another hit or blow to the child at the time.

DISCUSSION

When the approval of punishment is widespread and the array of phenomena regarded as maltreatment grows rapidly, a cultural tension is created in which potential child maltreatment disputes lie just beneath the surface of routine interaction. This study illustrates the interpersonal predicament that arises when strangers directly complain about deviant punishment in settings where interaction is typically shaped by noninvolvement. People in public are experts at maneuvering out of one another's way, minimizing expressivity, and conveying disinterest. They routinely make identities visible to strangers, and public identities usually go unchallenged (Lofland 1973). But situated identities are sacred and vulnerable (Felson 1978), and bold complaints about the mishandling of children challenge public identities of competent caretaker or loving parent. With an emphasis upon event patterns and claim themes, I have explored the interactive dynamics of this predicament as people negotiate the deviant import of wrongful punishment and unsolicited intervention.

Based on bystander intervention research, it seems that the interveners in this study took considerable risks. Like the crime interveners studied by Huston et al. (1981), these people became directly involved in naturally occurring situations where there appeared to be at least some physical risk. But the interveners in Huston et al. tended to be males with considerable training, in contrast to a matched comparison group. This contrasts sharply with the mostly female self-selecting sample in this study. Moreover, four out of five interveners in this study were parents, consistent with the NCPCA (1990) survey. And almost half the interveners in this study said they did not think any physical punishment was acceptable. These characteristics, no doubt, are partially explained by the way I obtained my sample. Should more systematic research on child maltreatment interveners indicate the same patterns, this would be consistent with the idea that feelings of closeness with victims facilitates intervention (Dovidio 1984:405).

Why are child maltreatment interventions predominantly woman-to-woman conflicts? Women perform more childcare than men, are more likely to do their childcare in public places (see Amato 1989), and are present in public settings where children are also present. They may be more vulnerable than men to deviant labels involving parenthood (Schur 1984). By default, they carry out the "work" of protecting other peoples' children. The ways in which public child maltreatment intervention by strangers reflects women's issues requires further study.

With respect to the micro-politics of informal control, when strangers in public initiate a face-to-face encounter with the wrongdoer, they do so as "intervention generalists" (Emerson and Messinger 1977) of the first order, lacking in recognized authority, formal intervention ideologies, and institutional support. In most instances, they step from the audience role just long enough to complain about the mishandling of the child, and to mange counter-claims that they have meddled. They quickly resume their audience status and return to routine activities feeling at once satisfied, shaken, and worried. Deviant punishment situations are rarely transformed by informal control encounters into formally designated deviance. The momentary nature of the violence, the vulnerability of strangers to counter-claims of deviant involvement, the lack of institutional resources, and the absence of institutionalized interaction rules make it likely that trouble definitions remain nebulous and tentative. But by halting traffic and attempting speedy remedies, they introduce what Aubert (1984:73) calls the third party's "unique moral standpoint in the little group."

Also relevant to the micro-politics of informal control, there is a common shift in interactive focus from the wrongful treatment of the child to the deviant involvement of the stranger. In the face of a complaint, the defense that the stranger has taken an undue interest in other people's business is probably one of a few basic *claim-shifts* at work when strangers self-mobilize as third parties to an interpersonal trouble. Such shifts in focus, allegations, and blame require further attention in the study of disputes in their early stages, when, according to Felstiner et al. (1981), events and

their meanings tend to be unstable, reactive, and incomplete. In addition to the conclusions I have drawn from retrospective data, direct observations of more commonplace interventions are needed to explore other claim-shift patterns.

In summary, though much maltreatment screening occurs in organizational contexts (Johnson 1986), audience members in public places routinely engage in screenings of their own. While most remain within the audience role, some directly complain. Like the size of the work force associated with the expanding domain of the child maltreatment movement, their numbers are probably increasing. Child maltreatment interveners can expect to receive a hostile response from the putative parent and mixed reactions from others. The data do not tell us whether a person should intervene, if one technique is more effective than another, or what the effective techniques might be. In the absence of any research on intervention's amplification effects, it seems reasonable for the time being to encourage community involvement in the social control of other peoples' caretaking that violates current standards. The fact that those standards are pluralistic and rapidly changing makes the intervener's predicament especially complex. There is a special need in future research to study the intervention experiences of parents, other caretakers, and children within unlabeled and labeled populations to uncover the meanings of their intervention experiences. How do interpretations of the intervener as meddlesome arise and shape the meaning of the encounter from the parent's perspective? What is their subjective estimate of the type and extent of its effects, if any, on their interaction with the child, including immediate and long term use of physical punishment? And what are the effects of intervention on caretaker self-esteem and children's emotions?

NOTES

1. In using the term "punishment" instead of abuse, I do not mean to beg the questions of interveners' definitions,

adults' intentions, or children's experiences of something nonabusive. The focus is on the problematic nature of definitions within everyday settings. The problem with the term "punishment," as Maurer (1974) notes in her discussion of semantics, is that its use typically assumes too much about the deserved nature of painful or unpleasant actions and the good intentions of the punishing person. This is similar to Straus, Gelles, and Steinmetz (1980) in their discussion of the spare-the-rod ideology.

2. Numbers at the end of quotes refer to the number assigned to interviewees as research progressed. Interviewees were not counted in the few tallies for this study if they did not initiate a face-to-face encounter. Thus some numbers associated with quotes are higher than 50.

3. This phrasing was used to encourage as many people as possible to consider responding, regardless of the severity of the force or violence, and whether or not they defined the actions as discipline or abuse. It is possible the phrasing dissuaded people from responding who intervened in what they felt were abuse situations. Given the saliency of abuse issues, however, it is likely any research announcement mentioning child punishment is automatically defined to include abuse, or is assumed to be about abuse.

4. Among other forms of discursive acts, Perinbanayagam (1991) discusses the symbolic features of complaints, demands, commands, and requests. Complaints appeal to shared standards. Demands, as imperative askings, assert an unequal power distribution and forestall friendly interaction. Commands imply a formal structure within which articulators claim they have status and power. Requests, as an importuning of the other, are more protective of the other's self.

5. This was the only instance involving a high degree of privatization by the intervener. It was also the least public of all the settings, even though the intervener had never seen the woman before at church and did not see her again. For a discussion of privatization in public places, see Lofland (1973).

6. Cahill (1990:394) notes strangers pay considerable attention to unaccompanied children in public places, and usually ask them where their mother is.

REFERENCES

Adler, Peter. 1981. Momentum. Newbury Park, Calif: Sage.

Amato, Paul. 1989. "Who cares for children in public places? Naturalistic observation of male and female caretakers." Journal of Marriage and the Family 51:981–990.

Aubert, Vilhelm. 1965. The Hidden Society. Totowa, NJ: Bedminster Press.

———. 1984. In Search of Law: Sociological Approaches to Law. Totowa, N.J.: Barnes and Noble.

Best, Joel. 1990. Threatened Children: Rhetoric and Concern about Child-Victims. University of Chicago Press.

Black, Donald, and M. P. Baumgartner. 1981. "Toward a theory of the third person." In Empirical Theories About Courts, ed. Lynn Mather and Keith Boyum, 84–114. New York: Longman.

Brown, Bruce. 1979. "Parent's discipline of children in public places." The Family Coordinator 28:67–71.

Cahill, Spencer. 1987. "Children and civility: Ceremonial deviance and the acquisition of ritual competence." Social Psychology Quarterly 50:312–321.

———. 1990. "Childhood and public life: Reaffirming biographical divisions." Social Problems 37:390–402.

Carson, Barbara. 1986. Parents Who Don't Spank: Deviation in the Legitimation of Physical Force. Ph.D. Diss., Department of Sociology, University of New Hampshire.

Celis, William. 1990. "Debate over school paddling grows amid rising concerns." The New York Times. August 16:1.

Davis, Phillip. 1990. "When adults hit children in public." Paper presented at the Annual Meeting of the Society for the Study of Social Problems, August, Washington, D.C.

Dovidio, John. 1984. "Helping behavior and altruism: An empirical and conceptual overview." In Advances in Experimental Social Psychology, ed. Leonard Berkowitz, 17:362–427. New York: Academic Press.

Edgerton, Robert. 1979. Alone Together: Social Order on an Urban Beach. Berkeley: University of California Press.

Emerson, Joan. 1970. "Nothing unusual is happening." In Human Nature and Collective Behavior: Papers in Honor of Herbert Blumer, ed. Tamotsu Shibutani, 208–222. Englewood Cliffs, N.J.: Prentice-Hall.

Emerson, Robert. 1981. "On last resorts." American Journal of Sociology 87:1–22.

Emerson, Robert, and Sheldon Messinger. 1977. "The micro-politics of trouble." Social Problems 25:121–134.

Felson, Richard. 1978. "Aggression as impression management" Social Psychology 41:205–213.

Felstiner, William, Richard Abel, and Austin Sarat. 1981. "The emergence and transformation of disputes." Law and Society Review 15:631–654.

Feshbach, Seymour, and Norma Feshbach. 1978. "Child advocacy and family privacy." Journal of Social Issues 34:168–78.

Fontana, Vincent. 1976. Child Abuse in the Name of Discipline. New York: New York Foundling Hospital Center for Parent and Child Development.

Geis, Gilbert, and Ted Huston. 1983. "Bystander intervention into crime: Public policy considerations." Policy Studies Journal 11:398–408.

Gelles, Richard. 1975. "The social construction of child abuse." American Journal of Orthopsychiatry 45:363–71.

———. 1987. The Violent Home: Updated Edition. Newbury Park, Calif.: Sage.

———. 1988. Intimate Violence. New York: Simon and Schuster.

Gil, David. 1970. Violence Against Children. Cambridge, Mass.: Harvard University Press.

Giovannoni, Jeanne, and Rosina Becerra. 1979. Defining Child Abuse. New York: Free Press.

Goffman, Erving. 1963. Behavior in Public Places. New York: Free Press.

———. 1971. Relations in Public. New York: Harper and Row.

Goode, William. 1971. "Force and violence in the family." Journal of Marriage and the Family 33:624–36.

Gulliver, P. H. 1979. Disputes and Negotiations. New York: Academic Press.

Harding, Christopher, and Richard Ireland. 1989. Punishment: Rhetoric, Rule, and Practice. New York: Routledge.

Huston, Ted, Mary Ruggiero, Ross Conner, and Gilbert Geis. 1981. "Bystander intervention into crime: A study based on naturally occurring episodes." Social Psychology Quarterly 44:14–23.

Johnson, John. 1986. "The changing concept of child abuse and its impact on the integrity of family life." In The American Family and the State, ed. Joseph Peden and Fred Glahe, 257–275. San Francisco, Calif.: Pacific Research Institute for Public Policy.

Kadushin, Alfred, and Judith Martin. 1981. Child Abuse: An Interactional Event. New York: Columbia University Press.

Korbin, Jill. 1980. "The cultural context of child abuse and neglect." Child Abuse and Neglect 4:3–13.

Latane, Bibb, and John Darley. 1970. The Unresponsive Bystander: Why Doesn't He Help? New York: Appleton-Century-Crofts.

Laslett, Barbara. 1973. "The family as a public and private institution: An historical perspective." Journal of Marriage and the Family August:480–492.

Lofland, Lyn. 1973. A World of Strangers: Order and Action in Urban Public Space. New York: Basic Books.

———. 1989. "Social life in the public realm: A review." Journal of Contemporary Ethnography 17:453–482.

Lyman, Stanford, and Marvin Scott. 1967. "Territoriality: A neglected sociological dimension." Social Problems 15:235–249.

Maurer, Adah. 1974. "Corporal punishment." American Psychologist 28:614–626.

Milgram, Stanley. 1970. "The experience of living in cities." Science 167:1461–1468.

National Center on Child Abuse and Neglect. 1980. Child Abuse and Neglect: State Reporting Laws. Department of Health, Education, and Welfare. Washington, D.C.: Government Printing Office. Publication Number 9(OHDS)80–30265.

National Committee for Prevention of Child Abuse. 1990. "Public attitudes and actions regarding child abuse and its prevention." Working Paper Number 840.

Perinbanayagam, R. S. 1991. Discursive Acts. New York: Aldine.

Rhodes, Richard. 1990. "Don't be a bystander." Parade. Sunday, October 14:4–7.

Robbins, Michael. 1990. "Sparing the child: How to intervene when you suspect abuse." New York 23:42–53.

Schur, Edwin. 1984. Labeling Women Deviant: Gender, Stigma, and Social Control. New York: Random House.

Shehan, Constance, and Gary Lee. 1990. "Roles and power." In Handbook of Family Measurement Techniques, ed. John Touliatos, Barry Perlmutter, and Murray Straus, 420–441. Newbury Park, Calif.: Sage.

Simms, Joanna. 1989. "Witness to child abuse." Parents
  May:90–94.
Straus, Murray, Richard Gelles, and Suzanne Steinmetz.
  1980. Behind Closed Doors: Violence in the American Family. New York: Doubleday.
Wauchope, Barbara, and Murray Straus. 1990. "Physical
  punishment and physical abuse of American chil-

dren: Incidence rates by age, gender, and occupa-
tional class." In Physical Violence in American
Families: Risk Factors and Adaptions to Violence in
8,145 Families, ed. Murray Straus and Richard
Gelles, 133–148. New Brunswick, N.J.: Transaction
Publishers.

Paranoia and the Dynamics of Exclusion

EDWIN M. LEMERT

The paranoid process begins with persistent inter-personal difficulties between the individual and his family, or his work associates and superiors, or neighbors, or other persons in the community. These frequently or even typically arise out of bona fide or recognizable issues centering upon some actual or threatened loss of status for the individual. This is related to such things as the death of relatives, loss of a position, loss of professional certification, failure to be promoted, age and physiological life cycle changes, mutilations, and changes in family and marital relationships. The status changes are distinguished by the fact that they leave no alternative acceptable to the individual, from whence comes their "intolerable" or "unendurable" quality. For example: the man trained to be a teacher who loses his certificate, which means he can never teach; or the man of 50 years of age who is faced with loss of promotion which is a regular order of upward mobility in an organization, who knows that he can't "start

Reprinted from *Sociometry*, Vol. 25, No. 1 (March 1962),
pp. 7–15, by permission of the author and the American Sociological Association.

The research for this paper was in part supported by a grant
from the California State Department of Mental Hygiene, arranged with the assistance of Dr. W. A. Oliver, Associate Superintendent of Napa State Hospital, who also helped as a
critical consultant and made the facilities of the hospital available.

over"; or the wife undergoing hysterectomy, which mutilates her image as a woman.

In cases where no dramatic status loss can be discovered, a series of failures often is present, failures which may have been accepted or adjusted to, but with progressive tension as each new status situation is entered. The unendurability of the current status loss, which may appear unimportant to others, is a function of an intensified commitment, in some cases born of an awareness that there is a quota placed on failures in our society. Under some such circumstances, failures have followed the person, and his reputation as a "difficult person" has preceded him. This means that he often has the status of a stranger on trial in each new group he enters, and that the groups or organizations willing to take a chance on him are marginal from the standpoint of their probable tolerance for his actions.

The behavior of the individual—arrogance, insults, presumption of privilege and exploitation of weaknesses in others—initially has a segmental or checkered pattern in that it is confined to status-committing interactions. Outside of these, the person's behavior may be quite acceptable—courteous, considerate, kind, even indulgent. Likewise, other persons and members of groups vary considerably in their tolerance for the relevant behavior, depending on the extent to which it threatens individual and organizational values, impedes functions, or sets in motion embarrassing sequences of social actions. In the early generic period, tolerance by others for the individual's aggressive behavior generally speaking is broad, and it is very likely to be interpreted as a variation of normal behavior, particularly in the absence of biographical knowledge of the person. At most, people observe that "there is something odd about him," or "he must be upset," or "he is just ornery," or "I don't quite understand him" [1].

At some point in the chain of interactions, a new configuration takes place in perceptions others have of the individual, with shifts in figure-ground relations. The individual, as we have already indicated, is an ambiguous figure, comparable to textbook figures of stairs or out-lined cubes which reverse themselves when studied intently. From a normal variant the person becomes "unreliable," "untrustworthy," "dangerous," or someone with whom others "do not wish to be involved." An illustration nicely apropos of this came out in the reaction of the head of a music department in a university when he granted an interview to a man who had worked for years on a theory to compose music mathematically:

When he asked to be placed on the staff so that he could use the electronic computers of the University I shifted my ground...when I offered an objection to his theory, he became disturbed, so I changed my reaction to "yes and no."

As is clear from this, once the perceptual reorientation takes place, either as the outcome of continuous interaction or through the receipt of biographical information, interaction changes qualitatively. In our words it becomes *spurious,* distinguished by patronizing, evasion, "humoring," guiding conversation onto selected topics, underreaction, and silence, all calculated either to prevent intense interaction or to protect individual and group values by restricting access to them. When the interaction is between two or more persons it is cued by a whole repertoire of subtle expressive signs which are meaningful only to them.

The net effects of spurious interaction are to:

1. stop the flow of information to ego;
2. create a discrepancy between expressed ideas and affect among those with whom he interacts;
3. make the situation or the group image an ambiguous one for ego, much as he is for others.

Needless to say this kind of spurious interaction is one of the most difficult for an adult in our society to cope with, because it complicates or makes decisions impossible for him and also because it is morally invidious.[1]

The process from inclusion to exclusion is by no means an even one. Both individuals and members of groups change their perceptions and reactions, and vacillation is common, depending upon the interplay of values, anxieties and guilt on both sides. Members of an excluding group may decide they have been unfair and seek to bring the individual back into their confidence. This overture may be rejected or used by ego as a means of further attack. We have also found that ego may capitulate, sometimes abjectly, to others and seek group reentry, only to be rejected. In some cases compromises are struck and a partial reintegration of ego into informal social relations is achieved. The direction which informal exclusion takes depends upon ego's reactions, the degree of communication between his interactors, the composition and structure of the informal groups, and the perceptions of "key others" at points of interaction which directly affect ego's status.

ORGANIZATIONAL CRISIS AND FORMAL EXCLUSION

Thus far we have discussed exclusion as an informal process. Informal exclusion may take place but leave ego's formal status in an organization intact. So long as this status is preserved and rewards are sufficient to validate it on his terms, an uneasy peace between him and others may prevail. Yet ego's social isolation and his strong commitments make him an unpredictable factor; furthermore the rate of change and internal power struggles, especially in large and complex organizations, means that preconditions of stability may be short lived.

Organizational crises involving a paranoid relationship arise in several ways. The individual may act in ways which arouse intolerable anxieties in others, who demand that "something be done." Again, by going to higher authority or making appeals outside the organization, he may set in motion procedures which leave those in power no other choice than to take action. In some situations ego remains relatively quiescent and does not openly attack the organization. Action against him is set off by growing anxieties or calculated motives of associates—in some cases his immediate superiors. Finally, regular organizational procedures incidental to promotion, retirement or reassignment may precipitate the crisis.

Assuming a critical situation in which the conflict between the individual and members of the organization leads to action to formally exclude him, several possibilities exist. One is the transfer of ego from one department, branch or division of the organization to another, a device frequently resorted to in the armed services or in large corporations. This requires that the individual be persuaded to make the change and that some department will accept him. While this may be accomplished in different ways, not infrequently artifice, withholding information, bribery, or thinly disguised threats figure conspicuously among the means by which the transfer is brought about. Needless to say, there is a limit to which transfers can be employed as a solution to the problem, contingent upon the size of the organization and the previous diffusion of knowledge about the transferee.

Solution number two we call encapsulation, which, in brief, is a reorganization and redefinition of ego's status. This has the effect of isolating him from the organization and making him directly responsible to one or two superiors who act as his intermediators. The change is often made palatable to ego by enhancing some of the material rewards of his status. He may be nominally promoted or "kicked upstairs," given a larger office, or a separate secretary, or relieved of onerous duties. Sometimes a special status is created for him.

This type of solution often works because it is a kind of formal recognition by the organization of ego's intense commitment to his status and in part a victory for him over his enemies. It bypasses them and puts him into direct communication with higher authority who may communicate with him in a more direct manner. It also relieves his associates of further need to connive against him. This solution is sometimes used to dispose of troublesome corporation executives, high-ranking military officers, and academic *personae non gratae* in universities.

A third variety of solutions to the problem of paranoia in an organization is outright discharge, forced resignation or non-renewal of appointment. Finally, there may be an organized move to have the individual in the paranoid relationship placed on sick leave, or to compel him to take psychiatric treatment. The extreme expression of this is pressure (as on the family) or direct action to have the person committed to a mental hospital.

The order of the enumerated solutions to the paranoid problem in a rough way reflects the amount of risk associated with the alternatives, both as to the probabilities of failure and of damaging repercussions to the organization. Generally, organizations seem to show a good deal of resistance to making or carrying out decisions which require expulsion of the individual or forcing hospitalization, regardless of his mental condition. One reason for this is that the person may have power within the organization, based upon his position, or monopolized skills and information,[2] and unless there is a strong coalition against him the general conservatism of administrative judgments will run in his favor. Herman Wouk's novel of *The Caine Mutiny* dramatizes some of the difficulties of cashiering a person from a position of power in an essentially conservative military organization. An extreme of this conservatism is illustrated by one case in which we found a department head retained in his position in an organization even though he was actively hallucinating as well as expressing paranoid delusions.[3] Another factor working on the individual's side is that discharge of a person in a position of power reflects unfavorably upon those who placed him there. Ingroup solidarity of administrators may be involved, and the methods of the opposition may create sympathy for ego at higher levels.

Even when the person is almost totally excluded and informally isolated within an organization, he may have power outside. This weighs heavily when the external power can be invoked in some way, or when it automatically leads to raising questions as to the internal workings of the organization. This touches upon the more salient reason for reluctance to eject an uncooperative and retaliatory person, even when he is relatively unimportant to the organization. We refer to a kind of negative power derived from the vulnerability of organizations to unfavorable publicity and exposure of their private lives that are likely if the crisis proceeds to formal hearings, case review or litigation. This is an imminent possibility where paranoia exists. If hospital commitment is attempted, there is a possibility that a jury trial will be demanded, which will force leaders of the organization to defend their actions. If the crisis turns into a legal contest of this sort, it is not easy to prove insanity, and there may be damage suits. Even if the facts heavily support the petitioners, such contests can only throw unfavorable light upon the organization.

THE CONSPIRATORIAL NATURE OF EXCLUSION

A conclusion from the foregoing is that organizational vulnerability as well as anticipations of retaliations from the paranoid person lay a functional basis for conspiracy among those seeking to contain or oust him. Probabilities are strong that a coalition will appear within the organization, integrated by a common commitment to oppose the paranoid person. This, the exclusionist group, demands loyalty, solidarity and secrecy from its members; it acts in accord with a common scheme and in varying degrees utilizes techniques of manipulation and misrepresentation.

Conspiracy in rudimentary form can be detected in informal exclusion apart from an organizational crisis. This was illustrated in an office research team in which staff members huddled around a water cooler to discuss the unwanted associate. They also used office telephones to arrange coffee breaks without him and employed symbolic cues in his presence, such as humming the Dragnet theme song when he approached the group. An office rule against extraneous conversation was introduced with the collusion of supervisors, ostensibly for everyone, actually to restrict the behavior of the isolated worker. In another case an interview schedule designed by a researcher was changed at a conference arranged without him. When he sought an explanation at a subsequent conference, his associates pretended to have no knowledge of the changes.

Conspiratorial behavior comes into sharpest focus during organizational crises in which the exclusionists who initiate action become an embattled group. There is a concerted effort to gain consensus for this view, to solidify the group and to halt close interaction with those unwilling to completely join the coalition. Efforts are also made to neutralize those who remain uncommitted but who can't be kept ignorant of the plans afoot. Thus an external appearance of unanimity is given even if it doesn't exist.

Much of the behavior of the group at this time is strategic in nature, with determined calculations as to "what we will do if he does this or that." In one of our cases, a member on a board of trustees spoke of the "game being played" with the person in controversy with them. Planned action may be carried to the length of agreeing upon the exact words to be used when confronted or challenged by the paranoid individual. Above all there is continuous, precise communication among exclusionists, exemplified in one case by mutual exchanging of copies of all letters sent and received from ego.

Concern about secrecy in such groups is revealed by such things as carefully closing doors and lowering of voices when ego is brought under discussion. Meeting places and times may be varied from normal procedures; documents may be filed in unusual places and certain telephones may not be used during a paranoid crisis.

The visibility of the individual's behavior is greatly magnified during this period; often he is the main topic of conversation among the exclusionists, while rumors of the difficulties spread to other groups, which in some cases may be drawn into the controversy. At a certain juncture steps are taken to keep the members of the ingroup continually informed of the individual's movements and, if possible, of his plans. In effect, if not in form, this amounts to spying. Members of one embattled group, for example, hired an outside person unknown to their accuser to take notes on a speech he delivered to enlist a community organization on his side. In another case, a person having an office opening onto that of a department head was persuaded to act as an informant for the nucleus of persons working to depose the head from his position of authority. This group also seriously debated placing an all-night watch in front of their perceived malefactor's house.

Concomitant with the magnified visibility of the paranoid individual, come distortions of his image, most pronounced in the inner coterie of exclusionists. His size, physical strength, cunning, and anecdotes of his outrages are exaggerated, with a central thematic emphasis on the fact that he is dangerous. Some individuals give cause for such beliefs in that previously they have engaged in violence or threats, others do not. One encounters characteristic contradictions in interviews on this point, such as: "No, he has never struck anyone around here—just fought with the policemen at the State Capitol," or "No, I am not afraid of him, but one of these days he will explode."

It can be said parenthetically that the alleged dangerousness of paranoid persons storied in fiction and drama has never been systematically demonstrated. As a matter of fact, the only substantial data on this, from a study of delayed admissions, largely paranoid, to a mental hospital in Norway, disclosed that "neither the paranoiacs nor paranoids have been dangerous, and most not particularly troublesome" [4]. Our interpretation of this, as suggested earlier, is that the imputed dangerousness of the paranoid individual does not come from physical fear but from the organizational threat he presents and the need to justify collective action against him.[4]

However, this is not entirely tactical behavior—as is demonstrated by anxieties and tensions which mount among those in the coalition during the more critical phases of their interaction. Participants may develop fears quite analogous to those of classic conspirators. One leader in such a group spoke of the period of the paranoid crisis as a "week of terror," during which he was wracked with insomnia and "had to take his stomach pills." Projection was revealed by a trustee who, during a school crisis occasioned by discharge of an aggressive teacher, stated that he "watched his shadows," and "wondered if all would be well when he returned home at night." Such tensional states, working along with a kind of closure of communication within the group, are both a cause and an effect of amplified group interaction which distorts or symbolically rearranges the image of the person against whom they act.

Once the battle is won by the exclusionists, their version of the individual as dangerous becomes a crystallized rationale for official action. At this point misrepresentation becomes part of a more deliberate manipulation of ego. Gross misstatements, most frequently called "pretexts," become justifiable ways of getting his cooperation, for example, to get him to submit to psychiatric examination or detention preliminary to hospital commitment. This aspect of the process has been effectively detailed by Goffman, with his concept of a "betrayal funnel" through which a patient enters a hospital [5]. We need not elaborate on this, other than to confirm its occurrence in the exclusion process, complicated in our cases by legal strictures and the ubiquitous risk of litigation.

THE GROWTH OF DELUSION

The general idea that the paranoid person symbolically fabricates the conspiracy against him is in our estimation incorrect or incomplete. Nor can we agree that he lacks insight, as is so frequently claimed. To the contrary, many paranoid persons properly realize that they are being isolated and excluded by concerted interaction, or that they are being manipulated. However, they are at a loss to estimate accurately or realistically the dimensions and form of the coalition arrayed against them.

As channels of communication are closed to the paranoid person, he has no means of getting feedback on consequences of his behavior, which is essential for correcting his interpretations of the social relationships and organization which he must rely on to define his status and give him identity. He can only read overt behavior without the informal context. Although he may properly infer that people are organized against him, he can only use confrontation or formal inquisitorial procedures to try to prove this. The paranoid person must provoke strong feelings in order to receive any kind of meaningful communication from others—hence his accusations, his bluntness, his insults. Ordinarily this is non-deliberate; nevertheless, in one complex case we found the person consciously provoking discussions to get readings from others on his behavior. This man said of himself: "Some people would describe me as very perceptive, others would describe me as very imperceptive."

The need for communication and the identity which goes with it does a good deal to explain the preference of paranoid persons for formal, legalistic, written communications, and the care with which many of them preserve records of their contracts with others. In some ways the resort to litigation is best interpreted as the effort of the individual to compel selected others to interact directly with him as equals, to engineer a situation in which evasion is impossible. The fact that the person is seldom satisfied with the outcome of his letters, his petitions, complaints and writs testifies to their function as devices for establishing contact and interaction with others, as well as "setting the record straight." The wide professional tolerance of lawyers for aggressive behavior in court and the nature of Anglo-Saxon legal institutions, which grew out of a revolt against conspiratorial or star-chamber justice, mean that the individual will be heard. Furthermore his charges must be answered; otherwise he wins by default. Sometimes he wins small victories, even if he loses the big ones. He may earn grudging respect as an adversary, and sometimes shares a kind of legal camaraderie with others in the courts. He gains an identity through notoriety. . . .

NOTES

1. The interaction in some ways is similar to that used with children, particularly the *"enfant terrible."* The function of language in such interactions was studied by Sapir [2] years ago.
2. For a systematic analysis of the organizational difficulties in removing an "unpromotable" person from a position see [3].
3. One of the cases in the first study.
4. *Supra*, p. 3.

REFERENCES

1. Cumming, E. and J. Cumming. 1957. *Closed Ranks.* Cambridge, Mass.: Harvard Press, Ch. 6.
2. Sapir, E. 1915. "Abnormal Types of Speech in Nootka." *Canada Department of Mines, Memoir 62* (5).
3. Levenson, B. 1961. "Bureaucratic Succession." In A. Etzioni (ed.), *Complex Organizations.* New York: Holt, Rinehart and Winston, pp. 362–395.
4. Ödegard, Ö. 1958. "A Clinical Study of Delayed Admissions to a Mental Hospital." *Mental Hygiene,* 42:66–67.
5. Goffman, E. 1959. "The Moral Career of the Mental Patient." *Psychiatry,* 22:127 ff.

The Moral Career of the Mental Patient

ERVING GOFFMAN

Traditionally the term *career* has been reserved for those who expect to enjoy the rises laid out within a respectable profession. The term is coming to be used, however, in a broadened sense to refer to any social strand of any person's course through life. The perspective of natural history is taken: unique outcomes are neglected in favor of such changes over time as are basic and common to the members of a social category, although occurring independently to each of them. Such a career is not a thing that can be brilliant or disappointing; it can no more be a success than a failure. In this light, I want to consider the mental patient, drawing mainly upon data collected during a year's participant observation of patient social life in a public mental hospital,[1] wherein an attempt was made to take the patient's point of view.

One value of the concept of career is its two-sidedness. One side is linked to internal matters held dearly and closely, such as image of self and felt identity; the other side concerns official position, jural relations, and style of life, and is part of a publicly accessible institutional complex. The concept of career, then, allows one to move back and forth between the personal and the public, between the self and its significant society, without having overly to rely for data upon what the person says he thinks he imagines himself to be.

This paper, then, is an exercise in the institutional approach to the study of self. The main concern will be with the *moral* aspects of career— that is, the regular sequence of changes that career entails in the person's self and in his framework of imagery for judging himself and others.[2]

Reprinted by special permission of the author and The William Alanson White Psychiatric Foundation, Inc., from *Psychiatry: Journal for the Study of Interpersonal Processes*, Vol. 22 (May 1959), pp. 123–135. Copyright © 1959 by The William Alanson White Psychiatric Foundation, Inc.

The category "mental patient" itself will be understood in one strictly sociological sense. In this perspective, the psychiatric view of a person becomes significant only in so far as this view itself alters his social fate—an alteration which seems to become fundamental in our society when, and only when, the person is put through the process of hospitalization.[3] I therefore exclude certain neighboring categories: the undiscovered candidates who would be judged "sick" by psychiatric standards but who never come to be viewed as such by themselves or others, although they may cause everyone a great deal of trouble;[4] the office patient whom a psychiatrist feels he can handle with drugs or shock on the outside; the mental client who engages in psychotherapeutic relationships. And I include anyone, however robust in temperament, who somehow gets caught up in the heavy machinery of mental hospital servicing. In this way the effects of being treated as a mental patient can be kept quite distinct from the effects upon a person's life of traits a clinician would view as psychopathological.[5] Persons who become mental hospital patients vary widely in the kind and degree of illness that a psychiatrist would impute to them, and in the attributes by which laymen would describe them. But once started on the way, they are confronted by some importantly similar circumstances and respond to these in some importantly similar ways. Since these similarities do not come from mental illness, they would seem to occur in spite of it. It is thus a tribute to the power of social forces that the uniform status of mental patient cannot only assure an aggregate of persons a common fate and eventually, because of this, a common character, but that this social reworking can be done upon what is perhaps the most obstinate diversity of human materials that can be brought together by society. . . . [6]

The career of the mental patient falls popularly and naturalistically into three main phases: the period prior to entering the hospital, which I shall call the *prepatient phase;* the period in the hospital, the *inpatient phase;* the period after discharge from the hospital, should this occur, namely, the *ex-patient phase.*[7] This paper will deal only with the first ...[phase].

THE PREPATIENT PHASE

A relatively small group of prepatients come into the mental hospital willingly, because of their own idea of what will be good for them, or because of wholehearted agreement with the relevant members of their family. Presumably these recruits have found themselves acting in a way which is evidence to them that they are losing their minds or losing control of themselves. This view of oneself would seem to be one of the most pervasively threatening things that can happen to the self in our society, especially since it is likely to occur at a time when the person is in any case sufficiently troubled to exhibit the kind of symptom which he himself can see. As Sullivan described it,

> What we discover in the self-system of a person undergoing schizophrenic changes or schizophrenic processes, is then, in its simplest form, an extremely fear-marked puzzlement, consisting of the use of rather generalized and anything but exquisitely refined referential processes in an attempt to cope with what is essentially a failure at being human—a failure at being anything that one could respect as worth being.[8]

Coupled with the person's disintegrative re-evaluation of himself will be the new, almost equally pervasive circumstance of attempting to conceal from others what he takes to be the new fundamental facts about himself, and attempting to discover whether others too have discovered them.[9] Here I want to stress that perception of losing one's mind is based on culturally derived and socially engrained stereotypes as to the significance of symptoms such as hearing voices, losing temporal and spatial orientation, and sensing that one is being followed, and that many of the most spectacular and convincing of these symptoms in some instances psychiatrically signify merely a temporary emotional upset in a stressful situation, however terrifying to the person at the time. Similarly, the anxiety consequent upon this perception of oneself, and the strategies devised to reduce this anxiety, are not a product of abnormal psychology, but would be exhibited by any person socialized into our culture who came to conceive of himself as someone losing his mind. Interestingly, subcultures in American society apparently differ in the amount of ready imagery and encouragement they supply for such self-views, leading to differential rates of *self*-referral; the capacity to take this disintegrative view of oneself without psychiatric prompting seems to be one of the questionable cultural privileges of the upper classes.[10]

For the person who has come to see himself—with whatever justification—as mentally unbalanced, entrance to the mental hospital can sometimes bring relief, perhaps in part because of the sudden transformation in the structure of his basic social situations; instead of being to himself a questionable person trying to maintain a role as a full one, he can become an officially questioned person known to himself to be not so questionable as that. In other cases, hospitalization can make matters worse for the willing patient, confirming by the objective situation what has theretofore been a matter of the private experience of self.

Once the willing prepatient enters the hospital, he may go through the same routine of experiences as do those who enter unwillingly. In any case, it is the latter that I mainly want to consider, since in America at present these are by far the more numerous kind.[11] Their approach to the institution takes one of three classic forms: they come because they have been implored by their family or threatened with the abrogation of family ties unless they go "willingly"; they come by force under police escort; they come under misapprehension purposely induced by others, this last restricted mainly to youthful prepatients.

The prepatient's career may be seen in terms of an extrusory model; he starts out with relationships and rights, and ends up, at the beginning of his hospital stay, with hardly any of either. The moral aspects of this career, then, typically begin with the experience of abandonment, disloyalty, and embitterment. This is the case even though to others it may be obvious that he was in need of treatment, and even though in the hospital he may soon come to agree.

The case histories of most mental patients document offense against some arrangement for face-to-face living—a domestic establishment, a work place, a semipublic organization such as a church or store, a public region such as a street or park. Often there is also a record of some *complainant,* some figure who takes that action against the offender which eventually leads to his hospitalization. This may not be the person who makes the first move, but it is the person who makes what turns out to be the first effective move. Here is the *social* beginning of the patient's career, regardless of where one might locate the psychological beginning of his mental illness.

The kinds of offenses which lead to hospitalization are felt to differ in nature from those which lead to other extrusory consequences—to imprisonment, divorce, loss of job, disownment, regional exile, noninstitutional psychiatric treatment, and so forth. But little seems known about these differentiating factors; and when one studies actual commitments, alternate outcomes frequently appear to have been possible. It seems true, moreover, that for every offense that leads to an effective complaint, there are many psychiatrically similar ones that never do. No action is taken; or action is taken which leads to other extrusory outcomes; or ineffective action is taken, leading to the mere pacifying or putting off of the person who complains. Thus, as Clausen and Yarrow have nicely shown, even offenders who are eventually hospitalized are likely to have had a long series of ineffective actions taken against them.[12]

Separating those offenses which could have been used as grounds for hospitalizing the offender from those that are so used, one finds a vast number of what students of occupation call career contingencies.[13] Some of these contingencies in the mental patient's career have been suggested, if not explored, such as socioeconomic status, visibility of the offense, proximity to a mental hospital, amount of treatment facilities available, community regard for the type of treatment given in available hospitals, and so on.[14] For information about other contingencies one must rely on atrocity tales: a psychotic man is tolerated by his wife until she finds herself a boyfriend, or by his adult children until they move from a house to an apartment; an alcoholic is sent to a mental hospital because the jail is full, and a drug addict because he declines to avail himself of psychiatric treatment on the outside; a rebellious adolescent daughter can no longer be managed at home because she now threatens to have an open affair with an unsuitable companion; and so on. Correspondingly there is an equally important set of contingencies causing the person to by-pass this fate. And should the person enter the hospital, still another set of contingencies will help determine when he is to obtain a discharge—such as the desire of his family for his return, the availability of a "manageable" job, and so on. The society's official view is that inmates of mental hospitals are there primarily because they are suffering from mental illness. However, in the degree that the "mentally ill" outside hospitals numerically approach or surpass those inside hospitals, one could say that mental patients *distinctively* suffer not from mental illness, but from contingencies.

Career contingencies occur in conjunction with a second feature of the prepatient's career— *the circuit of agents*—and agencies—that participate fatefully in his passage from civilian to patient status.[15] Here is an instance of that increasingly important class of social system whose elements are agents and agencies, which are brought into systemic connection through having to take up and send on the same persons.

Some of these agent-roles will be cited now, with the understanding that in any concrete circuit a role may be filled more than once, and a single person may fill more than one of them.

First is the *next-of-relation*—the person whom the prepatient sees as the most available of those upon whom he should be able to most depend in times of trouble; in this instance the last to doubt his sanity and the first to have done everything to save him from the fate which, it transpires, he has been approaching. The patient's next-of-relation is usually his next of kin; the special term is introduced because he need not be. Second is the *complainant,* the person who retrospectively appears to have started the person on his way to the hospital. Third are the *mediators*— the sequence of agents and agencies to which the prepatient is referred and through which he is relayed and processed on his way to the hospital. Here are included police, clergy, general medical practitioners, office psychiatrists, personnel in public clinics, lawyers, social service workers, school teachers, and so on. One of these agents will have the legal mandate to sanction commitment and will exercise it, and so those agents who precede him in the process will be involved in something whose outcome is not yet settled. When the mediators retire from the scene, the prepatient has become an inpatient, and the significant agent has become the hospital administrator.

While the complainant usually takes action in a lay capacity as a citizen, an employer, a neighbor, or a kinsman, mediators tend to be specialists and differ from those they serve in significant ways. They have experience in handling trouble, and some professional distance from what they handle. Except in the case of policemen, and perhaps some clergy, they tend to be more psychiatrically oriented than the lay public, and will see the need for treatment at times when the public does not.[16]

An interesting feature of these roles is the functional effects of their interdigitation. For example, the feelings of the patient will be influenced by whether or not the person who fills the role of complainant also has the role of next-of-relation—an embarrassing combination more prevalent, apparently, in the higher classes than in the lower.[17] Some of these emergent effects will be considered now.[18]

In the prepatient's progress from home to the hospital he may participate as a third person in what he may come to experience as a kind of *alienative coalition*. His next-of-relation presses him into coming to "talk things over" with a medical practitioner, an office psychiatrist, or some other counselor. Disinclination on his part may be met by threatening him with desertion, disownment, or other legal action, or by stressing the joint and explorative nature of the interview. But typically the next-of-relation will have set the interview up, in the sense of selecting the professional, arranging for time, telling the professional something about the case, and so on. This move effectively tends to establish the next-of-relation as the responsible person to whom pertinent findings can be divulged, while effectively establishing the other as the patient. The prepatient often goes to the interview with the understanding that he is going as an equal of someone who is so bound together with him that a third person could not come between them in fundamental matters; this after all, is one way in which close relationships are defined in our society. Upon arrival at the office the prepatient suddenly finds that he and his next-of-relation have not been accorded the same roles, and apparently that a prior understanding between the professional and the next-of-relation has been put in operation against him. In the extreme but common case the professional first sees the prepatient alone, in the role of advisor, while carefully avoiding talking things over seriously with them both together.[19] And even in those nonconsultative cases where public officials must forcibly extract a person from a family that wants to tolerate him, the next-of-relation is likely to be induced to "go along" with the official action, so that even here the prepatient may feel that an alienative coalition has been formed against him.

The moral experience of being third man in such a coalition is likely to embitter the prepatient, especially since his troubles have already probably led to some estrangement from his next-of-relation. After he enters the hospital, continued visits by his next-of-relation can give the patient the "insight" that his own best interests were being served. But the initial visits may temporarily strengthen his feeling of abandonment; he is likely to beg his visitor to get him out or at least to get him more privileges and to sympathize with the monstrousness of his plight—to which the visitor ordinarily can respond only by trying to maintain a hopeful note, by not "hearing" the requests, or by assuring the patient that the medical authorities know about these things and are doing what is medically best. The visitor then nonchalantly goes back into a world that the patient has learned is incredibly thick with freedom and privileges, causing the patient to feel that his next-of-relation is merely adding a pious gloss to a clear case of traitorous desertion.

The depth to which the patient may feel betrayed by his next-of-relation seems to be increased by the fact that another witnesses his betrayal—a factor which is apparently significant in many three-party situations. An offended person may well act forbearantly and accommodatively toward an offender when the two are alone, choosing peace ahead of justice. The presence of a witness, however, seems to add something to the implications of the offense. For then it is beyond the power of the offended and offender to forget about, erase, or suppress what has happened; the offense has become a public social fact.[20] When the witness is a mental health commission as is sometimes the case, the witnessed betrayal can verge on a "degradation ceremony."[21] In such circumstances, the offended patient may feel that some kind of extensive reparative action is required before witnesses, if his honor and social weight are to be restored.

Two other aspects of sensed betrayal should be mentioned. First, those who suggest the possibility of another's entering a mental hospital are not likely to provide a realistic picture of how in fact it may strike him when he arrives. Often he is told that he will get required medical treatment and a rest, and may well be out in a few months or so. In some cases they may thus be concealing what they know, but I think, in general, they will be telling what they see as the truth. For here there is a quite relevant difference between patients and mediating professionals; mediators, more so than the public at large, may conceive of mental hospitals as short-term medical establishments where required rest and attention can be voluntarily obtained, and not as places of coerced exile. When the prepatient finally arrives he is likely to learn quite quickly, quite differently. He then finds that the information given him about life in the hospital has had the effect of his having put up less resistance to entering than he now sees he would have put up had he known the facts. Whatever the intentions of those who participated in his transition from person to patient, he may sense they have in effect "conned" him into his present predicament.

I am suggesting that the prepatient starts out with at least a portion of the rights, liberties, and satisfactions of the civilian and ends up on a psychiatric ward stripped of almost everything. The question here is *how* this stripping is managed. This is the second aspect of betrayal I want to consider.

As the prepatient may see it, the circuit of significant figures can function as a kind of *betrayal funnel*. Passage from person to patient may be effected through a series of linked stages, each managed by a different agent. While each stage tends to bring a sharp decrease in adult free status, each agent may try to maintain the fiction that no further decrease will occur. He may even manage to turn the prepatient over to the next agent while sustaining this note. Further, through words, cues, and gestures, the prepatient is implicitly asked by the current agent to join with him in sustaining a running line of polite small talk that tactfully avoids the administrative facts of the situation, becoming, with each stage, progressively more at odds with these facts. The spouse would rather not have to cry to get the prepatient to visit a psychiatrist; psychiatrists would rather not have a scene when the prepatient learns that he and his spouse are being seen separately and in different ways; the police infrequently bring a prepatient to the hospital in a strait jacket, finding it much easier all around to give him a cigarette, some kindly words, and freedom to relax in the back seat of the patrol car; and finally, the admitting psychiatrist finds he can do his work better in the relative quiet and luxury of the "admission suite" where, as an incidental consequence, the notion can survive that a mental hospital is indeed a comforting place. If the prepatient heeds all of these implied requests and is reasonably decent about the whole thing, he can travel the whole circuit from home to hospital without forcing anyone to look directly at what is happening or to deal with the raw emotion that his situation might well cause him to express. His showing consideration for those who are moving him toward the hospital allows them to show consideration for him, with the joint result that these interactions can be sustained with some of the protective harmony characteristic of ordinary face-to-face dealings. But should the new patient cast his mind back over the sequence of steps leading to hospitalization, he may feel that everyone's *current* comfort was being busily sustained while his long-range welfare was being undermined. This realization may constitute a moral experience that further separates him for the time from the people on the outside.[22]

I would now like to look at the circuit of career agents from the point of view of the agents themselves. Mediators in the person's transition from civil to patient status—as well as his keepers, once he is in the hospital—have an interest in establishing a responsible next-of-relation as the patient's deputy or *guardian;* should there be no obvious candidate for the role, someone may be sought out and pressed into it. Thus while a person is gradually being transformed into a patient, a next-of-relation is gradually being transformed into a guardian. With a guardian on the scene, the whole transition process can be kept tidy. He is likely to be familiar with the prepatient's civil involvements and business, and can tie up loose ends that might otherwise be left to entangle the hospital. Some of the prepatient's abrogated civil rights can be transferred to him, thus helping to sustain the legal fiction that while the prepatient does not actually have his rights he somehow actually has not lost them.

Inpatients commonly sense, at least for a time, that hospitalization is a massive unjust deprivation, and sometimes succeed in convincing a few persons on the outside that this is the case. It often turns out to be useful, then, for those identified with inflicting these deprivations, however justifiably, to be able to point to the cooperation and agreement of someone whose relationship to the patient places him above suspicion, firmly defining him as the person most likely to have the patient's personal interest at heart. If the guardian is satisfied with what is happening to the new inpatient, the world ought to be.[23]

Now it would seem that the greater the legitimate personal stake one party has in another, the better he can take the role of guardian to the other. But the structural arrangements in society which lead to the acknowledged merging of two persons' interests lead to additional consequences. For the person to whom the patient turns for help—for protection against such threats as involuntary commitment—is just the person to whom the mediators and hospital administrators logically turn for authorization. It is understandable, then, that some patients will come to sense, at least for a time, that the closeness of a relationship tells nothing of its trustworthiness.

There are still other functional effects emerging from this complement of roles. If and when the next-of-relation appeals to mediators for help in the trouble he is having with the prepatient, hospitalization may not, in fact, be in his mind. He may not even perceive the prepatient as mentally sick, or, if he does, he may not consistently hold to this view.[24] It is the circuit of mediators, with their great psychiatric sophistication and their belief in the medical character of mental hospitals, that will often define the situation for the next-of-relation, assuring him that hospitalization is a possible solution and a good one, that it involves no betrayal, but is rather a medical action taken in the best interests of the prepatient. Here the next-of-relation may learn that doing his duty to the prepatient may cause the prepatient to distrust and even hate him for the time. But the fact that this course of action may have had to be pointed out and prescribed by professionals, and be defined by them as a moral duty, relieves the next-of-relation of some of the guilt he may feel.[25] It is a poignant fact that an adult son or daughter may be pressed into the role of mediator, so that the hostility that might otherwise be directed against the spouse is passed on to the child.[26]

Once the prepatient is in the hospital, the same guilt-carrying function may become a significant part of the staff's job in regard to the next-of-relation.[27] These reasons for feeling that he himself has not betrayed the patient, even though the patient may then think so, can later provide the next-of-relation with a defensible line to take when visiting the patient in the hospital and a basis for hoping that the relationship can be re-established after its hospital moratorium. And of course this position, when sensed by the patient, can provide him with excuses for the next-of-relation, when and if he comes to look for them.[28]

Thus while the next-of-relation can perform important functions for the mediators and hospital administrators, they in turn can perform important functions for him. One finds, then, an emergent unintended exchange or reciprocation of functions, these functions themselves being often unintended.

The final point I want to consider about the prepatient's moral career is its peculiarly *retroactive* character. Until a person actually arrives at the hospital there usually seems no way of knowing for sure that he is destined to do so, given the determinative role of career contingencies. And until the point of hospitalization is reached, he or others may not conceive of him as a person who is becoming a mental patient. However, since he will be held against his will in the hospital, his next-of-relation and the hospital staff will be in great need of a rationale for the hardships they are sponsoring. The medical elements of the staff will also need evidence that they are still in the trade they were trained for. These problems are eased, no doubt unintentionally, by the case-history construction that is placed on the patient's past life, this having the effect of demonstrating that all along he had been becoming sick, that he finally became very sick, and that if he had not been hospitalized much worse things would have happened to him—all of which, of course, may be true. Incidentally, if the patient wants to make sense out of his stay in the hospital, and, as already suggested, keep alive the possibility of once again conceiving of his next-of-relation as a decent, well-meaning person, then he too will have reason to believe some of this psychiatric workup of his past.

Here is a very ticklish point for the sociology of careers. An important aspect of every career is the view the person constructs when he looks backward over his progress; in a sense, however, the whole of the prepatient career derives from this reconstruction. The fact of having had a prepatient career, starting with an effective complaint, becomes an important part of the mental patient's orientation, but this part can begin to be played only after hospitalization proves that what he had been having, but no longer has, is a career as a prepatient....

NOTES

1. The study was conducted during 1955–56 under the auspices of the Laboratory of Socio-environmental Studies of the National Institute of Mental Health. I am grateful to the Laboratory Chief, John A. Clausen, and to Dr. Winfred Overholser, Superintendent, and the late Dr. Jay Hoffman, then First Assistant Physician of Saint Elizabeth's Hospital, Washington, D.C., for the ideal cooperation they freely provided. A preliminary report is contained in Goffman, "Interpersonal Persuasion," pp. 117–193; in *Group Processes: Transactions of the*

Third Conference, edited by Bertram Schaffner; New York, Josiah Macy, Jr. Foundation, 1957. A shorter version of this paper was presented at the Annual Meeting of the American Sociological Society, Washington, D.C., August, 1957.

2. Material on moral career can be found in early social anthropological work on ceremonies of status transition, and in classic social psychological descriptions of those spectacular changes in one's view of self that can accompany participation in social movements and sects. Recently new kinds of relevant data have been suggested by psychiatric interest in the problem of "identity" and sociological studies of work careers and "adult socialization."

3. This point has recently been made by Elaine and John Cumming, *Closed Ranks;* Cambridge, Commonwealth Fund, Harvard Univ. Press, 1957; pp. 101–102. "Clinical experience supports the impression that many people define mental illness as 'That condition for which a person is treated in a mental hospital.'...Mental illness, it seems, is a condition which afflicts people who must go to a mental institution, but until they do almost anything they do is normal." Leila Deasy has pointed out to me the correspondence here with the situation in white collar crime. Of those who are detected in this activity, only the ones who do not manage to avoid going to prison find themselves accorded the social role of the criminal.

4. Case records in mental hospitals are just now coming to be exploited to show the incredible amount of trouble a person may cause for himself and others before anyone begins to think about him psychiatrically, let alone take psychiatric action against him. See John A. Clausen and Marian Radke Yarrow, "Paths to the Mental Hospital," *J. Social Issues* (1955) 11:25–32; August B. Hollingshead and Frederick C. Redlich, *Social Class and Mental Illness;* New York, Wiley, 1958; pp. 173–174.

5. An illustration of how this perspective may be taken to all forms of deviancy may be found in Edwin Lemert, *Social Pathology;* New York, McGraw-Hill, 1951; see especially pp. 74–76. A specific application to mental defectives may be found in Stewart E. Perry, "Some Theoretic Problems of Mental Deficiency and Their Action Implications," *Psychiatry* (1954) 17:45–73; see especially p. 68.

6. [Goffman developed this point more fully as follows.] Whatever...the various patient's psychiatric diagnoses, and whatever the special ways in which social life on the "inside" is unique, the researcher can find that he is participating in a community not significantly different from any other he has studied. Conscientious objectors who voluntarily went to jail sometimes arrived at the same conclusion regarding criminal inmates. See, for example, Alfred Hassler, *Diary of a Self-made Convict;* Chicago, Regnery, 1954; p. 74.

7. This simple picture is complicated by the somewhat special experience of roughly a third of ex-patients—namely, readmission to the hospital, this being the recidivist or "repatient" phase.

8. Harry Stack Sullivan, *Clinical Studies in Psychiatry,* edited by Helen Swick Perry, Mary Ladd Gavel, and Martha Gibbon: New York, Norton, 1956; pp. 184–185.

9. This moral experience can be contrasted with that of a person learning to become a marihuana...[user], whose discovery that he can be "high" and still "op" effectively without being detected apparently leads to a new level of use. See Howard S. Becker, "Marihuana Use and Social Control," *Social Problems* (1955) 3:35–44; see especially pp. 40–41.

10. See Hollingshead and Redlich, *op. cit.,* p. 187, Table 6, where relative frequency is given of self-referral by social class grouping.

11. The distinction employed here between willing and unwilling patients cuts across the legal one, of voluntary and committed, since some persons who are glad to come to the mental hospital may be legally committed, and of those who come only because of strong familial pressure, some may sign themselves in as voluntary patients.

12. Clausen and Yarrow, *op. cit.*

13. An explicit application of this notion to the field of mental health may be found in Edwin M. Lemert, "Legal Commitment and Social Control," *Sociology and Social Research* (1946) 30:370–378.

14. For example, Jerome K. Meyers and Leslie Schaffer, "Social Stratification and Psychiatric Practice: A Study of an Outpatient Clinic," *Amer. Sociological Rev.* (1954) 19:307–310. Lemert, see footnote 5; pp. 402–403. *Patients in Mental Institutions, 1941;* Washington, D.C., Department of Commerce, Bureau of the Census, 1941; p. 2.

15. For one circuit of agents and its bearing on career contingencies, see Oswald Hall, "The Stages of a Medical Career," *Amer. J. Sociology* (1948) 53:327–336.

16. See Cumming and Cumming, *op. cit.;* p. 92.

17. Hollingshead and Redlich, *op. cit.;* p. 187.

18. For an analysis of some of these circuit implications for the inpatient, see Leila C. Deasy and Olive W. Quinn, "The Wife of the Mental Patient and the Hospital Psychiatrist," *J. Social Issues* (1955) 11:49–60. An interesting illustration of this kind of analysis may also be found in

Alan G. Gowman, "Blindness and the Role of Companion," *Social Problems* (1956) 4:68–75. A general statement may be found in Robert Merton, "The Role Set: Problems in Sociological Theory," *British J. Sociology* (1957) 8:106–120.

19. I have one case record of a man who claims he thought *he* was taking his wife to see the psychiatrist, not realizing until too late that his wife had made the arrangements.

20. A paraphrase from Kurt Riezler, "The Social Psychology of Shame," *Amer. J. Sociology* (1943) 48:458.

21. See Harold Garfinkel, "Conditions of Successful Degradation Ceremonies," *Amer. J. Sociology* (1956) 61:420–424.

22. Concentration camp practices provide a good example of the function of the betrayal funnel in inducing cooperation and reducing struggle and fuss, although here the mediators could not be said to be acting in the best interests of the inmates. Police picking up persons from their homes would sometimes joke good-naturedly and offer to wait while coffee was being served. Gas chambers were fitted out like delousing rooms, and victims taking off their clothes were told to note where they were leaving them. The sick, aged, weak, or insane who were selected for extermination were sometimes driven away in Red Cross ambulances to camps referred to by terms such as "observation hospital." See David Boder, *I Did Not Interview the Dead;* Urbana, Univ. of Illinois Press, 1949; p. 81; and Elie A. Cohen, *Human Behavior in the Concentration Camp;* London, Cape, 1954; pp. 32, 37, 107.

23. Interviews collected by the Clausen group at NIMH suggest that when a wife comes to be a guardian the responsibility may disrupt previous distance from in-laws, leading either to a new supportive coalition with them or to a marked withdrawal from them.

24. For an analysis of these nonpsychiatric kinds of perception, see Marian Radke Yarrow, Charlotte Green Schwartz, Harriet S. Murphy, and Leila Calhoun Deasy, "The Psychological Meaning of Mental Illness in the Family," *J. Social Issues* (1955) 11:12–24; Charlotte Green Schwartz, "Perspectives on Deviance—Wives' Definitions of Their Husbands' Mental Illness," *Psychiatry* (1957) 20:275–291.

25. This guilt-carrying function is found, of course, in other role-complexes. Thus, when a middle-class couple engages in the process of legal separation or divorce, each of their lawyers usually takes the position that his job is to acquaint his client with all of the potential claims and rights, pressing his client into demanding these, in spite of any nicety of feelings about the rights and honorableness of the ex-partner. The client, in all good faith, can then say to self and to the ex-partner that the demands are being made only because the lawyer insists it is best to do so.

26. Recorded in the Clausen data.

27. This point is made by Cumming, see *op. cit.;* p. 129.

28. There is an interesting contrast here with the moral career of the tuberculosis patient. I am told by Julius Roth that tuberculous patients are likely to come to the hospital willingly, agreeing with their next-of-relation about treatment. Later in their hospital career, when they learn how long they yet have to stay and how depriving and irrational some of the hospital rulings are, they may seek to leave, be advised against this by the staff and by relatives, and only then begin to feel betrayed.

PART TWO

THE FORMAL REGULATION OF DEVIANCE

In addition to typing on an informal, interpersonal level, much typing of deviants occurs on a formal or official level. In fact, complex societies such as ours invariably include formal agencies whose role it is to seek out, identify, and regulate deviance. Such agencies include the police, the courts, the federal Drug Enforcement Administration, the Department of the Treasury (whose agents deal with smuggling), county and state health and welfare agencies—the list could go on and on. When these agencies of social control take action against someone adjudged deviant, the effects can be dramatic. These may include a formal confirmation of deviant typing, induction into a deviant role, and launching on a deviant career. This turning point in the deviant's life can also bring about a radical redefinition of self. What the deviant may experience as a unique personal crisis, however, is usually merely organizational routine for the agent and the agency.

The controls that such agents and agencies can impose differ significantly from those available to lay people. In terms of power, for example, the political state stands behind many agencies, while informal labelers may be no more powerful than the deviant. Likewise, the agents' control is usually legitimized by the state, whereas labeling by other people may simply represent an opposing set of norms. Finally, agents of social control usually operate according to an elaborate set of rules that provide standardized ways of dealing with deviants; other people's actions against the deviant need not be based on any plan at all.

A special perspective, composed of rules, beliefs, and practices, underlies the formal processing of deviants. In the course of their work with deviant clients, agents of social control come to adopt this perspective. As they become more familiar with the agency's perspective, agents find that they can process their deviant clients more efficiently. And, as these conceptions become routine for agents, so does their processing of clients take on a routine character.

In this part of the book, we consider the basic premises reflected in the treatment and processing of deviants by various social control agencies. We take up, in sequence, how agencies dealing with the sick and the disabled define and respond to their clients, the special perspective police use in their work, the assumptions that court personnel make about the people whom they process, and the social conditions under which lay people adopt the perspectives of agencies of social control.

HELP AGENCIES AND THEIR THEORIES

When primary group controls break down (as noted in Part I), formal agencies of social control go into action on behalf of the larger society. Criminal justice agencies (such as police, court, and corrections) collect and process those deviants said to have broken the criminal law. Other agencies, broadly classified as helping agencies, take in clients who appear to be mentally or physically ill or whose long-standing handicaps make it difficult for them to fend for themselves. People become clients of these two different sets of control agencies under different circumstances. But in both cases people who work in either type of agency develop ideas about their clientele. Thus, criminal justice agents presume their clientele intended the harm they have allegedly done to others and do not voluntarily seek their official services. By contrast, helping agents presume their clientele did not intend the harm they have done to others or to themselves and that they may voluntarily seek the services of the helping agency.

Though the circumstances of entry may be involuntary in the criminal justice case or voluntary in the helping agency case, agents in either type of agency would be hard-pressed to perform their work without a shared body of ideas about their clientele. This collection of ideas, called here agency theories, underlies a number of very important organizational tasks. Not only do these theories help in categorizing the people who have come to the official attention of the agency but they also help in specifying which agents should do what and when, how, and why such action should be taken in the course of the client's career in the agency. Perhaps most important of all are those unwritten rules—derived from agency theories—that prescribe the kinds of treatment the clients may or may not receive. In effect, an etiquette of agency–client relations obtains. And clients often do not receive services until their behavior corresponds with the category into which the agents have assigned them. Further, categorization takes place as often if not more so in helping agencies as it does in criminal justice agencies and is equally consequential.

POLICE WORK

The police perspective—distinctly unlike other people's—is organized around "looking for trouble." Such "trouble" includes traffic violations, crimes, and observably eccentric or violent behavior. For police officers, trouble is defined by the penal code, by private citizens, and by experience with the kind of persons police define as de facto criminals.

Police culture combines legal and lay categories of deviance so as to be able to predict violations in advance. The police have advance notions of what suspects ought to look like, how they might make trouble, and how they should be typed. These routinized conceptions enable police to label suspects; thus they aid in the apprehension of deviants. In short, police perceive trouble in accordance with their working conceptions of it. Then they can regularize and deal with deviance in an orderly manner.

THE DEVIANT IN COURT

Police develop their categories of deviants from contact with a variety of suspects. When they make contact with a deviant, for example, their usual concern is the mechanics of arrest. Thus one way in which police type suspects is according to how hard or easy it will be to arrest them. By contrast, court personnel employ less pragmatic categories in dealing with suspects, because their roles are abstract and symbolic in accordance with the rules of law.

Court processing involves interaction (some of it behind the scenes) among judge, prosecuting attorney, defense attorney, bailiff, and sometimes a jury. To a very large extent it depends on legal terminology, court norms, and routine conceptions of defendants. Just as police fit suspects into a system of types, the court fits defendants into routine conceptions of typical cases. The use of these routine conceptions means that some persons who fit the court's conceptions of typical cases receive a prison sentence, while others who are guilty of the same offense (but who do not fit the court's conceptions of typical cases) may get lighter sentences or not get into court at all. Court work is rapid to the extent that court personnel can collaborate to make the facts fit their ideas of what typical cases look like.

THE EFFECTS OF CONTACT WITH CONTROL AGENTS

When a person comes into contact with an agency of social control, the agency may view the person solely in terms of a deviant label. Initial contact with such an agency may suffice to call into question the person's "good name." Additional contact may give the person a definitely bad reputation.

Thus deviant typing may not end with the person's experience with a given agency. When meeting a stranger, for example, people look for information to help them type the stranger. If they find out that s/he has been in a prison or mental hospital, they may type the person primarily on the basis of that past experience, assuming that a person who has had contact with an agency of social control is likely to repeat the behavior that originally led to that contact. Accordingly, lay people feel less inclined to trust such a person. The agency perspective is so powerful that a deviant label, once formally applied, can long outlive any evidentiary basis. Once formally labeled, the so-called deviant becomes defined as the kind of person who probably did perform the imputed behaviors, or at least would if given a chance. Both the deviant and others may then organize their social relations around this belief.

CHAPTER 5

HELP AGENCIES AND THEIR THEORIES

Helping agents develop a set of beliefs about their work and the clients whom they are charged with helping. These beliefs include notions about the nature of the problem, the moral character of clients presenting these problems, the kinds of help to give, and the conditions under which it may be given or withheld. The readings in this section show that regardless of the kind of help sought, agency demands and goals shape the agents' definitions of their clients and the kind of help they dispense. In the process of interaction between clients and helpers, typifications emerge which come to exert powerful influences on the way agents process those clients they have come to define as deviant.

In the first reading Robert Scott shows how contrasting theories in two agencies for the blind affect how they deal with their clients. Demie Kurz then shows how hospital emergency room staff's responses to identifying and intervening in cases involving battered women is related to their definition of the women and of whether this constitutes a legitimate medical concern. Finally, Leslie Margolin shows that in child abuse investigations, social workers assume the accused is guilty, and when they file reports, they construct a deviant label that will stick to the accused, disallowing any possibility of innocence.

The Making of Blind Men

ROBERT A. SCOTT

When a blind person first comes to an organization for the blind, he usually has some specific ideas about what his primary problems are and how they can be solved. Most new clients request services that they feel will solve or ameliorate the specific problems they experience because of their visual impairment. Many want only to be able to read better, and therefore request optical aids. Others desire help with mobility problems, or with special problems of dressing, eating, or housekeeping. Some need money or medical care. A few contact agencies for the blind in search of scientific discoveries that will restore their vision. Although the exact type of help sought varies considerably, many clients feel that the substance of their problems is contained in their specific requests....

The personal conceptions that blinded persons have about the nature of their problems are in sharp contrast with beliefs that workers for the blind share about the problems of blindness. The latter regard blindness as one of the most severe of all handicaps, the effects of which are long-lasting, pervasive, and extremely difficult to ameliorate. They believe that if these problems are to be solved, blind persons must understand them and all their manifestations and willingly submit themselves to a prolonged, intensive, and comprehensive program of psychological and restorative services. *Effective socialization of the client largely depends upon changing his views about his problem.* In order to do this, the client's views about the problems of blindness must be discredited. Workers must convince him that simplistic ideas about solving the problems of blindness by means of one or a few services are unrealistic.

Workers regard the client's initial definition of his problems as akin to the visible portion of an iceberg. Beneath the surface of awareness lies a tremendously complicated mass of problems that must be dealt with before the surface problems can ever be successfully solved.

Discrediting the client's personal ideas about his problems is achieved in several ways. His initial statements about why he has come to the organization and what he hopes to receive from it are euphemistically termed "the presenting problem," a phrase that implies superficiality in the client's views. During the intake interview and then later with the caseworker or psychologist, the client is encouraged to discuss his feelings and aspirations.... However, when concrete plans are formulated, the client learns that his personal views about his problems are largely ignored. A client's request for help with a reading problem produces a recommendation by the worker for a comprehensive psychological work-up. A client's inquiries regarding the availability of financial or medical aid may elicit the suggestion that he enroll in a complicated long-term program of testing, evaluation, and training. In short, blind persons who are acceptable to the agency for the blind will often find that intake workers listen attentively to their views but then dismiss them as superficial or inaccurate.... For most persons who have come this far in the process, however, dropping out is not a particularly realistic alternative, since it implies that the blind person has other resources open to him. For the most part, such resources are not available.

...[The] experiences a blind person has before being inducted into an agency make him vulnerable to the wishes and intentions of the workers who deal with them. The ability to withstand the pressure to act, think, and feel in conformity with the workers' concept of a model blind

Reprinted with permission from Scott, Robert A. 1969. *The Making of Blind Men: A Study of Adult Socialization.* New York: Russell Sage Foundation.

person is further reduced by the fact that the workers have a virtual monopoly on the rewards and punishments in the system. By manipulating these rewards and punishments, workers are able to pressure the client into rejecting personal conceptions of problems in favor of the worker's own definition of them. Much evaluative work, in fact, involves attempts to get the client to understand and accept the agency's conception of the problems of blindness.... In face-to-face situations, the blind person is rewarded for showing insight and subtly reprimanded for continuing to adhere to earlier notions about his problems. He is led to think that he "really" understands past and present experiences when he couches them in terms acceptable to his therapist....

Psychological rewards are not the only rewards at stake in this process. A fundamental tenet of work for the blind is that a client must accept the fact of his blindness and everything implied by it before he can be effectively rehabilitated. As a result, a client must show signs of understanding his problem in the therapist's terms before he will be permitted to progress any further in the program. Since most blind persons are anxious to move along in the program as rapidly as possible, the implications of being labeled "uncooperative" are serious. Such a label prevents him from receiving basic restorative services. The uncooperative client is assigned low priority for entering preferred job programs. Workers for the blind are less willing to extend themselves on his behalf. As a result, the alert client quickly learns to become "insightful," to behave as workers expect him to.

Under these circumstances, the assumptions and theories of workers for the blind concerning blindness and rehabilitation take on new significance, for what they do is to create, shape, and mold the attitudes and behavior of the client in his role as a blind person.... [It] is in organizations for the blind that theories and explicit and implicit assumptions about blindness and rehabilitation become actualized in the clients' attitudes and behavior. We can therefore gain an understanding about the behavior of clients as blind people by examining the theories and assumptions about blindness and rehabilitation held by workers for the blind.

THE PRACTICE THEORIES OF BLINDNESS WORKERS

The beliefs, ideologies, and assumptions about blindness and rehabilitation that make up practice theories of work for the blind are legion. They include global and limited theories about blindness, ethical principles, commonsense ideas, and an array of specific beliefs that are unrelated, and often contradictory, to one another. Contained in this total array of ideas are two basically different approaches to the problems of blindness. The first I will call the "restorative approach"; the most complete and explicit version of this approach is contained in the writings of Father Thomas Carroll.[1] The second I will call the "accommodative approach." This approach has never been formulated into a codified practice theory; rather, it is only apparent in the programs and policies of more orthodox agencies for the blind.

THE RESTORATIVE APPROACH

The basic premise of the restorative approach to blindness is that most blind people can be restored to a high level of independence enabling them to lead a reasonably normal life. However, these goals are attainable only if the person accepts completely the fact that he is blind, and only after he has received competent professional counseling and training....

Seven basic kinds of losses resulting from blindness are identified: (1) the losses to psychological security—the losses of physical integrity, confidence in the remaining senses, reality contact with the environment, visual background, and light security; (2) the losses of the skills of mobility and techniques of daily living; (3) the communication losses, such as the loss of ease of written and spoken communication, and of information about daily events in the world; (4) the losses of appreciation, which include the loss of the visual perception of the pleasurable and of the beautiful; (5) the losses of occupational and financial status, which consist of financial security, career, vocational goals, job opportunities, and ordinary recreational activities; (6) the resulting losses to the whole personality, including the loss of personal independence, social adequacy, self-esteem, and total personality organization; and (7) the concomitant losses of sleep, of physical tone of the body, and of decision, and the sense of control over one's life.[2]

Rehabilitation, in this scheme, is the process "whereby adults in varying stages of helplessness, emotional disturbance, and dependence come to gain new understanding of themselves and their handicap, the new skills necessary for their state, and a new control of their emotions and their environment."[3] This process is not a simple one; it involves the pain and recurrent crises that accompany the acceptance of the many "deaths" to sighted life. It consists of "restorations" for each of the losses involved in blindness. The final objective of total rehabilitation involves returning and integrating the blinded person in his society.

...The various restorations in each of these phases correspond to the losses the person has encountered. The loss of confidence in the remaining senses is restored through deliberate training of these senses; the loss of mobility is restored through training in the use of a long cane or a guide dog; the loss of ease of written communication is restored through learning braille; and so on. The goal of this process is to reintegrate the components of the restored personality into an effectively functioning whole....

[In] several rehabilitation centers and general agencies...the ideas contained in...[Father Carroll's] book are used as the basis for a formal course taught to blind people while they are obtaining services. The purpose of this course is to clarify for them what they have lost because they are blind, how they must change through the course of rehabilitation, and what their lives will

be like when rehabilitation has been completed. These ideas are given added weight by the fact that they are shared by all staff members who deal directly with the client and, in some agencies at least, by other nonservice personnel who have occasional contacts with clients....

We cannot assume that there is a necessary correspondence between these beliefs regarding the limits and potentialities imposed by blindness and the blind client's self-image. The question of the full impact of the former on the latter is an empirical one on which there are no hard data. Our analysis of the client's "set" when he enters an agency for the blind does suggest, however, that such beliefs probably have a profound impact on his self-image.... [When] the client comes to an agency, he is often seeking direction and guidance and, more often than not, he is in a state of crisis. Consequently, the authority of the system makes the client highly suggestible to the attitudes of those whose help he seeks.

There is evidence that some blind people resist the pressures of the environment of agencies and centers that adopt this philosophy by feigning belief in the workers' ideas for the sake of "making out" in the system.[4] In such cases, the impact of workers on the client's self-image will be attenuated. Despite this, he will learn only those skills made available to him by the agency or center. These skills, which the workers regard as opportunities for individual fulfillment, act also as limits. The choice of compensatory skills around which the theory revolves means the exclusion of a spectrum of other possibilities.

THE ACCOMMODATIVE APPROACH

A basic premise of the restorative approach is that most blind people possess the capacity to function independently enough to lead normal lives. Rehabilitation centers and general service agencies that have embraced this approach therefore gear their entire service programs toward achieving this goal. In other agencies for the blind, no disagreement is voiced about the desirability of blind people's attaining independence, but there is considerable skepticism as to whether this is a feasible goal for more than a small fraction of the client population.[5] According to this view, blindness poses enormous obstacles to independence—obstacles seen as insurmountable by a majority of people.... Settings and programs are designed to accommodate the helpless, dependent blind person.

The physical environment in such agencies is often contrived specifically to suit certain limitations inherent in blindness. In some agencies, for example, the elevators have tape recorders that report the floor at which the elevator is stopping and the direction in which it is going, and panels of braille numbers for each floor as well. Other agencies have mounted over their front doors special bells that ring at regular intervals to indicate to blind people that they are approaching the building. Many agencies maintain fleets of cars to pick up clients at their homes and bring them to the agency for services. In the cafeterias of many agencies, special precautions are taken to serve only food that blind people can eat without awkwardness. In one agency cafeteria, for example, the food is cut before it is served, and only spoons are provided.

Recreation programs in agencies that have adopted the accommodative approach consist of games and activities tailored to the disability. For example, bingo, a common activity in many programs, is played with the aid of a corps of volunteers who oversee the game, attending to anything the blind person is unable to do himself.

Employment training for clients in accommodative agencies involves instruction in the use of equipment specifically adapted to the disability. Work tasks, and even the entire method of production, are engineered with this disability in mind, so that there is little resemblance between an average commercial industrial setting and a sheltered workshop. Indeed, the blind person who has been taught to do industrial work in a training facility of an agency for the blind will acquire skills and methods of production that may be unknown in most commercial industries.

The general environment of such agencies is also accommodative in character. Clients are rewarded for trivial things and praised for performing tasks in a mediocre fashion. This superficial and overgenerous reward system makes it impossible for most clients to assess their accomplishments accurately. Eventually, since anything they do is praised as outstanding, many of them come to believe that the underlying assumption must be that blindness makes them incompetent.

The unstated assumption of accommodative agencies is that most of their clients will end up organizing their lives around the agency. Most will become regular participants in the agency's recreation programs, and those who can work will obtain employment in a sheltered workshop or other agency-sponsored employment program. The accommodative approach therefore produces a blind person who can function effectively only within the confines of the agency's contrived environment. He learns skills and behavior that are necessary for participating in activities and programs of the agency, but which make it more difficult to cope with the environment of the larger community. A blind person who has been fully socialized in an accommodative agency will be maladjusted to the larger community. In most cases, he does not have the resources, the skills, the means, or the opportunity to overcome the maladaptive patterns of behavior he has learned. He has little choice but to remain a part of the environment that has been designed and engineered to accommodate him.

This portrayal of accommodative agencies suggests that the workers in them, like those in restorative agencies, make certain assumptions about the limitations that blindness imposes, and that these assumptions are manifested in expectations about attitudes and behavior that people ought to have because they are blind....

Unfortunately, no hard data are available on socialization outcomes in agencies that adopt either of the two approaches I have described. However, the materials I collected from interviews with blind people suggest that a number of discernably patterned reactions occur.[6] Some clients and trainees behave according to workers' expectations of them deliberately and consciously in order to extract from the system whatever rewards it may have. Others behave according to expectations because they have accepted and internalized them as genuine qualities of character. The former are the "expedient" blind people, and the latter are the "true believers."

Expedient blind people consciously play a part, acting convincingly the way they sense their counselors and instructors want them to act. They develop a keen sense of timing that enables them to be at their best when circumstances call for it. When the circumstances change, the façade is discarded, much as the Negro discards his "Uncle Tomisms" in the absence of whites. As a rule, the expedient blind person is one who recognizes that few alternatives are open to him in the community; his response is an understandable effort to maximize his gains in a bad situation.

True believers are blind people for whom workers' beliefs and assumptions about blindness are unquestioned ideals toward which they feel impelled earnestly to strive. While this pattern is probably found in all agencies for the blind, it is most obvious in those which embrace the accommodative approach to blindness. Clients who become true believers in such agencies actually experience the emotions that workers believe they must feel. They experience and spontaneously verbalize the proper degree of gratitude, they genuinely believe themselves to be helpless, and they feel that their world must be one of darkness and dependency.

NOTES

1. Thomas J. Carroll, *Blindness: What It Is, What It Does, and How to Live with It,* Little, Brown & Company, Boston, 1961.
2. *Ibid.,* pp. 14–79.
3. *Ibid.,* pp. 96.
4. *Information Bulletin No. 59,* University of Utah, Regional Rehabilitation Research Institute, Salt Lake City, 1968.
5. Roger G. Barker et al., *Adjustment to Physical Handicap and Illness: A Survey of the Social Psychology of Physique and Disability,* Social Science Research Council, New York, 1953.
6. Most of this discussion applies to blind people who have been exposed to agencies that adopt an accommodative approach to rehabilitation. Little information could be gathered on those who have been trainees in restorative agencies, primarily because such agencies are comparatively few in number and recent in origin.

Emergency Department Responses to Battered Women

DEMIE KURZ

Sociologists concerned with the definition and construction of "social problems" and "deviant behaviors" argue that in recent decades a range of

Reprinted from "Emergency Department Responses to Battered Women: Resistance to Medicalization," *Social Problems,* Vol. 34, No. 1 (February 1987), pp. 70–82, by permission of the Society for the Study of Social Problems and the author.

The research for this paper was supported by NIMH Grant MH37180–02, and was conducted at the Philadelphia Health Management Corporation.

problems previously defined in moral or criminal terms, have been redefined as medical problems. Some now use the term "medicalization" to describe how the medical profession can label and gain jurisdiction over many areas of life which involve the workings of the body or mind such as drug addiction, alcohol, aging; birth control, pregnancy, and child birth; and child abuse (Conrad and Schneider, 1980a; Freidson, 1973; Zola, 1972, 1975). Those studying medicalization are particularly concerned with how the medicalization process can depoliticize "social" problems by redefining them as problems of individual pathology (Conrad, 1975; Kittrie, 1971).

This study examines a new area which reformers in the health care system are attempting to medicalize: the area of "battering," or the injury of women by husbands and boyfriends. Attempts to medicalize battering have their origins in a social movement on behalf of "battered women" which began in the early 1970s (Schecter, 1982; Tierney, 1982). The battered women's movement brought to public attention the fact that an estimated 1.5 million wives are injured each year by husbands (Strauss et al., 1980), and 1.5 million single, separated, and divorced women are injured by male intimates (Rosenberg et al., 1985). Supporters from within mental health, social service, and governmental organizations have joined advocates for battered women in bringing about the creation of a nationwide network of shelters and shelter services; legislation in most states increasing police powers and criminal penalties against abusers; government funding for programs and agencies for battered women; and increased data collection on the issues by public and private research organizations (Attorney General's Task Force, 1984; Dobash and Dobash, 1979; Schecter, 1982; Tierney, 1982). The battered women's movement and supporters in the health care system are now calling for the health care system to aid in the identification of battered women and their referral to appropriate sources of help.

From within the health care system, the Surgeon General of the United States (Koop, 1982, 1984), the American College of Physicians (1986), selected State and local health officials (New Jersey Department of Community Affairs, 1985), and a national network of nurses are among those calling for the health care system to play a role in addressing this problem. They argue that health care personnel should "diagnose" the battering "syndrome," consisting of specific injury and behavior patterns, and intervene on behalf of battered women. Some reformers have published articles in medical journals urging health care personnel to identify battering, and describing symptoms and signs of battering (Campbell and Humphreys, 1984; Finley, 1981; Goldberg and Carey, 1982; Greany, 1984; Klingbeil, 1986; Loraine, 1981; Petro et al., 1978). Others are holding conferences (Rich and Burgess, 1986) and developing protocols for use by health care personnel to identify battering (Helton, 1986). Reformers have succeeded in putting into place approximately 100 initiatives at the state and local levels to train hospital staff and other health care personnel about battering.[1]

Reformers argue that intervention in the health care system can result in the timely referral of battered women to sources of help, thus preventing further injury, and in the documentation of injuries on medical records for use by individual women and for the purpose of collecting statistics. They note that the potential benefit of reform is great in that large numbers of battered women come to the health care system. A survey of women in Texas estimated that 360,000 women had at some point in their lives required medical treatment because of abuse (Teske and Parker, 1983). Another study of battered women found that 80 percent of the women went to their physician for a battering injury (Dobash and Dobash, 1980). Stark et al. (1979) found that 19 percent of women trauma patients who came to the hospital emergency departments they studied were either confirmed as having been battered or very likely to have been battered.

The efforts of these groups are similar to those of earlier claims-makers who "discovered" specific injury patterns which they claimed were caused by child abuse (Pfohl, 1977). Child abuse reformers succeeded in having the identification of child abuse accepted as a legitimate medical concern and in passing legislation requiring the mandatory reporting of child abuse by physicians. The efforts to promote battering are more recent and less extensive than in the case of child abuse. Unlike child abuse, there are no medical specialties which lay claim to the problem of battering, nor is it expected that there will be legislation mandating that physicians report each individual case of battering. However, a few states have mandated the reporting of statistics of battering, and there is debate on other ways the health care system can help to stop battering (Rich and Burgess, 1986; Koop, 1984).

Since many current efforts are of a voluntary nature and since most future efforts will also require the cooperation of clinicians, it is essential to understand how clinicians will respond to battering. This paper reports on a participant observation study of responses of emergency department (ED) staff to battered women in four hospitals. In three of the hospitals there were one-time efforts to educate staff about battering and to encourage them to identify it. In the fourth hospital, due to the efforts of a reformer who believed in intervention with battered women in EDs, there were ongoing intervention efforts with staff to encourage them to view battering as a problem for medical attention, identify it, and make referrals. I compare the responses of ED staff in these two sets of EDs and analyze the factors which account for a greater response to battering in the fourth ED.

This study has implications both for our understanding of medicalization and for our understanding of the ED response to battering. Those studying medicalization typically focus on how medical professionals readily define emerging concerns as medical problems that belong within their professional domain (Conrad and Schneider, 1980a; Zola, 1972, 1975). Some argue further that, due to sexist attitudes in the medical system, women's problems are particularly likely to be "medicalized" or appropriated by the male medical establishment (Dreifus, 1978; Ehrenreich and English, 1975; Ruzek, 1978). In contrast, the medical staff I studied saw efforts to respond to battering as detracting from the proper performance of their work, not enhancing it. I further demonstrate that staff resistance to battering may be influenced by prevailing views of women, but that they are influenced more by other factors.

One previous study also suggests that health care personnel are reluctant to respond to battering. Based on an extensive review of medical records, Stark et al. (1979) found that staff in a New Haven hospital do not identify battering as such, but instead respond to battered women's psychosocial problems—e.g., depression, drug abuse, suicide attempts, or alcoholism—although the women's ED records indicate that these problems arose after the onset of battering. Stark et al. attribute this inclination to overlook battering to staff's adherence to the current medical paradigm, which does not view social factors as significant elements of medical problems. Whereas Stark et al. relied only on medical records, I present more direct, observational evidence on the reactions of ED staff to battered women.

METHODS

I used the following methods to collect data in four hospital EDs in a large metropolitan area: observations of interactions between battered women and staff; informal interviews with ED staff; and a review of medical records. The staff at each hospital ED during each eight-hour shift generally included one or two physicians, four or five nurses, and one or two orderlies or technicians. One or two interns were occasionally present as well. The staff members in all the hospitals are primarily white, the physicians primarily male, and the nurses primarily female. The patients represent a wide range of ethnic and class backgrounds.

Observers, who were graduate students in sociology and social work, followed the cases of all female trauma patients seen by health care professionals during different shifts. The observations extended over five months in two of the hospitals and two months in the other two.[2] A woman was considered battered if (1) the observer heard the women, or someone accompanying her, say that she had been injured by her husband or boyfriend, or (2) a staff member told the observer that the woman, or someone accompanying her, said she had been injured by a husband or boyfriend. Based on this definition, interactions between 104 battered women and ED staff were observed during this period.

Observers followed as much of the interaction between staff and women as possible and then immediately interviewed staff about what transpired in the interaction—i.e., what was said and done, what physical diagnosis was made, whether the staff thought battering had occurred, and what the staff's impression of the case was. Observers took verbatim field notes on all the interactions. Because of confidentiality agreements it was not possible for observers to speak directly to the female trauma patients.

During the informal interviewing observers questioned as many ED staff as possible about whether they saw battered women, what they were like, how they compared to other patients, or what staff thought could be done for them. Medical records of female trauma patients were reviewed for the same time period as the observation.

ED STAFF RESPONSES TO BATTERING

In this section I describe responses to battered women in the three EDs where staff had some knowledge of battering, but where there were no ongoing efforts to have ED staff respond to battering on a systematic basis. ED staff were informed about battering at meetings in which staff from the research project explained the purpose of the project: to understand more about battered women who come to EDs and to determine what EDs could do for battered women. Research staff presented battering as a problem which could be medically identified in the ED and for which there were appropriate referral sources. At the meeting, observers told ED staff that they were leaving cards in the ED with the telephone numbers of three hotlines for battered women, although from that point on observers did not mention the cards to staff. The fact that ED directors had allowed

these activities to take place was an indication to ED staff that the directors had granted some legitimacy to this issue. On the other hand, at no time did ED or hospital administrators set up procedures for identifying battered women or give any other indication that they viewed the issue as a priority.

Informally, staff knew about battered women from having seen them in the ED. Based on a record review, an average of one woman per day comes to each of these hospitals with injuries inflicted by husbands or boyfriends.[3] All staff who were asked about battered women expressed awareness of "these women." ED staff do not usually use the term "battered women," but refer to "the woman who was hit/beaten by her husband/boyfriend."[4] A major reason for staff's awareness of the presence of battered women is that in 75 percent of the cases the battered women volunteer that they have been injured by a husband or boyfriend. In the other 25 percent of the cases, it becomes known because a relative or the police tell the cause of the injury.

In the following section I describe the three major responses to battered women in the three EDs: "positive," "partial," and "no response." I describe the nature of the interactions in these categories and the reasons staff gave for their responses. Observers questioned as many staff members as possible about particular cases. All staff members were willing to describe the cases if they had time, and approximately half volunteered reasons for their responses.

POSITIVE RESPONSES

In 11 percent of the cases staff take a woman's battering seriously and view it as legitimately deserving of their time and attention. In addition to giving a battered woman medical treatment, staff note battering on the case record, speak to the woman about what happened, her current circumstances, her safety, and attempt to provide some assistance or give the card with hotline numbers. What distinguishes these responses from others is that staff attempt to follow through with a battered woman and ensure that when she leaves, something has been done for her. One nurse talked at length with a woman, and then arranged for her to talk with a policeman who had recently come to the ED. Several others tried to call hotline numbers and shelters, and waited for return calls if necessary. Some arranged to talk to women alone, who then told them they were battered.

The fairly small number of staff members involved in these interactions do not respond to all battered women in this way; their responses are contingent on several factors. First, staff respond to women they see as "true victims." The women have to be polite, have no discrediting attributes, and, in addition, staff members have to feel that some unfortunate event has happened to them. Staff members see women as "true victims" when they perceive them to be in immediate physical danger. As one medical student said,

> She wants to talk to someone about what to do and where she can go. It has happened five or six times before though she does not seem to have been seriously injured, but I mean this is pretty serious. He pulled a knife . . . she is really in a quandary as to what to do now.

Another resident said:

> Well, when I asked her today if she passed out last night when this happened, she said no. But then she said that two weeks ago, she passed out when he tried to strangle her. I couldn't believe it—this is really sick.

Secondly, staff members feel sympathetic towards women who say they are taking action to leave the violent relationship. Some women mention that they have contacted the police in order to press charges; some express their strong interest in leaving the relationship; some have already contacted an abuse agency or state their intention to do so; and some express strong interest in contacting hospital social services. One physician spoke approvingly of a patient who said: "He has beaten me the first time and this will be the last time." Staff have a genuine feeling for the predicament of these women.

Thirdly, if staff believe the woman has a pleasant personality, this influences how legitimately deserving of their time and attention they feel she is. In one ED many staff commented sympathetically about a particular woman. As the physician said:

> I told her completely off the record "you can do better." I mean she looks good, she seems to be nice. She shouldn't have to put up with that stuff. Do you know what that fool did? She was in here Wednesday night and that fool was telling her I want to get out of here. I mean he's nothing but a bastard. She doesn't need that.

A PARTIAL RESPONSE TO BATTERED WOMEN

In 49 percent of the cases, staff makes a "partial" response to the battering side of a case. They do similar things as those staff in the first category, such as asking the woman about her situation, giving her a card with the hotline phone numbers, calling the hotline numbers for the woman, or trying to arrange transportation home for the woman. However, staff members' involvement in these cases is brief and has a routine quality, and they do not typically think of different things they might do for a battered woman. They give a woman a small amount of their time, but give higher priority to other cases. Thus, the response may or may not be appropriate for that woman's condition. Staff may lose track of a woman who says she is in danger, or give extra time to a woman who does not appear to be in immediate danger.

In half of these cases, staff members gave reasons for their partial responses while describing their interactions with these battered women. The factor they mention most often is that the women are not responsive. In a few cases they described them as "not interested." An attending physician said directly to a couple: "So you don't want to talk about it," to which they replied, "That's right."

For the most part staff describe "unresponsive" women as "evasive," or purposely vague and inconsistent in describing how they were injured. In 16 percent of all cases in all four EDs, staff describe the women as evasive, hiding something, or unwilling to talk. In such interactions the women may say their injury was due to an accident. For example, one woman with a facial injury said only that she had been in a car accident. According to the nurse, "She wouldn't say a thing. She was completely non-communicative. I couldn't even get a history." The nurse initially believed the woman, "although it didn't really fit for a car accident. Her lip was split and that was all." The nurse, upon hearing that the woman's husband was waiting for her, went to speak to him. He immediately volunteered that the injury had occurred during an argument.

A staff person will become particularly irritated if he or she suspects battering, takes the time to ask the woman, and the woman will not give an answer. In one case, a nurse asked a woman with a broken jaw what she had been struck with. The woman replied, "a hand." The nurse then asked the woman if she had been struck by a "significant other," and the woman did not reply. The nurse offered the woman a card with phone numbers of battered women's agencies and asked her if she needed shelter. The woman said no, but that she would keep the card. The woman was admitted to the hospital with a broken jaw.

The second factor that staff mention in describing their interactions in cases of partial response is that the battered women have a condition which makes interacting with them difficult. Staff say these women are "AOB" (Alcohol on Breath), have taken drugs, act in ways staff believe are "crazy" or "inappropriate," or are "fighters." Staff describe 24 percent of all cases in all four EDs in terms of these stigmatized qualities.

Women who have been drinking, are generally assumed to be upset, vague, and difficult to understand. One badly beaten woman, with a high blood alcohol level, told four different stories about how she had been beaten. The following exchange reveals the typical staff attitude towards battered women with "AOB."

OBSERVER: What is your impression of this case?
NURSE: Somebody beat the shit out of her.
OBSERVER: Is is hard to nurse for these cases?
NURSE: She had "AOB." Do I feel sorry for her? No, I feel like if somebody drinks, at least they have control over that part of it.
OBSERVER: Does it make your job harder?
NURSE: Well, yes. For example, she can't remember what happened. Is that from the alcohol or the concussion? And she is dizzy—that could be from drinking too. Also, when people drink they let it all out. She is upset and maybe because of the alcohol it is more extreme.

Women labeled "AOB" are assumed to be all alike—unable and unwilling to cooperate with staff—although a review of "AOB" cases showed that over a third of these women became more cooperative and willing to talk in the ED as the effects of the alcohol wore off. Staff members perceived drug cases in a similar manner to "AOB" cases. When women act in a bizarre way, staff label them "crazy," express intense dislike for them, and view them as a waste of time. One "crazy" woman wouldn't stop talking, said inappropriate things, and would not sign her forms. Another talked about killing herself and her husband, and then stole valium from the ED.

A third aspect of these cases that staff members mention is the belief that they cannot help or produce "results" with these women. Staff develop an attitude summarized by the statement, "There's nothing much we can do." While staff can give a woman a card with the phone numbers of the battered women's hotlines, they do not know if their efforts will result in the woman's using the hotlines or getting help in some other way. Some staff would also like to be able to help a battered woman get into a shelter, but this is difficult to accomplish. As one nurse said, "There are so few shelters and so few vacancies that when we make a referral it's very difficult to find a place." On one occasion a woman wanted shelter and a staff person called the hotlines. No one answered.

STAFF DO NOT RESPOND

In 40 percent of the cases staff do not respond to the battering side of a case. The reason staff members most often give for not responding is the same reason given for "partial responses"—the women are "evasive." The second reason staff members give for "non-response" also parallels reasons for a "partial response": that the women have a stigmatizing trait—they are "AOB," have used drugs, or act "crazy." Third, staff members say they are sometimes too busy to respond. As one nurse said, "She had two bruised eyes. I had no time to spend with her. I was too busy." A doctor told the observer, "We couldn't get any more information about her. We were too rushed this morning."

The fourth reason staff members give for not responding is that they do not view battering as a legitimate medical concern. They question women patients about the cause of their injuries strictly to diagnose and treat their physical problems; once they ascertain, for example, that a woman was struck, staff do not ask who struck her. As one physician said, "I did not ask anything about her social situation. I only asked about how he hit her with the prong of the fork." Even if a woman volunteers the information about what happened to her, it is ignored.

NURSE: She has epigastral pain—tingling in her hands—that could be from hyperventilation. She has been upset about her husband . . . she was crying the whole time. She did not sleep last night.

OBSERVER: Did you ask if her pains were connected with this situation?

NURSE: It is not necessary. Since it could be coronary you have to be careful—she is in the age group. But I think it is emotional . She could even have been hyperventilating in her sleep.

OBSERVER: Do you see any direct links between her pain and her upset?

NURSE: Not really. She does not report any stabbing pain.

DOCTOR: She strikes me as being very upset. She says she had a fight with her husband. But we can not let that cloud our analysis.

Also, some staff view battering as a personal problem and define an inquiry about battering as an invasion into the patient's affairs. As one surgeon said, "It is none of my business who hit her. I am just here to treat her." One person mentioned a possible additional reason that staff do not respond. This staff person did not want to be legally responsible for bringing up the subject of battering, although she had no information about her legal liability. One staff person also mentioned fear of retaliation by a man if she got involved in a battering case.

NEGATIVE STEREOTYPES OF BATTERED WOMEN

In describing particular cases, staff members state that the demeanor of the women—their "evasiveness" and disruptive behavior—is a primary factor preventing their addressing the battering side of a case. In 40 percent of their interactions, staff members encounter women they believe possess "troublesome" traits. However, it is clear that ED staff believe the number of such women is higher. When questioned about their views of battered women generally, staff members indicated that battered women are a source of frustration, and some staff members held these women personally responsible for the batterings they received:

> It is difficult to feel sorry for these women as they have a choice to leave the situation (nurse).

> Why do anything for people who do not take responsibility for themselves? What good does it do when they won't come in and do something for themselves. Last night we had a battered woman. It took five hours for her to be convinced to come in by neighbors (cardiology resident).

When staff see a woman leave the ED with an abuser, this reinforces their view that the women are irresponsible. They remember these incidents:

> It is ridiculous because the women go back. We see it all the time. They are in the examining room. The man has gouged out her eye or stabbed her or something like that and she is in the ER and gets mad because we won't let the guy in (physician).

Others come to view battering as an inevitable problem of these women's social class.

> She is a blue collar worker. These people come from neighborhoods where husbands beat up their wives all the time. There is nothing much to say—it is a clear case (intern).

> I know battering takes place in middle class families but I do not associate it with middle class people such as myself.... I have only seen cases in [a poor section of the city]. There it is a way of life, one comes to expect that type of behavior and learns to live with it (physician).

> Well, it is normal for a woman to fight with a man in this area. What are you going to do about those women?... That is the culture in this area (nurse).

Occasionally staff members describe the problem as due to women's traits. They use popular negative social characterizations of women and battered women to describe the source of the problem. As one nurse said:

> A lot of women do things to provoke a man. Probably most of them do. I know there are some real crazy women around here.

Thus, many staff members treat battered women as "deliberate deviants" (Lorber, 1967), who have actively or willfully caused their own condition. Lorber demonstrates that medical personnel do not think that "deliberate deviants" are worthy of their time and attention. Staff members form this stereotype of battered women despite that fact that a great variety of battered women come to the ED—e.g., women who are about to take action to change their situation, those who

are actively thinking about what to do, or those who are afraid or unwilling to change their situation.

MEDICALIZATION EFFORTS IN ONE ED

This section describes the efforts of a physician assistant in the fourth ED to have other staff members identify and refer battered women. The physician assistant had begun to identify battering cases on her own, and then had made herself knowledgeable about it. She believes the battering aspect of a case is a legitimate medical concern and compatible with her own role. She refers to battering as a "syndrome" with distinct medical symptoms, and urges others to "diagnose" the condition. This physician assistant believes it is necessary to understand that battering is the cause of the injury in order to treat the injury physically, to see the related physical and social effects, and to take some preventive measures to ensure that it will not happen again. She argues that the fact that battering is "chronic" makes it a legitimate concern for the ED because women will repeatedly come back for treatment unless it is stopped.

In addition, the physician assistant is able to have productive encounters with women who are "evasive," "AOB," and "troublemakers." She views these behaviors not as illegitimate, but rather as behaviors expected of those under the stress of battering. For example, the physician assistant talked to one angry battered woman—who other staff members defined as a "troublemaker" that they wanted out of the ED as soon as possible— with a sympathetic tone. The woman began to respond calmly to the physician assistant and to reflect on her situation. From time to time the physician assistant did find a battered woman to be trouble, such as a woman who claimed to be uninterested in anything about battering. However, this physician assistant believes that most battered woman are not trouble.

The advocate made several changes in her ED. First, she developed and received approval for a file card system which all staff were to use to note the battering cases they identified. These cases would then be referred to the physician assistant or the ED social worker who was concerned about battering. The ED director put treatment of battering into the official ED manual, and also allowed the physician assistant to conduct training sessions on battering for new residents and interns.

As a result of the physician assistant's efforts, there was a much greater likelihood of "positive" responses to battered women in this ED. Forty-seven percent of the cases were in the "positive" category as opposed to 11 percent from the other three EDs. This high number of "positive" cases was mainly due to the actions of a group of eight ED staff members including a physician, several nurses, and a social worker. These staff members, influenced by the physician assistant, responded to battered women in a manner similar to her. They not only identified battering and referred the women, but briefly talked to the women and told them they didn't deserve such treatment. In a quarter of these cases the women were perceived to be "AOB," drug users, or "evasive," and yet staff members still responded in a "positive" manner.

The one difference between the advocate and other staff members is that the latter expressed frustration in several cases where they felt there was nothing they could do for the women. In a few cases the women had received help from the battering agencies but had returned home for lack of alternative places to live. Staff members also expressed frustration in a few cases where the women appeared to be "repeaters." As one nurse who helped many battered women said: "I mean now that she is here I want to give her good care. But it's just going to happen again."

In 21 percent of the cases in this ED, in contrast to 49 percent in the other three EDs, staff made a "partial" response. Their response was categorized as "partial" because they took only one action—they filled out cards for the physician assistant's card file system. However, even this response was somewhat different from those in the

other three EDs because these staff members did not view filling out a card as "trouble"; they accepted the identification of battered women as part of their role. Interestingly, the attitudes of staff members towards battered women in cases of "partial" response were similar to those of staff in the other three EDs. In half the cases the women were "AOB," used drugs, or were "evasive." Staff members were not anxious to spend time with these cases; they wanted to fill out a card for them and send them along as soon as possible. As one nurse said, "I think she's a little drunk and a little crazy. She says he threw her through three rooms. She's not like the women with no place to go."

Thirty-two percent of the cases in this ED fell in the third category, "no response," as compared to 40 percent in the other EDs. Staff members here gave reasons for their non-responsiveness that were similar to those mentioned by their counterparts in the other EDs. In half these cases, the women were "AOB" or had used drugs. As one nurse said, "She said she was on drugs as soon as she took her coat off. After that I wasn't even interested." In the other half of these cases, staff do not respond to battering because they did not think the women were interested; because they themselves were too busy or forgot to inquire about battering; or because they didn't see the social aspects of battering as part of their medical responsibilities.

DISCUSSION

I have described two sets of responses to battered women in EDs. In the three EDs with a minimal educational effort about battering, three factors affect staff response to battered women. First, staff respond to and form their images of battered women based on their evaluation of the women's demeanor. They respond positively to women who appear as "true victims" and with dislike to those seen to be "evasive" or possessing a stigmatized status such as "AOB." Second, staff feel there is not much they can do about battered women. Third, they don't believe that battering is a legitimate medical problem. Staff members' responses have significant consequences for women. Those staff who respond to women in a "partial" manner spend less time with women and may or may not find out the facts of their cases, determine whether they are in danger, or document battering on the medical record. Staff in the "non-response" category may ignore battering. In the case of women with "stigmatizing" traits, staff may not "see" battering at all. This is consistent with the conclusion of Stark et al. (1979) that staff diagnose and treat battered women not as battered, but as suffering from depression, drug abuse, suicide attempts, or alcoholism.

Staff members focus on demeanor—women's perceived lack of responsiveness and their stigmatizing qualities—because they feel these qualities determine whether and how they will be able to interact with battered women. There are few ways for ED staff to measure the success of their work, and they feel particularly unsure about "results" with battered women. Staff find those who seem like a "true victim" easiest to identify and help, and they find those who are "unresponsive" or "evasive" or have other stigmatized qualities, to be trouble.

The second and third factors affecting staff's lack of response—that they feel that there is little they can do, and that they don't see this as a legitimate medical problem—mean that staff feel that responding to battered women detracts from their "real" work. This, combined with their view of many battered women as trouble, results in staff viewing their treatment of battered women as a kind of "dirty work" (Hughes, 1971). As Roth (1972) and Sudnow (1967) have shown, ED staff consider those cases which are life-threatening and qualify as "real" emergencies as most legitimate and worthy of their time and attention; other cases are seen as belonging in medical clinics. Staff do respond to battered women whom they perceive to be in "serious" danger. These cases qualify as "real" emergencies and fit the most valued, "heroic," aspect of the medical role. However, while many

injuries due to battering are serious, they are seldom life-threatening. Furthermore, staff define battered women as "social" cases in which the women are responsible for their condition. Thus, in the majority of cases staff believe dealing with battered women is "dirty work," work which detracts from their ability to carry out their role, work which is symbolically degrading.

In contrast, the advocate in the fourth ED views her efforts to help battered women as "honorable work" which is central to their conception of her treatment role. A small number of other staff members also adopt and practice her orientation toward battered women. The majority of staff members accept the advocate system as legitimate, apart from whether or not they believe the women themselves are legitimate candidates for assistance. This is because the referral system enables the majority of staff members to be less concerned with demeanor. It makes them feel they have a clear, simple task—to get the information for the card—and that they are therefore less dependent on the woman's demeanor. Also, staff members are assured of some result or measure of success—a referral—and thus are not left with the sense, as in the other EDs, that there is "nothing they can do."

However, even with an advocate and a referral system, many staff members continue to view the evasive and stigmatized cases as trouble. Staff members' negative perceptions of women's demeanor still contribute to "partial" responses or "non-responses" in many cases. Staff members who respond "positively" have less difficulty with demeanor, but sometimes they question whether they are actually accomplishing anything with battered women.

Some feminist writers argue that sexist attitudes strongly affect the response of the health care system to women and that medical professionals are eager to "medicalize" women's issues, or appropriate these issues for their own uses (Dreifus, 1978; Ehrenreich and English, 1975; Ruzek, 1978). While I found that attitudes towards women were a factor in staff responses, the main reason staff members were not interested in appropriating battering was that they felt it difficult to make a successful intervention in such cases. One could argue that gender is still a major factor in ED treatment—that if women were more valued by the health care system, medical personnel would define the problem of battering as important. But then we need to reconceptualize more precisely how sexism affects the response to battered women. To do this we need further study of which of women's conditions become medicalized and which do not.

This study demonstrates the importance of looking at the role of clinicians in interpreting and carrying out concepts of medicalization originating from other advocates. First, it suggests a need to look at how conceptions of demeanor and trouble shape clinicians' responses to certain conditions. In theory, medicalization is supposed to mean that moral judgments, or attitudes of "badness" (Conrad and Schneider, 1980a) are replaced by concepts of illness; but this may not always be the case. Second, as Conrad and Schneider (1980b) note, medicalization takes place on three levels—conceptual, institutional, and interactional. This study shows the possibility of an appearance of medicalization on one level while moral judgments prevail on another, thus suggesting a need for more study of the relationship between different levels of the medicalization process.

CONCLUSION

What does this study suggest about the medicalization of battering in the future? The stereotypes of "troublesome" women and the individualistic orientation toward battering held by ED staff members are consistent with the position that these women should be referred to mental health services for treatment of their personal "problems." Accordingly, "medicalization" could come to mean referral to mental health professionals. An American College of Physicians (1986) position paper recommends that physicians refer battered women to social workers and mental health services. Whereas health care professionals may not intervene directly in cases of battering, they may be willing to serve as referral agents in a medicalized system that redefines battering as a problem of mental health.

However, at least in theory, advocacy or referral systems could develop strong connections with the battered women's movement and its programs. The physician assistant in this study was strongly oriented toward referring women to battered women's services rather than to the mental health system. The National Coalition on Domestic Violence (1985) provides materials on battering for health care personnel and urges them to train health care personnel about battering. Some health care reformers advocate working closely with shelters and hotlines sponsored by the battered women's movement (Rosenberg et al., 1985). Yet, it goes without saying that, in practice, the medical system has avoided close connections with popular movements (Freidson, 1973).

Thus, this study suggests that the orientation of advocacy and referral systems will be important in determining the course of the medicalization of battering. Those reform groups which mount the most extensive efforts to institute advocacy and referral programs will be able to shape the medical response to battering. However, in the absence of institutionalized advocacy and referral efforts, the response of the health care system to battering will not be long-lasting and medicalization will not take hold.

NOTES

1. Evan Stark, Nov. 16, 1986: personal communication.
2. In two of the hospitals there were two observation periods. The first was from December 1981 to February 1982; the second, from October to November, 1982. Three observers spent three five-hour shifts per week in the ED or 15 hours each, for a total of 45 hours a week. In the other two hospitals there was a period of observation for two months, April and May, 1983, and only two observers.

3. In the record review of female trauma cases collected during the course of the study, 7 percent of the cases were coded as "positive" for battering. These were cases where ED staff had indicated on the medical record that a woman was injured by her husband or boyfriend. Ten percent of the cases were coded as "suggestive" for battering. These were cases where a woman had been assaulted, but no assailant was recorded on the record. Thus, 17 percent of the female trauma cases are either "positive" or "suggestive" for battering. This is equivalent to one woman per day coming to each of these hospitals with injuries inflicted by husbands or boyfriends.

These figures are similar to those of Stark (1984). Using a slightly different coding system, Stark (1984) found that 10.6 percent of the cases were "positive." In 8.7 percent of these cases, where a full trauma history was taken, assault by a male intimate was recorded on the record, and an additional 2 percent were listed elsewhere in the record. Stark categorized 5.9 percent of the cases as "probables" (woman was assaulted, but no assailant was recorded, nor was a mugging recorded on the record), and 2.2 percent as "suggestives" (the recorded etiology of the injury did not seem to account adequately for the injury and there was contradictory information, such as woman fell downstairs and got two black eyes).

4. I use the term "battered women" throughout the paper as a short-hand term for "women injured by husbands and boyfriends." The term originated with the battered women's movement and names a social problem. My use of the term here is not meant to suggest that the view of battering as a social problem is uniformly defined or widespread.

REFERENCES

American College of Physicians. 1986. "Position statements of the American College of Physicians." Philadelphia Medicine 82:496.

Attorney General's Task Force. 1984. Attorney General's Task Force. Final Report. U.S. Department of Justice, September 1984.

Campbell, Jacquelyn, and Janice Humphreys. 1984. Nursing Care of Victims of Family Violence. Reston, VA: Reston Publishing.

Conrad, Peter. 1975. "The discovery of hyperkinesis: notes on the medicalization of deviant behavior." Social Problems 23:12–21.

Conrad, Peter, and Joseph W. Schneider. 1980a. Deviance and Medicalization: From Badness to Sickness. St. Louis: C. V. Mosby.

———. 1980b. "Looking at levels of medicalization: a comment on Strong's critique of the Theses of Medical Imperialism." Social Science and Medicine 14A:75–79.

Dobash, R. Emerson, and Russell Dobash. 1979. Violence Against Wives. New York: The Free Press.

Dreifus, C. 1978. Seizing Our Bodies: The Politics of Women's Health. New York: Vintage.

Ehrenreich, Barbara, and Deirdra English. 1979. For Her Own Good: 150 Years of the Experts' Advice to Women. Garden City, NY: Anchor.

Finley, Britt. 1981. "Nursing process with the battered woman." Nurse Practitioner 6:11–13, 29.

Freidson, Eliot. 1973. Profession of Medicine. New York: Dodd, Mead & Company.

Goffman, Erving. 1963. Stigma. Englewood Cliffs, NJ: Prentice-Hall.

Goldberg, Wendy, and Anne L. Carey. 1982. "Domestic violence victims in the emergency setting." Topics in Emergency Medicine 3:65–76.

Greany, Geraldine D. 1984. "Is she a battered woman?" American Journal of Nursing 84:725–27.

Helton, Anne S. 1986. Protocol of Care for the Battered Woman. Houston, TX: Texas Woman's University.

Hughes, Everett C. 1971. The Sociological Eye. Chicago: Aldine.

Kittrie, Nicholas N. 1971. The Right to be Different: Deviance and Enforced Therapy. Baltimore: Johns Hopkins University Press.

Klingbeil, Karil S. 1986. "Interpersonal violence: a hospital based model from policy to program." Response 9:6–9.

Koop, C. Everett. 1982. Family Violence: A Chronic Public Health Issue. Lecture to the Western Psychiatric Institute, Pittsburgh, November 9, 1982.

———. 1984. Testimony. Presented to the Attorney General's Task Force on Family Violence. Sacramento, February 15, 1984.

Loraine, Kaye. 1981. "Battered women: the ways you can help." RN 44:23–28.

Lorber, Judith. 1975. "Good patients and problem patients: conformity and deviance in a general hospital." Journal of Health and Social Behavior 16:213–25.

National Coalition Against Domestic Violence. 1985. Medical/Hospital Intervention and Domestic Violence. Washington, DC.

New Jersey Department of Community Affairs. 1985. Domestic Violence: A Guide for Emergency Medical Treatment. Division on Women.

Petro, Jane A., Patricia L. Quann, and William P. Graham. 1978. "Wife abuse: the diagnosis and implications." Journal of the American Medical Association 240:240–41.

Pfohl, Stephen J. 1977. "The 'discovery' of child abuse." Social Problems 24:310–23.

Rich, Robert F., and Ann W. Burgess. 1986. "NIMH report: panel recommends comprehensive program for victims of violent crime." Hospital and Community Psychiatry 37:437–39.

Riessman, Catherine K. 1983. "Women and medicalization: a new perspective." Social Policy 14:3–18.

Rosenberg, Mark L., Evan Stark, and Margaret A. Zahn. 1985. Interpersonal Violence: Homicide and Spouse Abuse. Pp. 4916–37 in J. Last (ed.), Public Health and Preventive Medicine, Twelfth edition. East Norwalk, CT: Appleton Century Crofts.

Roth, Julius, A. 1972. "Some contingencies of the moral evaluation and control of clientele: the case of the hospital emergency service." American Journal of Sociology 77:839–55.

Ruzek, Sheryl K. 1978. The Women's Health Movement: Feminist Alternatives to Medical Control. New York: Praeger.

Schecter, Susan. 1982. Women and Male Violence. Boston: South End Press.

Stark, Evan. 1984. The Battering Syndrome: Social Knowledge, Social Theory, and the Abuse of Women. Unpublished Ph.D. dissertation, SUNY, Binghamton, NY.

Stark, Evan, Anne Flitcraft, and William Frazier. 1979. "Medicine and patriarchal violence: the social construction of a 'private' event." International Journal of Health Services 9:461–93.

Strauss, Murray A., Richard J. Gelles, and Suzanne Steinmetz. 1980. Behind Closed Doors: Violence in the American Family. New York: Anchor.

Sudnow, David. 1967. Passing On: The Social Organization of Dying. Englewood Cliffs, NJ: Prentice-Hall.

Teske, R. H., and M. L. Parker. 1983. Spouse Abuse in Texas: A Study of Women's Attitudes and Experiences. Huntsville, TX: Criminal Justice Center, Sam Houston State University.

Tierney, Kathleen J. 1982. "The battered women movement and the creation of the wife beating problem." Social Problems 29:207–20.

Varvaro, Filomena F., and Patricia G. Cotman. 1986. "Domestic violence: a focus on the emergency room care of abused women." Pittsburgh: Women's Center and Shelter of Greater Pittsburgh.

Zola, Irving K. 1972. "Medicine as an institution of social control." Sociological Review 20:487–504.

———. 1975. "In the name of health and illness: on some socio-political consequences of medical influence." Social Science and Medicine 9:83–87.

Techniques for Labeling Child Abusers in Official Documents

LESLIE MARGOLIN

Some sociologists believe that wrong-doers have considerable capacity to defend and mollify attributions of deviance by offering excuses, apologies, and expressions of sorrow. For example,

Reprinted from "Deviance on Record: Techniques for Labeling Child Abusers in Official Documents," *Social Problems*, Vol. 39, No. 1 (February, 1992), pp. 58–70, by permission of the Society for the Study of Social Problems and the author.

The author is very grateful to Richard Hilbert for his many helpful insights and suggestions.

conceptual formulations such as Mill's (1940) "vocabularies of motive," Scott and Lyman's (1968) "accounts," Sykes and Matza's (1957) "techniques of neutralization," and Hewitt and Stokes' (1975) "disclaimers" reflect a belief in the almost limitless reparative potential of talk. In the parlance of these sociologists, deviant identities are negotiable because attributions of wrongdoing are seen to depend not only on an assessment of what the wrong-doer did but on an understanding of his or her mental state during and after the violation. As Douglas (1970:12) observes, "an individual is considered responsible for his actions if and only if . . . he has intended to commit those actions and knows the rules relevant to them. . . ."

Given these conditions, accused persons may argue that the violation in question was unanticipated, unplanned, and contrary to what they wished. Still, limited evidence exists that people win such arguments. Although account theorists (e.g., Scott and Lyman 1968:46–47) claim that "the timbers of fractured sociations" can be repaired through talk, investigators addressing the ways social control agents process putative deviants have found few instances of people talking their way out of deviant labels (cf. Margolin 1990). On the whole, social control agents tend to pigeon-hole clients fairly quickly. As Waegel (1981) has shown, the organizational demand to meet deadlines, process an expected number of cases, and turn out paperwork reduces the amount of time agents can give their clients. The more bureaucrats are hurried, the greater their need to rely on shorthand methods for dealing with clients, and thus, the greater the necessity to interpret people and situations by means of stereotypes. In this regard, stereotypical or "normal" case conceptions guide responses to homicide defendants (Swigert and Farrell 1977), juvenile delinquents (Piliavin and Briar 1964), clients in a public defender's office (Sudnow 1965), skid-row residents (Bittner 1967), and shoplifters (Steffensmeier and Terry 1973).

The paperwork demand has a second effect on the putative deviant's capacity to negotiate effectively. Because oral and written communication have different potentialities for conveying information and structuring argument, agencies emphasizing the creation of records place a proportional pressure on bureaucrats to note the "recordable" features of their clients' situations. By implication, the contingencies of a case which best lend themselves to being described in written language are given the most prominence in records, and those contingencies most difficult to capture on paper (those aspects of a case best understood through face-to-face interaction) are minimized or neglected.

Studies examining the types of information bureaucrats leave out of written accounts have shown that clients' feelings are often omitted because the inner life of the individual is not only difficult to defend as objective evidence, but it is difficult to defend as evidence in writing (Kahn 1953, Lemert 1969). In face-to-face encounters, however, feelings and intentions are available through a series of gestures, tonal changes, and bodily movements which accompany the other's words (Schutz and Luckmann 1973). There is continual exchange between words and gestures. Such reciprocity cannot be duplicated in written communication, particularly when the writing is part of an official document. This means that putative deviants' capacity to argue their cases is seriously reduced when cases must be made in writing.

While documents may be a poor medium for describing internal states, bureaucrats are also reluctant to designate deviance on something as indefinite as "feelings"—theirs or the client's. The primary risk of citing the client's mental state at the time of the violation as a criterion for labeling or not labeling is that it makes agents vulnerable to accusations of subjectivity and personal bias. Since records are permanently available to supervisory scrutiny, agents feel pressure to make written assessments defendable displays of bureaucratic competence (Meehan 1986). For this reason, agents must use records to display not only "what happened" but that they performed their jobs rationally and objectively (Garfinkel 1967, Zimmerman 1969). These practical considerations oblige agents whose decision processes are recorded to place singular emphasis on the tangible aspects of the case—what the putative deviant's behavior was and what harm resulted—at the same time giving relatively little weight to clients' excuses, apologies, and expressions of sorrow.

Conceptualizing the deviant identity, then, as a mosaic assembled out of imputations of behavior and intention, this study examines how such a mosaic is pieced together in written documents. I explore how the "deviant's" point of view is documented and displayed, and how evidence is organized on paper to create the appearance that "deviance" has occurred. These dynamics are addressed through the examination of 120 case records designating child abuse.

Since the documentary reality of child abuse provides the vehicle and substantive focus of the analysis, what follows shows how child care providers are constituted as intentionally harmful to children. Like other "dividing practices" which categorize people as either healthy/sick, law abiding/criminal, or sane/insane, the separation of child abusers from normals is seen as an accomplishment of asymmetric power relations (cf. Foucault 1965, 1973, 1977). This article focuses on the power imbalance between child abuse investigators and suspects and the means by which the former impose their version of reality on the latter. Since this imposition is an accomplishment of contemporary modes of discourse (cf. Foucault 1978), I focus on investigators' vocabularies, the structure of their arguments, and the types of common sense reasoning they utilize.

METHODS

The idea for this research emerged while I was involved in a study of child abuse by babysitters. As part of that study, I had to read "official" case records documenting that child abuse had occurred. The more records I read, the more it appeared that the social workers devoted a rather large portion of their writing to describing children's injuries, as well as the violent and sexual interactions which often preceded and followed them. By contrast, the alleged perpetrator's intentions, feelings, and interpretations of what happened appeared to occupy a relatively small portion of the documents. This imbalance roused

interest in view of the agency's formal regulations that social workers satisfy two criteria to establish that a caregiver committed child abuse: (1) They must establish that a caregiver performed acts which were damaging or exploitive to a child; (2) They must prove that the caregiver *intended* to damage or exploit the child—that the trauma was non-accidental. In the article I examine how social workers managed to label child abusers in a manner consistent with these regulations without appearing to give much weight to subjective factors such as suspects' excuses and justifications.

The sample consisted of 60 case records documenting physical abuse and 60 records documenting sexual abuse. They were randomly selected from all case records of child abuse by babysitters substantiated by a state agency during a two year period (N = 537). A babysitter was defined as someone who took care of a child who was not a member of the child's family, was not a boyfriend or girlfriend of the child's parent, and was not employed in a registered or licensed group care facility.

I do not treat these records as ontologically valid accounts of "what happened"; rather, I treat them as a "documentary reality" (Smith 1974), indicating the ways the social workers who constructed them want to be seen by their superiors. As such, the records provide evidence that the social workers utilized the unstated yet commonly known procedures which represent "good work." The following analysis attempts to make these procedures explicit and to show how the social workers who used them "prove" that child abuse took place by constructing good (bureaucratically sound) arguments supporting the view that a specific person intentionally damaged a child. I also explore the degree to which deviants' excuses, denials, and other accounts were incorporated into these decision processes. Finally, I look at how each type of information—descriptions of the injuries and accounts of what happened—was used as evidence that child abuse occurred and could have only been performed by the person who was labeled.

DISPLAYING VIOLENCE AND SEXUALITY

At the beginning of each record, the social worker described the physical injuries which were believed to have been inflicted on the child by the babysitter. These descriptions did not specify how the child's health or functioning were impaired but were presented as evidence that an act of transformative social import had occurred (cf. Denzin 1989). To illustrate this reporting style, one three-year-old who was spanked by his babysitter was described by the physician as having "a contusion to the buttocks and small superficial lacerations." However, the social worker who used these injuries as evidence of child abuse described them as follows:

> *The injuries gave the appearance of an ink blot, in that they were almost mirror images of each other, positioned in the center of each buttock. The bruising was approximately four inches long by about two and a half inches wide, and was dark red on the perimeter and had a white cast to the inside of the bruise. There was a long linear line running across the bottom of both buttocks extending almost the entire width of the child's buttock. There was lighter reddish bruising surrounding the two largest bruises on each buttock and faint bluish-red bruising extending up to the lower back. The bruising would be characterized as being red turning to a deeper reddish-purple than true bright red.*

This unusually graphic style of presentation gave the bruises a special status. They were no longer simply bruises but were now defined as out of the ordinary, strange, and grotesque. By removing the bruises from everyday experience, the stage was set for redefining the babysitter who supposedly did this to the child. In this manner, a person whose social status had been taken for granted could now be seen as potentially suspicious, foreign, and malevolent (Garfinkel 1956).

A parallel line of reportage was apparent in the sexual abuse cases. To the degree that the available information permitted, reports contained no obscurity in the descriptions of sexual interac-

tions. No detail of what happened appeared too small to be pursued, named, and included in the records as evidence (cf. Foucault 1978). This excerpt from a social worker's recorded interview with an eight-year-old girl illustrates:

S. W.: How did the bad touch happen? Can you think?
CHILD: I can't remember.
S. W.: Did you ever have to kiss?
CHILD: No.
S. W.: Anybody?
CHILD: Uh uh.
S. W.: Did you have to touch anybody?
CHILD: Yeah.
S. W.: Ah, you had to touch 'em. Where did you have to touch 'em?
CHILD: Down below.
S. W.: Oh, down below. Do you have a word for that body part?
CHILD: A thing-a-ma-jig.
S. W.: A thing-a-ma-jig. OK, let's look.... Is P [the suspect] a man?
CHILD: Yeah.
S. W.: OK, let's take a look at the man doll. Can you show me on the man doll what part you're talking about?
CHILD: This part.
S. W.: Oh, the part that sticks out in front. We have another word for that. Do you know the other word for that part?
CHILD: Dick.
S. W.: Yeah. Dick is another word for it. Another word is penis.
CHILD: Penis?
S. W.: Yeah.
CHILD: Oh.
S. W.: Can you tell me what—Did you see his body? Did you see his penis with your eyes?
CHILD: No.
S. W.: OK. Did he have his pants on or off?
CHILD: Unzipped.
S. W.: Unzipped. I see. How did his penis happen to come out of his pants?
CHILD: By the zipper.

S. W.: I see. Who took his penis out of his pants?

CHILD: He did.

S. W.: What did you have to touch his penis with?

CHILD: My fingers.

S. W.: I see. How did you know you had to do that?

CHILD: He told me to.

S. W.: What did he say?

CHILD: Itch it.

S. W.: Itch it. I see. Did he show you how to itch it? How did he have to itch it? One question at a time. Did he show you how to itch it?

CHILD: He said just go back.

S. W.: So you showed me that you're kind of scratching on it.

CHILD: Um hum.

S. W.: Did anything happen to his penis or his thing-a-ma-jig when you did that?

CHILD: No.

S. W.: OK. When he took his penis out of his pants, how did it look?

CHILD: Yucky.

S. W.: Yeah, I know you think it's yucky, but um, what does yucky mean? Can you tell me with some other words besides yucky?

CHILD: Slimy.

S. W.: Looked slimy. OK. Was it big?

CHILD: Yeah.

S. W.: Was it hard or soft.

CHILD: Soft and hard.

S. W.: OK. Explain how you mean that....

I offer this dialogue not as evidence that sexual abuse did or did not occur, but rather, to display the means by which equivocal behavior is translated into the "fact" of sexual abuse. Whatever it is that "really happened" to this child, we see that her experience of it is not a concern when "documentation" is being gathered. She is an object of inquiry, not a participant (Cicourel 1968, Smith 1974). Whatever reasons compel social workers to bring her to their offices and ask these questions are their reasons not hers. And as the child learns, even features of the "event"—such as the size, hardness, and overall appearance of a pe-

nis—can assume critical importance within interviewers' frames of reference.

While social workers used these details of sexual interactions and injuries to set the stage for the attribution of deviance, I noted four cases in which the analysis of the injuries themselves played a conspicuously larger role in determining who was responsible. In these cases the injured children were too young to explain how their injuries were caused, the babysitters denied causing the injuries, and there were no witnesses. This meant that the only way the investigators were able to label the babysitters as abusive was to argue that the injuries occurred during the time the suspects were taking care of the children. The parents of the injured children testified that the children were sent to the babysitters in good health, without any marks, but returned from the babysitters with a noticeable injury. This allowed the social workers to determine responsibility through the following method: if a babysitter cannot produce any plausible alternative explanation for the child's injuries, the babysitter must be responsible for the injuries.

Since children who had allegedly been sexually abused did not have conspicuous or easily described injuries, attributing sexual abuse on the absence of any plausible alternative explanation for the injury was, of course, impossible. This would appear to severely limit social workers' capacity to document that a babysitter committed sexual abuse when the babysitter denied the charges, when the child was too young to provide coherent testimony, and when there were no other witnesses. However, this was not always the case. Like the investigators described by Garfinkel (1967:18) who were able to determine the cause of death among possible suicides with only "*this* much; *this* sight; *this* note; *this* collection of whatever is at hand," child abuse investigators showed the capacity to "make do" with whatever information was available. In one case of sexual abuse, for example, there were no witnesses, no admission from the suspect, no physical evidence, and no charge from the alleged victim; still, "evidence" was summoned to establish a babysitter's guilt. Here, the social worker cited a four-year-old girl's fears, nightmares, and other "behavior consistent with that of a child who was sexually traumatized by a close family friend." Additionally, the babysitter in question was portrayed as a "type" capable of doing such things:

> Having no physical evidence, and no consistent statement from the alleged victim, I am forced to make a conclusion based on the credibility of the child as opposed to that of the perpetrator. This conclusion is supported by similar allegations against him from an independent source. It is also supported by behavioral indications and what we know of his history.

In a second case, a social worker showed that information pointing to the suspect's homosexuality and history of sexual victimization could be used to support charges of sexual abuse when other kinds of evidence were lacking:

> Although the babysitter denied having sexual contact with this child when interviewed, he did leave a note to the effect that he was attracted to males and thought that he was homosexual, and records indicate that he, himself, was sexually abused at the age of eight. Based on the interview done, the past history, and his own previous victimization, this worker feels that he did, in fact, penetrate and perpetrate himself upon the victim.

In most cases, however, portraying the suspect as a "type" was not critical to the finding of child abuse. The rationale for labeling was primarily constructed out of witnesses' testimony showing "who did what to whom."

USING WITNESSES TO DETERMINE WHO DID WHAT TO WHOM

Since the children and alleged child abusers often had different versions of what happened (40 cases), social workers needed a decision-rule to settle the question of who had the correct story. The rule used for resolving disagreements was

fairly simple: The child's version was considered the true one. The children were called "credible" witnesses when describing assaults which were done to them because it was assumed they had nothing to gain by falsely accusing the babysitter. The babysitters, on the other hand, were seen as "non-credible" (when they attempted to establish their innocence) because they had everything to gain by lying. Even children as young as two- and three-years-old were believed in preference to their adult babysitters. In fact, the main reason given for interpreting children as superior witnesses was precisely their youth, ignorance, and lack of sophistication. As one social worker observed, "It's my experience that a four-year-old would not be able to maintain such a consistent account of an incident if she was not telling the truth." Particularly in cases of sexual abuse, it was believed that the younger the witness, the more credible his or her testimony was. Social workers made the point that children who were providing details of sexual behavior would not know of such things unless they had been abused (cf. Eberle and Eberle 1986).

The children's accounts were rejected in only three instances. In one of these cases, two teenage boys claimed they witnessed a babysitter abuse a child as they peered through a window. Both the babysitter and the child said this was not true. The social worker did not feel it was necessary to explain why the babysitter would deny the allegations, but the child's denial was seen as problematic. Therefore, the social worker offered the following rationale for rejecting the child's account: "The child's refusal to say anything is not unusual because her mother was so verbally upset when she was informed of the allegations." A child's version of what happened (his denial of abuse) was rejected in a second case on the grounds that he was protecting a babysitter described as his "best friend." Finally, a 12-year-old female who repeatedly denied that anyone had touched her sexually was seen as non-credible because of her "modesty." As the social worker put it, "She did seem to have a very difficult time talking about it, and I feel she greatly minimized the incident due to her embarrassment about it."

In general, however, testimony from children was treated as the most credible source of evidence of what happened, since most social workers believe that children do not lie about the abuse done to them. By contrast, babysitters were presented as credible witnesses only when they agreed with the allegations made against them (56 cases). When they testified to the contrary, they were portrayed as biased. What does *not* happen, therefore, is the child implicating someone, the accused saying nothing happened, and the investigator siding with the accused. This suggests an underlying idealization that precedes and supports the ones operating on the surface of most cases: *the accused is guilty*. It goes without saying that this organizational stance runs roughly opposite to the Constitutional one of "innocent until proven guilty."

Here, it might be useful to draw an analogy between the child protection workers' "investigative stance" and that of welfare investigators responsible for determining applicants' eligibility (Zimmerman 1974). In both cases, investigators adopt a thorough-going skepticism designed "to locate and display the potential discrepancy between the applicant's [or suspect's] subjective and 'interested' claims and the factual and objective (i.e., rational) account that close observance of agency procedure is deemed to produce" (Zimmerman 1974:131). However, an important difference should be noted: during the conduct of welfare investigations, the investigated party is referred to as the "applicant," indicating that the investigation could end in a determination of either eligibility or ineligibility; by contrast, during the conduct of child abuse investigations, the investigated party is routinely identified as the "perpetrator," suggesting a previously concluded status. To illustrate, these notations documented one worker's activities during the first days of a child abuse investigation:

3/24: Home visit with police, interviewed parents, child not at home—perpetrator not in home.
3/26: Interview with detective J at Police station with CPI and child. Perpetrator arrested.

While babysitters accused of child abuse may in theory be only "suspects," at the level of practice, they are "perpetrators." This discrepancy between "theory" and "practice" is more than an example of how the formal structures of organizations are accompanied by unintended and unprogrammed structures (Bittner 1965). In this instance, child protection workers are formally enjoined to gather evidence about "perpetrators," not "suspects." Consider these guidelines from the agency's official handbook:

> *Information collected from the person [witness] should include precise description of size, shape, color, type, and location of injury. It may be possible to establish the credibility of the child, the responsible caretaker or the perpetrator as a source of this information.... The perpetrator and victim may be credible persons and need to be judged on the basis of the same factors as any other persons. (Italics added.)*

The implicit message is that the goal of the child abuse investigation is not to determine an individual's guilt or innocence but to find evidence to be used in recording or "documenting" what is already taken for granted, that parties initially identified as the "perpetrator" and "victim" are in fact the "perpetrator" and "victim." Strictly speaking, then, the goal is not to determine "who did what to whom," since that information is assumed at the outset, but rather, to document that agency rules have been followed, and that the investigation was conducted in a rational, impersonal manner.

DETERMINING INTENTIONALITY

A decision-rule was also needed to determine the babysitter's intentions. While babysitters were portrayed in the allegations as malicious or exploitive, many babysitters offered a different version of their motivations. Among the babysitters accused of physical abuse, 25 acknowledged hitting the children but also claimed they intended no harm. Three said they were having a bad day, were under unusual stress, and simply "lost it." They attributed their violence to a spontaneous, non-instrumental, expression of frustration. For example, one male caregiver took a two-year-old to the potty several times but the child did not go. Later he noticed that the child's diaper was wet; so he hurried him to the potty. However, just before being placed on the potty the child had a bowel movement. At that point the caregiver lost his temper and hit the child.

One woman who was labeled abusive claimed she was ill and never wanted to babysit in the first place. She only agreed to take care of a two-year-old girl because the girl's mother insisted. The mother had an unexpected schedule change at work and needed child care on an emergency basis. The abusive event occurred soon after the babysitter served lunch to the child. While the sitter rested on a couch in the living room, she observed the girl messing with her lunch. The sitter got up and tried to settle the child. When this did not work, she took away the girl's paper plate and threw it in the garbage. At that point the girl began to cry for her mother. The babysitter returned to the living room to lie down on the couch. But the girl followed her, wailing for her mother. When the girl reached the couch, the babysitter sat up and slapped her.

Other babysitters described their violence in instrumental terms: their goal was to discipline the children and not to hurt or injure them. They said that whatever injuries occurred were the accidental result of hitting (in one case, biting) the children harder than they meant to do. Some sitters indicated that the only reason children were injured during a disciplinary action was that the children moved just as they were being hit, exposing a sensitive part of the body to the blow. Others protested that the child's movements made it im-

possible to aim the blows accurately or to assess how hard they were hitting. In one case, the sitter said she was trying to hit the child across the buttocks with a stick, but the child put her hand across her buttocks to protect herself, receiving "non-intentional" bruising and swelling to the hand. A different sitter asked that the social worker consider that at the time of the violation he did not know it was against the law to beat a child with a belt. Another said he had been given permission to spank the child by the child's mother and was only following her orders. This was confirmed by the mother. After a two-and-a-half-year-old bit another child, his sitter bit him to show him "what it felt like." The sitter argued that she had done this in the past and had even told the child's mother. Thus, she believed that this was tacitly approved. Still another babysitter claimed that he struck the 11-year-old girl who was in his care in self-defense. He said that when he told her it was time for bed she began to bite and kick him. He said her injuries resulted from his efforts to calm and restrain her.

To sift out the babysitters' "official" intentions from the versions offered by the sitters themselves, several social workers explicitly invoked the following reasoning: Physical damage to the child would be considered "intentional" if the acts which produced them were intentional. Thus, a social worker wrote:

> I am concluding that this injury to the child was non-accidental in that the babysitter did have a purpose in striking the child, that purpose being to discipline her in hopes of modifying her behavior.

While close examination of this logic reveals an absurdity (the injury was seen as "intentional" despite the fact that it was produced by an act aimed at an entirely different outcome, "modifying her behavior"), the practical consequence of such a formula was a simple method for determining a suspect's intentions: If a babysitter was known to intentionally hit a child, causing an injury, the social worker could conclude the babysitter intended to cause the injury. Through such a formula, the most common excuse utilized by babysitters to account for their actions, that the injury was the accidental result of a disciplinary action, was interpreted as a confession of responsibility for physical abuse.

To give another example of how this formula provided a short-cut to determining intentionality, one social worker concluded her recording as follows:

> *Physical abuse is founded in that the caretaker did hit the child on the face because she was throwing a temper tantrum and left a bruise approximately one inch long under the right eye. This constitutes a non-accidental injury. The bruise is still visible after five days.*

In cases involving allegations of physical abuse, the problem of figuring out what the babysitter was really contemplating at the time of the violation never came up as a separate issue because the alleged perpetrator's motivation to injure the child was seen as the operational equivalent of two prior questions, "Does the child have an injury resulting from a blow?" and "Did the babysitter intentionally strike the child?" When each of these questions was answered affirmatively, intent to harm the child was inferred. Thus, it was possible for a social worker to observe, "It was this writer's opinion that the babysitter was surprised at the injury she left on the child by spanking the child," and later conclude, "the injury occurred as a result of a non-accidental incident."

One record included comments from witnesses which stated that a babysitter pushed a five-year-old boy after the child socked a cat. All agreed that the injury was not a direct consequence of the push but resulted when the child lost balance and fell over. Despite the social worker's explicit recognition that the child's injury was neither planned nor anticipated (she wrote that "the injury will probably not be repeated due to the sitter's awareness of the seriousness of disciplining a child by reacting rather than thinking"), the report of physical abuse was, nonetheless,

founded "due to the fact that the injury occurred in the course of a disciplinary action."

In another record, a male babysitter admitted to spanking a child, causing red marks on his buttocks. Although the child's father said he "did not believe the sitter meant to spank as hard as he did," and the police officer who was present concluded that "based on the information obtained in this investigation, I could find no intent on the sitter's part to assault this child," the social worker found the determination of physical abuse non-problematic. Since the child received the injury in the course of a spanking, child abuse occurred.

There were only two cases of sexual abuse in which the alleged abuser acknowledged touching the child in a manner consistent with the allegations, but at the same time denied sexual intent. In one of these cases, the alleged abuser said he only touched a 10-year-old boy's genitals in the process of giving him a bath. In the other case, the alleged abuser claimed he only touched the girl's body as part of an anatomy lesson, to show her where her rib and pelvic bones were located. Both of these accounts were dismissed as preposterous. The social workers expressed the opinion that sexual intent was the only possible reason anyone would enact the types of behavior attributed to the accused in the allegations. In short, an equation was drawn between specific behaviors attributed to the accused and their states of mind. If it was established that the babysitter behaved toward the child in ways commonly understood as sexual (e.g., fondling), establishing intent, as a separate dimension of the investigation, was seen as redundant. Thus, social workers were able to conclude their investigations of sexual abuse, as one investigator did, by utilizing the following formula: "The child, a credible witness, indicated that her babysitter did fondle her genitals. Therefore, this is a founded case of intent to commit sexual abuse."

To summarize, in cases of both physical and sexual abuse, the intent to commit these acts was seen as a necessary component of the specific behaviors used to accomplish them. Hitting which resulted in an injury was always treated as if it was a direct indicator of the motivation to injure. Similarly, behavior commonly known as "sexual" was always treated as if it was identical with the suspect's intent to sexually exploit. The fact that social workers sometimes described the suspects' surprise and horror at the physical damage their violence caused the child did not make the attribution of "intent to harm" more problematic because suspects' accounts were not organizationally defined as indicators of intent. Consistent with Mills' (1940), motives for child abuse are not features of the perpetrator's psyche, but rather, of the bureaucracy and profession. That 50 of the babysitters labeled as abusive denied performing the actions imputed to them, and another 14 were not interviewed at all (either because they could not be located or refused to speak to the social worker) demonstrated that it was possible to "officially" determine babysitters' intentions without confirmatory statements from the babysitters themselves.

DISCUSSION

Sociologists have often questioned official records on the grounds of their accuracy, reliability, and representativeness. However, the methods through which and by which deviance is routinely displayed in records have rarely been investigated (cf. Cicourel and Kitsuse 1963, Kitsuse and Cicourel 1963). This study has treated as problematic the standardized arguments and evidence which social workers use in official documents to prove that child abuse has taken place. In this regard, child abuse is seen as an accomplishment of a bureaucratic system in which members agree to treat specific phenomena as if they were "child abuse."

The proof of abuse was problematic since more than half of the suspects either denied the accusations or were not interviewed. Social workers "made do" without supportive testimony from suspects by routinely defining them as "non-credible" witnesses. Also, social workers managed to conform to agency regulations requiring proof that suspects intended to harm or exploit children by agreeing to treat specific observables as if they represented the intent to harm or exploit.

Thus, the designation of child abuse was simplified. Testimony from the person most likely to disagree with this label, the accused, did not have to be considered. This is not to say that testimony from the accused might overcome the processes of institutional sense-making. It is to suggest, rather, that defining the accused as non-credible makes the designation of child abuse more "cut and dried," defendable, and recordable, since abuse that might otherwise be denied, excused, or justified, either in whole or in part, can then be fully attributed to suspects.

While it can be argued that simplifying the means by which suspects are labeled is desirable for a society concerned about keeping dangerous people away from children, the negative consequences should be acknowledged. As already shown, individuals who assign child abuse labels have more power than suspects, making it impossible for parties at risk of being labeled to "negotiate" on an equal footing with labelers. Indeed, any disjuncture between suspects' and investigators' versions of "what really happened" do not have to be resolved prior to the attribution of child abuse (cf. Pollner 1987:77–81). Since investigators have the capacity to impose their versions of reality on suspects, the only "resolution" needed from the investigators' perspective entails finding ways to make their decisions defendable in writing.

As might also be expected, the personal, social, and legal stigma resulting from designating this label is enormous. Once the impression has been formed that a person is a child abuser, the expectation exists that he or she will continue to be abusive. Moreover, there is little a person can do to remove this label. It exists as part of a permanent record that can be recalled whenever a person's child care capacities or moral standing are questioned (cf. Rosenhan 1973). If, as Smith (1974:259) argues, the creation of written records "mediates relations among persons in ways analogous to how Marx conceived commodities mediating relations among individuals," then for the relations (and identities) constituted by records, there is no intersubjective world in which members share the passage of time, and, in the words of Schutz, "grow old together" (cited in Smith 1974:259). There is no interpersonal negotiation or becoming, but only "fact" as sedimented in the records themselves.

While most who write about child abuse are enmeshed in that system, either as practitioners or idealogues and so are strained to defend its existence, in recent years critics have shown concern about the growing numbers of people labeled as child abusers (Besharov 1986, Eberle and Eberle 1986, Elshtain 1985, Johnson 1985, Pride 1986, Wexler 1985). Most trace this "overattribution" of child abuse to professional and lay people's "emotionally charged desire to 'do something' about child abuse, fanned by repeated and often sensational media coverage" (Besharov 1986:19). However, Conrad and Schneider (1980:270) provide a more general explanation: "bureaucratic 'industries' with large budgets and many employees...depend for their existence on the acceptance of a particular deviance designation. They become 'vested interests' in every sense of the term." To take their analysis one step farther, "bureaucratic industries" have a vested interest not only in a label, but in a labeling process—specifically, in finding ways of reducing complexity and making labeling accomplishable.

Piven and Cloward's (1971) analysis of the regulating functions of welfare programs suggests why these bureaucracies have expanded in recent years. If income support programs expand and contract to control turmoil resulting from instability in labor markets, it is possible that social agencies geared to controlling child care grow in response to instability in the child care system. This hypothesis warrants attention if for no other reason than that mothers' dramatic increases in labor force participation over the last three decades, and the commensurate increase in young children's time in nonparental care, have closely paralleled the emergence of child abuse as a major social issue. However, this single causal mode of explanation would be more compelling if it were not that history reveals other periods in which institutional momentum developed around "saving children" under a variety of different conditions (Best 1990, Finestone 1976, Platt 1969). This suggests that any explanation of why such social movements wax and wane, taking their particular form at each point in history, needs to account for many interacting factors, including the prevailing moralities and family institutions as well as opportunities for effectively marketing these problems to a wide audience (cf. Best 1990).

To conclude, this study has shown some of the ways in which the construction of documents labels deviance. The main findings include bureaucrats' determination to translate sex and violence into endlessly accumulated verbal detail, to "make do" with whatever information is available, to fashion proofs of child abuse based on the new "common sense" that children's testimony is more credible than adults,' and to develop simple, accomplishable ways of imputing intentionality that are unaffected by suspects' accounts.

REFERENCES

Besharov, Douglas J. 1986. "Unfounded allegations—A new child abuse problem." The Public Interest 83:18–33

Best, Joel. 1990. Threatened Children: Rhetoric and Concern about Child-Victims. Chicago: The University of Chicago Press.

Bittner, Egon. 1965. "The concept of organization." Social Research 32:239–255.

———. 1967. "The police on skid row: A study of peace keeping." American Sociological Review 32:699–715.

Cicourel, Aaron V. 1968. The Social Organization of Juvenile Justice. New York: John Wiley and Sons.

Cicourel, Aaron V., and John I. Kitsuse. 1963. The Educational Decision-Makers. New York: Bobbs-Merrill.

Conrad, Peter, and Joseph W. Schneider. 1980. Deviance and Medicalization. St. Louis: C. V. Mosby.

Denzin, Norman K. 1989. Interpretive Interactionism. Newbury Park, Calif.: Sage.

Douglas, Jack D. 1970. "Deviance and respectability: The social construction of moral meanings." In Deviance and Respectability, ed. Jack D. Douglas, 3–30. New York: Basic Books.

Eberle, Paul, and Shirley Eberle. 1986. The Politics of Child Abuse. Secaucus, N. J.: Lyle Stuart.

Elshtain, Jean Bethke. 1985. "Invasion of the child savers: How we succumb to hype and hysteria." The Progressive 49:23–26.

Finestone, Harold. 1976. Victims of Change: Juvenile Delinquents in American Society. Westport, Conn.: Greenwood Press.

Foucault, Michel. 1965. Madness and Civilization. New York: Random House.

———. 1973. The Birth of the Clinic. New York: Pantheon.

———. 1977. Discipline and Punish. New York: Pantheon.

———. 1978. The History of Sexuality. Vol. 1. New York: Pantheon.

Garfinkel, Harold. 1956. "Conditions of successful degradation ceremonies." American Journal of Sociology 61:420–424.

———. 1967. Studies in Ethnomethodology. Englewood Cliff, N. J.: Prentice-Hall.

Hewitt, John P., and Randall Stokes. 1975. "Disclaimers." American Sociological Review 40:1–11.

Johnson, John M. 1985. "Symbolic salvation: The changing meanings of the child maltreatment movement." Studies in Symbolic Interaction 6:289–305.

Kahn, Alfred, J. 1953. A Court for Children. New York: Columbia University Press.

Kitsuse, John I., and Aaron V. Cicourel. 1963. "A note on the use of official statistics." Social Problems 11:131–139.

Lemert, Edwin M. 1969. "Records in juvenile court." In On Record: Files and Dossiers in American Life, ed. Stanton Wheeler, 355–389. New York: Russell Sage Foundation.

Margolin, Leslie. 1990. "When vocabularies of motive fail: The example of fatal child abuse." Qualitative Sociology 13:373–385.

Meehan, Albert J. 1986. "Record-keeping practices in the policing of juveniles." Urban Life 15:70–102.

Mills, C. Wright. 1940. "Situated actions and vocabularies of motive." American Sociological Review 5:904–913.

Piliavin, Irving, and Scott Briar. 1964. "Police encounters with juveniles." American Sociological Review 70:206–214.

Piven, Frances Fox, and Richard A. Cloward. 1971. Regulating the Poor: The Functions of Public Welfare. New York: Pantheon Books.

Platt, Anthony M. 1969. The Child Savers: The Invention of Delinquency. Chicago: The University of Chicago Press.

Pollner, Melvin. 1987. Mundane Reason: Reality in Everyday and Sociological Discourse. Cambridge: Cambridge University Press.

Pride, Mary. 1986. The Child Abuse Industry. Westchester, Ill.: Crossway.

Rosenhan, D. L. 1973. "On being sane in insane places." Science 179:250–258.

Schutz, Alfred, and Thomas Luckmann. 1973. The Structures of the Life-World. Translated by R. M. Zaner and H. T. Engelhardt, Jr. Evanston, Ill.: Northwestern University Press.

Scott, Marvin B., and Stanford M. Lyman. 1968. "Accounts." American Sociological Review 22:664–670.

Smith, Dorothy E. 1974. "The social construction of documentary reality." Sociological Inquiry 44:257–268.

Steffensmeier, Darrell J., and Robert M. Terry. 1973. "Deviance and respectability: An observational study of reactions to shoplifting." Social Forces 51:417–426.

Sudnow, David. 1965. "Normal crimes: Sociological features of the penal code in a public defender office." Social Problems 12:255–276.

Swigert, Victoria, and Ronald Farrell. 1977. "Normal homicides and the law." American Sociological Review 42:16–32.

Sykes, Gresham M., and David Matza. 1957. "Techniques of neutralization: A theory of delinquency." American Sociological Review 22:664–670.

Waegel, William B. 1981. "Case routinization in investigative police work." Social Problems 28:263–275.

Wexler, Richard. 1985. "Invasions of the child savers: No one is safe in the war against abuse." The Progressive 49:19–22.

Zimmerman, Don H. 1969. "Record-keeping and the intake process in a public welfare agency." In On Record: Files and Dossiers in American Life, ed. Stanton Wheeler, 319–354. New York: Russell Sage Foundation.

———. 1974. "Fact as a practical accomplishment." In Ethnomethodology, ed. Roy Turner, 128–143. Middlesex, Eng.: Penguin Books.

CHAPTER 6

POLICE WORK

In occupations that routinely deal with deviants, there are often guidelines for dealing with the deviants and for compiling and using official records about them. In some occupations, such as police work, these norms are so central that they often become second nature, followed almost by rote. They prescribe how police officers should relate to deviants, as well as the form their records should take.

In the first reading William Waegel shows that the typification of crimes, involved parties, and different types of residents comprise a large part of detectives' working knowledge, and these typifications make it possible for them to work only on cases which contain information they think is likely to lead to an arrest. In the next reading Jennifer Hunt shows how street cops arrive at a set of shared understandings about the use of legal, normal, and brutal force. Finally, Kenneth Stoddart shows how police underpursue women heroin users while they overpursue heroin users who violate the norms of police–heroin-user interaction.

Case Routinization in Investigative Police Work

WILLIAM B. WAEGEL

...In the police department studied,[1] detectives face two practical problems which substantially shape the manner in which cases are handled. They must satisfy the paperwork demands of the organization (referred to as "keeping the red numbers down") by classifying each case and producing a formal investigative report within two weeks after the case is assigned. Sanctions may be applied to those who fail to meet deadlines and who thus accumulate too many "red numbers." At the same time, the detectives are under the same pressure as other employees: they must produce. Specifically, detectives believe they must produce an acceptable level of arrests which will enhance their chances of remaining in the detective division and gaining promotion. While no arrest quota is formalized in the division, there is a shared belief that one should produce roughly two to three lock-ups per week. This arrest level is a practical concern for the detective because most wish to remain in the division and avoid transfer "back to the pit" (i.e., back into uniform in the patrol division). Moreover, the position of detective holds the highest status of any assignment in the department, and a transfer, therefore, generally entails a loss of status.

For the vast majority of cases handled, no explicit procedures exist to indicate what must be done on the case and how to go about doing it. As detectives go about the ordinary business of investigating and processing cases, they can select

Reprinted from "Case Routinization in Investigative Police Work," *Social Problems,* Vol. 28, No. 3 (February, 1981), pp. 263–275, by permission of the Society for the Study of Social Problems and the author.

An earlier version of this paper was presented at the annual meeting of the Society for the Study of Social Problems, Boston, 1979. The author would like to thank Gerry Turkel for his helpful comments. For correspondence about this article: Dept. of Sociology, Villanova University, Villanova, PA 19085.

strategies ranging from a *pro forma* victim interview comprising the total investigative activity devoted to the case, to a full-scale investigation involving extensive interviewing, physical evidence, the use of informants, interrogation, surveillance and other activities. The selection of a particular handling strategy in most cases is an informal process and not the direct result of formal organizational policy or procedure. This process of selection is grounded in practical solutions to concrete problems faced by the detective; it consists of an assignment of meaning to persons and events in ways that are regarded as proper because they have "worked" in previous cases.

A great deal of actual detective work may thus be seen as a process of mapping the features of a particular case onto a more general and commonly recognized *type* of case. The present work suggests that a detective's interpretation, classification, and handling of cases is guided by a set of occupationally shared typifications. The categorization schemes used by detectives center around specific configurations of information regarding the victim, the offense, and possible suspects. Information pertaining to these three elements constitutes the meaningful unit that detectives deal with: the case.

The most basic dimension of case categorization is that of the routine versus the nonroutine. Where a particular configuration of information regarding the victim, the offense, and possible suspects appears, the competent detective understands the case as a routine one—as an instance of a familiar type—and particular handling strategies are deemed appropriate. Such cases contrast with those which are viewed as nonroutine: that is, where no general type is available to which the case reasonably corresponds, and where the case is vigorously investigated and the detective attends to the unique features of the case. Case routinization is most characteristic for burglaries, which comprise the bulk of cases handled by detectives, but it is also exhibited in the handling of many assault, robbery, rape and homicide cases.

The categorization schemes used by detectives are derived from concrete experiences in working cases and are continually assessed for their relevance, adequacy, and effectiveness in handling one's caseload. It is because typificatory schemes serve as a solution to practical problems commonly faced by all detectives that they learn to share most of the content of these schemes. Both through direct experience in working cases and through interaction with other members, the detective learns to categorize and handle cases in ways that are regarded as proper by other detectives.

Routine case imageries serve as resources upon which detectives may draw to construct a solution to their problem of interpreting, investigating, and resolving their cases. The features of a specific case are compared with routine case imagery in a process of interpretive interplay. In some instances a correspondence is readily apparent, in others a fit is forced by the detective, and in still others the features of a specific case render the use of the typical imagery inappropriate. The interpretation and handling of a case may also change over the case's history; a routine case may come to be treated as nonroutine upon the receipt of additional information, and vice-versa.

THE ORGANIZATIONAL CONTEXT OF CASE ROUTINIZATION

In the department studied, detectives have no formal guidelines for allocating time and effort to different cases and there is little effective monitoring of daily activities by supervisors.[2] In conducting their work, detectives are, however, guided and constrained by two organizational imperatives: 1) the requirement to submit investigative reports, and 2) the requirement to produce arrests. In other words, the work is not organized by formal rules, but rather by the kinds of outcomes that are expected. Both of these expected outcomes

generate practical problems leading to routinized solutions.

An investigative report must be produced for each case assigned, and its submission within the prescribed time limit is viewed as a fundamental constraint on how vigorously different cases can be investigated. Departmental policy indicates that each investigative report submitted must be reviewed and signed by a supervisory lieutenant. However, in practice, these reports are often given only a cursory glance, and seldom is the content of a report questioned or challenged by a lieutenant. The primary concern of the supervisor is that the submission of reports comply with time deadlines.

The potential a case appears to hold for producing an arrest also has an important impact on how the case will be handled. Most detectives believe that the number of arrests they produce will be used as a basis for evaluating performance and, therefore, will affect decisions regarding promotions and transfers. Attempts to cope with the practical problems of meeting paperwork demands, while at the same time producing a satisfactory number of arrests, creates a situation in which one burglary case involving a $75 loss may receive less than five minutes investigative effort, yet another case with an identical loss may be worked on exclusively for two or three full days. These two concerns constitute central features of the work setting which structure case handling.

PAPERWORK

Formal organizational procedure demands that a case be investigated, classified, and a report produced within a specified time period after it is assigned. Detectives experience paperwork requirements and deadlines as central sources of pressure and tension in their job, and stories abound concerning former detectives who "could handle the job but couldn't handle the paperwork."

Most cases are assigned during the daily roll-call sessions. At this point, the information about the incident consists of an original report written by a patrol officer and any supplemental reports submitted by personnel in the evidence detection unit. Each case is stamped with a "red number" which supervisors use to monitor compliance with report deadlines.

Ordinary cases require the submission of two reports within specific time periods. A brief first-day report, consisting essentially of an interview with the victim, is formally required the day after the case is assigned. However, this deadline is generally ignored by supervisors and first-day reports are seldom submitted. The more meaningful deadline for detectives is the fourteen day limit for the submission of an investigative report. Here, the detective must provide a detailed accounting of the activities undertaken in investigating the incident and assign an investigative status to the case. Compliance with this second deadline is closely monitored; every Sunday a lieutenant draws up a list of each detective's overdue red numbers, and this list is read at the next roll call along with a caution to keep up with one's paperwork.

In the investigative report, the detective must classify the status of the investigation as suspended, closed arrest, or open. The ability to manipulate information about cases to fit them into these categories is of the utmost importance to detectives, for it is through such strategic manipulations that they are able to manage their caseloads effectively.

Of the total cases handled by a detective, a substantial majority are classified as suspended. This means that the steps already taken in the investigation (which may consist merely of a telephone interview with the victim) have not uncovered sufficient information to warrant continued investigation of the incident. Any number of acceptable reasons for suspending a case may be offered, ranging from a simple statement that the victim declines to prosecute up to a fairly elaborate report detailing contacts with the victim, the entry of serial numbers of stolen articles into the computerized crime files, the usefulness of ev-idence obtained from the scene, and a conclusion that the case must be suspended because there are no further investigative leads. Over 80 percent of the burglary cases assigned in the city are suspended; this percentage drops considerably for robbery cases and even more for assault, rape and homicide cases.[3]

An investigation is classified as closed when one or more arrests have been made pertaining to the incident and the detective anticipates no additional arrests. A case is classified as open when an investigation extends beyond the fourteen day limit but it is expected that an arrest eventually will be made. Generally, only major cases may remain classified as open after the fourteen day investigative period.

PRODUCING ARRESTS

As organizations become more bureaucratized and their procedures more formalized, there evolves a general tendency to develop quantitative indices or measures of individual performance. In the department studied, most detectives believe that the crude number of lock-ups they make is used as a basis for assessing their performance and competence in doing investigative work. Every arrest a detective makes is entered into a logbook, which is available for inspection by superiors and from which they can compare each detective's arrest level with that of others.

Ambitious detectives in particular are very conscious of producing a steady stream of arrests, feeling that this is an effective way to achieve recognition and promotion. One young detective boasted:

> I've made over forty lock-ups since the beginning of the year and eleven in April alone. Since I don't really have a godfather in here, I gotta' depend on making good lock-ups if I'm gonna' make sergeant.

This detective's use of the term "godfather" reveals a widely shared belief that some individuals are promoted not because of their performance but because they have a friend or relative in a position of power within the department.

Skimming off selected cases from one's workload is widely practiced as a means of achieving a steady stream of arrests. The practice of skimming refers to 1) selectively working only those cases that appear potentially solvable from information contained in the original report, and 2) summarily suspending the remainder of one's ordinary cases. Supervisors are certainly aware of both aspects of this practice, but they recognize its practical value in producing arrests. Moreover, supervisors, to a greater extent than working detectives, find their performance assessed in crude quantitative terms, and they are likely to be questioned by superiors if arrest levels begin to drop sharply. Supervisors support the practice of skimming even though they recognize that it ensures that a majority of ordinary cases will never receive a thorough investigation. The pragmatic work orientation of detectives is further revealed in the lack of attention given to conviction rates both by detectives and supervisors. Competence and productivity are judged by the arrests made, not by the proportion of cases which survive the scrutiny of the judicial process.

The recognition of potentially productive cases and of their utility in effectively managing one's caseload are among the earliest skills taught to the neophyte in the detective division. Moreover, newcomers are taught that their work on burglary cases is the primary basis upon which their performance will be judged. In a sizeable percentage of crimes against persons, the perpetrator is readily identified from information provided by the victim. Since no great investigative effort or acumen is involved, the same credit is not accorded an arrest in this type of case as in burglary cases. Detectives are expected to produce a steady flow of "quality" arrests: that is, arrests involving some effort and skill on the part of the investigator. Straightforward assaults cases involving acquainted parties, for example, are often handed out by supervisors along with a remark such as "Here's an easy one for you."

INTERPRETING CASES

The preceding observations have suggested that detectives are constrained in their conception and handling of cases not by the formal organization of their work or by supervisory surveillance, but rather by the bureaucratic pressure of writing reports and producing the proper number and quality of arrests. The process of interpreting cases in accordance with these pragmatic concerns may now be considered.

Data derived from observation of detective-victim interviews and from written case reports provide a basis for examining the interpretive schemes used by detectives. In the victim interview, the kinds of questions asked and the pieces of information sought out reveal the case patterns recognized as routine for the different offenses commonly encountered.[4] However, in attempting to make sense of the incident at hand, detectives attend to much more than is revealed in their explicit communications with the victim. Interpretation of the case is also based upon understanding of the victim's lifestyle, racial or ethnic membership group, class position, and possible clout or connections—especially as these factors bear upon such concerns as the likelihood of the victim inquiring into the progress of the investigation, the victim's intentions regarding prosecution, and the victim's competence and quality as a source of information.

The interpretive schemes employed also receive partial expression in the written investigative reports which must be produced for each case. These reports contain a selective accounting of the meaning assigned to a case, the information and understandings upon which this interpretation is based, and the reasonableness of the linkage between this particular interpretation of the case and the handling strategy employed.[5]

Several important features of the process of interpreting cases as routine or nonroutine may be seen in the following incidents.

CASE 1: ATTEMPTED HOMICIDE

A radio call was broadcast that a shooting had just occurred on the street in a working-class residential area. The victim, a white male, was still conscious when the detectives arrived, although he had been severely wounded in the face by a shotgun blast. He indicated that he had been robbed and shot by three black males, and provided a vague description of their appearance and clothing. This description was broadcast, an area search was initiated, the crime scene was cordoned off, and a major investigation was begun.

The following morning, the victim's employer brought into question the account of the incident that had been provided. He indicated his belief that the incident involved a "lover's triangle" situation between the victim, a male acquaintance of the victim, and a woman. All three were described as "hillbillies." The three parties were interviewed separately and each denied this version of the incident. After further questioning, the victim finally admitted that the story concerning three black males was false, but would say nothing more about the incident. Articles of the woman's clothing believed to show bloodstains and a weapon believed to have been used were obtained, but crime lab analysis would take at least three weeks. The case was now interpreted as a routine "domestic shooting" and little additional effort was devoted to it.

CASE 2: BURGLARY

A detective parked his car in front of an address in a public housing project and pulled out the original burglary report. A new member of the prosecutor's office was riding along to observe how detectives work. The detective read over the report, and after hesitating for awhile decided to go into the residence. He explained to the prosecutor that the loss was an inexpensive record player and

added, "This one's a pork chop, like most of the burglaries we get. But we gotta' go and interview the victim before suspending it." The detective asked the victim if she knew who might have committed the burglary or if she had heard about anyone committing burglaries in the area. Negative replies followed both questions. The entire encounter with the victim lasted less than two minutes.

CASE 3: ASSAULT AND ROBBERY

A robbery squad detective was waiting for two victims to come in the hall to be interviewed. Both were black, middle-aged, center-city residents who were described by the detective as "dead-end alcoholics." They had been robbed in their residence by a young male who had forced his way in, taken $20 from the pair, and cut the female victim on the hand with a knife. The victims were able to provide the detective with the name of their assailant, and they both picked his photograph out of a number of pictures they were shown. Several minutes later the detective handed them a photograph of a different individual, asking, "Are you sure this is the guy who robbed you?" After inspecting the picture they replied that they knew this person as well but he had not been the one who robbed them. At this point, the detective sat down and took a formal statement from the victims.

When the victims had left, the detective explained his views and usual handling of such "ghetto robberies": "In a case like this, what can we do? To tell you the truth, the only way this kind of thing is going to stop is for the victims or somebody they know to kill this guy off. My involvement in this case is minimal. If the two victims, those two old drunks, if they sober up and if they show up in court, we'll see how they do there. It's up to them here and not up to me."

CASE 4: BURGLARY

A detective entered the center-city residence of a burglary victim in a block where about one-fourth of the row houses were vacant. He examined a large hole in a basement wall that had been made to gain entry, and then sat down to compile a list of articles that had been stolen. The victim had literally been cleaned out, losing every easily transportable item of value she had owned. The woman explained that she worked during the day, that this was the fifth time she had been burglarized in the past four years, and that her coverage had been dropped by the insurance company. She added that she lived in the house for 21 years and was not about to move, and then asked, "What can I do to keep this from happening again?" The detective replied: "Ma'am, I don't know what to tell you. You're the only white family on this block. Most of the people around here work during the daytime, and a lot of these people, even if they saw somebody coming out of your house with some of your stuff, they're not going to call the cops anyhow. That's the way it is around here. It's a shame, but that's the way it is." The detective entered the serial numbers of some of the stolen articles into the computerized stolen property files, "to cover myself, just in case." The written report indicated that the pawn shop sheets had been checked but in fact this step was not taken. When the report deadline approached, the case was suspended.

CASE 5: HOMICIDES

Two homicides had occurred over the weekend. On Monday morning two detectives who were working on the different cases were discussing the status of their investigations. One detective, who was investigating a shooting death that occurred in a crowded bar in the presence of 100 persons noted that he was on the verge of making a lock-up even though none of the witnesses present had voluntarily come forward. The other detective was investigating the bludgeoning death of a male homosexual whose body had been found by firemen called to extinguish a small fire in the victim's residence. There were as yet no suspects in the case. The second detective took offense to remarks made by the other comparing the lack of progress in the second case to the nearly completed investigation in the barroom case. The second detective remarked, "Anybody can handle a killing like you've got. What we've got here is a murder, not a killing."

The above incidents illustrate detectives' use of a body of accumulated knowledge, beliefs, and assumptions which lead to the interpretation of certain case patterns as common, typical and routine. Cases are interpreted primarily using conceptions of 1) how identifiable the perpetrators seem to be; 2) the normal social characteristics of the victims; and 3) the settings involved, and behavior seen as typical in such settings. A detective's initial efforts on a case tend to focus on these three aspects, in the process of assigning meaning to the case and selecting an appropriate strategy for handling it.

1. Conceptions of how different kinds of offenses are typically committed—especially how identifiable the perpetrators seem to be—are routinely used in interpreting incidents. These imageries are specifically relevant to a detective's practical concerns. The ordinary burglary (Cases 2 and 4) is seen as involving a crude forced entry at a time of day or at a location where it is unlikely that anyone will witness the perpetrator entering or exiting. A burglary victim's ability or inability to provide information identifying a probable perpetrator constitutes the single feature of burglary cases which is given greatest interpretive significance. In roughly ten percent of these cases, the victim provides the name of a suspected perpetrator (commonly an ex-boyfriend, a relative or a neighboring resident), and vigorous effort is devoted to the case. For the remaining burglary cases, the initial inclination is to treat them as routine incidents deserving of only minimal investigative effort. In these routine cases the victim's race and class position have a decisive impact on whether the case will be summarily suspended or whether some minor investigative activities will be undertaken to impress the victim that "something is being done."

On the other hand, assault, rape, and homicide cases commonly occur in a face-to-face situation which affords the victim an opportunity to observe the assailant. Further, detectives recognize that many personal assault offenses involve acquainted parties. The earliest piece of information sought out and the feature of such cases given the greatest interpretive significance is whether the offense occurred between parties who were in some way known to one another prior to the incident. The interpretation and handling of the shooting incident in Case 1 changed markedly when it was learned that the victim and suspect were acquainted parties and that the offense reasonably conformed to a familiar pattern of domestic assaults. Where the victim and perpetrator are acquainted in assault, rape and homicide cases, the incident is seen as containing the core feature of the routine offense pattern for these cases. In such incidents a perfunctory investigation is usually made, for the identity of the perpetrator generally is easily learned from the victim or from persons close to the victim.

The barroom homicide in Case 5 was termed a "killing" and viewed as a routine case because the victim and perpetrator were previously acquainted and information linking the perpetrator to the crime could be easily obtained. The term "murder" is reserved for those homicides which do not correspond to a typical pattern.

A somewhat different pattern follows in the category of incidents which detectives refer to as "suspect rapes." Victims having certain social characteristics (females from lower-class backgrounds who are viewed as having low intelligence or as displaying some type of mental or emotional abnormality) are viewed as most likely to make a false allegation of rape. Where a victim so perceived reports a sexual assault by a person with whom she had some prior acquaintance, the initial orientation of the detective is to obtain information which either negates the crime of rape (the complainant actually consented) or warrants reducing the charge to a lesser offense. Where the victim and assailant were not previously acquainted, the case receives a vigorous investigative effort. The level of police resources devoted to the case varies according to the race and social standing of the victim.

2. Conceptions of the normal social characteristics of victims are also central to case routinization. Victims having different social characteristics are regarded as being more or less likely to desire or follow through with prosecution in the case, to be reliable sources of information about it, and to inquire as to the outcome of the investigation.

The treatment of the assault and robbery in Case 3 illustrates how a case may be interpreted and handled primarily in terms of the victim's class position, race, and presumed lifestyle and competencies. The case was cleared by arrest on the basis of information provided by the victims, but the handling of this "ghetto robbery" involved little actual police effort. No attempt was made to locate witnesses, gather evidence from the crime scene, or otherwise strengthen the case against the accused.

Poor and working-class people who are regarded as unlikely to make inquiries regarding the handling and disposition of the case are seen as typical of victims in the category of routine burglaries. Case 2 illustrates how the interpretation of an incident may be accomplished solely on the basis of information contained in the patrol report and prior to an actual interview with the victim. The interview was structured in this case by the detective's expectation of its outcome.

Case 4 illustrates how inconsistent elements in an otherwise routine pattern (in this instance the victim's social status and apparent interest in the handling of the case) are managed to suit the purposes of the detective. Detectives speak of a case "coming back on them" if a respectable victim contacts superiors regarding progress in the case when the incident has received little or no investigative effort. Informing the victim that the case was not solvable largely because of her neighbor's attitudes enabled the detective to suspend the case with minimal problems.

3. Routinization formulas, finally, contain conceptions of the settings in which different kinds

of offenses normally occur and the expected behavior of inhabitants of those settings. While assumptions about victims and perpetrators are
derived in part from the nature of the offense involved, the physical and social setting where the
incident occurred also contributes to a detective's
understanding of these parties. The fact that the
burglary in Case 2 occurred in a particular public
housing project told the detective much of what
he felt he had to know about the case. It should be
noted that none of these perceptions were communicated to the prosecutor observing the detective
work; they were part of the taken-for-granted
background upon which the detective based his
handling of the case.

With regard to actual and potential *witnesses,*
however, a detective's assumptions and beliefs are
based primarily on the offense setting, if the witness is seen as a normal inhabitant of that setting.
(This latter qualification simply recognizes that
detectives attribute different inclinations and sentiments to social workers or salesmen who may
have witnessed an incident than to residents of the
area who may have witnessed a crime.)

The impact of territorial conceptions may be
seen in the handling of Case 4. Routine burglaries
occur mainly in low-income housing projects, res-
idences in deteriorating center-city areas or, less
frequently, in commercial establishments in or
near these locations. Residents of these areas are
considered unlikely to volunteer that they have
witnessed a crime. Although official investigative
procedure dictates that neighboring residents be
interviewed to determine whether they saw or
heard anything that might be of value to the investigation, this step was not undertaken in Cases 2
or 4 because it was assumed that the residents
would be uncooperative.

Routine cases, then, may be seen as having
two components, one at the level of consciousness
and cognition, and the other at the level of observable behavior. A detective's interpretation of a
case as routine involves an assessment of whether
sufficient correspondence exists between the
current case and some typical pattern to warrant
handling it in the normal way. The criterion of

sufficient correspondence implies that not all the
elements of the typical pattern need be present for
a detective to regard a case as a routine one. Common elements are viewed and used as resources
which may be drawn upon selectively in accordance with one's practical concerns and objectives. Further, when certain elements in a case
appear inconsistent with the typical pattern, there
is a tendency to force and manage a sufficient fit
between the particular and the typical in ways that
help detectives deal with their caseload management problems and constraints.

These features of the interpretation process
mean that the assessments of the routine or nonroutine nature of a case take on more of the character of a dichotomy than a continuum. Once an
assessment is made, the case will be handled by
means of prescribed formulas unless additional
information changes the interpretation. It must be
emphasized that the routinization process is not a
matter of automatic or unreflective mapping of
case features onto more general conceptions of
criminal incidents. The interpretation of any particular case is shaped by a detective's understandings of what is required and expected and of how
to manage these concerns effectively.

CASE HANDLING

Case handling normally proceeds in accordance
with informal understandings shared among detectives. Routine case patterns are associated with
prescribed handling recipes. It is critical to an understanding of investigative police work that interpretation of criminal incidents as routine or
nonroutine largely determines which cases will be
summarily suspended, which will be investigated,
and how vigorous or extensive that investigation
will be.

The characteristic behavioral element of a
routine case is an absence of vigorous or thorough
investigative effort. Two distinct sets of circumstances are ordinarily encountered in routine cases
which lead to such a superficial or cursory investigative effort. The first, most common in burglary
and robbery cases, is that the available informa-

tion concerning the incident is seen as so meager or of so little utility that the possibility of making a quick arrest is virtually nonexistent. Viewing the case as nonproductive, and not wishing to expend effort on cases for which there are no formal rewards, the detective produces a brief investigative report detailing the routine features of the incident, concludes the case summary with "N.I.L." (no investigative leads were found), and classifies it as a suspended case.

The second set of circumstances associated with an absence of vigorous investigative effort involves assault, rape, and homicide cases which require some investigation because of their seriousness and the possibility of scrutiny by the judicial process. However, in many such incidents the facts of the case are so obvious and straightforward that little actual investigative work needs to be done. In these three types of offenses the victim and perpetrator are often known to one another, and it is not at all uncommon for the victim to name the assailant as soon as the police arrive. Cases in which a spouse or lover is still standing by the victim with weapon in hand when the police arrive, or in which the victim names the perpetrator before expiring, are not unusual. In essence, such cases are solved without any substantial police investigation. The detective is obligated to produce a comprehensive report on the incidence, and the investigation is generally classified as closed in this report if the perpetrator has been apprehended. Indeed, in such obvious and straightforward cases the detective's only difficult task may be that of locating the perpetrator.[6]

Handling recipes associated with routine cases have a practical and instrumental character, reflecting the objective circumstances surrounding the investigation of many criminal events. After all, in the great majority of burglary cases the probability of ascertaining the identity of the perpetrator is rather small. Yet, handling recipes reflect certain *beliefs* and *assumptions* on the part of detectives concerning such matters as a victim's willingness to cooperate fully in the case, whether persons in particular sections of the city are likely

to volunteer information about a crime, or the kind of impression a victim or witness would make in court. Such beliefs and assumptions constitute integral features in the construction of cases as routine or nonroutine, and they represent a pivotal linkage between specific features of cases and particular handling recipes.

The following incident illustrates the extent to which case handling may be guided by the detective's beliefs and assumptions about the nature of an incident and the parties involved:

CASE 6:

A detective was assigned a case in which a man had stabbed his common-law wife in the arm with a kitchen knife. The patrol report on the incident indicated that the woman had been taken to City Hall to sign an arrest warrant, while the man had been arrested by patrol officers on the charge of felony assault and released on his own recognizance. Nominally, the detective was required to collect additional information and evidence relating to the incident and to write a detailed and comprehensive report which would be used in prosecuting the case. However, the detective's interpretation of the incident, based on his understanding of the area in which it occurred and the lifestyles of the persons involved, led him to view any further investigative effort on his part as futile. He remarked: "These drunks, they're always stabbing one another over here. Then you see 'em the next day and they're right back together again. She won't show up in court anyhow. Why waste my time and everybody else's on it." The handling of the case involved only the production of a brief report which concluded: "The victim in this complaint wishes no further investigation by the police department. This complaint is to be classified as closed."

The interpretive schemes used by detectives are not based solely on their experiences as police investigators, but also on their accumulated experiences as everyday social actors; they thus reflect commonsense social knowledge. Categorizations made by detectives about race, class, ethnicity, sex, and territory parallel wider cultural evaluations of morality and worth. None of the features of the formal organization of detective work substantially reduce this reliance on commonsense knowledge and its typical biases, prejudices and interpretations.

SUMMARY AND IMPLICATIONS

Some general features of case routinization may now be noted in an attempt to clarify the interpretive activities through which detectives achieve order and predictability in their handling of cases and their encounters with victims and other relevant actors.

1. Shortly after receipt of a case, specific pieces of information are sought out and attended to for use in assessing the typicality of the incident. That is, the fundamental case-working orientation of detectives involves an attempt to establish commonalities between an actual case and typical case patterns. Incidents having typical features are interpreted and constructed as some variety of routine case. The orientation to typify and routinize cases is partly traceable to bureaucratic pressures and constraints to meet paperwork deadlines and produce a certain quantity and quality not of convictions but of arrests.

2. The interpretation of an incident is accomplished by attending to case features having commonly recognized utility as indicators of the type of case at hand. Detectives use such routinization schemes unless some problematic feature of an actual case brings into question their applicability and appropriateness. The interpretation of a case as routine or nonroutine essentially determines whether the case will be quickly closed or suspended or whether it will receive a more vigorous and extensive investigation. However, this initial assignment of meaning is provisional and subject to revision or modification upon receipt of additional information. Most importantly, the handling of cases is directed by these informal categoriza-

tion schemes and is not the result of formal organizational policy or procedures. These schemes constitute a taken-for-granted background of decision making.

3. The interpretive schemes shared by detectives represent "successful" solutions to common practical problems, based on experience and shared understandings about the nature of urban crime and about types of urban residents, lifestyles and territories. These understandings are rooted in socially distributed as well as role-specific knowledge, for both provide a basis for constructing solutions to work problems. Occupationally specific knowledge provides a set of instructions for interpreting case patterns in ways which enable a detective to successfully manage organizational constraints and demands. Commonsense social knowledge provides an understanding of the typical characteristics, attitudes and action patterns of persons encountered. Identities may be readily assigned to persons by drawing on this stock of knowledge. Such identity assignments structure case handling along race, class, age, sex and territorial lines in ways that are intended to minimize case handling problems. Because of this reliance on general social knowledge, the treatment of different types of urban residents tends to reflect wider cultural evaluations of social worth.

4. The essential nature of these interpretive processes is phenomenological rather than mechanical or rule-guided. In formulating a particular case, the operative process involves a determination of whether sufficient correspondence exists between the actual case and the paradigmatic case to warrant handling the incident in routine, low-effort ways. Sufficient correspondence assessments are accomplished in ways that serve the practical purposes of detectives, especially those of paper-work compliance and productivity.

5. Accordingly, routine cases are not constituted as a single determinant pattern. A variety of combinations of case features may result in routine handling of the case. For each offense, a core feature or set of features gets maximum interpretive significance. When a core feature is recognized in a particular case, other features which are ambiguous or even contradictory tend to be interpreted in a manner consistent with the identified core feature. Additional interpretive features, particularly the social status of the victim, are used as resources in selecting a safe and workable handling strategy.

6. In highly routinized case patterns, there is a tendency to squeeze great indicativeness out of a few case features. Detectives often rely upon assumptions to add detail to a case rather than actually gather information to further specify the type of case at hand. In other words, it is frequently taken for granted that certain investigative procedures will have predictable outcomes. Frequently, this process manifests itself in the fudging, doctoring and manipulation of formal organizational reports.

It is likely that interpretive schemes having similar features will be found in all bureaucratically organized enterprises where large numbers of clients or cases are processed (e.g., social service centers, public hospitals, and other agencies in the criminal justice system). Whenever we find an organizational setting where members deal with similar events time and again, and where there are no features in the formal organization of the work which act to counter stereotyping, we may expect to find routinization schemes in use. These schemes will be used to categorize the population and apply standard patterns of treatment to each category.

These observations have significant implications for the study of decision making by legal agents. Decision making by bureaucratic agents inevitably involves discretion on the part of the agent who must fit general rules to particular cases. This discretionary latitude will be reflected in different forms of decision making in different kinds of organizational settings. The work of Roth (1977), Scheff (1978), Sudnow (1965) and others suggests that caseload size, amount of information readily available about the person or event, the nature of the body of knowledge used, and the expectation of future interaction with the person are crucial features governing the nature of the decision-making process. Where caseloads are high, continued interaction is not anticipated, minimal information is available, and the body of knowledge used by the agent is imprecise—stereotypes tend to become the operative and binding basis for decision making. Accordingly, detective work, presentence casework, public defender work, and medical practice in clinics or emergency rooms may be seen as lying toward the end of a continuum where typifications act as essentially final judgments.

At the other end of the continuum are settings where caseload sizes are smaller, more detailed information about the person is available, future interaction is anticipated, and decision making is grounded in a more substantial body of knowledge. In such settings, typificatory schemes are likely to be used only as provisional hypotheses, to be amplified and modified over the course of the encounter. Thus in probation work, some types of social service work, and the practice of general medicine, we might expect to find interaction only tentatively structured by stereotypic understandings. As interaction proceeds in these latter settings, typifications will begin to fade in importance as the basis for decision making.

NOTES

1. The description and the analysis presented here are based on nine months of participant observation field work in a city police detective division. Further information about access agreements, characteristics of the city and department, the field role adopted, and problems encountered during the research is available from the author.

2. An exception to this general observation occurs where a supervisor imposes a "major case" definition on an incident. In highly publicized or nonroutine homicide or rape cases, especially those involving higher status victims, a supervisor frequently takes an active part in the investigation and more closely monitors and directs the activities of detectives. With regard to the influence of the victim's social status on case handling, see Wilson's (1968:27) analysis of police perceptions of the legitimacy of complaints made by middle-class versus lower-class victims.

3. Official nationwide clearance rates are listed as 17.6% for burglary, 27.3% for robbery, 63.4% for felonious assault, 51.1% for rape, and 79.9% for homicide (Hindelang *et al.*, 1977).

4. Cf. Sudnow's (1965) argument that public defenders use their first interview with a client to gain an initial sense of the defendant's place in the social structure as well as the typicality or lack thereof of the offense with which the person has been charged.

5. Garfinkel (1967:186–207) argues that organizational records are not to be treated as accurate or mirror reflections of the actual handling of a client or case by organizational members. However, these records can be employed to examine how members go about constructing a meaningful conception of a client or case and use it for their own practical purposes. Any valid sociological use of such records requires detailed knowledge on the part of the researcher regarding the context in which the records are produced, background understandings of members, and organizationally relevant purposes and routines.

6. Reiss (1971) makes a similar observation. He found that a great deal of detective work in the department studied merely involves attempting to locate identified perpetrators. The Rand survey of investigative practices in 153 police departments draws conclusions similar to those presented here. It was found that substantially more than half of all serious reported crimes receive no more than superficial attention from investigators (Greenwood and Petersilia, 1975).

REFERENCES

Garfinkel, Harold. 1967. Studies in Ethnomethodology. Englewood Cliffs, N. J.: Prentice-Hall.

Greenwood, Peter W. and Joan Petersilia. 1975. The Criminal Investigation Process, Volume I. Santa Monica, Calif.: The Rand Corporation.

Hindelang, M., M. Gottfredson, C. Dunn and N. Parisi. 1977. Sourcebook of Criminal Justice Statistics. Washington, D.C.: National Criminal Justice Information and Statistics Service.

Reiss, Albert. 1971. Police and the Public. New Haven: Yale University Press.

Roth, Julius. 1977. "Some contingencies of the moral evaluation and control of clients." American Journal of Sociology 77 (October):830–56.

Scheff, Thomas. 1978. "Typification in rehabilitation agencies." Pp. 172–175 in E. Rubington and M. S. Weinberg (eds.), Deviance: The Interactionist Perspective. New York: Macmillan.

Sudnow, David. 1965. "Normal crimes: Sociological features of the penal code in a public defender's office." Social Problems 12 (3):255–276.

Wilson, James Q. 1968. Varieties of Police Behavior. Cambridge, Mass.: Harvard University Press.

Normal Force

JENNIFER HUNT

The police are required to handle a variety of peacekeeping and law enforcement tasks including settling disputes, removing drunks from the street, aiding the sick, controlling crowds, and

Excerpt from Jennifer Hunt, "Police Accounts of Normal Force," *Urban Life,* Vol. 13, No. 4 (January 1985), pp. 315–341. Copyright © 1985 Sage Publications. Inc. Reprinted by permission of Sage Publications, Inc.

The author is deeply indebted for both substantive and editorial assistance to Michael Brown and Robert M. Emerson. She would also like to thank Peter Manning, Bill DiFazio, Jim Birch, and Marie DeMay Della Guardia for their comments on an earlier draft of this article.

pursuing criminals. What unifies these diverse activities is the possibility that their resolution might require the use of force. Indeed, the capacity to use force stands at the core of the police mandate (Bittner, 1980).

The bulk of the sociological literature on the use of force by police is concerned with analyzing the objective causes of "excessive" force. Some social scientists, for example, suggest that the incidence of extra-legal force correlates with characteristics of individual officers—in particular, their authoritarianism, age, or length of service

(Niederhoffer, 1967; Blumberg, 1983). Others emphasize the relevance of the behavior and characteristics of the target population, including demeanor, sex, race, and class (Reiss, 1970; Friedrich, 1980; Lee, 1981). Still others investigate the legal and organizational roots of force. They are concerned with how formal rules and/or subcultural norms may influence the police officer's decision to employ force (Fyfe, 1983; Waegel, 1984).

Although representing diverse perspectives, these approaches share a similar underlying orientation to use of force by police. First, they all specify, in advance of study, formal or legal definitions of permissible force, definitions that are then used to identify deviations legally classifiable as brutal or "excessive." This procedure disregards the understandings and standards police officers actively employ in using and evaluating force in the course of their work. Second, these studies are primarily concerned with identifying the objective conditions held to determine "excessive" force defined in this way. As a result, they minimize the active role of consciousness in police decisions to use force, tending to depict such decisions as mere passive responses to external determinants.

In contrast, sociologists working within the symbolic interactionist tradition have displayed particular interest in the police officer's own assessment of what constitutes necessary force. This research has varied in how such assessments are conceptualized. Rubinstein (1973: 302), for example, suggests that police use force instrumentally to control persons whom they perceive as presenting a physical threat. In contrast, Van Maanen (1978) explores how police, in reacting to others, are highly attentive to symbolic violation of their authority, dispensing harsh treatment to categories of persons who commit such violations.

The following research departs from and seeks to extend the symbolic interactionist concern with police officers' own assessments of the use of force. It explores how police themselves classify and evaluate acts of force as either legal, normal, or excessive. Legal force is that coercion necessary to subdue, control, and restrain a suspect in order to take him into custody. Although force not accountable in legal terms is technically labelled excessive by the courts and the public, the police perceive many forms of illegal force as normal. Normal force involves coercive acts that specific "cops" on specific occasions formulate as necessary, appropriate, reasonable, or understandable. Although not always legitimated or admired, normal force is depicted as a necessary or natural response of normal police to particular situational exigencies.

Most officers are expected to use both legal and normal force as a matter of course in policing the streets. In contrast, excessive force or brutality exceeds even working police notions of normal force.... Brutality is viewed as illegal, illegitimate, and often immoral violence, but the police draw the lines in extremely different ways and at different points than do either the court system or the public.

These processes of assessing...the use of force, with special reference to the critical distinction between normal and excessive force as drawn by the police, will be explored in what follows.

The article is based on approximately eighteen months of participant observation in a major urban police department referred to as the Metro City P.D. I attended the police academy with male and female recruits and later rode with individual officers in one-person cars on evening and night shifts in high crime districts.[1] The female officers described in this research were among the first 100 women assigned to the ranks of uniformed patrol as a result of a discrimination suit filed by the Justice Department and a policewoman plaintiff.

NORMAL FORCE

The police phrase "it's not done on the street the way that it's taught at the academy" underscores the perceived contradiction between the formal world of the police academy and the informal world of the street. This contradiction permeates the police officer's construction of his world, particularly his view of the rational and moral use of force.

In the formal world of the police academy, the recruit learns to account for force by reference to legality. He or she is issued the regulation instruments and trained to use them to subdue, control, and restrain a suspect. If threatened with great bodily harm, the officer learns that he can justifiably use deadly force and fire his revolver. Yet the recruit is taught that he cannot use his baton, jack, or gun, unnecessarily to torture, maim, or kill a suspect.

When recruits leave the formal world of the academy and are assigned to patrol a district, they are introduced to an informal world in which police recognize normal as well as legal and brutal force. Through observation and instruction, rookies gradually learn to apply force and account for its use in terms familiar to the street cop. First, rookies learn to adjust their arsenals to conform to street standards. They are encouraged to buy the more powerful weapons worn by veteran colleagues as these colleagues point out the inadequacy of a wooden baton or compare their convoy jacks to vibrators. They quickly discover that their department-issued equipment marks them as new recruits. At any rate, within a few weeks, most rookies have dispensed with the wooden baton and convoy jack and substituted them with the more powerful plastic nightstick and flat headed slapjack.[2]

Through experience and informal instruction, the rookie also learns the street use of these weapons. In school, for example, recruits are taught to avoid hitting a person on the head or neck because it could cause lethal damage. On the street, in contrast, police conclude that they must hit wherever it causes the most damage in order to incapacitate the suspect before they themselves are harmed. New officers also learn that they will earn the respect of their veteran coworkers not by observing legal niceties in using force, but by being "aggres-

sive" and using whatever force is necessary in a given situation.

Peer approval helps neutralize the guilt and confusion that rookies often experience when they begin to use force to assert their authority. One female officer, for example, learned she was the object of a brutality suit while listening to the news on television. At first, she felt so mortified that she hesitated to go to work and face her peers. In fact, male colleagues greeted her with a standing ovation and commented, "You can use our urinal now." In their view, any aggressive police officer regularly using normal force might eventually face a brutality suit or civilian complaint. Such accusations confirm the officer's status as a "street cop" rather than an "inside man" who doesn't engage in "real police work."[3]

Whereas male rookies are assumed to be competent dispensers of force unless proven otherwise, women are believed to be physically weak, naturally passive, and emotionally vulnerable.[4] Women officers are assumed to be reluctant to use physical force and are viewed as incompetent "street cops" until they prove otherwise. As a result, women rookies encounter special problems in learning to use normal force in the process of becoming recognized as "real street cops." It becomes crucial for women officers to create or exploit opportunities to display their physical abilities in order to overcome sexual bias and obtain full acceptance from coworkers. As a result, women rookies are encouraged informally to act more aggressively and to display more machismo than male rookies. Consider the following incident where a young female officer reflects upon her use of force during a domestic disturbance:

And when I get there, if goddamn, there isn't a disturbance going on. So Tom comes, the guy that I went to back up. The male talks to him. I take the female and talk to her. And the drunk (cop) comes and the sergeant comes and another guy comes. So while we think we have everything settled, and we have the guy calmed down, he turns around and says to his sister, no less, that's who it is, "Give me the keys to my car!" And with that, she rips them out of her pocket and throws them at him. Now, he goes nuts. He goes into a Kung fu stance and says he's gonna kill her. The drunk cop says, "Yo, knock it off!" and goes to grab him and the guy punches him. So Mike (the drunk cop) goes down. Tommy goes to grab him and is wrestling with him. And all the cops are trying to get in there. So I ran in with my stick and I stick the guy in the head. But I just missed Tommy's face and opened him (the suspect) up. So all of a sudden everybody's grabbin' him and I'm realizing that if we get him down, he won't hurt anybody. So I pushed the sergeant out of the way and I got my stick under the guy's legs and I pulled his legs out from under him and I yelled, "Tommy, take him down." I pulled his legs and he went down and I sat on him. So Tommy says, "Well, cuff him." And I says, "I can't find my goddamned cuffs." I molested my body trying to get my cuffs. . . .

So, when I [finally] get my cuffs, we cuff him. And we're sitting there talking. And Tommy, he has no regard for me whatsoever. . . . The guy's opened up and he bled all over Tommy's shirt. And I turned around and said, "Tommy, look at your shirt. There's blood all over your shirt." He said, "Who the hell almost clobbered me?" I said, "I'm sorry Tom, that was me." He said, "You're the one that opened him up?" And I said, "Yeh. I'm sorry, I didn't mean to get so close to you." . . .

So when the sergeant came out he said, "And you, what do you mean telling me to get outta the way." He said, "Do you know you pushed me outta your way. . . ." And I said, "I didn't want you to get hurt . . . and I was afraid he was gonna kick one of you." And he says, "I still can't believe you pushed me outta your way. You were like a little dynamo." And I found after that I got respect from the sergeant. He doesn't realize it but he treated me differently after that.

Her colleagues' reactions provided informal instruction in the use of normal force, confirming that her actions under these circumstances were reasonable and even praiseworthy.

For a street cop, it is often a graver error to use too little force and develop a "shaky" reputation than it is to use too much force and be told to calm down. Thus officers, particularly rookies, who do not back up their partners in appropriate

ways or who hesitate to use force in circumstances where it is deemed necessary are informally instructed regarding their aberrant ways. If the problematic incident is relatively insignificant and his general reputation is good, a rookie who "freezes" one time is given a second chance before becoming generally known as an untrustworthy partner. However, such incidents become the subject of degrading gossip, gossip that pressures the officer either to use force as expected or risk isolation. Such talk also informs rookies about the general boundaries of legal and normal force.

For example, a female rookie was accused of "freezing" in an incident that came to be referred to as a "Mexican standoff." A pedestrian had complained that "something funny is going on in the drugstore." The officer walked into the pharmacy where she found an armed man committing a robbery. Although he turned his weapon on her when she entered the premises, she still pulled out her gun and pointed it at him. When he ordered her to drop it, claiming that his partner was behind her with a revolver at her head, she refused and told him to drop his.[5] He refused, and the stalemate continued until a sergeant entered the drugstore and ordered the suspect to drop his gun.

Initially, the female officer thought she had acted appropriately and even heroically. She soon discovered, however, that her hesitation to shoot had brought into question her competence with some of her fellow officers. Although many veterans claimed that "she had a lot a balls" to take her gun out at all when the suspect already had a gun on her, most contended "she shoulda shot him." Other policemen confirmed that she committed a "rookie mistake"; she had failed to notice a "lookout" standing outside the store and hence had been unprepared for an armed confrontation. Her sergeant and lieutenant, moreover, even insisted that she had acted in a cowardly manner, despite her reputation as a "gung-ho cop," and cited the incident as evidence of the general inadequacy of policewomen.

In the weeks that followed, this officer became increasingly depressed and angry. She was particularly outraged when she learned that she would not receive a commendation, although such awards were commonly made for "gun pinches" of this nature. Several months later, the officer vehemently expressed the wish that she had killed the suspect and vowed that next time she would "shoot first and ask questions later." The negative sanctions of supervisors and colleagues clearly encouraged her to adopt an attitude favorable to using force with less restraint in future situations.

Reprimand, gossip, and avoidance constitute the primary means by which police try to change or control the behavior of coworkers perceived as unreliable or cowardly. Formal accusations, however, are discouraged regardless of the seriousness of the misconduct. One male rookie, for example, earned a reputation for cowardice after he allegedly had to be "dragged" out of the car during an "assist officer." Even then, he apparently refused to help the officers in trouble. Although no formal charges were filed, everyone in the district was warned to avoid working with this officer.

Indeed, to initiate formal charges against a coworker may discredit the accuser. In one incident a male rookie, although discouraged by veteran officers and even his district captain, filed charges of cowardice against a female rookie. The rookie gained the support of two supervisors and succeeded in having the case heard before the Board of Inquiry. During the trial he claimed the woman officer failed to aid him in arresting a man who presented physical resistance and had a knife on his person. In rebuttal, the woman testified that she perceived no need to participate in a physical confrontation because she saw no knife and the policeman was hitting the suspect. In spite of conflicting testimony, she was found guilty of "Neglect of Duty." Although most veterans thought the woman was "flaky" and doubted her competence, they also felt the male rookie had exaggerated his story. Moreover, they were outraged that he filed formal charges and he quickly found himself ostracized.

At the same time that male and female rookies are commended for using force under appropriate circumstances, they are reprimanded if their participation in force is viewed as excessive or inappropriate. In this way, rookies are instructed that although many acts of coercion are accepted and even demanded, not everything goes. They thereby learn to distinguish between normal and brutal force. In the following incident, for example, a policewoman describes how she instructed a less experienced officer that her behavior was unreasonable and should be checked. Here, the new officer is chastised for misreading interactional cues and overreacting to minor affronts when treating a crazy person involved in a minor dispute as if he were a serious felon.[6]

But like I said, when I first heard about it (another fight) I'd wondered if Mary had provoked it any because we'd gone on a disturbance and it was a drunk black guy who called to complain that the kid who lived upstairs keeps walking through his apartment. The kid to me looks wacky. He's talking crazy. He's saying they shoulda sent men. What are you women going to do. Going on and on. And to me it was a bullshit job. But Mary turns around and says, "We don't have to take that from him. Let's lock him up." I said, "Mary forget it." And the kid has numchuck sticks on him and when he turned his back . . . he had them in his back pocket. So, as he's pulling away saying you're scared, like a little kid, I turned around and said, "I've got your sticks." And I go away. Mary . . . so Mary was . . . I looked at her and she was so disappointed in me . . . like I'd turned chicken on her. So I tried to explain to her, I said, "Mary, all we have is disorderly conduct. That's a summary offense. That's bullshit." I said, "Did you want to get hurt for a summary offense?" I said, "The guy was drunk who called to complain. It wasn't even a legit complaint." I said, "It's just . . . You've got to use discretion. If you think I'm chicken think of the times when a 'man with a gun' comes over the air and I'm the first car there." I said, "When it's worth it, I'll do anything. When it's not worth it, I'll back off." And I think she tries to temper herself some because Collette and her, they finally had a talk about why they hated each other. And Collette said to her, "I think you're too physical. I think you look for fights." And I think maybe Mary

hearing it twice, once from me and once from Col-
lette, might start to think that maybe she does pro-
voke. Instead of going up...I always go up to
them friendly and then if they act shitty I get shitty.

In summary, when rookies leave the academy, they begin to familiarize themselves with
street weapons and to gain some sense of what
kinds of behavior constitute too little or too much
force. They also begin to develop an understanding of street standards for using and judging appropriate and necessary force. By listening to and
observing colleagues at work and by experiencing
a variety of problematic interactions with the public, newcomers become cognizant of the occasions and circumstances in which to use various
degrees and kinds of force....

ACCOUNTING FOR NORMAL FORCE

...Police justify force [of] two analytically distinct kinds...situational and abstract. In the
former, the officer represents force as a response
in some specific situation needed to restore immediate control or to reestablish the local order of
power in the face of a threat to police authority. In
contrast, abstract accounts justify force as a morally appropriate response to certain categories of
crime and criminals who symbolize a threat to the
moral order.... [A]bstract justification does not
highlight processes of interactional provocation
and threats to immediate control, but rather legitimates force as a means of obtaining some higher
moral purpose, particularly the punishment of heinous offenders. Mixed accounts involving situational and abstract justifications of force are also
frequent: force may be depicted as necessary to
regain control when an officer is physically assaulted; but at the same time it may also be justified as punishment appropriate to the kind of
morally unworthy person who would challenge an
officer's authority.

Officers...justify force as normal by reference to interactional situations in which an officer's authority is physically or symbolically

threatened. In such accounts, the use of force is
justified instrumentally—as a means of regaining
immediate control in a situation where that control has become tenuous. Here, the officer depicts
his primary intent for using force as a need to reestablish immediate control in a problematic encounter, and only incidentally as hurting or
punishing the offender.

Few officers will hesitate to assault a suspect
who physically threatens or attacks them. In one
case, an officer was punched in the face by a prisoner he had just apprehended for allegedly attempting to shoot a friend. The incident occurred
in the stationhouse and several policemen observed the exchange. Immediately, one officer hit
the prisoner in the jaw and the rest immediately
joined the brawl.

Violations of an officer's property such as his
car or hat may signify a more symbolic assault on
the officer's authority and self, thus justifying a
forceful response to maintain control. Indeed, in
the police view, almost any person who verbally
challenges a police officer is appropriately subject
to force.[7] In the following extract, a female officer
accounts in these ways for a colleague's use of
force against an escaping prisoner:

> *And so Susan gets on the scene (of the fight). They*
> *cuff one of the girls, and she throws her in the back*
> *seat of the car. She climbs over the back seat,*
> *jumps out of the car with cuffs on and starts run-*
> *ning up the stairs. Susan and Jane are trying to*
> *cuff the other girl and all of a sudden Susan looks*
> *up and sees her cuffs running away. She (Jane)*
> *said Susan turned into an animal. Susan runs up*
> *the steps grabs the girl by the legs. Drags her*
> *down the five steps. Puts her in the car. Kicks her*
> *in the car. Jane goes in the car and calls her every*
> *name she can think of and waves her stick in her*
> *face.[8]*

On rare occasions, women officers encounter
special problems in these regards. Although most
suspects view women in the same way as policemen, some seem less inclined to accord female officers de facto and symbolic control in street
encounters, and on a few occasions seem deter-

mined to provoke direct confrontations with such officers, explicitly denying their formal authority and attempting none too subtly to sexualize the encounter. Women officers, then, might use force as a resource for rectifying such insults and for establishing control over such partially sexualized interactions. Consider the following...

Well, the day before the lieutenant had a roll-call announcement that there had been a pursuit in one of the districts and, as a result, a fireman was killed. And he said, "Why pursue them? In court nothing is gonna happen anyway and being as it was a taxi cab that was involved it would be returned." He said, "What I'm trying to say..." So one of the guys said, "What's a pursuit?" He said, "Exactly."

So Goddamn, if not the next day, about three o'clock in the morning, three thirty, I heard Anne got out with a carstop at Second and Madison. And I heard Joan back her up, and she (Anne) ran the car through (the computer) and I heard, "Hold me out for TVRs (traffic tickets)." So, I'm sitting at Second Street, Second and Nassau, writing curfews up. And this silver Thunderbird (the same car) blows right by a stop sign where I'm sitting. And I look up and think to myself, "Now, do I want to get involved." And I figure, it was really belligerent doing it right in front of me. So I take off after him, put my lights on and he immediately pulls over. So he jumps out of the car. I jump out of the car right away and I say, "I'm stopping you for that stop sign you just blew through." And he says, "Aw come on, I just got stopped. I'm sick of this shit." So I said to him, "Look, I don't care how many times you got stopped." He said, "Well, I'm sick of this shit." And I said, "I'm stopping you right now for this stop sign you went through at Second and Nassau. Let me see your cards please." Then he starts making these lip smacking noises at me everytime he begins to talk. He said, (smack) "The only way you're seeing my cards is if you lock me up and the only way you're gonna lock me up is if you chase me." And I said to him, "Well, look, I will satisfy you on one account. Now go to your car because I will lock you up.... And just sit in your car. I'll be right with you." He smacks his lips, turns around and goes to his car

and he sits. And I call a wagon at Second and Nassau. They ask me what I have. I say, "I've got one to go." So as the wagon acknowledges, the car all of a sudden tears out of its spot. And I get on the air and say, "I'm in pursuit." And I give them a description of the car and the direction I'm going. And I heard a couple of other cars coming in and they're comin' in. And all of a sudden he pulls over about a block and a half after I started the pursuit. So I got on the air and I said, "I got him at Second and Washington." I jumped out of my car and as I jumped out he tears away again. Now I'm ready to die of embarrassment. I have to get back on the air and say no I don't have him. So I got on the air and said, "Look, he's playing games with me now. He took off again." I said, "I'm still heading South on Second street." He gets down to Lexington. He pulls over again. Well, this time I pulled the police car in front of him. I jumped out of the car and as I'm jumping out of the car I hear two female voices screaming, "Lock him up, lock him up!" I go over to the car and I hear him lock the doors. I pull out my gun and I put it right in his window. I say, "Unlock that door." Well, he looked at the gun. He nearly like to shit himself. He unlocked the door. I holster my gun. I go to grab his arms to pull him out and all of a sudden I realize Anne's got him. So we keep pulling him out of the car. Throw him on the trunk of his car and kept pounding him back down on the trunk. She's punching his head. I'm kicking him. Then I take out my blackjack. I jack him across the shoulder. Then I go to jack him in the head and I jack Anne's fingers. We're being so rough. Then the wagon comes and we're kicking the shit out of him. Trying to... dragging him over to the wagon. This poor sucker don't have a chance. The next thing they know is we're throwing him bodily into the wagon. And they said, "Did you search him?" We go to the wagon, drag him out again. Now we're tearing through his pockets throwing everything on the ground. Pick him up bodily again, threw him in.... So I straightened it out with the sergeant and he said, "By the way what were you doing?" I said, "I was in a pursuit." (He said) "A pursuit! Thank God the Lieutenant wasn't there. He said there's no such thing as a pursuit." I said, "I tried to call it another name but I couldn't think of any other name to call it. All I know of it is as a pursuit. I'm following some guy at fast speed who refuses to pull over." So I said, "What did you want me to do? Let any citizen on the street get stopped and pull away and that's the end of it?"

In this instance, a male suspect manages to convey a series of affronts to the officer's authority. These affronts become explicitly and insultingly sexual,[9] turning the challenge from the claim that "no cop will stop me" to the more gender specific one, "no woman cop will stop me." Resistance ups the ante until the suspect backs down in the face of the officer's drawn revolver. The force to which the culprit was then subjected is normalized through all the accounts considered to this point—it is...a means to reestablish and maintain immediate and symbolic control in a highly problematic encounter and it is...[seen] as a natural, collective outburst following resolution of a dangerous, tension-filled incident....

Police also justify the use of extreme force against certain categories of morally reprehensible persons. In this case, force is not presented as an instrumental means to regain control that has been symbolically or physically threatened. Instead, it is justified as an appropriate response to particularly heinous offenders. Categories of such offenders include: cop haters who have gained notoriety as persistent police antagonizers; cop killers or any person who has attempted seriously to harm a police officer (Westley, 1970: 131); sexual deviants who prey on children and "moral women";[10] child abusers; and junkies and other "scum" who inhabit the street. The more morally reprehensible the act is judged, the more likely the police are to depict any violence directed toward its perpetrator as justifiable. Thus a man who exposes himself to children in a playground is less likely to experience police assault than one who rapes or sexually molests a child.

"Clean" criminals, such as high level mafiosi, white collar criminals, and professional burglars, are rarely subject to abstract force. Nor are perpetrators of violent and nonviolent street crimes who prey on adult males, prostitutes, and other categories of persons who belong on the street.[11] Similarly, the "psycho" or demented person is perceived as so mentally deranged that he is not responsible for his acts and hence does not merit abstract, punitive force (Van Maanen, 1978: 233–4).

Police justify abstract force by invoking a higher moral purpose that legitimates the violation of commonly recognized standards.[12] In one case, for example, a nun was raped by a 17-year-old male adolescent. When the police apprehended the suspect, he was severely beaten and his penis put in an electrical outlet to teach him a lesson. The story of the event was told to me by a police officer who, despite the fact that he rarely supported the use of extralegal force, depicted this treatment as legitimate. Indeed, when I asked if he would have participated had he been present, he responded, "I'm Catholic. I would have participated."

EXCESSIVE FORCE AND PEER RESPONSES

...[T]he concept of normal force is useful because it suggests that there are specific circumstances under which police officers will not condone the use of force by themselves or colleagues as reasonable and acceptable. Thus, officer-recognized conceptions of normal force are subject to restrictions of the following kinds:

1. Police recognize and honor some rough equation between the behavior of the suspect and the harmfulness of the force to which it is subject. There are limits, therefore, to the degree of force that is acceptable in particular circumstances. In the following incident, for example, an officer reflects on a situation in which a "symbolic assailant" (Skolnick, 1975:45) was mistakenly subject to more force than he "deserved" and almost killed:

One time Bill Johnson and I, I have more respect for him than any other policeman.... He and I, we weren't particularly brutal. If the guy deserved it, he got it. It's generally the attitude that does it. We had a particularly rude drunk one day. He was re-

ally rude and spit on you and he did all this stuff and we even had to cuff him lying down on the hard stretcher, like you would do an epileptic.... We were really mad at this guy. So, what you normally do with drunks is you take them to the district cell.... So we were really mad. We said let's just give him one or two shots...slamming on the brakes and having him roll. But we didn't use our heads. He's screaming and hollering "You lousy cops" and we slammed on the brakes and we didn't use our heads and we heard the stretcher go nnnnnnBam and then nothing. We heard nothing and we realized we had put this man in with his head to the front so when we slammed on the brakes this stretcher.... I guess it can roll four foot. Well, it was his head that had hit the front of it and we heard no sounds and my God, I've never been so scared. Me and Bill we thought we killed him. So I'm saying "Bill, what are we gonna do? How are we gonna explain this one." The guy's still saying nothing. So, we went to Madison Street and parked. It's a really lonely area. And we unlocked the wagon and peeked in. We know he's in there. We were so scared and we look in and there's not a sound and we see blood coming in front of the wagon and think "Oh my God we killed this man. What am I gonna do? What am I gonna tell my family?" And to make a long story short, he was just knocked out. But boy was I scared. From then on we learned, feet first.

2. Although it is considered normal and natural to become emotional and angry in highly charged, taut encounters, officers nonetheless prefer to minimize the harmful consequences of the use of force. As a result, officers usually acknowledge that emotional reactions that might lead to extreme force should be controlled and limited by coworkers if at all possible. In the following..., for example, an officer justified the use of force as a legitimate means to regain situational control when physically challenged. Nonetheless, he expressed gratitude to his partner for stopping him from doing serious harm when he "snapped out" and lost control:

Well, I wasn't sure if she was a girl until I put my hand on her shoulder and realized it was a

woman's shoulder. I was trying to stop her. But it happened when she suddenly kicked me in the balls. Then everything inside of me exploded and I grabbed her and pushed her against the car and started pressing her backwards and kept pressing her backwards. All of a sudden something clicked inside of me because I noticed her eyes changed and her body caved in and she looked frightened because she knew that I was gonna kill her. And I stopped. I think I stopped because Susan was on the scene. She must have said something. But anyway she (Susan) told me later that I should calm down. And I snapped at her and told her to mind her own business because she didn't know what happened. The girl kicked me in the balls. But she was right about it. I mean it was getting to me. I'd never hit a woman before.

3. Similarly, even in cases where suspects are seen as deserving some violent punishment, this force should not be used randomly and without control. Thus, in the following incident, an officer who "snapped out" and began to beat a child abuser clearly regarded his partners attempt to stop the beating as reasonable.

We get a call "meet complainant" and I drive up and there's a lady standing out in front of the house and she's saying, "Listen officer, I don't know what the story is but the neighbors in there. They're screaming and hollering and there's kicking going on in there and I can't take it. I can't sleep. There's too much noise." Nothing unusual about that. Just a typical day in the district. So the next thing you do is knock on the door and tell them to please keep the noise down or whatever you do. You say to yourself it's probably a boy friend–girl friend fight. So I knock on the door and a lady answers just completely hysterical. And I say, "Listen, I don't know what's going on in here," but then I hear this, just this screeching. You know. And I figure well I'm going to find out what's going on so I just go past the lady and what's happening is that the husband had.... The kid was being potty trained and the way they were potty training this kid, this two-year-old boy, was that the boyfriend of this girl would pick up this kid and he would sit him down on top of the stove. It was their method of potty training. Well, first of *all you think of your own kids. I mean afterwards you do. I mean I've never been this mad in my whole life. You see this little two-year-old boy seated on top of the stove with rings around it being absolutely scalding hot. And he's saying "I'll teach you to go...." It just triggered something. An uncontrollable.... It's just probably the most violent I ever got. Well you just grab that guy. You hit him ten, fifteen times...you don't know how many. You just get so mad. And I remember my partner eventually came in and grabbed me and said, "Don't worry about it. We got him. We got him." And we cuffed him and we took him down. Yeah that was bad.*

It is against this background that patrol officers identify excessive force and the existence of violence-prone peers. Some officers become known for recurrently committing acts of coercion that exceed working notions of normal force.... In contrast to the officer who makes a "rookie mistake" and uses excessive force from inexperience, the brutal cop does not honor the practices of normal force. Such an officer is also not effectively held in check by routine means of peer control. As a result, more drastic measures must be taken to prevent him from endangering the public and his colleagues.

One rookie gained a reputation for brutality from frequent involvement in "unnecessary" fights. One such incident was particularly noteworthy: Answering a call on a demented male with a weapon, he came upon a large man pacing the sidewalk carrying a lead pipe. The officer got out of the patrol car and yelled in a belligerent tone of voice, "What the fuck are you doing creep?" At this point "the creep" attacked the officer and tried to take away his gun. A policewoman arrived on the scene, joined the fight, called an assist, and rescued the patrolman. Although no one was hurt, colleagues felt the incident was provoked by the officer who aggressively approached a known crazy person who should have been assumed to be unpredictable and nonresponsive.

When colleagues first began to doubt this officer's competence, he was informally instructed

to moderate his behavior by veteran and even rookie partners. When his behavior persisted, confrontations with fellow officers became explosive. When peers were unable to check his behavior, complaints were made to superiors. Officially, colleagues indicated they did not want to work with him because of "personality problems." Informally, however, supervisors were informed of the nature of his provocative and dangerous behavior. The sergeant responded by putting the rookie in a wagon with a responsible partner whom he thought might succeed in controlling him. When this strategy proved unsuccessful, he was eventually transferred to the subway unit. Such transfers to "punishment districts," isolated posts, "inside units," or the subway are typical means of handling police officers deemed dangerous and out of control.

As this discussion indicates, the internal control of an exceptionally or inappropriately violent police officer is largely informal. With the exception of civilian complaints and brutality suits, the behavior of such officers rarely becomes the subject of formal police documents. However, their reputations are often well known throughout the department and the rumors about their indiscretions educate rookies about how the line between normal force and brutality is drawn among working police officers.

It takes more than one incident of excessively violent behavior for a police officer to attain a brutal reputation. The violent officer is usually involved in numerous acts of aggressive behavior that are not accountable as normal force either because of their frequency or because of their substance. However, once identified as "brutal," a "head beater," and so on, an officer's use of force will be condemned by peers in circumstances in which competent officers would be given the benefit of the doubt. For example, one officer gained national notoriety during a federal investigation into a suspicious shooting. Allegedly, a local resident had thrown an ax at the patrol wagon. According to available accounts, the police pursued the suspect inside a house and the officer in question shot him in the head. Although witnesses claimed the victim was unarmed, the officer stated that he fired in self defense. The suspect reportedly attacked him with a metal pipe. This policeman had an established reputation for being "good with his hands," and many colleagues assumed he had brutally shot an unarmed man in the aftermath of a pursuit.[13] . . .

NOTES

1. Nonetheless, masculine pronouns are generally used to refer to the police in this article, because the Metro P.D. remained dominated by men numerically, in style and in tone. My fieldwork experience is discussed in detail in a forthcoming paper (Hunt, 1984).

2. Some officers also substitute a large heavy duty flashlight for the nightstick. If used correctly, the flashlight can inflict more damage than the baton and is less likely to break when applied to the head or other parts of the body.

3. For a discussion of the cultural distinction between "inside men" who handle desk and administrative tasks and "real cops" who work outside on the street, see Hunt (1984).

4. As the Metro City Police Commissioner commented in an interview: "In general, they (women) are physically weaker than males. . . . I believe they would be inclined to let their emotions all to [sic] frequently overrule their good judgment . . . there are periods in their life when they are psychologically unbalanced because of physical problems that are occurring within them."

5. The woman officer later explained that she did not obey the suspect's command because she saw no reflection of the partner in the suspect's glasses and therefore assumed he was lying.

6. Patrol officers do not view demented people as responsible for their acts and therefore do not hold them strictly culpable when they challenge an officer's authority (see Van Maanen, 1978: 231). In dealing with such persons, coercion other than that narrowly required for control and self-protection tends to be viewed as inappropriate and unjustifiable.

7. According to Van Maanen (1978: 224), such persons tend to be labeled "assholes." The "asshole," who symbolically challenges an officer's control and thereby defies his definition of a situation, provokes the officer's wrath and becomes a likely candidate for street justice (Van Maanen, 1978: 224).

8. Note that this account employs both the justifications of reestablishing real and symbolic control, and the excuse of emotionally snapping out in response to this symbolic challenge and to the resulting pursuit.

9. Again, such affronts arise with different frequency and have different impact depending upon gender. Although policemen are occasionally subjected to sexual insults by women and teenage girls, this kind of harassment is more commonly experienced by women and thus constitutes a special type of affront to the female officer.

10. For a discussion of the significance of "the moral woman," see Hunt (1984).

11. The categories of persons who merit violence are not unique to the police. Prisoners, criminals, and hospital personnel appear to draw similar distinctions between morally unworthy persons; on the latter, see Sudnow (1967: 105).

12. Abstract force constitutes what Emerson (1969: 149) calls a "principled justification":

> Here one depicts the act as an attempt to realize some absolute moral or social value that has precedence over the value violated by the act.

13. The suspect was known to other officers from prior encounters as a slightly demented cop antagonizer. Consequently, the officer's actions appeared completely unnecessary because he was not dealing with an unpredictable stranger. The suspect's neighbors depicted him as a mentally disturbed person who was deathly afraid of the police because he had been a frequent target of harassment.

REFERENCES

Bittner, E. 1980. *The Functions of the Police in Modern Society.* Cambridge, MA: Oelgeschlager, Gunn & Hain.

Blumberg, M. 1983. "The Use of Firearms by Police Officers: The Impact of Individuals, Communities, and Race." Ph.D. dissertation. School of Criminal Justice, State University of New York at Albany.

Emerson, R. M. 1969. *Judging Delinquents: Context and Process in Juvenile Court.* Chicago: Aldine.

Friedrich, R. 1980. "Police Use of Force: Individuals, Situations, and Organizations." *The Annals,* 452: 82–97.

Fyfe, J. J. 1983. "Police Shootings: Environment, License and Individuals." Presented at the Annual Meeting of the American Society of Criminology.

Hunt, J. Forthcoming. "The Development of Rapport Through the Negotiation of Gender in Field Work Among Police." *Human Organization.*

Lee, J. A. 1981. "Some Structural Aspects of Police Deviance in Relation to Minority Groups." In C. D. Shearing (ed.), *Organizational Police Deviance.* Toronto: Butterworths.

Niederhoffer, A. 1967. *Behind the Shield: The Police in Urban Society.* Garden City, NY: Anchor-Doubleday.

Reiss, A. J. 1970. "Police Brutality—Answers to Key Questions." In A. Niederhoffer and A. S. Blumberg (eds.), *The Ambivalent Force: Perspectives on the Police.* Toronto: Xerox College Publishing.

Scott, M. B. and S. M. Lyman 1968. "Accounts." *American Sociological Review,* 33:46–62.

Skolnick, J. 1975. *Justice Without Trial.* New York: Wiley.

Sudnow, D. 1967. *Passing On: The Social Organization of Dying.* Englewood Cliffs, NJ: Prentice-Hall.

Sykes, G. M. and D. Matza 1957. "Techniques of Neutralization: A Theory of Delinquency." *American Sociological Review,* 22:664–70.

Van Maanen, J. 1978 "The asshole." In P. K. Manning and J. Van Maanen (eds.), *Policing: A View from the Street.* Santa Monica, CA: Goodyear.

Waegel, W. B. 1984. "The Use of Deadly Force by Police: The Effect of Statutory Change." *Crime and Delinquency,* 30:121–140.

Westley, W. A. 1970. *Violence and the Police: A Sociological Study of Law, Custom and Morality.* Cambridge, MA: MIT.

Narcotics Enforcement in a Canadian City

KENNETH STODDART

INTRODUCTION

Attempts to answer fundamental questions relating to the extent and distribution of non-medical drug use have often used some version of an officially-produced case register as a major data source, such as the one provided by Canada's Bureau of Dangerous Drugs. Traditionally the examination and analysis of official statistical records has been regarded as amongst the most valuable ways of uncovering features of the activity's volume and morphology.

From "The Enforcement of Narcotics Violations in a Canadian City: Heroin Users' Perspectives on the Production of Official Statistics," *Canadian Journal of Criminology,* Vol. 23, No. 4 (October 1982), pp. 425–438.

Financial support for the research reported herein was provided by the Social and Epidemiological Research Division of the non-Medical use of Drugs Directorate (Irving Rootman, Chief). The author is solely responsible for the interpretations presented.

During the past fifteen years, however, a considerable amount of social scientific research focussing on arrest situations and decision-making by police—major contributors to official statistics—has called into question the utility of such records in general. Basically, the discovery that police activity introduces systematic distortions rather than random, self-cancelling ones, has suggested that official statistics may be more an artifact of enforcement procedures and routines, etc. than a reliable index of community law-breaking. That this is likely the case for statistical portrayals of non-medical drug use has been claimed for a variety of jurisdictions: analyses of the Canadian situation, however, are conspicuous in their absence.

In the hope of partially filling this gap the present report offers a set of materials descriptive of some of the police activities that contribute to official portrayals of the volume and morphology of heroin use in a large city in the Canadian West. Drawing on data produced via a program of unstructured interviews with heroin users residing in Western City, this report examines the potential significance for official heroin use statistics of two police-related matters: (1) the responsiveness of crucial decision-making to certain features of narcotics violators and (2) the organization of policework.

VIOLATOR FEATURES

As has been documented in numerous investigations, the law is *unevenly enforced* by personnel charged with the task. Rather than as a program to be applied uniformly over all situations enforcement personnel confront the law as a scheme of interpretation that they can invoke or not invoke for a variety of reasons. Indeed, an increasing volume of research, which describes how persons are assembled by police for induction into the criminal justice process, suggests that *however* that assembly occurs, it is inadequately depicted as proceeding via the "matching" of observed conduct with prospectively defined illegal conduct. Study after study has shown that a meeting of legal specifications for arrest is merely *one of* the criteria informing the decision to arrest, not exhaustive of them. Unsurprisingly, police assembly is revealed as responsive in unknown measure to a host of other considerations. As Bittner [1] and others have suggested, policemen ". . . often make decisions based on reasons that the law probably does not recognize as valid." Some of these "reasons" relate to the policeman's perception of the violator. For example—independent of technical possibility—arrests may or may not be made because of the violator's social status in the community [2], appearance and demeanor [3], etc.

This section explores the influence of such "violator features" on two police decisions which are routine to the narcotics enforcement process: the decision to arrest and the decision to pursue a heroin user as a candidate for arrest.

THERE'S NO WAY YOU CAN TALK THEM OUT OF IT: THE RESTRICTED RELEVANCE OF EXTRALEGAL CONSIDERATIONS

In line with other research findings regarding decision-making in the criminal justice system and hopeful of uncovering the potential influence of violator features on official portrayals of community heroin use informants were queried about their own encounters with enforcement personnel. Perhaps not surprisingly, their accounts revealed that—unlike other kinds of violations—narcotics violations were enforced, in their words, "to the letter of the law." Indeed, some informants found *incredulous* the suggestion that police suspended the relevance of legal considerations and did not arrest a violator when it was technically possible. On occasion, variations of the question:

> *Have there ever been any times when they got the dope but didn't pinch you for it?*

were greeted with ridicule. For example:

I: Have there ever been any times when they got the dope but didn't pinch you for it?

R: You mean just let you go or something?

I: Yeah, something like that.

R: Fuck, you gotta be kidding. Once they got it outa you you're pinched and that's it. No two ways about it, you're fuckin' pinched. You gotta be crazy to think they'd let you off just like that, fuck no, that's not the way it happens.

As suggested in the following excerpts from interviews, that such a thing was beyond the realm of possibility, was typically formulated as due to either police contempt of heroin users or the difficulty they experienced in apprehending them.

> *Once they've got ya, it's a good catch for them, they got some brownie points, y'know. They just don't say "well that's a bad habit you've got, sonny" and forget it cause for one thing its a lot of work for them, y'know. We put them through their paces, believe me.*

The bulls hate us junkies. The more of us they pinch the happier they are.

Whatever the underlying reason, however, informants suggest that after police have obtained evidence sufficient to warrant an arrest, legal considerations are afforded priority over all others. According to this portrayal, the police systematically employ the law to decide a course of action. Informants maintained that this was the case, virtually independent of anything that one might do, say, or be. Unlike the situation with other violations, any and all features of the violator—save one, as will be indicated below—seem irrelevant vis-à-vis the decision to make an arrest for a narcotics offence. In the following excerpt from an interview, a woman recently arrested for the first time relates her "surprise" that this is the case. As she discovered, "traditional" ways of altering the probability of arrest were thoroughly ineffective:

The way the narco bulls operate is different from other kinds. They're harder...Like I was pinched for boosting, shoplifting a couple of times and you know I'd just start bawlin' about things. What's gonna happen to my baby if I go to jail, what's gonna happen.... They'd say "okay, we'll give you a break"...Try that with the fuckin' narco bulls and they'll tell you to shut your fuckin' mouth. There's no way you can talk them out of it.

Should a violator be "let off", it was held that it would be because of an offer to perform as an informant:

The only way they're gonna let you off once they've got you is if you offer to go rat for them.

In general, the likelihood of altering one's fate after evidence had been obtained, was received as virtually non-existent; from informants' point-of-view, "...there's no way you can talk them out of it." This alleged overriding priority attributed to legal considerations is a matter of some importance to those interested in the research utility of official rates of heroin use. For example, the observation that the successfully detected cohort appears to pass into official records in its intact version suggests that underreporting due to the operation of other-than-legal considerations is minimal.

SOME PEOPLE HAVE A BETTER CHANCE ON THE STREET: SOCIAL CATEGORIES AND ENFORCEMENT

Though informants asserted that legally irrelevant considerations were virtually uninfluential upon police decision-making after a successful investigation, they claimed that such considerations played an important role in determining who would be selected as a candidate for investigation in the first place. They saw the likelihood of being pursued by police as dependent on somewhat *more* than the "mere fact" that one was known to be in possession of heroin. While being in possession made one liable for pursuit, it did not guarantee it:

I: So every time you score you're taking a chance of getting pinched or at least having them come after you.

R: Oh yeah, the chance is there, but there's more to it than that, y'know.

Indeed, informants were of the opinion that not all heroin users in possession were equally likely to be selected as candidates for pursuit:

I: So does pretty well everybody have the same chance of getting followed after they score, or what?

R: Oh no, no. Some people have got a better chance on the street.

In part these differential probabilities were structured by the responsiveness of enforcement personnel to a variety of legally-irrelevant factors.

One's membership in certain *social categories* was portrayed by community members as prominent amongst those factors. For example, a heroin user identified as a "rat", i.e., a provisioner of information to the police is obviously unlikely to be selected for pursuit. As one informant puts it:

Well if somebody's rattin' to the bulls they're not gonna pinch him, are they?

It was suggested that women, too, enjoyed "...a better chance on the street".

I: Do the police give the women as bad a time, as rough a time as they give the men?

R: Well they're pretty rough all around, y'know. I don't think they go after the chicks as much as the guys, though. Not that they leave us alone or anything, but they don't come after us as much.

Informants were not united regarding *why* women were selected as candidates for investigation less frequently than men. Some suggested that the police perceived female heroin users as less threatening to society than their male counterparts:

Well, the bulls leave the working girls pretty much alone, usually. I guess they figure "what the fuck, they're workin' for their money, providin' a service and so on." We're not stealin' or nothin, y'know.

I guess they figure its the guys that are the ones to get 'cause of what they do, steal and the like.

Others accounted for the difference by referring to the practical problems women pose for investigative work carried out primarily by males:

A lot of girls carry dope internally, y'know, so it's a lot of trouble for the bulls. They gotta take you down to (the public safety building) and wait for a qualified doctor to come and give you an internal search. That could take hours.

What is paramount among the theories advanced to explain the lesser likelihood of pursuit enjoyed by women, however, was the notion that enforcement personnel perceived female heroin users as having "female" and not "heroin user" status. Despite their use of heroin they were understood to be *women* first and foremost. This itself was portrayed as creating a practical problem for police. Indeed, a notable feature of their regard for female heroin users in this way, it was asserted, was a reduction in the amount of physical vigour applied to obtain arrest-producing evidence. Informants attributed to police sensibilities

that did not permit them to be egalitarian in their treatment of the sexes. As one informant put it:

They're not...they don't beat the shit outa chicks the way they do with the guys. Sure, they're rough alright, but the guys've got it worse.

Informants claimed, however, that the difference enjoyed by women in general, was enjoyed to a greater extent by particular types of women. Other types, it was told, were treated "...just like the guys."

Well some broads they treat just like the guys. I've seen lots with broken teeth from handcuffs going down their throats, scars.... They beat the shit outa them to get the dope, just like they'd do to a guy.

It was suggested that the woman who had "... a better chance on the street" were those with an appearance and demeanour approximating those of "ordinary", i.e. non-heroin using, women. For informants, a woman's "better chance" eroded precisely to the extent that her presentation *strayed* from the one just suggested, as:

the bulls don't mind beatin' on an old douche-bag with rotten teeth and dirty hair. Some chicks let themselves get so scraggy, its no wonder they take shit.

One informant formulated the effect of a conventional presentation as functionally equivalent to an adaptive strategy:

I: So what do you spend all that money on. Besides junk.

R: Well there's clothes and groceries. Getting my hair done and stuff. Makeup. You gotta keep yourself up, y'know.

I: Keep yourself up?

R: Yeah, its not good if you let yourself go like some chicks do.

I: Its no good to....

R: Let yourself go, get...be a slob about yourself. I don't like gettin' that way, I never have. Its a personal thing. But if you look like shit you're gonna get treated that way too, y'know.

I: By who?

R: By everybody.

I: By the cops?

R: Oh yeah. If you look like a decent person they're not gonna bother you as much as if you walk around lookin' like a fuckin' dirty junkie asshole. Broads who do that are just askin' for it.

I: Okay, so what you're saying then is that if you look like a... if you look pretty good then you're not gonna get the hassle you would if you didn't. Is that right or am I missing something?

R: No, that's about it. If a chick looks good the bulls are definitely not gonna... they're probably not gonna give her the usual shit.

These observations appear massively relevant to research and policy decisions based on officially-located heroin users. Consider, for example, the issue of *who*—in the sense of social type—*gets assembled into official statistics*. Indeed, notation of the pre-investigation significance of such presentational considerations as demeanour, appearance, etc., underscore the fact that an *official* heroin user—as opposed to a person who "merely" uses heroin—is the product of a social judgement made by the police. To paraphrase Piliavin and Briar [3], he or she is a heroin user because someone in authority has defined him/her as one, often on the basis of the public face presented to officials rather than the kind of offence committed. Quite obviously, if similar "public faces" are being assembled, heroin users start to look alike, a fact of no little clinical relevance.

IF THEY WANT YA, THEY'RE GONNA GET YA: THE PARTICULARIZATION OF ENFORCEMENT

For informants, however, category membership did not exhaust the list of extra-legal factors potentially influential upon the choice of *who* from a range of possibles might be pursued as a candidate for investigation. Indeed, they asserted the relevance of a number of other considerations. For example, they claimed that "for personal rea-

sons", enforcement personnel singled out some heroin users for vigorous pursuit. When members of the community realized that this was the case in their situation, i.e. that they had been selected for special investigation attention, they characterized the police as "having a burn" for them:

R: ... well if they've got a burn for you for some reason...

I: How do you mean have a burn?

R: Well if they really want you bad, y'know. Really want to see you pinched.

They suggested that this state-of-affairs would eventually result in their arrest, as "if they want ya, they're gonna get ya..."

> Once they've got a burn for ya, y'might as well start sayin' goodbye to everybody 'cause you'll be in jail before ya know it. If they want ya, they're gonna get ya, no two ways about it.

Informants indicated that one could become attractive as an enforcement target for a variety of reasons. In general, their own and their colleagues' experience suggested that anything one might do to further alienate the police, i.e., "...to make them hate you even more than they do," stood to heighten the probability of investigative pursuit and, eventually, arrest.

> If you fuck them around, treat them...if you don't play it right they're gonna be after you. If you do anything that...anything to make them hate you even more than they do, then watch out 'cause that's it for you.

It was held that further alienation of enforcement personnel could be accomplished by irritating them in any number of ways. One could, for example, make their work more difficult by interfering with it:

R: Well I did what you might call a stupid thing, what I think's a stupid thing anyway.

I: What? What kind of stupid thing did you do?

R: Well I got the narco bulls mad at me, but I couldn't help it. I couldn't just...I couldn't hold myself back.

I: Well what was the stupid thing?

R: Well one of my buddies—she's in here now as a matter of fact. She was gettin' roughed up a little and I was pissed off. I started screamin' at 'em, callin' them dumb fuckers and so forth. Kickin'. They told me to fuck off and mind my own business but I just got more frantic, y'know. After I thought about it I thought "Fuck, these guys are gonna be after me now for makin' them so fuckin' mad and all." So then I got pinched.

I: This last time?

R: Yeah, just before Christmas. Anyway when I got pinched one of them said "that'll teach you to keep your fuckin' nose outa other people's business." So there ya go. If I'd ... if I'd just turned away I'd probably still be on the street, y'know.

Also, one could refuse to cooperate:

I: Have the police ever approached you, ever asked you to rat for them? Like be an informant or something?

R: Not in any kind of a formal way or nothing! Like offering me money. One time they asked me, on the street just out of the blue ... asked me to tell them who's doin' things. I said just forget it and they said "things have been known to happen to guys like you. You'd better watch out from now on."

I: What was that supposed to mean?

R: Well they were tellin' me in so many words that they'd be watching me a little bit closer for the next while.

I: Did they?

R: Fuckin' right they did. I got jumped three times the next week.

Informants claimed that one could irritate the police—and thus potentially cause them to "have a burn for you" by, persistently frustrating their attempts at successful, arrest-producing investigation. The following excerpt from an interview provides an example:

R: I know they were after me 'cause they told me they were.

I: Oh yeah, they told you?

R: Oh yeah, it was just a matter of time. I haven't taken a pinch for years, y'know and its not 'cause they haven't tried. I just been smarter than them and they were pissed off. ... So every time I scored I figured "well its gonna be this time, this time they're gonna get me" so I was pretty careful, y'know. And they tried but I kept outsmartin' the fuckers. "We're gonna get ya," they said, "we're gonna get ya." I was ... hurtin' their pride I guess, always outsmartin' em like that.

Irritating the police by verbally abusing them or by suggesting the superiority of a deviant lifestyle were portrayed as making them "... hate you even more than they do" and thereby increasing the likelihood of being selected as a candidate for pursuit. For example:

> These young kids you see on the street, they think they're smart callin' the bulls names, dirty pig and all that. All they're doin' by that is makin' it worse for themselves cause they'll be harder on 'em and bug 'em.

R: You can be on the street for a long time with no trouble then all of a sudden something happens and bingo, you're pinched.

I: Like what can happen, for example.

R: Well you do somethin' stupid. Like I started makin' fun of a bull, one bull in particular. I told him one day that I was savin' up for a downpayment on a house and he said "oh yeah, how long'll that take ya?" I said "Oh, about a month or so." And he said "fuck, it'll take you five years." So every time I saw him I said "well are ya still savin'?" Fuck he got pissed off.

I: He couldn't take a joke. ...

R: I guess not 'cause he was sure after me for a while. I couldn't go on the street without gettin' some hassle. I was a real heatbag.

Informants indicated that the likelihood of being singled out for special investigative attention was increased by one's ignoring recent court orders:

The judge told me that I had 48 hours to get out of the Province of British Columbia and the bulls knew it, things get around. So when I scored they just naturally came right after me. Figured I'd really get the book thrown at me, what with gettin' it for possession when I shoulda been out of town.

THE ORGANIZATION OF POLICEWORK

In addition to violator features there are, of course, numerous other considerations which influence narcotics enforcement and—ultimately—official portrayals of community drug use. This section discusses the potential impact of changes in size of the enforcement unit and quality and style of enforcement on official rates.

THEY'RE BETTER AND THERE'S MORE OF THEM: ASSERTED CHANGES IN THE SIZE AND QUALITY OF THE ENFORCEMENT UNIT

Notations of change in the rate of a given deviant behaviour presume—among other things—that the number and quality of personnel assigned to deal with the behaviour have remained static. Black [4] explains how crime rates and size of enforcement units influence each other:

Crime rates that are produced in proactive police operations, such as arrests for...narcotics violation, directly correlate with police manpower allocation. Until a point of total detection is reached and holding all else constant, these vice rates increase as the number of policemen assigned to vice control is increased.

The influence of enhanced *quality* of enforcement is more difficult to establish. It is the case, however, that since the early 1970's recruits to all municipal police departments in the province have been receiving narcotics investigation training through the Western Province Police College. The putative "spread" of heroin use from metropolis to hinterland thus becomes potentially more related to the diffusion of knowledge than narcotics. Some informants added documentation to this

notion via their complaints about the declining number of places thought to be "safe" for engaging in drug-relevant activities. Consider the following excerpts from an interview with a drug trafficker who used to conduct business in such places... "before it got too hot."

I: So what happened after that?

R: Well after that I started to stay out of town pretty much. I'd take a half-a-dozen bundles or so and go up through the Interior and places like that. There was always people lookin' for dope up here and there wasn't the heat.

I: This was when.

R: Oh, shit, 10–12 years ago or so.

I: So you'd stay out of town.

R: Yeah. I'd head up to the Interior. That was before it got too hot. The bulls are all wise now, not like before.

I: They used to be...

R: They didn't know what dope was, not at all. Then you could even go out to the Russell Hotel in (a municipality adjacent to Western City). Cops didn't know what was goin' on.

I: Now they do?

R: Oh yeah, they're wise all over now. Nowhere's safe anymore, like it used to be.

Undercover operations, too, were portrayed as increasingly more sophisticated. One informant insisted that "...the bulls are getting smarter" and documented this assertion with observations of the changed appearance and manner of personnel attempting to infiltrate the heroin community:

R: Oh yeah, the bulls are gettin' smarter, there's no doubt about it.... Look at the guys they send down now, the undercover bulls. They used to be big healthy lookin' assholes with size 12 shoes, hangin' around bein' a bit too pushy. Now they get these guys who look so much like dope fiends y'could never tell. Y'wonder how they ever got to be cops...They're cooler, too. Take their time gettin' in.

THEY DON'T DO THINGS THE WAY THEY DID BEFORE: ASSERTED CHANGES IN THE STYLE OF NARCOTICS ENFORCEMENT

As potentially influential upon drug use statistics as the number and quality of enforcement personnel, is the *style* of enforcement. Informants were virtually unanimous in asserting that enforcement procedures and priorities had undergone dramatic stylistic revisions, that they appeared different from the way they did at an early period in the history of the local community. One informant expressed recognition of such changes in the following way:

> The bulls don't do things the way they did before. Older people like me—not necessarily old but who've been around, y'know.... I can remember when the bulls did things very differently from the way your average one is now.

She continues, specifying the character of the stylistic changes:

> Well for one thing you knew where you stood, they played by the rules. And they weren't as chickenshit about things.

Informants frequently spoke of current enforcement practices as "chickenshit" or "petty." For them, this implied an emphasis on the letter of the law, on offences of small magnitude, on "...things that you wouldn't get busted for before." For example, informants suggested that unlike an earlier period in the history of the local community, police would *now* attempt to arrest a person for being in possession of any heroin-using paraphernalia that might bear a minute trace of the substance—in their words, "...anything that might analyze...."

R: The bulls are chickenshit now. They're out to pinch you for anything that might analyze—a spoon, a fit, an empty cup. That's what I got it on, a fuckin' cap for fuck sake, a fuckin' cap with hardly anythin' in it.

I: Just a cap?

R: Yeah, fuck, there was...I'd used better than three-quarters of it, more than that and they got it outa my purse.

Also, consider the following excerpt from an interview, wherein an informant describes the activity that resulted in her imprisonment for trafficking in narcotics:

I: So what was the offence that landed you in here this time?

R: Trafficking, they say I put out to an undercover bull.

I: But you didn't?

R: No. Its a bum rap. I just passed it to him. I wasn't puttin' out at the time. I was just with somebody when it happened.

I: Tell me what happened.

R: Well I was just in my car with this person I know and he was going to—He was putting out some stuff. This Rick guy—you've heard about him—he was gonna score from my friend. He was talkin' to him. My friend's next to me in the passenger seat. So he takes the joint out and Rick goes around to the driver's side where I am—right out in the road—and my friend passes the joint to me and I give it to Rick. He just did that so he could get two busts at once.

Though informants characterized their adversaries as going to great lengths to enforce narcotics laws, i.e.,

> the bulls'll do anything to make a pinch,

they reasonably expected enforcement to be constrained by proprieties they sometimes called the "rules of the game":

R: Its just a game, cops and junkies.

I: Games have got rules.

R: So's this one, believe me. If you don't go by the rules of the game you're fucked. Even the bulls go by rules.

In short, informants had a sense of activities that the police *would* and *would not* engage in

"...to make a pinch." This notion was informed in part by an understanding of them as not only policemen but as well citizens, members-of-society, persons possessing sensibilities uncongenial to doing literally *anything* to enforce narcotics laws. Recently however, informants claim that the latitude of personally-congenial behaviours has widened considerably. Some related this widening to the presence in enforcement units of more *committed* personnel. In the words of an informant:

> They've got bulls now who don't give a shit about nothin' except makin' pinches. Nothin'...

For informants, the following excerpt from an interview would exemplify this new, *liberated* enforcement style. In the late 1970's the events it relates were being spread—rumour like—throughout the heroin-using community.

I: What about this guy Fred, the narc who was just under.
R: Oh that asshole.
I: Did you ever run into him?
R: Oh, for sure. Everybody knew him. He was always around. Fuckin' earring on, just one, y'know. Big nigger hairdo. Fuckin' weird he looked. Leather jacket. Everybody knew the prick. People figured he was solid. He even had me fooled, which is why I'm fuckin' here.
I: So everybody knew him.
R: Oh yeah. He was really into it. Only went home once in the eight fuckin' months he was on the street. That's dedication. I knew girls.... Well he was with a couple of girls. They were supportin' him, turnin' tricks for fuck sake. He was their old man. They were keepin' him fixed.
I: Keeping him fixed?
R: Fuck yes. He was wired up. He had to spend a whole week in the hospital afterwards. He was fuckin' wired up.

Another stylistic change cited by some informants was a refusal on the part of enforcement personnel to make "deals" with violators particularly on occasions where a detected offence in-volved more than one party. Solomon [5] provides an observation of the sort of deal in question:

> *(Name) boots in the bathroom door, knocking the girl inside into the bathtub. (Name) fishes into the sink for the needle in the midst of the scramble. They find the needle and take them both into the station. The guy had just shot up and was just about to fix his chick. He says he'll cop the rap if they let her go. The police agree to this deal.*

An informant related an instance of the contemporary suspension of this practice:

I: So where's your husband now?
R: Oh he's over there (in the men's unit of the provincial prison), we got pinched together.
I: Two for the price of one.
R: Oh yeah, shit. He woulda taken the rap 'cause I was pregnant at the time, but the bulls wouldn't let him. He tried, though.

From informants' point-of-view, narcotics enforcement patterns in Western City have undergone dramatic revisions in terms of quality and style. Time and time again in interviews and casual conversation heroin users characterized current police strategies as "better" and stylistically "different" than they were at an earlier period.

That a number of changes appear to have occurred in enforcement activities is a matter of more than passing interest to those concerned with the quality of official statistical portrayals of the volume, and volume trends of narcotics use. Indeed, the changes tend to erode one's faith in a reasonable correspondence between the portrayals and their referents. For example, the enforcement revisions appear to be *patterned,* suggesting not only the presence of systematic—rather than random and self-cancelling—error influences in the statistics, but the possibility as well that recent assertions of increases in the number of heroin users may be more an artifact of the revisions than a reflection of what is happening in the community. Taken together the changes in style and quality of enforcement provide for the appearance of an enlarged population independent of any *actual* enlargement.

The influence of enhanced quality of enforcement upon official portrayals of narcotic use is virtually self-announcing. Quite obviously, better enforcement increases the probability of arrest and thereby "builds in" an apparent increase in the number of drug users. Furthermore—as suggested earlier—it provides for the "spread" of drug-related activity to previously untainted communities.

Stylistic changes, too, suggest a potentially artificial swelling of community size. For example, the alleged refusal on the part of police to charge only one person in a multiple violator situation stands to inflate the number of arrests in unknown but potentially significant ways. Similarly, informants' characterization of enforcement personnel as newly "chickenshit" suggests not only that previously unnoticed offences are now being recorded but as well that the official records include arrests for violations that are technically but not socially valid.

CONCLUDING REMARKS

A continuing debate in the sociology of deviant behaviour concerns the degree to which official statistics accurately depict the actual volume and morphology of community deviance. At issue is not *whether* official portrayals depart from perfect correspondence with their referents: indeed, that they are somehow biased, somehow incomplete is widely acknowledged. Instead, debate centers on another question, specifically: can official statistics be taken as standing in some determinable relationship to the actual volume and morphology of a given activity or are the departures such that official statistics are essentially useless?

Commonly, sociologists have endeavoured to make the relationship determinable by attempting to identify the *source* of acknowledged bias, incompleteness, etc. Potentially more important than knowing the sources of such errors, however, is knowing their *character*. Indeed, the utility of official rates of deviant behaviour for research and policy design persists only when it can be demonstrated that factors which might erode the correspondence between such rates and their referents display a *random* character, thereby cancelling each other out.

This report has examined some of the enforcement activities that produce official portrayals of the volume and morphology of heroin use in and around a large city in the Canadian West.

Using data obtained via a program of unstructured interviews with heroin users resident in Western City, this report has described some of the ways in which police activity potentially influences official portrayals of the volume and morphology of non-medical drug use. In general, the data suggest a *pattern* and an unevenness of enforcement over time.

That the enforcement component of the narcotics environment cannot be presumed to be *static* is hardly a revelation. It remains the case, however, that many who use official statistics for research, policy, and political purposes attribute an unchanging nature to police procedures.

Recognition that a situation of uneven enforcement exists has numerous implications for users of official statistics. Some of these have been indicated here, though many more await explication. In general, however, the data presented suggest the rationality of a decreased reliance on official statistics as indicators of the extent and distribution of community heroin use.

REFERENCES

1. Bittner, Egon. 1967. "The Police on Skid-Row: A Study of Peace Keeping." *American Sociological Review, 32.*

2. Cicourel, Aaron V. 1968. *The Social Organization of Juvenile Justice.* New York: Wiley.

3. Piliavin, Irving and Scott Briar. "Police Encounters with Juveniles." *American Journal of Sociology, 70.*

4. Black, Donald J. 1970. "Production of Crime Rates," *American Sociological Review, 35.*

5. Solomon, Robert. 1970. Fieldnotes prepared for the Commission of Inquiry into the Non-Medical Use of Drugs. Unpublished manuscript.

CHAPTER 7

THE DEVIANT IN COURT

The court is one of the important stations through which many deviants pass during their deviant careers. Like the police, court personnel have working conceptions to help them process deviants.

Reporting on the public defender, David Sudnow shows how cases are handled according to stereotypes of different kinds of crimes and criminals. In the second section Lisa Frohman describes the logic of prosecutors' decisions to take sexual assault cases to court. In the final section Jack Spencer shows how probation officers make sentence recommendations on the basis of defendants' answers to questions during presentence interviews.

Normal Crimes

DAVID SUDNOW

Two stances toward the utility of official classificatory schema for criminological research have been debated for years. One position, which might be termed that of the "revisionist" school, has it that the categories of the criminal law, e.g., "burglary," "petty theft," "homicide," etc., are not "homogeneous in respect to causation."[1] From an inspection of penal code descriptions of crimes, it is argued that the way persons seem to be assembled under the auspices of criminal law procedure is such as to produce classes of criminals who are, at least on theoretical grounds, as dissimilar in their social backgrounds and styles of activity as they are similar. The entries in the penal code, this school argues, require revision if sociological use is to be made of categories of crime and a classificatory scheme of etiological relevance is to be developed. Common attempts at such revision have included notions such as "*white collar* crime," and "*systematic* check forger," these conceptions constituting attempts to institute sociologically meaningful specifications which the operations of criminal law procedure and statutory legislation "fail" to achieve.

The other major perspective toward the sociologist's use of official categories and the criminal statistics compiled under their heading derives less from a concern with etiologically useful schema than from an interest in understanding the actual operations of the administrative legal system. Here, the categories of the criminal law are not regarded as useful or not, as objects to be either adopted, adapted, or ignored; rather, they are seen as constituting the basic conceptual equipment with which such people as judges, lawyers, policemen, and probation workers organize their everyday activities. The study of the actual use of official classification systems by actually employed administrative personnel regards the penal code as data, to be preserved intact; its use, both in organizing the work of legal representation, accusation, adjudication, and prognostication, and in compiling tallies of legal occurrences, is to be examined as one would examine any social activity. By sociologically regarding, rather than criticizing, rates of statistics and the categories employed to assemble them, one learns, it is promised, about the "rate producing agencies" and the assembling process.[2]

While the former perspective, the "revisionist" position, has yielded several fruitful products, the latter stance (commonly identified with what is rather loosely known as the "labelling" perspective), has been on the whole more promissory than productive, more programmatic than empirical. The present report will examine the operations of a Public Defender system in an effort to assess the warrant for the continued theoretical and empirical development of the position argued by Kitsuse and Cicourel. It will address the question: what of import for the sociological analysis of legal administration can be learned by describing the actual way the penal code is employed in the daily activities of legal representation? First, I shall consider the "guilty plea" as a way of handling criminal cases, focusing on some features of the penal code as a description of a population of defendants. Then I shall describe the Public Defender operation with special attention to the way defendants are represented. The place of the guilty plea and penal code in this representation will be

Reprinted from "Normal Crimes: Sociological Features of the Penal Code in a Public Defender Office," *Social Problems*, Vol. 12, No. 3 (Winter 1965), pp. 255–264, 269–270, by permission of the Society for the Study of Social Problems and the author.

This investigation is based on field observations of a Public Defender Office in a metropolitan California community. The research was conducted while the author was associated with the Center for the Study of Law and Society, University of California, Berkeley.

examined. Lastly, I shall briefly analyze the fashion in which the Public Defender prepares and conducts a "defense." The latter section will attempt to indicate the connection between certain prominent organizational features of the Public Defender system and the penal code's place in the routine operation of that system.

GUILTY PLEAS, INCLUSION, AND NORMAL CRIMES

It is a commonly noted fact about the criminal court system generally, that the greatest proportion of cases are "settled" by a guilty plea.[3] In the county from which the following material is drawn, over 80 per cent of all cases "never go to trial." To describe the method of obtaining a guilty plea disposition, essential for the discussion to follow, I must distinguish between what shall be termed "necessarily-included-lesser-offenses" and "situationally-included-lesser-offenses." Of two offenses designated in the penal code, the lesser is considered to be that for which the length of required incarceration is the shorter period of time. *Inclusion* refers to the relation between two or more offenses. The "necessarily-included-lesser-offense" is a strictly legal notion:

> *Whether a lesser offense is included in the crime charged is a question of law to be determined solely from the definition and corpus delicti of the offense charged and of the lesser offense.... If all the elements of the corpus delicti of a lesser crime can be found in a list of all the elements of the offense charged, then only is the lesser included in the greater.*[4]

Stated alternatively:

> *The test in this state of necessarily included offenses is simply that where an offense cannot be committed without necessarily committing another offense, the latter is a necessarily included offense.*[5]

The implied negative is put: could Smith have committed A and not B? If the answer is yes, then B is not necessarily included in A. If the answer is no, B is necessarily included. While in a given case a battery might be committed in the course of a robbery, battery is not necessarily included in robbery. Petty theft is necessarily included in robbery but not in burglary. Burglary primarily involves the "intent" to acquire another's goods illegally (e.g., by breaking and entering); the consummation of the act need not occur for burglary to be committed. Theft, like robbery, requires that some item be stolen.

I shall call *lesser* offenses that are not necessarily but "only" *actually* included, "situationally-included-lesser-offenses." By statutory definition, necessarily included offenses are "actually" included. By actual here, I refer to the "way it occurs as a course of action." In the instance of necessary inclusion, the "way it occurs" is irrelevant. With situational inclusion, the "way it occurs" is definitive. In the former case, no particular course of action is referred to. In the latter, the scene and progress of the criminal activity would be analyzed.

The issue of necessary inclusion has special relevance for two procedural matters:

1. A man cannot be charged and/or convicted of two or more crimes any one of which is necessarily included in the others, unless the several crimes occur on separate occasions.

If a murder occurs, the defendant cannot be charged and/or convicted of both "homicide" and "intent to commit a murder," the latter of which is necessarily included in first degree murder. If, however, a defendant "intends to commit a homicide" against one person and commits a "homicide" against another, both offenses may be properly charged. While it is an extremely complex question as to the scope and definition of "in the course of," in most instances the rule is easily applied.

2. The judge cannot instruct the jury to consider as alternative crimes of which to find a defendant guilty, crimes that are not necessarily included in the charged crime or crimes.

If a man is charged with "statutory rape" the judge may instruct the jury to consider as a possible alternative conviction "contributing to the delinquency of a minor," as this offense is necessarily included in "statutory rape." He cannot however suggest that the alternative "intent to commit murder" be considered and the jury cannot find the defendant guilty of this latter crime, unless it is charged as a distinct offense in the complaint.

It is crucial to note that these restrictions apply only to (a) the relation between several charged offenses in a formal allegation, and (b) the alternatives allowable in a jury instruction. At any time before a case "goes to trial," alterations in the charging complaint may be made by the district attorney. The issue of necessary inclusion has no required bearing on (a) what offense(s) will be charged initially by the prosecutor, (b) what the relation is between the charge initially made and "what happened," or (c) what modifications may be made after the initial charge and the relation between initially charged offenses and those charged in modified complaints. It is this latter operation, the modification of the complaint, that is central to the guilty plea disposition.

Complaint alterations are made when a defendant agrees to plead guilty to an offense and thereby avoid a trial. The alteration occurs in the context of a "deal" consisting of an offer from the district attorney to alter the original charge in such a fashion that a lighter sentence will be incurred with a guilty plea than would be the case if the defendant were sentenced on the original charge. In return for this manipulation, the defendant agrees to plead guilty. The arrangement is proposed in this following format: "if you plead guilty to this new lesser offense, you will get less time in prison than if you plead not guilty to the original, greater charge and lose the trial." The decision must then be made whether or not the chances of obtaining complete acquittal at trial are great enough to warrant the risk of a loss and higher sentence if found guilty on the original

charge. As we shall see below, it is a major job of the Public Defender, who mediates between the district attorney and the defendant, to convince his "client" that the chances of acquittal are too slight to warrant this risk.

If a man is charged with "drunkenness" and the Public Defender and Public Prosecutor (hereafter P.D. and D.A.) prefer not to have a trial, they seek to have the defendant agree to plead guilty. While it is occasionally possible, particularly with first offenders, for the P.D. to convince the defendant to plead guilty to the originally charged offense, most often it is felt that some "exchange" or "consideration" should be offered, i.e., a lesser offense charged.

To what offense can "drunkenness" be reduced? There is no statutorily designated crime that is necessarily included in the crime of "drunkenness." That is, if any of the statutorily required components of drunk behavior (its corpus delicti) are absent, there remains no offense of which the resultant description is a definition. For drunkenness there is, however, an offense that while not necessarily included is "typically-situationally-included," i.e., "typically" occurs as a feature of the way drunk persons are seen to behave—"disturbing the peace." The range of possible sentences is such that of the two offenses, "disturbing the peace" cannot call for as long a prison sentence as "drunkenness." If, in the course of going on a binge a person does so in such a fashion that "disturbing the peace" may be employed to describe some of his behavior, it would be considered as an alternative offense to offer in return for a guilty plea. A central question for the following analysis will be: in what fashion would he have to behave so that disturbing the peace would be considered a suitable reduction?

If a man is charged with "molesting a minor," there are not any necessarily included lesser offenses with which to charge him. Yet an alternative charge—"loitering around a schoolyard"—is often used as a reduction. As above, and central to our analysis the question is: what would the defendant's behavior be such that "loitering around a schoolyard" would constitute an appropriate alternative?

If a person is charged with "burglary," "petty theft" is not necessarily included. Routinely, however, "petty theft" is employed for reducing the charge of burglary. Again, we shall ask: what is the relation between burglary and petty theft and the *manner in which the former occurs* that warrants this reduction?

Offenses are regularly reduced to other offenses the latter of which are not necessarily or situationally included in the former. As I have already said the determination of whether or not offense X was situationally included in Y involves an analysis of the course of action that constitutes the criminal behavior. I must now turn to examine this mode of behavioral analysis.

When encountering a defendant who is charged with "assault with a deadly weapon," the P.D. asks: "what can this offense be reduced to so as to arrange for a guilty plea?" As the reduction is only to be proposed by the P.D. and accepted or not by the D.A., his question becomes "what reduction will be allowable?" (As shall be seen below, the P.D. and D.A. have institutionalized a common orientation to allowable reductions.) The method of reduction involves, as a general feature, the fact that the particular case in question is scrutinized to decide its membership in a class of similar cases. But *the penal code does not provide the reference for deciding the correspondence between the instant event and the general case; that is, it does not define the classes of offense types.* To decide, for purposes of finding a suitable reduction, if the instant case involves a "burglary," reference is not made to the statutory definition of "burglary." To decide what the situationally included offenses are in the instant case, the instant case is not analyzed as a *statutorily* referable course of action; rather, reference is made to a *non-statutorily* conceived class "burglary" and offenses that are typically situationally included in it, taken as a class of behavioral events. Stated again: in searching an instant case to decide what to *reduce it to,* there is no analysis of the statutori-

ly referable elements of the instant case; instead, its membership in a class of events, the features of which cannot be described by the penal code, must be decided. An example will be useful. If a defendant is charged with burglary and the P.D. is concerned to propose a reduction to a lesser offense, he might search the elements of the burglary at hand to decide what other offenses were committed. The other offenses he might "discover" would be of two sorts: those necessarily and those situationally included. In attempting to decide those other offenses situationally included in the instant event, the instant event might be analyzed as a statutorily referable course of action. Or, as is the case with the P.D., the instant case might be analyzed to decide if it is a "burglary" in common with other "burglaries" conceived of in terms other than those provided by the statute.

Burglaries are routinely reduced to petty theft. If we were to analyze the way burglaries typically occur, petty theft is neither situationally nor necessarily included; when a burglary is committed, money or other goods are seldom illegally removed from some person's body. If we therefore analyzed burglaries, employing the penal code as our reference, and then searched the P.D.'s records to see how burglaries are reduced in the guilty plea, we could not establish a rule that would describe the transformation between the burglary cases statutorily described and the reductions routinely made (i.e., to "petty theft"). The rule must be sought elsewhere, in the character of the non-statutorily defined class of "burglaries," which I shall term *normal burglaries.*

NORMAL CRIMES

In the course of routinely encountering persons charged with "petty theft," "burglary," "assault with a deadly weapon," "rape," "possession of marijuana," etc., the P.D. gains knowledge of the typical manner in which offenses of given classes are committed, the social characteristics of the persons who regularly commit them, the features of the settings in which they occur, the types of victims often involved, and the like. He learns to speak knowledgeably of "burglars," "petty thieves," "drunks," "rapists," "narcos," etc., and to attribute to them personal biographies, modes of usual criminal activity, criminal histories, psychological characteristics, and social backgrounds. The following characterizations are illustrative:

> Most ADWs [assault with deadly weapon] start with fights over some girl.

> These sex fiends [child molestation cases] usually hang around parks or schoolyards. But we often get fathers charged with these crimes. Usually the old man is out of work and stays at home when the wife goes to work and he plays around with his little daughter or something. A lot of these cases start when there is some marital trouble and the woman gets mad.

> I don't know why most of them don't rob the big stores. They usually break into some cheap department store and steal some crummy item like a $9.95 record player you know.

> Kids who start taking this stuff [narcotics] usually start out when some buddy gives them a cigarette and they smoke it for kicks. For some reason they always get caught in their cars, for speeding or something.

They can anticipate that point when persons are likely to get into trouble:

> Dope addicts do O.K. until they lose a job or something and get back on the streets and, you know, meet the old boys. Someone tells them where to get some and there they are.

> In the springtime, that's when we get all these sex crimes. You know, these kids play out in the schoolyard all day and these old men sit around and watch them jumping up and down. They get their ideas.

The P.D. learns that some kinds of offenders are likely to repeat the same offense while others are not repeat violators or, if they do commit crimes frequently, the crimes vary from occasion to occasion:

> You almost never see a check man get caught for anything but checks—only an occasional drunk charge.

> Burglars are usually multiple offenders, most times just burglaries or petty thefts. Petty thefts get started for almost anything—joy riding, drinking, all kinds of little things.

> These narcos are usually through after the second violation or so. After the first time some stop, but when they start on the heavy stuff, they've had it.

I shall call *normal crimes* those occurrences whose typical features, e.g., the ways they usually occur and the characteristics of persons who commit them (as well as the typical victims and typical scenes), are known and attended to by the P.D. For any of a series of offense types the P.D. can provide some form of proverbial characterization. For example, *burglary* is seen as involving regular violators, no weapons, low-priced items, little property damage, lower class establishments, largely Negro defendants, independent operators, and a non-professional orientation to the crime. *Child molesting* is seen as typically entailing middle-aged strangers or lower class middle-aged fathers (few women), no actual physical penetration or severe tissue damage, mild fondling, petting, and stimulation, bad marriage circumstances, multiple offenders with the same offense repeatedly committed, a child complainant, via the mother, etc. *Narcotics* defendants are usually Negroes, not syndicated, persons who start by using small stuff, hostile with police officers, caught by some form of entrapment technique, etc. *Petty thefts* are about 50–50 Negro-white, unplanned offenses, generally committed on lower class persons and don't get much money, don't often employ weapons, don't make living from thievery, usually younger defendants with long juvenile assaultive records, etc. *Drunkenness* offenders are lower class white and Negro, get drunk on wine and beer, have long histories of repeated drunkenness, don't hold down jobs, are usually arrested on the streets, seldom violate other penal code sections, etc.

Some general features of the normal crime as a way of attending to a category of persons and events may be mentioned:

1. The focus, in these characterizations, is not on particular individuals, but offense types. If asked "What are burglars like?" or "How are burglaries usually committed?", the P.D. does not feel obliged to refer to particular burglars and burglaries as the material for his answer.

2. The features attributed to offenders and offenses are often not of import for the statutory conception. In burglary, it is "irrelevant" for the statutory determination whether or not much damage was done to the premises (except where, for example, explosives were employed and a new statute could be invoked). Whether a defendant breaks a window or not, destroys property within the house or not, etc., does not affect his statutory classification as a burglar. While for robbery the presence or absence of a weapon sets the degree, whether the weapon is a machine gun or pocket knife is "immaterial." Whether the residence or business establishment in a burglary is located in a higher income area of the city is of no issue for the code requirements. And, generally, the defendant's race, class position, criminal history (in most offenses), personal attributes, and in particular style of committing offenses are features specifically not definitive of crimes under the auspices of the penal code. For deciding "Is this a 'burglary' case I have before me," however, the P.D.'s reference to this range of non-statutorily referable personal and social attributes, modes of operation, etc., is crucial for the arrangement of a guilty plea bargain.

3. The features attributed to offenders and offenses are, in their content, specific to the community in which the P.D. works. In other communities and historical periods the lists would presumably differ. Narcotics violators in certain areas, for example, are syndicated in dope rackets or engage in systematic robbery as professional criminals, features which are not commonly encountered (or, at least, evidence for which is not systematically sought) in this community. Bur-

glary in some cities will more often occur at large industrial plants, banking establishments, warehouses, etc. The P.D. refers to the population of defendants in the county as "our defendants" and qualifies his prototypical portrayals and knowledge of the typically operative social structures, "for our county." An older P.D., remembering the "old days," commented:

> *We used to have a lot more rapes than we do now, and they used to be much more violent. Things are duller now in. . . .*

4. Offenses whose normal features are readily attended to are those which are routinely encountered in the courtroom. This feature is related to the last point. For embezzlement, bank robbery, gambling, prostitution, murder, arson, and some other uncommon offenses, the P.D. cannot readily supply anecdotal and proverbial characterizations. While there is some change in the frequencies of offense-type convictions over time, certain offenses are continually more common and others remain stably infrequent. . . . Troubles (are) created for the P.D. when offenses whose features are not readily known occur, and whose typicality is not easily constructed. . . .

5. Offenses are ecologically specified and attended to as normal or not according to the locales within which they are committed. The P.D. learns that burglaries usually occur in such and such areas of the city, petty thefts around this or that park, ADWs in these bars. Ecological patterns are seen as related to socio-economic variables and these in turn to typical modes of criminal and non-criminal activities. Knowing where an offense took place is thus, for the P.D., knowledge of the likely persons involved, the kind of scene in which the offense occurred, and the pattern of activity characteristic of such a place:

> *Almost all of our ADWs are in the same half a dozen bars. These places are Negro bars where laborers come after hanging around the union halls trying to get some work. Nobody has any money and they drink too much. Tempers are high and almost anything can start happening.*

6. One further important feature can be noted at this point. . . . The P.D. office consists of a staff of twelve full time attorneys. Knowledge of the properties of offense types of offenders, i.e., their normal, typical, or familiar attributes, constitutes the mark of any given attorney's competence. A major task in socializing the new P.D. deputy attorney consists in teaching him to recognize these attributes and to come to do so naturally. The achievement of competence as a P.D. is signalled by the gradual acquisition of professional command not simply of local penal code peculiarities and courtroom folklore, but, as importantly, of relevant features of the social structure and criminological wisdom. His grasp of that knowledge over the course of time is a key indication of his expertise. Below, in our brief account of some relevant organizational properties of the P.D. system, we shall have occasion to reemphasize the competence-attesting aspects of the attorney's proper use of established sociological knowledge. Let us return to the mechanics of the guilty plea procedure as an example of the operation of the notion of normal crimes.

Over the course of their interaction and repeated "bargaining" discussions, the P.D. and D.A. have developed a set of unstated recipes for reducing original charges to lesser offenses. These recipes are specifically appropriate for use in instances of normal crimes and in such instances alone. "Typical" burglaries are reduced to petty theft, "typical" ADWs to simple assault, "typical" child molestation to loitering around a schoolyard, etc. The character of these recipes deserves attention.

The specific content of any reduction, i.e., what particular offense class X offenses will be reduced to, is such that the reduced offense may bear no obvious relation (neither situationally nor necessarily included) to the originally charged offense. The reduction of burglary to petty theft is an example. The important relation between the reduced offense and the original charge is such that the reduction from one to the other is considered "reasonable." At this point we shall only state what seems to be the general principle involved in deciding this reasonableness. The underlying premises cannot be explored at the present time, as that would involve a political analysis beyond the scope of the present report. *Both P.D. and D.A. are concerned to obtain a guilty plea wherever possible and thereby avoid a trial. At the same time, each party is concerned that the defendant "receive his due." The reduction of offense X to Y must be of such a character that the new sentence will depart from the anticipated sentence for the original charge to such a degree that the defendant is likely to plead guilty to the new charge and, at the same time, not so great that the defendant does not "get his due."*

In a homicide, while battery is a necessarily included offense, it will not be considered as a possible reduction. For a conviction of second degree murder a defendant could receive a life sentence in the penitentiary. For a battery conviction he would spend no more than six months in the county jail. In a homicide, however, "felony manslaughter," or "assault with a deadly weapon," whatever their relation to homicide as regards inclusion, would more closely approximate the sentence outcome that could be expected on a trial conviction of second degree murder. These alternatives would be considered. For burglary, a typically situationally included offense might be "disturbing the peace," "breaking and entering" or "destroying public property." "Petty theft," however, constitutes a reasonable lesser alternative to burglary as the sentence for petty theft will often range between six months and one year in the county jail and burglary regularly does not carry higher than two years in the state prison. "Disturbing the peace" would be a thirty-day sentence offense.

While the present purposes make the exposition of this calculus unnecessary, it can be noted and stressed that the particular content of the reduction does not necessarily correspond to a relation between the original and altered charge that could be described in either the terms of necessary or situational inclusion. Whatever the relation between the original and reduced charge, its essential feature resides in the spread between sentence likelihoods and the reasonableness of that spread, i.e., the balance it strikes between the defendant "getting his due" and at the same time "getting something less than he might so that he will plead guilty."

The procedure we want to clarify now, at the risk of some repetition, is the manner in which an instant case is examined to decide its membership in a class of "crimes such as this" (the category *normal crimes*). Let us start with an obvious case, burglary. As the typical reduction for burglary is petty theft and as petty theft is neither situationally nor necessarily included in burglary, the examination of the instant case is clearly not undertaken to decide whether petty theft is an appropriate statutory description. The concern is to establish the relation between the instant burglary and the normal category "burglaries" and, having decided a "sufficient correspondence," to now employ petty theft as the proposed reduction.

In scrutinizing the present burglary case, the P.D. seeks to establish that "this is a burglary just like any other." If that correspondence is not established, regardless of whether or not petty theft in fact was a feature of the way the crime was enacted, the reduction to petty theft would not be proposed. *The propriety of proposing petty theft as a reduction does not derive from its in-fact-existence in the present case, but is warranted or not by the relation of the present burglary to "burglaries," normally conceived.*

In a case of "child molestation" (officially called "lewd conduct with a minor"), the concern is to decide if this is a "typical child molestation case." While "loitering around a schoolyard" is frequently a feature of the way such crimes are instigated, establishing that the present defendant *did in fact loiter around a schoolyard* is secondary to the more general question "Is this a typical child molestation case?" What appears as a contradiction must be clarified by examining the status of "loitering around a schoolyard" as a typical

feature of such child molestations. The typical character of "child molesting cases" does not stand or fall on the fact that "loitering around a schoolyard" is a feature of the way they are in fact committed. It is *not* that "loitering around a schoolyard" as a *statutorily referable behavior sequence* is part of typical "child molesting cases" but that "loitering around a schoolyard" as a *socially distinct mode of committing child molestations typifies the way such offenses are enacted.* "Strictly speaking," i.e., under the auspices of the statutory *corpus delicti,* "loitering around a schoolyard," requires *loitering, around, a schoolyard;* if one loiters around a ball park or a public recreation area, he "cannot," within a proper reading of the statute, be charged with loitering around a *schoolyard.* Yet "loitering around a schoolyard," as a feature of the typical way such offenses as child molestations are committed, has the status not of a description of the way in *fact (fact,* statutorily decided) it occurred or typically occurs, but "the kind-of-social-activity-typically-associated-with-such-offenses." It is not its statutorily conceived features but its socially relevant attributes that gives "loitering around a schoolyard" its status as a feature of the class "normal child molestations." Whether the defendant loitered around a schoolyard or a ball park, and whether he loitered or "was passing by," "loitering around a schoolyard" as a reduction will be made if the defendant's activity was such that "he was hanging around some public place or another" and "was the kind of guy who hangs around schoolyards." As a component of the class of normal child molestation cases (of the variety where the victim is a stranger), "loitering around a schoolyard" typifies a mode of committing such offenses, the class of "such persons who do such things as hang around schoolyards and the like." A large variety of actual offenses could thus be nonetheless reduced to "loitering" if, as kinds of social activity, "loitering," conceived of as typifying a way of life, pattern of daily activity, social psychological circumstances, etc., characterized the conduct of the defendant. The young P.D. who would object

"You can't reduce it to 'loitering'—he didn't really 'loiter,'" would be reprimanded: "Fella, you don't know how to use that term; he might as well have 'loitered'—it's the same kind of case as the others...."

...The P.D. awaits to see if, how far, and in what ways the instant case is deviant. If the defendant is charged with burglary and a middle class establishment was burglarized, windows shattered, a large payroll sought after and a gun used, then the reduction to petty theft, generally employed for "normal burglaries," would be more difficult to arrange.

Generally, the P.D. doesn't have to discover the atypical kinds of cases through questioning. Rather, the D.A., in writing the original complaint, provides the P.D. with clues that the typical recipe, given the way the event occurred, will not be allowable. Where the way it occurs is such that it does not resemble normal burglaries and the routinely used penalty would reduce it *too far* commensurate with the way the crime occurred, the D.A. frequently charges various situationally included offenses, indicating to the P.D. that the procedure to employ here is to suggest "dropping" some of the charges, leaving the originally charged greatest offense as it stands.

In the general case he doesn't charge all those offenses that he legally might. He might charge "child molesting" and "loitering around a schoolyard" but typically only the greater charge is made. The D.A. does so, so as to provide for a later reduction that will appear particularly lenient in that it seemingly involves a *change* in the charge. Were he to charge both molesting and loitering, he would be obliged, moreover, should the case come to trial, to introduce evidence for both offenses. The D.A. is thus always constrained not to set overly high charges or not situationally included multiple offenses by the possibility that the defendant will not plead guilty to a lesser offense and the case will go to trial. Of primary importance is that he doesn't charge multiple offenses so that the P.D. will be in the best position vis-à-

vis the defendant. He thus charges the first complaint so as to provide for a "setup."

The alteration of charges must be made in open court. The P.D. requests to have a new plea entered:

P.D.: Your honor, in the interests of justice, my client would like to change his plea of not guilty to the charge of burglary and enter a plea of guilty to the charge of petty theft.

JUDGE: Is this new plea acceptable to the prosecution?

D.A.: Yes, your honor.

The prosecutor knows beforehand that the request will be made, and has agreed in advance to allow it.

I asked a P.D. how they felt about making such requests in open court, i.e., asking for a reduction from one offense to another when the latter is obviously not necessarily included and often (as is the case in burglary-to-petty theft) not situationally included. He summarized the office's feeling:

> ...in the old days, ten or so years ago, we didn't like to do it in front of the judge. What we used to do when we made a deal was that the D.A. would dismiss the original charge and write up a new complaint altogether. That took a lot of time. We had to re-arraign him all over again back in the muni court and everything. Besides, in the same courtroom, everyone used to know what was going on anyway. Now, we just ask for a change of plea to the lesser charge regardless of whether it's included or not. Nobody thinks twice about asking for petty theft on burglary or drunkenness on car theft, or something like that. It's just the way it's done.

Some restrictions are felt. Assaultive crimes (e.g., ADW, simple assault, attempted murder, etc.) will not be reduced to or from "money offenses" (burglary, robbery, theft) unless the latter involve weapons or some violence. Also, victimless crimes (narcotics, drunkenness) are not reduced to or from assaultive or "money offenses," unless there is some factual relation, e.g., drunkenness with a fight might turn out to be simple assault reduced to drunkenness.

For most cases that come before their courts, the P.D. and D.A. are able to employ reductions that are formulated for handling typical cases. While some burglaries, rapes, narcotics violations and petty thefts are instigated in strange ways and involve atypical facts, some manipulation in the way the initial charge is made can be used to set up a procedure to replace the simple charge-alteration form of reducing. . . .

NOTES

1. D. R. Cressey, "Criminological Research and the Definition of Crimes," *American Journal of Sociology,* Vol. 61 (No. 6), 1951, p. 548. See also J. Hall, *Theft, Law and Society,* second edition, Indianapolis: Bobbs-Merrill, 1952; and E. Sutherland, *Principles of Criminology,* New York: Lippincott, 1947, p. 218. An extensive review of "typological developments" is available in D. C. Gibbons and D. L. Garrity, "Some Suggestions for the Development of Etiological and Treatment Theory in Criminology," *Social Forces,* Vol. 38 (No. 1), 1959.

2. The most thorough statement of this position, borrowing from the writings of Harold Garfinkel, can be found in the recent critical article by J. I. Kitsuse and A. V. Cicourel, "A Note on the Official Use of Statistics," *Social Problems,* Vol. 11, No. 2 (Fall, 1963), pp. 131–139.

3. See D. J. Newman, "Pleading Guilty for Considerations," *The Journal of Criminal Law, Criminology and Police Science,* Vol. 46, No. 6 (March–April, 1956), pp. 780–790. Also, M. Schwartz, *Cases and Materials on Professional Responsibility and the Administration of Criminal Justice,* San Francisco: Matthew Bender and Co., 1961, esp. pp. 79–105.

4. C. W. Fricke, *California Criminal Law,* Los Angeles: The Legal Book Store, 1961, p. 41.

5. People v. Greer, 30 Cal. 2d, 589.

Sexual Assault

LISA FROHMANN

Case screening is the gateway to the criminal court system. Prosecutors, acting as gatekeepers, decide which instances of alleged victimization will be passed on for adjudication by the courts. A recent study by the Department of Justice (Boland et al. 1990) suggests that a significant percentage of felony cases never get beyond this point, with only cases characterized as "solid" or "convictable" being filed (Stanko 1981, 1982; Mather 1979). This

Reprinted from "Discrediting Victims' Allegations of Sexual Assault: Prosecutorial Accounts of Case Rejections," *Social Problems,* Vol. 38, No. 2 (May, 1991), by permission of the Society for the Study of Social Problems and the author.

An earlier version of this paper was presented at the American Sociological Association, August 1990. The author would like to thank Jack Katz, Janet A. Gilboy, Elizabeth A. Stanko, Nancy A. Matthews, James A. Holstein, Timothy Diamond, Kate Gilbert, and the anonymous reviewers of *Social Problems* for their comments on earlier drafts. She is indebted to Robert M. Emerson for his reading of numerous drafts, ever insightful comments, and continuing guidance and support.

paper will examine how prosecutors account for the decision to reject sexual assault cases for prosecution and looks at the centrality of discrediting victims' rape allegations in this justification.

A number of studies on sexual assault have found that victim credibility is important in police decisions to investigate and make arrests in sexual assault cases (LaFree 1981; Rose and Randall 1982; Kerstetter 1990; Kerstetter and Van Winkle 1990). Similarly, victim credibility has been shown to influence prosecutors' decisions at a number of stages in the handling of sexual assault cases (LaFree 1980, 1989; Chandler and Torney 1981; Kerstetter 1990).

Much of this prior research has assumed, to varying degrees, that victim credibility is a phenomenon that exists independently of prosecutors' interpretations and assessments of such credibility. Particularly when operationalized in terms of quantitative variables, victim credibility is treated statistically as a series of fixed, objective features of cases. Such approaches neglect the processes whereby prosecutors actively assess and negotiate victim credibility in actual, ongoing case processing.

An alternative view examines victim credibility as a phenomenon constructed and maintained through interaction (Stanko 1980). Several qualitative studies have begun to identify and analyze these processes. For example, Holmstrom and Burgess's (1983) analysis of a victim's experience with the institutional handling of sexual assault cases discusses the importance of victim credibility through the prosecutor's evaluation of a complainant as a "good witness." A "good witness" is someone who, through her appearance and demeanor, can convince a jury to accept her account of "what happened." Her testimony is "consistent," her behavior "sincere," and she cooperates in case preparation. Stanko's (1981, 1982) study of felony case filing decisions similarly emphasizes prosecutors' reliance on the notion of the "stand-up" witness—someone who can appear to the judge and jury as articulate and credible. Her work emphasizes the centrality of victim credibility in complaint-filing decisions.

In this article I extend these approaches by systematically analyzing the kinds of accounts prosecutors offer in sexual assault cases to support their complaint-filing decisions. Examining the justifications for decisions provides an understanding of how these decisions appear rational, necessary, and appropriate to decision-makers as they do the work of case screening. It allows us to uncover the inner, indigenous logic of prosecutors' decisions and the organizational structures in which those decisions are embedded (Garfinkel 1984).

I focus on prosecutorial accounting for case rejection for three reasons. First, since a significant percentage of cases are not filed, an important component of the case-screening process involves case rejection. Second, the organization of case filing requires prosecutors to justify case rejection, not case acceptance, to superiors and fellow deputies. By examining deputy district attorneys' (DDAs') reasons for case rejection, we can gain access to what they consider "solid" cases, providing further insight into the case-filing process. Third, in case screening, prosecutors orient to the rule—when in doubt, reject. Their behavior is organized more to avoiding the error of filing cases that are not likely to result in conviction than to avoiding the error of rejecting cases that will probably end in conviction (Scheff 1966). Thus, I suggest that prosecutors are actively looking for "holes" or problems that will make the victim's version of "what happened" unbelievable or not convincing beyond a reasonable doubt, hence unconvictable (see Miller [1970], Neubauer [1974], and Stanko [1980, 1981] for the importance of conviction in prosecutors' decisions to file cases). This bias is grounded within the organizational context of complaint filing.

DATA AND METHODS

The research was part of an ethnographic field study of the prosecution of sexual assault crimes by deputy district attorneys in the sexual assault units of two branch offices of the district attorney's offices in a metropolitan area on the West Coast.[1] Research was conducted on a full-time basis in 1989 for nine months in Bay City and on a full-time basis in 1990 for eight months in Center Heights. Three prosecutors were assigned to the unit in Bay City, and four prosecutors to the unit in Center Heights. The data came from 17 months of observation of more than three hundred case screenings. These screenings involved the presentation and assessment of a police report by a sexual assault detective to a prosecutor, conversations between detectives and deputies regarding the "filability"/reject status of a police report, interviews of victims by deputies about the alleged sexual assault, and discussions between deputies regarding the file/reject status of a report. Since tape recordings were prohibited, I took extensive field notes and tried to record as accurately as possible conversation between the parties. In addition, I also conducted open-ended interviews with prosecutors in the sexual assault units and with investigating officers who handled these cases. The accounts presented in the data below include both those offered in the course of negotiating a decision to reject or file a case (usually to the investigating officer [IO] but sometimes with other prosecutors or to me as an insider), and the more or less fixed accounts offered for a decision already made (usually to me). Although I will indicate the context in which the account occurs, I will not emphasize the differences between accounts in the analysis.

The data were analyzed using the constant comparison method of grounded theory (Glaser and Strauss 1967). I collected all accounts of case rejection from both offices. Through constant comparison of the data, I developed coding schema which provide the analytic framework of the paper.

The two branches of the district attorney's office I studied cover two communities differing in socioeconomic and racial composition. Bay City is primarily a white middle-to-upper-class community, and Center Heights is primarily a black and Latino lower-class community. Center Heights has heavy gang-drug activity, and most of the cases brought to the district attorney were assumed to involve gang members (both the complainant and the assailant) or a sex-drug or sex-money transaction. Because of the activities that occur in this community, the prior relationships between the parties are often the result of gang affiliation. This tendency, in connection with the sex-drug and sex-money transactions, gives a twist to the "consent defense" in "acquaintance" rapes. In Bay City, in contrast, the gang activity is much more limited and the majority of acquaintance situations that came to the prosecutors' attention could be categorized as "date rape."

THE ORGANIZATIONAL CONTEXT OF COMPLAINT FILING

Several features of the court setting that I studied provided the context for prosecutors' decisions.

These features are prosecutorial concern with maintaining a high conviction rate to promote an image of the "community's legal protector," and prosecutorial and court procedures for processing sexual assault cases.

The promotion policy of the county district attorney's (DA) office encourages prosecutors to accept only "strong" or "winnable" cases for prosecution by using conviction rates as a measure of prosecutorial performance. In the DA's office, guilty verdicts carry more weight than a conviction by case settlement. The stronger the case, the greater likelihood of a guilty verdict, the better the "stats" for promotion considerations. The inducement to take risks—to take cases to court that might not result in conviction—is tempered in three ways: First, a pattern of not-guilty verdicts is used by the DA's office as an indicator of prosecutorial incompetency. Second, prosecutors are given credit for the number of cases they reject as a recognition of their commitment to the organizational concern of reducing the case load of an already overcrowded court system. Third, to continually pursue cases that should have been rejected outright may lead judges to question the prosecutor's competence as a member of the court.

Sexual assault cases are among those crimes that have been deemed by the state legislature to be priority prosecution cases. That is, in instances where both "sex" and "nonsex" cases are trailing (waiting for a court date to open), sexual assault cases are given priority for court time. Judges become annoyed when they feel that court time is being "wasted" with cases that "should" have been negotiated or rejected in the first place, especially when those cases have been given priority over other cases. Procedurally, the prosecutor's office handles sexual assault crimes differently from other felony crimes. Other felonies are handled by a referral system; they are handed from one DDA to another at each stage in the prosecution of the case. But sexual assault cases are vertically prosecuted; the deputy who files the case remains with it until its disposition, and therefore is closely connected with the case outcome.

ACCOUNTING FOR REJECTION BECAUSE OF "DISCREPANCIES"

Within the organizational context, a central feature of prosecutorial accounts of case rejection is the discrediting of victims' allegations of sexual assault. Below I examine two techniques used by prosecutors to discredit victim's complaints: discrepant accounts and ulterior motives.

USING OFFICIAL REPORTS AND RECORDS TO DETECT DISCREPANCIES

In the course of reporting a rape, victims recount their story to several criminal justice officials. Prosecutors treat consistent accounts of the incident over time as an indicator of a victim's credibility. In the first example two prosecutors are discussing a case brought in for filing the previous day.

> *DDA TAMARA JACOBS: In the police report she said all three men were kissing the victim. Later in the interview she said that was wrong. It seems strange because there are things wrong on major events like oral copulation and intercourse . . . , for example whether she had John's penis in her mouth. Another thing wrong is whether he forced her into the bedroom immediately after they got to his room or, as the police report said, they all sat on the couch and watched TV. This is something a cop isn't going to get wrong, how the report started. (Bay City)*

The prosecutor questions the credibility of the victim's allegation by finding "inconsistencies" between the complainant's account given to the police and the account given to the prosecutor. The prosecutor formulates differences in these accounts as "discrepancies" by noting that they involve "major events"—events so significant no one would confuse them, forget them, or get them wrong. This is in contrast to some differences that may involve acceptable, "normal inconsistencies" in victims' accounts of sexual assault. By "normal inconsistencies," I mean those that are expected and explainable because the victim is confused, upset, or shaken after the assault.

The DDA also discredited the victim's account by referring to a typification of police work. She assumes that the inconsistencies in the accounts could not be attributed to the incorrect writing of the report by the police officer on the grounds that they "wouldn't get wrong how the report started." Similarly, in the following example, a typification of police work is invoked to discredit the victim's account. Below the DDA and IO are discussing the case immediately after the victim interview.

> *DDA SABRINA JOHNSON: [T]he police report doesn't say anything about her face being swollen, only her hand. If they took pictures of her hand, wouldn't the police have taken a picture of her face if it was swollen? (Bay City)*

The prosecutor calls the credibility of the victim's complaint into question by pointing to a discrepancy between her subsequent account of injuries received during the incident and the notation of injuries on the police reports taken at the time incident was reported. Suspicion of the complainant's account is also expressed in the prosecutor's inference that if the police went to the trouble of photographing the victim's injured hand they would have taken pictures of her face had it also shown signs of injury.

In the next case the prosecutor cites two types of inconsistencies between accounts. The first set of inconsistencies is the victim's accounts to the prosecutor and to the police. The second set is between the account the victim gave to the prosecutor and the statements the defendants gave to the police. This excerpt was obtained during an interview.

> *DDA TRACY TIMMERTON: The reason I did not believe her [the victim] was, I get the police report first and I'll read that, so I have read the police report which recounts her version of the facts but it also has the statement of both defendants. Both defendants were arrested at separate times and give[n] separate independent statements that were virtually the same. Her story when I had her recount it to me in the DA's office, the number of acts*

changed, the chronological order of how they happened has changed. (Bay City)

When the prosecutor compared the suspects' accounts with the victim's account, she interpreted the suspects' accounts as credible because both of their accounts, given separately to police, were similar. This rests on the assumption that if suspects give similar accounts when arrested together, they are presumed to have colluded on the story, but if they give similar accounts independent of the knowledge of the other's arrest, there is presumed to be a degree of truth to the story. This stands in contrast to the discrepant accounts the complainant gave to law enforcement officials and the prosecutor.

USING OFFICIAL TYPIFICATIONS OF RAPE-RELEVANT BEHAVIOR

In the routine handling of sexual assault cases prosecutors develop a repertoire of knowledge about the features of these crimes.[2] This knowledge includes how particular kinds of rape are committed, post-incident interaction between the parties in an acquaintance situation, and victims' emotional and psychological reactions to rape and their effects on victims' behavior. The typifications of rape-relevant behavior are another resource for discrediting a victim's account of "what happened."

Typifications of Rape Scenarios

Prosecutors distinguish between different types of sexual assault. They characterize these types by the sex acts that occur, the situation in which the incident occurred, and the relationship between the parties. In the following excerpt the prosecutor discredits the victim's version of events by focusing on incongruities between the victim's description of the sex acts and the prosecutor's knowledge of the typical features of kidnap-rape. During an interview a DDA described the following:

DDA TRACY TIMMERTON: [T]he only act she complained of was intercourse, and my experience has been that when a rapist has a victim cornered for a long period of time, they engage in multiple acts and different types of sexual acts and very rarely do just intercourse. (Bay City)

The victim's account is questioned by noting that she did not complain about or describe other sex acts considered "typical" of kidnap-rape situations. She only complained of intercourse. In the next example the DDA and IO are talking about a case involving the molestation of a teenage girl.

DDA WILLIAM NELSON: Something bothers me, all three acts are the same. She's on her stomach and has her clothes on and he has a "hard and long penis." All three times he is grinding his penis into her butt. It seems to me he should be trying to do more than that by the third time. (Center Heights)

Here the prosecutor is challenging the credibility of the victim's account by comparing her version of "what happened" with his typification of the way these crimes usually occur. His experience suggests there should be an escalation of sex acts over time, not repetition of the same act.

Often the typification invoked by the prosecutor is highly situational and local. In discussion a drug-sex-related rape in Center Heights, for example, the prosecutor draws on his knowledge of street activity in that community and the types of rapes that occur there to question whether the victim's version of events is what "really" happened. The prosecutor is describing a case he received the day before to an investigating officer there on another matter.

DDA KENT FERNOME: I really feel guilty about this case I got yesterday. The girl is 20 going on 65. She is real skinny and gangly. Looks like a cluck-head [crack addict]—they cut off her hair. She went to her uncle's house, left her clothes there, drinks some beers and said she was going to visit a friend in Center Heights who she said she met at a drug rehab program. She is not sure where this friend Cathy lives. Why she went to Center Heights after midnight, God knows? It isn't clear what she was doing between 12 and 4 a.m. Some gang bangers came by and offered her a ride. They picked her up on the corner of Main and Lincoln. I think she was turning a trick, or looking for a rock, but she wouldn't budge from her story.... There are lots of conflicts between what she told the police and what she told me. The sequence of events, the sex acts performed, who ejaculates. She doesn't say who is who.... She's beat up, bruises on face and a laceration on her neck. The cop and doctor say there is no trauma—she's done by six guys. That concerns me. There is no semen that they see. It looks like this to me—maybe she is a strawberry, she's hooking or looking for a rock, but somewhere along the line it is not consensual.... She is [a] real street-worn woman. She's not leveling with me—visiting a woman with an unknown address on a bus in Center Heights—I don't buy it.... (Center Heights)

The prosecutor questioned the complainant's reason for being in Center Heights because, based on his knowledge of the area, he found it unlikely that a woman would come to this community at midnight to visit a friend at an unknown address. The deputy proposed an alternative account of the victim's action based on his knowledge of activities in the community—specifically, prostitution and drug dealing—and questioned elements of the victim's account, particularly her insufficiently accounted for activity between 12 and 4 a.m., coming to Center Heights late at night to visit a friend at an unknown address, and "hanging out" on the corner.

The DDA uses "person-descriptions" (Maynard 1984) to construct part of the account, describing the complainant's appearance as a "cluckhead" and "street-worn." These descriptions suggested she was a drug user, did not have a "stable" residence or employment, and was probably in Center Heights in search of drugs. This description is filled in by her previous "participation in a drug rehab program," the description of her activity as "hanging out" and being "picked up" by gang bangers, and a medical report which states that no trauma or semen was found when she was "done by six guys." Each of these features of the account suggests that the complainant is a prostitute or

"strawberry" who came to Center Heights to trade sex or money for drugs. This alternative scenario combined with "conflicts between what she told the police and what she told me" justify case rejection because it is unlikely that the prosecutor could get a conviction.

The prosecutor acknowledges the distinction between the violation of women's sexual/physical integrity—"somewhere along the line it wasn't consensual"—and prosecutable actions. The organizational concern with "downstream consequences" (Emerson and Paley, forthcoming) mitigate against the case being filed.

Typifications of Post-incident Interaction

In an acquaintance rape, the interaction between the parties after the incident is a critical element in assessing the validity of a rape complaint. As implied below by the prosecutors, the typical interaction pattern between victim and suspect after a rape incident is not to see one another. In the following cases the prosecutor challenges the validity of the victims' allegations by suggesting that the complainants' behavior runs counter to a typical rape victim's behavior. In the first instance the parties involved in the incident had a previous relationship and were planning to live together. The DDA is talking to me about the case prior to her decision to reject.

DDA SABRINA JOHNSON: I am going to reject the case. She is making it very difficult to try the case. She told me she let him into her apartment last night because she is easily influenced. The week before this happened [the alleged rape] she agreed to have sex with him. Also, first she says "he raped me" and then she lets him into her apartment. (Bay City)

Here the prosecutor raises doubt about the veracity of the victim's rape allegation by contrasting it to her willingness to allow the suspect into her apartment after the incident. This "atypical" behavior is used to discredit the complainant's allegation.

In the next excerpt the prosecutor was talking about two cases. In both instances the parties knew each other prior to the rape incident as well as having had sexual relations after the incident. As in the previous instance, the victims' allegations are discredited by referring to their atypical behavior.

> DDA SABRINA JOHNSON: *I can't take either case because of the women's behavior after the fact. By seeing these guys again and having sex with them they are absolving them of their guilt. (Bay City)*

In each instance the "downstream" concern with convictability is indicated in the prosecutor's talk—"She is making it very difficult to try the case" and "By seeing these guys again and having sex with them they are absolving them of their guilt." This concern is informed by a series of common-sense assumptions about normal heterosexual relations that the prosecutors assume judges and juries use to assess the believability of the victim: First, appropriate behavior within ongoing relationships is noncoercive and nonviolent. Second, sex that occurs within the context of ongoing relationships is consensual. Third, if coercion or violence occurs, the appropriate response is to sever the relationship, at least for a time. When complainants allege they have been raped by their partner within a continuing relationship, they challenge the taken-for-granted assumptions of normal heterosexual relationships. The prosecutors anticipate that his challenge will create problems for the successful prosecution of a case because they think that judges and jurors will use this typification to question the credibility of the victim's allegation. They assume that the triers of fact will assume that if there is "evidence" of ongoing normal heterosexual relations–she didn't leave and the sexual relationship continued—then there was no coercive sex. Thus the certitude that a crime originally occurred can be retrospectively undermined by the interaction between complainant and suspect after the alleged incident. Implicit in this is the assumed primacy of the normal heterosexual relations typification as the standard on which to assess the victim's credibility even though an allegation of rape has been made.

Typifications of Rape Reporting

An important feature of sexual assault cases is the timeliness in which they are reported to the police (see Torrey, forthcoming). Prosecutors expect rape victims to report the incident relatively promptly: "She didn't call the police until four hours later. That isn't consistent with someone who has been raped." If a woman reports "late," her motives for reporting and the sincerity of her allegation are questioned if they fall outside the typification of officially recognizable/explainable reasons for late reporting. The typification is characterized by the features that can be explained by Rape Trauma Syndrome (RTS). In the first excerpt the victim's credibility is not challenged as a result of her delayed reporting. The prosecutor describes her behavior and motives as characteristic of RTS. The DDA is describing a case to me that came in that morning.

> DDA TAMARA JACOBS: *Charlene was in the car with her three assailants after the rape. John (the driver) was pulled over by the CHP [California Highway Patrol] for erratic driving behavior. The victim did not tell the officers that she had just been raped by these three men. When she arrived home, she didn't tell anyone what happened for approximately 24 hours. When her best friend found out from the assailants (who were mutual friends) and confronted the victim, Charlene told her what happened. She then reported it to the police. When asked why she didn't report the crime earlier, she said that she was embarrassed and afraid they would hurt her more if she reported it to the police. The DDA went on to say that the victim's behavior and reasons for delayed reporting were symptomatic of RTS. During the trial an expert in Rape Trauma Syndrome was called by the prosecution to explain the "normality" and commonness of the victim's reaction. (Bay City)*

Other typical motives include "wanting to return home first and get family support" or "wanting to talk the decision to report over with family and friends." In all these examples, the victims sustained injuries of varying degrees in addition to the trauma of the rape itself, and they reported the crime within 24 hours. At the time the victims reported the incident, their injuries were still visible, providing corroboration for their accounts of what happened.

In the next excerpt we see the connection between atypical motives for delayed reporting and ulterior motives for reporting a rape allegation. At this point I focus on the prosecutors' use of typification as a resource for discrediting the victim's account. I will examine ulterior motives as a technique of discrediting in a later section. The deputy is telling me about a case she recently rejected.

> DDA SABRINA JOHNSON: *She doesn't tell anyone after the rape. Soon after this happened she met him in a public place to talk business. Her car doesn't start, he drives her home and starts to attack her. She jumps from the car and runs home. Again she doesn't tell anyone. She said she didn't tell anyone because she didn't want to lose his business. Then the check bounces, and she ends up with VD. She has to tell her fiance so he can be treated. He insists she tell the police. It is three weeks after the incident. I have to look at what the defense would say about the cases. Looks like she consented, and told only when she had to because of the infection and because he made a fool out of her by having the check bounce. (Bay City)*

The victim's account is discredited because her motives for delayed reporting—not wanting to jeopardize a business deal—fall outside those considered officially recognizable and explicable.

Typifications of Victim's Demeanor

In the course of interviewing hundreds of victims, prosecutors develop a notion of a victim's comportment when she tells what happened. They distinguish between behavior that signifies "lying" versus "discomfort." In the first two exchanges the DDA and IO cite the victim's behavior as an indication of lying. Below, the deputy and IO are discussing the case immediately after the intake interview.

IO NANCY FAUTECK: I think something happened. There was an exchange of body language that makes me question what she was doing. She was yawning, hedging, fudging something.

DDA SABRINA JOHNSON: Yawning is a sign of stress and nervousness.

IO NANCY FAUTECK: She started yawning when I talked to her about her record earlier, and she stopped when we finished talking about it. (Bay City)

The prosecutor and the investigating officer collaboratively draw on their common-sense knowledge and practical work experience to interpret the yawns, nervousness, and demeanor of the complainant as running counter to behavior they expect from one who is "telling the whole truth." They interpret the victim's behavior as a continuum of interaction first with the investigating officer and then with the district attorney. The investigating officer refers to the victim's recurrent behavior (yawning) as in indication that something other than what the victim is reporting actually occurred.

In the next excerpt the prosecutor and IO discredit the victim's account by referencing two typifications—demeanor and appropriate rape-victim behavior. The IO and prosecutor are telling me about the case immediately after they finished the screening interview.

IO DINA ALVAREZ: One on one, no corroboration.

DDA WILLIAM NELSON: She's a poor witness, though that doesn't means she wasn't raped. I won't file a one-on-one case.

IO DINA ALVAREZ: I don't like her body language.

DDA WILLIAM NELSON: She's timid, shy, naive, virginal, and she didn't do all the right things. I'm not convinced she is even telling the truth. She's not even angry about what happened to her. . . .

DDA WILLIAM NELSON: Before a jury if we have a one on one, he denies it, no witnesses, no physical evidence or medical corroboration they won't vote guilty.

IO DINA ALVAREZ: I agree, and I didn't believe her because of her body language. She looks down, mumbles, crosses her arms, and twists her hands.

DDA WILLIAM NELSON: ...She has the same mannerisms and demeanor as a person who is lying. A jury just won't believe her. She has low self-esteem and self-confidence.... (Center Heights)

The prosecutor and IO account for case rejection by characterizing the victim as unbelievable and the case as unconvictable. They establish their disbelief in the victim's account by citing the victim's actions that fall outside the typified notions of believable and expected behavior—"she has the same mannerisms and demeanor as a person who is lying," and "I'm not convinced she is even telling the truth. She isn't even angry about what happened." They assume that potential jurors will also find the victim's demeanor and post-incident behavior problematic. They demonstrate the unconvictability of the case by citing the "holes" in the case—a combination of a "poor witness" whom "the jury just won't believe" and "one on one, [with] no corroboration" and a defense in which the defendant denies anything happened or denies it was nonconsensual sex.

Prosecutors and investigating officers do not routinely provide explicit accounts of "expected/honest" demeanor. Explicit accounts of victim demeanor tend to occur when DDAs are providing grounds for discrediting a rape allegation. When as a researcher I pushed for an account of expected behavior, the following exchange occurred. The DDA had just concluded the interview and asked the victim to wait in the lobby.[3]

IO NANCY FAUTECK: Don't you think he's credible?

DDA SABRINA JOHNSON: Yes.

LF: What seems funny to me is that someone who said he was so unwilling to do this talked about it pretty easily.

IO NANCY FAUTECK: Didn't you see his eyes, they were like saucers.

DDA SABRINA JOHNSON: And [he] was shaking too. (Bay City)

This provides evidence that DDAs and IOs are orienting to victims' comportment and could pro-

vide accounts of "expected/honest" demeanor if necessary. Other behavior that might be included in this typification are the switch from looking at to looking away from the prosecutor when the victim begins to discuss the specific details of the rape itself; a stiffening of the body and tightening of the face as though to hold in tears when the victim begins to tell about the particulars of the incident; shaking of the body and crying when describing the details of the incident; and a lowering of the voice and long pauses when the victim tells the specifics of the sexual assault incident.

Prosecutors have a number of resources they call on to develop typification related to rape scenarios and reporting. These include how sexual assaults are committed, community residents and activities, interactions between suspect and defendants after a rape incident, and the way victims' emotional and psychological responses to rape influence their behavior. These typifications highlight discrepancies between prosecutors' knowledge and victims' accounts. They are used to discredit the victims' allegation of events, justifying case rejection.

As we have seen, one technique used by prosecutors to discredit a victim's allegations of rape as a justification of case rejection is the detection of discrepancies. The resources for this are official documents and records and typifications of rape scenarios and rape reporting. A second technique prosecutors use is the identification of ulterior motives for the victim's rape allegation.

ACCOUNTING FOR REJECTION BY "ULTERIOR MOTIVE"

Ulterior motives rest on the assumption that a woman consented to sexual activity and for some reason needed to deny it afterwards. These motives are drawn from the prosecutor's knowledge of the victim's personal history and the community in which the incident occurred. They are elaborated and supported by other techniques and knowledge prosecutors use in the accounting process.

I identify two types of ulterior motives prosecutors use to justify rejection: The first type suggests the victim has a reason to file a false rape complaint. The second type acknowledges the legitimacy of the rape allegation, framing the motives as an organizational concern with convictability.

KNOWLEDGE OF VICTIM'S
CURRENT CIRCUMSTANCES

Prosecutors accumulate the details of victims' lives from police interviews, official documents, and filing interviews. They may identify ulterior motives by drawing on this information. Note that unlike the court trial itself, where the rape incident is often taken out of the context of the victim's life, here the DDAs call on the texture of a victim's life to justify case rejection. In an excerpt previously discussed, the DDA uses her knowledge of the victim's personal relationship and business transactions as a resource for formulating ulterior motives for the rape allegation—disclosure to her fiance about the need to treat a sexually transmitted disease, and anger and embarrassment about the bounced check. Both of these are motives for making a false complaint. The ulterior motives are supported by the typification for case reporting. Twice unreported sexual assault incidents with the same suspect, a three-week delay in reporting, and reporting only after the fiance insisted she do so are not within the typified behavior and reasons for late reporting. Her atypical behavior provides plausibility to the alternative version of the events—the interaction was consensual and only reported as a rape because the victim needed to explain a potentially explosive matter (how she contracted venereal disease) to her fiance. In addition she felt duped on a business deal.

Resources for imputing ulterior motives also come from the specifics of the rape incident. Below, the prosecutor's knowledge of the residents and activities in Center Heights supply the reason: the type of activity the victim wanted to cover up

from her boyfriend. The justification for rejection is strengthened by conflicting accounts between the victim and witness on the purpose for being in Center Heights. The DDA and IO are talking about the case before they interview the complainant.

DDA WILLIAM NELSON: A white girl from Addison comes to buy dope. She gets kidnapped and raped.

IO BRANDON PALMER: She tells her boyfriend and he beats her up for being so stupid for going to Center Heights.... The drug dealer positively ID's the two suspects, but she's got a credibility problem because she said she wasn't selling dope, but the other two witnesses say they bought dope from her....

LF: I see you have a blue sheet [a sheet used to write up case rejections] already written up.

IO BRANDON PALMER: Oh yes. But there was no doubt in my mind that she was raped. But do you see the problems?

DDA WILLIAM NELSON: Too bad because these guys really messed her up.... She has a credibility problem. I don't think she is telling the truth about the drugs. It would be better if she said she did come to buy drugs. The defense is going to rip her up because of the drugs. He is going to say, isn't it true you had sex with these guys but didn't want to tell your boyfriend, so you lied about the rape like you did about the drugs, or that she had sex for drugs.... (Center Heights)

The prosecutor expresses doubt about the victim's account because it conflicts with his knowledge of the community. He uses this knowledge to formulate the ulterior motive for the victim's complaint—to hide from her boyfriend the "fact" that she trading sex for drugs. The victim, "a white woman from Addison," alleges she drove to Center Heights "in the middle of the night" as a favor to a friend. She asserted that she did not come to purchase drugs. The DDA "knows" that white people don't live in Center Heights. He assumes that whites who come to

Center Heights, especially in the middle of the night, are there to buy drugs or trade sex for drugs. The prosecutor's scenario is strengthened by the statements of the victim's two friends who accompanied her to Center Heights, were present at the scene, and admitted buying drugs. The prosecutor frames the ulterior motives as an organizational concern with defense arguments and convictability. This concern is reinforced by citing conflicting accounts between witnesses and the victim. He does not suggest that the victim's allegation was false—"there is no doubt in my mind she was raped"; rather, the case isn't convictable—"she has a credibility problem" and "the defense is going to rip her up."

CRIMINAL CONNECTIONS

The presence of criminal connections can also be used as a resource for identifying ulterior motives. Knowledge of a victim's criminal activity enables prosecutors to "find" ulterior motives for her allegation. In the first excerpt the complainant's presence in an area known by police as "where prostitutes bring their clients" is used to formulate an ulterior motive for her rape complaint. This excerpt is from an exchange in which the DDA was telling me about a case he had just rejected.

> DDA WILLIAM NELSON: *Young female is raped under questionable circumstances. One on one. The guy states it is consensual sex. There is no corroboration, no medicals. We ran the woman's rap sheet, and she has a series of prostitution arrests. She's with this guy in the car in a dark alley having sex. The police know this is where prostitutes bring their customers, so she knew she had better do something fast unless she is going to be busted for prostitution, so, lo and behold, she comes running out of the car yelling "he's raped me." He says no. He picked her up on Long Beach Boulevard, paid her $25 and this is "where she brought me." He's real scared, he has no record. (Center Heights)*

Above, the prosecutor, relying on police knowledge of a particular location, assumes the woman

is a prostitute. Her presence in the location places her in a "suspicious" category, triggering a check on her criminal history. Her record of prostitution arrests is used as the resource for developing an ulterior motive for her complaint: To avoid being busted for prostitution again, she made a false allegation of rape. Here the woman's record of prostitution and the imminent possibility of arrest are used to provide the ulterior motive to discredit her account. The woman's account is further discredited by comparing her criminal history—"a series of prostitution arrests" with that of the suspect, who "has no record," thus suggesting that he is the more credible of the two parties.

Prosecutors and investigating officers often decide to run a rap sheet (a chronicle of a person's arrests and convictions) on a rape victim. These decisions are triggered when a victim falls into certain "suspicious" categories, categories that have a class/race bias. Rap sheets are not run on women who live in the wealthier parts of town (the majority of whom are white) or have professional careers. They are run on women who live in Center Heights (who are black and Latina), who are homeless, or who are involved in illegal activities that could be related to the incident.

In the next case the prosecutor's knowledge of the victim's criminal conviction for narcotics is the resource for formulating an ulterior motive. This excerpt was obtained during an interview.

> DDA TRACY TIMMERTON: *I had one woman who had claimed that she had been kidnapped off the street after she had car trouble by these two gentlemen who locked her in a room all night and had repeated intercourse with her. Now she was on a cocaine diversion [a drug treatment program where the court places persons convicted of cocaine possession instead of prison], and these two guys' stories essentially were that the one guy picked her up, they went down and got some cocaine, had sex in exchange for the cocaine, and the other guy comes along and they are all having sex and all doing cocaine. She has real reason to lie, she was doing cocaine, and because she has then violated the terms of her diversion and is now subject to criminal prosecution for her possession of cocaine*

charge. She is also supposed to be in a drug program which she has really violated, so this is her excuse and her explanation to explain why she has fallen off her program. (Bay City)

The prosecutor used the victim's previous criminal conviction for cocaine and her probation conditions to provide ulterior motives for her rape allegation—the need to avoid being violated on probation for the possession of cocaine and her absence from a drug diversion program. She suggests that the allegation made by the victim was false.

Prosecutors develop the basis for ulterior motives from the knowledge they have of the victim's personal life and criminal connections. They create two types of ulterior motives, those that suggest the victim made a false rape complaint and those that acknowledge the legitimacy of the complaint but discredit the account because of its unconvictability. In the accounts prosecutors give, ulterior motives for case rejection are supported with discrepancies in victims' accounts and other practitioners' knowledge.

CONCLUSION

Case filing is a critical stage in the prosecutorial process. It is here that prosecutors decide which instances of alleged victimization will be forwarded for adjudication by the courts. A significant percentage of sexual assault cases are rejected at this stage. This research has examined prosecutorial accounts for case rejection and the centrality of victim discreditability in those accounts. I have elucidated the techniques of case rejection (discrepant accounts and ulterior motives), the resources prosecutors use to develop these techniques (official reports and records, typifications of rape-relevant behavior, criminal connections, and knowledge of a victim's personal life), and how these resources are used to discredit victims' allegations of sexual assault.

This examination has also provided the beginnings of an investigation into the logic and organization of prosecutors' decisions to reject/ accept cases for prosecution. The research suggests that prosecutors are orienting to a "downstream" concern with convictability. They are constantly "in dialogue with" anticipated defense arguments and anticipated judge and juror responses to case testimony. These dialogues illustrate the intricacy of prosecutorial decision-making. They make visible how prosecutors rely on assumptions about relationships, gender, and sexuality (implicit in this analysis, but critical and requiring of specific and explicit attention) in complaint filing of sexual assault cases. They also make evident how the processes of distinguishing truths from untruths and the practical concerns of trying cases are central to these decisions. Each of these issues, in all its complexity, needs to be examined if we are to understand the logic and organization of filing sexual assault cases.

The organizational logic unveiled by these accounts has political implications for the prosecution of sexual assault crimes. These implications are particularly acute for acquaintance rape situations. As I have shown, the typification of normal heterosexual relations plays an important role in assessing these cases, and case conviction is key to filing cases. As noted by DDA William Nelson: "There is a difference between believing a woman was assaulted and being able to get a conviction in court." Unless we are able to challenge the assumptions on which these typification are based, many cases of rape will never get beyond the filing process because of unconvictability.

NOTES

1. To protect the confidentiality of the people and places studied, pseudonyms are used throughout this article.
2. The use of practitioners' knowledge to inform decision making is not unique to prosecutors. For example, such practices are found among police (Bittner 1967; Rubinstein 1973), public defenders (Sudnow 1965), and juvenile court officials (Emerson 1969).

3. Unlike the majority of rape cases I observed, this case had a male victim. Due to lack of data, I am unable to tell if this made him more or less credible in the eyes of the prosecutor and police.

REFERENCES

Bittner, Egon A. 1967. "The police on skid-row: A study of peace keeping." *American Sociological Review* 32:699–715.

Boland, Barbara, Catherine H. Conly, Paul Mahanna, Lynn Warner, and Ronald Sones. 1990. *The Prosecution of Felony Arrests, 1987.* Washington, D.C.: Bureau of Justice Statistics, U.S. Department of Justice.

Chandler, Susan M., and Martha Torney. 1981. "The decision and the processing of rape victims through the criminal justice system." *California Sociologist* 4:155–69.

Emerson, Robert M. 1969. *Judging Delinquents: Context and Process in Juvenile Court.* Chicago: Aldine Publishing Co.

Emerson, Robert M., and Blair Paley. Forthcoming. "Organizational horizons and complaint-filing." In *The Uses of Discretion,* ed. Keith Hawkins. Oxford: Oxford University Press.

Garfinkel, Harold. 1984. *Studies in Ethnomethodology.* Cambridge, Eng.: Polity Press.

Glaser, Barney, and Anselm Strauss. 1967. *The Discovery of Grounded Theory.* Chicago: Aldine Publishing Co..

Holmstrom, Lynda Lytle, and Ann Wolbert Burgess. 1983. *The Victim of Rape: Institutional Reactions.* New Brunswick, N.J.: Transaction Books.

Kerstetter, Wayne A. 1990. "Gateway to justice: Police and prosecutorial response to sexual assaults against women." *Journal of Criminal Law and Criminology* 81:267–313.

Kerstetter, Wayne A., and Barrik Van Winkle. 1990. "Who decides? A study of the complainant's decision to prosecute in rape cases." *Criminal Justice and Behavior* 17:268–83.

LaFree, Gary D. 1980. "Variables affecting guilty pleas and convictions in rape cases: Toward a social theory of rape processing." *Social Forces* 58:833–50.

———. 1981. "Official reactions to social problems: Police decisions in sexual assault cases." *Social Problems* 28:582–94.

———. 1989. *Rape and Criminal Justice: The Social Construction of Sexual Assault.* Belmont, Calif.: Wadsworth Publishing Co.

Mather, Lynn M. 1979. *Plea Bargaining or Trial? The Process of Criminal-Case Disposition.* Lexington, Mass.: Lexington Books.

Maynard, Douglas W. 1984. *Inside Plea Bargaining: The Language of Negotiation.* New York: Plenum Press.

Miller, Frank. 1970. *Prosecution: The Decision to Charge a Suspect with a Crime.* Boston: Little, Brown.

Neubauer, David. 1974. *Criminal Justice in Middle America.* Morristown, N.J.: General Learning Press.

Rose, Vicki M., and Susan C. Randall. 1982. "The impact of investigator perceptions of victim legitimacy on the processing of rape/sexual assault cases." *Symbolic Interaction* 5:23–36.

Rubinstein, Jonathan. 1973. *City Police.* New York: Farrar, Straus & Giroux.

Scheff, Thomas. 1966. *Being Mentally Ill: A Sociological Theory.* Chicago: Aldine Publishing Co.

Stanko, Elizabeth A. 1980. "These are the cases that try themselves: An examination of the extra-legal criteria in felony case processing." Presented at the Annual Meetings of the North Central Sociological Association, December. Buffalo, N.Y.

———. 1981. "The impact of victim assessment on prosecutor's screening decisions: The case of the New York District Attorney's Office." *Law and Society Review* 16:225–39.

———. 1982. "Would you believe this woman? Prosecutorial screening for "credible" witnesses and a problem of justice." In *Judge, Lawyer, Victim, Thief,* ed. Nicole Hahn Rafter and Elizabeth A. Stanko, 63–82. Boston: Northeastern University Press.

Sudnow, David. 1965. "Normal crimes: Sociological features of the penal code in a public defenders office." *Social Problems* 12:255–76.

Torrey, Morrison. Forthcoming. "When will we be believed? Rape myths and the idea coming of a fair trial in rape prosecutions." U.C. Davis Law Review.

Waegel, William B. 1981. "Case routinization in investigative police work." *Social Problems* 28:263–75.

Williams, Kristen M. 1978a. *The Role of the Victim in the Prosecution of Violent Crimes.* Washington D.C.: Institute for Law and Social Research.

———. 1978b. *The Prosecution of Sexual Assaults.* Washington D.C.: Institute for Law and Social Research.

Probation Officer—Defendant Negotiations

JACK W. SPENCER

One of the principal concerns of sociologists and criminologists has been how criminal defendants are sentenced for their crimes. Probation officers (POs) play a significant role in the sentencing process because they make sentencing recommendations to the courts. Therefore, an examination of how POs make their recommendations is crucial for a full understanding of this sentencing process. Previous research has failed to examine important aspects of the processes whereby POs arrive at these recommendations.

Historically, the dominant approach to the study of criminal behavior has been deterministic. Thus, most of the researchers and theorists in this area have been concerned with delineating the causal factors associated with the occurrence of crime (Bonger, 1916; Cloward and Ohlin, 1960; Merton, 1957; Sellin, 1938). Since the 1930s, other sociologists and criminologists have reacted to this deterministic approach by stressing the importance of examining the processes of formal social reaction to criminal behavior (Becker, 1963; Cicourel, 1968; Lemert, 1951; Schur, 1971; Tannenbaum, 1938). These theorists have argued that it is the operation of the criminal justice system which defines or labels criminal behavior. In the mid-1970s, research on the criminal justice system began to take a deterministic approach. That is, this research examined the causal factors associated with criminal justice outcomes. Much of this research was concerned with the influence of legal vs. extra-legal variables on sentencing decisions (Bernstein *et al.*, 1977; Burke and Turk, 1975; Chiricos and Waldo, 1975).

This same approach has dominated research on decision-making by POs. That is, researchers have examined the variables which determine the decision which POs make (Carter, 1967; Dembo, 1972; Hagan, 1977; Reed and King, 1966).[1] One of these decisions is the sentence recommendation that POs make to the courts. While this approach has led to important insights it has left an important gap in our understanding of how POs arrive at these recommendations.

What has been left relatively unexamined are the *processes* whereby POs first interview defendants and then make recommendations. Previous research has found that a defendant's attitude is an important factor in these recommendations (Carter, 1967; Gross, 1967). However, we know little about the presentencing interview within which POs assess defendants' attitudes, nor how POs link this information with other factors in deciding what recommendation to make.

This paper is intended to bridge this gap. First, I discuss a set of factors—defendant's subjective orientations to criminal behavior—which includes defendants' attitudes. Next, I examine how POs assess these subjective orientations during presentence interviews. Finally, I discuss how these assessments affect the ways POs label defendants for the purpose of making sentence recommendations.

METHOD

In 1981, I spent nine months collecting data on the organizational processing of criminal defendants at a county probation department in the Midwestern United States. This project was part of my dissertation research. The present study is based on part of that data, and consists of: (1) field notes of observations; (2) interviews with POs; and (3) tape recordings of presentencing interviews.

Reprinted from "Accounts, Attitudes, and Solutions: Probation Officer-Defendant Negotiations of Subjective Orientations," *Social Problems,* Vol. 30, No. 5 (June, 1983), pp. 570–581, by permission of the Society for the Study of Social Problems and the author.

The probation department I studied comprised four divisions: felony, misdemeanor, juvenile, and substance-abuse. The staff consisted of a chief PO, three division heads, six POs, two substance-abuse counselors, and various support staff. I excluded the juvenile and substance-abuse division from the study early in the research.[2] The chief and all the POs in the felony and misdemeanor divisions agreed to participate in the research. Before each presentencing interview I identified myself, explained the nature of my research to the defendant involved, and obtained his or her written consent to record the interaction. No defendants refused to be included in the study.

The POs were extremely helpful, allowing me access to most sources of information that I needed, offering important ethnographic data during informal conversations, and discussing particular cases which I included in the study. After a short time my presence in the department became taken for granted: I was allowed to occupy a desk while not observing presentencing interviews and, when needed, would answer the telephones and run errands.

I collected data on 23 presentencing interviews in the following manner. After obtaining written consent from the defendant, I went to a corner of the room and started the tape recorder. During the interview I noted characteristics of the defendant and salient aspects of the interaction not captured by the tape recorder, such as nonverbal behavior. After the interview was completed and the defendant had left the room, I interviewed the POs about their perception of the interaction, the defendant, and the offense.

The method I used to analyze the data closely resembles Glaser and Strauss's (1967) grounded theory approach. Thus, I formulated theoretical propositions and constructs from the data, modifying these by comparing them with subsequent data, and developing hypotheses which accounted for the relationships between these constructs. I also used Cicourel's (1975, 1978, 1980) model of discourse processes which stresses the relationship between these processes, various predicates of knowledge which participants possess, and how the participants articulate or link that knowledge with information which emerges in the interactive setting.

DEFENDANTS' SUBJECTIVE ORIENTATIONS

Most previous research on sentencing recommendations has divided input factors into legal and extra-legal categories, in the process either ignoring such factors as attitudes or categorizing them as extra-legal. The POs I studied considered attitudes and other related factors in making sentencing recommendations. However, such factors were relatively distinct from those traditionally designated extra-legal (e.g., race, age, employment stability) both in how they were elicited in presentencing interviews and how they affected sentence recommendations. This finding led me to formulate a third category of factors, which I call defendant's subjective orientations to their criminal behavior. I found four subjective orientations to be relevant: (1) accounts for the offenses; (2) attitudes toward the offenses; (3) attitudes toward the consequences of the offenses; and (4) attitudes toward changing their behavior. I discuss each of these in turn.

ACCOUNTS FOR THE OFFENSES

According to Scott and Lyman (1968:46) an account is "a statement made by a social actor to explain unanticipated or untoward behavior." In my data the defendants' accounts consisted of two elements: the factors involved in the commission of the offense and the degree of intent involved.

There were generally two types of *factors:* motivating and causal. Motivating factors involved problematic situations in which the defendants sought to accomplish some particular goal and to which the commission of the offenses presented a solution. Causal factors, on the other hand, led to the commission of the offenses, in spite of the conscious intentions of the defendants.

The degree of responsibility the defendants claimed decided the type of factor.

The amount of prior planning by the defendant determined the *degree of intent*. Relevant components of this element included the point at which defendants had decided to commit the offense and whether they had considered the method by which it would be committed. Of primary importance to the POs was whether the offense was spontaneous or calculated. Combining these two elements—the factors and the degree of intent—results in a four-fold typology of accounts, of which only two will concern us here: rational and non-rational accounts.[3]

Rational accounts were ones in which defendants claimed some degree of prior planning and in which they had been in control of their actions. For example, one rational account for shoplifting involved a defendant who claimed to have desired an item yet, lacking sufficient money, decided to steal it. *Non-rational accounts* were those in which defendants claimed they committed the offense relatively spontaneously and because of some identifiable factor which was beyond their immediate control. For example, one defendant claimed he had assaulted someone because he had been drunk and their argument had gotten "out of hand."

Defendants' accounts were important for sentencing recommendations for four reasons: (1) The POs believed planned offenses deserved more severe sanctions than those which were more spontaneous. (2) POs sometimes regarded a causal factor as a mitigating circumstance deserving a more lenient recommendation. (3) The type of account could affect the type of recommendation. For example, in some cases a claim that alcohol or drugs led to the commission of an offense encouraged the PO to recommend counseling rather than incarceration. (4) In lieu of information to the contrary, POs did not usually accept non-rational accounts since they mitigate some of the defendant's responsibility. Thus, defendants who offered rational accounts were generally viewed as cooperative and responsible; those who

made (unwarranted) claims to non-rational accounts were seen as presenting a "line."

ATTITUDES TOWARD THE OFFENSE

POs generally viewed any offense which resulted in a conviction as a serious affair. For example, POs viewed with concern the theft of even a few inexpensive items from a store because such losses to stores create higher prices for customers. Similarly, pranks were defined as serious since they usually involved theft or property damage, or both.

POs regarded as relevant two basic components of defendants' attitudes toward their offense—their attitude toward the wrongfulness of the act and toward the seriousness of the act. Defendants who accepted that their behavior was wrong or illegal, and who shared the PO's definition that their behavior was serious, were viewed as holding an acceptable attitude. In addition, POs regarded defendants' attitudes as indicators of underlying character or behavior traits. Thus, defendants who exhibited acceptable attitudes were viewed as possessing some generally redeeming traits which made them less likely to commit subsequent offenses. POs viewed unacceptable attitudes, however, as cause for more severe sanctions, since they believed that such defendants were more likely to become recidivists.[4] In addition, defendants who did not even pay lip service to acceptable attitudes in presenting interviews were seen as not taking the proceedings seriously—in effect, an improper demeanor.

ATTITUDES TOWARD THE CONSEQUENCES

POs expected defendants to anticipate the effects of their behavior. That is, if a certain behavioral option was expected to have negative consequences, this was supposed to act as at least a partial deterrent to that behavior. Thus, POs regarded defendants' attitudes toward the consequences of their behavior as related to their likelihood of recidivism. Two sets of consequences are relevant: (1) the possible legal sanctions; and (2) the nonlegal, negative effects of a criminal record on current or future endeavors. In both instances, POs considered an acceptable attitude one in which the defendant expressed concern about these consequences. This concern included both an awareness of the likelihood of the consequences and of their adverse nature.

ATTITUDES TOWARD CHANGING THEIR BEHAVIOR

POs believed that people do not engage in serious violations of the law under normal circumstances. The corollary of this maxim was that serious violations were the result or manifestation of some problem, to which there was an identifiable solution. In this regard, POs viewed as relevant nonlegal solutions which defendants could pursue. In an important sense, POs viewed how defendants felt about these solutions as an indication of their attitudes toward changing their criminal behavior. When defendants offered non-rational accounts for their offenses, solutions were sought for the particular causal factor. For example, if an offense was caused by a defendant's alcoholism, the PO addressed solutions which the defendant could pursue and which would alleviate the problem, such as counseling. However, when rational accounts were offered, the POs located the problem in the defendant's choices of behaviors, and attention was focused on identifying more appropriate (legal) alternatives. For example, one defendant accounted for his theft of food by saying he was out of money and hadn't eaten in two days. The PO tried to point out to the defendant that there were legal alternatives available, such as welfare, which would have solved his problem. In either case, if defendants expressed a willingness to pursue a solution, they were viewed as possessing acceptable attitudes toward changing their behavior.

POs viewed as acceptable three attitudes by defendants toward changing their behavior. (1) Defendants were expected to express concern about the particular factor (causal or motivating) which had been identified. (2) They were expected to express an awareness of an appropriate solu-

tion. (3) They were expected to express a willingness to pursue these solutions—that is, demonstrate that these solutions were viewed as both feasible and desirable. POs viewed defendants who expressed these acceptable attitudes as less likely to commit further offenses, since they were more likely to solve the problem and thus change their behavior. In these cases, sentence recommendations were less severe, since legal sanctions were less necessary as a deterrent.

NEGOTIATIONS BETWEEN PROBATION OFFICERS AND DEFENDANTS

In addition to legal and extra-legal factors, POs took into account defendants' subjective orientations to criminal behavior in deciding what sentence to recommend. POs elicited most information about legal and extra-legal factors by asking defendants simple questions. However, POs elicited information about subjective orientations in a more complex way. They engaged defendants in a process of negotiation aimed at reaching a shared agreement which at least approximated the POs' notions of propriety or acceptability. In conducting these negotiations, POs used a variety of interactional strategies to seek desired responses in each of the four subjective orientations.[5]

ACCOUNTS FOR THE OFFENSES

The POs generally viewed rational accounts as more reasonable and acceptable than nonrational accounts. Therefore, when they requested accounts from defendants, their questions implied or assumed a request for a rational account. The POs used two strategies in requesting such accounts.

1. They asked a question which implied a decision-making process on the part of the defendant (D).

   PO: Why'dja decide to take the motorcycle?

2. They asked a series of indirect questions in an attempt to establish the conditions for a rational account.

PO: You knew you were on probation when you did this.

D: Uh huh.

PO: Did that concern you at all? Did you think about that?

Through either of these strategies, the POs attempted to elicit a rational account from the defendants. If the defendants' responses confirmed the POs' assumptions about such an account, the negotiation was concluded. However, when responses did not confirm that assumption, the negotiation took a different format.

The defendants were viewed by POs as more likely to offer a non-rational account, in the hope of mitigating some responsibility on their part. Due to this, the POs responded to such accounts with an additional request to establish specific conditions for a rational account.

PO: Why'dja decide to take the motorcycle?

D: Uh, its stupidity. We were messing around and then—and we didn't have no reason.

PO: What were you gonna do with it?

If the response to this request still contained a claim to a non-rational account, the PO turned to a series of questions in an attempt to establish conditions for that type of account.

PO: What were you gonna do with [the motorcycle]?

D: I don't know.

PO: How drunk or high were ya?

D: I was still aware of what was goin on.

PO: What did you have to drink or smoke that night?

D: Uhm, we'd been drinking beer and smoking marijuana; and going around to different parties all that night.

Only when such conditions were established did the PO accept a non-rational account.

While the POs accepted claims to rational accounts unconditionally, claims to non-rational accounts were not so readily accepted. Further, while they made direct requests for rational ac-

counts, requests for non-rational accounts were only approached in a piecemeal fashion which did not allow the defendant to make a singular, direct claim to that type of account.

ATTITUDES TOWARD THE OFFENSES

While the POs defined defendants' offenses as wrong and serious enough to be concerned about, defendants did not always share this definition. The POs used four strategies in trying to obtain defendants' agreement with their definition of criminal offenses.

1. The POs would request examples of behaviors which defendants felt were subsumed under the latters' definition. The PO would then show the defendants that these behaviors were actually examples of the POs definition of the offense.

D: I realize there's a difference between stealing and a college prank.

PO: Give me another example of a college prank—a legitimate college prank.

D: Another thing [people on] my [dormitory] floor have done, which I think is worse than the thing that I did, and that's paintin' a bridge outside of the front of the dorm, which is not the dorm's property. It's university property. That's permanently defacing it. I would say [this] is a college prank that was worse than the one I did.

PO: So there's somethin' you would call a prank that you admitted was wrong. It's probably a criminal offense, yet you think they're mainly college pranks.

The effectiveness of this strategy lay in the POs ability to convince the defendants that, since these examples can be subsumed under the PO's definition, so could the defendants' current offenses.

2. The POs pointed out the seriousness of the offenses' potential or actual harm to others. For example, one defendant was convicted of shoplifting after eating candy while shopping and not paying for it.

PO: Why didn't you pay for [the candy]?

D: Where I come from, people do this all the time—"try it before you buy it." I've always done it. Everyone does it where I come from. No one considers it a crime. It's like spitting or littering; there's some obscure law against it.

PO: Ya know, if everybody did that the store is out a lot of money and they're gonna pass that loss on to the customers. I'm not real happy about the prospects of paying higher prices so you can eat the candy.

This strategy pointed out to defendants that their behaviors were not isolated events, but rather had consequences for other people. In this way, the POs attempted to validate their claim to the definition of offenses as serious and wrong.

3. The POs argued that other aspects of the defendants' behaviors associated with the commission of the offenses were wrong and, in some cases, could also have been charged as criminal offenses. They did this in the hope of convincing the defendants that the acts they had been charged with were wrong and worthy of concern. For example, a teenage university student and his friends were drinking late one night. They decided to climb over the fence surrounding the university football stadium and "play some football." To prove they had been there, they decided to take a soft drink canister back to the dormitory. The defendant was subsequently arrested and convicted of theft. Throughout the presentencing interview, the defendant steadfastly denied that what he had done was wrong or should have been charged as a criminal offense.

PO: Did ya know that you were also doing what's known as criminal trespass? What'd you do, climb over the fence?

D: Yeah. I considered that a college prank, too.

PO: Ya know that's another Class A misdemeanor. That's another year in jail if they charge you with that. You were committing a crime just by being there. Then you chose to steal something. You were drinking beer—that's another offense [since you were underage]. I mean you were doing a whole series of things here which resulted in your getting arrested.

4. The POs pointed out the potential legal consequences of a conviction. For example, one defendant presented a particularly cavalier attitude toward both his current and previous offenses. The PO seemed to think that this attitude was bolstered by the fact that the defendant had reached a plea agreement with the prosecutor. According to the agreement, in exchange for the defendant's guilty plea, the prosecutor would not argue for a severe sentence at the sentencing hearing. In addition, the PO thought the defendant "was high on something" during the interview.

PO: Do you have any prior criminal record as a juvenile?

D: Yes. I don't know what it all is. It's not very much, probably four charges—stupid charges like common nuisance, vandalism, vehicle theft, and I don't know what. Probably one or two more after that.

PO: Do you know that with a [class] C Felony you can get eight years?

D: I know.

PO: You realize if you get probation, which [there] is no guarantee you will, that plea agreement don't mean nothin' till its accepted, alright?

D: Uh huh.

PO: Only thing this plea agreement does.... Look, you're looking at two-to-eight [years], OK? All this plea agreement's gonna do—instead of the prosecutor getting up there and wanting your ass for eight years he's gonna stand mute. He's not gonna argue anything one way or another, but you can still be given the full amount. Do you understand that?

D: Yes, sir.

PO: Where they'll send ya ain't like boy's school. You're an adult now and you're gonna be treated as such.

The POs generally felt that this strategy was effective, even when other strategies had failed, since the prospects of incarceration and/or a substantial fine was enough "to get the attention of most of the people."

ATTITUDES TOWARD CONSEQUENCES

Often the defendants had not considered the specific consequences of their convictions. The strategies the POs used in negotiating these attitudes were indirect and based on a lay version of cognitive dissonance theory (Festinger, 1957). The POs believed that if the defendants came to express acceptable attitudes "on their own, it [would] mean more to them," and they would be more inclined to act according to these acceptable attitudes than if the POs had directly presented these attitudes for their consideration. To this end the POs used two strategies.

1. The POs used defendants' expressions of an appropriate orientation to address another orientation.

D: So, I mean, I'm really scared this is on my record, 'cause I want to go to law school, ya know, like my old man, and I've heard that you can't get into law school if you have a criminal record.

PO: Does the possible sentence worry you any?

D: I couldn't care less about the sentence.

PO: Could you care less about a year of your life in jail?

D: I would be concerned about that, yes.

PO: So you are concerned about the sentence?

D: Yeah, I'm concerned about the sentence. I wanna go to school, ya know, and I don't want my dad to know.

The POs used this strategy to indicate to defendants that the attitude they expressed toward the first topic was also appropriate for the second one.

2. The POs linked background information about the defendants to the topic currently under negotiation.

PO: Have you thought about what [your conviction] is gonna do to your chances of getting into med school?

D: From the second I got out of the [store].

PO: And?

D: It's, it's gonna hurt me bad. There's a real good possibility they'd kick me out.

In this example, the defendant had been convicted of shoplifting. The PO had learned in a previous part of the interview that the defendant planned to go to medical school and used this information in negotiating his attitudes toward the consequences of his offense. This strategy was particularly effective; it pointed out to defendants that the things they valued had been placed in jeopardy by their behavior.

ATTITUDES TOWARD CHANGING THEIR BEHAVIOR

The POs used three indirect strategies in trying to get defendants to change their behavior. Which strategy the POs used was determined by the outcome of the negotiations over accounts.

1. When the POs and the defendants had reached agreement on a rational account, the POs used strategies which addressed alternative courses of action, ones which would have allowed the defendants to achieve their goal without breaking the law. In other words, the POs tried to make the defendants aware of legal (and, therefore, more desirable) alternatives to the particular courses of action they had chosen. The goal was to find solutions to the problem of the defendant's criminal behavior. A typical question in this strategy was:

PO: Think there might've been a way to avoid this?

2. When a non-rational account had been agreed upon, the POs used a strategy which allowed the defendants to consider courses of action which would alleviate or overcome the causal factor responsible for the offense. In addition, since a non-rational account mitigated some of the defendant's responsibility, the POs attempted to get the defendants to take some responsibility in solving the problem itself.

PO: Do you think alcohol is the root of your problems?

D: Yeah. I think its got a lot to do with it because I don't have no juvenile record at all or nothin'. It's only been while I've been drinking.

PO: What have you done to work on your drinking problem?

D: I tried to get away from it but I can't. It's just like on Sunday night. [The bar] opens up about noon and I can't wait to go up there and start drinkin'.

PO: If you knew this was a problem, why didn't you go get some help?

3. When no mutually satisfactory account had been agreed upon, the POs addressed this orientation in a different way. Since no problem had been identified, rather than addressing solutions, the POs addressed the defendant's risk of recidivism. They challenged the defendants to offer reasons why they would not be likely to commit a crime in the future. In this way, the defendants were asked to provide prospective accounts for their behavior.

PO: Why don't you tell me what you would like the judge to know about you; why you did these [crimes]; and what's to convince us you're not gonna keep stealing. Sounds to me like you've got sticky fingers.

D: Uhm, I know I won't do it again.

PO: Why not?

D: 'Cause ya know, I'm doin' too much for myself now, lots of things that I wouldn't want to lose. I have a full time job and friends that I admire are trying to teach me to stay out of trouble.

NEGOTIATING LABELS

[Accounts] presuppose an identifiable speaker and audience. The particular identities of the interactants must often be established as part of the encounter in which the account is presented. In other words, people generate role identities for one an- *other in social situations.... Every account is a manifestation of underlying negotiation of identities (Scott and Lyman, 1968:58).*

I have argued that defendants' accounts of their offenses, as well as other subjective orientations, are subject to negotiation during presentencing interviews. Analysis revealed that these subjective orientations are one of the central components of a typology of defendants which POs possessed and used in making sentence recommendations. I posit, therefore, that *in the process of negotiating subjective orientations, the PO and the defendant were simultaneously negotiating the particular defendant type that the former would use to define the latter.*

In the bureaucratic processing of defendants this type can be conceptualized as a *label* which POs attached to defendants for the purpose of making sentence recommendations. Thus, the POs did not so much process individuals as they *processed types of individuals who had been labeled in particular ways.* The particular label attached to an individual defendant depended on the POs' linking of characteristics of the individual with characteristics of the general category or type.[6]

Ethnographic data revealed that, in making sentence recommendations, POs used a threefold typology of criminal defendants which was based on the defendants' risk of recidivism.

1. Low-risk defendants were usually in trouble with the criminal justice system for the first time, were between the ages of 18 and 25, and were either attending university or had a steady job. These defendants, therefore, had much to lose by possessing a criminal record and they took their current involvement with the courts seriously. As one PO put it, "These people have made one screwy mistake and it's shaken them up so much we'll probably never see them again." For example, one defendant had been convicted of attempted theft after he had altered a sales receipt to obtain items he hadn't paid for. This defendant was unusually cooperative during the interview and expressed concern about the fact that business associates and local bankers would find out about the criminal record he now possessed. His PO told me, "I don't think we'll see him come through here again. This was his first offense and I think it really made an impression on him."

2. High-risk defendants usually had at least two prior arrests and convictions, little formal education, and were seen as unwilling or unable to hold a steady job. Often, they were perceived as not taking their involvement with the courts seriously. For these reasons, POs saw these defendants as likely to be in and out of trouble for much of their adult lives. For example, a defendant had been convicted of burglary and had several other theft-related convictions. In addition, he had never held a job for more than three months at a time. The PO who handled the case told me:

> *This [defendant] is just too lazy to work.... He commits these burglaries because of that. I'll bet ya we see this guy again. He's definitely [high-risk] material.*

3. The final category of defendants consisted of individuals whose risk of recidivism was neither definitely high nor low, but was seen as problematic. Some of these defendants had been in trouble with the law before, generally involving minor offenses such as shoplifting. Others possessed characteristics such as alcoholism or a "bad attitude" which POs considered likely to be related to future criminal behavior. While there was no specific set of characteristics which defined this category of defendants, POs pointed out that what they did share was the potential for "heading for trouble." For example, a defendant had been convicted of theft and had two prior theft-related offenses. However, he also was working two jobs to pay off a student loan and return to the university. The PO described the defendant's risk of recidivism in the following way:

> *Its hard to tell with him. He's got these [prior offenses], but he's got these things [two jobs, a car] going for him. If he was in a situation where he could steal, I don't know.*

What was important for POs was that, whatever the problem, these defendants were "workable." As one PO put it:

> *I spend the most time with these [defendants]. I try to make them aware of alternatives ... or refer them for heavy-duty counseling, or do some things myself so hopefully they won't get in trouble again.*

By the time POs began negotiations with defendants, they already possessed information about their criminal records and background. Thus, they had already formed initial impressions of the defendants, and had attached to them a provisional label on the basis of available information. What remained to be accomplished in the interview was to attach an unambiguous label upon which a sentence recommendation could be based.

The initial label was provisional for three reasons: (1) POs only possessed partial information about defendants. (2) Labels based on prior information could be misleading. Thus, some defendants had all the "objective" indicators of a low-risk defendant, yet may have exhibited unacceptable attitudes associated with problematic or high-risk defendants. The converse was also true. (3) In some cases the background information may have been too ambiguous to allow even a provisional labeling. For example, a defendant may have had the criminal record of a high-risk defendant, yet also have had low-risk characteristics such as a steady job or a college degree. In these cases, the determining characteristics may have been the defendants' subjective orientations.

POs used various strategies in negotiating reasonable or acceptable responses with defendants for each subjective orientation. At the aggregate level of types, however, with each verbal expression of an orientation, defendants were making claim to a certain defendant type. Thus, expressing concern about the consequences of the offense functioned as a claim to a low-risk defendant, while an unwillingness to accept the POs' definition of the offense as serious and wrong served as a claim to a high-risk defendant. These claims to defendant types were always relative to the initial impression the PO had of a defendant. A defendant initially labeled as high risk who expressed consistently acceptable orientations was (in the eyes of the PO) making claim to a type of defendant whose risk was problematic (a change in label from high-risk to low-risk being unlikely). On the other hand, a defendant initially labeled low-risk who offered unacceptable orientations was seen as jeopardizing that label in favor of one of the others. For example, a defendant with various characteristics of a low-risk defendant (university student, relatively wealthy background, no prior record) presented consistently unacceptable orientations. After the negotiations, the PO labeled the defendant as one whose risk of recidivism was problematic, based largely on his "bad attitude."

While POs and defendants negotiated the labels that the former attached to the latter, this was not accomplished directly. Rather, it was accomplished piecemeal by negotiating the individual components of that label. Consider the following example.

PO: Didn't the time that you spent a day in jail over the [shoplifting] thing have any impact on you when you decided to steal the motorcycle? Didn't you think about that at all? Did you think about what might happen if you got caught?

D: To be truthful, as far as I remember, I didn't even think about that.

PO: You didn't even consider it. Did you realize you can go to prison for four years?

D: I do now, yes.

PO: How does that feel?

D: I wouldn't want that to happen.

PO: Do you realize that's a possibility?

D: Yes.

PO: Was it worth it?

D: No, not at all.

On the surface level, the PO and the defendant were negotiating the latter's attitude toward the consequences of his offense. However, at the aggregate level of types of defendants, the PO's strategies functioned to say, "By saying this, you are claiming to be a high-risk defendant; if you are that type, how do you feel about this?" In most cases, POs closed the negotiations when they reached a point where they could accomplish an unambiguous labeling of the defendants which made sense, given their linking of the defendant's characteristics with those characteristics of the more general type which was being assigned to the case. As Cicourel (1978:28) argues, this linking or articulation is accomplished by using abductive reasoning, that is, the "... inferential step that occurs in first stating and then reflecting upon a hypothesis that would choose among several possible explanations of some set of facts."

CONCLUSIONS

My findings suggest three implications for future research on POs. First, I have argued that research on POs has failed to recognize the existence of a third set of factors—defendants' subjective orientations—in sentencing recommendations. My findings suggest that POs treat the components of this set of factors in ways qualitatively different from other sets of factors. They elicited these factors in different ways. These factors affected the impression the PO formed of the defendant. They also affected the particular sentencing recommendation made by the PO. A consideration of this set of factors is important for a full explanation of the outcome of this particular aspect of the criminal justice system.

Second, my findings point to the need for research on the interaction between POs and defendants. I believe that one of the reasons subjective orientations have been largely ignored in the past is that they are only directly accessible through a detailed analysis of this discourse between POs and defendants. When such factors as attitudes have been considered in previous research, they have been treated as stable entities rather than as entities subject to manipulation, as I have found. More generally, a lack of understanding about these negotiations leaves us with a lack of understanding about one of the crucial aspects of the *processes* involved in presentencing interviews.

Finally, my findings point to the need to include ethnographic data in studies of criminal justice processes. In this paper, I focused on both actual discourse processes as well as background ethnographic data. Much of my analysis would have been speculative had it not been for the insights I gained from detailed ethnographic information.[7] Knowledge of the categories POs use is crucial for understanding their actions and decisions concerning defendants and probationers, since these categories are involved in a process of typing in which POs subsume individual cases under more general categories.

NOTES

1. There are, of course, exceptions. For example, Cicourel (1968) empirically examined the routine practices of police and POs in the processing of juvenile cases. Prus and Stratton (1976) delineate a process model of how parole officers move from individual definitions to official action.

2. I excluded the juvenile division because of the high degree of confidentiality surrounding juvenile cases in the county. I would not have been allowed access to certain data, and POs anticipated some difficulty in obtaining consent from the juveniles' parents. Substance-abuse was excluded because its goals and focus (clinical evaluation and counseling) were distinct from the rest of the divisions' goals of sentencing recommendations and supervision. While this data would have been valuable for comparative analysis, the lack of sufficient time and other resources precluded such an expansion of the present study.

3. These two types of accounts, and two others (opportunistic and pathological), form a typology of accounts obtained by intersecting the types of factors with degree of intent. Thus, an opportunistic account involved motivating factors and no prior planning, while a pathological account was one in which defendants claimed the offense was due to causal factors but in which they engaged in prior planning. While these latter two types of accounts are logical possibilities, they rarely occurred in the data and, thus, were not particularly important for this study.

4. I am not aware of any research which addresses this issue. However, the POs held this view because unacceptable attitudes were common among defendants who were, or became, recidivists.

5. It should be noted that these negotiations were primarily invoked by POs when defendants expressed unreasonable or unacceptable orientations. When a defendant expressed an acceptable or reasonable orientation the need for negotiation on that point was precluded and the POs introduced another topic. The majority of strategies discussed below were used by POs in attempting to change (or assess the possibility of changing) defendants' orientations when they were deemed unacceptable.

6. Sudnow (1965) makes the same argument regarding public defenders and their processing of clients. He argues that the goal of their interactions with clients is an assessment of the applicability of characteristics of "normal crimes" with an instant case.

7. See Corsaro (1982) for a detailed discussion of the importance of ethnography in the analysis of discourse processes.

REFERENCES

Becker, Howard S. 1963. *Outsiders: Studies in the Sociology of Deviance.* New York: Free Press.

Bernstein, Ilene, William Kelly, and Patricia Doyle. 1977. "Social Reactions to Deviants: The Case of Criminal Defendants." *American Sociological Review* 42(5):743–755.

Bonger, Willem. 1916. *Criminality and Economic Conditions.* Translated by Henry P. Horton. Boston: Little, Brown.

Burke, Peter and Austin Turk. 1975. "Factors Affecting Post-arrest Dispositions: A Model for Analysis." *Social Problems* 22(3):313–332.

Carter, Robert. 1967. "The Presentence Report and the Decision-making Process." *Journal of Research in Crime and Delinquency* 4(2):203–211.

Chiricos, Theodore and Gordon Waldo. 1975. "Socioeconomic Status and Criminal Sentencing: An Empirical Assessment of a Conflict Proposition." *American Sociological Review* 40(6):753–772.

Cicourel, Aaron. 1968. The Social Organization of Juvenile Justice. New York: Wiley and Sons.

———. 1975. "Discourse and Text: Cognitive and Linguistic Processes in Studies of Social Structure."

Versus: Quaderni di studi Semiotica (September–December): 33–84.

———. 1978. "Language and Society: Cognitive, Cultural, and Linguistic Aspects of Language Use." *Social wissenschaftliche Annalen Band* 2, Seite B25–B58. Physica-Verlag, Wien.

———. 1980. "Three Models of Discourse Analysis: The Role of Social Structure." *Discourse Processes* 3(2):102–132.

Cloward, Richard, and Lloyd Ohlin. 1960. *Delinquency and Opportunity: A Theory of Delinquent Gangs.* Glencoe, Ill.: Free Press.

Corsaro, William. 1982. "Something Old and Something New: The Importance of Prior Ethnography in the Collection and Analysis of Audiovisual Data." *Sociological Methods and Research* 11(2):145–166.

Dembo, Richard. 1972. "Orientations and Activities of Parole Officers." *Criminology* 10(4):193–215.

Festinger, Leon. 1957. *A Theory of Cognitive Dissonance.* Evanston, Ill.: Row, Peterson.

Glaser, Barney and Anselm Strauss. 1967. *The Discovery of Grounded Theory.* Chicago: Aldine.

Gross, Seymour. 1967. "The Prehearing Juvenile Report: Probation Officers' Conceptions." *Journal of Research in Crime and Delinquency* 4(2):212–217.

Hagan, John. 1977. "Criminal Justice in Rural and Urban Communities: A Study of the Bureaucratization of Justice." *Social Forces* 55(3):597–612.

Lemert, Edwin. 1951. *Social Pathology.* New York: McGraw-Hill.

Merton, Robert. 1957. *Social Theory and Social Structure.* Glencoe, Ill.: Free Press.

Prus, Robert and John Stratton. 1976. "Parole Revocation Decision-making: Private Typings and Official Designations." *Federal Probation* 40(1):48–53.

Reed, John and Charles King. 1966. "Factors in the Decision-making of North Carolina Probation Officers." *Journal of Research in Crime and Delinquency* 3(2):120–128.

Schur, Edwin. 1971. *Labeling Deviant Behavior.* New York: Harper & Row.

Scott, Marvin and Stanford Lyman. 1968. "Accounts." *American Sociological Review* 33(1):46–62.

Sellin, Thorsten. 1938. *Culture, Conflict, and Crime.* New York: Social Science Research Council.

Sudnow, David. 1965. "Normal Crimes: Sociological Features of the Penal Code." *Social Problems* 12(3):255–276.

Tannenbaum, Frank. 1938. *Crime and the Community.* Boston: Ginn.

CHAPTER 8

THE EFFECTS OF CONTACT WITH CONTROL AGENTS

The careers of many deviants take them through correctional or treatment institutions. Some are arrested, charged, tried, sentenced, and sent to prison. Others are processed through a network of health and welfare agencies. Passage through such institutions can have both dramatic and subtle effects. Once it is known, for example, that a person has had contact with such institutions, other persons may regard that person as permanently suspect.

In the first reading D. L. Rosenhan shows the difficulty mental patients have in disproving the label of insanity. William Chambliss then shows that deviant labels are more often applied to lower-class than to middle-class adolescents and that this differential application markedly affects the life-chances of the adolescents. Richard Schwartz and Jerome Skolnick then show that prospective employers may discriminate against persons who have been accused of a crime, even though later found innocent; thus they illustrate how a deviant status may transcend time, organizational setting, and factual basis.

Being Sane in Insane Places

D. L. ROSENHAN

If sanity and insanity exist, how shall we know them?

The question is neither capricious nor itself insane. However much we may be personally convinced that we can tell the normal from the abnormal, the evidence is simply not compelling. It is commonplace, for example, to read about murder trials wherein eminent psychiatrists for the defense are contradicted by equally eminent psychiatrists for the prosecution on the matter of the defendant's sanity. More generally, there are a great deal of conflicting data on the reliability, utility, and meaning of such terms as "sanity," "insanity," "mental illness," and "schizophrenia" [1]. Finally, as early as 1934, Benedict suggested that normality and abnormality are not universal [2]. What is viewed as normal in one culture may be seen as quite aberrant in another. Thus, notions of normality and abnormality may not be quite as accurate as people believe they are.

To raise questions regarding normality and abnormality is in no way to question the fact that some behaviors are deviant or odd. Murder is deviant. So, too, are hallucinations. Nor does raising such questions deny the existence of the personal anguish that is often associated with "mental illness." Anxiety and depression exist. Psychological suffering exists. But normality and abnormality, sanity and insanity, and the diagnoses that flow from them may be less substantive than many believe them to be.

At its heart, the question of whether the sane can be distinguished from the insane (and whether degrees of insanity can be distinguished from each other) is a simple matter: do the salient characteristics that lead to diagnoses reside in the patients themselves or in the environments and contexts in which observers find them?...[T]he belief has been strong that patients present symptoms, that those symptoms can be categorized, and, implicitly, that the sane are distinguishable from the insane. More recently, however, this belief has been questioned.... [T]he view has grown that psychological categorization of mental illness is useless at best and downright harmful, misleading, and pejorative at worst. Psychiatric diagnoses, in this view, are in the minds of the observers and are not valid summaries of characteristics displayed by the observed [3–5].

Gains can be made in deciding which of these is more nearly accurate by getting normal people (that is, people who do not have, and have never suffered, symptoms of serious psychiatric disorders) admitted to psychiatric hospitals and then determining whether they were discovered to be sane and, if so, how. If the sanity of such pseudopatients were always detected, there would be prima facie evidence that a sane individual can be distinguished from the insane context in which he is found.... If, on the other hand, the sanity of the pseudopatients were never discovered, serious difficulties would arise for those who support traditional modes of psychiatric diagnosis. Given that the hospital staff was not incompetent, that the pseudopatient had been behaving as sanely as he had been outside of the hospital, and that it had never been previously suggested that he belonged in a psychiatric hospital, such an unlikely outcome would support the view that psychiatric diagnosis betrays little about the patient but much about the environment in which an observer finds him.

This article describes such an experiment. Eight sane people gained secret admission to 12 different hospitals [6]. Their diagnostic experiences constitute the data of the first part of this ar-

Reprinted from *Science*, Vol. 179 (January 1973), pp. 250–258, by permission of the publisher and author. Copyright 1973 by the American Association for the Advancement of Science.

ticle; the remainder is devoted to a description of their experiences in psychiatric institutions. . . .

PSEUDOPATIENTS AND THEIR SETTINGS

The eight pseudopatients were a varied group. One was a psychology graduate student in his 20's. The remaining seven were older and "established." Among them were three psychologists, a pediatrician, a psychiatrist, a painter, and a housewife. Three pseudopatients were women, five were men. All of them employed pseudonyms, lest their alleged diagnoses embarrass them later. Those who were in mental health professions alleged another occupation in order to avoid the special attentions that might be accorded by staff, as a matter of courtesy or caution, to ailing colleagues [7]. With the exception of myself (I was the first pseudopatient and my presence was known to the hospital administrator and chief psychologist and, so far as I can tell, them alone), the presence of pseudopatients and the nature of the research program was not known to the hospital staffs [8].

The settings were similarly varied. In order to generalize the findings, admission into a variety of hospitals was sought. The 12 hospitals in the sample were located in five different states on the East and West coasts. Some were old and shabby, some were quite new. Some were research-oriented, others not. Some had good staff-patient ratios, others were quite understaffed. Only one was a strictly private hospital. All of the others were supported by state or federal funds or, in one instance, by university funds.

After calling the hospital for an appointment, the pseudopatient arrived at the admissions office complaining that he had been hearing voices. Asked what the voices said, he replied that they were often unclear, but as far as he could tell they said "empty," "hollow," and "thud." The voices were unfamiliar and were of the same sex as the pseudopatient. . . .

Beyond alleging the symptoms and falsifying name, vocation, and employment, no further alterations of person, history, or circumstances were made. The significant events of the pseudopatient's life history were presented as they had actually occurred. Relationships with parents and siblings, with spouse and children, with people at work and in school, consistent with the aforementioned exceptions, were described as they were or had been. Frustrations and upsets were described along with joys and satisfactions. These facts are important to remember. If anything, they strongly biased the subsequent results in favor of detecting sanity, since none of their histories or current behaviors were seriously pathological in any way.

Immediately upon admission to the psychiatric ward, the pseudopatient ceased simulating *any* symptoms of abnormality. In some cases, there was a brief period of mild nervousness and anxiety, since none of the pseudopatients really believed that they would be admitted so easily. Indeed, their shared fear was that they would be immediately exposed as frauds and greatly embarrassed. Moreover, many of them had never visited a psychiatric ward; even those who had, nevertheless had some genuine fears about what might happen to them. Their nervousness, then, was quite appropriate to the novelty of the hospital setting, and it abated rapidly.

Apart from that short-lived nervousness, the pseudopatient behaved on the ward as he "normally" behaved. The pseudopatient spoke to patients and staff as he might ordinarily. Because there is uncommonly little to do on a psychiatric ward, he attempted to engage others in conversation. When asked by staff how he was feeling, he indicated that he was fine, that he no longer experienced symptoms. He responded to instructions from attendants, to calls for medication (which was not swallowed), and to dining-hall instructions. Beyond such activities as were available to him on the admissions ward, he spent his time writing down his observations about the ward, its patients, and the staff. Initially these notes were written "secretly," but as it soon became clear that no one much cared, they were subsequently written on standard tablets of paper in such public places as the dayroom. No secret was made of these activities.

The pseudopatient, very much as a true psychiatric patient, entered a hospital with no foreknowledge of when he would be discharged. Each was told that he would have to get out by his own devices, essentially by convincing the staff that he was sane. The psychological stresses associated with hospitalization were considerable, and all but one of the pseudopatients desired to be discharged almost immediately after being admitted. They were, therefore, motivated not only to behave sanely, but to be paragons of cooperation. That their behavior was in no way disruptive is confirmed by nursing reports, which have been obtained on most of the patients. These reports uniformly indicate that the patients were "friendly," "cooperative," and "exhibited no abnormal indications."

THE NORMAL ARE NOT DETECTABLY SANE

Despite their public "show" of sanity, the pseudopatients were never detected. Admitted, except in one case, with a diagnosis of schizophrenia [9], each was discharged with a diagnosis of schizophrenia "in remission." The label "in remission" should in no way be dismissed as a formality, for at no time during any hospitalization had any question been raised about any pseudopatient's simulation. Nor are there any indications in the hospital records that the pseudopatient's status was suspect. Rather, the evidence is strong that, once labeled schizophrenic, the pseudopatient was stuck with that label. If the pseudopatient was to be discharged, he must naturally be "in remission"; but he was not sane, nor, in the institution's view, had he ever been sane.

The uniform failure to recognize sanity cannot be attributed to the quality of the hospitals.... Nor can it be alleged that there was simply not enough time to observe the pseudopatients. Length of hospitalization ranged from 7 to 52 days, with an average of 19 days. The pseudopatients were not, in fact, carefully observed, but this failure clearly speaks more to traditions within psychiatric hospitals than to lack of opportunity.

Finally, it cannot be said that the failure to recognize the pseudopatients' sanity was due to the fact that they were not behaving sanely. While there was clearly some tension present in all of them, their daily visitors could detect no serious behavioral consequences—nor, indeed, could other patients. It was quite common for the patients to "detect" the pseudopatients' sanity.... "You're not crazy. You're a journalist, or a professor [referring to the continual note-taking]. You're checking up on the hospital." While most of the patients were reassured by the pseudopatient's insistence that he had been sick before he came in but was fine now, some continued to believe that the pseudopatient was sane throughout his hospitalization [10]. The fact that the patients often recognized normality when staff did not raises important questions.

Failure to detect sanity during the course of hospitalization may be due to the fact that ... physicians are more inclined to call a healthy person sick ... than a sick person healthy.... The reasons for this are not hard to find: it is clearly more dangerous to misdiagnose illness than health. Better to err on the side of caution, to suspect illness even among the healthy.

But what holds for medicine does not hold equally well for psychiatry. Medical illnesses, while unfortunate, are not commonly pejorative. Psychiatric diagnoses, on the contrary, carry with them personal, legal, and social stigmas [11]. It was therefore important to see whether the tendency toward diagnosing the sane insane could be reversed. The following experiment was arranged at a research and teaching hospital whose staff had heard these findings but doubted that such an error could occur in their hospital. The staff was informed that at some time during the following 3 months, one or more pseudopatients would attempt to be admitted into the psychiatric hospital. Each staff member was asked to rate each patient who presented himself at admissions or on the ward according to the likelihood that the patient was a pseudopatient....

Judgments were obtained on 193 patients who were admitted for psychiatric treatment. All staff who had had sustained contact with or primary responsibility for the patient—attendants, nurses, psychiatrists, physicians, and psychologists—were asked to make judgments. Forty-one patients were alleged, with high confidence, to be pseudopatients by at least one member of the staff. Twenty-three were considered suspect by at least one psychiatrist. Nineteen were suspected by one psychiatrist *and* one other staff member. Actually, no genuine pseudopatient (at least from my group) presented himself during this period.

The experiment is instructive. It indicates that the tendency to designate sane people as insane can be reversed when the stakes (in this case, prestige and diagnostic acumen) are high. But what can be said of the 19 people who were suspected of being "sane" by one psychiatrist and another staff member? Were these people truly "sane?"... There is no way of knowing. But one thing is certain: any diagnostic process that lends itself so readily to massive errors of this sort cannot be a very reliable one.

THE STICKINESS OF PSYCHODIAGNOSTIC LABELS

Beyond the tendency to call the healthy sick—a tendency that accounts better for diagnostic behavior on admission than it does for such behavior after a lengthy period of exposure—the data speak to the massive role of labeling in psychiatric assessment. Having once been labeled schizophrenic, there is nothing the pseudopatient can do to overcome the tag. The tag profoundly colors others' perceptions of him and his behavior.

From one viewpoint, these data are hardly surprising, for it has long been known that elements are given meaning by the context in which they occur.... Once a person is designated abnormal, all of his other behaviors and characteristics are colored by that label. Indeed, that label is so powerful that many of the pseudopatients' normal behaviors were overlooked entirely or profoundly misinterpreted. Some examples may clarify this issue.

Earlier I indicated that there were no changes in the pseudopatient's personal history and current status beyond those of name, employment, and, where necessary, vocation. Otherwise, a veridical description of personal history and circumstances was offered. Those circumstances were not psychotic. How were they made consonant with the diagnosis of psychosis? Or were those diagnoses modified in such a way as to bring them into accord with the circumstances of the pseudopatient's life, as described by him?

As far as I can determine, diagnoses were in no way affected by the relative health of the circumstances of a pseudopatient's life. Rather, the reverse occurred: the perception of his circumstances was shaped entirely by the diagnosis. A clear example of such translation is found in the case of a pseudopatient who had had a close relationship with his mother but was rather remote from his father during his early childhood. During adolescence and beyond, however, his father became a close friend, while his relationship with his mother cooled. His present relationship with his wife was characteristically close and warm. Apart from occasional angry exchanges, friction was minimal. The children had rarely been spanked. Surely there is nothing especially pathological about such a history.... Observe, however, how such a history was translated in the psychopathological context, this from the case summary prepared after the patient was discharged.

> This white 39-year-old male...manifests a long history of considerable ambivalence in close relationships, which began in early childhood. A warm relationship with his mother cools during his adolescence. A distant relationship to his father is described as becoming very intense. Affective stability is absent. His attempts to control emotionality with his wife and children are punctuated by angry outbursts and, in the case of the children, spankings. And while he says that he has several good friends, one senses considerable ambivalence embedded in those relationships also....

The facts of the case were unintentionally distorted by the staff to achieve consistency with a popular theory of the dynamics of a schizophrenic reaction [12]. Nothing of an ambivalent nature had been described in relations with parents, spouse, or friends.... Clearly, the meaning ascribed to his verbalizations (that is, ambivalence, affective instability) was determined by the diagnosis: schizophrenia. An entirely different meaning would have been ascribed if it were known that the man was "normal."

All pseudopatients took extensive notes publicly. Under ordinary circumstances, such behavior would have raised questions in the minds of observers, as, in fact, it did among patients. Indeed, it seemed so certain that the notes would elicit suspicion that elaborate precautions were taken to remove them from the ward each day. But the precautions proved needless. The closest any staff member came to questioning these notes occurred when one pseudopatient asked his physician what kind of medication he was receiving and began to write down the response. "You needn't write it," he was told gently. "If you have trouble remembering, just ask me again."

If no questions were asked of the pseudopatients, how was their writing interpreted? Nursing records for three patients indicate that the writing was seen as an aspect of their pathological behavior.... Given that the patient is in the hospital, he must be psychologically disturbed. And given that he is disturbed, continuous writing must be a behavioral manifestation of that disturbance, perhaps a subset of the compulsive behaviors that are sometimes correlated with schizophrenia.

One tacit characteristic of psychiatric diagnosis is that it locates the sources of aberration within the individual and only rarely within the complex of stimuli that surrounds him. Consequently, behaviors that are stimulated by the environment are commonly misattributed to the patient's disorder. For example, one kindly nurse found a pseudopatient pacing the long hospital corridors. "Nervous, Mr. X?" she asked. "No, bored," he said.

The notes kept by pseudopatients are full of patient behaviors that were misinterpreted by well-intentioned staff. Often enough, a patient would go "berserk" because he had, wittingly or unwittingly, been mistreated by, say, an attendant. A nurse coming upon the scene would rarely inquire even cursorily into the environmental stimuli of the patient's behavior. Rather, she assumed that his upset derived from his pathology, not from his present interactions with other staff members.... [N]ever were the staff found to assume that one of themselves or the structure of the hospital had anything to do with a patient's behavior. One psychiatrist pointed to a group of patients who were sitting outside the cafeteria entrance half an hour before lunchtime. To a group of young residents he indicated that such behavior was characteristic of the oral acquisitive nature of the syndrome. It seemed not to occur to him that there were very few things to anticipate in a psychiatric hospital besides eating.

A psychiatric label has a life and an influence of its own. Once the impression has been formed that the patient is schizophrenic, the expectation is that he will continue to be schizophrenic. When a sufficient amount of time has passed, during which the patient has done nothing bizarre, he is considered to be in remission and available for discharge. But the label endures beyond discharge, with the unconfirmed expectation that he will behave as a schizophrenic again. Such labels, conferred by mental health professionals, are as influential on the patient as they are on his relatives and friends, and it should not surprise anyone that the diagnosis acts on all of them as a self-fulfilling prophecy. Eventually, the patient himself accepts the diagnosis, with all of its surplus meanings and expectations, and behaves accordingly [5]. ...

POWERLESSNESS AND DEPERSONALIZATION

Eye contact and verbal contact reflect concern and individuation; their absence, avoidance and depersonalization. The data I have presented do not do justice to the rich daily encounters that grew up around matters of depersonalization and avoidance. I have records of patients who were beaten by staff for the sin of having initiated verbal contact. During my own experience, for example, one patient was beaten in the presence of other patients for having approached an attendant and told him, "I like you." Occasionally, punishment meted out to patients for misdemeanors seemed so excessive that it could not be justified by the most radical interpretations of psychiatric canon. Nevertheless, they appeared to go unquestioned. Tempers were often short. A patient who had not heard a call for medication would be roundly excoriated, and the morning attendants would often wake patients with, "Come on, you m----- f-----s, out of bed!"

Neither anecdotal nor "hard" data can convey the overwhelming sense of powerlessness which invades the individual as he is continually exposed to the depersonalization of the psychiatric hospital. . . .

Powerlessness was evident everywhere. The patient is deprived of many of his legal rights by dint of his psychiatric commitment [13]. He is shorn of credibility by virtue of his psychiatric label. His freedom of movement is restricted. He cannot initiate contact with the staff, but may only respond to such overtures as they make. Personal privacy is minimal. Patient quarters and possessions can be entered and examined by any staff member, for whatever reason. His personal history and anguish is available to any staff member (often including the "grey lady" and "candy striper" volunteer) who chooses to read his folder, regardless of their therapeutic relationship to him. His personal hygiene and waste evacuation are often monitored. The [toilets] may have no doors.

At times, depersonalization reached such proportions that pseudopatients had the sense that they were invisible, or at least unworthy of account. Upon being admitted, I and other pseudopatients took the initial physical examinations in a semipublic room, where staff members went about their own business as if we were not there.

On the ward, attendants delivered verbal and occasionally serious physical abuse to patients in the presence of other observing patients, some of whom (the pseudopatients) were writing it all down. Abusive behavior, on the other hand, terminated quite abruptly when other staff members were known to be coming. Staff are credible witnesses. Patients are not.

A nurse unbuttoned her uniform to adjust her brassiere in the presence of an entire ward of viewing men. One did not have the sense that she was being seductive. Rather, she didn't notice us. A group of staff persons might point to a patient in the dayroom and discuss him animatedly, as if he were not there.

One illuminating instance of depersonalization and invisibility occurred with regard to medications. All told, the pseudopatients were administered nearly 2100 pills. . . . Only two were swallowed. The rest were either pocketed or deposited in the toilet. The pseudopatients were not alone in this. Although I have no precise records on how many patients rejected their medications, the pseudopatients frequently found the medications of other patients in the toilet before they deposited their own. As long as they were cooperative, their behavior and the pseudopatients' own in this matter, as in other important matters, went unnoticed throughout.

Reactions to such depersonalization among pseudopatients were intense. Although they had come to the hospital as participant observers and were fully aware that they did not "belong," they nevertheless found themselves caught up in and fighting the process of depersonalization. . . .

THE CONSEQUENCES OF LABELING AND DEPERSONALIZATION

Whenever the ratio of what is known to what needs to be known approaches zero, we tend to invent "knowledge" and assume that we understand more than we actually do. We seem unable to acknowledge that we simply don't know. The needs for diagnosis and remediation of behavioral and emotional problems are enormous. But rather than acknowledge that we are just embarking on understanding, we continue to label patients "schizophrenic," "manic-depressive," and "insane," as if in those words we had captured the essence of understanding. The facts of the matter are that we have known for a long time that diagnoses are often not useful or reliable, but we have nevertheless continued to use them. We now know that we cannot distinguish insanity from sanity. It is depressing to consider how that information will be used.

Not merely depressing, but frightening. How many people, one wonders, are sane but not recognized as such in our psychiatric institutions? How many have been needlessly stripped of their privileges of citizenship, from the right to vote and drive to that of handling their own accounts? How many have feigned insanity in order to avoid the criminal consequences of their behavior, and, conversely, how many would rather stand trial than live interminably in a psychiatric hospital—but are wrongly thought to be mentally ill? How many have been stigmatized by well-intentioned, but nevertheless erroneous, diagnoses?. . . [P]sychiatric diagnoses are rarely found to be in error. The label sticks, a mark of inadequacy forever.

Finally, how many patients might be "sane" outside the psychiatric hospital but seem insane in it—not because craziness resides in them, as it were, but because they are responding to a bizarre setting, one that may be unique to institutions which harbor nether people? Goffman [4] calls the process of socialization to such institutions "mortification"—an apt metaphor that includes the processes of depersonalization that have been described here. And while it is impossible to know whether the pseudopatients' responses to these processes are characteristic of all inmates—they were, after all, not real patients—it is difficult to believe that these processes of socialization to a psychiatric hospital provide useful attitudes or habits of response for living in the "real world."

REFERENCES AND NOTES

1. P. Ash, *J. Abnorm. Soc. Psychol.* 44, 272 (1949); A. T. Beck, *Amer. J. Psychiat.* 119, 210 (1962); A. T. Boisen, *Psychiatry* 2, 233 (1938); N. Kreitman, *J. Ment. Sci.* 107, 876 (1961); N. Kreitman, P. Sainsbury, J. Morrisey, J. Towers, J. Scrivener, *ibid.,* p. 887; H. O. Schmitt and C. P. Fonda, *J. Abnorm. Soc. Psychol.* 52, 262 (1956); W. Seeman, *J. Nerv. Ment. Dis.* 118, 541 (1953). For an analysis of these artifacts and summaries of the disputes, see J. Zubin, *Annu. Rev. Psychol.* 18, 373 (1967); L. Phillips and J. G. Draguns, *ibid.,* 22, 447 (1971).

2. R. Benedict, *J. Gen. Psychol.* 10, 59 (1934).

3. See in this regard H. Becker, *Outsiders: Studies in the Sociology of Deviance* (Free Press, New York, 1963); B. M. Braginsky, D. D. Braginsky, K. Ring, *Methods of Madness: The Mental Hospital as a Last Resort* (Holt, Rinehart & Winston, New York, 1969); G. M. Crocetti and P. V. Lemkau, *Amer. Sociol. Rev.* 30, 577 (1965); E. Goffman, *Behavior in Public Places* (Free Press, New York, 1964); R. D. Laing, *The Divided Self: A Study of Sanity and Madness* (Quadrangle, Chicago, 1960); D. L. Phillips, *Amer. Sociol. Rev.* 28, 963 (1963); T. R. Sarbin, *Psychol. Today* 6, 18 (1972); E. Schur, *Amer. J. Sociol.* 75, 309 (1969); T. Szasz, *Law, Liberty and Psychiatry* (Macmillan, New York, 1963); *The Myth of Mental Illness: Foundations of a Theory of Mental Illness* (Hoeber Harper, New York, 1963). For a critique of some of these views, see W. R. Gove, *Amer. Sociol. Rev.* 35, 873 (1970).

4. E. Goffman, *Asylums* (Doubleday, Garden City, N.Y., 1961).

5. T. J. Scheff, *Being Mentally Ill: A Sociological Theory* (Aldine, Chicago, 1966).

6. Data from a ninth pseudopatient are not incorporated in this report because, although his sanity went undetected, he falsified aspects of his personal history, including his marital status and parental relationships. His experimental behaviors therefore were not identical to those of the other pseudopatients.

7. Beyond the personal difficulties that the pseudopatient is likely to experience in the hospital, there are legal and social ones that, combined, require considerable attention before entry. For example, once admitted to a psychiatric institution, it is difficult, if not impossible, to be discharged on short notice, state law to the contrary notwithstanding. I was not sensitive to these difficulties at the outset of the project, nor to the personal and situational emergencies that can arise, but later a writ of habeas corpus was prepared for each of the entering pseudopatients and an attorney was kept "on call" during every hospitalization. I am grateful to John Kaplan and

Robert Bartels for legal advice and assistance in these matters.

8. However distasteful such concealment is, it was a necessary first step to examining these questions. Without concealment, there would have been no way to know how valid these experiences were; nor was there any way of knowing whether whatever detections occurred were a tribute to the diagnostic acumen of the staff or to the hospital's rumor network. Obviously, since my concerns are general ones that cut across individual hospitals and staffs, I have respected their anonymity and have eliminated clues that might lead to their identification.

9. Interestingly, of the 12 admissions, 11 were diagnosed as schizophrenic and one, with the identical symptomatology, as manic-depressive psychosis. This diagnosis has a more favorable prognosis, and it was given by the only private hospital in our sample. On the relations between social class and psychiatric diagnosis, see A. B. Hollingshead and F. C. Redlich, *Social Class and Mental Illness: A Community Study* (Wiley, New York, 1958).

10. It is possible, of course, that patients have quite broad latitudes in diagnosis and therefore are inclined to call many people sane, even those whose behavior is patently aberrant. However, although we have no hard data on this matter, it was our distinct impression that this was not the case. In many instances, patients not only singled us out for attention, but came to imitate our behaviors and styles.

11. J. Cumming and E. Cumming, *Community Ment. Health* 1, 135 (1965); A. Farina and K. Ring, *J. Abnorm. Psychol.* 70, 47 (1965); H. E. Freeman and O. G. Simmons, *The Mental Patient Comes Home* (Wiley, New York, 1963); W. J. Johannsen, *Ment. Hygiene* 53, 218 (1969); A. S. Linsky, *Soc. Psychiat.* 5, 166 (1970).

12. For an example of a similar self-fulfilling prophecy, in this instance dealing with the "central" trait of intelligence, see R. Rosenthal and L. Jacobson, *Pygmalion in the Classroom* (Holt, Rinehart & Winston, New York, 1968).

13. D. B. Wexler and S. E. Scoville, *Ariz. Law Rev.* 13, 1 (1971).

The Saints and the Roughnecks

WILLIAM J. CHAMBLISS

Eight promising young men—children of good, stable, white upper-middle-class families, active in school affairs, good pre-college students—were some of the most delinquent boys at Hanibal High School. While community residents and parents knew that these boys occasionally sowed a few wild oats, they were totally unaware that sowing wild oats completely occupied the daily routine of these young men. The Saints were constantly occupied with truancy, drinking, wild driving, petty theft and vandalism. Yet not one was officially arrested for any misdeed during the two years I observed them.

Reprinted by permission of Transaction, Inc. from *Society*, Vol. 11, No. 1 (November/December 1973), pp. 24–31. Copyright © 1973 by Transaction, Inc.

This record was particularly surprising in light of my observations during the same two years of another gang of Hanibal High School students, six lower-class white boys known as the Roughnecks. The Roughnecks were constantly in trouble with police and community even though their rate of delinquency was about equal with that of the Saints. What was the cause of this disparity? The result? The following consideration of the activities, social class and community perceptions of both gangs may provide some answers.

THE SAINTS FROM MONDAY TO FRIDAY

The Saints' principal daily concern was with getting out of school as early as possible. The boys managed to get out of school with minimum danger that they would be accused of playing hookey through an elaborate procedure for obtaining "legitimate" release from class. The most common procedure was for one boy to obtain the release of another by fabricating a meeting of some committee, program or recognized club. Charles might raise his hand in his 9:00 chemistry class and ask to be excused—a euphemism for going to the bathroom. Charles would go to Ed's math class and inform the teacher that Ed was needed for a 9:30 rehearsal of the drama club play. The math teacher would recognize Ed and Charles as "good students" involved in numerous school activities and would permit Ed to leave at 9:30. Charles would return to his class, and Ed would go to Tom's English class to obtain his release. Tom would engineer Charles' escape. The strategy would continue until as many of the Saints as possible were freed. After a stealthy trip to the car (which had been parked in a strategic spot), the boys were off for a day of fun.

Over the two years I observed the Saints, this pattern was repeated nearly every day. There were variations on the theme, but in one form or another, the boys used this procedure for getting out of class and then off the school grounds. Rarely did all eight of the Saints manage to leave school at the same time. The average number avoiding school on the days I observed them was five.

Having escaped from the concrete corridors the boys usually went either to a pool hall on the other (lower-class) side of town or to a cafe in the suburbs. Both places were out of the way of people the boys were likely to know (family or school officials), and both provided a source of entertainment. The pool hall entertainment was the generally rough atmosphere, the occasional hustler, the sometimes drunk proprietor and, of course, the game of pool. The cafe's entertainment was provided by the owner. The boys would "accidentally" knock a glass on the floor or spill cola on the counter—not all the time, but enough to be sporting. They would also bend spoons, put salt in sugar bowls and generally tease whoever was working in the cafe. The owner had opened the cafe recently and was dependent on the boys' business which was, in fact, substantial since between the horsing around and the teasing they bought food and drinks.

THE SAINTS ON WEEKENDS

On weekends, the automobile was even more critical than during the week, for on weekends the Saints went to Big Town—a large city with a population of over a million, 25 miles from Hanibal. Every Friday and Saturday night most of the Saints would meet between 8:00 and 8:30 and would go into Big Town. Big Town activities included drinking heavily in taverns or nightclubs, driving drunkenly through the streets, and committing acts of vandalism and playing pranks.

By midnight on Fridays and Saturdays the Saints were usually thoroughly high, and one or two of them were often so drunk they had to be carried to the cars. Then the boys drove around town, calling obscenities to women and girls; occasionally trying (unsuccessfully so far as I could tell) to pick girls up; and driving recklessly through red lights and at high speeds with their lights out. Occasionally they played "chicken." One boy would climb out the back window of the car and across the roof to the driver's side of the car while the car was moving at high speed (between 40 and 50 miles an hour); then the driver would move over and the boy who had just crawled across the car roof would take the driver's seat.

Searching for "fair game" for a prank was the boys' principal activity after they left the tavern. The boys would drive alongside a foot patrolman and ask directions to some street. If the policeman leaned on the car in the course of answering the question, the driver would speed away, causing him to lose his balance. The Saints were careful to play this prank only in an area where they were not going to spend much time and where they could quickly disappear around a corner to avoid having their license plate number taken.

Construction sites and road repair areas were the special province of the Saints' mischief. A soon-to-be-repaired hole in the road inevitably invited the Saints to remove lanterns and wooden barricades and put them in the car, leaving the hole unprotected. The boys would find a safe vantage point and wait for an unsuspecting motorist to drive into the hole. Often, though not always, the boys would go up to the motorist and commiserate with him about the dreadful way the city protected its citizenry.

Leaving the scene of the open hole and the motorist, the boys would then go searching for an appropriate place to erect the stolen barricade. An "appropriate place" was often a spot on a highway near a curve in the road where the barricade would not be seen by an oncoming motorist. The boys would wait to watch an unsuspecting motorist attempt to stop and (usually) crash into the wooden barricade. With saintly bearing the boys might offer help and understanding.

A stolen lantern might well find its way onto the back of a police car or hang from a street lamp. Once a lantern served as a prop for a reenactment of the "midnight ride of Paul Revere" until the "play," which was taking place at 2:00 A.M. in the center of a main street of Big Town, was interrupted by a police car several blocks away. The boys ran, leaving the lanterns on the street, and managed to avoid being apprehended.

Abandoned houses, especially if they were located in out-of-the-way places, were fair game for destruction and spontaneous vandalism. The boys would break windows, remove furniture to the yard and tear it apart, urinate on the walls and scrawl obscenities inside.

Through all the pranks, drinking and reckless driving the boys managed miraculously to avoid being stopped by police. Only twice in two years was I aware that they had been stopped by a Big City policeman. Once was for speeding (which they did every time they drove whether they were drunk or sober), and the driver managed to convince the policeman that it was simply an error. The second time they were stopped they had just left a nightclub and were walking through an alley. Aaron stopped to urinate and the boys began making obscene remarks. A foot patrolman came into the alley, lectured the boys and sent them home. Before the boys got to the car one began talking in a loud voice again. The policeman, who had followed them down the alley, arrested this boy for disturbing the peace and took him to the police station where the other Saints gathered. After paying a $5.00 fine, and with the assurance that there would be no permanent record of the arrest, the boy was released.

The boys had a spirit of frivolity and fun about their escapades. They did not view what they were engaged in as "delinquency," though it surely was by any reasonable definition of that word. They simply viewed themselves as having a little fun and who, they would ask, was really hurt by it? The answer had to be no one, although this fact remains one of the most difficult things to explain about the gang's behavior. Unlikely though it seems, in two years of drinking, driving, carousing and vandalism no one was seriously injured as a result of the Saints' activities.

THE SAINTS IN SCHOOL

The Saints were highly successful in school. The average grade for the group was "B," with two of the boys having close to a straight "A" average. Almost all of the boys were popular and many of them held offices in the school. One of the boys was vice-president of the student body one year. Six of the boys played on athletic teams.

At the end of their senior year, the student body selected ten seniors for special recognition as the "school wheels"; four of the ten were Saints. Teachers and school officials saw no problem with any of these boys and anticipated that they would all "make something of themselves."

How the boys managed to maintain this impression is surprising in view of their actual behavior while in school. Their technique for covering truancy was so successful that teachers did not even realize that the boys were absent from school much of the time. Occasionally, of course, the system would backfire and then the boy was on his own. A boy who was caught would be most contrite, would plead guilty and ask for mercy. He inevitably got the mercy he sought.

Cheating on examinations was rampant, even to the point of orally communicating answers to exams as well as looking at one another's papers. Since none of the group studied, and since they were primarily dependent on one another for help, it is surprising that grades were so high. Teachers contributed to the deception in their admitted inclination to give these boys (and presumably others like them) the benefit of the doubt. When asked how the boys did in school, and when pressed on specific examinations, teachers might admit that they were disappointed in John's performance, but would quickly add that they "knew he was capable of doing better," so John was given a higher grade than he had actually earned. How often this happened is impossible to know. During the time that I observed the group, I never saw any of the boys take homework home. Teachers may have been "understanding" very regularly.

One exception to the gang's generally good performance was Jerry, who had a "C" average in his junior year, experienced disaster the next year and failed to graduate. Jerry had always been a little more nonchalant than the others about the liberties he took in school. Rather than wait for someone to come get him from class, he would offer his own excuse and leave. Although he probably did not miss any more classes than most of the others in the group, he did not take the requisite pains to cover his absences. Jerry was the only Saint whom I ever heard talk back to a teacher. Although teachers often called him a "cut up" or a "smart kid," they never referred to him as a troublemaker or as a kid headed for trouble. It seems likely, then, that Jerry's failure his senior year and his mediocre performance his junior year were consequences of his not playing the game the proper way (possibly because he was disturbed by

his parents' divorce). His teachers regarded him as "immature" and not quite ready to get out of high school.

THE POLICE AND THE SAINTS

The local police saw the Saints as good boys who were among the leaders of the youth in the community. Rarely, the boys might be stopped in town for speeding or for running a stop sign. When this happened the boys were always polite, contrite and pled for mercy. As in school, they received the mercy they asked for. None ever received a ticket or was taken into the precinct by the local police.

The situation in Big City, where the boys engaged in most of their delinquency, was only slightly different. The police there did not know the boys at all, although occasionally the boys were stopped by a patrolman. Once they were caught taking a lantern from a construction site. Another time they were stopped for running a stop sign, and on several occasions they were stopped for speeding. Their behavior was as before: contrite, polite and penitent. The urban police, like the local police, accepted their demeanor as sincere. More important, the urban police were convinced that these were good boys just out for a lark.

THE ROUGHNECKS

Hanibal townspeople never perceived the Saints' high level of delinquency. The Saints were good boys who just went in for an occasional prank. After all, they were well dressed, well mannered and had nice cars. The Roughnecks were a different story. Although the two gangs of boys were the same age, and both groups engaged in an equal amount of wild-oat sowing, everyone agreed that the not-so-well-dressed, not-so-well-mannered, not-so-rich boys were heading for trouble. Townspeople would say, "You can see the gang members at the drugstore night after night, leaning against the storefront (sometimes drunk) or slouching around inside buying cokes, reading magazines, and probably stealing old Mr. Wall blind. When they are outside and girls walk by, even respectable girls, these boys make suggestive remarks. Sometimes their remarks are downright lewd."

From the community's viewpoint, the real indication that these kids were in for trouble was that they were constantly involved with the police. Some of them had been picked up for stealing, mostly small stuff, of course, "but still it's stealing small stuff that leads to big time crimes." "Too bad," people said. "Too bad that these boys couldn't behave like the other kids in town; stay out of trouble, be polite to adults, and look to their future."

The community's impression of the degree to which this group of six boys (ranging in age from 16 to 19) engaged in delinquency was somewhat distorted. In some ways the gang was more delinquent than the community thought; in other ways they were less.

The fighting activities of the group were fairly readily and accurately perceived by almost everyone. At least once a month, the boys would get into some sort of fight, although most fights were scraps between members of the group or involved only one member of the group and some peripheral hanger-on. Only three times in the period of observation did the group fight together: once against a gang from across town, once against two blacks and once against a group of boys from another school. For the first two fights the group went out "looking for trouble"—and they found it both times. The third fight followed a football game and began spontaneously with an argument on the football field between one of the Roughnecks and a member of the opposition's football team.

Jack had a particular propensity for fighting and was involved in most of the brawls. He was a prime mover of the escalation of arguments into fights.

More serious than fighting, had the community been aware of it, was theft. Although almost everyone was aware that the boys occasionally stole things, they did not realize the extent of the activity. Petty stealing was a frequent event for the Roughnecks. Sometimes they stole as a group and coordinated their efforts; other times they stole in pairs. Rarely did they steal alone.

The thefts ranged from very small things like paperback books, comics and ballpoint pens to expensive items like watches. The nature of the thefts varied from time to time. The gang would go through a period of systematically lifting items from automobiles or school lockers. Types of thievery varied with the whim of the gang. Some forms of thievery were more profitable than others, but all thefts were for profit, not just thrills.

Roughnecks siphoned gasoline from cars as often as they had access to an automobile, which was not very often. Unlike the Saints, who owned their own cars, the Roughnecks would have to borrow their parents' cars, an event which occurred only eight or nine times a year. The boys claimed to have stolen cars for joy rides from time to time.

Ron committed the most serious of the group's offenses. With an unidentified associate the boy attempted to burglarize a gasoline station. Although this station had been robbed twice previously in the same month, Ron denied any involvement in either of the other thefts. When Ron and his accomplice approached the station, the owner was hiding in the bushes beside the station. He fired both barrels of a double-barreled shotgun at the boys. Ron was severely injured; the other boy ran away and was never caught. Though he remained in critical condition for several months, Ron finally recovered and served six months of the following year in reform school. Upon release from reform school, Ron was put back a grade in school, and began running around with a different gang of boys. The Roughnecks considered the new gang less delinquent than themselves, and during the following year Ron had no more trouble with the police.

The Roughnecks, then, engaged mainly in three types of delinquency: theft, drinking and fighting. Although community members perceived that this gang of kids was delinquent, they mistakenly believed that their illegal activities were primarily drinking, fighting and being a nuisance to passersby. Drinking was limited among the gang members, although it did occur, and theft was much more prevalent than anyone realized.

Drinking would doubtless have been more prevalent had the boys had ready access to liquor. Since they rarely had automobiles at their disposal, they could not travel very far, and the bars in town would not serve them. Most of the boys had little money, and this, too, inhibited their purchase of alcohol. Their major source of liquor was a local drunk who would buy them a fifth if they would give him enough extra to buy himself a pint of whiskey or a bottle of wine.

The community's perception of drinking as prevalent stemmed from the fact that it was the most obvious delinquency the boys engaged in. When one of the boys had been drinking, even a casual observer seeing him on the corner would suspect that he was high.

There was a high level of mutual distrust and dislike between the Roughnecks and the police. The boys felt very strongly that the police were unfair and corrupt. Some evidence existed that the boys were correct in their perception.

The main source of the boys' dislike for the police undoubtedly stemmed from the fact that the police would sporadically harass the group. From the standpoint of the boys, these acts of occasional enforcement of the law were whimsical and uncalled for. It made no sense to them, for example, that the police would come to the corner occasionally and threaten them with arrest for loitering when the night before the boys had been out siphoning gasoline from cars and the police had been nowhere in sight. To the boys, the police were stupid on the one hand, for not being where they should have been and catching the boys in a serious offense, and unfair on the other hand, for trumping up "loitering" charges against them.

From the viewpoint of the police, the situation was quite different. They knew, with all the confidence necessary to be a policeman, that these

boys were engaged in criminal activities. They knew this partly from occasionally catching them, mostly from circumstantial evidence ("the boys were around when those tires were slashed"), and partly because the police shared the view of the community in general that this was a bad bunch of boys. The best the police could hope to do was to be sensitive to the fact that these boys were engaged in illegal acts and arrest them whenever there was some evidence that they had been involved. Whether or not the boys had in fact committed a particular act in a particular way was not especially important. The police had a broader view: their job was to stamp out these kids' crimes; the tactics were not as important as the end result.

Over the period that the group was under observation, each member was arrested at least once. Several of the boys were arrested a number of times and spent at least one night in jail. While most were never taken to court, two of the boys were sentenced to six months' incarceration in boys' schools.

THE ROUGHNECKS IN SCHOOL

The Roughnecks' behavior in school was not particularly disruptive. During school hours they did not all hang around together, but tended instead to spend most of their time with one or two other members of the gang who were their special buddies. Although every member of the gang attempted to avoid school as much as possible, they were not particularly successful and most of them attended school with surprising regularity. They considered school a burden—something to be gotten through with a minimum of conflict. If they were "bugged" by a particular teacher, it could lead to trouble. One of the boys, Al, once threatened to beat up a teacher and, according to the other boys, the teacher hid under a desk to escape him.

Teachers saw the boys the way the general community did, as heading for trouble, as being uninterested in making something of themselves.

Some were also seen as being incapable of meeting the academic standards of the school. Most of the teachers expressed concern for this group of boys and were willing to pass them despite poor performance, in the belief that failing them would only aggravate the problem.

The group of boys had a grade point average just slightly above "C." No one in the group failed either grade, and no one had better than a "C" average. They were very consistent in their achievement or, at least, the teachers were consistent in their perception of the boys' achievement.

Two of the boys were good football players. Herb was acknowledged to be the best player in the school and Jack was almost as good. Both boys were criticized for their failure to abide by training rules, for refusing to come to practice as often as they should, and for not playing their best during practice. What they lacked in sportsmanship they made up for in skill, apparently, and played every game no matter how poorly they had performed in practice or how many practice sessions they had missed.

TWO QUESTIONS

Why did the community, the school and the police react to the Saints as though they were good, upstanding, nondelinquent youths with bright futures but to the Roughnecks as though they were tough, young criminals who were headed for trouble? Why did the Roughnecks and the Saints in fact have quite different careers after high school—careers which, by and large, lived up to the expectations of the community?

The most obvious explanation for the differences in the community's and law enforcement agencies' reactions to the two gangs is that one group of boys was "more delinquent" than the other. Which group *was* more delinquent? The answer to this question will determine in part how we explain the differential responses to these groups by the members of the community and, particularly, by law enforcement and school officials.

In sheer number of illegal acts, the Saints were the more delinquent. They were truant from school for at least part of the day almost every day of the week. In addition, their drinking and vandalism occurred with surprising regularity. The Roughnecks, in contrast, engaged sporadically in delinquent episodes. While these episodes were frequent, they certainly did not occur on a daily or even a weekly basis.

The difference in frequency of offenses was probably caused by the Roughnecks' inability to obtain liquor and to manipulate legitimate excuses from school. Since the Roughnecks had less money than the Saints, and teachers carefully supervised their school activities, the Roughnecks' hearts may have been as black as the Saints', but their misdeeds were not nearly as frequent.

There are really no clear-cut criteria by which to measure qualitative differences in antisocial behavior. The most important dimension of the difference is generally referred to as the "seriousness" of the offenses.

If seriousness encompasses the relative economic costs of delinquent acts, then some assessment can be made. The Roughnecks probably stole an average of about $5.00 worth of goods a week. Some weeks the figure was considerably higher, but these times must be balanced against long periods when almost nothing was stolen.

The Saints were more continuously engaged in delinquency but their acts were not for the most part costly to property. Only their vandalism and occasional theft of gasoline would so qualify. Perhaps once or twice a month they would siphon a tankful of gas. The other costly items were street signs, construction lanterns and the like. All of these acts combined probably did not quite average $5.00 a week, partly because much of the stolen equipment was abandoned and presumably could be recovered. The difference in cost of stolen property between the two groups was trivial, but the Roughnecks probably had a slightly more expensive set of activities than did the Saints.

Another meaning of seriousness is the potential threat of physical harm to members of the community and to the boys themselves. The Roughnecks were more prone to physical violence; they not only welcomed an opportunity to fight; they went seeking it. In addition, they fought among themselves frequently. Although the fighting never included deadly weapons, it was still a menace, however minor, to the physical safety of those involved.

The Saints never fought. They avoided physical conflict both inside and outside the group. At the same time, though, the Saints frequently endangered their own and other people's lives. They did so almost every time they drove a car, especially if they had been drinking. Sober, their driving was risky; under the influence of alcohol it was horrendous. In addition, the Saints endangered the lives of others with their pranks. Street excavations left unmarked were a very serious hazard.

Evaluating the relative seriousness of the two gangs' activities is difficult. The community reacted as though the behavior of the Roughnecks was a problem, and they reacted as though the behavior of the Saints was not. But the members of the community were ignorant of the array of delinquent acts that characterized the Saints' behavior. Although concerned citizens were unaware of much of the Roughnecks' behavior as well, they were much better informed about the Roughnecks' involvement in delinquency than they were about the Saints'.

VISIBILITY

Differential treatment of the two gangs resulted in part because one gang was infinitely more visible than the other. This differential visibility was a direct function of the economic standing of the families. The Saints had access to automobiles and were able to remove themselves from the sight of the community. In as routine a decision as to where to go to have a milkshake after school, the Saints stayed away from the mainstream of community life. Lacking transportation, the Roughnecks could not make it to the edge of town. The

center of town was the only practical place for them to meet since their homes were scattered throughout the town and any noncentral meeting place put an undue hardship on some members. Through necessity the Roughnecks congregated in a crowded area where everyone in the community passed frequently, including teachers and law enforcement officers. They could easily see the Roughnecks hanging around the drugstore.

The Roughnecks, of course, made themselves even more visible by making remarks to passersby and by occasionally getting into fights on the corner. Meanwhile, just as regularly, the Saints were either at the cafe on one edge of town or in the pool hall at the other edge of town. Without any particular realization that they were making themselves inconspicuous, the Saints were able to hide their time-wasting. Not only were they removed from the mainstream of traffic, but they were almost always inside a building.

On their escapades the Saints were also relatively invisible, since they left Hanibal and travelled to Big City. Here, too, they were mobile, roaming the city, rarely going to the same area twice.

DEMEANOR

To the notion of visibility must be added the difference in the responses of group members to outside intervention with their activities. If one of the Saints was confronted with an accusing policeman, even if he felt he was truly innocent of a wrongdoing, his demeanor was apologetic and penitent. A Roughneck's attitude was almost the polar opposite. When confronted with a threatening adult authority, even one who tried to be pleasant, the Roughneck's hostility and disdain were clearly observable. Sometimes he might attempt to put up a veneer of respect, but it was thin and was not accepted as sincere by the authority.

School was no different from the community at large. The Saints could manipulate the system by feigning compliance with the school norms. The availability of cars at school meant that once free from the immediate sight of the teacher, the boys could disappear rapidly. And this escape was well enough planned that no administrator or teacher was nearby when the boys left. A Roughneck who wished to escape for a few hours was in a bind. If it were possible to get free from class, downtown was still a mile away, and even if he arrived there, he was still very visible. Truancy for the Roughnecks meant almost certain detection, while the Saints enjoyed almost complete immunity from sanctions.

BIAS

Community members were not aware of the transgressions of the Saints. Even if the Saints had been less discreet, their favorite delinquencies would have been perceived as less serious than those of the Roughnecks.

In the eyes of the police and school officials, a boy who drinks in an alley and stands intoxicated on the street corner is committing a more serious offense than is a boy who drinks to inebriation in a nightclub or a tavern and drives around afterwards in a car. Similarly, a boy who steals a wallet from a store will be viewed as having committed a more serious offense than a boy who steals a lantern from a construction site.

Perceptual bias also operates with respect to the demeanor of the boys in the two groups when they are confronted by adults. It is not simply that adults dislike the posture affected by boys of the Roughneck ilk; more important is the conviction that the posture adopted by the Roughnecks is an indication of their devotion and commitment to deviance as a way of life. The posture becomes a cue, just as the type of the offense is a cue, to the degree to which the known transgressions are indicators of the youths' potential for other problems.

Visibility, demeanor and bias are surface variables which explain the day-to-day operations of the police. Why do these surface variables operate as they do? Why did the police choose to disregard the Saints' delinquencies while breathing down the backs of the Roughnecks?

The answer lies in the class structure of American society and the control of legal institutions by those at the top of the class structure. Obviously, no representative of the upper class drew up the operational chart for the police which led them to look in the ghettoes and on streetcorners—which led them to see the demeanor of lower-class youth as troublesome and that of upper-middle-class youth as tolerable. Rather, the procedures simply developed from experience—experience with irate and influential upper-middle-class parents insisting that their son's vandalism was simply a prank and his drunkenness only a momentary "sowing of wild oats"—experience with cooperative or indifferent, powerless, lower-class parents who acquiesced to the laws' definition of their son's behavior.

ADULT CAREERS OF THE SAINTS AND THE ROUGHNECKS

The community's confidence in the potential of the Saints and the Roughnecks apparently was justified. If anything, the community members underestimated the degree to which these youngsters would turn out "good" or "bad."

Seven of the eight members of the Saints went on to college immediately after high school. Five of the boys graduated from college in four years. The sixth one finished college after two years in the army, and the seventh spent four years in the air force before returning to college and receiving a B.A. degree. Of these seven college graduates, three went on for advanced degrees. One finished law school and is now active in state politics, one finished medical school and is practicing near Hanibal, and one boy is now working for a Ph.D. The other four college graduates entered submanagerial, managerial or executive training positions with larger firms.

The only Saint who did not complete college was Jerry. Jerry had failed to graduate from high school with the other Saints. During his second senior year, after the other Saints had gone on to college, Jerry began to hang around with what

several teachers described as a "rough crowd"—
the gang that was heir apparent to the Roughnecks. At the end of his second senior year, when
he did graduate from high school, Jerry took a job
as a used-car salesman, got married and quickly
had a child. Although he made several abortive
attempts to go to college by attending night
school, when I last saw him (ten years after high
school) Jerry was unemployed and had been living on unemployment for almost a year. His wife
worked as a waitress.

Some of the Roughnecks have lived up to
community expectations. A number of them were
headed for trouble. A few were not.

Jack and Herb were the athletes among the
Roughnecks and their athletic prowess paid off
handsomely. Both boys received unsolicited athletic scholarships to college. After Herb received
his scholarship (near the end of his senior year),
he apparently did an about-face. His demeanor became very similar to that of the Saints. Although
he remained a member in good standing of the
Roughnecks, he stopped participating in most activities and did not hang on the corner as often.

Jack did not change. If anything, he became
more prone to fighting. He even made excuses for
accepting the scholarship. He told the other gang
members that the school had guaranteed him a
"C" average if he would come to play football—
an idea that seems far-fetched, even in this day of
highly competitive recruiting.

During the summer after graduation from
high school, Jack attempted suicide by jumping
from a tall building. The jump would certainly
have killed most people trying it, but Jack survived. He entered college in the fall and played
four years of football. He and Herb graduated in
four years, and both are teaching and coaching in
high schools. They are married and have stable
families. If anything, Jack appears to have a more
prestigious position in the community than does
Herb, though both are well respected and secure
in their positions.

Two of the boys never finished high school.
Tommy left at the end of his junior year and went
to another state. That summer he was arrested and
placed on probation on a manslaughter charge.
Three years later he was arrested for murder; he
pleaded guilty to second degree murder and is
serving a 30-year sentence in the state penitentiary.

Al, the other boy who did not finish high
school, also left the state in his senior year. He is
serving a life sentence in a state penitentiary for
first degree murder.

Wes is a small-time gambler. He finished
high school and "bummed around." After several
years he made contact with a bookmaker who employed him as a runner. Later he acquired his own
area and has been working it ever since. His position among the bookmakers is almost identical to
the position he had in the gang; he is always
around but no one is really aware of him. He
makes no trouble and he does not get into any.
Steady, reliable, capable of keeping his mouth
closed, he plays the game by the rules, even
though the game is an illegal one.

That leaves only Ron. Some of his former
friends reported that they had heard he was "driving a truck up north," but no one could provide
any concrete information.

REINFORCEMENT

The community responded to the Roughnecks as
boys in trouble, and the boys agreed with that perception. Their pattern of deviancy was reinforced,
and breaking away from it became increasingly
unlikely. *Once the boys acquired an image of
themselves as deviants,* [italics added], they selected new friends who affirmed that self-image.
As that self-conception became more firmly en-
trenched, they also became willing to try new and
more extreme deviances. With their growing
alienation came freer expression of disrespect and
hostility for representatives of the legitimate society. This disrespect increased the community's
negativism, perpetuating the entire process of
commitment to deviance. Lack of a commitment
to deviance works the same way. In either case,
the process will perpetuate itself unless some

event (like a scholarship to college or a sudden failure) external to the established relationship intervenes. For two of the Roughnecks (Herb and Jack), receiving college athletic scholarships created new relations and culminated in a break with the established pattern of deviance. In the case of one of the Saints (Jerry), his parents' divorce and his failing to graduate from high school changed some of his other relations. Being held back in school for a year and losing his place among the Saints had sufficient impact on Jerry to alter his self-image and virtually to assure that he would not go on to college as his peers did. Although the experiments of life can rarely be reversed, it seems likely in view of the behavior of the other boys who did not enjoy this special treatment by the school that Jerry, too, would have "become something" had he graduated as anticipated. For Herb and Jack outside intervention worked to their advantage; for Jerry it was his undoing.

Selective perception and labelling—finding, processing and punishing some kinds of criminali-

ty and not others [italics added]—means that visible, poor, nonmobile, outspoken, undiplomatic "tough" kids will be noticed, whether their actions are seriously delinquent or not. Other kids, who have established a reputation for being bright (even though underachieving), disciplined and involved in respectable activities, who are mobile and monied, will be invisible when they deviate from sanctioned activities. They'll sew their wild oats—perhaps even wider and thicker than their lower-class cohorts—but they won't be noticed. When it's time to leave adolescence most will follow the expected path, settling into the ways of the middle class, remembering fondly the delinquent but unnoticed fling of their youth. The Roughnecks and others like them may turn around, too. It is more likely that their noticeable deviance will have been so reinforced by police and community that their lives will be effectively channelled into careers consistent with their adolescent background.

Legal Stigma

RICHARD D. SCHWARTZ and JEROME H. SKOLNICK

Legal thinking has moved increasingly toward a sociologically meaningful view of the legal system. Sanctions, in particular, have come to be regarded in functional terms.[1] In criminal law, for instance, sanctions are said to be designed to prevent recidivism by rehabilitating, restraining, or executing the offender. They are also said to deter others from the performance of similar acts and, sometimes, to provide a channel for the expression of retaliatory motives. In such civil actions as tort or contract, monetary awards may be intended

Reprinted from "Two Studies of Legal Stigma," *Social Problems,* Vol. 10 No. 2 (Fall 1962), pp. 133–38, by permission of the Society for the Study of Social Problems and the authors.

as retributive and deterrent, as in the use of punitive damages, or may be regarded as a *quid pro quo* to compensate the plaintiff for his wrongful loss.

While these goals comprise an integral part of the rationale of law, little is known about the extent to which they are fulfilled in practice. Lawmen do not as a rule make such studies, because their traditions and techniques are not designed for a systematic examination of the operation of the legal system in action, especially outside the courtroom. Thus, when extra-legal consequences—e.g., the social stigma of a prison sentence—are taken into account at all, it is through the discretionary actions of police, prosecutor, judge, and jury. Systematic information on a variety of unanticipated outcomes, those which benefit the accused as well as those which hurt him, might help to inform these decision makers and perhaps lead to changes in substantive law as well. The present paper is an attempt to study the consequences of stigma associated with legal accusation....

THE EFFECTS OF A CRIMINAL COURT RECORD ON THE EMPLOYMENT OPPORTUNITIES OF UNSKILLED WORKERS

In [a] field experiment, four employment folders were prepared, the same in all respects except for the criminal court record of the applicant. In all of the folders he was described as a thirty-two year old single male of unspecified race, with a high school training in mechanical trades, and a record of successive short term jobs as a kitchen helper, maintenance worker, and handyman. These characteristics are roughly typical of applicants for unskilled hotel jobs in the Catskill resort area of New York State where employment opportunities were tested.[2]

The four folders differed only in the applicant's reported record of criminal court involvement. The first folder indicated that the applicant had been convicted and sentenced for assault; the second, that he had been tried for assault and acquitted; the third, also tried for assault and acquitted, but with a letter from the judge certifying the finding of not guilty and reaffirming the legal presumption of innocence. The fourth folder made no mention of any criminal record.

A sample of one hundred employers was utilized. Each employer was assigned to one of four "treatment" groups.[3] To each employer only one folder was shown; this folder was one of the four kinds mentioned above, the selection of the folder being determined by the treatment group to which the potential employer was assigned. The employer was asked whether he could "use" the man described in the folder. To preserve the reality of the

situation and make it a true field experiment, employers were never given any indication that they were participating in an experiment. So far as they knew, a legitimate offer to work was being made in each showing of the folder by the "employment agent."

The experiment was designed to determine what employers would do in fact if confronted with an employment applicant with a criminal record. The questionnaire approach used in earlier studies[4] seemed ill-adapted to the problem since respondents confronted with hypothetical situations might be particularly prone to answer in what they considered a socially acceptable manner. The second alternative—studying job opportunities of individuals who had been involved with the law—would have made it very difficult to find comparable groups of applicants and potential employers. For these reasons, the field experiment reported here was utilized.

Some deception was involved in the study. The "employment agent"—the same individual in all hundred cases—was in fact a law student who was working in the Catskills during the summer of 1959 as an insurance adjuster. In representing himself as being both an adjuster and an employment agent, he was assuming a combination of roles which is not uncommon there. The adjuster role gave him an opportunity to introduce a single application for employment casually and naturally. To the extent that the experiment worked, however, it was inevitable that some employers should be led to believe that they had immediate prospects of filling a job opening. In those instances where an offer to hire was made, the "agent" called a few hours later to say that the applicant had taken another job. The field experimenter attempted in such instances to locate a satisfactory replacement by contacting an employment agency in the area. Because this procedure was used and since the jobs involved were of relatively minor consequence, we believe that the deception caused little economic harm.

As mentioned, each treatment group of twenty-five employers was approached with one type of folder. Responses were dichotomized: those who expressed a willingness to consider the applicant in any way were termed positive, those who made no response or who explicitly refused to consider the candidate were termed negative. Our results consist of comparisons between positive and negative responses, thus defined, for the treatment groups.

Of the twenty-five employers shown the "no record" folder, nine gave positive responses. Subject to reservations arising from chance variations in sampling, we take this as indicative of the "ceiling" of jobs available for this kind of applicant under the given field conditions. Positive responses by these employers may be compared with those in the other treatment groups to obtain an indication of job opportunities lost because of the various legal records.

Of the twenty-five employers approached with the "convict" folder, only one expressed interest in the applicant. This is a rather graphic indication of the effect which a criminal record may have on job opportunities. Care must be exercised, of course, in generalizing the conclusions to other settings. In this context, however, the criminal record made a major difference.

From a theoretical point of view, the finding leads toward the conclusion that conviction constitutes a powerful form of "status degradation"[5] which continues to operate after the time when, according to the generalized theory of justice underlying punishment in our society, the individual's "debt" has been paid. A record of conviction produces a durable if not permanent loss of status. For purposes of effective social control, this state of affairs may heighten the deterrent effect of conviction—though that remains to be established. Any such contribution to social control, however, must be balanced against the barriers imposed upon rehabilitation of the convict. If the exprisoner finds difficulty in securing menial kinds of legitimate work, further crime may become an increasingly attractive alternative.[6]

Another important finding of this study concerns the small number of positive responses elicited by the "accused but acquitted" applicant. Of the twenty-five employers approached with this folder, three offered jobs. Thus, the individual accused but acquitted of assault has almost as much trouble finding even an unskilled job as the one who was not only accused of the same offense, but also convicted.

From a theoretical point of view, this result indicates that permanent lowering of status is not limited to those explicitly singled out by being convicted of a crime. As an ideal outcome of American justice, criminal procedure is supposed to distinguish between the "guilty" and those who have been acquitted. Legally controlled consequences which follow the judgment are consistent with this purpose. Thus, the "guilty" are subject to fine and imprisonment, while those who are acquitted are immune from these sanctions. But deprivations may be imposed on the acquitted, both before and after victory in court. Before trial, legal rules either permit or require arrest and detention. The suspect may be faced with the expense of an attorney and a bail bond if he is to mitigate these limitations on his privacy and freedom. In addition, some pre-trial deprivations are imposed without formal legal permission. These may include coercive questioning, use of violence, and stigmatization. And, as this study indicates, some deprivations not under the direct control of the legal process may develop or persist after an official decision of acquittal has been made.

Thus two legal principles conflict in practice. On the one hand, "a man is innocent until proven guilty." On the other, the accused is systematically treated as guilty under the administration of criminal law until a functionary or official body—police, magistrate, prosecuting attorney or trial judge—decides that he is entitled to be free. Even then, the results of treating him as guilty persist and may lead to serious consequences.

The conflict could be eased by measures aimed at reducing the deprivations imposed on the accused, before and after acquittal. Some legal attention has been focused on pre-trial deprivations.

The provision of bail and counsel, the availability of habeas corpus, limitations on the admissibility of coerced confessions, and civil actions for false arrest are examples of measures aimed at protecting the rights of the accused before trial. Although these are often limited in effectiveness, especially for individuals of lower socioeconomic status, they at least represent some concern with implementing the presumption of innocence at the pretrial stage.

By contrast, the courts have done little toward alleviating the post-acquittal consequences of legal accusation. One effort along these lines has been employed in the federal courts, however. Where an individual has been accused and exonerated of a crime, he may petition the federal courts for a "Certificate of Innocence" certifying this fact.[7] Possession of such a document might be expected to alleviate post-acquittal deprivations.

Some indication of the effectiveness of such a measure is found in the responses of the final treatment group. Their folder, it will be recalled, contained information on the accusation and acquittal of the applicant, but also included a letter from the judge addressed "To whom it may concern" certifying the applicant's acquittal and reminding the reader of the presumption of innocence. Such a letter might have had a boomerang effect, by reemphasizing the legal involvement of the applicant. It was important, therefore, to determine empirically whether such a communication would improve or harm the chances of employment. Our findings indicate that it increased employment opportunities, since the letter folder elicited six positive responses. Even though this fell short of the nine responses to the "no record" folder, it doubled the number for the "accused but acquitted" and created a significantly greater number of job offers than those elicited by the convicted record. This suggests that the procedure merits consideration as a means of offsetting the occupational loss resulting from accusation. It should be noted, however, that repeated use of this device might reduce its effectiveness.

The results of the experiment are summarized in Table 1. The differences in outcome found there indicate that various types of legal records are systematically related to job opportunities. It seems fair to infer also that the trend of job losses corresponds with the apparent punitive intent of the authorities. Where the man is convicted, that intent is presumably greatest. It is less where he is accused but acquitted and still less where the court makes an effort to emphasize the absence of a finding of guilt. Nevertheless, where the difference in punitive intent is ideally greatest, between conviction and acquittal, the difference in occupational harm is very slight....

TABLE 1   Effect of Four Types of Legal Folder on Job Opportunities (in per cent)

	NO RECORD	ACQUITTED WITH LETTER	ACQUITTED WITHOUT LETTER	CONVICTED	TOTAL
	($N = 25$)	($N = 25$)	($N = 25$)	($N = 25$)	($N = 100$)
Positive response	36	24	12	4	19
Negative response	64	76	88	96	81
Total	100	100	100	100	100

NOTES

1. Legal sanctions are defined as changes in life conditions imposed through court action.

2. The generality of these results remains to be determined. The effects of criminal involvement in the Catskill area are probably diminished, however, by the temporary nature of employment, the generally poor qualifications of the work force, and the excess of demand over supply of unskilled labor there. Accordingly, the employment differences among the four treatment groups found in this study are likely, if anything to be *smaller* than would be expected in industries and areas where workers are more carefully selected.

3. Employers were not approached in pre-selected random order, due to a misunderstanding of instructions on the part of the law student who carried out the experiment during a three and one-half week period. Because of this flaw in the experimental procedure, the results should be treated with appropriate caution. Thus, chi-squared analysis may not properly be utilized. (For those used to this measure, $P < .05$ for Table 1.)

4. Sol Rubin, *Crime and Juvenile Delinquency,* New York: Oceana, 1958, pp. 151–56.

5. Harold Garfinkel, "Conditions of Successful Degradation Ceremonies," *American Journal of Sociology,* 61 (March, 1956), pp. 420–24.

6. Severe negative effects of conviction on employment opportunities have been noted by Sol Rubin, *Crime and Juvenile Delinquency,* New York: Oceana, 1958. A further source of employment difficulty is inherent in licensing statutes and security regulations which sometimes preclude convicts from being employed in their pre-conviction occupation or even in the trades which they may have acquired during imprisonment. These effects, may, however, be counteracted by bonding arrangement, prison associations, and publicity programs aimed at increasing confidence in, and sympathy for, exconvicts. See also, B. F. McSally, "Finding Jobs for Released Offenders," *Federal Probation,* 24 (June, 1960), pp. 12–17; Harold D. Lasswell and Richard C. Donnelly, "The Continuing Debate over Responsibility: An Introduction to Isolating the Condemnation Sanction," *Yale Law Journal,* 68 (April, 1959), pp. 869–99; Johs Andenaes, "General Prevention—Illusion or Reality?" *J. Criminal Law, Criminology and Police Science,* 43 (July–August, 1952), pp. 176–98.

7. 28 United States Code, Secs, 1495, 2513.

PART THREE

DEVIANT SUBCULTURES

Despite popular stereotype, deviant careers are not unilinear; nor do they have fixed and inevitable stages. Some people who commit deviant acts may never be typed as deviant and/or may discontinue those acts, while others may become "hard-core" career deviants. And even those who do become career deviants may do so through widely different routes. Thus there is no single natural history of deviant careers; there are many career histories. One hypothetical deviant career might proceed as follows. A person lives in a culture where certain acts are viewed as deviant. This person is believed, rightly or wrongly, to have committed such deviance. Someone (e.g., teacher, neighbor) types the person as a certain type of deviant. The person comes to the attention of an official agency (e.g., juvenile authorities) and becomes an official case. This social processing propels the person into organized deviant life (e.g., the person is now a "hoodlum"—ostracized by "good kids" and accepted only in disreputable circles). Finally, in self-redefinition, the person assumes the deviant role (i.e., actually becomes a "hood"), thus confirming the initial typing.

This, however, is only one developmental model. Another hypothetical deviant career (which is probably more characteristic of certain kinds of deviance such as professional crime) might proceed along opposite lines. First, the person defines himself or herself as a certain kind of deviant, then enters a deviant world to confirm that identity, comes to official notice, becomes an official case, and engages in more persistent and patterned deviations, thus reinforcing the system of social types. Still other types of deviant careers may require different models. In fact, deviant careers vary so widely that a person might enter the deviance process at any one of the various stages and move forward, backward, or out of the process completely.

Perhaps a visual image will help. Suppose we visualize deviant careers as a long corridor. Each segment of the corridor represents one stage in a deviant career, with doors that allow people to directly enter into or exit from that stage. Some people can enter the deviance corridor from a side door, without previous experience in a deviant career. Others can leave by a side door, thus terminating their deviant careers. Finally, there are some who will enter at one end of the corridor and proceed through all the stages to the other end. The diagram on page 246 shows how the traffic of deviance may flow.

The dotted lines represent the invisible boundaries marking stages of a person's deviant career. At each of these symbolic boundaries there are defining agents who speed certain people farther along the corridor and usher others out the side doors or back to where they started.

The rate and direction of a person's progress through the corridor are based largely on the person's responses to others' symbolic definitions of him or her. In addition to con-

The deviance corridor

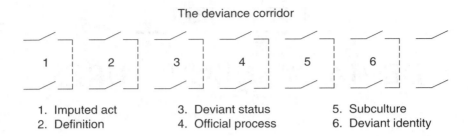

1. Imputed act   3. Deviant status   5. Subculture
2. Definition   4. Official process   6. Deviant identity

ventional people, those who type and respond to the deviant often include members of the deviant subculture; thus these people can be an important influence in solidifying a person's deviant career.

The fact that a person has been assigned a deviant label does not mean that s/he will automatically be drawn into a deviant subculture. Nonetheless, dilettantes in deviance and career deviants alike are likely to become involved with a deviant subculture at some time. Thus Part III of this book examines the rise and nature of deviant subcultures. It then goes on to examine how people enter deviant worlds, and how they learn subcultural traditions. Finally, it considers social variations within and among deviant subcultures.

THE RISE AND NATURE OF DEVIANT SUBCULTURES

A subculture is apt to come into being when people are in contact with one another, suffer a common fate, and have common interests. These common interests generally arise from their social situation and are shared because these people face more or less the same dilemma.

The general dilemma for the persons who ultimately become involved in deviant subcultures is that they want to continue activities that the society labels deviant but at the same time they want to avoid punishment. When enough people become aware that they share such a problem, a deviant subculture can arise to provide a solution.

When these people are especially concerned with continuing their activities, the deviant group forms on the basis of a common attraction; an example would be the gay subculture. When people are thrust together because of official typing, on the other hand, the deviant group forms on the basis of shared punishment; the prison subculture is one example. Finally, if it is merely by chance that the persons engage together in deviant activities, they do not actually form a subculture. Race riots provide an example.

ENTRY AND ACCULTURATION

Entry refers to the ways in which a person comes to participate in and gain admittance to a deviant subculture. *Acculturation* refers to the new ways and meanings a person acquires from that subculture. Entry can be clearly defined (where a person clearly is or is not a member of the subculture), or it can be rather loose in character. Likewise, acculturation can be highly specialized or casual and offhand. Like colleges, subcultures vary in how hard they are to get into and how hard they are to stay in. Much of this depends on the complexity of the activities involved, on how much commitment others in the subculture expect from newcomers, and on how much they must rely on them for their own safety and welfare. With a team of pickpockets, for example, entry and socialization are rigorous. On the other hand, admission and socialization to a Skid Row bottle gang are relatively simple. Here all a person needs is a few coins to "go in on a bottle," and there is relatively little to learn.

SUBCULTURAL VARIATIONS

Some deviants become highly involved in deviant subcultures, but this is not true for all deviants. Within a particular subculture (e.g., a youth subculture) some people may be highly immersed while others (e.g., weekend visitors) may participate only occasionally. Also, some forms of deviance lend themselves to more involvement in a subculture than do others. Because they have to be highly mobile, check forgers, for example, may be marginal to any kind of social group, conventional or deviant. Skid Row drunks, on the other hand, are freer to immerse themselves in a subculture. In addition, covert deviants (e.g., "closet queens") are generally less engulfed in an unconventional way of life and engage in the deviant subculture sporadically and secretly. Overt deviants (e.g., gay activists) ordinarily find themselves more involved in an unconventional way of life that stipulates a regular schedule of activities and a circle of intimate and deviant acquaintances.

Sanctions that deviants bring against one another are also important. Social control operates in deviant ways of life just as it does in the conventional world. How well do deviant groups control members? In general, it seems that in some subcultures (e.g., organized crime) members are subject to more social control than in others (e.g., the gay subculture). Also, it seems that within a subculture more social control is exerted over some members (e.g., a novice) than over others (e.g., a leader in the group).

Subcultures have beliefs, values, and norms that are supposed to regulate conduct. These prescriptions contribute to a form of social order. Deviant groups vary in the extent to which they organize their activities and define them by subcultural rules: some have elaborate rules that specify beliefs and actions; others have simpler codes. A simple, tightly organized code leads to one set of consequences, a complex, loosely organized code to another. In addition, some deviant subcultures have rules and beliefs that protect and dignify their members while others spawn normlessness, induce exploitation, and set deviants against one another.

Within a subculture some members show more commitment to the deviant way of life than do others. How dependent the person is on the deviant subculture, the person's identity, how much the person shares the viewpoints of others in the subculture—all these seem to be factors influencing a person's commitment to the subculture.

CHAPTER 9

THE RISE AND NATURE
OF DEVIANT SUBCULTURES

In most cases a so-called deviant is not unique or alone. There are often many other people who have been similarly typed; they may also have been similarly punished (e.g., imprisoned) for their alleged deviance and thus further differentiated from conventional society. If such people come into contact with one another, they may form their own subculture, thereby gaining acceptance and support. Also, when they are interested in continuing their "deviant ways," a subculture may arise to offer good opportunities for them to do so. These conditions and others discussed in the readings to follow, then, may lead to the rise of deviant subcultures.

In the first reading Earl Rubington points out that deviants develop through the process of social interaction a set of shared solutions to the various problems they face. This body of problem-solving devices—what they think and do—make up their subculture. In the second reading J. L. Simmons describes the sociological character of these groups. In the final reading Nancy Herman illustrates Simmons' points with research on ex-psychiatric patients.

Theory of Deviant Subcultures

EARL RUBINGTON

"Subculture," as a concept, has gained widespread currency in lay as well as sociological circles. Usually it refers to beliefs, values, and norms which are different from, yet supportive of, conventional traditions. Ethnic groups in the United States, who eat different foods, are bilingual, and dress differently, are examples. Beliefs, values, and norms shared by people who violate conventional traditions have come to be referred to as "deviant subcultures." Hippies, punks, Skid Row bums, and junkies are some examples of persons who are seen to be in deviant subcultures.

Three questions about deviant subcultures which sociologists have raised are: Under what social conditions do these subcultures come into existence? How do they function for those people who participate in them? And how do people who behave the same way yet are not in the subculture differ from those who are? Albert K. Cohen[1] has perhaps done the most to develop some systematic answers to such questions. We turn now to a brief exposition of his views.

Albert Cohen says that all behavior is problem-solving. The genesis of deviant subcultures follows from that general principle; that is, people in a given social situation face social-psychological problems of adjustment. Given an appropriate sequence of events, a subculture can emerge. The result of its emergence, of course, is that it provides a solution to the common problem experienced by all people in the situation. The reason why there aren't more subcultures, conventional or deviant, follows from a natural history model of how subcultures emerge.

As Cohen sees it, there are five stages in the development of a subculture: (1) experiencing a problem, (2) communicating about it with someone else in the same situation, (3) interacting on the basis of the problem, (4) developing a solution, and (5) sustaining and passing on the tradition.

Experiencing a problem is a necessary but not sufficient condition for the development of a subculture. Although people without problems are not likely to create and sustain a special subculture, experiencing a problem cannot lead to the emergence of a subculture if people do not talk about their common problem. If they do communicate with one another about their shared problem, then the chances of the next step (namely, that they will come to interact with one another on the basis of their shared problem) being taken become that much better. Out of this focused interaction, they come to forge a solution to their common problem. They apply their solution, it works, and soon a few others in the same situation join up with them. The last stage comes when they practice and pass on the tradition they have just developed.

According to Cohen (1955), the delinquent subculture emerged in the following way. First, working class youth came to sense difficulties in their competition for status in school. Their parents could not train them as well to compete for the middle class values the school distributed. A few of them began talking about the way they felt. Soon others came to express similar feelings. In the course of subsequent meetings, they focused in their interaction on their common fate. Unable to compete successfully for these values, they rejected them, turned them around, and became malicious, negativistic, and nonutilitarian. A few of them hit upon some joint activities that captured their imagination, such as breaking school windows after school was out. This activity only led to similar kinds of negativistic acts. It soon became a pattern, and after a while they found a number of recruits who wanted to join up with them and engage in similar activities. In effect, they invented a new game—juvenile delinquency—in which they were able to achieve status.

Critics argue that Cohen's theory requires all gang participants to respond to the same set of unconscious motives when they form a delinquent gang. Kitsuse and Dietrick (1959), for example, argue that a reactive theory of delinquent subculture formation is more plausible; that is, when working class youths engage in delinquent behavior, they are responding to an almost infinite variety of motives for participation. The sense of rejection and alienation from middle class values, they say, happens after these youths have been caught, punished, and stigmatized. The common fate they experience is that of being singled out and treated as deviants by their teachers and classmates. According to Kitsuse and Dietrick, the punitive reaction isolates them from middle-class values and their representatives in schools and thrusts them into the company of all the others who have been tarred with the same brush. The rejection of middle-class values follows from sharing the common fate of social punishment and becomes the basis for delinquent gang formation. Unlike Cohen, Kitsuse and Dietrick argue that the shared status problem has little to do with failure to compete for success and status in the school's social system. Rather, having now been defined as outsiders by the authorities, they react with group vengeance against their social punishment. These actions only trigger another acting out—social punishment cycle. In the interaction between authorities and youth, the delinquent subculture is born.

Whether the deviant subculture arises out of deviant motivation or in response to a process of social differentiation, Cohen's main point still holds. In either case, people who feel rejected, as well as people who have actually experienced rejection, have an acute problem of social-psychological adjustment. Under whatever conditions the deviant subculture emerges, people who share in it sustain it and live by it so long as it helps them to manage these problems.

A deviant subculture, then, consists of a body of shared solutions to the problems of social deviance. Three areas in which a variety of problems may develop include the act, partners, and the consequences of the act. A subculture of deviants of whatever kind will make available to its constituents ways of organizing and executing the deviant act, a set of rules of associating with one's partners in deviance, and some means for either avoiding or managing the consequences of deviance. The subculture of drug addicts provides a useful example (Rubington, 1967).

Once addicted, drug users require another shot some four hours after their last injection, if they are to avoid severe withdrawal symptoms. Awareness of this necessity generates a set of fairly regular activities. The cycle of activities the addict engages in includes obtaining a supply of drugs, having the drug experience, managing the aftermath, and then starting the cycle all over again. The cycle begins with a "hustle." This includes selling drugs, engaging in prostitution, and stealing goods and then fencing them for money. Once the addict has the price, the next step is to "cop" (obtain a supply of drugs). The third step is to find a "shooting gallery" (a place where one can take drugs in safety) and then "fix" (inject the dose). The fourth step is either "going on the nod" (falling asleep) or just "feeling normal." After a few hours, the cycle is reactivated, and the addict goes out to "hustle," "cop," and "fix" all over again.

At each juncture of the cycle, addicts go through all of the steps required before they can administer the needed dosage. In the process, there are always problems connected with obtaining drugs, interacting with an assortment of role-partners, and avoiding capture. Through the process of interaction with other addicts, they learn, share, and employ a set of collective solutions to every one of these problems, all of which are contingent on their status as drug addicts.

Addict subculture, learned in intimate interaction with other addicts, provides solutions to problems that arise at any of the phases of the addict's cycle of activities. Thus the behavior patterns center on the administration of drugs in order to obtain the desired drug experience. The norms specify rules for how to conduct oneself when in the company of other addicts, dealers, undercover agents, the police, and so on.... And the ideology contains justifications for the drug experience, along with a body of ideas about the social world of nonusers. In addition, it is the main repository of collective definitions of the range of situations in which addicts may expect to find themselves. In summary, then, the beliefs, values, and norms of the addict subculture provide information on how to think, feel, and act like an addict. This subculture affords to each of its participants answers to the central question of drug addiction: what to think, feel, say, and do while having drug experiences and coping with their social and psychological consequences.

Culture for deviants such as drug addicts is essentially the same as it is for conventional people. The main difference, of course, is that the content of deviant subcultures is illegal, immoral, or both. The content provides knowledge and skills on how to execute deviant activities and further the interests of those who engage in such activities. Because the activities are stigmatized, those who engage in them place themselves in opposition to the dominant culture. Their resistance to conventionality requires them to develop justifications for their activities. The ideology of the deviant subculture supplies these justifications. Without them, it is questionable whether these actions could continue, given the necessity that people understand the meaning of their own conduct.

The major difference between social deviants and solitary deviants is that social deviants draw upon a stock of collective solutions to the problems their deviance creates for them. By contrast, solitary deviants proceed by trial-and-error and fashion private solutions to the problems of deviance. Being a member of a group, albeit a deviant one, the social deviant experiences the benefits as well as the costs of group membership. As with all groups, however, the benefits of membership are contingent on the members paying the price of conformity. Considering the hazards attached to the situation of most social deviants, they are usually more than willing to pay this price. The group, as is the case with any group, prescribes norms for its members to follow. By adhering to the group's code of conduct, members satisfy their deviant motives.

Solitary deviants lack guidelines, not to mention social support. Lacking both a membership and a reference group of similarly situated other people, they also lack a set of consistent definitions for the range of unpredictable and hazardous situations in which they may become implicated. In these isolated circumstances, solitary deviants cannot achieve consensus about the meaning of their activities and how best to pursue their interest in deviance.

NOTE

1. Albert K. Cohen, *Delinquent Boys: The Culture of the Gang,* New York: The Free Press, 1955.

The Nature of Deviant Subcultures

J. L. SIMMONS

..."Deviant subculture" is a stripped-down scientific abstraction for a very real and concrete

From J. L. Simmons, *Deviants* (Berkeley, Calif.: The Glendessary Press, 1969), pp. 88–92. Copyright © 1969 by The Glendessary Press.

thing—most deviants live in connection with other deviants and "sympathizers," even if this be only half a dozen people in a little Midwestern town. And such subcultures evolve their own little communities or social worlds, each with its own local myths (the county attorney goes easy with us cause he's an old head himself), its own legendary heroes (remember Max—what a crazy one he was), its own honorary members (Blaine the druggist or Sophie at the cafe), its own scale of reputations (Garth's all right, he's just a little slow about some things), and its own social routine (probably see you at the Totem later on tonight).

The term is useful because it points to something important; deviants tend to get together. There are deviant traditions and ideologies, deviant prestige systems, commitment and conformity to deviant codes, deviant recruitment and missionary work, and deviant utopian dreams.

But the social scientists have also been taken in by their own word game. My conclusion from field research with two rural delinquent gangs, a health food coterie, two mystic groups, several beatnik and hippie groups, and various student fringe groups is that "deviant subcultures" are in actuality far from the tightly-knit, highly cohesive, clearly structured entities they are pictured to be in social science literature, police records, or the press. These misconceptions are projected onto what, in reality, is usually no more than a bunch of people with ever-shifting, over-lapping relationships. Such groups are amorphous and quite unstable through time. Goals and purposes, moral codes, and even memberships are often only semi-conscious. Commitment and loyalties to the group wax and wane, and they are seldom dependable. I recall the remark of a mischievous teenager in Cedar Rapids, Iowa: "I had no idea I belonged to a delinquent gang until the cops told me."

The notion of "deviant subcultures" therefore, is itself a stereotype which is partly true but also false in several important respects. Lewis Yablonsky's concept, "near-group"—a collectivity of people whose degree of cohesion and organization falls somewhere between a mob and a true group—applies, I think, far more accurately to the realities of deviants associating together. There are shared understandings among the participants, but their interpersonal relations are also shot through with many misunderstandings and miscarried intentions. Any "organization" is usually informal, uncrystallized and unstable beyond a few weeks.

With a few notable exceptions, such as the Hell's Angels, the commitment of the participants to one another and to the group as a whole is tenuous and half-hearted. For individual "members" it varies. On one occasion it may be an intense brotherhood; on the next the individuals may be willing to sell each other out to save themselves or to obtain some small personal gain. (Sometimes this personal gain may be no more than the undivided attention of a reporter or a bit of flattery from an investigator.)

Membership itself is often vague, and the line between "us" and "them" wavers and changes.... The dichotomy of members and non-members is oversimple; usually a few core members are unequivocally committed, a larger circle of part-time members drift back and forth between conventionality and deviance, and an even larger circle are only tangentially acquainted or involved. These last two circles, and sometimes even the few at the core, constantly move in and out of the subculture. They are occupied with a variety of conventional as well as deviant activities and commitments. Rather than being the essential part of their lives, the deviance may be only a casual weekend thing or the result of an occasional spree.

The supposed members are often not very clear in their own minds on what the group is about, who else is in it, and what it attempts to accomplish. And different members will give conflicting views on these matters.

Even leadership and other designations of functions are vague and constantly changing. Factionalism and incessant internal shifts in personal status are the rule rather than the exception. Internal statuses tend to be negotiated and temporary, so control of individual members by the group isn't really all that extensive.

These vagaries are why drug use or black radicalism or homosexuality can't be eradicated by dealing with the supposed leaders. There are eminent people in these and similar fringe movements but there is no "head to lop off." A teacher in one of the depressed schools of Wichita, Kansas, exclaimed after the assassination of Martin Luther King, "Good, that'll be the end of all this trouble and unrest." I could only feel sorry for her on various counts.

We mustn't, however, err in the opposite direction by suggesting that the whole subculture notion is false. A deviant's closer associates are statistically most likely to be other fringe people. There are discernible deviant social worlds, partially insulated and estranged from the society at large, each with its subterranean traditions, its own literature and slang, its own beliefs and ways of looking at things. All these things exist but in varying degrees, not as hard and fast characteristics.

The ambivalence of the participants is the main thing that keeps deviant subcultures from becoming more solid. Most members are of two minds about deviating and most of them still have many conventional commitments. My observations suggest that the vast majority of deviants inhabit dual worlds of deviance/conventionality and when things aren't going well in the one they turn to the other. They vacillate between the two as situations and opportunities shift....

A visible deviant group is the symptom and surface of some larger and more widespread fringe drift within the society. The Women's Christian Temperance Union, for instance, was only the organized spearhead of a Prohibition backlash against the perceived moral decline of urbanism—the Prohibition mood was felt by far more people than were members of this organization, and it spread beyond a fight against liquor into action against illicit drugs, sex, political liberalism and so on. Delinquent gangs were only the more spectacular aspects of the failure of the huge metropolis to take humane care of its inhabitants. The hippies are only the more far out examples of the pervasive unrest and disillusionment of a whole generation of youth with standard-brand America. And the Black Panthers are but a more vocal and visible swell on the surface of a deep militant thrust of twenty million blacks for a place in the sun.

Sometimes changes in these fringe drifts will leave particular deviant groups aground to flounder and finally expire for lack of underlying support. This seems to be the fate of the old Marxist radicals in the United States, younger radicals have gone beyond Communism as well as capitalism....

More often there is a number of different ... groups expressing a range of different positions in the fringe drift. Most such groups are more fleeting and unstable than the underlying deviant subcultural drift that spawned them. Wife-swapping clubs, sexual freedom leagues ... are only facets of the erotic revolution in our time.

Societal condemnation gives powerful support to the creation and continuation of those deviant groups. Even when the members don't altogether agree with or even like each other they are thrown together because they may have nowhere else to turn for help and support. But just about everything else is against them. Unlike conventional associations, deviant groups must solve their internal conflicts and problems without any supports from the larger society....

"Mixed Nutters," "Looney Tuners," and "Daffy Ducks"

NANCY J. HERMAN

In response to society's disapproval and harassment, deviants usually band together with others in the same plight. Beyond the ties of similar interests and views ... deviants find that establishing fairly stable relationships with other deviants does much to ease procurement and coping problems and to provide a more stable and reliable source of direct support and interaction. In these indirect ways, society's condemnation "creates" the deviant subculture (Simmons, 1969:88).

INTRODUCTION

This sociological study on subcultures of chronic ex-mental patients was stimulated by the observation that a wealth of sociological research has been conducted on such various deviant subcultures as: delinquent gangs (Cohen, 1979; Demotte, 1984; Yablonsky, 1959), the drug subculture (Burr, 1984; Johnson, 1980; Lipton and Johnson, 1980; Ray, 1961), the prison subculture (Webb, 1984), religious subcultures (Lofland, 1966; Melville, 1972; Shupe and Bromley, 1980), the skid row subculture (Rubington, 1968; Wallace, 1965), the motorcycle gang subculture (Hopper and Moore, 1993), and even the subculture of female impersonators (Tewksbury, 1995).

Despite the preponderance of sociological research on such diverse, deviant groups, and the concomitant theoretical approaches[1] used to explain such phenomena, no systematic research has centered on subcultures of ex-psychiatric patients.[2]

This is an expanded and updated version of Nancy J. Herman, "Mixed Nutters and Looney Tuners: The Emergence, Development, Nature and Functions of Two Informal, Deviant Subcultures of Chronic, Ex-psychiatric Patients," *Deviant Behavior* 8, 235–258, 1987. Reprinted with permission of the author.

Since the advent of the movement toward deinstitutionalization and development of community psychiatry, some thirty years ago, there has been a marked shift *away* from the hospital *to* the community.[3] As a result of the movement toward deinstitutionalization, hundreds of thousands of persons once institutionalized for long periods of time in mental hospitals in the United States, Canada, and Great Britain, have been released into the community. Moreover, with this shift in policy and treatment of the mentally ill, newly diagnosed or defined psychiatric patients are no longer being sent directly to the government or state institutions, but rather, are being treated primarily on an out-patient basis in community mental health centers or are admitted on a short-term basis to psychiatric wards in general hospital facilities, and are only admitted to mental institutions or "tertiary care facilities" as a last resort.

Further, what research has been conducted on discharged or deinstitutionalized psychiatric patients has been done largely from a psychiatric, social work, or psychological perspective.[4] With the exception of a few studies (Cheadle et al., 1978; Dear et al., 1980; Estroff, 1981; Reynolds and Farberow, 1977), little sociological research has focused on the effects of deinstitutionalization from the perspectives of the ex-patients themselves. No published work has documented the origins, development, and functions of informal deviant subcultures of chronic[5] ex-psychiatric patients.

It is the purpose of this paper, then, to fill such a void. Specifically, it seeks to examine the effects of deinstitutionalization from the perspectives of chronic discharged psychiatric patients, individuals who are directly affected by this shift in treatment, housing, and policies. Adopting a symbolic interactionist perspective, this study seeks to discover the social meanings that the ex-patients define and determine to be important and real. Specifically, this paper examines the ex-patient subculture[6]—one major organizational adaptive response former chronic ex-patients develop and utilize to deal with their "deviantness"—the structural and interactional factors giving rise to this formation, its characteristic traits, and the various functions it serves for its members.

METHODOLOGY, SAMPLE AND SETTINGS

For the purposes of this study, data were collected from December 1981 to June 1984, and from November 1987 to April 1990 largely by means of participant observation and informal interviewing with one hundred and thirty-nine chronic ex-psychiatric patients living in three large cities in southern Ontario, Canada, and in central Michigan.

In the case of the Canadian cohort, as part of a larger, ongoing study, the researcher initially obtained a disproportionate, stratified random sample[7] of two hundred and eighty-five chronic and non-chronic ex-psychiatric patients living in eight communities in southern Ontario. Through semiformal and informal interviewing with the respondents, this researcher came upon, quite by accident, the discovery of two informal ex-psychiatric patient subcultures, referred to here as the "Mixed Nutters" and "Looney Tuners."[8]

In terms of the Mixed Nutters, this cultural formation is comprised of forty-nine members (thirty-six males and thirteen females) living in rooming houses, boarding homes, and cheap hotels in the southwest section of a large metropolitan city of 2.5 million. Subjects ranged in age from twenty-one to forty-two, were predominantly from working-class backgrounds and were poorly educated, with a mean level of educational attainment being grade seven.

In terms of the Looney Tuners, this subculture is comprised of forty-eight members (twenty-six males and twenty-two females) living in boarding homes, rooming houses, in missions, or

simply on the streets in the northern section of a smaller city of 300,000 in southern Ontario. Similar to the Mixed Nutters, the Looney Tuners were also poorly educated with a mean level of educational attainment being grade eight, were from working and middle-class backgrounds, and ranged in age from twenty-two to forty-five. In terms of their "moral careers" as mental patients, the mean number of years that the Mixed Nutters and Looney Tuners were institutionalized was nine years. The mean number of occasions upon which such persons were institutionalized was seven.

The Daffy Duck subculture is an all-male group comprised of forty-two members. These individuals were living in downtown missions, rooming houses, flop hotels, on their own in one-room apartments, or simply on the streets of a large city of 250,000 in central Michigan. In terms of their psychiatric history, the mean number of years the Daffy Ducks were institutionalized was ten years and the mean number of occasions upon which they were hospitalized throughout their life was twelve. Unlike the Mixed Nutter and Looney Tuner groups, which were comprised almost exclusively by Caucasian members, the Daffy Ducks was made up of 75 percent African Americans, 15 percent Hispanics, and only 10 percent Caucasians.

THE EMERGENCE OF THREE INFORMAL EX-PSYCHIATRIC PATIENT SUBCULTURES

Early subcultural theorists (Gans, 1962; Gillen, 1955; Lewis, 1961) contended that deviant subcultures emerge largely in response to particular problems or social situations. Speaking on the subculture of poverty, Lewis (1961:27) argues that:

> *Many of the traits of the subculture of poverty can be viewed as attempts at local solutions for problems not met by existing institutions and agencies because the people are not eligible for them, cannot afford them, or are suspicious of them.*

In a similar vein, Gans (1962:248) argues:

> Each subculture is an organized set of related responses that has developed out of people's efforts to cope with the opportunities, incentives, and rewards, as well as the deprivations, prohibitions, and pressures which the natural environment and society—that complex of coexisting and competing subcultures—offer to them.

Reacting against this primary emphasis on *response* to the neglect of secondary role of *interaction* as having importance for the development of subcultures, other theorists (Becker, 1963; Cohen, 1955; Hughes, 1961; Shibutani, 1955; and Wallace, 1965), proposed an alternative explanation that places equal importance on *both* factors for subcultural development. Wallace (1965:149), speaking on the emergence of the skid row subculture, for example, states:

> One effect of the self and community imposed isolation [of skid row persons] has been the emergence of skid row subculture. Skid rowers share similar problems of adjustment to their deviance and are in effective interaction with one another.

Cohen (1955), in his systematic attempt to develop a theory of subcultures, states that the following conditions are important in the development of this cultural form: (1) experiencing a problem or set of problems; (2) communicating such problems; (3) effectively interacting over an extended period of time with like others on the basis of such problems; and (4) developing solutions to these common problems.

In the case of the Mixed Nutters, Looney Tuners, and Daffy Ducks, the data suggest that these ex-psychiatric patient subcultures emerged in 1978, 1980, and 1987 respectively.[9] Prior to their formation, chronic ex-psychiatric patients were experiencing a number of post-hospital problems. These problems included: abandonment; the stigma of mental illness; physical, mental, and sexual exploitation; social isolation; poverty; and coping. Speaking on the problems of isolation and poverty, a Mixed Nutter states:

> You think it's bad in the hospital but on the outside it's a lot worse. You're all alone in the world, no one gives a fucking damn; you're trying to survive on a few measly bucks a month and most goes to the landlord.... People in this society care more about their pets, what's going on in South Africa or the Middle East.... America has really let us mentals down!

A Daffy Duck, addressing the problems of the stigma of mental illness and sexual exploitation remarks:

> Mary [another patient] and I have a lot of problems on the outside.... The biggest ones center on people taking advantage of us sexually—I mean, the bosses of the boarding homes expect *you* to screw 'em. If you say no, they rough you up real bad and threaten to throw you out on the street—they also threaten to give you an OD of your meds. They have all the power—you have to do what they want. But where can we go; no one wants to take in a mental—your friends and so-called family all treat you like you've got AIDS!

The three ex-psychiatric patient subcultures studied originated when the individuals began communicating with one another and realizing that they had a number of problems in common, they shared a common fate of being "in the same boat." Commenting on her discovery of others experiencing the same problems in the community, Sally says:

> Nobody organized us or anything. We all just got together on a fluke. Each one of us, for a long time, thought we were the only ones going through the shit of being an ex-mental. But gradually we found out, by talking and bitching to a couple of others, that we were all in the "same leaky lifeboat" trying not to drown in the choppy sea of society.

Analysis of the data indicates that, subsequent to this initial communication of their problem(s) with others, individuals began interacting with one another over an extended period of time on the basis of their newly discovered shared fate:

> It wasn't like we started a formal club but we would first get together 'cause we realized that we

had this common bond—we all shared the same blight of humanity. We'd just get together once in a while and listen to other's problems and tribulations.... We gradually realized that we were benefitting and then decided to make it a twice a week thing at the Mall over in the Food Court Area.

Out of this semi-regular interaction with others of their own kind, chronic ex-psychiatric patients attempt to develop solutions to the various problems they are collectively experiencing. Three young male members of the Daffy Ducks, discussing their attempts to develop solutions to the problem of poverty, comment:

We first thought about pooling our money together and buying lotto tickets, but we realized that that would be a waste.... We moved to some thoughts about illegal activities.... B and E and even thought about carjacking.... In the end, we decided that these ventures were too dangerous, that we didn't have any experience, so we decided on collecting cans to add to our income and doing odd jobs for people and sometimes even playing our guitar in the park.

In short then, the data reveal that certain interactional and structural factors contribute to the rise of the ex-mental patient subculture. This subcultural formation arises essentially in response to the various problems and negative post-hospital situations collectively faced by a number of chronic ex-patients, insofar as they are able to effectively communicate and interact with one another over an extended period of time. Given that, upon discharge, these ex-psychiatric patients are "placed" in rooming houses, boarding homes, and "approved homes" in specific geographical sections of the city, such concentrated placement in specific neighborhoods increases the probability of social interaction among ex-patients. When ex-psychiatric patients have the opportunity to interact with one another, they are likely to develop a subculture to deal with such specific problems as abandonment, poverty, sexual, physical and emotional exploitation, stigma, social isolation, and in general, with problems developing out of the discrepancies between their personal perceptions of mental illness and mental patients and the stereotypical perceptions held by society.

THE SOCIAL CHARACTERISTICS OF THE MIXED NUTTERS, LOONEY TUNERS AND DAFFY DUCKS

As mentioned previously, chronic ex-psychiatric patients have one thing in common: their deviant attribute (and the problems associated with it). Such things give chronic ex-patients a sense of a common fate. It is from this feeling of a shared fate that the Mixed Nutters, Looney Tuners and Daffy Ducks have developed subcultures consisting of: a set of perspectives or world-view about the nature of society, its members, and how to deal with each other, and a set of activities based on this world-view, some of which are specifically centered on providing solutions to the problems associated with the attribute of mental illness. These deviant subcultures possess four major characteristics to which attention will now turn.

BEHAVIORAL PATTERNS

The ex-mental patient subculture generally focuses its attention, interests, and activities around their deviant attribute and the problems associated with it. Specifically, the Mixed Nutters and Looney Tuners participate in three major activities referred to by the subjects as: (1) "hanging around"; (2) "shrink sessions"; and (3) "schooling." The data indicate that a major portion of the chronic ex-patients' day is usually spent at a specified location such as a park, parking lot, at the riverfront, shopping mall, street corner, donut shop or hospital canteen:

Most of us live at the mission, in a boarding home and a couple of us live in the streets. If you live in one of those places, they got strict rules and we're kicked out early in the day...which leaves a lot of time to 'kill' before we can go back to eat or sleep.... So the guys and me meet up in the park and then we go to 'our table' at the mall and we kill five or six hours.

In a similar vein, a member of the Mixed Nutters, discussing the activity of "hanging around" remarks:

> There's three, four or sometimes even six of us that meet every day. It's not always the same crowd though. Each day, different faces show up at the Delicious Donut Shop.... It's our second home and that's why we do our hanging around there. We scrape up our money and drink coffee until we got no more left and Gus, the owner, "invites" us to leave.

In order to be allowed to "hang around" in such locations as donut shops or hospital canteens, it is a prerequisite that ex-patients purchase (and continue to purchase) food and/or drink. For those ex-patients unable to purchase items on their own, other group members make contributions, thus enabling them to remain with the others:

> 'Chipping in' is the name of the game.... Everyone in the group knows this...you give what you got, you ante up. If you don't got nothin' this time, maybe you will put in double next time. The group will let you ride and pull up the slack 'cause they know that you will come through for them when they are short of cash.

The activity of "hanging around" or being in the company of other ex-psychiatric patients serves to combat feelings of alienation, social isolation, and fear experienced by such persons. As one middle-aged Looney Tuner put it:

> It makes me feel a million times better when I meet up with the guys; it really lifts me up mentally.... I don't feel so alone.... They're my brothers and they'd do anything for me. I don't have to be scared when I'm with them.

Similarly, a second chronic ex-patient adds:

> We're a tight network of buddies, more like family than friends, out to help each other any way we can. We can count on them any time.... We can also learn from each other—how to combat people being shitty to us, our anxiety about being alone and things like that.

Another activity (somewhat related to the first) in which chronic ex-psychiatric patients frequently engage are "shrink sessions." Shrink sessions, or informal self-help meetings, usually occur (in the case of the Mixed Nutters) at the hospital canteen where ex-patients frequent, at a drop-in center for discharged patients (in the case of the Looney Tuners), or at the mall (in the case of the Daffy Ducks). Such meetings vary in duration from half an hour up to four hours with members coming and going throughout. The data indicate that the sessions begin when an individual initiates the topic of conversation and petitions others for advice. During these sessions, members of the subculture complain about such problems as fear, anxiety, stress, the stigma of mental illness, depression, deteriorating psychiatric conditions, poor follow-up care by psychiatric professionals, and the negative side-effects of their maintenance medications. During these sessions, some air such problems while other ex-patient "experts" supportively respond. Speaking of post-hospital anxiety and stress in his life and the helpful suggestions proposed by the group, one chronic male remarks:

> When we sit down and start "shrinking" each other, I sometimes talk about how tense and nervous I get being out [discharged]. Everything is moving at such a fast pace that it freaks me out. There's too much stress for me.... When I talked about it to the other guys, it felt so good to let it all out, and the guys really helped me get a handle on it.... They really know about these things, because, after all, they've been through it themselves a hundred times before.

Another ex-patient speaking of airing, to the group, the problems he was experiencing with respect to his deteriorating mental condition, drug side-effects, and his condemnation of the type of psychiatric aftercare (or lack thereof), states:

> It's real shitty.... I feel that I'm getting sicker each day...but where is my social worker. She's supposed to be assigned to me but I haven't seen her in months. The drugs they got me are dozing me

up—they make me so confused that I can't function—I'm like I'm moving in slow motion. The times that I've gone over the _____ Clinic (outpatient psychiatric facility), they tell me to get lost. Telling the group about these problems made me feel better, and they gave me some good advice on how to handle things.

These "shrink sessions," then, serve a three-fold function for the ex-psychiatric patients: (1) disclosure of concerns and complaints in a cathartic fashion serves to alleviate a portion of the burden of their loads; (2) ex-patients are given social support and helpful suggestions to deal with various problems; and (3) they are presented with an ideology and positive self-image of ex-psychiatric patients that refutes stereotypical beliefs about mental patients held by conventional society, thereby elevating their self-esteem.

Just as chronic ex-psychiatric patients frequently engage in the activities of "hanging around" and "shrink sessions," so too do they participate in one other activity referred to by the subjects as "schooling." Schooling involves ex-patients teaching each other various methods for "making it on the outside" or how to capitalize[10] on their deviant identities. By making it on the outside, ex-patients, through informal interaction with other subcultural members, learn how to make the most of their deviant identities. They are taught such things as: where, how, and when they can pick up "quick cash," or "free eats," the art of begging, and where to get a "free place to crash." So, for example, neophytes entering the ex-patient subculture are taught that they can pick up "quick cash" by selling their "meds" and their bodies for money (not only where to sell these commodities, but for how much), and they are given a set of rationalizations justifying such actions:

When I first started hanging around with those guys, they showed me the ropes. I was pretty green about things, and I never had any money. But they told me that if I ran short of bucks, I could pick up an extra twenty or fifty by selling my meds. They even pointed out this group of young boys who would be willing to buy the stuff.

Margo, a Mixed Nutter adds:

We're not prosties, we only sell ourselves when it's absolutely necessary. We don't turn tricks. It's only done when it's a matter of life and death, like getting some cash for food or to pay rent or for a place to sleep. Mavis and Flo was the ones who turned me on to the idea. They'd been doing it for five years. It's a way to survive out here.

Moreover, in the context of the ex-patient subculture, members learn which religious and social agencies give "hand-outs"—where such agencies are located, how much they may give, and how to approach them:

You learn from your friends how to go about getting what you want and which agencies is good for it, which want you to sign your life away, which want to "religicize" you or sign away your soul. These guys sure pointed me in the right direction to help me get what I need with no hassle.

Another chronic ex-patient, discussing the skills and knowledge about various agencies she acquired through interaction with others in the subculture, remarks:

If it wasn't for my friends, I would be out in the cold. I wouldn't know nothing about where to get a hand-out when I really needed it. They took me by the hand when I met them and pointed out each and every one of them in the area, and not only that, they teached me to dress poorly, muss up my hair and cry a lot when I went to them.

Further, ex-patients learn through participation in their subculture which agencies, missions, and restaurants provide such things as free food, clothing, and shelter:

At first, I didn't know nothing. But my friends taught me where I could get free food whenever I wanted it, like down at the Lakeside Mission. You gotta put up with their praying and singing, but that's O.K. They also showed me where to go to this church if I needed new threads and some lady will give you whatever you want.

Speaking on his major source of free food from one fast-food restaurant, a middle-aged male says:

Moe was the one who wised me up about the free eats from Burger Town. A couple of times the manager caught us snatching leftovers from the garbage and we told him how hungry we were and really laid it on thick to him. He felt sorry for us, I guess, so he told me to come back near closing and we get a lot of the hamburgers and fries that they don't sell.

Through participation in such groups as the Mixed Nutters, Looney Tuners, and Daffy Ducks, individuals not only learn the "ins and outs" of the system and how to use it to their advantage but also learn how to capitalize on their deviant identities by becoming "professional crazies":

Look, if you've got the curse of psychosis or manic depression, or even schizophrenia, I've learned that you might as well make the most of it.... I mean, you take advantage of what you've got.... So we often go right into the downtown area and beg for money. We tell 'em a sad tale—that we're mentally ill and need money for our treatment. Sometimes we hit the jackpot—like from decked-out businessmen or old ladies, especially if the cops don't chase us away.

A second ex-patient, speaking on the capitalization of his deviant identity says:

There are places where a mental can make a killing.... Like standing outside of St. Mark's right after Sunday services. People are usually in a charitable mood and if you approach them with the proper spiel about being a sick mental person, they will usually fork over a few bucks.

In short then, these three behavioral patterns serve to combat the social isolation ex-patients are experiencing, provide a therapeutic function, enhance their self-esteem, provide pragmatic solutions to various problems, and equip ex-patients with important knowledge and skills for "making it on the outside."

ARGOT

The Mixed Nutters, Looney Tuners, and Daffy Ducks communicate with their respective members by means of an argot, a distinctive vocabulary that demarcates not only outsiders from insiders but also neophytes from veterans. Speaking on the role of argot, one Mixed Nutter remarks:

Our way of rapping with each other is real cool. You can be in any public place and talking about whatever and nobody eavesdropping has a clue about what the hell you're saying.

In a similar vein, a member of the Daffy Ducks adds:

It's them against us. Having a special language all our own protects us.... You can clearly tell who is one of us and who isn't. You can test them by using a few code words. If they don't understand you, they ain't part of the group and are not to be trusted.

Moreover, their argot prescribes symbols for cognition and communication regarding matters of interest to chronic ex-psychiatric patients. So, for example, "shaking it" refers to the act of sexual solicitation; "plucking the rooster" refers to receiving hand-outs from clergy or social agency members; "going to a banquet" refers to individuals discovering a place giving out large amounts of free food; and "doing the groceries" refers to shop-lifting various foodstuffs.

In an effort to maintain some sense of order and stability, all social groups make evaluations of its members. So, for example, in the case of the Looney Tuners, at certain times, usually when "hanging around," members will talk about "cheapers," those ex-patients who violated the norm of reciprocity. So, too, do they speak about "dozers," those individuals who were caught committing a deviant act. The Mixed Nutters also refer to members being "turncoats" or "fruitcakes." The former term refers to those ex-patients who have violated norms of trust and confidentiality. The latter term refers to individuals with little common sense. Moreover, they use the terms "oldies" and "shit-kid" to make distinction between veterans and novices.

In their demarcation between themselves and outsiders, the Daffy Ducks use such terms as the "pigs" or "terminators," while the Mixed Nutters refer to outsiders as "Nazis"—individuals who reject or stigmatize them; the term "moron" refers to unacceptable ex-patients who do not meet the standards for acceptance into the group. Similarly, the Looney Tuners use such terms as "head shrinkers" and "cop patrols" to refer to psychiatric professionals and social workers respectively.

BOUNDARIES

Similar to other subcultural groups such as the nudist (Weinberg, 1966) and motorcycle gang (Hopper and Moore, 1993) subcultures, which have territorial boundaries, the data indicate that the ex-psychiatric patient subcultures also have sharply defined territorial boundaries, within which they carry out their daily rounds. In the case of the Looney Tuners, members live and carry out their daily activities in a territorial area of approximately 2.5 to 3.0 square miles. This territory contains a mixture of residential housing and commercial and service-oriented properties. The Mixed Nutters live and carry out their activities in a somewhat larger territorial area of approximately 3.0 to 4.0 square miles. This territory contains a mixture of commercial and service-oriented properties, residential housing, and some light industries. The Daffy Ducks, by contrast, have a still larger territorial area of approximately 5.5 square miles, consisting of commercial and service-oriented industries/businesses, low-rent housing, and many abandoned buildings.

During the five years this researcher studied these three groups, individuals rarely stepped outside their respective territories. The territories of these three subcultures essentially provide ex-patients with everything they need to "get by on." Remaining inside imaginary boundaries brings the world down to size and makes life more manageable for the ex-patients. The individuals come to know every inch of their territory—a knowledge that gives them a sense of security:

This is my world cut down to size. The guys and me know everything about it and everybody living there. There are no real surprises for me. You get to know it like the back of you hand, inside out.

IDEOLOGY

Similar to other deviant subcultures, the ex-psychiatric subcultures develop an ideology: a perspective on themselves and on their relations with other societal members, a set of ideas repudiating conventional, stereotypical attitudes about their deviant attribute, and a set of justifications for engaging in deviant/illegal activities.

The ideology of the Mixed Nutters, Looney Tuners and Daffy Ducks provides their members with a set of ideas about the mentally ill, about "normals" in society, and about the relations between the two groups. Normals are generally perceived as evil, cruel, untrustworthy, uncaring, dangerous, and unknowledgeable about mental illness, an ideology prescribing avoidance on the part of ex-patients. As one member of the Daffy Ducks puts it:

It's terrible to be mentally ill. The world doesn't care one iota about us. We're lumped in with the homeless, serial killers and druggies. Society is so mean to us—they're not kind and caring; they won't give us a break. They just want us to fall down and slip between one of those cracks and disappear from sight.

Moreover, the ideology of these ex-psychiatric patient subcultures refutes stereotypical perceptions about mental patients and mental illness generally held by conventional society. Members are provided with a set of excuses for their illnesses mitigating their blameworthiness,[11] thereby enabling ex-patients to redefine themselves in a more positive, although still deviant, light. According to one male Looney Tuner:

The group taught me that I'm not to blame for my illness. It was something genetic and I couldn't stop it. I am not responsible, therefore, I should not be ashamed or feel bad.

Similarly, a Mixed Nutter remarks:

My friend told me that I wasn't responsible for my situation. How could I be? It's not my own fault. . . . They helped me to see that my sickness was caused by others, and that's what I try to convince other [ex-patients] of. It makes them feel less guilt and really picks them up mentally.

Just as the ideology of the subculture provides ex-patients with ideas about normal others and a set of excuses holding others accountable for their deviant attribute, so too, does it function in one final respect: specifically, it provides members with a set of justifications for carrying out deviant/illegal acts. This self-justifying rationale then, furnishes ex-patients with "sound" reasons for engaging in such activities as prostitution, selling their medication, and shoplifting:

We're not doing anything that's really wrong. We don't murder or rob or things like that. We only take a few groceries once in a while from the A & P store. And we only do that when it's absolutely necessary. Other people who have lots of money do it all the time, and they take things much bigger than we do. We do it for medical reasons—our health, but they just do it for greed.

In a similar vein, another ex-patient discussing her rationale for engaging in prostitution, says:

The world is against us patients and we got to get by somehow. And we can't make ends meet on a disability pension. The boarding home takes most of the monthly cheque and we're only left with a few bucks for the whole month. There is nothing wrong with what we do. Most patients do it to survive. So, what the hell, we "work under the covers" once in a while. It's not that we do it for pleasure, it's necessary. No one will give me a "normal" job because of my sickness, so this is my only option. You look down the big streets and avenues and see lots of girls doing it anyway. It's just another way to make a buck!

In short then, the chronic ex-patients in this study develop and utilize an ideology: a set of ideas that suit their own interests, justify their post-hospital actions, and hold others accountable

for their mental illness. Moreover, this ideology contains a set of ideas and judgments about others in society and provides ex-patients with specific prescriptions for action.

SUMMARY AND DISCUSSION

The results of this study have indicated that this subcultural formation emerged when ex-patients began experiencing a number of problems (created by the deinstitutionalization of mental health services and societal attitudes toward the mentally ill), communicating such problems to other discharged chronic ex-patients, subsequently interacting with like others on the basis of their problems, and attempting to provide solutions to their difficulties. Ex-psychiatric patient subcultures were characterized by crystallized patterns of behavior centered around their social plights, a set of clearly defined norms and values, and an ideology: a set of ideas developed to suit their own interests and justify their actions.

Analysis of the data revealed that the ex-psychiatric patient subcultures provided a number of functions for their members. First, through subcultural participation, ex-patients established social relationships with understanding others—a relationship that was supportive in nature and served to combat feelings of fear and social isolation. Second, group activities, in particular "shrink sessions," allowed members to discuss problems of anxiety, stress, depression, stigma, and the like, and ask fellow group members for advice on how to deal with such problems. Through such "shrink sessions" ex-patients were able to disclose various concerns and dilemmas in a cathartic fashion; by so doing, they were able to alleviate a portion of the burden of their loads, thereby elevating their self-esteem. Moreover, in the context of their daily interactions, in general, and during "shrink sessions" specifically, fellow members provided "expert advice" and practical strategies for mitigating the stigma potential of mental illness on their daily rounds. Given that others in the subculture had experienced the stigma of mental illness on numerous occasions during the post-patient phase of their careers, such persons had indeed become "expert managers"—they had a great deal of advice on the "dos and don'ts" of avoiding stigma associated with their discreditable attribute. In the context of this subcultural formation, various stigma management strategies were imparted upon new charges. Third, in the context of participating in the ex-mental patient subcultures, members were provided with an ideology, a set of justifications or "sound" rationales about their deviant attribute. The ideology of the Mixed Nutters, Looney Tuners, and Daffy Ducks provided ex-patients with a set of rationalizations which mitigated their blameworthiness; instead, blame was placed upon various others, ranging from spouses, children, teachers, parents, to society, in general. By placing blame on others for their discreditable attribute, this enables ex-patients to redefine themselves in a more positive, although still deviant, light. Further, the ideology that normals were untrustworthy, callous, and uneducated about mental illness—an ideology that prescribed "avoidance of normals" to members of the subculture. Also, the ideology of the ex-patient subcultures furnished members with a self-justifying rationale for engaging in various deviant/illegal activities. Ex-patients, through subcultural participation, were provided with a set of "sound" reasons for engaging in such activities as selling drugs, shoplifting, and prostitution, enabling them to maintain positive self-images. A final function of the ex-psychiatric patient subcultures was that they provided members with various practical stratagems for "making formal sense," how to capitalize on their deviant identities, specifically, by selling their bodies, selling their medication, locations where to get "free eats" or a "free place to crash." In short, in the context of this subcultural form, individuals were taught how to make the most of their attributes by becoming "professional crazies."

This is not to say, however, that ex-psychiatric patients experienced only positive consequences from participation in the subcultures. In fact, on a number of occasions the author observed situations of conflict surrounding authority, verbal abuse among members, stolen wallets, tobacco, cigarettes and various articles of clothing. However, the positive consequences of subcultural participation far outweighed the negative effects:

> Overall, I think that this group has help(ed) me tremendously, but society is also threatened by people that group themselves together. This is what happened in our area. The neighborhood got up in arms, spit on us as we walked by, the kids threw garbage at us, and one of our guys, Frank, was found beaten to death in the alley.... That was a grim message that we weren't wanted.

According to the ideology behind the movement toward deinstitutionalization of mental health services, individuals would be released or discharged from the institution. However, "stone walls do not a prison make, nor iron bars a cage." Many chronic ex-psychiatric patients, even though discharged, remain imprisoned in a metaphorical sense with their guards and wardens being the family, friends, potential employers, and society in general who are unable to tolerate mental illness. The term, "deinstitutionalization" is defined by chronic ex-patients as a form of "social segregation and reinstitutionalization in *certain* areas in the community." Such persons are *in* but not *of* the community. Ex-patients, for the most part, are confined in "institutions without walls, bars or locks," living lives of frustration, disappointment, fear, exploitation, and poverty. In response to their undesirable social situations, these persons (similar to other stigmatized deviants in society), have developed and entered into deviant subcultures or "informal self-help groups"—an "expressive group exist[ing] primarily to furnish activities for members" (Gordon and Babchuk, 1959:25), including evading stigma.

NOTES

1. See Cloward and Ohlin (1964); Cohen (1955); Gorden (1964); Kitsuse and Dietrick (1959); Matza (1964); Sykes and Matza (1957); Wallace (1965); and Wolfgang and Ferracuti (1967).

2. See Anspach (1979)and Landy and Singer (1961) for discussions of *formal* social organizations for ex-mental patients.

3. For detailed discussions concerning the origins and development of the movement toward deinstitutionalization of psychiatric services, consult: Bassuk and Gerson (1978); Bellak (1964); Brown (1979); Chu and Trotter (1974); Herman (1986a); Leifer (1967); Ralph (1980); and Scull (1977).

4. For an extensive review of the body of literature which examines the ideological foundations, background philosophies, treatment programs, the medical and psychological consequences of such treatments, and the aftercare programs for discharged patients, the reader may consult Herman (1986a).

5. For the purposes of this study, the term "chronic" is defined *not* in diagnostic terms, i.e., "chronic schizophrenic"; rather it is defined in terms of duration, continuity and frequency of hospitalizations. Specifically, chronicity refers to those individuals institutionalized on a continual basis, or those institutionalized on five or more occasions.

6. Following Rubington (1982), the concept of deviant subculture is defined in this paper as: "the shared ways of thinking, feeling, and acting that members of a deviant group have developed for engaging in deviant behavior, organizing relations among themselves, and defending themselves against social punishment."

7. For specific details concerning the sample, consult Herman (1986a).

8. The names used here to refer to the three subcultures are pseudonyms that closely approximate the actual names that the groups call themselves.

9. In contrast to the Mixed Nutters who had been in existence for three years prior to the beginning of this research project, the researcher was able to directly follow the development of the Looney Tuners and Daffy Ducks shortly following their inception.

10. See Goffman (1963) and Scott (1969) for related discussions on the capitalization of the visually impaired.

11. See Sykes and Matza (1957) for a discussion of similar neutralizing techniques employed by juvenile delinquents.

REFERENCES

Anspach, Renee. 1975. "From Stigma to Identity Politics: Political Activism among the Physically Disabled and Former Mental Patients." *Social Science and Medicine* 13A: 765–773.

Bassuk, Ellen L., and Samuel Gerson. 1978. "Deinstitutionalization and Mental Health Services." *Scientific American* 238: 46–53.

Becker, Howard S. 1963. *Outsiders: Studies in the Sociology of Deviance.* New York: Free Press.

Bellak, Leopold. 1964. "Community Psychiatry: The Third Psychiatric Revolution." In L. Bellak (ed.), *Handbook of Community Psychiatry and Community Mental Health.* New York: Grune and Stratton.

Brown, Philip. 1979. "The Transfer to Care: U.S. Mental Health Policy Since World War II." *International Journal of Health Services* 9: 645–662.

Burr, Angela. 1984. "The Illicit Non-Pharmaceutical Heroin Market and Drug Scene in Kensington Market." *British Journal of Addiction* 79 (3): 337–343.

Cheadle, A. J., H. Freeman, and J. Korer. 1978. "Chronic Schizophrenics in the Community." *British Journal of Psychiatry* 132: 221–227.

Chu, F. D., and S. Trotter. 1974. *The Madness Establishment: Ralph Nader's Study Group Report on the National Institute of Mental Health.* New York: Grossman.

Cloward, R. A., and L. E. Ohlin. 1964. *Delinquency and Opportunity.* New York: Free Press.

Cohen, Albert. 1955. *Delinquent Boys.* Glencoe, Illinois: Free Press.

Cohen, Jere. 1979. "High-School Subcultures and the Adult World." *Adolescence* 14 (55): 491–502.

Dear, Michael, L. Bayne, G. Boyd, E. Callaghan, and E. Goldstein. 1980. *Coping in the Community: The Needs of Ex-Psychiatric Patients.* Mental Health Hamilton Project.

Demotte, Charles. 1984. "Conflicting Worlds of Meaning: Juvenile Delinquency in 19th Century Manchester." *Deviant Behavior* 5: 193–215.

Estroff, Sue E. 1981. *Making It Crazy: An Ethnography of Psychiatric Clients in an American Community."* Berkeley: University of California Press.

Gans, Herbert. 1962. *The Urban Villagers.* New York: Free Press.

Gillen, John. 1955. "National and Regional Cultural Values in the United States." *Social Forces* (Dec.): 110–115.

Goffman, Erving. 1963. *Stigma.* Englewood Cliffs, New Jersey: Prentice-Hall.

Gordon, C. Wayne, and Nicholas Babchuk. 1959. "A Typology of Voluntary Associations." *American Sociological Review* 24 (February): 22–29.

Gordon, Milton M. 1964. *Assimilation in American Life.* London: Oxford University Press.

Herman, Nancy J. 1993. "Return to Sender: The Reintegrative Stigma-Management Strategies of Ex-Psychiatric Patients." *Journal of Contemporary Ethnography* 22 (3): 295–330.

———. 1986a. *Crazies in the Community: An Ethnographic Study of Ex-Psychiatric Clients in Canadian Society.* Unpublished Ph.D, dissertation, McMaster University, Hamilton, Ontario, Canada.

———. 1986b. "The Chronically Mentally Ill in Canada." Pp. 111–123 in B. Havens and E. Rathbone-McCuan, eds., *The North American Elders: A Comparison of U.S. and Canadian Issues.* New Hampshire: Greenwood.

———. 1987. "Mixed Nutters and Looney Tuners: The Emergence, Development, Nature and Functions of Two Informal, Deviant Subcultures of Chronic, Ex-Psychiatric Patients." *Deviant Behavior* 8, 235–258.

Hopper, Columbus, and J. Moore. 1993. "Women in Outlaw Motorcycle Gangs." Pp. 389–400 in Patricia A. Adler and Peter Adler, *Constructions of Deviance.* Belmont, California: Wadsworth.

Hughes, Everett Cherington. 1961. *Students' Culture and Perspectives: Lectures on Medical and General Education.* Lawrence, Kansas: University of Kansas Law School.

Humphreys, L., and B. Miller. 1980. "Identities in the Emerging Gay Culture." In J. Marmor (ed.), *Homosexual Behavior: A Modern Reappraisal.* New York: Basic Books.

Irwin, John. 1970. *The Felon.* Englewood Cliffs, New Jersey: Prentice-Hall.

Johnson, Bruce. 1980. "Towards a Theory of Drug Subculture." Paper presented at the annual meetings of the Society for the Study of Social Problems.

Kitsuse, J. I., and D. C. Dietrick. 1959. "Delinquent Boys: A Critique." *American Sociological Review* 24: 213–215.

Leifer, Rod. 1959. "Community Psychiatry and Social Power." *Social Problems* 14: 16–22.

Lewis, Oscar. 1961. *The Children of Sanchez.* New York: Vintage Books.

Landy, David and Sara Singer. 1961. "The Social Organization and Culture of a Club for Former Mental Patients." *Human Relations* 14: 31–40.

Lipton, D. S., and B. D. Johnson. 1980. "Control at the Subcultural Interface: Heroin vs. Methadone." Paper presented at the annual meetings of the Society for the Study of Social Problems.

Lofland, John. 1966. *Doomsday Cult.* Englewood Cliffs, New Jersey: Prentice-Hall.

Matza, David. 1964. *Delinquency and Drift.* New York: Wiley.

Melville, K. 1972. *Communes in the Counter Culture.* New York: Morrow.

Partridge, W. L. 1973. *The Hippie Ghetto. The Natural History of a Subculture.* New York: Holt, Rinehart and Winston.

Platt, Stephen D. 1985. "A Subculture of Parasuicide?" *Human Relations* 38 (4): 257–297.

Ralph, Diana. 1980. "Where Did Community Psychiatry Come From? The Labour Theory of Community Psychiatry." Mimeo. University of Regina, Saskatchewan, Canada.

Ray, Marsh B. 1961. "Abstinence Cycles and Heroin Addicts." *Social Problems* 9: 132–140.

Reynolds, David K., and Norman Farberow. 1977. *Endangered Hope: Experiences in Psychiatric Aftercare Facilities.* Berkeley: University of California Press.

Rubington, Earl. 1968. "The Bottle Gang." *Quarterly Journal of Studies on Alcohol* 29: 943–955.

———. 1982. "Deviant Subcultures." In M. Michael Rosenberg, R. Stebbins, and A. Turowetz (eds.), *The Sociology of Deviance.* New York: St. Martin's, pp. 42–70.

Scott, Robert. 1969. *The Making of Blind Men: A Study of Adult Socialization.* New York: Russell Sage Foundation.

Scull, Andrew. 1977. *Decarceration: Community Treatment and the Deviant: A Radical View.* New Jersey: Prentice-Hall.

Shupe, Anson, and David Bromley. 1980. "Some Continuities in American Religion: Witches, Moonies and Accusations of Evil." In Thomas Robbins and Dick Anthony (eds.), *God We Trust: New Patterns of American Religious Pluralism.* New Jersey: Transaction.

Simmons, J. L. 1969. *Deviants.* Berkeley: The Glendessary Press.

Shibutani, Tamotsu. 1955. "Reference Groups as Perspectives." *American Journal of Sociology* (May): 565–566.

Sykes, G. M. and D. Matza. 1957. "Techniques of Neutralization: A Theory of Delinquency." *American Sociological Review* 22: 124–136.

Tewksbury, Richard. 1995. "Constructing Women and Their World: The Subculture of Female Impersonation." In Nancy J. Herman (ed.), *Creating Deviance*. Dix Hills, New York: General Hall.

Wallace, Samuel E. 1965. *Skid Row as a Way of Life*. New York: Harper Torchbook.

Webb, Gary. 1984. "The Inmate Subculture: A Case Study." Paper presented at the Western Social Science Association Meetings.

Weinberg, Martin S. 1966. "Becoming a Nudist." *Psychiatry: Journal for the Study of Interpersonal Processes* 29 (1): 15–24.

Wolfgang, Marvin, and Franco Ferracuti. 1967. *The Subculture of Violence*. London: Tavistock.

Yablonsky, Lewis. 1959. "The Delinquent Gang as a Near Group." *Social Problems* 7 (2): 108–117.

CHAPTER 10

GETTING INTO DEVIANT SUBCULTURES

Getting into deviant subcultures is rarely simple or automatic. People usually have to come into frequent contact with deviants and have some lengthy exposure to their traditions before gaining initial acceptance. In addition, factors that initially bring people into contact with deviants are often not the same ones that sustain that contact.

In the first reading Martin Weinberg deals with how people become nudists and how segmental that involvement remains. Next, Martin Sanchez Jankowski describes how joining a gang is a two-way process: young men seek membership for a variety of reasons while gangs recruit and offer incentives, or sometimes, force people to join when they are threatened by other gangs or are experiencing a decline in members. In the last reading John Lofland highlights the processes by which people gradually become converted to a religious cult.

Becoming a Nudist

MARTIN S. WEINBERG

In order to better understand deviant life-styles and the meanings they have for those engaged in them, it is often useful to conceptualize a lifestyle as a career, consisting of various stages. We can then study the interpersonal processes that draw and sustain people at each of these various stages. In this way, we can appreciate the motivations, perceptions, and experiences that characterize involvement in that way of life at various points in time—e.g., these may differ for novices, "veterans," etc.

Using such a career model, this paper deals with the interpersonal processes and phases involved in nudist camp membership. Specifically, it deals with the processes by which people come to contemplate a visit to a nudist camp, attend for the first time, and then continue attending over a period of time. The data come from three sources—101 interviews with nudists in the Chicago area; two successive summers of participant observation in nudist camps; and 617 mailed questionnaires completed by nudists located throughout the United States and Canada.[1]

PRENUDIST ATTITUDES TOWARD NUDISM

Most people seldom give much thought to the subject of nudism.[2] Responses in the interviews indicated that nudism is not a prominent object of thought even for many persons who will later become nudists. Thus when nudist members were

Reprinted by special permission of The William Alanson White Psychiatric Foundation, Inc., from *Psychiatry: Journal for the Study of Interpersonal Processes,* Vol. 29, No. 1 (February 1966), pp. 15–24. Copyright 1966 by The William Alanson White Psychiatric Foundation, Inc.

This investigation was supported in part by a Public Health Service fellowship (No. 7–F1–MH–14, 660–01A1 BEH) from the National Institute of Mental Health, and in part by contributions from Mr. O. B. E. and from the National Nudist Council.

asked what they had thought of nudism before visiting a camp, many stated that they had never really given it any thought. Until their initial experience, the interviewees' conceptions of nudism had been vague stereotypes, much like those held by the general public. In the words of a now active nudist:

> I never gave it too much thought. I thought it was a cult—a nut-eating, berry-chewing bunch of vegetarians, doing calisthenics all day, a gymno-physical society. I thought they were carrying health to an extreme, being egomaniacs about their body.

Many of those who had thought about the subject conceived of nudists' camps as more exclusive, luxurious, and expensive than they actually are. Others had different conceptions:

> I'm afraid I had the prevailing notion that they were undignified, untidy places populated (a) by the very poor, and (b) by languishing bleached blonds, and (c) by greasy, leering bachelors.

Table 1 sums up the attitudes that nudists reported themselves to have taken before their affiliation.

TABLE 1   Prenudist Attitudes Toward Nudism*

ATTITUDE	PERCENTAGE OF INTERVIEWEES
Positive	35
Live and let live	16
Negative	19
Very negative	1
Does not know	29

*For coding purposes, "positive" was defined as a desire to participate in nudism or to become a nudist. "Live and let live" included those who did not desire participation in nudism, but did not think ill of those who did participate; however, some of these respondents would have imposed social distance from nudists, and some would not.

THE INITIAL INTEREST IN NUDISM

If prenudist attitudes are of the nature indicated by Table 1, how does one become interested enough to make a first visit to a nudist camp? As shown in Table 2, the highest percentage of men mentioned magazines as the source of their interest, and the next largest source was other persons (exclusive of parents or parents-in-law). For women, the pattern was different; the highest percentage were first informed about nudism by their husbands. In 78 percent of the families, the husband had been more interested in visiting a camp. In all other cases both spouses had equally wanted to go. There were no cases in which the wife had wanted to go more than the husband.

The fact that the overwhelming majority of women became interested in nudism through their relationships with other people, rather than through the mass media which played such an important part with men, was reflected in the finding that interpersonal trust had to be sustained in order to evoke the women's interest.[3] This was indicated in the content of many interviews. The interviews also indicated that commonsense justifications and "derivations"[4] were important in overcoming the women's anxieties.

The following quotation is from an interview with a woman who became interested in nudism after being informed about it by a male friend. Here she was describing what her feelings would have been prior to that time. (In this quotation, as in others in this paper, *Q* is used to signify a neutral probe by the interviewer that follows the course of the last reply—such as "Could you tell me some more about that?" or "How's that?" or "What do you mean?" Other questions by the interviewer are given in full.)

...[Whether or not I would go to a nudist camp would] depend on who asked me. If a friend, I probably would have gone along with it.... [Q] If an acquaintance, I wouldn't have been interested. [Q] I don't know, I think it would depend on who was asking me to go. [Q] If it was someone you liked or had confidence in, you'd go along with it. If you didn't think they were morally upright you probably wouldn't have anything to do with it.

A man described how he had persuaded his wife to become interested in nudism:

I expected difficulty with my wife. I presented it to her in a wholesome manner. [Q] I had to convince her it was a wholesome thing, and that the people there were sincere.... [Q] That they were sincere in efforts to sunbathe together and had only good purposes in mind when they did that. [Q] All the things that nudism stands for: a healthy body and a cleansed mind by killing sex curiosities.

The anxieties that enter into the anticipation of public nudity were described in the following interview excerpts:

I was nervous.... [Q] It's different. It's not a daily practice.... I'm heavy, that added to the nervousness.

They said they were ashamed of their builds. They think everyone there is perfection. [Q] They think everyone will look at them.

He [a friend] said he'd never go, but that he could understand it. He saw nothing wrong in it. [Q] He said he wouldn't want other men looking at his wife.

Even though they had enough confidence to make the decision to visit a camp, the respondents did not necessarily anticipate becoming nudists themselves. For many the first trip was merely a joke, a lark, or a new experience, and the main motivation was curiosity. They visited the camp

TABLE 2   Source of Initial Interest in Nudism

SOURCE	MALE	FEMALE
Magazines	47%	14%
Movies	6	6
Newspapers	6	0
Spouse	0	47
Parents or parents-in-law	2	8
Other person	31	23
Medical advice from physician	0	2
Other source	8	0

as one might make a trip to the zoo, to see what it was like and what kind of characters would belong to such a group. There was also curiosity, on the part of many of the respondents, about seeing nude members of the opposite sex.

> The original thought was that we were going to see a bunch of nuts. It was a joke going out there.

> I thought they must be a little nutty. Eccentric. I didn't think there'd be so many normal people.... [Q] I felt that people that are nudists are a little bohemian or strange. [Q] I don't feel that way now. I thought we'd be the only sane people there. I thought it was kind of an adventure.... [Q] I like feeling I'm doing something unusual that no one knows about. It's a big secret.... [Q] The novelty, the excitement of driving up in the car; no one knew we were going....

Table 3 presents the motivations given by interviewees for their first trip to a nudist camp.

THE FIRST VISIT

The first trip to camp was frequently accompanied by extreme nervousness. Part of this might be attributed simply to the experience of entering a new group. The visitors did not know the patterns common to the group, and they were uncertain about their acceptance by group members. For example, a nudist said, referring to his participation in a nudist camp in which he was not well known:

> I guess I'm a little nervous when I get there, 'cause I'm not recognized as a member of the group.[5]

But, in the instance of a first visit to a nudist camp, this anxiety on entering a new group was considerably heightened by the unknown nature of the experience that lay ahead. Mead, in his discussion of the "social psychology of the act," has described how people, in planning an action, imaginatively rehearse it and its anticipated consequences.[6] The nudist camp, however, presents a totally unfamiliar situation; the person planning a visit has no past of similar situations, and usually no one has effectively described the situation to him in advance. This gap in effective imagination produces apprehension, anxiety, and nervousness.

> [On the trip up] I was very nervous. [Q] Because the idea was foreign. [Q]...The unknown factor. Just seeing a lot of people without clothes on is an unusual situation. Different or new experiences make one nervous.

> You're nervous and apprehensive. You don't know what to expect.... I was very nervous.... I thought of everything under the sun.... I didn't know what to expect.

> I felt a little inferior at first, because I had no knowledge of nudist camps.... I started to enjoy myself, but I couldn't quite feel comfortable. [Q] In the nude. In front of a lot of people. A lack of confidence, self-confidence. [Q] By not having a complete knowledge. I really didn't know what to expect.

> I was afraid of the unknown. I didn't know what to expect. If we had known nudists, I wouldn't have had those fears.

In most instances, the initial nervousness dissipated soon after the newcomer's arrival. Forty-six percent of the interviewees said that they were not nervous at all after arriving at camp. An additional 31 percent felt at ease in less than three hours. Thus most visitors adjusted rapidly to the nudist way of life. Seventy-one percent of those

TABLE 3 Motivations for the First Visit to a Nudist Camp

MOTIVATION	MALE	FEMALE
Curiosity over what it was like	33%	25%
Sexual curiosity	16	2
To satisfy spouse or relative	2	38
Combination of curiosity and to satisfy spouse	0	13
For relaxation	2	4
For health	12	6
To sunbathe	8	2
To make friends	6	0
Other	21	10

interviewed reported that *no* major adjustment was necessary. Sixteen percent of the residual group reported that undressing for the first time, or becoming used to being nude, was the only adjustment. Of these people who had to adjust, only 15 percent found the adjustment to be difficult.

> I really was afraid and shy and I didn't feel too well. We had discussed going, but when the time came to go I couldn't sleep that night.... Once we got nude then everything just seemed to come natural. I was surprised at how at ease I felt.

A variety of other response patterns, which I shall not discuss in detail, were characteristic of the initial visit. For example, one pattern related to the visitor's socioeconomic position.[7] Because facilities in many camps are relatively primitive, those used to more comfortable circumstances were likely to be disappointed. One professional man said:

> I was disappointed to see it was as rustic and unkempt as it was.... If people wore clothes and nothing else changed it would be a fourth-class resort. [Q] Everything there is shabby and not well cared for.

THE ADOPTION OF NUDISM AS A WAY OF LIFE

COACHING AND SOCIAL VALIDATION

The newcomers to camps received no formal indoctrination in the nudist perspective, but acquired it almost imperceptibly as the result of a subtle social process. Informal coaching, either prior to or after arrival, appears to have eased adjustment problems.[8]

> My husband said the men are gentlemen. He told me I'd have fun, like play in the sun, play games, and swim.

> She didn't want to undress.... [Q] I tried to talk to her and her husband did; she finally got convinced. [Q] I told her you feel better with them off, and that no one will pay any attention.

The consensus of 95 percent of the interviewees was that, as one of them put it, "Things run along very smoothly when you first become a nudist." Asked if they ever had any doubts that becoming a nudist was the right decision, once they had made up their minds, 77 percent reported that they had never had any doubts. Fourteen percent had doubts at the time of the interview. The following quotations illustrate the process of social validation that tends to quell doubts:[9]

> I do and I don't [have doubts], because of my religion. [Q] Nobody knows about it, and I wonder about that. [Q] Whether it's the right thing. But as I read the pamphlets [nudist literature] I realize it's up to the individual. God made Adam and Eve and they had no clothes. You don't have to be ashamed of your body. Some are fat and some are thin, but it doesn't matter; it's your personality that matters. I don't know, if my minister found out, I'd defend it. We don't use bad language. Sometimes I wonder, but down underneath I think it's all right. We've just been taught to hide our bodies. Sometimes I wonder, but then I think what the pamphlets say. [Q: At what time do you have these doubts?] When I'm in church. [Q] Yes, when I get to thinking about religion. Not very often. Sometimes I just wonder. [Q: Do you ever have these doubts while at camp?] No, I forget about everything. I'm having too much fun. I remind myself that this is something good for the children. My children won't become Peeping Toms or sex maniacs.

> [At first] I felt ridiculous. I thought all those people looked so funny. [Q: Why's that?] All your life you've seen people with their clothes on; now they all have them off. After a while, you feel ridiculous with your clothes on. [Q] I liked the people. They were all very nice. They came from nice families. It couldn't just be something anyone would do, or just people from a lower class.

The nudist way of life becomes a different reality, a new world:

> It seems like a different world from the world we live in every day. No washing, ironing, worries. You feel so free there. The people are friendly there, interested in each other. But not nosy. You can relax among them more easily than in the city.

And this new reality imposes a different meaning on the everyday life of the outside world:

> My daughter told us today the boys and girls don't sit together at school, but it makes no difference to her. Several times they're out playing and the boys get excited when they see their panties. My children don't understand that. They have a different state of mind toward different sexes.

MOTIVES FOR BECOMING A NUDIST

Persons who became nudists—that is, became members of a camp and conceived of themselves as nudists—usually demonstrated an autonomy of motives,[10] in the sense that their motives for doing so differed from their motives for first visiting a camp. That is to say, participation in different stages of the "nudist career" were usually characterized by different sets of motives. Hence the curiosity that had often been the overriding motive for initial visits was satisfied, and the incentive for affiliating with a nudist camp was based on the person's experiences at the camp, experiences which may not have been anticipated before visiting the camp.[11] It should be noted, however, that the decision was sometimes prompted by the owner's insistence that visitors join if they wished to return. As Table 4 shows, there was a considerable change, after the first visit, in the pattern of male versus female desire to attend the camp.

TABLE 4   Comparative Desires of Male and Female Members of Couples to Visit a Nudist Camp*

	MALE WANTED TO GO MORE	MALE AND FEMALE WANTED TO GO EQUALLY	FEMALE WANTED TO GO MORE
First visit	79%	21%	0%
Return visits	40	51	9

*Two unmarried couples are included in these data.

The following quotations are illustrative of the autonomous motives of respondents for the first and subsequent visits:

> [Q: What was your main reason for wanting to attend camp the first time?] Curiosity. [Q] To see how people behave under such circumstances, and maybe also looking at the girls. [Q] Just that it's interesting to see girls in the nude. [Q: What is the main reason you continue to attend?] I found it very relaxing. [Q] It's more comfortable to swim without a wet suit, and not wearing clothes when it's real warm is more comfortable and relaxing.

> [I went up the first time] to satisfy my husband. He wanted me to go and I fought it. But he does a lot for me, so why not do him a favor. [She had told him that people went to nudist camps only for thrills and that she would divorce him before she would go. Although he talked her into it, she cried all the way to camp. Asked why she continued to attend, she looked surprised and replied:] Why, because I thoroughly enjoy it!

This last quotation describes a common pattern for women, which appears also in the following recollection:

> [I went the first time] because my husband wanted me to go. [Q: What is the main reason that you continue to attend?] Because we had fun...and we met a lot of nice people.

The interviewees were asked what they liked most about nudism, with the results shown in Table 5. Three of the benefits cited are of special sociological interest—the concept of nudist freedom, the family-centered nature of the recreation, and the emphasis on friendliness and sociability.

"Freedom"

Echoing the nudist ideology, many respondents mentioned "freedom"—using the term in various contexts—as a major benefit. There were varied definitions of this freedom and its meaning for the participant. Some defined it in terms of free body action, of being unhindered by clothing.

TABLE 5 What Interviewees Liked Most About Nudism

	PERCENT OF SAMPLE MENTIONING THE ITEM
Friendliness, sociability	60%
Relaxation, getting away from the city	47
Enjoyment of outdoors and sports	36
Freedom	31
Sunbathing	26
Physical health	26
Children becoming informed about the human body	11
Mental health	8
Economical vacations	4
Family recreation, keeping family together	4
Seeing people nude	1
Other aspects	15

Nudism . . . gives me an opportunity to be in the sunshine and fresh air. Also to take a swim nude gives me free expression of body. [Q] I'm not hindered by clothes, a freedom of body movement and I can feel the water all over my body.

Nothing was binding; no socks, no tight belt, nothing clothing-wise touching me.

You don't have garter belts or bras. Your body can breathe.

With perspiration your clothes start to bind and you develop rashes. [Q] You just feel more relaxed when you're nude, and more comfortable from hot, sticky clothing.

Others interpreted freedom from clothing in a different way:

Freedom from a convention of society. It's a relief to get away from it. [Q] A physical relief in that wearing clothes is something you must do. I hate wearing a choking tie at a dinner party, but I have to because it is a society convention.

You don't have to dress appropriate for the occasion. You aren't looking for the smartest slacks and sports clothes.

The freedom. . . . You don't have to worry about the way you're dressed. You don't try to outdo someone with a thirty-dollar bathing suit.

For others, freedom meant the absence of routine and restraint:

A nudist camp has a lot more freedom [than a summer resort]. You do just as you want. . . . [Q] Just to do what you want to do, there is nothing you have to do. At a resort you have to participate in activities.

The freedom. [Q] You can do as you please. [Q] I can read or just lay in the sun.

The freedom. [Q] You can go any place you want in the camp. You can walk anywhere nude.

The range of conceptions of freedom is indicated by the following examples:

I felt free in the water. No one staring at you.

I like the complete freedom of . . . expression. With nudist people, I find them more frank and outspoken, not two-faced. You don't have to be cagey and worry about saying the wrong thing.

Feeling free with your body. [Q] I can't really explain it. Feeling more confident, I guess.

The varying constructions of nudist freedom support Schutz's model of man as a commonsense actor.[12] According to Schutz, man lives very naively in his world; clear and distinct experiences are mixed with vague conjectures, and "cookbook" descriptions of experiences are uncritically adopted from others. When these standard descriptions are vague, and are called into question—for example, by an interviewer who asks what is meant by "freedom"—a wide variety of constructions is elicited from respondents. Nudists, as devotees to a "cause," resemble other commonsense actors in their frequent inability to understand their stock answers critically.

Family Cohesion

As shown in Table 5, some respondents gave, as the feature of nudism they like most, its function in providing family recreation. One of the interview sample expressed this as follows:

> Nudism tends to keep the family together. In the nonnudist society the family tends to split into different organizations; all have different interests. You can still do different things in camp, but you still have a common interest. And all your plans are made together.

One would expect that nudism would lead to family cohesiveness, as a result of this common interest, and also as a result of a tendency for the family members to conceal their nudist involvements in their dealings with the outside world. In regard to the element of secrecy, Simmel has pointed out how a group's intensified seclusion results in heightened cohesiveness.[13] Participation in nudism did not, however, always lead to increased family cohesiveness. For example, if one spouse did not appreciate the experience, the family's continued participation resulted in increased strain. And although nudist ideology claims that nudist participation brings the family closer together, 78 percent of the interviewees, and 82 percent of the questionnaire respondents, reported no change in their family relationships.

Relationships with Others

Friendliness and sociability were the characteristics of the nudist experience mentioned most often by interviewees. In addition, nudists extended the concept of "family" to include fellow nudists; they cited a "togetherness" that is rare in the clothed society. Some insight into this cohesiveness was displayed in the following remarks by an interviewee:

> Camaraderie and congeniality...comes in any minority group that supports an unpopular position. [Q] Feelings develop by these in-groups because you are brought together by one idea which you share. On the street you may run into people you share no ideas with.

The interviewees were asked how the camp situation would change if everything remained constant except that clothes were required. Most of them anticipated that their bond would be dissolved.

> They would lose the common bond. They have a bond that automatically is a bond. They are in a minority. They are glad you're here. You are welcome there; they're glad you're one of us.

> I think the people would be less friendly. When you're all nude you feel the same as them. You all came here to be nude.... [Q] Everybody feels the other is the same; you have something in common to be doing this unusual thing.

A number of interviewees, supporting the nudist contention that social distinctions diminish in the nudist camp, believed that class distinctions would reappear if clothing were donned.[14] A 19-year-old respondent cited both class and age distinctions:

> You would have...your classes, and age. [Q] I wouldn't feel as close to B and G.

> There is a great age difference. Knowing them this way, though, gives us a common bond. You just don't think about their ages or anything else about them.

Several blue-collar workers remarked that one of the things they liked about nudism was that, without their uniforms or customary clothes, they and their families could associate with a better class of people. Status striving decreases with the removal of these important props of impression management.

> [If everyone in the camp wore clothes] everything I detest about country clubs I've seen would immediately become manifest. Namely: (1) social climbing with all its accompanying insincerity and ostentation; (2) wolves tracking down virgins; (3) highly formalized activities such as golf; (4) gambling and drinking; (5) embarrassment of having to swim under the appraising gaze of a gallery full of people sipping cocktails. This is the paradox, the curious thing; it doesn't embarrass

me to swim at...[a nudist camp] whereas I can't be coaxed into the swimming pool at the country club in my hometown. [Q] I think that the reason is the fact that so much in that country club is so calculated to make tableaux or pictures, in which only the young and the handsome can really be a part. That's terribly true.

Another interviewee, when asked what he liked most about social nudism, replied:

It is the best way to relax. [Q] Once you take your clothes off, people are on the same basis. [Q] Everyone is a person. There are no distinctions between a doctor or a mechanic because of clothing. [Q]...It's hard to describe. It's just that all have an equal basis, no distinctions because of clothing. That helps you to relax.

Although these statements may be somewhat idealized, the nudist camp does effectively break down patterns common to country clubs, resorts, and other settings in the outside society. Sex, class, and power lose much of their relevance in the nudist camp, and the suspension of the barriers they create effects a greater unity among the participants. This is not to say, however, that there is no social hierarchy—a point to which I shall return shortly.

The suspension of clothing modesty reinforces the atmosphere of "one big family" in another way. Clothing modesty is a *ceremony* of everyday life that sustains a nonintimate definition of relationships, and with its voluntary suspension relationships are usually defined as closer in character. However, for this to occur, trust must not be called into question, and each person must take for granted that he is differentiated from other social objects. Camp relationships usually meet these conditions. For example, they are differentiated from relationships elsewhere; being undressed in front of others is still out of the ordinary, since nudists do not appear nude among outsiders.

The social effect was significant enough to prompt members to describe the nudist way of life as a discovery that had brought new meaning to their lives. The experience provided many of them

with "a sense of belonging." As one respondent put it:

...you feel like you're part of a whole family. You feel very close. That's how I feel.

The feeling of being part of "one big family" was, of course, more common to the smaller camps. But even in the large camps, participants in camp activities felt themselves to be a part of a special group.

As I have suggested, however, the "togetherness" of nudists is exaggerated. Personality clashes, cliques, and intergroup disagreements exist, and social stratification remains in evidence. In the words of an unmarried neophyte:

Sometimes I think there is a hierarchy at...[a large nudist camp]. [Q] In any organization there are cliques. [Q] These cliques I believe are formed by seniority. [Q] Those who have been there the longest. [Q: What makes you think this?] Something that is in the air. [Q] Just an impression you get. It's hard to say; it's just a feeling. [Q] As a newcomer I felt not at ease. [Q] There is an air of suspicion; people are not really friendly. [Q] They are not really unfriendly, just suspicious, I suppose, of single men.... They suspect single men are coming for Peeping Tom purposes. [Q] Just to see the nude women.... Single men, I think, are the lowest class at camp.

This attitude was borne out in the interviews with other single men; rarely did they describe nudism in *gemeinschaftlich* terms. The meaning of a person's experiences still depends on his social position.

Furthermore, it is doubtful that many people find a Utopia in nudism. The nudists interviewed were asked how seriously they felt that they would be affected if nudist camps were closed. As Table 6 shows, 30 percent of the interviewees considered that they would be relatively unaffected. When they were asked to identify their three best friends, almost half of the interviewees did not name another nudist.[15] Table 7 details this information, as well as the degree of social involvement with other nudists, as rated by coders.

TABLE 6   The Degree to Which the Closing of Nudist Camps Would Affect Interviewees*

CLOSING CAMPS WOULD AFFECT RESPONDENT	PERCENT OF RESPONDENTS
Very much	43
Somewhat	26
Not too much	17
Not at all	13

*Vague categories, such as those presented in this table, were occasionally used for their descriptive value in grossly delineating some point. In this case, respondents were asked to classify themselves (after completing their open-end response). In other cases, the coders used a large group of indicators in constructing such gross scales. Although these scales lacked intrinsic rigor, reliability between coders was high.

NUDISTS AND THE CLOTHED SOCIETY

Nudists envision themselves as being labeled deviant by members of the clothed society. In both the interviews and the questionnaires, the respondents were asked to conceptualize the view of nudists taken by the general public, and by their parents. No consistent difference was found between the views of the two groups, as described by the nudists.[16] Approximately one-third of the respondents conceptualized a live-and-let-live attitude on the part of parents and public. Two-thirds conceptualized a negative or very negative attitude.

They think we're fanatics. [Q] That we go overboard on something. That we're out of line.

If I went by what the guys say at work, you'd have to be pretty crazy, off your head a little bit. [Q] They think you almost have to be . . . a sex fiend or something like that. They think there's sex orgies, or wife-swapping, or something.

They think we're a bunch of nuts. [Q] They just think that anyone who runs around without clothes is nuts. If they stopped to investigate, they'd find we weren't.

People think the body should be clothed and not exposed at any time. They associate that with vulgarity, indecency, and abnormality. [Q] Vulgarity is something that is unacceptable to the general public. [Q] Indecency in this respect would be exposing portions of the body which normally we hide. [Q] Abnormality? Well, the general public feels it's abnormal for the body to be undressed around other people, in a social group.

The fact that nudists were able to participate in a group which they viewed as stigmatized (and also the sense of belonging they claimed to have found in nudism) suggested that nudists might be

TABLE 7   Social Involvement with Other Nudists*

	DEGREE OF SOCIAL INVOLVEMENT						
Best Friends Who Are Nudists	Very Low	Moderately Low	Neither High Nor Low	Moderately High	Very High		Totals
None	13	9	12	5	7	46	(47%)
One	3	2	6	9	5	25	(26%)
Two		1	3	3	10	17	(18%)
Three					9	9	(9%)
Total	16	12	21	17	31	97	(100%)
	(16%)	(12%)	(22%)	(18%)	(32%)		

*The data on the number of best friends who are nudists were drawn from the replies of interviewees. The degree of social involvement was rated by coders on the basis of the following instructions: Code the degree of social involvement with nudists throughout the year on the basis of answers to Question 40 (b and c). Think of this as a scale or continuum: (1) Very low involvement (no contact at all); (2) moderately low involvement (just write or phone occasionally); (3) neither low nor high involvement (get together every couple of months—or attend New Year's party or splash party together); (4) moderately high involvement (visit once a month); (5) very high involvement (visit every week or two).

TABLE 8 Frequency of Informal Group Participation

	NUDISTS	GENERAL POPULATION
At least twice a week	17%	30%
Every 4 or 5 days	4	35
Once a week	12	16
Less often or never	67	19

isolated in the larger society. If they were isolated they could more easily participate in such a deviant group, being insulated from social controls.

A comparison of nudist interviewees with a sample of the general population[17] did show the nudists to fall substantially below the general population in frequency of informal association, [18] as shown in Table 8. Further, while members of the general population got together most often with relatives, nudists got together most often with friends,[19] as Table 9 indicates. The fact that 34 percent of the nudist sample got together with relatives less than once a month may reflect a considerable insulation from informal controls, since it is relatives who would probably provide the greatest pressure in inhibiting participation in such deviant groups.[20]

The degree to which nudists were isolated in the clothed society was found to be related to the length of time they had been nudists. As shown in Table 10, the longer a person had been in nudism, the more likely he was to be isolated. This may be interpreted in different ways. For example, there may be a tendency to become more isolated with continued participation, perhaps to avoid sanctions. (Yet, in regard to formal organizations nudists did *not* drop out or become less active.) Or, in the past it is likely that nudism was considered even more deviant than it is today and therefore it may have appealed primarily to more isolated types of people.

Regardless of which interpretation is correct, as previously discussed, many nudists found a sense of belonging in nudism.[21]

> *People are lonely. It gives them a sense of belonging.*
>
> *Until I started going out...[to camp] I never felt like I was part of a crowd. But I do out there. I was*

TABLE 10 Social Isolation of Nudists According to Their Length of Time in Nudism

Degree of Social Isolation*	YEARS IN NUDISM			
	1–2	3–5	6–9	10 and Over
Moderately or very isolated	22%	38%	44%	54%
Neither isolated nor active	39	31	25	35
Very or moderately active	39	31	32	12

*As rated by coders.

TABLE 9 Frequency of Association with Several Types of Informal Groups

	RELATIVES		FRIENDS		NEIGHBORS		CO-WORKERS	
	Nudists	General Population	Nudists	General Population	Nudists	General Population	Nudists	General Population
At least once a week	38%	51%	49%	29%	26%	30%	17%	13%
A few times a month	16	13	21	20	11	9	10	8
About once a month	11	13	8	19	6	9	7	15
Less often	34	23	20	32	56	52	63	65

surprised. [Q] Well, like I said, I was never part of a crowd.... I had friends, but never outstanding. My wife and I were [camp] King and Queen.

However, while the nudist experience helps solve this life problem for some, it creates this same problem for others. For the latter group, nudism may only ease the problem that it creates—that is, the isolation that results from concealing one's affiliation with a deviant group.[22]

NOTES

1. Interviews were the primary source of data, and all of the quotations and quantifications in this paper, unless otherwise specified, are drawn from interviews. All known nudists in the vicinity of Chicago were contacted for an interview; the mean interview time was three and one-half hours. Approximately one hundred camps were represented in the interviews and questionnaires. A detailed discussion of my methodology may be found in "Sex, Modesty, and Deviants," Ph.D. Dissertation, Northwestern University, June, 1965.

2. This statement is based on the results of a questionnaire study of social response to nudism.

3. My thanks are due to James L. Wilkins for initially pointing this pattern out in his analysis of the additional data on the response of college students to nudists.

4. For a discussion of Pareto's concept of derivation, see Talcott Parsons, *The Structure of Social Action* (second edition); Glencoe, Ill., Free Press, 1949; pp. 198 *ff.*

5. It is this very fact of an established social system, however, that prevents a disruption of social order in nudist camps. Traditions and norms are stabilized, and even neophytes who think of themselves as leader-types are forced to fall into the pattern or be rejected. (For a small-group experiment that studies this phenomenon, see Ferenc Merei, "Group Leadership and Institutionalization," *Human Relations* [1949] 2:23–39.) In another paper I have shown how some of these traditions function to sustain a nonsexual definition of the nudist situation. See Martin S. Weinberg, "Sexual Modesty, Social Meanings, and the Nudist Camp," *Social Problems* (1965) 12:311–318.

6. Anselm Strauss, editor, *The Social Psychology of George Herbert Mead;* Chicago, Univ. of Chicago Press, 1956; p. xiii.

7. At the time of the interviews, the interviewers, making a commonsense judgment, placed 54 percent of the nudist respondents in the lower-middle class. This was the modal and median placement.

8. For a discussion of "coaching" relationships, see Anselm Strauss, *Mirrors and Masks: The Search for Identity;* New York, Free Press, 1959; pp. 109–118.

9. By "social validation," I mean the process by which the subjective comes to be considered objective—that is, true. The views of others (especially those considered to have more extensive knowledge) provide a social yardstick by which to measure truth. Pareto reaches a similar view of objectivity. Note the following statement: "...we apply the term 'logical actions' to actions that logically conjoin means to ends not only from the standpoint of the subject performing them, but from the standpoint of other persons who have more extensive knowledge—in other words, to actions that are logical both subjectively and objectively in the sense just explained." See Vilfredo Pareto, *The Mind and Society,* Vol. 1; New York, Harcourt, Brace, 1935; p. 77.

10. This concept was developed by Gordon Allport, "The Functional Autonomy of Motives," *Amer. J. Psychology* (1937) 50:141–156.

11. Attendance is usually confined to summer weekends, and sexual curiosity may arise again between seasons.

12. See Alfred Schutz, "The Dimensions of the Social World," in *Collected Papers, II: Studies in Social Theory,* edited by Arvid Broderson; The Hague, Martinus Nijhoff, 1964; pp. 48 *ff.*

13. Kurt H. Wolff, *The Sociology of Georg Simmel;* New York, Free Press, 1950; see Part IV.

14. For discussions of clothes as "sign equipment," see Erving Goffman, "Symbols of Class Status," *British J. Sociology* (1951) 2:294–304; and *The Presentation of Self in Everyday Life;* Garden City, N.Y., Doubleday, 1959; pp. 24 *ff.* Also see Gregory Stone, "Appearance and the Self," in *Human Behavior and Social Processes: An Interactionist Approach,* edited by Arnold Rose; Boston, Houghton Mifflin, 1962; pp. 86–118.

15. Although 59 percent of the interviewees had been nudists for over two years, and 27 percent of this group had been nudists for over ten years, involvement did not appear to be particularly high. Also, an estimated 17 percent of the membership drops out every year.

16. Although a positive versus negative differentiation of parents and general public was not found, there was a difference in the character of the typifications involved. In the case of parents, the typifications were derived from a

history of experiences with an acting personality and were relatively concrete. In contrast, typifications of the general public were highly anonymous. Because such a collectivity could never be experienced directly, there was a much larger region of taken-for-granteds. This is due to the great number of substrata typifications underlying the general whole. This phenomenon is discussed by Alfred Schutz (see footnote 12).

17. In this comparison, Axelrod's data on a sample of the general population in the Detroit area were used. See Morris Axelrod, "Urban Structure and Social Participation," *Amer. Sociol. Review* (1956) 21:13–18.

18. A major limitation in this comparison, however, is that Axelrod has collapsed frequencies of association that are less than once a week into the category of "less often or never."

19. Axelrod finds this greater participation with friends only for members of his sample with high income or high educational or social status.

20. Also the absolute frequency of association with friends includes association with nudist friends. This reduces the apparent social-control function of their friendship associations.

Curiously, members of the nudist sample belonged to more formal organizations than did members of Axelrod's sample of the general population. The comparison was as follows: Membership in no group—general population, 37 percent; nudists, 18 percent. One group—general population, 31 percent; nudists, 27 percent. Two groups—general population, 16 percent; nudists, 19 percent.

21. Some nudists also viewed themselves as members of an elite, superior to clothed society because they had suspended the body taboo.

22. For a discussion of information control, see Erving Goffman, *Stigma: The Management of Spoiled Identity;* Englewood Cliffs, N.J., Prentice-Hall, 1963; pp. 41–104.

Getting into Gangs

MARTIN SANCHEZ JANKOWSKI

Earlier, I argued that one of the most important features of gang members was their defiant individualist character. I explained the development of defiant individualism by locating its origins in the material conditions—the competition and conflict over resource scarcity—of the low-income neighborhoods of most large American cities. These conditions exist for everyone who lives in such neighborhoods, yet not every young person joins a gang. Although I have found that nearly all those who belong to gangs do exhibit defiant individualist traits to some degree, not all those who possess such traits join gangs. This...[section] explores who joins a gang and why in more detail.

From Chapter Two, "Gang Involvement," in Martin Sanchez Jankowski, *Islands in the Street: Gangs and American Urban Society* (Berkeley: University of California Press, 1991). Copyright © 1991 The Regents of the University of California. Reprinted by permission of the publisher.

Many studies offer an answer to why a person joins a gang, or why a group of individuals start a gang. These studies can be divided into four groupings. First, there are those that hold the "natural association" point of view. These studies argue that people join gangs as a result of the natural act of associating with each other.[1] Their contention is that a group of boys, interrelating with each other, decide to formalize their relationship in an attempt to reduce the fear and anxiety associated with their socially disorganized neighborhoods. The individual's impetus to join is the result of his desire to defend against conflict and create order out of the condition of social disorganization.

The second group of studies explains gang formation in terms of "the subculture of blocked opportunities": gangs begin because young males experience persistent problems in gaining employment and/or status. As a result, members of poor communities who experience the strain of these blocked opportunities attempt to compensate for socioeconomic deprivation by joining a gang and establishing a subculture that can be kept separate from the culture of the wider society.[2]

The third group of studies focuses on "problems in identity construction." Within this broad group, some suggest that individuals join gangs as part of the developmental process of building a personal identity or as the result of a breakdown in that process.[3] Others argue that some individuals from low-income families have been blocked from achieving social status through conventional means and join gangs to gain status and self-worth, to rebuild a wounded identity.[4]

A recent work by Jack Katz has both creatively extended the status model and advanced the premise that sensuality is the central element leading to the commission of illegal acts. In Katz's "expressive" model, joining a gang, and being what he labels a "badass," involves a process whereby an individual manages (through transcendence) the gulf that exists between a sense of self located within the local world (the here) and a reality associated with the world outside (the there). Katz argues that the central elements in various forms of deviance, including becoming involved in a gang and gang violence, are the moral emotions of humiliation, righteousness, arrogance, ridicule, cynicism, defilement, and vengeance. "In each," he says, "the attraction that proves to be most fundamentally compelling is that of overcoming a personal challenge to moral—not material—existence."[5]

Most of these theories suffer from three flaws. First, they link joining a gang to delinquency, thereby combining two separate issues. Second, they use single-variable explanations. Third, and most important, they fail to treat joining a gang as the product of a rational decision to maximize self-interest, one in which both the individual and the organized gang play a role. This is especially true of Katz's approach, for two reasons. First, on the personal level, it underestimates the impact of material and status conditions in establishing the situations in which sensual needs/drives (emotions) present themselves, and overestimates/exaggerates the "seductive" impact of crime in satisfying these needs. Second, it does not consider the impact of organizational dynamics on the thought and action of gang members.

In contrast, the data presented here will indicate that gangs are composed of individuals who join for a variety of reasons. In addition, while the individual uses his own calculus to decide whether or not to join a gang, this is not the only deciding factor. The other deciding factor is whether the gang wants him in the organization. Like the individual's decision to join, the gang's decision to permit membership is based on a variety of factors. It is thus important to understand that who becomes a gang member depends on two decision-making processes: that of the individual and that of the gang.

THE INDIVIDUAL AND THE DECISION TO BECOME A MEMBER

Before proceeding, it is important to dismiss a number of the propositions that have often been advanced. The first is that young boys join gangs because they are from broken homes where the father is not present and they seek gang membership in order to identify with other males—that is, they have had no male authority figures with whom to identify. In the ten years of this study, I found that there were as many gang members from homes where the nuclear family was intact as there were from families where the father was absent.[6]

The second proposition given for why individuals join gangs is related to the first: it suggests that broken homes and/or bad home environments force them to look to the gang as a substitute family. Those who offer this explanation often quote gang members' statements such as "We are like a family" or "We are just like brothers" as indications of this motive. However, I found as many members who claimed close relationships with their families as those who denied them.

The third reason offered is that individuals who drop out of school have fewer skills for getting jobs, leaving them with nothing to do but join a gang. While I did find a larger number of members who had dropped out of school, the number was only slightly higher than those who had finished school.

The fourth reason suggested, disconfirmed by my data, is a modern version of the "Pied Piper" effect: the claim that young kids join gangs because they are socialized by older kids to aspire to gang membership and, being young and impressionable, are easily persuaded. I found on the contrary that individuals were as likely to join when they were older (mid to late teens) as when they were younger (nine to fifteen). I also found significantly more who joined when they were young who did so for reasons other than being socialized to think it was "cool" to belong to a gang. In brief, I found no evidence for this proposition.

What I did find was that individuals who live in low-income neighborhoods join gangs for a variety of reasons, basing their decisions on a rational calculation of what is best for them at that particular time. Furthermore, I found that they use the same calculus (not necessarily the same reasons) in deciding whether to stay in the gang, or, if they happen to leave it, whether to rejoin.

REASONS FOR DECIDING TO JOIN A GANG

Most people in the low-income inner cities of America face a situation in which a gang already exists in their area. Therefore the most salient question facing them is not whether to start a gang or not, but rather whether to join an existing one. Many of the reasons for starting a new gang are related to issues having to do with organizational development and decline—that is, with the existing gang's ability to provide the expected services, which include those that individuals considered in deciding to join.... This section deals primarily, although not exclusively, with the question of what influences individuals to join an existing gang. However, many of these are the same influences that encourage individuals to start a new gang.

MATERIAL INCENTIVES

Those who had joined a gang most often gave as their reason the belief that it would provide them with an environment that would increase their chances of securing money. Defiant individualists constantly calculate the costs and benefits associated with their efforts to improve their financial well-being (which is usually not good). Therefore, on the one hand, they believe that if they engage in economic ventures on their own, they will, if successful, earn more per venture than if they acted as part of a gang. However, there is also the belief that if one participates in economic ventures with a gang, it is likely that the amount earned will be more regular, although perhaps less per venture. The comments of Slump, a sixteen-year-old member of a gang in the Los Angeles area, represent this belief:

> Well, I really didn't want to join the gang when I was a little younger because I had this idea that I could make more money if I would do some gigs [various illegal economic ventures] on my own. Now I don't know, I mean, I wasn't wrong. I could make more money on my own, but there are more things happening with the gang, so it's a little more even in terms of when the money comes in.... Let's just say there is more possibilities for a more steady amount of income if you need it.

It was also believed that less individual effort would be required in the various economic ventures in a gang because more people would be involved. In addition, some thought that being in a gang would reduce the risk (of personal injury) associated with their business ventures. They were aware that if larger numbers of people had knowledge of a crime, this would increase the risk that if someone were caught, others, including themselves, would be implicated. However, they countered this consideration with the belief that they faced less risk of being physically harmed when they were part of a group action. The comments of Corner, a seventeen-year-old resident of a poor Manhattan neighborhood, represent this consideration. During the interview, he was twice approached about joining the local gang. He said:

> I think I am going to join the club [gang] this time. I don't know, man, I got some things to decide, but I think I will.... Before I didn't want to join because when I did a job, I didn't want to share it with the whole group—hell, I was never able to make that much to share.... I would never have got enough money, and with all those dudes [other members of the gang] knowing who did the job, you can bet the police would find out.... Well, now my thinking is changed a bit 'cause I almost got hurt real bad trying something the other day and so I'm pretty sure I'll join the gang 'cause there's more people involved and that'll keep me safer. [He joined the gang two weeks later.]

Others decided to join the gang for financial security. They viewed the gang as an organization that could provide them or their families with money in times of emergency. It represented the combination of a bank and a social security system, the equivalent of what the political machine had been to many new immigrant groups in American cities.[7] To these individuals, it provided both psychological and financial security in an economic environment of scarcity and intense competition. This was particularly true of those who were fifteen and younger. Many in this age group often find themselves in a precarious position. They are in need of money, and although social services are available to help during times of economic hardship, they often lack legal means of access to these resources. For these individuals, the gang can provide an alternative source of aid. The comments of Street Dog and Tomahawk represent these views. Street Dog was a fifteen-year-old Puerto Rican who had been in a New York gang for two years:

> Hey, the club [the gang] has been there when I needed help. There were times when there just wasn't enough food for me to get filled up with. My family was hard up and they couldn't manage all of their bills and such, so there was some lean

meals! Well, I just needed some money to help for awhile, till I got some money or my family was better off. They [the gang] was there to help. I could see that [they would help] before I joined, that's why I joined. They are there when you need them and they'll continue to be.

Tomahawk was a fifteen-year-old Irishman who had been in a gang for one year:

> Before I joined the gang, I could see that you could count on your boys to help in times of need and that meant a lot to me. And when I needed money, sure enough they gave it to me. Nobody else would have given it to me; my parents didn't have it, and there was no other place to go. The gang was just like they said they would be, and they'll continue to be there when I need them.

Finally, many view the gang as providing an opportunity for future gratification. They expect that through belonging to a gang, they will be able to make contact with individuals who may eventually help them financially. Some look to meet people who have contacts in organized crime in the hope of entering that field in the future. Some hope to meet businessmen involved in the illegal market who will provide them with money to start their own illegal businesses. Still others think that gang membership will enable them to meet individuals who will later do them favors (with financial implications) of the kind fraternity brothers or Masons sometimes do for each other. Irish gang members in New York and Boston especially tend to believe this.

RECREATION

The gang provides individuals with entertainment, much as a fraternity does for college students or the Moose and Elk clubs do for their members. Many individuals said they joined the gang because it was the primary social institution of their neighborhood—that is, it was where most (not necessarily the biggest) social events occurred. Gangs usually, though not always, have some type of clubhouse. The exact nature of the clubhouse varies according to how much money the gang has to support it, but every clubhouse offers some form of entertainment. In the case of some gangs with a good deal of money, the clubhouse includes a bar, which sells its members drinks at cost. In addition, some clubhouses have pin-ball machines, soccer-game machines, pool tables, ping pong tables, card tables, and in some cases a few slot machines. The clubhouse acts as an incentive, much like the lodge houses of other social clubs.[8]

The gang can also be a promoter of social events in the community, such as a big party or dance. Often the gang, like a fraternity, is thought of as the organization to join to maximize opportunities to have fun. Many who joined said they did so because the gang provided them with a good opportunity to meet women. Young women frequently form an auxiliary unit to the gang, which usually adopts a version of the male gang's name (e.g., "Lady Jets"). The women who join this auxiliary do so for similar reasons—that is, opportunities to meet men and participate in social events.[9]

The gang is also a source of drugs and alcohol. Here, most gangs walk a fine line. They provide some drugs for purposes of recreation, but because they also ban addicts from the organization, they also attempt to monitor members' use of some drugs.[10]

The comments of Fox and Happy highlight these views of the gang as a source of recreation.[11] Fox was a twenty-three-year-old from New York and had been in a gang for seven years:

> Like I been telling you, I joined originally because all the action was happening with the Bats [gang's name]. I mean, all the foxy ladies were going to their parties and hanging with them. Plus their parties were great. They had good music and the herb [marijuana] was so smooth.... Man, it was a great source of dope and women. Hell, they were the kings of the community so I wanted to get in on some of the action.

Happy was a twenty-eight-year-old from Los Angeles, who had been a gang member for eight years:

> I joined because at the time, Jones Park [gang's name] had the best clubhouse. They had pool tables and pinball machines that you could use for free. Now they added a video game which you only have to pay like five cents for to play. You could do a lot in the club, so I thought it was a good thing to try it for awhile [join the gang], and it was a good thing.

A PLACE OF REFUGE AND CAMOUFLAGE

Some individuals join a gang because it provides them with a protective group identity. They see the gang as offering them anonymity, which may relieve the stresses associated with having to be personally accountable for all their actions in an intensely competitive environment. The statements of Junior J. and Black Top are representative of this belief. Junior J. was a seventeen-year-old who had been approached about becoming a gang member in one of New York's neighborhoods:

> I been thinking about joining the gang because the gang gives you a cover, you know what I mean? Like when me or anybody does a business deal and we're members of the gang, it's difficult to track us down 'cause people will say, oh, it was just one of those guys in the gang. You get my point? The gang is going to provide me with some cover.

Black Top was a seventeen-year-old member of a Jamaican gang in New York:

> Man, I been dealing me something awful. I been doing well, but I also attracted me some adversaries. And these adversaries have been getting close to me. So joining the brothers [the gang] lets me blend into the group. It lets me hide for awhile, it gives me refuge until the heat goes away.

PHYSICAL PROTECTION

Individuals also join gangs because they believe the gang can provide them with personal protection from the predatory elements active in low-income neighborhoods. Nearly all the young men who join for this reason know what dangers exist for them in their low-income neighborhoods.

These individuals are not the weakest of those who join the gang, for all have developed the savvy and skills to handle most threats. However, all are either tired of being on the alert or want to reduce the probability of danger to a level that allows them to devote more time to their effort to secure more money. Here are two representative comments of individuals who joined for this reason. Chico was a seventeen-year-old member of an Irish gang in New York:

> When I first started up with the Steel Flowers, I really didn't know much about them. But, to be honest, in the beginning I just joined because there were some people who were taking my school [lunch] money, and after I joined the gang, these guys laid off.

Cory was a sixteen-year-old member of a Los Angeles gang:

> Man I joined the Fultons because there are a lot of people out there who are trying to get you and if you don't got protection you in trouble sometimes. My homeboys gave me protection, so hey, they were the thing to do.... Now that I got some business things going I can concentrate on them and not worry so much. I don't always have to be looking over my shoulder.

A TIME TO RESIST

Many older individuals (in their late teens or older) join gangs in an effort to resist living lives like their parents'. As Joan Moore, Ruth Horowitz, and others have pointed out, most gang members come from families whose parents are underemployed and/or employed in the secondary labor market in jobs that have little to recommend them.[12] These jobs are low-paying, have long hours, poor working conditions, and few opportunities for advancement; in brief, they are dead ends.[13] Most prospective gang members have lived through the pains of economic deprivation and the stresses that such an existence puts on a family. They desperately want to avoid following in their parents' path, which they believe is exactly what awaits them. For these individuals, the gang is a way to resist the jobs their parents held and, by extension, the life their parents led. Deciding to become a gang member is both a statement to society ("I will not take these jobs passively") and an attempt to do whatever can be done to avoid such an outcome. At the very least, some of these individuals view being in a gang as a temporary reprieve from having to take such jobs, a postponement of the inevitable. The comments of Joey and D. D. are representative of this group. Joey was a nineteen-year-old member of an Irish gang in Boston:

> Hell, I joined because I really didn't see anything in the near future I wanted to do. I sure the hell didn't want to take that job my father got me. It was a shit job just like his. I said to myself, "Fuck this!" I'm only nineteen, I'm too young to start this shit.... I figured that the Black Rose [the gang] was into a lot of things and that maybe I could hit it big at something we're doing and get the hell out of this place.

D. D. was a twenty-year-old member of a Chicano gang in Los Angeles:

> I just joined the T-Men to kick back [relax, be carefree] for awhile. My parents work real hard and they got little for it. I don't really want that kind of job, but that's what it looked like I would have to take. So I said, hey, I'll just kick back for a while and let that job wait for me. Hey, I just might make some money from our dealings and really be able to forget these jobs.... If I don't [make it, at least] I told the fuckers in Beverly Hills what I think of the jobs they left for us.

People who join as an act of resistance are often wrongly understood to have joined because they were having difficulty with their identity and the gang provided them with a new one. However, these individuals actually want a new identity less than they want better living conditions.

COMMITMENT TO COMMUNITY

Some individuals join the gang because they see participation as a form of commitment to their community. These usually come from neighborhoods where gangs have existed for generations. Although the character of such gangs may have changed over the years, the fact remains that they have continued to exist. Many of these individuals have known people who have been in gangs, including family members—often a brother, but even, in a considerable number of cases, a father and grandfather. The fact that their relatives have a history of gang involvement usually influences these individuals to see the gang as a part of the tradition of the community. They feel that their families and their community expect them to join, because community members see the gang as an aid to them and the individual who joins as meeting his neighborhood obligation. These attitudes are similar to attitudes in the larger society about one's obligation to serve in the armed forces. In a sense, this type of involvement represents a unique form of local patriotism. While this rationale for joining was present in a number of the gangs studied, it was most prevalent among Chicano and Irish gangs. The comments of Dolan and Pepe are representative of this line of thinking. Dolan was a sixteen-year-old member of an Irish gang in New York:

> I joined because the gang has been here for a long time and even though the name is different a lot of the fellas from the community have been involved in it over the years, including my dad. The gang has helped the community by protecting it against outsiders so people here have kind of depended on it. . . . I feel it's my obligation to the community to put in some time helping them out. This will help me to get help in the community if I need it some time.

Pepe was a seventeen-year-old member of a Chicano gang in the Los Angeles area:

> The Royal Dons [gang's name] have been here for a real long time. A lot of people from the community have been in it. I had lots of family in it so I guess I'll just have to carry on the tradition. A lot of people from outside this community wouldn't understand, but we have helped the community whenever they've asked us. We've been around to help. I felt it's kind of my duty to join 'cause every-

body expects it. . . . No, the community doesn't mind that we do things to make some money and raise a little hell because they don't expect you to put in your time for nothing. Just like nobody expects guys in the military to put in their time for nothing.

In closing this section on why individuals join gangs, it is important to reemphasize that people choose to join for a variety of reasons, that these reasons are not exclusive of one another (some members have more than one), that gangs are composed of individuals whose reasons for joining include all those mentioned, that the decision to join is thought out, and that the individual believes this was best for his or her interests at the moment.

ORGANIZATIONAL RECRUITMENT

Deciding whether or not to join a gang is never an individual decision alone. Because gangs are well established in most of these neighborhoods, they are ultimately both the initiators of membership and the gatekeepers, deciding who will join and who will not.

Every gang that was studied had some type of recruitment strategy. A gang will frequently employ a number of strategies, depending on the circumstances in which recruitment is occurring. However, most gangs use one particular style of recruitment for what they consider a "normal" period and adopt other styles as specific situations present themselves. The three most prevalent styles of recruitment encountered were what I call the fraternity type, the obligation type, and the coercive type.

THE FRATERNITY TYPE OF RECRUITMENT

In the fraternity type of recruitment, the gang adopts the posture of an organization that is "cool," "hip," the social thing to be in. Here the gang makes an effort to recruit by advertising through word of mouth that it is looking for members. Then many of the gangs either give a party or circulate information throughout the neighborhood, indicating when their next meeting will be held and that those interested in becoming members are invited. At this initial meeting, prospective members hear a short speech about the gang and its rules. They are also told about the gang's exploits and/or its most positive perks, such as the dances and parties it gives, the availability of dope, the women who are available, the clubhouse, and the various recreational machinery (pool table, video games, bar, etc.). In addition, the gang sometimes discusses, in the most general terms, its plans for creating revenues that will be shared among the general membership. Once this pitch is made, the decision rests with the individual. When one decides to join the gang, there is a trial period before one is considered a solid member of the group. This trial period is similar, but not identical, to the pledge period for fraternities. There are a number of precautions taken during this period to check the individual's worthiness to be in the group. If the individual is not known by members of the gang, he will need to be evaluated to see if he is an informant for one of the various law enforcement agencies (police, firearms and alcohol, drug enforcement). In addition, the individual will need to be assessed in terms of his ability to fight, his courage, and his commitment to help others in the gang.

Having the *will* to fight and defend other gang members or the "interest" of the gang is considered important, but what is looked upon as being an even more important asset for a prospective gang member is the *ability* to fight and to carry out group decisions. Many researchers have often misinterpreted this preference by gangs for those who can fight as an indication that gang members, and thus gangs as collectives, are primarily interested in establishing reputations as fighters.[14] They interpret this preoccupation as being based on adolescent drives for identity and the release of a great deal of aggression. However, what is most often missed are the functional aspects of fighting and its significance to a gang. The prospective member's ability to fight well is not looked upon by the organization simply as an additional symbol of status. Members of gangs want to know if a potential member can fight because if any of them are caught in a situation where they are required to fight, they want to feel confident that everyone can carry his or her own responsibility. In addition, gang members want to know if the potential gang member is disciplined enough to avoid getting scared and running, leaving them vulnerable. Often everyone's safety in a fight depends on the ability of every individual to fight efficiently. For example, on many occasions I observed a small group of one gang being attacked by an opposing gang. Gang fights are not like fights in the movies: there is no limit to the force anybody is prepared to use—it is, as one often hears, "for all the marbles." When gang members were attacked, they were often outnumbered and surrounded. The only way to protect themselves was to place themselves back to back and ward off the attackers until some type of help came (ironically, most often from the police). If someone cannot fight well and is overcome quickly, everyone's back will be exposed and everyone becomes vulnerable. Likewise, if someone decides to make a run for it, everyone's position is compromised. So assessing the potential member's ability to fight is not done simply to strengthen the gang's reputation as "the meanest fighters," but rather to strengthen the confidence of other gang members that the new member adds to the organization's general ability to protect and defend the collective's interests. The comments of Vase, an eighteen-year-old leader of a gang in New York, highlight this point:

> When I first started with the Silk Irons [gang's name], they checked me out to see if I could fight. After I passed their test, they told me that they didn't need anybody who would leave their butts uncovered. Now that I'm a leader I do the same thing. You see that guy over there? He wants to be in the Irons, but we don't know nothing about whether he can fight or if he got no heart [courage]. So we going to check out how good he is and whether he going to stand and fight. 'Cause if he ain't got good heart or skills [ability to fight], he could leave some of the brothers [gang members]

real vulnerable and in a big mess. And if [he] do that, they going to get their asses messed up!

As mentioned earlier, in those cases where the gang has seen a prospective member fight enough to know he will be a valuable member, they simply admit him. However, if information is needed in order to decide whether the prospective gang member can fight, the gang leadership sets up a number of situations to test the individual. One favorite is to have one of the gang members pick a fight with the prospective member and observe the response. It is always assumed that the prospective member will fight; the question is, how well will he fight? The person selected to start the fight is usually one of the better fighters. This provides the group with comparative information by which to decide just how good the individual is in fighting.[15] Such fights are often so intense that there are numerous lacerations on the faces of both fighters. This test usually doubles as an initiation rite, although there are gangs who follow up this test phase with a separate initiation ritual where the individual is given a beating by all those gang members present. This beating is more often than not symbolic, in that the blows delivered to the new members are not done using full force. However, they still leave bruises.

Assessing whether a prospective gang member is trustworthy or not is likewise done by setting up a number of small tests. The gang members are concerned with whether the prospective member is an undercover agent for law enforcement. To help them establish this, they set up a number of criminal activities (usually of medium-level illegality) involving the individual(s); then they observe whether law enforcement proceeds to make arrests of the specific members involved. One gang set up a scam whereby it was scheduled to commit an armed robbery. When a number of the gang members were ready to make the robbery, the police came and arrested them— the consequence of a new member being a police informer. The person responsible was identified and punished. Testing the trustworthiness of new

recruits proved to be an effective policy because later the gang was able to pursue a much more lucrative illegal venture without the fear of having a police informer in the organization.

Recruiting a certain number of new members who have already established reputations as good fighters does help the gang. The gang's ability to build and maintain a reputation for fighting reduces the number of times it will have to fight. If a gang has a reputation as a particularly tough group, it will not have as much trouble with rival gangs trying to assume control over its areas of interest. Thus, a reputation acts as an initial deterrent to rival groups. However, for the most part, the gang's concern with recruiting good fighters for the purpose of enhancing its reputation is secondary to its concern that members be able to fight well so that they can help each other.

Gangs who are selective about who they allow in also scrutinize whether the individual has any special talents that could be useful to the collective. Sometimes these special talents involve military skills, such as the ability to build incendiary bombs. Some New York gangs attempted to recruit people with carpentry and masonry skills so that they could help them renovate abandoned buildings.

Gangs that adopt a "fraternity recruiting style" are usually quite secure within their communities. They have a relatively large membership and have integrated themselves into the community well enough to have both legitimacy and status. In other words, the gang is an organization that is viewed by members of the community as legitimate. The comments of Mary, a 53-year-old garment worker who was a single parent in New York, indicate how some community residents feel about certain gangs:

> *There are a lot of young people who want in the Bullets, but they don't let whoever wants to get in in. Those guys are really selective about who they want. Those who do get in are very helpful to the whole community. There are many times that they have helped the community...and the community appreciates that they have been here for us.*

Gangs that use fraternity style recruitment have often become relatively prosperous. Having built up the economic resources of the group to a level that has benefited the general membership, they are reluctant to admit too many new members, fearing that increased numbers will not be accompanied by increases in revenues, resulting in less for the general membership. Hackman, a twenty-eight-year-old leader of a New York gang, represented this line of thought:

> Man, we don't let all the dudes who want to be let in in. We can't do that, or I can't, 'cause right now we're sitting good. We gots a good bank account and the whole gang is getting dividends. But if we let in a whole lot of other dudes, everybody will have to take a cut unless we come up with some more money, but that don't happen real fast. So you know the brothers ain't going to dig a cut, and if it happens, then they going to be on me and the rest of the leadership's ass and that ain't good for us.

THE OBLIGATION TYPE OF RECRUITMENT

The second recruiting technique used by gangs is what I call the "obligation type." In this form, the gang contacts as many young men from its community as it can and attempts to persuade them that it is their duty to join. These community pressures are real, and individuals need to calculate how to respond to them, because there are risks if one ignores them. In essence, the gang recruiter's pitch is that everyone who lives in this particular community has to give something back to it in order to indicate both appreciation of and solidarity with the community. In places where one particular gang has been in existence for a considerable amount of time (as long as a couple of generations), "upholding the tradition of the neighborhood" (not that of the gang) is the pitch used as the hook. The comments of Paul and Lorenzo are good examples. Paul was a nineteen-year-old member of an Irish gang in New York:

> Yeah, I joined this group of guys [the gang] because they have helped the community and a lot of us have taken some serious lumps [injuries] in do-

> ing that.... I think if a man has any sense of himself, he will help his community no matter what. Right now I'm talking to some guys about joining our gang and I tell them that they can make some money being in the gang, but the most important thing is they can help the community too. If any of them say that they don't want to get hurt or something like that, I tell'm that nobody wants to get hurt, but sometimes it happens. Then I tell them the bottom line, if you don't join and help the community, then outsiders will come and attack the people here and this community won't exist in a couple of years.

Lorenzo was a 22-year-old Chicano gang member from Los Angeles. Here he is talking to two prospective members:

> I don't need to talk to you dudes too much about this [joining a gang]. You know what the whole deal is, but I want you to know that your barrio [community] needs you just like they needed us and we delivered. We all get some battle scars [he shows them a scar from a bullet wound], but that's the price you pay to keep some honor for you and your barrio. We all have to give something back to our community.[16]

This recruiting pitch is primarily based on accountability to the community. It is most effective in communities where the residents have depended on the gang to help protect them from social predators. This is because gang recruiters can draw on the moral support that the gang receives from older residents.

Although the power of this recruiting pitch is accountability to the community, the recruiter can suggest other incentives as well. Three positive incentives generally are used. The first is that gang members are respected in the community. This means that the community will tolerate their illegal business dealings and help them whenever they are having difficulty with the police. As Cardboard, a sixteen-year-old member of a Dominican gang, commented:

> Hey, the dudes come by and they be putting all this shit about that I should do my part to protect

the community, but I told them I'm not ready to join up. I tell you the truth, I did sometimes feel a little guilty, but I still didn't think it was for me. But now I tell you I been changing my mind a little. I thinking more about joining.... You see the dudes been telling me the community be helping you do your business, you understand? Hey, I been thinking, I got me a little business and if they right, this may be the final straw to get me, 'cause a little help from the community could be real helpful to me. [He joined the gang three weeks later.]

The second incentive is that some members of the community will help them find employment at a later time. (This happens more in Irish neighborhoods.) The comments of Andy, a seventeen-year-old Irish-American in Boston, illustrate this view:

The community has been getting squeezed by some developers and there's been a lot of people who aren't from the community moving in, so that's why some of the Tigers [gang's name] have come by while we've been talking. They want to talk to me about joining. Just like they been saying, the community needs their help now and they need me. I really was torn because I thought there might be some kind violence used and I don't really want to get involved with that. But the other day when you weren't here, they talked to me and told me that I should remember that the community remembers when people help and they take care of their own. Well, they're right, the community does take care of its own. They help people get jobs all the time 'cause they got contacts at city hall and at the docks, so I been thinking I might join. [He joined three weeks later.]

The third incentive is access to women. Here the recruiter simply says that because the gang is a part of the community and is respected, women look up to gang members and want to be associated with them. So, the pitch continues, if an individual wants access to a lot of women, it will be available through the gang. The comments of Topper, a fifteen-year-old Chicano, illustrate the effectiveness of this pitch:

Yeah, I was thinking of joining the Bangers [a gang]. These two homeboys [gang members] been coming to see me about joining for two months now. They've been telling me that my barrio really needs me and I should help my people. I really do want to help my barrio, but I never really made up my mind. But the other day they were telling me that the mujeres [women] really dig homeboys because they do help the community. So I was checking that out and you know what? They really do! So, I say, hey, I need to seriously check the Bangers out. [One week later he joined the gang.]

In addition to the three positive incentives used, there is a negative one. The gang recruiter can take the tack that if a prospective member decides not to join, he will not be respected as much in the community, or possibly even within his own family. This line of persuasion can be successful if other members of the prospective recruit's family have been in a gang and/or if there has been a high level of involvement in gangs throughout the community. The suggestion that people (including family) will be disappointed in him, or look down on his family, is an effective manipulative tool in the recruiting process in such cases. The comments of Texto, a fifteen-year-old Chicano, provide a good example:

I didn't want to join the Pearls [gang's name] right now 'cause I didn't think it was best for me right now. Then a few of the Pearls came by to try to get me to join. They said all the stuff about helping your barrio, but I don't want to join now. I mean I do care about my barrio, but I just don't want to join now. But you heard them today ask me if my father wanted me to join. You know I got to think about this, I mean my dad was in this gang and I don't know. He says to me to do what you want, but I think he would be embarrassed with his friends if they heard I didn't want to join. I really don't want to embarrass my dad, I don't know what I'm going to do. [He joined the gang one month later.]

The "obligation method of recruitment" is similar to that employed by governments to secure recruits for their armed services, and it meets with only moderate results. Gangs using this method realized that while they would not be able to recruit all the individuals they made contact with, the obligation method (sometimes in combination with the coercive method) would enable them to recruit enough for the gang to continue operating.

This type of recruitment was found mostly, although not exclusively, in Irish and Chicano communities where the gang and community had been highly integrated. It is only effective in communities where a particular gang or a small number of gangs have been active for a considerable length of time.

THE COERCIVE TYPE OF RECRUITMENT

A third type of recruitment involves various forms of coercion. Coercion is used as a recruitment method when gangs are confronted with the need to increase their membership quickly. There are a number of situations in which this occurs. One is when a gang has made a policy decision to expand its operations into another geographic area and needs troops to secure the area and keep it under control. The desire to build up membership is based on the gang's anticipation that there will be a struggle with a rival gang and that, if it is to be successful, it will be necessary to be numerically superior to the expected adversary.

Another situation involving gang expansion also encourages an intense recruitment effort that includes coercion. When a gang decides to expand into a geographic area that has not hitherto been controlled by another gang, and is not at the moment being fought for, it goes into the targeted area and vigorously recruits members in an effort to establish control. If individuals from this area are not receptive to the gang's efforts, then coercion is used to persuade some of them to join. The comment of Bolo, a seventeen-year-old leader of a New York gang, illustrates this position:

Let me explain what just happened. Now you might be thinking, what are these dudes doing beating up on somebody they want to be in their gang? The answer is that we need people now, we can't be waiting till they make up their mind. They don't have to stay for a long time, but we need them now.... We don't like to recruit this way 'cause it ain't good for the long run, but this is necessary now because in order for us to expand our business in this area we got to get control, and in order to do that we got to have members who live in the neighborhood. We can't be building no structure to defend ourselves against the Wings [the rival gang in the area], or set up some communications in the area, or set up a connection with the community. We can't do shit unless we got a base and we ain't going to get any base without people. It's that simple.

A third situation where a gang feels a need to use a coercive recruiting strategy involves gangs who are defending themselves against a hostile attempt to take over a portion of their territory. Under such conditions, the gang defending its interests will need to bolster its ranks in order to fend off the threat. This will require that the embattled gang recruit rapidly. Often, a gang that normally uses the fraternity type of recruitment will be forced to abandon it for the more coercive type. The actions of these gangs can be compared to those of nation-states when they invoke universal conscription (certainly a form of coercion) during times when they are threatened and then abrogate it when they believe they have recruited a sufficient number to neutralize the threat, or, more usually, when a threat no longer exists. The comments of M. R. and Rider represent those who are recruited using coercion. M. R. was a nineteen-year-old ex–gang member from Los Angeles:[17]

I really didn't want to be in any gang, but one day there was this big blowout [fight] a few blocks from here. A couple of O Streeters who were from another barrio came and shot up a number of the Dukes [local gang's name]. Then it was said that the O Streeters wanted to take over the area as theirs, so a group of the Dukes went around asking people to join for awhile till everything got secure.

They asked me, but I still didn't want to get involved because I really didn't want to get killed over something that I had no interest in. But they said they wanted me and if I didn't join and help they were going to mess me up. Then the next day a couple of them pushed me around pretty bad, and they did it much harder the following day. So I thought about it and then decided I'd join. Then after some gun fights things got secure again and they told me thanks and I left.

Rider was a sixteen-year-old member of an Irish gang from New York:

Here one day I read in the paper there was fighting going on between a couple of gangs. I knew that one of the gangs was from a black section of the city. Then some of the Greenies [local Irish gang] came up to me and told me how some of the niggers from this gang were trying to start some drugs in the neighborhood. I didn't want the niggers coming in, but I had other business to tend to first. You know what I mean? So I said I thought they could handle it themselves, but then about three or four Greenies said that if I didn't go with them that I was going to be ground meat and so would members of my family. Well, I know they meant business because my sister said they followed her home from school and my brother said they threw stones at him on his way home. So they asked me again and I said OK . . . then after we beat the niggers' asses, I quit. . . . Well, the truth is that I wanted to stay, but after the nigger business was over, they didn't want me. They just said that I was too crazy and wouldn't work out in the group.

This last interview highlights the gang's movement back to their prior form of recruitment after the threat was over. Rider wanted to stay in the gang but was asked to leave. Many of the members of the gang felt Rider was too crazy, too prone to vicious and outlandish acts, simply too unpredictable to trust. The gang admired his fighting ability, but he was the kind of person who caused too much trouble for the gang. As T. R., an eighteen-year-old leader of the gang, said:

There's lots of things we liked about Rider. He sure could help us in any fight we'd get in, but he's just too crazy. You just couldn't tell what he'd do. If we

kept him, he'd have the police on us all the time. He just had to go.

There is also a fourth situation in which coercion is used in recruiting. Sometimes a gang that has dominated a particular area has declined to such an extent that it can no longer control all its original area. In such situations, certain members of this gang often decide to start a new one. When this occurs, the newly constituted gang often uses coercive techniques to recruit members and establish authority over its defined territory. Take the comments of Rob and Loan Man, both of whom were leaders of two newly constituted gangs. Rob was a sixteen-year-old gang member from Los Angeles:

There was the Rippers [old gang's name], but so many of their members went to jail that there really wasn't enough leadership people around. So a number of people decided to start a new gang. So then we went around the area to check who wanted to be in the gang. We only checked out those we really wanted. It was like pro football scouts, we were interested in all those that could help us now. Our biggest worry was getting members, so when some of the dudes said they didn't want to join, we had to put some heavy physical pressure on them; because if you don't get members, you don't have anything that you can build into a gang. . . . Later after we got established we didn't need to pressure people to get them to join.

Loan Man was a twenty-five-year-old member of a gang in New York:

I got this idea to start a new gang because I thought the leaders we had were all fucked up. You know, they had shit for brains. They were ruining everything we built up and I wasn't going to go down with them and lose everything. So I talked to some others who didn't like what was going on and we decided to start a new club [gang] in the neighborhood we lived in. So we quit. . . . Well, we got new members from the community, one way or the other . . . you know we had to use a little persuasive muscle to build our membership and let the community know we were able to take control and hold it, but after we did get control, then we only took brothers who wanted us [they used the fraternity type of recruiting].

In sum, the coercive method of recruitment is used most by gangs that find their existence threatened by competitor gangs. During such periods, the gang considers that its own needs must override the choice of the individual and coercion is used to induce individuals to join their group temporarily.

NOTES

1. See Thrasher, *The Gang;* Suttles, *Social Order of the Slum;* Hagedorn, *People and Folks.*
2. Of course, some of the studies cited here overlap these categories, and I have therefore placed them according to the major emphasis of the study. See Cloward and Ohlin, *Delinquency and Opportunity;* Hagedorn, *People and Folks;* Moore, *Homeboys;* Short and Strodtbeck, *Group Process and Gang Delinquency.*
3. Here again it is important to restate that many of these studies overlap the categories I have created, but I have attempted to identify them by what seems to be their emphasis. See Block and Niederhoffer, *The Gang;* Yablonsky, *The Violent Gang.*
4. See the qualifying statement in nn. 2 and 3 above. See Horowitz, *Honor and the American Dream;* Cohen, *Delinquent Boys;* Miller, "Lower Class Culture as a Generating Milieu of Gang Delinquency"; Vigil, *Barrio Gangs.*
5. See Jack Katz, *The Seduction of Crime: Moral and Sensual Attractions in Doing Evil* (New York: Basic Books, 1988), p. 9.
6. Although the present study is not a quantitative study, the finding reported here and the ones to follow are based on observations of, and conversations and formal interviews with, hundreds of gang members.
7. For a discussion of the political machine's role in providing psychological and financial support for poor immigrant groups, see Robert K. Merton, *Social Theory and Social Structure* (New York: Free Press, 1968), pp. 126–36. Also see William L. Riordan, *Plunkitt of Tammany Hall* (New York: Dutton, 1963).
8. There are numerous examples throughout the society of social clubs using the lodge or clubhouse as one of the incentives for gaining members. There are athletic clubs for the wealthy (like the University Club and the Downtown Athletic Club in New York), social clubs in ethnic

neighborhoods, the Elks and Moose clubs, the clubs of various veterans' associations, and tennis, yacht, and racket ball clubs.
9. See Anne Campbell, *Girls in the Gang* (New York: Basil Blackwell, 1987).
10. For the use of drugs as recreational, see Vigil, *Barrio Gangs;* and Fagan, "Social Organization of Drug Use and Drug Dealing among Urban Gangs," who reports varying degrees of drug use among various types of gangs. For studies that report the monitoring and/or prohibition of certain drugs by gangs, see Vigil, *Barrio Gangs,* on the prohibition of heroin use in Chicano gangs; and Thomas Mieczkowski, "Geeking Up and Throwing Down: Heroin Street Life in Detroit," *Criminology* 24 (November 1986): 645–66.
11. See Thrasher, *The Gang,* pp. 84–96. He also discusses the gang as a source of recreation.
12. See Moore, *Homeboys,* ch. 2.; Horowitz, *Honor and the American Dream,* ch. 8; Vigil, *Barrio Gangs;* and Hagedorn, *People and Folks.*
13. For a discussion of these types of jobs, see Michael J. Piore, *Notes for a Theory of Labor Market Stratification,* Working Paper no. 95 (Cambridge, Mass.: Massachusetts Institute of Technology, 1972).
14. See Horowitz, *Honor and the American Dream;* and Ruth Horowitz and Gary Schwartz, "Honor, Normative Ambiguity and Gang Violence," *American Sociological Review* 39 (April 1974): 238–51. There are many other studies that could have been cited here. These two are given merely as examples.
15. The testing of potential gang members as to their fighting ability was also observed by Vigil. See his *Barrio Gangs,* pp. 54–55.
16. This quotation was recorded longhand, not tape-recorded.
17. I first met M. R. when he was in one of the gangs that I was hanging around with. He subsequently left the gang, and I stayed in touch with him by talking to him when our paths crossed on the street. This quotation is from a long conversation that I had with him during one of our occasional encounters.

REFERENCES

Bloch, Herbert A., and Arthur Niederhoffer. *The Gang: A Study in Adolescent Behavior.* New York: Philosophical Library, 1958.

Campbell, Anne. *Girls in the Gang.* New York: Basil Blackwell, 1987.

Cloward, Richard A., and Lloyd B. Ohlin, *Delinquency and Opportunity: A Theory of Delinquent Gangs.* New York: Free Press, 1960.

Cohen, Albert K. *Delinquent Boys: The Culture of the Gang.* Glencoe, Ill.: Free Press, 1955.

Fagan, Jeffery. "The Social Organization of Drug Use and Drug Dealing among Urban Gangs." *Criminology* 27, no. 4 (November 1989): 633–70.

Hagedorn, John M. *People and Folks: Gangs, Crime and the Underclass in a Rustbelt City.* Chicago: Lakeview Press, 1988.

Horowitz, Ruth. *Honor and the American Dream: Culture and Identity in a Chicano Community.* New Brunswick: Rutgers University Press, 1983.

Horowitz, Ruth and Gary Schwartz. "Honor, Normative Ambiguity and Gang Violence." *American Sociological Review* 39 (April 1974): 238–51.

Katz, Jack. *The Seduction of Crime: Moral and Sensual Attractions in Doing Evil.* New York: Basic Books, 1988.

Merton, Robert K. *Social Theory and Social Structure.* New York: Free Press, 1968.

Mieczkowski, Thomas. "Geeking Up and Throwing Down: Heroin Street Life in Detroit." *Criminology* 24 (November 1986): 645–66.

Miller, Walter B. "Lower Class Culture as a Generating Milieu of Gang Delinquency." *Journal of Social Issues* 14, no. 3 (Fall): 5–19.

Moore, Joan W. *Homeboys: Gangs, Drugs, and Prisons in the Barrios of Los Angeles.* Philadelphia: Temple University Press, 1978.

Piore, Michael J. *Notes for a Theory of Labor Market Stratification.* Working Paper no. 95. Cambridge, Mass.: Massachusetts Institute of Technology, 1972.

Riordan, William L. *Plunkitt of Tammany Hall.* New York: Dutton, 1963.

Short, James F., Jr., and Fred L. Strodtbeck. *Group Process and Gang Delinquency.* Chicago: University of Chicago Press, 1965.

Suttles, Gerald D. *The Social Order of the Slum: Ethnicity and Territory in the Inner City.* Chicago: University of Chicago Press, 1968.

Thrasher, Frederic. *The Gang: A Study Of 1303 Gangs in Chicago.* Chicago: University of Chicago Press, 1928.

Vigil, James Diego. *Barrio Gangs: Street Life and Identity in Southern California.* Austin: University of Texas Press, 1988.

Yablonsky, Lewis. *The Violent Gang.* New York: Macmillan, 1966.

Conversion to the Doomsday Cult

JOHN LOFLAND

The logical and methodological structure of . . . [this] analysis is based on a developmental conception.[1] That is, I will offer a series of more or less successively accumulating factors, which in their total combination would seem to account for conversion to the DP's [Divine Precepts]. Seven such factors will be presented, all of which together seem both necessary and sufficient causes for conversion to occur. . . .

From John Lofland, *Doomsday Cult: A Study of Conversion, Proselytization, and Maintenance of Faith,* Englewood Cliffs, N.J.: Prentice-Hall, © 1966. Excerpt from pp. 31–62. Reprinted by permission of the author.

A MODEL OF CONVERSION

To account for the process by which persons come to be world savers for the DP, I shall be concerned with two types of conditions or factors. The first type, which may be called *predisposing conditions,* comprises attributes of persons *prior* to their contact with the cult. . . .

The second type of conditions concerns . . . the contingencies of social situations. By *situational contingencies* I refer to those conditions that develop through direct confrontation and interaction between the potential convert and DP members, conditions that can lead to the successful recruitment of persons already well disposed toward the enterprise. Many of those who qualified for conversion on the basis of predispositional factors entered into interpersonal relationships with the DP's, but because the proper situational conditions were not met, they did not convert.

Let us now turn to a discussion of each of the factors operating within these two classes.

TENSION

It would seem that no model of human conduct entirely escapes some concept of tension, strain, frustration, deprivation, or the like, as a factor in accounting for action. And not surprisingly, even the most cursory examination of the life situations of converts over the years before they embraced the DP reveals that they labored under what they at least *perceived* to be considerable tension.

This tension is best characterized as a felt discrepancy between some imaginary, ideal state of affairs and the circumstances in which they actually saw themselves. It is suggested that such acutely felt tension is a necessary, but far from sufficient condition for conversion. It provides some disposition to act. But tension may be resolved in a number of ways (or remain unresolved). Hence to know that these people were in a tension situation says little about *what* action they might take. . . .

It would appear that problems we find among [pre-converts]. . . are not *qualitatively* different or distinct from those presumably experienced by a significant, albeit unknown, proportion of the general population. Their peculiarity, if any, appears to be *quantitative;* that is, preconverts felt their problems to be acute and experienced high levels of tension concerning them over rather long periods of time.

It might in fact be said that from the point of view of an outside observer, their circumstances were in general not massively oppressive. One can probably find among the general population large numbers of people laboring under tensions that would seem to be considerably more acute and prolonged.

Perhaps the strongest qualitative characterization of tension supportable by the data is that pre-converts felt themselves frustrated in their various aspirations and *experienced* the tension rather more acutely and over longer periods than most do. . . .

TYPES OF PROBLEM-SOLVING PERSPECTIVES

On the basis of the first factor alone, only those without enduring, acute tensions are ruled out as potential DP converts. Since conversion is hardly the only response to problems, it is important to ask what else these people could have done, and why they didn't.

It seems likely that there were very few converts to the DP's for the simple reason that people have a number of conventional and readily available alternative ways of defining and coping with their problems. By this I mean that they have alternative perspectives, or rhetorics, that specify the nature and sources of problems and offer some program for their resolution. There are many such alternatives in modern society, but I shall briefly describe three particular types: the *psychiatric,* the *political,* and the *religious.* In the first, the origin of problems is typically traced to the psyche, and manipulation of the self is advocated as a resolution to problems. Political solutions, mainly radical, locate the sources of problems in the social structure and advocate its reorganization as a solution. The religious perspective tends to see both sources and solutions to difficulties as emanating from an unseen, and in principle unseeable, realm.

The first two rhetorics are both secular and are the most often used in contemporary society. It is no longer appropriate to regard recalcitrant and aberrant actors as possessed of devils. Indeed, modern religious institutions, in significant measure, offer secular, frequently psychiatric rhetorics concerning problems in living. The predominance of secular definitions of tension is a major source of loss of potential converts to the DP. Most people with acute tensions "get the psychiatric word" especially, either by defining themselves as grist for its mill or by being forced into it. Several persons met other conditions of the model but had adopted a psychiatric definition of their tensions and failed to convert....

All pre-converts seemed surprisingly uninformed about conventional psychiatric and political perspectives for defining their problems. Perhaps largely because of their backgrounds (many were from small towns and rural communities), they had long been accustomed to defining the world in religious terms. Although conventional religious outlooks had been discarded by all pre-converts as inadequate, "spiritless," "dead," etc., prior to contact with the DP's, *the general propensity to impose religious meaning on events had been retained.*

Even within these constrictions in the available solutions for acutely felt problems, a number of alternative responses still remain. First, it must be recognized that people can persist in stressful situations and do little or nothing to reduce their discomfort. This is something that students of social life too often tend to underestimate....

Second, people often take specifically problem-directed action to change those portions of their lives that are troublesome, without at the same time adopting a different world view to interpret them....

Third, there exists a range of maneuvers that "put the problem out of mind." In general these constitute compensations for, or distractions from, problems in living. Such maneuvers include addiction to the mass media, preoccupation with childrearing, or immersion in work. More spectacular bypass routes are alcoholism, suicide, promiscuity, and the like....

In any event, it may be assumed not only that many people with tensions explore these strategies, but also that some succeed and hence become unavailable as potential DP recruits.[2]

RELIGIOUS SEEKERSHIP

Whatever the reasons, pre-converts failed in their attempts to find a successful way out of their difficulties through any of the strategies outlined above. Thus their need for solutions persisted, and their problem-solving perspective was restricted to a religious outlook. However, all pre-converts found that conventional religious institutions failed to provide adequate solutions. Subsequently, each came to see himself as a seeker, a person searching for some satisfactory system for interpreting and resolving his discontent. Given their generally religious view of the world, all pre-converts had, to a greater or lesser extent, defined themselves as looking for an adequate religious perspective and had taken some action to achieve this end.

Some went from church to church and prayer group to prayer group, routing their religious seeking through relatively conventional institutions....

The necessary attributes of pre-converts stated thus far could all have persisted for some time before these people encountered the DP and can be thought of as background factors, or predispositions. Although they appeared to have arisen and been active in the order specified, they are important here as accumulated and simultaneously active factors during the development of succeeding conditions.

THE TURNING POINT

We now turn to situational factors in which timing becomes significant. The first of these is the striking universal circumstance that at the time when they first encountered the DP, all pre-converts had reached or were about to reach what they perceived as a turning point in their lives. That is, each had come to a moment when old lines of action were complete, had failed, or had been or were about to be disrupted, and when they were faced with the opportunity or necessity for doing something different with their lives.[3]...

Turning points in general derived from having recently migrated, lost or quit a job...or graduated from, failed in, or quit an educational institution. Perhaps because most converts were young adults, turning points involving educational institutions were relatively frequent....

The significance of...[the] various kinds of turning points lies in their having produced an increased awareness of and desire to take some action on their problems, *combined with a new opportunity to do so*. Turning points were circumstances in which old obligations and lines of action had diminished, and new involvements had become desirable and possible.

CULT-AFFECTIVE BONDS

We come now to the moments of contact between a potential recruit and the DP's. In order for persons who meet all four of the previously activated steps to be further drawn down the road to full conversion, an affective bond must develop or already exist between the potential recruit and one or more of the DP members. The development or presence of some positive, emotive, interpersonal response seems necessary to bridge the gap between first exposure to the message and coming to accept its truth. That is, persons developed affective ties with the group or some of its members while they still regarded the DP perspective as problematic, or even "way out." In a manner of speaking, final conversion was coming to accept the opinions of one's friends.[4]...

It is particularly important to note that conversions frequently moved through *pre-existing* friendship pairs or nets....

The building of bonds that were unsupported by previous friendships with a new convert often took the form of a sense of instant and powerful rapport with a believer....

It is suggested, then, that although potential converts might have difficulty in taking up the DP perspective, when the four previous conditions *and* an affective tie were present, they came to consider the DP seriously and to begin to accept it as their personal construction of reality.

EXTRA-CULT-AFFECTIVE BONDS

It may be supposed that non-DP associates of the convert-in-process would not be entirely neutral to the now live possibility of his taking up with the DP's. We must inquire, then, into the conditions under which extra-cult controls in the form of emotional attachments are activated, and how they restrain or fail to restrain persons from DP conversion.

By virtue of recent migration, disaffection with geographically distant families and spouses, and very few proximate, extra-cult acquaintances, a few converts were "social atoms" in the classic sense. For them extra-cult attachments were irrelevant....

More typically, converts were effectively without opposition because, although they were acquainted with persons, no one was intimate enough with them to become aware that a conversion was in progress, or, if they knew, did not feel that there was a sufficient mutual attachment to justify intervention....

Ironically, in many cases positive extra-cult attachments were to other religious seekers, who, even though not yet budding converts themselves, provided impetus to continue investigation or entertainment of the DP rather than exercising a countervailing force. Indeed, such extra-cult persons might only be slightly behind their friend or friends in their own conversion process....

In the relatively few cases where there were positive attachments between conventional extra-cult persons and a convert-in-process, control was minimized or not activated because of geographical distance and intentional avoidance of contact or communication about the topic during the period when the convert was solidifying his faith....

When there were emotional attachments to extra-cult, nonseeking persons, and when these persons were physically present and cognizant of the incipient transformation, conversion became a nip and tuck affair. Pulled upon by competing emotional loyalties and their discordant versions of reality, pre-converts were thrown into intense emotional strain....

When extra-cult bonds withstood the period of affective and ideological flirtation with the DP's, conversion failed to be consummated. However, most converts did not seem to have the kind of external affiliations in which the informal control over belief that is exerted among close friends could be exercised. They were so effectively unintegrated into any network of conventional people that for the most part they could simply fall out of relatively routine society virtually unnoticed and take their co-seeker friends (if any) with them.

INTENSIVE INTERACTION

The combination of the six previous factors seems sufficient to bring a person to *verbal conversion* to the DP, but one more contingency must be met if he is to become a deployable agent[5] or what I have termed a *total convert*.

...[Most,] but not all, verbal converts ultimately put their lives at the disposal of the cult. It is suggested that such commitment took place as a result of intensive interaction with DP's and failed to result when such interaction was absent. By intensive interaction is meant actual daily, and even hourly physical accessibility to DP total converts. Such intense exposure offers the opportunity to reinforce and elaborate upon the initial, tentative assent that has been granted the DP world view. It is in such prolonged association that the perspective comes alive as a device for interpreting the moment-to-moment events in the verbal convert's life.

The DP doctrine has a variety of resources for explaining the most minor everyday events and for relating them to a cosmic battle between good and evil spirits in a way that places the convert at the center of this war. Since all DP interpretations point to the imminence of the end, to participate in these explanations of daily life is more and more to come to see the necessity of one's personal participation as a totally committed agent in this cosmic struggle.[6]

The need to make other converts and to support the cause in all ways was the main theme of verbal exchanges between the tentatively accepting and the total converts—and, indeed, among the total converts themselves. Without this close association with those already totally committed, such an appreciation of the need for one's transformation into a total convert failed to develop. In recognition of this fact, the DP's gave greatest priority to attempting to get verbal converts (and even the merely interested) to move into the cult's communal dwellings....

Thus it is that verbal conversion and resolutions to reorganize one's life for the DP's are not automatically translated into total conversion. One must be intensively exposed to the group supporting these new standards of conduct. The DP's did not find proselytizing, the primary task of total converts, a very easy activity to perform. But in the presence of people who supported one another and balmed their collective wounds, such a transformation became possible. Those who accepted the truth of the doctrine but lacked intensive interaction with the core group remained partisan spectators and failed to play an active part in the battle to usher in God's kingdom....

CONCLUDING REMARK

In view of the character of the set of conditions outlined, it might be wondered what competitive advantage the DP's had over other unusual religious groups. In terms of background conditions, I am suggesting that they had little, if any, advantage. In terms of situational conditions, their advantage lay merely in the fact that they got there and actually made their pitch, developed affective bonds, and induced people into intensive interaction. As with so much in life one may say that "there but for the grace of God go I"—within the limits of the conditions specified. It is to be hoped that the present effort will contribute to dispelling the tendency to think that there must be some deep, almost mystical connection between world views and their carriers. Like conceptions which hold that criminals and delinquents must be different from others, so our thinking about other types of deviants has too often assumed some extensive characterological conjunction between participant and pattern of participation.

NOTES

1. Cf. Ralph Turner, "The Quest for Universals in Sociological Research," *American Sociological Review,* Vol. XVIII (December, 1953), 604–611; Howard S. Becker, *Outsiders* (New York: The Free Press of Glencoe, Inc., 1963), esp. pp. 22–25; and, Neil J. Smelser, *Theory of Collective Behavior* (New York: The Free Press of Glencoe, Inc., 1963), pp. 12–21.

2. It perhaps needs to be noted that this discussion is confined to isolating the elements of the conversion sequence. Extended analysis would have to give attention to the factors that *in turn* bring each conversion condition into existence—that is, to develop a theory for each of the seven elements, specifying the conditions under which they develop. On the form that this would likely take see Ralph Turner's discussion of "the intrusive factor," *op. cit.,* 609–611.

3. Everett C. Hughes, *Men and Their Work* (New York: The Free Press of Glencoe, Inc., 1958), Chap. 1; Anselm Strauss, "Transformations of Identity," in Arnold Rose, ed., *Human Behavior and Social Processes* (Boston: Houghton Mifflin Company, 1962), pp. 67–71. Cf. the oft-noted "cultural dislocation" and migration pattern found in the background of converts to many groups, especially cults.

4. Cf. Tamotsu Shibutani, *Society and Personality* (Englewood Cliffs, N.J.: Prentice-Hall, Inc., 1961), pp. 523–532, 588–592. Edgar Schein reports that in prison "the most potent source of influence in coercive persuasion was the identification which arose between a prisoner and his more reformed cellmate" [*Coercive Persuasion* (New York: W. W. Norton & Company, Inc., 1961), p. 277]. See also Alan Kerckhoff, Kurt Back, and Norman Miller, "Sociometric Patterns in Hysterical Contagion," *Sociometry,* Vol. XXVIII (March, 1965), 2–15.

5. On the concept of the "deployable agent" or "deployable personnel" in social movements, see Philip Selznick, *The Organizational Weapon* (New York: The Free Press of Glencoe, Inc., 1959), pp. 18–29.

6. Cf. Schein, *op. cit.,* pp. 136–139, 280–282.

CHAPTER 11

LEARNING THE CULTURE

Deviant subcultures have their own distinctive traditions; these include ways of thinking, feeling, and behaving. Newcomers must learn these traditions, and deviant groups must work to sustain their ideas against the countervailing influences of the dominant culture.

In the first selection Barbara Heyl describes a brothel specifically devoted to training new prostitutes. Next, Martin Weinberg describes the norms nudists learn and how these norms sustain the official nudist perspective. Kenneth Stoddart then shows how LSD users learn from members of their drug-using community how to interpret and control the drug experience.

The Training of House Prostitutes

BARBARA SHERMAN HEYL

Although the day of the elaborate and conspicuous high-class house of prostitution is gone, houses still operate throughout the United States in a variety of altered forms. The business may be run out of trailers and motels along major highways, luxury apartments in the center of a metropolis or run-down houses in smaller, industrialized cities. (Discussions of various aspects of house prostitution include: Gagnon and Simon, 1973:226–27; Hall, 1973:115–95; Heyl, 1974; Jackson, 1969:185–92; Sheehy, 1974:185–204; Stewart, 1972; and Vogliotti, 1975:25–80.) Madams sometimes find themselves teaching young women how to become professional prostitutes. This paper focuses on one madam who trains novices to work at the house level. I compare the training to Bryan's (1965) account of the apprenticeship of call girls and relate the madam's role to the social organization of house prostitution.

Bryan's study of thirty-three Los Angeles call girls is one of the earliest interactionist treatments of prostitution. His data focus on the process of entry into the occupation of call girl and permit an

From "The Madam as Teacher: The Training of House Prostitutes," *Social Problems,* Vol. 24, No. 5 (June 1977), pp. 545–551, 554–555, and in *The Madam as Entrepreneur* by Barbara Sherman Heyl (New Brunswick, NJ: Transaction Books, 1979), pp. 113–128. Reprinted with permission of the Society for the Study of Social Problems and the author.

Author's Note: This study analyzes the training provided by one madam for women entering house prostitution in a moderate-sized city. The data include taped training sessions, observations of the madam's teaching techniques, and repeated interviews with the madam. The content and structure of the training is compared to that reported in Bryan's (1965) study of the apprenticeship of call girls. The madam's training reflects aspects of the social organization of house prostitution, especially the close interaction of prostitutes in the house that requires a common set of work rules and practices.

analysis of the structure and content of a woman's apprenticeship. He concluded that the apprenticeship of call girls is mainly directed toward developing a clientele, rather than sexual skills (1965:288, 296–7). But while Bryan notes that pimps seldom train women directly, approximately half of his field evidence in fact derives from pimp-call girl apprenticeships. Thus, in Bryan's study (as well as in subsequent work on entry into prostitution as an occupation) there is a missing set of data on the more typical female trainer-trainee relationship and on the content and process of training at other levels of the business in nonmetropolitan settings. This paper attempts to fill this gap.

ANN'S TURN-OUT ESTABLISHMENT

A professional prostitute, whether she works as a streetwalker, house prostitute, or call girl, can usually pick out one person in her past who "turned her out," that is, who taught her the basic techniques and rules of the prostitute's occupation.[1] For women who begin working at the house level, that person may be a pimp, another "working girl," or a madam. Most madams and managers of prostitution establishments, however, prefer not to take on novice prostitutes, and they may even have a specific policy against hiring turn-outs (see Erwin (1960:204–5) and Lewis (1942:222)). The turn-out's inexperience may cost the madam clients and money; to train the novice, on the other hand, costs her time and energy. Most madams and managers simply do not want the additional burden.

It was precisely the madam's typical disdain for turn-outs that led to the emergence of the house discussed in this paper—a house specifically devoted to training new prostitutes. The madam of this operation, whom we shall call Ann, is forty-one years old and has been in the prostitution world twenty-three years, working primarily at the house level. Ann knew that pimps who manage women at this level have difficulty placing novices in houses. After operating several houses staffed by professional prostitutes, she decided to run a school for turn-outs partly as a strategy for acquiring a continually changing staff of young women for her house. Pimps are the active recruiters of new prostitutes, and Ann found that, upon demonstrating that she could transform the pimps' new, square women into trained prostitutes easily placed in professional houses, pimps would help keep her business staffed.[2] Ann's house is a small operation in a middle-sized, industrial city (population 300,000), with a limited clientele of primarily working-class men retained as customers for ten to fifteen years and offered low rates to maintain their patronage.

Although Ann insists that every turn-out is different, her group of novices is remarkably homogeneous in some ways. Ann has turned out approximately twenty women a year over the six years while she has operated a training school. Except for one Chicano, one black and one American Indian, the women were all white. They ranged in age from eighteen to twenty seven. Until three years ago, all the women she hired had pimps. Since then, more women are independent (so-called "outlaws"), although many come to Ann sponsored by a pimp. That is, in return for being placed with Ann, the turn-out gives the pimp a percentage of her earnings for a specific length of time. At present eighty percent of the turn-outs come to Ann without a long-term commitment to a pimp. The turn-outs stay at Ann's on the average of two to three months. This is the same average length of time Bryan (1965:290) finds for the apprenticeship in his call-girl study. Ann seldom has more than two or three women in training at any one time. Most turn-outs live at the house, often just a large apartment near the older business section of the city.

THE CONTENT OF THE TRAINING

The data for the following analysis are of three kinds. First, tape recordings from actual training sessions with fourteen novices helped specify the structure and content of the training provided. Second, lengthy interviews with three of the novices and multiple interviews with Ann were conducted to obtain data on the training during the novice's first few days at the house before the first group training sessions were conducted and recorded by Ann. And third, visits to the house on ten occasions and observations of Ann's interaction with the novices during teaching periods extended the data on training techniques used and the relationship between madam and novice. In addition, weekly contact with Ann over a four-year period allowed repeated review of current problems and strategies in training turn-outs.

Ann's training of the novice begins soon after the woman arrives at the house. The woman first chooses an alias. Ann then asks her whether she has ever "Frenched a guy all the way," that is, whether she has brought a man to orgasm during the act of fellatio. Few of the women say they have. By admitting her lack of competence in a specialized area, the novice has permitted Ann to assume the role of teacher. Ann then launches into instruction on performing fellatio. Such instruction is important to her business. Approximately eighty percent of her customers are what Ann calls "French tricks." Many men visit prostitutes to receive sexual services, including fellatio, their wives or lovers seldom perform. This may be particularly true of the lower- and working-class clientele of the houses and hotels of prostitution (Gagnon and Simon, 1973:230). Yet the request for fellatio may come from clients at all social levels; consequently, it is a sexual skill today's prostitute must possess and one she may not have prior to entry into the business (Bryan, 1965:293; Winick and Kinsie, 1971:180, 207; Gray, 1973:413).

Although Ann devotes much more time to teaching the physical and psychological techniques of performing fellatio than she does to any other sexual skill, she also provides strategies for coitus and giving a "half and half"—fellatio followed by coitus. The sexual strategies taught are frequently a mixture of ways for stimulating the client sexually and techniques of self-protection during the sexual acts. For example, during coitus, the woman is to move her hips "like a go-go dancer's" while keeping her feet on the bed and tightening her inner thigh muscles to protect herself from the customer's thrust and full penetration. Ann allows turn-outs to perform coitus on their backs only, and the woman is taught to keep one of her arms across her chest as a measure of self-defense in this vulnerable position.

After Ann has described the rudimentary techniques for the three basic sexual acts—fellatio, coitus, and "half and half"—she begins to explain the rules of the house operation. The first set of rules concerns what acts the client may receive for specific sums of money. Time limits are imposed on the clients, roughly at the rate of $1 per minute; the minimum rate in this house is $15 for any of the three basic positions. Ann describes in detail what will occur when the first client arrives: he will be admitted by either Ann or the maid; the women are to stand and smile at him, but not speak to him (considered "dirty hustling"); he will choose one of the women and go to the bedroom with her. Ann accompanies the turn-out and the client to the bedroom and begins teaching the woman how to check the man for any cuts or open sores on the genitals and for any signs of old or active venereal disease. Ann usually rechecks each client herself during the turn-out's first two weeks of work. For the first few days Ann remains in the room while the turn-out and client negotiate the sexual contract. In ensuing days Ann spends time helping the woman develop verbal

skills to "hustle" the customer for more expensive sexual activities.

The following analysis of the instruction Ann provides is based on tape recordings made by Ann during actual training sessions in 1971 and 1975. These sessions took place after the turn-outs had worked several days but usually during their first two weeks of work. The tapes contain ten hours of group discussion with fourteen different novices. The teaching tapes were analyzed according to topics covered in the discussions, using the method outlined in Barker (1963) for making such divisions in the flow of conversation and using Bryan's analysis of the call girl's apprenticeship as a guide in grouping the topics. Bryan divides the content of the training of call girls into two broad dimensions, one philosophical and one interpersonal (1965:291–4). The first emphasizes a subcultural value system and sets down guidelines for how the novice *should* treat her clients and her colleagues in the business. The second dimension follows from the first but emphasizes actual behavioral techniques and skills.

The content analysis of the taped training sessions produced three major topics of discussion and revealed the relative amount of time Ann devoted to each. The first two most frequently discussed topics can be categorized under Bryan's dimension of interpersonal skills; they were devoted to teaching situational strategies for managing clients. The third topic resembles Bryan's value dimension (1965:291–2).

The first topic stressed physical skills and strategies. Included in this category were instruction on how to perform certain sexual acts and specification of their prices, discussion of particular clients, and instruction in techniques for dealing with certain categories of clients, such as "older men" or "kinky" tricks. This topic of physical skills also included discussion of, and Ann's demonstration of, positions designed to provide the woman maximum comfort and protection from the man during different sexual acts. Defense tactics, such as ways to get out of a sexual position and out of the bedroom quickly, were practiced by the novices. Much time was devoted to analyzing past encounters with particular clients. Bryan finds similar discussions of individual tricks among novice call girls and their trainers (1965:293). In the case of Ann's turn-outs these discussions were often initiated by a novice's complaint or question about a certain client and his requests or behavior in the bedroom. The novice always received tips and advice from Ann and the other women present on how to manage that type of bedroom encounter. Such sharing of tactics allows the turn-out to learn what Gagnon and Simon call "patterns of client management" (1973:231).

Ann typically used these discussions of bedroom difficulties to further the training in specific sexual skills she had begun during the turn-out's first few days at work. It is possible that the addition of such follow-up sexual training to that provided during the turn-out's first days at the house results in a more extensive teaching of actual sexual skills than that obtained either by call girls or streetwalkers. Bryan finds that in the call-girl training—except for fellatio—"There seems to be little instruction concerning sexual techniques as such, even though the previous sexual experience of the trainee may have been quite limited" (1965:293). Gray (1973:413) notes that her sample of streetwalker turn-outs were rarely taught specific work strategies:

> They learned these things by trial and error on the job. Nor were they schooled in specific sexual techniques: usually they were taught by customers who made the specific requests.

House prostitution may require more extensive sexual instruction than other forms of the business. The dissatisfied customer of a house may mean loss of business and therefore loss of income to the madam and the prostitutes who work there. The sexually inept streetwalker or call girl does not hurt business for anyone but herself; she may actually increase business for those women in the area should dissatisfied clients choose to

avoid her. But the house depends on a stable clientele of satisfied customers.

The second most frequently discussed topic could be labeled: client management—verbal skills. Ann's primary concern was teaching what she calls "hustling." "Hustling" is similar to what Bryan terms a "sales pitch" for call girls (1965:292), but in the house setting it takes place in the bedroom while the client is deciding how much to spend and what sexual acts he wishes performed. "Hustling" is designed to encourage the client to spend more than the minimum rate.[3] The prominence on the teaching tapes of instruction in this verbal skill shows its importance in Ann's training of novices.

On one of the tapes Ann uses her own turning-out experience to explain to two novices (both with pimps) why she always teaches hustling skills as an integral part of working in a house.

Ann as a Turn-out[4]

ANN: Of course, I can remember a time when I didn't know that I was supposed to hustle. So that's why I understand that it's difficult to *learn* to hustle. When I turned out it was $2 a throw. They came in. They gave me their $2. They got a hell of a fuck. And that was it. Then one Saturday night I turned *forty-four* tricks! And Penny [the madam] used to put the number of tricks at the top of the page and the amount of money at the bottom of the page—she used these big ledger books. Lloyd [Ann's pimp] came in at six o'clock and he looked at that book and he just *knew* I had made all kinds of money. Would you believe I had turned forty-two $2 tricks and two $3 tricks—because two of 'em got generous and gave me an extra buck! [Laughs] I got my ass whipped. And I was so tired—I thought I was going to die—I was 15 years old. And I got my ass whipped for it. [Ann imitates an angry Lloyd:] "Don't you know you're supposed to ask for more money?!"

No, I didn't. Nobody told me that. All they told me was it was $2. So that is learning it the *hard* way. I'm trying to help you learn it the *easy* way, if there is an easy way to do it.

In the same session Ann asks one of the turn-outs (Linda, age eighteen) to practice her hustling rap.

Learning the Hustling Rap

ANN: I'm going to be a trick. You've checked me. I want you to carry it from there. [Ann begins role-playing: she plays the client; Linda, the hustler.]

LINDA: [mechanically] What kind of party would you like to have?

ANN: That had all the enthusiasm of a wet noodle. I really wouldn't *want* any party with that because you evidently don't want to give me one.

LINDA: What kind of party would you *like* to have?

ANN: I usually take a half and half.

LINDA: Uh, the money?

ANN: What money?

LINDA: The money you're supposed to have! [loudly] 'Cause you ain't gettin' it for free!

ANN: [upset] Linda, if you *ever*, ever say that in my joint...Because that's fine for street hustling. In street hustling, you're going to have to hard-hustle those guys or they're not going to come up with anything. Because they're going to *try* and get it for free. But when they walk in here, they *know* they're not going to get it for free to begin with. So try another tack—just a little more friendly, not quite so hard-nosed. [Returning to role-playing:] I just take a half and half.

LINDA: How about fifteen [dollars]?

ANN: You're leading into the money too fast, honey. Try: "What are you going to spend?" or "How much money are you going to spend?" or something like that.

LINDA: How much would you like to spend?

ANN: No! Not "like." 'Cause they don't *like* to spend anything.

LINDA: How much *would* you like to spend?

ANN: Make it a very definite, positive statement: "How much are you going to spend?"

Ann considers teaching hustling skills her most difficult and important task. In spite of her lengthy discussion on the tapes of the rules and techniques for dealing with the customer sexually, Ann states that it may take only a few minutes to "show a girl how to turn a trick." A substantially longer period is required, however, to teach her to hustle. To be adept at hustling, the woman must be mentally alert and sensitive to the client's response to what she is saying and doing and be able to act on those perceptions of his reactions. The hustler must maintain a steady patter of verbal coaxing, during which her tone of voice may be more important than her actual words.

In Ann's framework, then, hustling is a form of verbal sexual aggression. Referring to the problems in teaching novices to hustle, Ann notes that "taking the aggressive part is something women are not used to doing; particularly young women." No doubt, hustling is difficult to teach partly because the woman must learn to discuss sexual acts, whereas in her previous experience, sexual behavior and preferences had been negotiated nonverbally (see Gagnon and Simon, 1973:228). Ann feels that to be effective, each woman's "hustling rap" must be her own—one that comes naturally and will strike the clients as sincere. All of that takes practice. But Ann is aware that the difficulty in learning to hustle stems more from the fact that it involved inappropriate sex-role behavior. Bryan concludes that it is precisely this aspect of soliciting men on the telephone that causes the greatest distress to the novice call girl (1965:293). Thus, the call girl's income is affected by how much business she can bring in by her calls, that is, by how well she can learn to be socially aggressive on the telephone. The income of the house prostitute, in turn, depends heavily on her hustling skills in the bedroom. Ann's task, then, is to train the novice, who has recently come from a culture where young women are not expected to be sexually aggressive, to assume that role with a persuasive naturalness.

Following the first two major topics—client management through physical and verbal skills—the teaching of "racket" (prostitution world) values was the third-ranking topic of training and discussion on the teaching tapes. Bryan notes that the major value taught to call girls is "that of maximizing gains and minimizing effort, even if this requires transgressions of either a legal or moral nature" (1965:291). In her training, however, Ann avoids communicating the notion that the novices may exploit the customers in any way they can. For example, stealing or cheating clients is grounds for dismissal from the house. Ann cannot afford the reputation among her tricks that they risk being robbed when they visit her. Moreover, being honest with clients is extolled as a virtue. Thus, Ann urges the novices to tell the trick if she is nervous or unsure, to let him know she is new to the business. This is in direct contradiction to the advice pimps usually give their new women to hide their inexperience from the trick. Ann asserts that honesty in this case usually means that the client will be more tolerant of mistakes in sexual technique, be less likely to interpret hesitancy as coldness, and be generally more helpful and sympathetic. Putting her "basic principle" in the form of a simple directive, Ann declares: "Please the trick, but at the same time get as much money for pleasing him as you possibly can." Ann does not consider hustling to be client exploitation. It is simply the attempt to sell the customer the product with the highest profit margin. That is, she would defend hustling in terms familiar to the businessman or sales manager.

That Ann teaches hustling as a value is revealed in the following discussion between Ann and Sandy—a former hustler and long-time friend of Ann. Sandy, who married a former trick and still

lives in town, has come over to the house to help instruct several novices in the hustling business.

Whores, Prostitutes and Hustlers

ANN: [To the turn-outs:] Don't get up-tight that you're hesitating or you're fumbling, within the first week or even the first five years. Because it takes that long to become a good hustler. I mean you can be a whore in one night. There's nothing to that. The first time you take money you're a whore.

SANDY: This girl in Midtown [a small, Midwestern city] informed me—I had been working there awhile—that I was a "whore" and she was a "prostitute." And I said: "Now what the hell does that mean?" Well the difference was that a prostitute could pick her customer and a whore had to take anybody. I said: "Well honey, I want to tell you something. I'm neither one." She said: "Well, you *work*." I said: "I know, but I'm a *hustler.* I make *money* for what I do."

ANN: And this is what I turn out—or try to turn out—hustlers. Not prostitutes. Not whores. But hustlers.

For Ann and Sandy the hustler deserves high status in the prostitution business because she has mastered a specific set of skills that, even with many repeat clients, earn her premiums above the going rate for sexual acts.

In the ideological training of call girls Bryan finds that "values such as fairness with other working girls, or fidelity to a pimp, may occasionally be taught" (1965:291–2); the teaching tapes revealed Ann's affirmation of both these virtues. When a pimp brings a woman to Ann, she supports his control over that woman. For example, if during her stay at the house, the novice breaks any of the basic rules—by using drugs, holding back money (from either Ann or the pimp), lying or seeing another man—Ann will report the infractions to the woman's pimp. Ann notes: "If I don't do that and the pimp finds out, he knows I'm not training her right, and he won't bring his future ladies to me for training." Ann knows she is dependent on the pimps to help supply her with turn-outs. Bryan, likewise, finds a willingness among call-girls' trainers to defer to the pimps' wishes during the apprenticeship period (1965:290).

Teaching fairness to other prostitutes is particularly relevant to the madam who daily faces the problem of maintaining peace among competing women at work under one roof. If two streetwalkers or two call girls find they cannot get along, they need not work near one another. But if a woman leaves a house because of personal conflicts, the madam loses a source of income. To minimize potential negative feelings among novices, Ann stresses mutual support, prohibits "criticizing another girl," and denigrates the "prima donna"—the prostitute who flaunts her financial success before the other women.

In still another strategy to encourage fair treatment of one's colleagues in the establishment, Ann emphasizes a set of rules prohibiting "dirty hustling"—behavior engaged in by one prostitute that would undercut the business of other women in the house. Tabooed under the label of "dirty hustling" are the following: appearing in the line-up partially unclothed; performing certain disapproved sexual positions, such as anal intercourse; and allowing approved sexual extras without charging additional fees. The norms governing acceptable behavior vary from house to house and region to region, and Ann warns the turn-outs to ask about such rules when they begin work in a new establishment. The woman who breaks the work norms in a house, either knowingly or unknowingly, will draw the anger of the other women and can be fired by a madam eager to restore peace and order in the house.

Other topics considered on the tapes—in addition to physical skills, "hustling" and work values—were instruction on personal hygiene and grooming, role-playing of conversational skills with tricks on topics not related to sex or hustling ("living room talk"), house rules not related to hustling (such as punctuality, no perfume, no drugs), and guidelines for what to do during an arrest. There were specific suggestions on how to handle personal criticism, questions and insults from clients. In addition, the discussions on the tapes provided the novices with many general strategies for becoming "professionals" at their work, for example, the importance of personal style, enthusiasm ("the customer is always right"), and sense of humor. In some ways these guidelines resemble a beginning course in salesmanship. But they also provide clues, particularly in combination with the topics on handling client insults and the emphasis on hustling, on how the house prostitute learns to manage a stable and limited clientele and cope psychologically with the repetition of the clients and the sheer tedium of the physical work (Hughes, 1971:342–5).

. . . Although Ann feels strongly that training is required to become a successful hustler at the house level, the function served by the training can be seen more as a spin-off of the structure of the occupation at that level: madams of establishments will often hire only trained prostitutes. Novices who pose as experienced hustlers are fairly easily detected by those proficient in the business working in the same house; to be found out all she need do is violate any of the expected norms of behavior: wear perfume, repeatedly fail to hustle any "over-money" or engage in dirty hustling. The exposure to racket values, which the training provides, may be more critical to the house prostitute than to the call girl. She must live and work in close contact with others in the business. Participants in house prostitution are more integrated into the prostitution world than are call girls, who can be and frequently are "independent"—working without close ties to pimps or other prostitutes. Becoming skilled in hustling is also less important for the call girl, as her minimum fee is usually high, making hustling for small increments less necessary. The house prostitute who does not know how to ask for more money, however, lowers the madam's income as well—another reason why madams prefer professional prostitutes.

The training of house prostitutes, then, reflects two problems in the social organization of house prostitution: (1) most madams will not hire untrained prostitutes; and (2) the close interaction of prostitutes operating within the confines of a house requires a common set of work standards and practices. These two factors differentiate house prostitution from call-girl and streetwalking operations and facilitate this madam's task of turning novices into professional prostitutes. The teaching madam employs a variety of coaching techniques to train turn-outs in sexual and hustling skills and to expose them to a set of occupational rules and values. Hers is an effort to prepare women with conventional backgrounds for work in the social environment of a house of prostitution where those skills and values are expected and necessary.

NOTES

1. This situation-specific induction into prostitution may be contrasted with the "smooth and almost imperceptible" transition to the status of poolroom "hustler" noted by Polsky (1969:80–81).
2. In the wider context of the national prostitution scene, Ann's situation reflects the "minor league" status of her geographical location. In fact, she trains women from other communities who move on to the more lucrative opportunities in the big city. See the stimulating applications of the concept of "minor league" to the study of occupations in Faulkner (1974).
3. The term "hustling" has been used to describe a wide range of small-time criminal activities. Even within the world of prostitution, "hustling" can refer to different occupational styles; see Ross' description of the "hustler" who "is distinguished from ordinary prostitutes in frequently engaging in accessory crimes of exploitation," such as extortion or robbery (1959:16). The use of the term here is thus highly specific, reflecting its meaning in Ann's world.
4. The indented sections (for example, "Ann as a Turn-out" and "Learning the Hustling Rap") are transcriptions from the teaching tapes. Redundant expressions have been omitted, and the author's comments on the speech tone or delivery are bracketed. Words italicized indicate emphasis by the speaker.

REFERENCES

Barker, Roger G. (ed.). 1963. *The Stream of Behavior: Explorations of Its Structure and Content.* New York: Appleton-Century-Crofts.

Bryan, James H. 1965. "Apprenticeships in Prostitution." *Social Problems,* 12 (Winter): 287–297.

———. 1966. "Occupational Ideologies and Individual Attitudes of Call Girls." *Social Problems,* 13 (Spring): 441–450.

Erwin, Carol. 1960. *The Orderly Disorderly House.* Garden City, N.Y.: Doubleday.

Faulkner, Robert R. 1974. "Coming of Age in Organizations: A Comparative Study of Career Contingencies and Adult Socialization." *Sociology of Work and Occupations,* 1 (May): 131–173.

Gagnon, John H. and William Simon. 1973. *Sexual Conduct: The Social Sources of Human Sexuality.* Chicago: Aldine.

Gray, Diana. 1973. "Turning-out: A Study of Teenage Prostitution." *Urban Life and Culture,* 1 (January): 401–425.

Hall, Susan. 1973. *Ladies of the Night.* New York: Trident Press.

Heyl, Barbara S. 1974. "The Madam as Entrepreneur." *Sociological Symposium,* 11 (Spring): 61–82.

Hughes, Everett C. 1971. "Work and Self." In *The Sociological Eye: Selected Papers.* Chicago: Aldine-Atherton, pp. 338–347.

Jackson, Bruce. 1969. *A Thief's Primer.* Toronto, Ontario: Macmillan.

Kinsey, Alfred C., Wardell B. Pomeroy, and Clyde E. Martin. 1948. *Sexual Behavior in the Human Male.* Philadelphia: W. B. Saunders.

Lewis, Gladys Adelina (ed.). 1942. *Call House Madam: The Story of the Career of Beverly Davis.* San Francisco: Martin Tudordale.

Polsky, Ned. 1969. *Hustlers, Beats and Others.* Garden City, N.Y.: Doubleday.

Ross, H. Laurence. 1959. "The 'Hustler' in Chicago." *Journal of Student Research,* 1: 13–19.

Sheehy, Gail. 1974. *Hustling: Prostitution in Our Wide-Open Society.* New York: Dell.

Stewart, George I. 1972. "On First Being a John." *Urban Life and Culture,* 1 (October): 255–274.

Vogliotti, Gabriel R. 1975. *The Girls of Nevada.* Secaucus, New Jersey: Citadel Press.

Winick, Charles and Paul M. Kinsie. 1971. *The Lively Commerce: Prostitution in the United States.* Chicago: Quadrangle Books.

The Nudist Management of Respectability

MARTIN S. WEINBERG

Public nudity is taboo in our society. Yet there is a group who breach this moral rule. They call themselves "social nudists."

A number of questions may be asked about these people. For example, how can they see their behavior as morally appropriate? Have they constructed their own morality? If so, what characterizes this morality and what are its consequences?[1]

This article will attempt to answer these questions through a study of social interaction in nudist camps. The data come from three sources: two summers of participant observation in nudist camps; 101 interviews with nudists in the Chicago area; and 617 mailed questionnaires completed by nudists in the United States and Canada.[2]

THE CONSTRUCTION OF SITUATED MORAL MEANINGS: THE NUDIST MORALITY

The construction of morality in nudist camps is based on the official interpretations that camps provide regarding the moral meanings of public heterosexual nudity. These are (1) that nudity and sexuality are unrelated, (2) that there is nothing shameful about the human body, (3) that nudity promotes a feeling of freedom and natural pleasure, and (4) that nude exposure to the sun promotes physical, mental, and spiritual well-being.

This official perspective is sustained in nudist camps to an extraordinary degree, illustrating the extent to which adult socialization can affect traditional moral meanings. (This is especially true with regard to the first two points of the nudist perspective, which will be our primary concern since these are its "deviant" aspects.) The assump-

Reprinted from *Sex Research: Studies from the Kinsey Institute* by Martin S. Weinberg, pp. 217–232. Copyright © 1976 by The Kinsey Institute for Research in Sex, Gender, and Reproduction. Reprinted by permission of Oxford University Press, Inc.

tion in the larger society that nudity and sexuality are related, and the resulting emphasis on covering the sexual organs, make the nudist perspective a specifically situated morality. My field work, interview, and questionnaire research show that nudists routinely use a special system of rules to create, sustain, and enforce this situated morality.

STRATEGIES FOR SUSTAINING A SITUATED MORALITY

The first strategy used by the nudist camp to anesthetize any relationship between nudity and sexuality[3] involves a system of organizational precautions regarding who can come into the camp. Most camps, for example, regard unmarried people, especially single men, as a threat to the nudist morality. They suspect that singles may indeed see nudity as something sexual. Thus, most camps either exclude unmarried people (especially men), or allow only a small quota of them. Camps that do allow single men may charge them up to 35 percent more than they charge families. (This is intended to discourage single men, but since the cost is still relatively low compared with other resorts, this measure is not very effective. It seems to do little more than create resentment among the singles, and by giving formal organizational backing to the definition that singles are not especially desirable, it may contribute to the segregation of single and married members in nudist camps.)

Certification by the camp owner is another requirement for admission to camp grounds, and three letters of recommendation regarding the applicant's character are sometimes required. These regulations help preclude people whom members regard as a threat to the nudist morality.

[The camp owner] invited us over to see if we were desirable people. Then after we did this, he invited

us to camp on probation; then they voted us into camp. [Q: Could you tell me what you mean by desirable people?] Well, not people who are inclined to drink, or people who go there for a peep show. Then they don't want you there. They feel you out in conversation. They want people for mental and physical health reasons.

Whom to admit [is the biggest problem of the camp]. [Q][4] Because the world is so full of people whose attitudes on nudity are hopelessly warped. [Q: Has this always been the biggest problem in camp?] Yes. Every time anybody comes, a decision has to be made. [Q]...The lady sitting at the gate decides about admittance. The director decides on membership.

A limit is sometimes set on the number of trial visits a non-member may make to camp. In addition, there is usually a limit on how long a person can remain clothed. This is a strategy to mark guests who may not sincerely accept the nudist perspective.

The second strategy for sustaining the nudist morality involves norms of interpersonal behavior. These norms are as follows:

No Staring. This rule controls overt signs of overinvolvement. As the publisher of one nudist magazine said, "They all look up to the heavens and never look below." Such studied inattention is most exaggerated among women, who usually show no recognition that the male is unclothed. Women also recount that they had expected men to look at their nude bodies, only to find, when they finally did get up the courage to undress, that no one seemed to notice. As one woman states: "I got so mad because my husband wanted me to undress in front of other men that I just pulled my clothes right off thinking everyone would look at me." She was amazed (and appeared somewhat disappointed) when no one did.

The following statements illustrate the constraints that result:

[Q: Have you ever observed or heard about anyone staring at someone's body while at camp?] I've heard stories, particularly about men that

stare. Since I heard these stories, I tried not to, and have even done away with my sunglasses after someone said, half-joking, that I hide behind sunglasses to stare. Toward the end of the summer I stopped wearing sunglasses. And you know what, it was a child who told me this.

[Q: Would you stare...?] Probably not, 'cause you can get in trouble and get thrown out. If I thought I could stare unobserved I might. They might not throw you out, but it wouldn't do you any good. [Q] The girl might tell others and they might not want to talk to me.... [Q] They disapprove by not talking to you, ignoring you, etc.

[Someone who stares] wouldn't belong there. [Q] If he does that he is just going to camp to see the opposite sex. [Q] He is just coming to stare. [Q] You go there to swim and relax.

I try very hard to look at them from the jaw up—even more than you would normally.[5]

No Sex Talk. Sex talk, or telling "dirty jokes," is uncommon in camp. The owner of a large camp in the Midwest stated: "It is usually expected that members of a nudist camp will not talk about sex, politics, or religion." Or as one single male explained: "It is taboo to make sexual remarks here." During my field work, it was rare to hear "sexual" joking such as one hears at most other types of resort. Interview respondents who mentioned that they had talked about sex qualified this by explaining that such talk was restricted to close friends, was of a "scientific nature," or, if a joke, was a "cute sort."

Asked what they would think of someone who breached this rule, respondents indicated that such behavior would cast doubt on the situated morality of the nudist camp:

One would expect to hear less of that at camp than at other places. [Q] Because you expect that the members are screened in their attitude for nudism—and this isn't one who prefers sexual jokes.

I've never heard anyone swear or tell a dirty joke out there.

No. Not at camp. You're not supposed to. You bend over backwards not to.

They probably don't belong there. They're there to see what they can find to observe. [Q] Well, their mind isn't on being a nudist, but to see so and so nude.

No Body Contact.   Although the extent to which this is enforced varies from camp to camp, there is at least some degree of informal enforcement in nearly every camp. Nudists mention that they are particularly careful not to brush against anyone or have any body contact for fear of how it might be interpreted:

I stay clear of the opposite sex. They're so sensitive, they imagine things.

People don't get too close to you. Even when they talk. They sit close to you, but they don't get close enough to touch you.

We have a minimum of contact. There are more restrictions [at a nudist camp]. [Q] Just a feeling I had. I would openly show my affection more readily someplace else.

And when asked to conceptualize a breach of this rule, the following response is typical:

They are in the wrong place. [Q] That's not part of nudism. [Q] I think they are there for some sort of sex thrill. They are certainly not there to enjoy the sun.

Also, in photographs taken for nudist magazines, the subjects usually have only limited body contact. One female nudist explained: "We don't want anyone to think we're immoral." Outsiders' interpretations, then, can also constitute a threat.

Associated with the body contact taboo is a prohibition of nude dancing. Nudists cite this as a separate rule. This rule is often talked about by members in a way that indicates organizational strain—that is, the rule itself makes evident that a strategy is in operation to sustain their situated morality.

This reflects a contradiction in our beliefs. But it's self-protection. One incident and we'd be closed.

No Alcoholic Beverages in American Camps. This rule guards against breakdowns in inhibition, and even respondents who admitted that they had "snuck a beer" before going to bed went on to say that they fully favor the rule.

Yes. We have [drunk at camp]. We keep a can of beer in the refrigerator since we're out of the main area. We're not young people or carousers.... I still most generally approve of it as a camp rule and would disapprove of anyone going to extremes. [Q] For commonsense reasons. People who overindulge lose their inhibitions, and there is no denying that the atmosphere of a nudist camp makes one bend over backwards to keep people who are so inclined from going beyond the bounds of propriety.

Anyone who drinks in camp is jeopardizing their membership and they shouldn't. Anyone who drinks in camp could get reckless. [Q] Well, when guys and girls drink they're a lot bolder—they might get fresh with someone else's girl. That's why it isn't permitted, I guess.

Rules Regarding Photography.   Photography in a nudist camp is controlled by the camp management. Unless the photographer works for a nudist magazine, his (or her) moral perspective is sometimes suspect. One photographer's remark to a woman that led to his being so typed was, "Do you think you could open your legs a little more?"

Aside from a general restriction on the use of cameras, when cameras are allowed, it is expected that no pictures will be taken without the subject's permission. Members blame the misuse of cameras especially on single men. As one nudist said: "You always see the singles poppin' around out of nowhere snappin' pictures." In general, control is maintained, and any infractions that take place are not blatant or obvious. Overindulgence in picture-taking communicates an overinvolvement in the subjects' nudity and casts doubt on the assumption that nudity and sexuality are unrelated.

Photographers dressed only in cameras and light exposure meters. I don't like them. I think they only go out for pictures. Their motives should be questioned.

Photographers for nudist magazines recognize the signs that strain the situated morality that characterizes nudist camps. As one such photographer commented:

> I never let a girl look straight at the camera. It looks too suggestive. I always have her look off to the side.

Similarly, a nudist model showed the writer a pin-up magazine to point out how a model could make a nude picture "sexy"—through the use of various stagings, props, and expressions—and in contrast, how the nudist model eliminates these techniques to make her pictures "natural." Although it may be questionable that a nudist model completely eliminates a sexual perspective for the non-nudist, the model discussed how she attempts to do this.

> It depends on the way you look. Your eyes and your smile can make you look sexy. The way they're looking at you. Here, she's on a bed. It wouldn't be sexy if she were on a beach with kids running around. They always have some clothes on too. See how she's "looking" sexy? Like an "oh dear!" look. A different look can change the whole picture.

> Now here's a decent pose.... Outdoors makes it "nature." Here she's giving you "the eye," or is undressing. It's cheesecake. It depends on the expression on her face. Having nature behind it makes it better. Don't smile like "come on honey!" It's that look and the lace thing she has on.... Like when you half-close your eyes, like "oh baby," a Marilyn Monroe look. Art is when you don't look like you're hiding it halfway.

The element of trust plays a particularly strong role in socializing women to the nudist perspective. Consider this in the following statements made by another model for nudist magazines. She and her husband had been indoctrinated in the nudist ideology by friends. At the time of the interview, however, the couple had not yet been to camp, although they had posed indoors for nudist magazines.

> [Three months ago, before I was married] I never knew a man had any pubic hairs. I was shocked when I was married.... I wouldn't think of getting undressed in front of my husband. I wouldn't make love with a light on, or in the daytime.

With regard to being a nudist model, this woman commented:

> None of the pictures are sexually seductive. [Q] The pose, the look—you can have a pose that's completely nothing, till you get a look that's not too hard to do. [Q: How do you do that?] I've never tried. By putting on a certain air about a person; a picture that couldn't be submitted to a nudist magazine—using _____ [the nudist photographer's] language.... [Q: Will your parents see your pictures in the magazine?] Possibly. I don't really care.... My mother might take it all right. But they've been married twenty years and she's never seen my dad undressed.[6]

No Accentuation of the Body. Accentuating the body is regarded as incongruent with the nudist morality. Thus, a woman who had shaved her pubic area was labeled "disgusting" by other members. There was a similar reaction to women who sat in a blatantly "unladylike" manner.

> I'd think she was inviting remarks. [Q] I don't know. It seems strange to think of it. It's strange you ask it. Out there, they're not unconscious about their posture. Most women there are very circumspect even though in the nude.

> For a girl,...[sitting with your legs open] is just not feminine or ladylike. The hair doesn't always cover it. [Q] Men get away with so many things. But, it would look dirty for a girl, like she was waiting for something. When I'm in a secluded area I've spread my legs to sun, but I kept an eye open and if anyone came I'd close my legs and sit up a little. It's just not ladylike.

> You can lay on your back or side, or with your knees under your chin. But not with your legs spread apart. It would look to other people like you're there for other reasons. [Q: What other reasons?]...To stare and get an eyeful...not to enjoy the sun and people.

No Unnatural Attempts at Covering the Body.

"Unnatural attempts" at covering the body are ridiculed since they call into question the assumption that there is no shame in exposing any area of the body. If such behavior occurs early in one's nudist career, however, members usually have more compassion, assuming that the person just has not yet fully assimilated the new morality.

It is how members interpret the behavior, however, rather than the behavior per se, that determines whether covering up is disapproved.

If they're cold or sunburned, it's understandable. If it's because they don't agree with the philosophy, they don't belong there.

I would feel their motives for becoming nudists were not well founded. That they were not true nudists, not idealistic enough.

A third strategy that is sometimes employed to sustain the nudist reality is the use of communal toilets. Not all the camps have communal toilets, but the large camp where I did most of my field work did have such a facility, which was marked, "Little Girls Room and Little Boys Too." Although the stalls had three-quarter-length doors, this combined facility still helped to provide an element of consistency; as the owner said, "If you are not ashamed of any part of your body or any of its natural functions, men and women do not need separate toilets." Thus, even the physical ecology of the nudist camp was designed to be consistent with the nudist morality. For some, however, communal toilets were going too far.

I think they should be separated. For myself it's all right. But there are varied opinions, and for the satisfaction of all, I think they should separate them. There are niceties of life we often like to maintain, and for some people this is embarrassing.... [Q] You know, in a bowel movement it always isn't silent.

THE ROUTINIZATION OF NUDITY

In the nudist camp, nudity becomes routinized; its attention-provoking quality recedes, and nudity becomes a taken-for-granted state of affairs. Thus, when asked questions about staring ("While at camp, have you ever stared at anyone's body? Do you think you would stare at anyone's body?") nudists indicate that nudity generally does not invoke their attention.

Nudists don't care what bodies are like. They're out there for themselves. It's a matter-of-fact thing. After a while you feel like you're sitting with a full suit of clothes on.

To nudists the body becomes so matter-of-fact, whether clothed or unclothed, when you make it an undue point of interest it becomes an abnormal thing. [Q: What would you think of someone staring?] I would feel bad and let down. [Q] I have it set up on a high standard. I have never seen it happen.... [Q] Because it's not done there. It's above that; you don't stare.... If I saw it happen, I'd be startled. There's no inclination to do that. Why would they?

There are two types—male and female. I couldn't see why they were staring. I wouldn't understand it.

In fact, these questions about staring elicit from nudists a frame of possibilities in which what is relevant to staring is ordinarily not nudity itself. Rather, what evokes attention is something unusual, something the observer seldom sees and thus is not routinized to.[7]

There was a red-haired man. He had red pubic hair. I had never seen this before.... He didn't see me. If anyone did, I would turn the other way.

Well, once I was staring at a pregnant woman. It was the first time I ever saw this. I was curious, her stomach stretched, the shape.... I also have stared at extremely obese people, cripples. All this is due to curiosity, just a novel sight. [Q]...I was discreet. [Q] I didn't look at them when their eyes were fixed in a direction so they could tell I was.

[Q: While at camp have you ever stared at someone's body?] Yes. [Q] A little girl. She had a birthmark on her back, at the base of her spine.

[Q: Do you think you would ever stare at someone's body while at camp?] No. I don't like that. I

think it's silly.... What people are is not their fault if they are deformed.

I don't think it would be very nice, very polite. [Q] I can't see anything to stare at, whether it's a scar or anything else. [Q] It just isn't done.

I've looked, but not stared. I'm careful about that, because you could get in bad about that. [Q] Get thrown out by the owner. I was curious when I once had a perfect view of a girl's sex organs, because her legs were spread when she was sitting on a chair. I sat in the chair across from her in perfect view of her organs. [Q] For about ten or fifteen minutes. [Q] Nobody noticed. [Q] It's not often you get that opportunity.[8]

[Q: How would you feel if you were alone in a secluded area of camp sunning yourself, and then noticed that other nudists were staring at your body?] I would think I had some mud on me. [Q]...I would just ask them why they were staring at me. Probably I was getting sunburn and they wanted to tell me to turn over, or maybe I had a speck of mud on me. [Q] These are the only two reasons I can think of why they were staring.

In the nudist camp, the arousal of attention by nudity is usually regarded as *unnatural*. Thus, staring is unnatural, especially after a period of grace in which to adjust to the new meanings.

If he did it when he was first there, I'd figure he's normal. If he kept it up I'd stay away from him, or suggest to the owner that he be thrown out. [Q] At first it's a new experience, so he might be staring. [Q] He wouldn't know how to react to it. [Q] The first time seeing nudes of the opposite sex. [Q] I'd think if he kept staring, that he's thinking of something, like grabbing someone, running to the bushes and raping them. [Q] Maybe he's mentally unbalanced.

He just sat there watching the women. You can forgive it the first time, because of curiosity. But not every weekend. [Q] The owner asked him to leave.

These women made comments on some men's shapes. They said, "He has a hairy body or ugly bones," or "Boy his wife must like him because he's hung big." That was embarrassing.... I

thought they were terrible. [Q] Because I realized they were walking around looking. I can't see that.

ORGANIZATIONS AND THE CONSTITUTION OF NORMALITY

The rules-in-use of an organization *and the reality they sustain* form the basis on which behaviors are interpreted as "unnatural."[9] Overinvolvement in nudity, for example, is interpreted by nudists as unnatural (and not simply immoral). Similarly, erotic stimuli or responses, which breach the nudist morality, are defined as unnatural.

They let one single in. He acted peculiar.... He got up and had a big erection. I didn't know what he'd do at night. He might molest a child or anybody.... My husband went and told the owner.

I told you about this one on the sundeck with her legs spread. She made no bones about closing up. Maybe it was an error, but I doubt it. It wasn't a normal position. Normally you wouldn't lay like this. It's like standing on your head. She had sufficient time and there were people around.

She sat there with her legs like they were straddling a horse. I don't know how else to describe it. [Q] She was just sitting on the ground. [Q] I think she's a dirty pig. [Q] If you sit that way, everyone don't want to know what she had for breakfast. [Q] It's just the wrong way to sit. You keep your legs together even with clothes on.

[Q: Do you think it is possible for a person to be modest in a nudist camp?] I think so. [Q] If a person acts natural.... An immodest person would be an exhibitionist, and you find them in nudism too.... Most people's conduct is all right.

When behaviors are constituted as *unnatural*, attempts to understand them are usually suspended, and reciprocity of perspectives is called into question. (The "reciprocity of perspectives" involves the assumption that if one changed places with the other, one would, for all practical purposes, see the world as the other sees it.[10])

[Q: What would you think of a man who had an erection at camp?] Maybe they can't control them-

selves. [Q] Better watch out for him. [Q] I would tell the camp director to keep an eye on him. And the children would question that. [Q: What would you tell them?] I'd tell them the man is sick or something.

[Q: What would you think of a Peeping Tom—a nonnudist trespasser?] They should be reported and sent out. [Q] I think they shouldn't be there. They're sick. [Q] Mentally. [Q] Because anyone who wants to look at someone else's body, well, is a Peeping Tom, is sick in the first place. He looks at you differently than a normal person would. [Q] With ideas of sex. [A trespasser]...is sick. He probably uses this as a source of sexual stimulation.

Such occurrences call into question the taken-for-granted character of nudity in the nudist camp and the situated morality that is officially set forth.

INHIBITING BREAKDOWNS IN THE NUDIST MORALITY

Organized nudism promulgates a nonsexual perspective toward nudity, and breakdowns in that perspective are inhibited by (1) controlling erotic actions and (2) controlling erotic reactions. Nudity is partitioned off from other forms of "immodesty" (e.g., verbal immodesty, erotic overtures). In this way, a person can learn more easily to attribute a new meaning to nudity.[11] When behaviors occur that reflect other forms of "immodesty," however, nudists often fear a voiding of the nonsexual meaning that they impose on nudity.

This woman with a sexy walk would shake her hips and try to arouse the men.... [Q] These men went to the camp director to complain that the woman had purposely tried to arouse them. The camp director told this woman to leave.

Nudists are sensitive to the possibility of a breakdown in the nudist morality. Thus, they have a low threshold for interpreting acts as "sexual."

Playing badminton, this teenager was hitting the birdie up and down and she said, "What do you think of that?" I said, "Kind of sexy." _____ [the president of the camp] said I shouldn't talk like that, but I was only kidding.

Note the following description of "mauling":

I don't like to see a man and a girl mauling each other in the nude before others.... [Q: Did you ever see this at camp?] I saw it once.... [Q: What do you mean by mauling?] Just, well, I never saw him put his hands on her breasts, but he was running his hands along her arms.

This sensitivity to "sexual" signs also sensitizes nudists to the possibility that certain of their own acts, although not intended as "sexual," might nonetheless be interpreted that way.

Sometimes you're resting and you spread your legs unknowingly. [Q] My husband just told me not to sit that way. [Q] I put my legs together.

Since "immodesty" is defined as an unnatural manner of behavior, such behaviors are easily interpreted as being motivated by "dishonorable" intent. When the individual is thought to be in physical control of the "immodest" behavior and to know the behavior's meaning within the nudist scheme of interpretation, sexual intentions are assigned. Referring to a quotation that was presented earlier, one man said that a woman who was lying with her legs spread may have been doing so unintentionally, "but I doubt it. [Q] It wasn't a normal position. Normally you wouldn't lay like this. It's like standing on your head."

Erotic reactions, as well as erotic actions, are controlled in camp. Thus, even when erotic stimuli come into play, erotic responses may be inhibited.

When lying on the grass already hiding my penis, I got erotic thoughts. And then one realizes it can't happen here. With fear there isn't much erection.

Yes, once I started to have an erection. Once. [Q] A friend told me how he was invited by some young lady to go to bed. [Q] I started to picture the situation and I felt the erection coming on; so I immediately jumped in the pool. It went away.

I was once in the woods alone and ran into a woman. I felt myself getting excited. A secluded spot in the bushes which was an ideal place for procreation. [Q] Nothing happened, though.

When breaches of the nudist morality do occur, other nudists' sense of modesty may inhibit sanctioning. The immediate breach may go un-sanctioned. The observers may feign inattention or withdraw from the scene. The occurrence is usually communicated, however, via the grape-vine, and it may reach the camp director.

> We were shooting a series of pictures and my wife was getting out of her clothes. _____ [the photog-rapher] had an erection but went ahead like noth-ing was happening. [Q] It was over kind of fast.... [Q] Nothing. We tried to avoid the issue.... Later we went to see _____ [the camp director] and _____ [the photographer] denied it.

> [If a man had an erection] people would probably pretend they didn't see it.

> [Q: What do you think of someone this happens to?] They should try to get rid of it fast. It don't look nice. Nudists are prudists. They are more prudish. Because they take their clothes off they are more careful. [Q] They become more prudish than people with clothes. They won't let anything out of the way happen.

As indicated in the remark, "nudists are prud-ists," nudists may at times become aware of the fragility of their situated moral meanings.

> At _____ [camp], this family had a small boy no more than ten years old who had an erection. Mrs. _____ [the owner's wife] saw him and told his parents that they should keep him in check, and tell him what had happened to him and to watch himself. This was silly, for such a little kid who didn't know what happened.

DEVIANCE AND MULTIPLE REALITIES

There are basic social processes that underlie re-sponses to deviance. Collectivities control thresh-olds of response to various behaviors, determining the relevance, meaning, and importance of the be-havior. In the nudist camp, as pointed out previ-ously, erotic overtures and erotic responses are regarded as unnatural, and reciprocity of perspec-tives is called into questions by such behaviors.

> We thought this single was all right, until others clued us in that he had brought girls up to camp.

> [Then we recalled that]...he was kind of weird. The way he'd look at you. He had glassy eyes, like he could see through you.[12]

Such a response to deviance in the nudist camp is a result of effective socialization to the new system of moral meanings. The deviant's be-havior, on the other hand, can be construed as re-flecting an ineffective socialization to the new system of meanings.

> I think it's impossible [to have an erection in a nudist camp]. [Q] In a nudist camp you must have some physical contact and a desire to have one.

> He isn't thinking like a nudist. [Q] The body is wholesome, not...a sex object. He'd have to do that—think of sex.

> Sex isn't supposed to be in your mind, as far as the body. He doesn't belong there. [Q] If you go in thinking about sex, naturally it's going to happen.... You're not supposed to think about go-ing to bed with anyone, not even your wife.

As these quotes illustrate, the unnaturalness or deviance of a behavior is ordinarily determined by relating it to an institutionalized scheme of in-terpretation. Occurrences that are "not under-standable" in the reality of one collectivity may, however, be quite understandable in the reality of another collectivity.[13] Thus, what are "deviant" occurrences in nudist camps probably would be regarded by members of the clothed society as natural and understandable rather than unnatural and difficult to understand.

Finally, a group of people may subscribe to different and conflicting interpretive schemes. Thus, the low threshold of nudists to anything "sexual" is a function of their marginality; the fact that they have not completely suspended the moral meanings of the clothed society is what leads them to constitute many events as "sexual" in purpose.

NOTES

1. In my previous papers, I have dealt with other ques-tions that are commonly asked about nudists. How per-sons become nudists is discussed in my "Becoming a

Nudist," *Psychiatry,* XXIX (February, 1966), 15–24. A report on the nudist way of life and social structure can be found in my article in *Human Organization,* XXVI (Fall, 1967), 91–99.

2. Approximately one hundred camps were represented in the interviews and questionnaires. Interviews were conducted in the homes of nudists during the off season. Arrangements for the interviews were initially made with these nudists during the first summer of participant observation; selection of respondents was limited to those living within a one-hundred-mile radius of Chicago. The questionnaires were sent to all members of the National Nudist Council. The different techniques of data collection provided a test of convergent validation.

3. For a discussion of the essence of such relationships, see Alfred Schutz, *Collected Papers: The Problem of Social Reality,* Maurice Natanson, ed. (The Hague: Nijhoff, 1962), I, 287 ff.

4. [Q] is used to signify a neutral probe by the interviewer that follows the course of the last reply, such as "Could you tell me some more about that?" or "How is that?" or "What do you mean?" Other questions by the interviewer are given in full.

5. The King and Queen contest, which takes place at conventions, allows for a patterned evasion of the staring rule. Applicants stand before the crowd in front of the royal platform, and applause is used for selecting the winners. Photography is allowed during the contest, and no one is permitted to enter the contest unless willing to be photographed. The major reason for this is that this is a major camp event, and contest pictures are used in nud-

ist magazines. At the same time, the large number of photographs sometimes taken by lay photographers (that is, not working for the magazines), makes many nudists uncomfortable by calling into question a nonsexual definition of the situation.

6. I was amazed at how many young female nudists described a similar pattern of extreme clothing modesty among their parents and in their own married life. Included in this group was another nudist model, one of the most photographed of nudist models. Perhaps there are some fruitful data here for cognitive-dissonance psychologists.

7. Cf. Schutz, *op. cit.,* p. 74.

8. For some respondents, the female genitals, because of their hidden character, never become a routinized part of camp nudity; thus their visible exposure does not lose an attention-provoking quality.

9. Compare Harold Garfinkel, "A Conception of, and Experiments with, 'Trust' as a Condition of Stable Concreted Actions," in O. J. Harvey, ed., *Motivation and Social Interaction* (New York: Ronald, 1963).

10. See: Schutz, *op. cit.,* I, 11, for his definition of reciprocity of perspectives.

11. This corresponds with the findings of learning-theory psychologists.

12. For a study of the process of doublethink, see James L. Wilkins, "Doublethink: A Study of Erasure of the Social Past," unpublished doctoral dissertation, Northwestern University, 1964.

13. Cf. Schutz, *op. cit.,* pp. 229 ff.

The Facts of Life About LSD

KENNETH STODDART

KINDS OF DOPE

Participants in the community under study maintained that a grasp of LSD's location in the local schema of pharmacological classification was

Excerpt from Kenneth Stoddart, "The Facts of Life about Dope: Observations of a Local Pharmacology," *Urban Life and Culture,* Vol. 3, No. 2 (July 1974), pp. 182–204. Copyright © 1974 Sage Publications, Inc. Reprinted by permission of Sage Publications, Inc.

Financial support for the research reported herein was provided by the Commission of Inquiry into the Non-Medical Use of Drugs, Gerald LeDain, O.C., Chairman.

central to the achievement of desirable experiences with the substance. For them, any encountered drug was classifiable into one of two categories, namely "mind drugs" and "body drugs." As one experienced user put it: "When you get right down to it there's only two kinds of drugs. Anything's gotta be a mind drug or a body drug." Such substances as heroin, barbiturates, amphetamines, and so forth, are classified as "body drugs" while LSD, mescaline, and so forth, are properly spoken of as "mind drugs."

SINGLE VERSUS MULTIPLE DETERMINANTS

Obviously, mind and body drugs are named by reference to the principal locus of their effects, that is, "mind" and "body." But they are contrasted by users in a way less obvious and more important than locus. Through their talk about past drug experiences, their planning of future ones, their advice given to colleagues, and their common talk about a variety of topics, participants in the . . . community revealed that the most significant difference between the two categories of substance resides in the manner in which their effects are generated. While "body drug" effects were seen as effects produced primarily by the action of drug upon ingestor, "mind drug" effects were understood as not merely the result of such action, but instead as the result of a number of determining factors, some irrelevant to that action. A grasp of the fact of multiple determining factors, a knowledge of them, and attendance to them were seen by participants in the pub scene community as central to the achievement of desirable experiences with LSD.

USER-ASSERTED DETERMINANTS OF THE CHARACTER OF THE LSD EXPERIENCE

Users endorse as significant in the determination of the character of an LSD experience at least five relatively distinct sets of circumstances. The following discussion will reveal that only one (chemical composition) makes reference to features of the drug ingested: the remainder formulate as relevant features of the user—his "state of mind," recent history of general drug use, and cumulative experience with LSD and features of the setting in which the drug experience takes place.

STATE OF MIND

Included in the . . . corpus of knowledge about drugs is the notion that the effects of psychedelic substances are related to their ingestor's "state of mind" or "psychological condition." The determinant significance of one's "head" is expressed via the attribution of the quality of a psychedelic experience to "What people think when they take acid. What's in their head when they drop." Specifically, it is asserted that LSD intensifies a felt state of mind and heightens the experience of it without engendering an alteration of its "basic nature." A self-styled "connoisseur" of the substance put it this way: "Acid doesn't change the way you're feeling, like other dope does. It just makes you feel more that way." Basing their reasoning in this belief, . . . drug users claim that they attenuate the possibility of an adverse reaction or "bad trip" if they ingest LSD when—and only when—in a "good frame of mind."[1] An expressed "desire" to drop acid can be lent a rational appearance by referring to a felt experience of joy or happiness:

> Henri told me that he'd just met the girl he wanted to marry. I ordered two beers to celebrate the occasion. When they came, Henri raised his glass in a toast to "Fran, the girl of my dreams." He sighed dramatically and remarked that he wished he had some acid to drop. I asked him why he wanted to drop acid at this particular moment and he said: "I feel great because I'm in love and the trip would be beautiful for me."

The asserted relationship between state of mind and the expected effects of LSD ingestion was encountered as advice extended by drug users to colleagues who voiced the intention to drop acid at what was construed to be a "bad psychological time."

> Gerry had been commenting that I "looked sad" or "worried about something." I told him that I had a few things on my mind and assured him that it was nothing serious. Later, I purchased a tablet of apparently high-grade "Pink Berkeley" acid from Gino, a dealer well-known for the quality of his merchandise. As I was examining the tablet, Gerry said he hoped I was going to "wait a little while" before taking it. I looked at him rather quizzically and asked him why it should matter whether I took the acid now or later. He put his hand on my shoulder and said, in what appeared to be a sincere, concerned manner: "It's just that you shouldn't be dropping acid when you're uptight. I wouldn't want you to freak out on us or have a bummer."

Jocko was going on and on about how poorly life had been going for him since he lost his job, how depressed he was, how the future looked no brighter than the present, and so forth. When he finished his rather sorry-sounding recitation, Jocko shrugged his shoulders and announced that he felt like getting "some good acid" to "take all this shit off my mind." At this point, Lou—who had been listening sympathetically to Jocko's woes—said to him: "You're just asking for a bad trip if you drop now, with your head in that kind of shape. Wait till you're feeling better about things. Now is a bad psychological time."

Thus, their understanding of the likely consequences of ingesting LSD when in a depressed or anxious state of mind advises drug users to postpone ingestion until such states of mind "pass.". . . It is further claimed that LSD is thoroughly incompatible with the "character structure" possessed by some people. Thus, one can say of a colleague known to have experienced an inordinate number of "bad trips": "He's the kind of person who shouldn't do acid. His head's fucked."

SETTING

The film EASY RIDER (Fonda et al., 1970:103) contains a scene wherein one of the central characters is extended this advice: "When you get to the right place, with the right people—quarter this." Such advice, occasioned by the gift of what turned out to be a tablet of LSD or some other hallucinogenic chemical, is illustrative of the culturally-asserted relationship between setting and quality of drug experience. That is: in the community under study, the effects of psychedelic substances are seen as partially dependent upon the social and physical aspects of the setting in which they are experienced. Or, as one young drug user commented: "Half of acid is where you're at and who you're with. The place and the people." As noted earlier, . . . drug users entertain a conception of psychedelic substances in general, and LSD in particular, as intensifiers of the received world. Consistent with that understanding, they maintain

that the likelihood of an adverse reaction or "bad trip" is dramatically increased if they experience the effects of such substances in settings that are, for whatever reason, received as "bad": "If you drop in a bad situation, you're just asking for it. You're bound to have a bad trip because acid just brings out what's around you." And conversely, a pleasant trip can be anticipated if the substance is experienced in a "good" situation. . . .

. . . Drug users characterize settings as good or bad places to trip relative to the anxiety they would encounter there while operating "normally" and in accordance with the view of LSD as an experience-intensifier. Thus:

Any place you like ordinarily (that is, when not under the influence of LSD) is a good place to drop 'cause you're gonna like it even better when you're tripping. And the other way around. The places you hate get worse.

I told Freddie that he was "wasting" his acid trip by having it in the dark and dingy Alcatraz beer-parlor. This place, I noted, is surely the worst in the world for experiencing acid. Freddie said that I was nuts and informed me that "This is a great place to trip. I can really get off here. All my friends are with me and there's nice music on the jukebox. It's great."

The drug user's corpus of knowledge specifies as well the relevance of a setting's social features. One . . . [user] stated their relevance in the following manner:

The people you're with can make or break a trip. There's some people I just wouldn't trip with because they're complete assholes. They just get me by the way they act and it unnerves me.

Indeed, the behavior of other persons in a setting is a feature that . . . drug users insist is a determinant of any setting's anxiety-producing potential. Thus, as the following suggests, a setting conceived of as "good" on other grounds may be avoided as a place to have a psychedelic experience because of what the drug user knows about the behavior of the people who routinely populate it:

In his enumeration of things that had "changed" in Pacific City since the beginning of the summer, Henri made reference to the demise of two local beaches as "good places to drop acid." He said that those places had been "spoiled by all the bikers and greasers who go down there and hassle people."...

EXPERIENCE

The following report introduces a further "fact" that is included in the...corpus of knowledge about psychedelic drugs and their effects:

I was standing in front of the beer parlor watching Singh as he attempted to sell LSD to passersby. Two long-haired males in their mid-teens responded to his solicitations and asked him the price of his acid and whether it was "good stuff." With regard to their latter question, Singh told them that he'd been dropping acid "for years" and was able to "really get off on a tab of this stuff." His customers decided that they'd take one tablet, saying that it would probably be sufficient to get them both "off" since they'd only dropped acid a few times. Yes, agreed Singh, half a tab each should be more than enough. After they left, Singh told me that "a full tab of this stuff would freak anybody who wasn't really used to acid."

The field-note describes the common belief that the amount of LSD required to produce recognizably psychedelic effects varies directly with any person's experience with the substance.[2] Or: "The more acid you take, the more you need to take to get off. People who've taken a lot of acid need more to get off than before."

Pub scene drug users offer two interpretations of this phenomenon. According to both interpretations, frequent use of LSD creates within the user a situation that permits the full experience of its effects only when the amount ingested is larger than amounts ingested in the recent past. The interpretations collide on the issue of whether the effects actually diminish. In one interpretation, the effects of LSD are regarded as merely appearing to diminish. What "really" diminishes, it is held, is the frequent user's appreciation of those effects.

The following field-notes, wherein acid-users report they increased their per-occasion dosage because they were "used to" or tired of the effects of previous amounts, are illustrative of these interpretations.

Rory joined us at our table and, much to everyone's surprise, bought a round of beer. He told us that he'd panhandled seven dollars at the bus depot and wanted to share it with us by buying some beer. Also, he said he wanted to buy two tabs of acid and treat himself to a "really fine trip." "Why two tabs?" I asked. "Can't you get off on one?" Rory said that yes, he could get off on one tab but it was "kind of boring" to him. "I've had so many trips that one tab is just like nothing to me."

Henri told me that for the first ten-or-so times he dropped acid one tab was enough to produce an interesting experience. Since that time, though, he claims that he's had to increase his dose twice to one-and-a-half and then to two, which he takes now in order to have "a halfway decent trip." He said that after a while "your head gets used to what happens when you take one tab."

In the second interpretation of the necessity of increasing dosage, the effects of LSD are seen as actually diminishing as a consequence of frequent use. One young drug user referred to this attenuation as a "loss of sensitivity" and offered the common claim that it is the result of a concentration of acid "in the brain": "What it is is that you lose your sensitivity to the chemicals in acid that make you trip. Acid builds up in your brain and you get sort of immune to it so it takes more and more to get you off." Such a concentration of LSD, resulting in "immunity," is frequently cited as the reason motivating increased dosage....

CHEMICAL COMPOSITION

From the point of view of...drug users, the character of an LSD experience—considered in all its phases—is partially dependent upon the proportion and kind of adulterant mixed with the "acid" they ingest. Members "know" the acid they purchase in the illicit marketplace will be "impure" insofar as it has been adulterated with a variety of other substances. It is expected that anything offered for sale as "acid" will regularly be a combination of LSD and amphetamine. Furthermore, they expect that what is bought as "acid" will occasionally contain LSD in combination with atropine or strychnine. The following notes report...claims and expectations regarding the presence of such substances and the chemical composition of "acid" in general.

> In the course of asking various people about the local availability of speed I was told repeatedly that "most of the speed is in the acid." Barry, a former speed-freak, held this belief so strongly that he refused, since voluntarily "quitting" speed, to drop acid. He said that "the acid you can buy around here" makes him "yenny for bigger and better things," meaning that the amphetamine-content of LSD makes him desirous of the substance of his former "addiction." According to Barry, he'd drop acid if and only if he could obtain it from a "reliable medical source." "It's impossible to buy street acid without speed," he added.

> Grace was telling Rory, Bert, and I that her first acid trip consisted mainly of "seeing brightness" in colors and little else. She said that she was expecting much more, given all she'd heard of acid's powers. Rory asked if she'd experienced a rush and Grace replied that she did indeed. Rory told her that what she dropped was probably a combination of atropine and speed, with no acid at all. Grace said she was "pissed off" at being burned by a guy she knew. Rory said that at least she got a trip out of it and added that "a lot of acid has got atropine in it, to make the visual part of it better."

> I was approached by a dealer whose face was familiar and asked if I wanted to buy some acid. I told him that I'd just bought a tab from somebody. The dealer wanted to know "who?" I told him I didn't know, and, as he left our table he said "It's probably full of rat poison." Rory laughed. I asked him "what's this about rat poison?" He replied: "Well, sometimes you get a tab of acid that's a little heavy on the strychnine, you know."

...[D]rug users believe that one can recognize the adulterant mixed with the acid by the type of "down" and/or "rush" it produces: "Henry told me that all the acid offered for sale around the Pacific City pubs was 'loaded with speed.' He said that he knew this because 'the rush is so strong it almost explodes your heart' and the down brings with it severe depression and the shakes." The character of the psychedelic experience, too, is held to be indicative of the chemical composition of the substance ingested:

> According to many of the people around the beer parlor, a lot of the acid is merely atropine, speed, and a filler compound. They say that they can tell it's mainly atropine because the trip it produces is thoroughly visual. Acid, they say, would give an experience that was tactile and auditory as well as visual.

Prior to actually ingesting whatever acid they purchase "on the street," however, the dealer's testimony is the only information pub scene drug users have regarding its chemical composition. They recognize that dealers often misrepresent their wares and suggest that one "know" a dealer before making a purchase from him:

> Rory told me that I shouldn't have bought acid from a "guy I'd never seen before." He said that "the only smart way to do it" is to "buy from Lou, or somebody else who's always around so if something goes wrong you'll know who to see." According to Rory, if I find myself burned or poisoned I've only got myself to blame.

The preceding comments are not intended to suggest that the members of the community under study prefer "pure" LSD and seek to avoid its adulterated versions. In their ordinary talk,...drug users contrast "good acid" with "bad acid" not in terms of the presence or absence of adulterants but in terms of the relative proportion of those adulterants. That is, "good acid" is not necessarily "pure" or unadulterated, for it is held that "To be any good, acid's gotta have something in it beside acid." Thus, acid may be regarded as good because it contains the "right amount" of speed:

> Why, I asked, is the brand of acid known as "Pink Berkeley" so highly regarded by all? "Well," said

Harvey, "*real Pink Berkeley has got just the right amount of speed in it.*" *He went on to tell me that it gives you a nice rush and doesn't "let you down hard" at the end of the trip.*

Or the "right amount" of strychnine:

I wondered aloud about the kind of chemist who would adulterate his acid with rat poison. Bobby told me that it was really nothing to worry about unless you ingested some acid that contained it in a large quantity. Rat poison, he said, despite its toxicity, contributes to the experience insofar as it makes the trip "more physical." A little rat poison, said Bobby, "makes for a fine rush."

DRUG INTERACTION

...[D]rug users maintain that the effects of LSD are partially dependent upon the kind and quantity of other substances ingested immediately prior to or during an anticipated psychedelic experience. In their common talk and behavior they expressed a special concern for the "mixing" of LSD and those substances thought to inhibit or diminish its effects. Given the high cost of acid relative to their financial resources, members were anxious to avoid substances they saw as attenuating its effects and thereby "wasting" a trip.

Virtually without exception,...drug users mix LSD and beer. It is held that drinking beer shortly before or after dropping acid will put one in a physically and psychologically "relaxed" state, thus enabling him to have a better psychedelic experience. Such a belief, as illustrated in the following field-note is consistent with the culturally-asserted relationship between "state of mind" and the quality of the trip:

Alex put the tab of acid in his mouth and washed it down with a gulp of the beer he'd been drinking. He raised his glass in a toast "to a good trip" and emptied it. Alex told me that it was good to drink "a bit of beer" before you get off on acid because it relaxes you and makes you "less uptight."

Similarly, beer or any depressant is recommended as an aid to those who find the final or "down" phase of an acid trip particularly disquieting. The user whose claims are reported above followed such a strategy:

Alex talked further about beer, and told me that he generally has a few glasses when he's coming down from acid. He said that "the down you get from the acid around here is like a speed down" and added that he experienced severe nervousness towards the end of an LSD trip. The beer, said Alex, "makes me feel better." I asked him if a downer would do the same thing and he told me that it would, laughingly adding that "beer tastes better."

...[D]rug users believe, however, that alcoholic beverages and barbiturates consumed in large quantities will inhibit the effects of LSD:

An interview in a public park with David, a former pub scene regular, was interrupted by one of his hobo-alcoholic friends. Upon hearing that we were talking about acid, he told us that he took it once and "it didn't do anything for me." Laughing, David pushed him over on the grass and said: "You were probably sloshed out of your head when you dropped it. Acid doesn't work when you've got too much booze in your body." Later, I asked David to explain this statement to me. He told me that "too much booze or too many downers" tend to "numb your body and head" making one "not feel acid."

While...drug users attempt in general to avoid substances whose interaction with LSD diminishes or blocks its effects, there are some situations wherein such attenuation is deliberately sought. For example, the experiencing of a bad trip is seen as an occasion calling for the ingestion of a "downer":

I told Rick that I was curious about taking acid, but had so far avoided it because of a fear of having a bad trip. Rick said that that was always a possibility, but nothing to be really afraid of. He said that you can bring yourself out of any bad trip by dropping a couple of downers.

While depressants such as alcohol and barbiturates are seen as at most "blocking" or "neutralizing" any effects of LSD, other substances are understood as specifically incompatible with acid.

Speed is one of these and, as indicated below, the mixing of it with acid is portrayed as the "cause" of some people's bad trips:

> I asked Henri why he thought Bert had such a bad trip two evenings ago. He told me that one of the reasons was "probably" the fact that Bert had injected himself with speed while he was getting off on the acid.

> Joan, who earlier told us that she'd dropped a tab of "white lightening" acid, came over to our table and said that her former boyfriend had taken her into "the men's can" and injected her with speed. Eileen was standing behind Joan shaking her head in a somewhat disgusted and definitely disapproving manner. Later, when Joan was in the midst of a particularly adverse reaction, Eileen said that it was "all she could expect, mixing acid and speed like that."

CONCLUDING REMARKS

Participant observation in a community where drug use was a focal concern detected a corpus of knowledge about LSD and its effects that members of the community appreciated and attended to as *factual*. The corpus was encountered by the researcher (and presumably by "ordinary" participants as well) in a variety of ways: as advice given by experienced drug users to their novice counterparts...,as grounds for "timing" the ingestion of LSD relative to diverse objective factors, as explanations of good or bad experiences with LSD, and so on.

Over the course of time, participants' talk revealed a conception of LSD effects as effects whose character was determined by a number of diverse factors. Indeed, far from being seen as merely "programmed" by the action of drug upon ingestor—as is the case with "body drugs"—the character of the LSD experience is understood by users as variably constituted by a *variety* of personal and environmental factors.

The corpus of knowledge described in this report proposes for participants in the community studied a set of *facts* about the effects of LSD and the contingencies bearing on their generation. For those who appreciate it *as* factual the corpus they call the "facts of life about dope" is understood as constituting the truth about LSD and LSD effects and hence as formulating a set of conditions properly attended to by all those who wish to consume LSD *rationally,* that is, with the hope of achieving desirable outcomes.

NOTES

1. In contrast, as the following suggests, marijuana is regarded as an antidote to depression: "Henri told Rory and I that he was quite depressed because of a recent fight with Joan, the love of his life. Rory put his hand on Henri's shoulder and said: 'Look, I'll get us a joint. That'll make you feel better. There's nothing like a few tokes on some good grass to make a guy feel right again.' Henri nodded in agreement and Rory went to look for 'the guy who's selling joints for four-bits a piece.'"
2. Marijuana is regarded in exactly the opposite fashion: it is held that the more experience one has with it, the less grass it takes to get "stoned." Thus, it is common for experienced users to claim intoxication after inhaling only a small quantity of marijuana, and equally as common for novices to fail to get "stoned" after smoking a large quantity. See Becker (1963). In passing it is interesting to note that in social worlds where alcohol is the main drug of intoxication, these persons who become "stoned" on small amounts are negatively regarded.

REFERENCES

Becker, H. S. 1963. "Becoming a Marijuana User." In *Outsiders: Studies in the Sociology of Deviance.* New York: Free Press.

Fonda, P. et al. 1970. *Easy Rider.* New York: Dell.

CHAPTER 12

SUBCULTURAL VARIATIONS

While some deviants engage in solitary deviance, many are involved in deviance for which there is a definite subculture—what we call *subcultural deviance*. Even among those engaging in subcultural deviance, though, there is a great deal of variation. The deviants may differ in their backgrounds and social situations. Some may participate in the subculture more than others. And they may differ in the activities, both deviant and conventional, that they engage in. Associated with these variations are other differences—e.g., in the ways people perform deviant roles.

In this chapter the selections explore some of these subcultural variations. In the first reading Charles Faupel argues that variations in access to drugs, and in the stability of life routines, generate four types of heroin addicts, and correspondingly, different degrees of conformity with subcultural norms. Paul Higgins then shows the character of two distinct social segments in the deaf community—those who use sign language and those who don't. Finally, James Inciardi, Dorothy Lockwood, and Anne Pottieger show how social settings shape prostitute-client transactions and that the sequences which comprise them vary markedly depending on whether street rules or crackhouse rules regulate them.

A Typology of Heroin Addicts

CHARLES E. FAUPEL

A widely shared belief in American society holds that increased heroin addiction inevitably results in moral degeneracy. According to the "dope fiend mythology" (Lindesmith, 1940), as the addict becomes hopelessly enslaved to this deadliest of all drugs, all ethical restraints dissolve. In the words of a vice squad officer interviewed by Gould and his associates:

> These junkies become so degenerate it is sad. They live in such filth. You should see some of the apartments I've been in. What's more, junkies have no consideration for their families and their friends.... I think the drug does something basic to a person. I don't know what it is. I'm not an expert on that sort of thing, but it seems as if drug users just don't have any morals left after a while. (Gould et al., 1974:71).

As this statement indicates, many believe that addicts will indiscriminately victimize anyone they know or encounter. One San Francisco journalist flatly asserts:

> He's after that money; he needs it to buy heroin. And he'll take it from you if you are his nearest and dearest friend, even if he has to kill you to do it (quoted in Silver and Aldrich, 1979:42).

Similarly, the "dope peddler" is commonly depicted as an unscrupulous entrepreneur with a penchant for turning young children on to drugs (Anslinger and Tompkins, 1953; Ashley, 1972; Eldridge, 1967; Lindesmith, 1940; Rubington,

Reprinted from Social Problems, Vol. 34, No. 1 (February 1987), pp. 54–63, by permission of the Society for the Study of Social Problems and the author.
This research was supported in part by DHEW grant 1 RO1 DA 01827 from the Division of Research, National Institute on Drug Abuse. Views expressed are my own and do not necessarily reflect the position of the National Institute on Drug Abuse. I would like to thank Robert M. Emerson for his many helpful comments throughout the various drafts of this article.

1967). "Every addict," say Anslinger and Tompkins (1953:272), "knowing himself to be a moral and social outcast, delights in bringing others into the outcast fold."

Recent research has openly questioned this assumption of the inevitable and totally morally destructive effects of heroin use. Studies by Ashley (1972), Bullington (1977), Coombs (1981), Hanson et al. (1985), Hughes (1977), Preble and Casey (1969), Reese (1975), Rosenbaum (1981a, 1981b), Waldorf (1973), and Zinberg (1984) suggest that most heroin addicts maintain a sense of ethical responsibility in the social world in which they function. Contrary to the popular imagery, this research has consistently reported that heroin addicts are not indiscriminate with regard to whom they will victimize. Rosenbaum (1981a:54) found, for example, not only that addicts espouse a distinct code of ethics, but also that the inclination and ability to adhere to this code varies with an addict's standing in the street world of heroin use:

> A code of ethics is, in fact, a part of the stratification system in the addict world. Theft, for example, is graduated. The more impersonal the target of stealing, the better; the closer to home, the worse the addicts feels about it. While it is seen as all right, even courageous and bold, to steal from a large store or a person unknown to the addict, stealing from friends, family, and to a lesser extent, other addicts is not sanctioned.

Ethnographic studies have also failed to support the image of the addict as promiscuously turning on the young and vulnerable. Most young users were first turned on by close friends who were themselves just beginning to experiment with drugs (Ashley, 1972; Blum, 1972; Blumer et al., 1976; Crawford et al., 1983; Eldridge, 1967; Hughes, 1977; Sutter, 1969). Moreover, Sutter (1969:807) insists that "turning someone on" *is an expression of trust, friendship and acceptance. Most lower strata youth were introduced to drugs by a close friend or relative. After they learned to use drugs for pleasure, being turned on and turning others on became an established social practice, similar to the convention of buying a friend a drink or offering a drink to a guest when he comes to your house.*

In spite of this body of research, however, we know that most addicts have at times engaged in behaviors that violated the standards and ideals of their own subculture. Despite ethical protestations to the contrary, young neophytes may be turned on to drugs by experienced addicts, and addicts may victimize those nearest and dearest to them. It is not sufficient simply to note that addicts engage in such norm-violating behaviors. Situational exceptions to idealized cultural standards can frequently be observed throughout various sectors of the population. Consequently, we should expect that there will also be times, places, and circumstances when normative standards in the heroin subculture will fail to invoke strict conformity. The more important consideration is the circumstances under which these standards are violated and the stance that addicts take toward these violations and the values they represent. For as Meier (1981:14) has argued:

> *The concept of norm...does not require a correspondence between what persons say and what they do; discrepancies are to be expected.... [B]ecause norms identify behavior that "ought" or "ought not" to occur, behavior may (and often does) depart from norms.... The more relevant consideration includes the conditions under which this potential for deviance is realized and the conditions under which norms guide specific conduct.*

The subculture of heroin use provides an excellent opportunity to examine the situational contingencies affecting departure from or conformity to such subcultural normative standards. Heavily involved heroin addicts experience a daily demand for high-cost drugs, a harsh reality that may indeed come to overshadow all other concerns in the addict's life. This article seeks to identify and

analyze those conditions that tend to undermine conformity to espoused subcultural ideals.

METHODOLOGY

The present study was conducted in 1980–1981 as part of a larger, ongoing research project that examined the relationship between drug use and crime among hard-core heroin users. In an effort to explore more thoroughly the dynamics of the drugs-crime nexus, I conducted in-depth life histories with a subsample of 30 so-called hard-core heroin addicts[1] in the Wilmington, Delaware, area. Women addicts were deliberately overrepresented, constituting 12 of the 30 respondents. Ethnically, 22 of the respondents were black and 8 were white. There is no Hispanic representation in this sample due to the lack of a sizable Hispanic drug-using population in the Wilmington area. The interviews ranged from 10 to 25 hours in length and, with one exception, were tape recorded. Respondents were paid $5 per hour contributing to a 100 percent response rate. Respondents were selected on the basis of extensive involvement in the heroin subculture, limiting the generalizability of the data to heavily involved, hard-core urban addicts.

A number of relevant "focal areas" emerged early in the research, including early childhood experiences, peer group associations, patterns of initiation into drug use and crime, techniques of committing crimes, and the nature of encounters with the criminal justice system and with treatment agencies. I also talked with these addicts about the normative structure of the heroin subculture and the processes by which it was internalized. This line of inquiry often produced quite idealized accounts of addict ethics and behavior. My efforts to get addicts to specify these ideals and, occasionally, to confront them with discrepancies in their testimonies led to further discussion of the vicissitudes of daily life on the street and of the circumstances under which subcultural norms had been ignored and violated. The interviews were conducted in an unstructured, open-ended format, which provided maximum flexibility in interviewee response.

All of the respondents had prior contact with the criminal justice system and most (24) were incarcerated at the time of interview. Most of the incarcerated respondents were enrolled in the prison drug-treatment program. The six street respondents had also had contact with treatment programs, either by direct court order, voluntary involvement, or through close personal relationships with treatment personnel or graduates of treatment programs. Both street and incarcerated respondents were selected with the aid of treatment personnel who were carefully instructed regarding the goals of the research and selection criteria. This strategy proved invaluable for two reasons. First, by utilizing treatment personnel in the screening process, I was able to avoid the time-consuming task of establishing the appropriateness of respondents for the purpose of this research; the treatment personnel were already intimately familiar with the drug-using and criminal histories of the respondents. Second, the treatment personnel had an unusually positive relationship with the population of drug users from which the respondents were selected. Addicts regarded the treatment counselor in the prison system as a highly trustworthy ally in the quest for better living conditions, appeals for early release, and so on. His frequent confrontations with prison authorities over prisoner rights and privileges enhanced his reputation among inmates considerably. Similarly, the treatment counselor who aided in the selection of street respondents had longstanding multifaceted relations with Wilmington-area addicts and had been instrumental in bringing about reforms in area treatment agencies.

Clearly, this sample of respondents does not necessarily represent the population of heroin users in the Wilmington community. In particular, the heavy reliance on incarcerated respondents warrants caution in the interpretation of the data. Furthermore, these respondents, who had not been active in the subculture for a period of time ranging from several weeks to over two years, neces-

sarily had to reconstruct their previous drug-using and criminal activities, much of which had occurred at earlier points in time. Johnson et al. (1985) note that with the passage of time such respondents have a tendency to overestimate the magnitude of their drug and crime involvement, seemingly forgetting days they were incapable of hustling and scoring successfully. As to their reported ethical dynamics and related street behavior, however, the incarcerated respondents I interviewed did not differ appreciably from the street respondents in this and similar ethnographic studies.

DRUG AVAILABILITY AND LIFE STRUCTURE

The situational character of addict ethics must be understood in the context of addict careers. As Crawford et al. (1983) and Rubington (1967) point out, heroin-using careers are not an inevitable result of heroin use, but are shaped by external career contingencies. Two contingencies that have a profound influence both on the direction of addicts' careers and on their conformity to or departure from subcultural norms of behavior are *drug availability* and *life structure* (Faupel, 1981). *Availability* refers in the broadest sense to the extent to which heroin is accessible to any particular addict. At issue here is more than mere access to sellers of heroin who have quantities of the drug to sell, although this is certainly an important aspect of availability. Availability is also a function of the fluctuating cost of heroin, the resources and opportunities to obtain the drug in nonmonetary ways (for example, see Goldstein, 1981; Johnson et al., 1985), possession of the conventional and/or criminal skills necessary to provide money to purchase heroin, and the knowledge and techniques necessary to actually use heroin. In short, availability is a product of all of those opportunities and obstacles that may influence a heroin user's prospects for ultimately introducing a quantity of the drug into his or her bloodstream.

This feature of heroin-using careers has profound implications for the ethical behavior of addicts. Ready availability of drugs affords the addict the luxury of maintaining a comfortable level of consumption without engaging in many of the "low-down" or desperate tactics characteristic of less fortunate users. Rosenbaum (1981b:77) notes, for example, that

> the addict who occupies the top of the stratification system—the successful dealer or hustler—does not have to resort to those activities more characteristic of poorer addicts. Such addicts do not have to become unscrupulous and without values or morals. However, those addicts who are sick from withdrawal and penniless find themselves in a situation that forces them to get money by whatever means possible [emphasis in the original].

These moral dynamics are not, of course, limited to the experience of heroin addicts. Hughes (1971), for example, has observed a "moral division of labor" in the legal and medical professions where, because of their relative position in the professional hierarchy, some lawyers and physicians end up doing the "dirty work" enabling those of higher status to "stay clean."

Life structure refers to the regularly occurring patterns of domestic, recreational, work, and criminal activity that shape and constrain the daily life of heroin users. Recent ethnographic accounts of street heroin use in several major cities reveal that, like their "straight" counterparts, most addicts maintain reasonably predictable daily routines (Beschner and Brower, 1985; Walters, 1985). Throughout their lives all of the respondents in my study fulfilled conventional as well as criminal and other subcultural roles, both of which serve to structure the addict's daily routine. Indeed, although conventional roles are frequently overlooked in accounts of street addicts, the individuals I interviewed typically spent more time engaged in conventional activities than in criminal or deviant ones. Several worked conventional jobs. Women with children performed routine housekeeping and child-rearing duties. Many leisure-time activities did not differ from those of nonaddicts. These hard-core addicts spent time grocery shopping, tinkering with cars, visiting relatives, talking with friends and watching television in totally unremarkable fashion.

Criminal activity, too, is an important source of life structure for the addicts I interviewed. Burglars spend time "casing" residential areas and business establishments. Shoplifters typically establish "runs," more or less stable sequences of targeted stores from which to "boost" during late morning, noon, and early afternoon hours, fencing their goods later in the afternoon. Most prostitutes keep a regular evening and nightime schedule; mornings are usually spent sleeping and afternoons are typically occupied with conventional duties.

Although the source of these daily routines (conventional versus criminal) may have important implications for drug availability—as I shall point out momentarily—the degree of life structure exerts a significant force independently of its source. Durkheim's (1897) observation of the impact of economic disruption on suicide behavior is pertinent here; it is during such periods of instability that the usual structures of restraint lose their relevance, resulting in a state of "anomie." Lacking a routinized life structure, the heroin addict, too, finds himself or herself in an anomic condition. Under such conditions, when routine conventional and subcultural roles that serve to guide and constrain drug-using and criminal behavior are abandoned or suddenly altered, addicts typically find themselves in normative limbo. The problems of adjustment entailed in the shift from heroin to methadone maintenance, particularly as such a change disrupted the structuring of daily routine, provide a recurrent theme in the life histories. For example, "Belle," an older female addict who attempted to replace her heroin-using lifestyle with the use of "crank" (amphetamines), recalled:

> It was just like day and night between the person I had been when I was using heroin and the person I was when I got on this meth and crank...doing things in my home I had never done before; and taking things from my home that I had never done before. It was always a no-no touching my home in any way...and this last period—whew! it was really abominable.

This brief behavioral aberration, which lasted several weeks, captures the anomic reality encountered by addicts who experience an abandonment or sudden alteration of normal daily routine. In this respect, life structure exercises an important stabilizing force that helps regulate an otherwise insatiable appetite and provides the addict with a meaningful normative context.

Finally, drug availability and life structure are dynamically interrelated. Availability, for example, is often considerably enhanced when a beginning user abandons or curtails conventional routines for more lucrative criminal roles. Similarly, an addict may suffer reduced availability to drugs if he or she has a falling out with a connection (dealer), if his or her connection is arrested, or if a dealer decides to appreciably raise prices. Such eventualities may force the addict to abandon or alter normal routines in order to raise more money to obtain higher-priced drugs or to accommodate to lowered availability. Other factors, such as loss of a job, divorce, or problems from the police may result in an abandonment of normal routines, which in turn may have direct implications for an addict's ability to secure a stable supply of heroin. Consequently, the careers of addicts are characterized by periods of structured routine and relative ease of availability and by periods of disruption in routine and/or difficulty in obtaining drugs.

TYPES OF HEROIN USE AND THE CONTINGENCIES OF ETHICAL BEHAVIOR

Figure 1 depicts four "heroin use types" that reflect the drug-use patterns produced by different combinations of drug availability and life structure. Since drug availability and life structure involve dynamic and fluctuating contingencies, these types do not represent static descriptions of particular addicts. Rather, any specific addict is likely to have experienced varying constellations of availability and structure at different times during his or her career. Furthermore, addicts do not necessarily move through these types in any sort of linear career path. Although some addicts did

Availability	Life Structure	
	High	Low
High	The Stabilized Junkie	The Free-Wheeling Junkie
Low	The Occasional User	The Street Junkie

FIGURE 1   A Typology of Heroin Use

indeed seem to follow the sequence that will be discussed, others moved in different patterns or skipped types entirely. Moreover, it was not uncommon for there to be movement back and forth between types as the circumstances of an addict's life situation changed. Each heroin use type does represent, however, certain critical constraints and opportunities that profoundly affect addicts' inclinations and/or abilities to maintain the ethical ideals of the subculture.

THE OCCASIONAL USER

Initiates into the heroin-using subculture typically fall into this category, characterized by high life structure and low drug availability. A number of factors limit the availability of heroin to beginning users. They have not spent enough time in the subculture to have developed extensive connections for "copping dope." Moreover, their level of income is probably not capable of supporting substantial levels of heroin consumption inasmuch as successful hustling takes time to learn technique, to establish patterns, and to develop necessary connections within the subculture.

Corresponding to low levels of availability, this early period of drug use usually takes place within a structure of more conventional roles. In many cases, individuals experimenting with drugs are young and involved in school and related activities. Adolescents experimenting with drugs are also typically tied into a family structure. Conventional adult roles similarly serve to structure heroin consumption. Ron, an older black addict who had an unusually long period of occasional use, was shooting an average of only $10–$15 in street dope a day for eight years. During this eight-year period he was working a full-time job. At the same time he was living with his mother, who did not allow drug use in her home. At the end of this eight years he became a "tester" for a local dealer, a job that entailed injecting drug samples to test for quality. At that same time he lost his job and moved out of his mother's home. Hence, in addition to having more drugs available as a tester, Ron no longer maintained the rigorous daily routine that had been crucial in controlling his heroin use for eight years. His consumption escalated dramatically over a few short weeks as he quickly came to assume the "stabilized junkie" status.

All of the addicts I interviewed can be characterized as occasional users during the early period of their involvement in the subculture. Indeed, recent research by Zinberg (1984) suggests that there is a sizable number of users who never advance beyond such "controlled" use. Just beginning their careers as heroin users, many occasional users have not spent sufficient time in the subculture to internalize its normative expectations. Consequently, many of the respondents admitted to having violated commonly espoused subcultural standards during this phase of their careers. For example, a number of the addicts I interviewed turned friends on to heroin in a way analogous to that described by Sutter (1969). It was also during this period as young initiates that these individuals most frequently reported dipping into the family's petty cash box for some extra "spending" money. The following remarks by a veteran female addict, however, suggest that such behavior is not so much a violation of an internalized ethic, but rather a manifestation of inadequate socialization at this early point in one's career.

> *When you're real young...you don't have the same kind of ethics as when you get older.... All you think about in the beginning is just getting the money. But after a while as you go through the years...you begin to see that this is not the right way.*

THE STABILIZED JUNKIE

Often, though not necessarily, the occasional user moves directly to the status of "stabilized junkie," characterized by a high level of availability and high, though usually modified, life structure. As occasional users, emerging addicts become socialized into the life of the subculture. Not only do they learn and internalize the normative expectations of the subculture, they also learn the essentials of copping (locating and purchasing), cooking (preparing), and spiking (injecting) themselves—all factors that, in effect, increase the availability of heroin. It was not uncommon for the addicts I interviewed, for example, to experience a sharp increase in their heroin consumption after they learned to inject themselves. They were no longer dependent on the presence of more experienced drug using friends to "get off."

In addition to enhancing these fundamental skills as a drug user, the stabilized junkie increases drug availability by upgrading copping skills and connections. The addict who must rely on the lower-quality, more expensive "street bag," who gets "ripped" by paying high prices for "bad dope," or who is totally dependent on the quality or quantity of heroin a single supplier happens to have available, does not have access to regularly available, high-quality heroin. As Belle explains, gaining such access usually requires extending and developing contacts in the drug subculture:

> *You got to start associating with different people. You got to be in touch with different people for the simple reason that not just one person has it all the time. You got to go from one person to the other, find out who's got the best bag and who hasn't.... You want to go where the best bag is for your money.... You got to mingle with so many different people.*

Not only must the aspiring stabilized junkie learn the essentials of shooting and copping, but the expensive nature of heroin usually requires that the addict become familiar with the art of hustling. Hustling provides an alternative basis for life structure capable of accommodating higher levels of drug use. Unlike the adolescent in school or some types of conventional jobs, the hustler role provides a daily structure capable of incorporating periodic visits to a copping connection to secure a "fix." At the same time, however, hustling does provide a routine structure that serves to limit one's habit and prevent it from "getting out of hand." Most hustles, for example, require regular commitments of time and patience, and must be practiced within certain unavoidable constraints. Just as important, however, the hustler role provides the addict with increased income that facilitates the ready availability of heroin without compromising the normative and ethical ideals of the subculture. "Little Italy," a young male addict in his early twenties, reports that his ready access to dependable supplies of heroin was crucial in maintaining ethical respectability:

> I just kept right at it [using heroin] because...I had it in my possession every day.... I could go get it and that's just the way it was. With that in order, I didn't have to go out and burglarize. No one had to worry about me stealing from them.... I had money. I didn't have to beat anybody.

For this reason, the stabilized junkie, which often represents a dominant phase in the career of the hard-core addict, is characterized by a high degree of *conformity* to subcultural norms and most closely reflects the recent ethnographic accounts of the normative structure of drug use.

THE FREE-WHEELING JUNKIE

In contrast to the stabilized junkie, the free-wheeling junkie lacks a daily structure to guide and constrain his or her consumption. A number of factors may undermine the stable life structure characteristic of the stabilized junkie. Addicts place particular importance on the inevitable vicissitudes of the hustler routine. Here it is not so much the hard times or difficulties in raising money that are critical. Addicts can often accommodate themselves to such lean periods by adjusting the level of their heroin use, substituting other drugs for heroin, or working longer and harder at hustling without undue disruption or abandonment of daily routine.

"You can adjust yourself to a certain amount of drugs a day," explains Belle, "that you don't have to have but just that much." On the contrary, it is the unusual success, the "big sting," that distinctively undermines the stabilized junkie's high level of life structure. Often, in the course of hustling, addicts will confront an opportunity to make a score so big that they will not have to hustle so rigorously for a period of time. If successful, such a score brings a dramatic change in daily routine. Consider the experience of a burglar named Harry. Harry was working residential areas full time and supporting a modest habit. An associate stopped by one day with a roll of bills worth several thousand dollars and asked Harry if he would like to be partners in a new and more profitable hustle. Harry agreed and began holding up local grocery stores. His profits increased dramatically, and with his bigger earnings he started using drugs on a grand scale; not only did he increase his heroin use, but began using cocaine heavily as well.

However, the robberies brought a critical disjuncture to his normal daily routine. Harry no longer had to work eight hours a day for his copping money, but could secure a much more sizable income working only two or three hours per day three days a week. Harry now marvels that he was not even aware of the extensiveness of his habit until he voluntarily quit robberies because of the risk and returned once again to burglaries. All of these changes took place over a six-month period.

With drugs available, the free-wheeling junkie typically experiences a sharp escalation of his or her drug use. Moreover, because normal daily routine is suspended at least temporarily, the lifestyle of the addict tends to be erratic and often out of control. The free-wheeling junkie quite often resembles the sometimes stereotyped "flashy" junkie (often associated with pimps), engaged in seemingly uncontrolled conspicuous consumption with a greatly expanded wardrobe, expensive cars, and extreme generosity; in short, the free-wheeling junkie typically finds himself or herself in a state of anomie, lacking the structures of restraint characteristic of the stabilized junkie.

The anomic condition peculiar to the free-wheeling junkie, however, relates specifically to patterns of personal consumption. The windfalls that catapult the addict to this type of heroin use usually allow him or her to maintain ethical integrity. As he mentally relives a particularly lucrative period of drug dealing, Little Italy recalls the following:

> So I'm a junkie now. But I'm not one of those scrub junkies, where I got to steal from my family.... I'm dealing. And I'm paying for my habit thataway. And man, listen here, don't you know that everybody that didn't know me, knew me now. Because I'm uptown on the Main Street Strip. You can drive by in your pretty car, blow at the girls. I had flashy clothes and the whole bit.

Provided that the free-wheeling junkie has not severed connections or alienated himself or herself in some way from the subculture, he or she may be able to rebuild the necessary daily routine and accommodate to new and lower levels of drug availability. Insofar as this can be managed the free-wheeling junkie may resume a stabilized junkie lifestyle. In many cases, however, the "big sting" has the effect of isolating the free-wheeling junkie from the subculture by decreasing the need to participate in the copping and hustling aspects of the subculture. Where this occurs the free-wheeling junkie is particularly susceptible to change toward the "street junkie" type.

THE STREET JUNKIE

The street junkie, characterized by low drug availability and minimal life structure, is the basis for the commonly held "junkie" stereotype. With drugs not freely available, the street junkie must typically cop his or her dope from the nearest street dealer who may be willing to provide credit on a bag or two. The cost is much higher on the street, and often the street junkie can afford only enough to take the edge off his or her "jones" (withdrawal) temporarily.

> After I stopped going back and forth to New York, the street copping cost a lot more, too.... I might not have been shooting as much as I was [before] but I was spending a hell of a lot more money.

Under these conditions, the street junkie lives from one "fix" to the next, often unable to maintain the most rudimentary routine. Personal hygiene and regular eating habits may be abandoned as the addict desperately seeks to scrape up enough money for his or her next shot. Not uncommonly, the street junkie will also abandon normal hustling routine, impulsively committing crimes that "happen" along, often in response to a felt need for dope due to withdrawal sickness. This happened to "Little Italy" who, after cutting himself off from his wholesale connection, turned to robberies to support his use. Lacking experience and technique, Little Italy staged these robberies largely on impulse:

> I know today, I can say that if you don't have a plan you're gonna fuck up, man.... Now those robberies weren't no plan. They didn't fit in nowhere...just by the spur of the moment, you know what I mean? I had to find something to take that place so that income would stand off properly, 'cause I didn't have a plan or didn't know anything about robbery.

The street junkie type might be precipitated by structural factors as well, particularly those that lead to the relinquishing of conventional roles. Some addicts, for example, report that "things started going downhill" after a divorce or the death of a loved one. Another common precipitator is the loss of conventional jobs. It is not uncommon for the stabilized junkie to be working a part-time job in addition to carrying out regular hustling activities. If an employer learns about drug use, the addict may well be fired. The emerging street junkie loses not only income, but also the high degree of daily routine provided by conventional employment. Desperately seeking to maintain even the most meager level of consumption to keep the edge off his or her "jones," the street junkie is forced to take chances that would ordinarily be quite unthinkable. Moreover, under those conditions, the street junkie becomes difficult to live with and family relationships become strained or perhaps even severed. Again, the addict faces a state of anomie, but this time without the luxury of easy access to drugs. This "down and out junkie" who has by now probably lost all semblance of respect and perhaps has been disenfranchised even by peers has little stake in the moral order of the subculture. The addict in these desperate straits is likely to consider the possibility of "beating" friends or even family members for money to cop a street bag. Sylvia, a black woman in her twenties, explains:

> After the money is coming in like that...and it gets to the point where their habit is worked up like that, then they might do anything [if they're cut off] and they have to find a new way of making their money. They might do anything.

Rosenbaum (1981a:60) also reflects the dynamics of this situation for the female addict when she writes:

> The woman addict's self-respect is at least temporarily damaged when, due to the fluidity of the money-stratification system, she finds herself down and out, with no way to earn money legally. It is at this point that she becomes temporarily unscrupulous and may rip off a personal friend, even family. It is important to note that this unscrupulousness is temporary *and that in some way, most addicts become unscrupulous in some form, at some point in their careers. [emphasis in the original].*

Similarly, the street junkie who has lost access to a stable network of copping connections is the most likely candidate to turn on a stranger (perhaps even a novice), introducing him or her to a dealer acquaintance in return for a bag of dope. Such a situation almost always creates a dilemma for the street junkie. Rose had recently lost her copping connection and had to rely on a young neophyte to cop for her. Unfortunately for Rose, the young girl was not willing to make the purchase without compensation in drugs. Rose ex-

plained how she attempted to resolve her ethical dilemma:

> I gave her the least amount I figured she'd feel with a whole bunch of water so it would look like she had a lot.... It wasn't that I was trying to cheat her...it's just that I didn't want her to really get into it.

Lacking a daily routine and with drugs difficult to obtain, the street junkie must take more chances than would otherwise be the case. Under these circumstances addicts will engage in criminal hustles at which they are not adept. Unless their life circumstances change, arrest is virtually inevitable. Although not universally the case, it is the street junkie who typically encounters the criminal justice system. As Fiddle (1967:12–13) has observed,

> The police see junkies at their worst. They see them under the spur of need or pseudo-need ...they see them violating even their own negative codes. The police rarely see the addict engaging in a purely voluntary humane act.

Moreover, that population of addicts most available to the media as well as to researchers are those who have been apprehended. For this reason, the image of the heroin addict generally available to the public is that of the stereotyped "street junkie." It is important to recognize, however, that the street junkie represents but one phase in the addict's career. For substantial portions of their careers, most addicts lead relatively stable, though fast-paced, lives. Far from being an inevitable result of the physiological dynamics of heroin use, the behavior of the street junkie, with all of its stereotyped ethical compromises, only emerges in response to the career contingencies that limit accessibility and disrupt established patterns of behavior.

CONCLUSIONS

Drug using careers, like other careers, are subject to external constraints that affect the maintenance of ideal normative standards.[2] The testimony of the addicts I interviewed points to the importance of the career contingencies of drug availability and life structure in affecting their lifestyles. Most important, although most addicts generally proceed from a period of occasional use to more extensive stabilized use and often to the stereotyped down and out street junkie, these career contingencies are themselves affected by numerous factors in the addict's social environment so as to preclude a simple linear career model. Due to circumstances entirely beyond his or her control, for example, the stabilized junkie may lose access to a main connection, thereby reducing availability. If this unfortunate situation coincides with tighter law enforcement, forcing abandonment of usual hustling routine, the addict finds himself or herself in the situation of the street junkie without the benefit of "free wheeling." Similarly, it is not uncommon for free-wheeling junkies to reorganize their lives sufficiently by engaging in new or previous hustling role activities, thereby assuming once again the status of the stabilized junkie.

Regardless of the specific turns that an individual's drug using career may take, however, ethical conduct in the heroin subculture is dependent upon and sustained by the constraints and opportunities imposed by drug availability and life structure. That addict ethics are situated in this manner is hardly remarkable; the situational character of social behavior has long been documented in other contexts as well, particularly in the areas of racial attitudes and behavior (Deutscher, 1966; Kutner et al., 1952; LaPiere, 1934; Linn, 1965), classroom behavior (Freeman and Ataov, 1960; Henry 1959), and drinking behavior (Warriner, 1958), among others. Nevertheless, unlike individuals in these other contexts who fail to adhere to their stated principles, the failure of heroin addicts consistently to maintain ethical integrity is commonly understood to be evidence for a lack of any normative sensitivity whatsoever.

The testimony of the individuals reported here would suggest otherwise. These hard-core addicts readily articulated their ethical standards, often in a most forceful manner. Moreover, even

as they failed to maintain their ethical standards behaviorally, addicts acknowledged and asserted the legitimacy of the very norms they violated. Many, like "Joy," expressed deep regret at their behavior during these desperate times:

> I felt bad...doing the things I was doing.... I didn't want to take nobody's check that I know [they] only get once a month and they probably got kids—and I know they did have kids or else they wouldn't be on welfare.

At other times these addicts used various sorts of excuses and rationalizations to mitigate or neutralize their culpability (see Sykes and Matza, 1957), as in Belle's emphasis on the deleterious effect of methamphetamines on her behavior. Then, too, some addicts attempted to lessen the impact of their indiscretion by pointing to the even more serious violations of actual or hypothetical peers. As one female addict put it, "There's things I've done that I've been ashamed of...but there's things that...I know I could have done that I didn't do."

In short, the credibility of the system of ethics embraced by street addicts cannot be measured by absolute behavioral conformity any more than the credibility of business ethics can be assessed in terms of the absolute absence of fraud. As Meier (1981:14) reminds us once again, "because norms identify behavior that ought or ought not to occur, behavior may (and often does) depart from norms." The legitimacy of these street ethics is rather established by the addict's reaction to their violation. The regrets expressed, and the very necessity of offering excuses, rationalizations, and moral comparisons, all acknowledge the legitimacy of those norms that have been breached. Through these sorts of statements and reactions, then, addicts honor and reaffirm their own indigenous standards of conduct, even in pointing to and acknowledging their violation on particular occasions. In this way addict subculture is sustained and preserved in much the same way that interactional order, as Goffman (1967) reminds us, is sustained and preserved by displays of embarrassment at moments of incompetence performance.

NOTES

1. One of the respondents used methamphetamine heavily but heroin only marginally. This respondent was especially insightful, however, and is included in the final sample because of her close association with the heroin subculture.

2. Such career contingencies are not, of course, limited to drug-using careers. Career contingencies have been discussed in relation to the fate of idealism in medical school (Becker and Geer, 1958); in nursing school (Psathas, 1968); and in dental school (Morris and Sherlock, 1971). Similarly, Cressey (1953) has discussed those external contingencies that are conducive to embezzlement among otherwise respectable businessmen. More generally, Lofland (1969) has specified a number of external conditions affecting the direction of deviant careers.

REFERENCES

Anslinger, H. J. and W. F. Tompkins (1953) The Traffic in Narcotics. New York: Funk and Wagnalls.

Ashley, R. (1972) Heroin: The Myths and the Facts. New York: St. Martin's.

Becker, H. S. and B. Geer (1958) "The fate of idealism in medical school." Amer. Soc. Rev. 23:50–56.

Beschner, G. M. and W. Brower (1985) "The scene," pp. 19–29 in B. Hanson et al. (eds.) Life with Heroin: Voices from the Inner City. Lexington, MA: D. C. Heath.

Blum, R. (1972) The Dream Sellers. San Francisco: Jossey-Bass.

Blumer, H., A. Sutter, R. Smith, and S. Ahmed (1976) "Recruitment into drug use," in R. Coombs et al. (eds.) Socialization in Drug Use. Cambridge, MA: Schenkman.

Bullington, B. (1977) Heroin Use in the Barrio. Lexington, MA: D. C. Heath.

Coombs, R. H. (1981) "Drug abuse as career." J. of Drug Issues 11:369–387.

Crawford, G. A., M. C. Washington, and E. C. Senay (1983) "Careers with heroin." Intl. J. of the Addictions 18:701–715.

Cressey, D. R. (1953) Other People's Money. Glencoe, IL: Free Press.

Deutscher, I. (1966) "Words and deeds: social science and social policy." Social Problems 13:235–254.

Durkheim, E. (1897) Suicide (trans., 1951) New York: Free Press.

Eldridge, W. B. (1967) Narcotics and the Law: A Critique of the American Experiment in Narcotic Drug Control. Chicago: Univ. of Chicago Press.

Faupel, C. E. (1981) "Understanding the relationship between heroin use and crime: contributions of the life history technique." Presented at the thirty-third Annual Meeting of the American Society of Criminology, Washington, DC.

Fiddle, S. (1967) Portraits from a Shooting Gallery. New York: Harper & Row.

Freeman, L. C. and T. Ataov (1960) "Invalidity of indirect and direct measures toward cheating." J. of Personality 28:443–447.

Goffman, E. (1967) "Embarrassment and social organization," pp. 97–112 in E. Goffman (ed.) Interaction Ritual: Essays on Face to Face Behavior. Chicago: Aldine.

Goldstein, P. J. (1981) "Getting over: economic alternatives to predatory crime among street drug users," pp. 67–84 in J. A. Inciardi (ed.) The Drugs-Crime Connection. Beverly Hills, CA: Sage.

Gould, L., A. L. Walker, L. E. Crane, and C. W. Lidz (1974) Connections: Notes from the Heroin World. New Haven, CT: Yale Univ. Press.

Hanson, B., G. Beschner, J. W. Walters, and E. Bovelle (1985) Life with Heroin: Voices from the Inner City. Lexington, MA: D. C. Heath.

Henry, J. (1959) "Spontaneity, initiative and creativity in suburban classrooms." Amer. J. of Orthopsychiatry 29:266–279.

Hughes, E. C. (1971) The Sociological Eye: Selected Papers. Chicago: Aldine-Atherton.

Hughes, P. H. (1977) Behind the Wall of Respect. Chicago: Univ. of Chicago Press.

Johnson, B. D., P. J. Goldstein, E. Preble, J. Schmeidler, D. S. Lipton, B. Spunt, and T. Miller (1985) Taking Care of Business: The Economics of Crime by Heroin Abusers. Lexington, MA: D. C. Heath.

Kutner, B., C. Wilkins, and P. R. Yarrow (1952) "Verbal attitudes and overt behavior involving racial prejudice." J. of Abnormal and Social Psychology 47:649–652.

LaPiere, R. T. (1934) "Attitudes vs. actions." Social Forces 13:230–237.

Lindesmith, A. (1940) "'Dope fiend' mythology." J. of Criminal Law and Criminology 31:199–208.

Linn, L. S. (1965) "Verbal attitude and overt behavior: a study of racial discrimination." Social Forces 43:353–364.

Lofland, J. (1969) Deviance and Identity. Englewood Cliffs, NJ: Prentice-Hall.

Meier, R. F. (1981) "Norms and the study of deviance: a proposed research strategy." Deviant Behavior 3: 1–25.

Morris, R. and B. Sherlock (1971) "Decline of ethics and the rise of cynicism in dental school." J. of Health and Social Behavior 12:290–299.

Preble, E. and J. J. Casey (1969) "Taking care of business—the heroin user's life on the street." Intl. J. of the Addictions 4:1–24.

Psathas, G. (1968) "The fate of idealism in nursing school." J. of Health and Social Behavior 9:52–64.

Reese, A. (1975) "An addict's view of drug abuse," pp. 5–19 in R. H. Coombs (ed.) Junkies and Straights. Lexington, MA: D. C. Heath.

Rosenbaum, M. (1981a) Women on Heroin, New Brunswick, NJ: Rutgers Univ. Press.

Rosenbaum, M. (1981b) "Women addicts' experience of the heroin world: risk, chaos and inundation." Urban Life 10:65–91.

Rubington, E. (1967) "Drug addiction as a deviant career." Intl. J. of the Addictions 2:3–20.

Silver, G. and M. Aldrich (1979) The Dope Chronicles: 1850–1950. New York: Harper & Row.

Sutter, A. G. (1969) "Worlds of drug use on the street scene," pp. 802–829 in D. R. Cressey and D. A. Ward (eds.) Delinquency, Crime and Social Process. New York: Harper & Row.

Sykes, G. M. and D. Matza (1957) "Techniques of neutralization: a theory of delinquency." Amer. Soc. Rev. 22:664–670.

Waldorf, D. (1973) Careers in Dope. Englewood Cliffs, NJ: Prentice-Hall.

Walters, J. M. (1985) "'Taking care of business' updated: a fresh look at the daily routine of the heroin user," pp. 31–48 in B. Hanson et al. (eds.) Life with Heroin: Voices from the Inner City. Lexington, MA: D. C. Heath.

Warriner, C. K. (1958) "The nature and functions of official morality." Amer. J. of Sociology 64:165–168.

Zinberg, N. (1984) Drug Set and Setting: The Basis for Controlled Intoxicant Use. New Haven, CT: Yale Univ. Press.

Outsiders in a Hearing World

PAUL C. HIGGINS

Much of everyday life is based on the assumption that people can hear and speak. We communicate through telephones, radios, television, intercom systems and loudspeakers. Warning signals are often buzzers, sirens or alarms. Time is structured by bells and whistles. And, of course, people talk. Our world is an oral-aural one in which deaf people are typically left out (Higgins, 1978). They are *outsiders* in a hearing world (Becker, 1963). And like other outsiders, they are likely to create and

Excerpt from Paul C. Higgins, "Outsiders in a Hearing World—The Deaf Community," *Urban Life*, Vol. 8, No. 1 (April 1979), pp. 3–22. Copyright © 1979 Sage Publications, Inc. Reprinted by permission of Sage Publications, Inc.

maintain their own communities in order to survive and even thrive within an often hostile world.

In this article I explore the deaf community. Unlike many other disabled populations—who often only establish self-help groups (Sagarin, 1969)—the deaf are not merely a statistical aggregate. For example, 85% of deaf people who lost their hearing before the age of 19 have hearing-impaired spouses (Schein and Delk, 1974:40).[1] Through marriage, friendships, casual acquaintances, clubs, religious groups, magazines published by and for themselves and sign language, the deaf create and maintain communities in the hearing world. Though scattered throughout a metropolitan area, members of the deaf community primarily confine their social relations to other members (Schein, 1968:74). Membership within those deaf communities and the organization of the relationships among members are the foci of this article. Each of these aspects of deaf communities revolves around the deaf being outsiders in a hearing world.

METHODS

This article is part of a larger study in Chicago which investigated the identity, interaction and community of the deaf in a hearing world (Higgins, 1977). I draw on materials from in-depth interviews with 75 hearing-impaired people and 15 counselors or friends of the deaf. My sample was developed through a snowballing technique. Two well-known deaf people in Chicago provided me with names of deaf people. I contacted those people who in turn provided me other names and so on. I supplemented my interviews with observations of a club for the deaf in Chicago, a winter carnival sponsored by a deaf-run organization and several meetings and outings of a senior citizen's club for the deaf in Chicago. National publications by and for the deaf, published writings of deaf individuals and articles or monographs about the deaf proved helpful. My research and analysis was primarily limited to the white deaf community. I soon learned that there was little interaction between white and black deaf. They form separate communities.

As I will discuss later, members of the deaf community are often suspicious and wary of hearing people (just as outsiders in general are of "normals"). They are reluctant to share their lives with the hearing. I overcame that potential reluctance in several ways. First, my parents are deaf. I am a "wise" hearing person (Goffman, 1963). Several people I interviewed knew them and therefore were happy to talk with me. Others approached me at a club for the deaf because of my name. One hearing woman of deaf parents told

me that her husband was concerned that I would be interviewing her while she was alone. She told her husband that I had deaf parents (though she did not know them personally) and therefore everything would be alright. Second, I was mistaken for being deaf during my research due to my signing skills, though I did not intentionally try to pass as deaf. Finally, by contacting potential respondents through referrals (snowball technique) or through having first met them at a club for the deaf, I reduced potential problems of establishing my identity and intentions. Only five people refused to be interviewed and two of those may never have received my letter asking to meet them.

It is a lack of trust which typically has led outsiders to distort the information they give to members of the larger society. For example, black respondents give more "docile" and "subservient" replies to white interviewers than to black interviewers (Sattler, 1970:151). Through all the ways noted above, I believe I gained the trust of those members of the deaf community who shared their lives with me.

MEMBERSHIP

More than 13 million people in America have some form of hearing impairment. Almost 2 million are deaf. Of those 2 million approximately 410,000 are "prevocationally" deaf; they suffered their hearing losses before the end of adolescence (Schein and Delk, 1974).[2] It is from this latter group, the prevocationally deaf, that members of deaf communities are likely to come. I neither met nor heard of members of the Chicago-area deaf community who lost their hearing after adolescence. Surely some exist, but they are few. It will become evident later why that is so.

Deafness is not a sufficient condition for membership in deaf communities, though some degree of hearing impairment is a necessary condition as I will examine later. Deafness does not make "its members part of a natural community" (Furth, 1973:2). Membership in deaf communities must be *achieved*. It is not an ascribed status (Markowicz and Woodward, 1975). Membership in a deaf community is achieved through (1) *identification* with the deaf world, (2) *shared experiences* of being hearing impaired, and (3) *participation* in the community's activities. Without all three characteristics one cannot be nor would one choose to be a member of a deaf community.

IDENTIFICATION

A deaf community is in part a "moral" phenomenon. It involves:

> a sense of identity and unity with one's group and a feeling of involvement and wholeness on the part of the individual [Poplin, 1972:7].

A deaf woman, her hearing impaired since childhood, dramatically describes the realization in her late teens and early twenties that she was part of the deaf world:

> I didn't think I was very deaf myself. But when I saw these people (at a deaf organization) I knew I belonged to their world. I didn't belong to the hearing world. Once you are deaf, you are deaf, period. If you put something black in white paint, you can't get the black out. Same with the deaf. Once you are deaf, you're always deaf.

While it is problematic both physiologically and in terms of identification that "once you are deaf, you are always deaf," the woman's remarks express her commitment to the deaf world.[3] Whether members dramatically realize it or not, what is important is their commitment to and identification with the deaf. Other members, who attended schools and classes for the deaf since childhood and continued their interaction in the deaf world as adults, may, on looking back, find no dramatic moment when they realized that they had become part of a deaf community.

Members of the deaf community feel more comfortable with deaf people than they do with hearing people. They feel a sense of belonging. A young deaf woman explained:

> At a club for the deaf, if I see a deaf person whom I don't know, I will go up to that person and say, "Hi! What's your name?" I would never do that to a hearing person.

Not all deaf or hearing-impaired people, though, identify with the deaf world. Those who lost their hearing later in life through an accident, occupational hazard or presbycusis (i.e., aging process) do not seek to become members of deaf communities. Rather, as Goffman (1963) notes, they are likely to stigmatize members of deaf communities in the same way that those with normal hearing stigmatize them. Others, impaired from birth or from an early age, may never have developed such an identification. They probably had hearing parents and were educated in schools for the hearing. Some may participate in activities of deaf communities, but are not members. They are tolerated, though not accepted by the members. While audiologically they are deaf, socially they are not.

A hearing-impaired man, who participates in a deaf religious organization, but is not part of the deaf community, explained his self-identity in the following way:

> In everyday life I consider myself a hearing person. (His hearing impaired wife interjected that she did too.) I usually forget it that I have a hearing problem. Sometimes I'm so lost (absorbed) in the hearing world; I mean I don't even realize I have a hearing problem. It seems automatic. I don't know what it is. I feel I'm hearing people to the deaf and hearing. I don't feel hearing impaired not even if I have a hard time to understand somebody. Still I don't feel I'm deaf because I couldn't hear you or understand you.

This man and his hearing-impaired wife are on the fringe of the deaf community. They participate in some community activities "just to show that we care" and "because they (the deaf) need help."

Hearing-impaired people like this man and his wife are often a source of both ill feelings and amusement for members of deaf communities. They are a source of ill feelings because their behavior does not respect the identity of the deaf community. Thus, this same hearing-impaired man was severely criticized for having someone at a board meeting of a religious group interpret his spoken remarks into sign language rather than signing himself. As I will explain later, signing skill and communication preference are indications of one's commitment to the deaf community. Those who are opposed to signing or who do not sign are not members of the community.

They are a source of amusement for trying to be what members of deaf communities feel they are not—hearing. A deaf couple were both critical and amused at the attempt of the same hearing-impaired man's wife to hide her deafness. As they explained:

A hearing woman who signs well came up to her (the wife) at a religious gathering, and assuming that she was deaf, which she is, began to sign to her. The wife became flustered, put her own hands down and started talking.

Such hearing-impaired people serve as examples that members of deaf communities use in explaining to others what their community is like and in reaffirming to themselves who they are. These hearing-impaired people help to define for the members the boundary of their community and their identity as deaf people. The members reject the feelings of these "misguided" hearing-impaired people; feelings which deny their deafness. And in rejection, the members affirm who they are and what their community is.

SHARED EXPERIENCES

In developing an identification with the deaf world, members of deaf communities share many similar experiences. Those experiences relate particularly to the everyday problems of navigating in a hearing world (Higgins, 1978) and to being educated in special programs for the deaf.

Since childhood, members of deaf communities have experienced repeated frustration in making themselves understood, embarrassing misunderstandings and the loneliness of being left out by family, neighborhood acquaintances and others. Such past and present experiences help to strengthen a deaf person's identification with the deaf world. A *typical* instance of these experiences, remarkable only because it is so routine, was described by a deaf man:

Most of my friends are deaf. I feel more comfortable with them. Well, we have the same feelings. We are more comfortable with each other. I can communicate good with hearing people, but in a group, no. For example, I go bowling. Have a league of hearing bowlers. Four of them will be talking, talking, talking and I will be left out. Maybe if there was one person I would catch some by lipreading, but the conversation passes back and forth so quickly. I can't keep up. I just let it go; pay attention to my bowling. Many things like that.

Yet, to be a member of a deaf community, one need not actually be deaf. Some members have lesser degrees of hearing impairment. As children, though, they were processed through educational programs for the deaf. These children were not necessarily mislabeled, though certainly some were. Rather, often no local programs for "hard of hearing" children were available. Children with various degrees of impairment were educated together. Through such processing, these children developed friendships with deaf children and an identification with the deaf world. As adults, they moved comfortably into deaf communities. With amplification these members of deaf communities are often able to use the telephone successfully, if also somewhat haltingly. Some converse with hearing people reasonably well. Yet, due to that childhood processing as deaf, these hearing-impaired people choose to live their lives within deaf communities. Audiologically they are not deaf; socially they are (Furfey and Harte, 1964, 1968; Schein, 1968).

Other members of a deaf community may have once been deaf, but through surgery or fortuitous circumstances they have regained some hearing. Though no longer severely hearing impaired, they remain active in the deaf community where their identity as a person developed. A dramatic case is that of a now slightly hearing-impaired man. He went to the state school for the deaf in Illinois. His childhood friends were deaf. During World War II, though, he regained much of his hearing while working in a munitions plant; the loud blasts from testing the bombs apparently improved his hearing. Consequently, his speech also improved. Only his modest hearing aid indicates that he has a slight impairment. Yet his wife is deaf, most of their friends are deaf, and he is active in a state organization for the deaf. As he explained:

(As your speech got better, did you continue to associate with your deaf friends in _____ town?) Oh, yeh, I'm more involved with the deaf community now than I was back then (WW II). To me they are still my family. I feel more at home when I walk into a room with 1,000 deaf people; more so than walking into a room with 1,000 hearing people, non-deaf. I feel at home. I can relate to them. We had something in common; our childhood, our education, our problems, and all that.

Since membership in a deaf community is based on shared experiences of being deaf and identification with the deaf world, it is difficult for hearing individuals to be members of such communities. A deaf woman put it simply: "Hearing people are lost in the deaf world just as deaf people are lost in the hearing world."

Outsiders are often wary and resentful of "normals": blacks of whites, gays of straights and so on. Likewise, deaf people are skeptical of hearing people's motives and intentions. A deaf man remarked:

When a hearing person starts to associate with the deaf, the deaf begin to wonder why that hearing person is here. What does that hearing person want?

When a "hard of hearing" woman, who for years had associated exclusively with the hearing, started a north shore club for the deaf, her motives and behavior were questioned by some of the deaf members. I was warned myself by two deaf leaders to expect such skepticism and resistance by members of the deaf community. I encountered little in my research, but having deaf parents and

clearly establishing my intentions probably allayed members' suspicions.

Outsider communities may grant courtesy membership to "wise" people who are not similarly stigmatized (Goffman, 1963). These individuals are "normal," yet they are familiar with and sympathetic to the conditions of outsiders. For example, gay communities grant courtesy membership to "wise" heterosexuals: heterosexual couples or single females known as "fag hags" (Warren, 1974:113). Researchers are often granted that status. Yet, that courtesy membership represents only a partial acceptance by the outsiders of the "normals."

Some hearing individuals are courtesy members of deaf communities. They may be educators, counselors, interpreters or friends of the deaf. Often they have deafness in their families: deaf parents, siblings, children or even spouses. Yet, their membership is just that, a courtesy, which recognizes the fundamental fact that no matter how empathetic they are, no matter that there is deafness in their families, they are not deaf and can never "really" know what it means to be deaf.[4]

Not surprisingly, hearing-impaired individuals who through their actions and attitudes would otherwise be part of a deaf community may be rejected by some members because they hear and speak too well. A hearing-impaired woman who speaks well and with amplification uses the telephone, who went to a state school for the deaf since childhood and to a college for the deaf and who is married to a deaf man is such an individual.

Yet, hearing-impaired people like that woman do receive some acceptance from those members who tend to reject them. They are called upon to act as go-betweens with the hearing world. This clearly differentiates these impaired people from the hearing. As the hearing-impaired woman mentioned above noted:

They (deaf people) can rely on me to do the talking for them (e.g., telephoning). And in that sense they do accept me because I am somebody who can help them. Because they don't really want to turn around to a hearing person and ask them to do something.

The hearing and speech ability of this hearing-impaired woman creates a barrier between her and some members of the deaf community, but simultaneously allows her some acceptance by those who reject her. She is almost hearing; therefore, some members reject her. She is not quite hearing, though; therefore, members will rely on her for help in navigating through the hearing world. It is often only with greatest reluctance that members of deaf communities rely on hearing people for such assistance.[5]

PARTICIPATION

Active participation in the deaf community is the final criteria for being a member. Participation, though, is an outgrowth of identification with the deaf world and of sharing similar experiences in being hearing impaired. In that respect, then, it is the least important characteristic for being a member of the deaf community. Yet the deaf community is not merely a symbolic community of hearing-impaired people who share similar experiences. It is also created through marriages, friendships, acquaintances, parties, clubs, religious organizations and published materials. The activities provide the body of the community, whereas the identification and shared experiences provide the soul.

Thus, a deaf couple, who lived in the Chicago area for years, were not warmly received when they began to attend a deaf, Protestant congregation. The members of the congregation wondered where they had been all these years. Members interpreted that lack of participation as a lack of identification with themselves and a lack of commitment to the deaf community.

Participation, though, varies among the members of deaf communities. Involvement in community activities is tempered by outside commitments such as work, family and traveling time to and from activities as well as individual preference. More importantly, what activities one participates in and with whom one associates help to organize relationships among members of the deaf community.

SOCIAL ORGANIZATION

While normals may often treat outsiders as a homogeneous group, the outsiders themselves create distinctions among one another. Gays distinguish among "elite," "career" and "deviants" (Warren, 1972). Lower-class blacks may vilify middle-class blacks for being Uncle Toms (Pettigrew, 1964). The deaf community, too, is heterogeneous. Through differential participation with other members and in various activities of the deaf community, members organize their relationships with one another.

Members of the deaf community use several major characteristics in organizing relationships with one another. Some of these characteristics operate in much the same way as in the hearing world. Outsiders, whether they be deaf or not, live within a larger world. Some are not born as outsiders, but only later acquire that status. All are socialized to some degree within the dominant culture. Consequently, communities of outsiders and their subculture are continuous with the dominant culture of the larger society (Plummer, 1975:157). Therefore, it is not surprising that some characteristics which members of the dominant culture use to differentiate each other are also used by members of communities of outsiders. Sex, race, religion and sophistication (as often indicated by educational attainment) differentiate members in the deaf community as they do in the hearing world. Consequently, they will not receive special attention here.

Age, however, adds a special dimension to deaf communities. Unlike ethnic or racial outsiders, there are few deaf children in the deaf community. Less than 10% of deaf people have deaf parents (Schein and Delk, 1974:35). Consequently, deaf communities are actually adult deaf communities. As children, most members of the community were probably isolated in a hearing world except while attending educational programs for the deaf. The same holds true today, though deaf children may participate in such activities as religious worship where deaf adults are present. The intriguing question becomes: how are deaf children and adolescents socialized into the adult deaf community? I did not address this issue which clearly needs attention.

COMMUNICATION

Other characteristics which members of an outsider community use to organize their relationships with one another are related to their unique position within the dominant world. For example, within the black community skin color has played an important but diminishing role (Udry et al., 1971). Within the deaf community, communication preference and skill, the relative emphasis that members give to signing and speaking, is an important basis on which relationships are organized. I will examine this characteristic closely, because it is crucial for understanding the deaf community in a hearing world.

There are two general modes of communication used among the deaf. One is called the oral method; the other is the manual method. The oral method in its "purest" form is composed of speaking and lipreading. Manual communication is sign language and fingerspelling. Put very simply, sign language is a concept-based language of signs (i.e., various movements of the hands in relationship to one another and to the body in which the hands themselves take various shapes) that has a different structure from English, but one that is not yet fully understood (Stokoe et al., 1975). Within the deaf community there are oralists and manualists who I will refer to as *speakers* and *signers*.[6]

Speakers. Speakers rely primarily on speaking and lipreading when communicating with fellow oralists. When communicating with signers, they may often accompany their speaking with signs, but they do not sign fluently. Those who are "pure" oralists in philosophy or communicative behavior are not part of the deaf community. A small number of these "pure" oralists are members of an oral association of the deaf; whereas, others go it alone in the hearing world (Oral Deaf Adults Section Handbook, 1975). Of course, the

distinction between a "pure" oralist and a speaker is arbitrary. Speakers may accept as a member of the community an oralist who signers reject as too orally oriented to be a fellow member. Speakers are likely to have had hearing parents and attended day schools and classes for the deaf where signing was not permitted.

Signers. Signers sign and fingerspell when communicating to their deaf friends. For many signers their first language is sign language. They are native signers. Some have unintelligible speech and poor lipreading skills. Yet, others speak and lipread well, even better than speakers. Signers, though, prefer signing as compared to speech or lipreading when communicating with one another. Rarely will they use their voices or even move their mouths with other signers. Those who do may be teased. Signers reason that speaking and lipreading are for navigating in the hearing world, but they are not necessary among fellow signers.

Varieties of sign language exist. Many of those are due to the mixing of sign language and English. American Sign Language is least influenced by English. The use of varieties of sign language displays the social organization of the deaf community. The more educated the deaf individual is, the more likely that individual will be familiar with varieties which approximate English. Varieties of sign language which approximate English are more likely to be used at formal occasions (e.g., at a conference) than at informal ones. Social, educational, regional and ethnic (particularly black-white) variations in signing exist much as they do in English (Stokoe and Battison, 1975).

Becoming a signer follows no single path. Those who have deaf parents who sign most likely grew up as signers themselves. Others became signers in residential schools. Although signing often was not permitted in the classrooms of such schools, it was often allowed outside of the classrooms in the dorms and on the playgrounds. After leaving *oral* day school programs, many deaf individuals began to use signs which they learned from deaf adults. The hand rapping and monetary fines which were (and in some cases still are) administered to them when they were caught using their hands to communicate were not forgotten. The frustration and bitterness from failing to understand and to learn through the oral approach is still felt.[7] Consequently, these converts are often the most adamantly opposed to oral education because they are the self-perceived victims of it.

Others who did not immediately seek out signers often found that their speech and lipreading skills did not gain them easy entrance into the hearing world. They were misunderstood and in turn misunderstood hearing people. Such experiences influenced these deaf individuals to become signers.

CLEAVAGE BETWEEN SIGNERS AND SPEAKERS

Signers and speakers are members of the same deaf community. They may attend the same religious organization, social club or community gala. They also marry one another. In such marriages the speaker typically becomes a signer. Yet, through their feelings toward each other and their differential involvement with each other, strong divisions and at times antagonisms are created. That cleavage within the deaf community relates historically to the deaf's position within a hearing world. Particularly, it is an outgrowth of how educators of the deaf have traditionally felt it best to teach deaf children.

Historically, throughout the United States and especially in Chicago, Boston, and a few other places, the oral method of instruction has been dominant in schools and classes for the deaf. Only since the early 1970s has the Chicago area begun to emphasize manual communication in the classroom. The combination of the two approaches along with writing and any other effective means of communication has been called total communication (O'Rourke, 1972).

The oral philosophy was stressed in the hope and desire that deaf children, trained in such a method, would be able to move easily into the hearing world as adults. Perhaps more important-

ly, it was also stressed due to the fear that deaf children were allowed to sign and fingerspell with one another, especially in often isolated residential schools, then as adults they would marry one another and form deaf communities within, but apart from, the hearing world. Alexander Graham Bell, whose wife was deaf and who was an influential supporter of the oral philosophy, voiced such fears in an 1883 paper, "Upon the Formation of a Deaf Variety of the Human Race" (Boese, 1971). This emphasis of hearing educators on oralism and their suppression of signing among deaf children has not gone unnoticed by the deaf.

Through formal organizations as well as friendships and informal relations, signers and speakers organize the deaf community according to communication skill and preference. For example, a national fraternal organization for the deaf has several divisions in the Chicago area. One is attended by speakers; the other two by signers. Though the oral division has a dwindling membership, its members insist on being separate from the larger, manually oriented divisions. Further, respondents noted that most, if not all, of their friends had similar communication preferences as their own, be they manual or oral. Each group is not quite comfortable with the other's mode of communication. Speakers explain that it is difficult to follow fast signers, especially when the signers do not move their mouths. Signers complain that it is difficult to lipread the oralists or understand their modest or minimal signing.

The conflict between signing and speaking also disrupts family relationships. It is not unusual for deaf children who sign to communicate little with their parents who do not sign. As adults, their relationships with their parents may be bitter. Deaf siblings, too, can be divided by communication differences. For example, two deaf sisters in the Chicago area rarely see each other. Both grew up in the oral tradition but the older married a speaker while the younger married a signer. The younger sister has retained her oral skills, but has become more involved with signers. Rather than join the oral fraternal division at her sister's request, she remains in the larger, manual division where her friends are.

Although signing is not a basis for membership in deaf communities, it is clearly an outgrowth of becoming a member.[8] Signing is an indication of one's identity as a deaf person and one's commitment to the deaf world. It is perhaps the most obvious indication to hearing people that one is deaf. Because deafness is a relatively invisible impairment, deaf people would often go unnoticed in everyday, impersonal activities except for their signing to one another. Also, signing often attracts stares, unflattering imitations and ridicule from the hearing. Therefore, "pure" oralists are viewed by members of deaf communities, particularly by signers, as outsiders to the deaf world. Further, some signers wonder if speakers are ashamed of being deaf. Signers may interpret the speakers' not fully embracing signing as an indication that speakers are either trying to hide their deafness or are still hopelessly under the influence of misguided, hearing educators. Either way, the speakers' commitment to the deaf world becomes questioned. That commitment is partially based on the conviction that hearing people have too long dominated deaf people's lives; in education, in jobs, in even telling them how to communicate with each other.

CONCLUSION

Within the larger society, outsiders often create and maintain communities. Some of these communities are located within well-defined geographical areas of the city: ethnic neighborhoods, black ghettos or Mexican-American barrios. Other communities of outsiders may not be quite so geographically bounded. Through marriages (both legal and symbolic), friendships, clubs, formal organizations, publications and a special argot, outsiders who are scattered throughout a metropolitan area *create* their community. The deaf community is such a creation.

Membership in deaf communities, though, is neither granted to nor sought by all who are deaf.

Rather, it is achieved through identification with the deaf world, shared experiences of being hearing impaired and involvement with other members. Most people who are audiologically deaf never become members. Some with lesser degrees of hearing impairment have been members for as long as they can remember.

Although the deaf community may appear to be homogeneous to the hearing, members of the community create distinctions among one another. These distinctions are used in organizing relationships within the community. Some of these distinguishing characteristics, such as sex, are used within the hearing world as well. Yet, due to the unique (historical and present) position of the deaf as outsiders in a hearing world, members of the community distinguish among one another based on communication preference. Signers and speakers find it easier to communicate with those who have preferences similar to their own. More importantly, speaking to fellow members is a vestige of the hearing's domination of and paternalism toward the deaf. Therefore, not fully embracing and using sign language may call into question one's identification with and commitment to the deaf community.

Within deaf communities the members seldom face the difficulties and frustrations which arise when they navigate through the hearing world. A sense of belonging and wholeness is achieved which is not found among the hearing. *Among* fellow members there is no shame in being deaf and being deaf does not mean being odd or different. Deafness is taken for granted. Within deaf communities those who cannot "turn a deaf ear" now become the outsiders.

NOTES

1. Ghettos for the blind have existed in the past in China and in many European cities. In 1935, a prominent worker in the field of blindness proposed establishing self-contained communities of the blind (Chevigny and Braverman, 1950). Few blind people, though, have blind spouses (Best, 1934).

A predominantly self-contained village of 400 physically disabled adults has been created by rehabilitation specialists in the Netherlands (Zola, unpublished). To what extent it is a community and to what extent it is merely an extension of a long-term care facility is not clear.

2. Prevocationally deaf people were defined as those "who could not hear and understand speech and who had lost (or never had) that ability prior to 19 years of age" (Schein and Delk, 1974:2). A self-report hearing scale was used to determine the respondent's hearing ability. Schein (1968) discusses the factors (e.g., chronicity, age of onset and degree of loss) involved in defining deafness and examines previous definitions.

3. Most "coming out" among homosexuals, a process of defining oneself as gay, seems to occur in interaction with other homosexuals. Gays too feel that being gay is a permanent condition (Dank, 1971; Warren, 1974).

4. While members of deaf communities grant courtesy membership to "wise" hearing people, those members often subtly indicate that those hearing people are still not "one of them" (Markowicz and Woodward, 1975). When signing to a hearing person, the deaf may slow the speed of their signing or speak while signing. They would rarely do that when communicating with a fellow member.

5. This desire of the deaf to be independent from and their skeptical attitude toward help offered by the hearing has been documented in the more general situation of disabled-nondisabled relations (Ladieu et al., 1947).

6. It is difficult to estimate the relative proportion of oralists and manualists within deaf communities. Both the relative membership within the oral and manual divisions of a deaf fraternal organization (in Chicago) and the proportion of the prevocationally, adult deaf population who use signs (Schein, 1968; Schein and Delk, 1974) indicate that oralists are a numerical minority within deaf communities. Further, their numbers are likely to decline in the future as signing becomes more extensively employed in educational programs for the deaf.

7. On academic achievement tests, deaf children score several years behind their hearing counterparts (Trybus and Karchmer, 1977).

8. Some researchers have viewed deaf communities as language communities where American Sign Language use is necessary for membership (Markowicz and Woodward, 1975; Schlesinger and Meadow, 1972). This approach is too restrictive because it excludes speakers as well as many signers who are not ASL users from being members of deaf communities. Yet, speakers, nonnative signers and native signers associate with each other, marry one another and recognize each other as part of the same community while also maintaining distinctions among one another.

REFERENCES

Becker, H. S. 1963. *Outsiders: Studies in the Sociology of Deviance.* New York: Free Press.

Best, H. 1934. *Blindness and the Blind in the United States.* New York: Macmillan.

Boese, R. J. 1971. "Native Sign Language and the Problem of Meaning." Ph.D. dissertation, University of California—Santa Barbara (unpublished).

Chevigny, H. and S. Braverman. 1950. *The Adjustment of the Blind.* New Haven, CT: Yale Univ. Press.

Dank, B. M. 1971. "Coming Out in the Gay World." *Psychiatry,* 34:180–197.

Furfey, P. H. and T. J. Harte. 1968. *Interaction of Deaf and Hearing in Baltimore City, Maryland.* Washington, DC: Catholic University Press.

———. 1964. *Interaction of Deaf and Hearing in Frederick County, Maryland.* Washington, DC: Catholic University of America Press.

Furth, H. G. 1973. *Deafness and Learning: A Psychosocial Approach.* Belmont, CA: Wadsworth.

Goffman, E. 1963. *Stigma: Notes on the Management of Spoiled Identity.* Englewood Cliffs, NJ: Prentice-Hall.

Higgins, P. C. 1978. "Encounters Between the Disabled and the Nondisabled: Bringing the Impairment Back In." American Sociological Association Meetings, San Francisco.

———. 1977. "The Deaf Community: Identity and Interaction in a Hearing World." Ph.D. dissertation, Northwestern University (unpublished).

Ladieu, G., E. Haufman, and T. Dembo. 1947. "Studies in Adjustment to Visible Injuries: Evaluation of Help by the Injured." *Journal of Abnormal and Social Psychology,* 42:169–192.

Markowicz, H. and J. Woodward. 1975. "Language and the Maintenance of Ethnic Boundaries in the Deaf Community." Conference on Culture and Communication, Temple University, March 13–15.

Oral Deaf Adults Section Handbook. 1975. Washington, DC: Alexander Graham Bell Association for the Deaf.

O'Rourke, T. J. (ed.). 1972. *Psycholinguistics and Total Communication: The State of the Art.* Washington, DC: American Annals of the Deaf.

Pettigrew, T. F. 1964. *A Profile of the Negro American.* Princeton, NJ: D. Van Nostrand.

Plummer, K. 1975. *Sexual Stigma: An Interactionist Account.* London: Routledge and Kegan Paul.

Poplin, D. E. 1972. *Communities: A Survey of Theories and Methods of Research.* New York: Macmillan.

Sagarin, E. 1969. *Odd Man In: Societies of Deviants in America.* Chicago: Quadrangle.

Sattler, J. M. 1970. "Racial 'Experimenter Effects' in Experimentation, Testing, Interviewing, and Psychotherapy." *Psychological Bulletin,* 73:137–160.

Schein, J. D. 1968. *The Deaf Community: Studies in the Social Psychology of Deafness,* Washington, DC: Gallaudet College Press.

Schein, J. D. and M. T. Delk, Jr. 1974. *The Deaf Population of the United States.* Silver Spring, MD: National Association of the Deaf.

Schlesinger, H. S. and K. P. Meadow. 1972. *Sound and Sign: Childhood Deafness and Mental Health.* Berkeley: Univ. of California Press.

Stokoe, W. C. and R. M. Battison. 1975. "Sign Language, Mental Health, and Satisfying Interaction." First National Symposium on the Mental Health Needs of Deaf Adults and Children. Chicago: David T. Siegel Institute for Communicative Disorders, Michael Reese Hospital and Medical Center, June 12–14.

Stokoe, W. C., C. G. Casterline, and C. G. Croneberg (eds.). 1975. *A Dictionary of American Sign Language on Linguistic Principles.* Washington, DC: Gallaudet College Press.

Trybus, R. J. and M. A. Karchmer. 1977. "School Achievement Scores of Hearing Impaired Children: National Data on Achievement Status and Growth Patterns." *American Annals of the Deaf,* 122(2):62–69.

Udry, J. R., K. E. Bauman, and C. Chase. 1971. "Skin Color, Status, and Mate Selection." *American Journal of Sociology,* 76:722–733.

Warren, C. A. B. 1974. *Identity and Community in the Gay World.* New York: Wiley.

———. 1972. "Observing the Gay Community." In J. D. Douglas (ed.), *Research on Deviance.* New York: Random House, pp. 139–163.

Zola, I. K. "To Find the Missing Piece." (Unpublished.)

Prostitution and Crack-House Sex

JAMES A. INCIARDI, DOROTHY LOCKWOOD, and ANNE E. POTTIEGER

... [W]omen who trade sex for drugs, or money to buy drugs, drift in and out of both drug use and prostitution. Due to the instability of their lifestyles, it is impossible to group them by either their drug use or their sexual practices. However, *drug use and prostitution do often vary according*

to where they occur. In crack houses, prostitution takes on a very different character than soliciting on the streets. In the crack house a barter system exists in which sex and crack are the currency. Moreover, in the descriptions that follow, it becomes readily clear that there are a number of very real differences between *prostitutes who use crack* and *crack users who exchange sex for drugs.* . . .

Although there are many similarities between trading sex on the streets and in a crack house, the differences resulting from the unique nature of crack addiction and the crack-house environment are central to understanding crack addiction among women. The crack-house environment affects every aspect of the business of providing sexual services—the setting, the solicitation, the negotiation, the payment, the actual exchange of either money or drugs for sex, as well as the violence and cheating endemic to both the street and crack-house environments.

THE SETTING

On the streets, sex usually occurs in cars, and less frequently in motels or rooming houses. This is confirmed by a study of 20 full-time career prostitutes in Camden, New Jersey, who were interviewed five times a day over a seven-month period.[1] For them, contact with customers was made on the streets and most sex was performed in the customer's vehicle. The Miami street prostitutes described similar arrangements....

Most women providing sexual services on the street have a specific area in which they work. Case studies of street prostitution in the United States, Europe, and Australia indicate that it is common for prostitutes to consider a particular territory as their own and one that other street workers should respect.[2] These arrangements are certainly the case in Miami, with several prostitutes working the same area under an informal agreement.

Crack-house sex occurs in different locations. In some houses, sex is restricted to a specific room, often called the freak room. The owner of the crack house—the "kingrat," "rock master," or "house man"—charges for use of this room, usually $5 to $10 paid by the customer, with a limit of thirty minutes to an hour. The freak room may be used by street prostitutes who visit crack houses solely as places to trick. They bring their own dates and stay only long enough to have sex....

In other crack houses sex occurs not only in freak rooms but also in the common areas where everyone else is smoking. During one visit to a crack house in 1989,[3] the main smoking area was

observed to be a large living room/dining room combination covering about 1,000 square feet. There were 16 people in the room. Three men and four women were sitting or lying down by themselves, in various parts of the room—some were sitting on the floor in corners or by doorways, a few were just stretched out on the floor. Only two were smoking crack; the others appeared to be resting, or waiting, or watching what was going on elsewhere in the room. In a corner farthest away from the entrance, two men were sitting at opposite ends of a couch. Both were smoking and receiving oral sex from two women. Periodically, one of the women would interrupt her "chicken-heading"[4] to have a hit from the man's crack pipe. In another corner, two women were totally naked, with one straddling the other's face, receiving oral sex. They were "freaking" for crack. That is, they were being paid in crack to perform. Close by, a solitary man was watching them intently, smoking a cigarette with one hand, masturbating with the other.

Elsewhere, in a large bean-bag chair by a flickering television set a woman was removing her clothes. She was alone, smoking crack. She kept complaining about the heat, that clothing and "base" just didn't mix and made her skin "crawl," and that she preferred to smoke in the nude. After she was fully undressed, she continued to complain about the heat and her skin. In the midst of these activities, one of the operators of the house looked around from his post at the doorway to make sure that things were in order.

This scene continued for almost an hour. New customers would come and go—purchase crack, smoke crack, watch sex, engage in sex. Some would just look around and disappear into other rooms. The two men on the couch never spoke to each other, to the women, or to anyone else. Since they couldn't seem to climax or even maintain a complete erection, they just kept nudging the women on. The man who was masturbating and watching the two freaking women eventually got up and had vaginal sex with one of them—the one who had been on top, the straddler, the recipient.

The other wiped her mouth, lit a cigarette, and watched—disinterested in all of the goings-on. The woman in the bean-bag chair eventually settled into a quiet smoking session. At one point a new visitor tried to solicit her for sex, but she waved him off. Later he was observed in another room engaging in vaginal intercourse with a young woman who apparently lived in the house and represented a "free service" of the house—freely available to anyone who regularly purchased sufficient amounts of crack, or who brought new customers to the house....

In addition to the freak rooms and the smoking rooms, there are other locations where crack-house sex might occur—in bathrooms and closets, on porches and rooftops, in cars parked nearby, and, as one male customer noted, even in empty swimming pools.

Another aspect of crack-house sex is that there are some territorial issues that decide who tricks in one crack house as opposed to another. When the house is a residence in which only a small circle of friends or acquaintances are permitted to smoke, there are a few rules. Strangers aren't allowed, but they can be brought in as tricks by any member of the group. For these, there may be a freak room that can be used. For example:

> Oh boy, I had a house, a nice big house. Everybody liked to come over to my house for some reason, to party or something. So they would come over there. Every room in my house I could lock with one key. I had freak rooms. It was crucial. I would lock people up in the freak room so they were alone. I would lock them up so no one would get in. I would give them thirty minutes for $10 in the freak room. It was nice. Thursday and Friday nights I would take my kids next door to the neighbor. As long as they [crack smokers] gonna use the house they give me drugs. It was like we all hit together, you make one hit you pass around, all around. You share the shit, we were friends. It's my house and I keep my house secure. If you were strung out and get in an argument, you gotta go.

In the more commercialized houses, territorial constraints are generally absent. Street prostitutes are permitted to solicit johns, as long as someone pays for the use of a room. Crack users soliciting or providing sex in the smoking rooms are permitted to do so as long as they have paid their entry fee to the house. In general, it is the crack-house owners who ultimately decide who tricks and who doesn't. And, too, although some women work in several crack houses, most focus on one or two.

THE SOLICITATION

On the streets and in the crack houses, soliciting customers is primarily a matter of waiting. Prostitution is often portrayed as a "lively commerce,"[5] a colorful and exciting part of urban night life. However, for most prostitutes it can be extremely monotonous. Street prostitutes "hang out" on certain corners or "stroll" particular streets until approached by a potential customer....

It is at this point of solicitation that women on the street decide whether to pursue a situation and begin to negotiate the actual exchange of sexual services. The prostitutes encountered during the course of this study have been street-wise for quite some time and have developed a sense of whether situations are unsafe....

One concern of these women is the plain-clothes police, the vice squad.... In *Working Women*, Arlene Carmen and Howard Moody of the Judson Memorial Church in New York City have explored the relationship and interchange between police and prostitutes.[6] They discuss the unpredictable and illogical patterns of arrest as well as the frequent excessive force and violence used by police. They also indicate that most prostitutes are arrested when they begin working new areas. Similar to the comments made by the street-walkers in Miami, the prostitutes in this New York City study quickly learned who were police officers and how to avoid them.

In contrast with the streetwalkers, women who exchange sex for crack in crack houses usually initiate the exchange when they are in need of a hit or rock. This solicitation is often informal and nonverbal. The women offer sexual services implicitly by sharing drugs bought by a man. . . .

However, it is also not unusual for a man to approach a woman for the purpose of having a sex partner throughout a smoking encounter. Some men will enter a crack house, purchase enough rocks for two people for several hours, and then make it clear to every woman in the house what he has in mind. Usually someone will take him up on it. If not, someone else eventually comes by. In any case, the potential for soliciting an undercover police officer is not the problem in the crack house that it is on the street. Streetwalkers, crack-house prostitutes, and police officers alike all agree that vice cops don't work crack houses. . . .

THE NEGOTIATION

Although much of the soliciting in the sex industry is simply a matter of being in a particular place—on certain streets or in the crack houses—sex negotiations differ dramatically between the two settings. On the streets, prostitutes are active participants, if not the lead players, in the negotiating process. During the deliberations, the price and type of sex are determined. . . . [T]o avoid vice arrests, street prostitutes insist that the customers quote the price.[7] Prostitutes also have prices to which they generally adhere. For the most part, if the customer is unwilling to pay her set price, then no business is conducted. . . .

Other street workers, however, for a variety of reasons, are more flexible in their negotiations:

> If you are really lookin' good, haven't lost your good looks, an' you're out there just prancin' like some foxy bitch, sure you can hold your price. But when I need the money I'm bad up, I'm gonna go for $5.

In the crack house, on the other hand, there seems to be an expectation that if a man wants to have sex with a woman, she will not oppose the offer. The expectations are implicit. Everyone involved—the house owner, the male user/customer, and the female user/prostitute are all aware of what is expected. Because the rules and the roles are known to all parties, there is little negotiating. As mentioned above, it is also implied that if a woman uses the drugs bought by a man, she has agreed to provide sexual services—typically oral or vaginal sex but sometimes anal sex or participation in freaking or a sex show. . . .

PAYMENT AND EXCHANGE

On the street, payment is received before services are rendered. Moreover, money is preferred and frequently demanded by street prostitutes. Although some will accept drugs in exchange for sex, most will not hear of it, feeling that they receive less for their services, particularly when the drug is crack. Other studies of prostitution confirm the existence of this preference.[8]

In the crack house, payment occurs before, during, and after the sexual service, and is usually a piece or hit of crack. Infrequently, a woman is paid with an entire rock. This barter system also defines the monetary exchange rate, which is much lower in the crack house than it is on the streets. The going rate for oral sex on the streets of Miami in the early 1990s was $20 or $25. In the crack house, it was $5 or $10, approximately the cost of a rock. As crack-house women become more desperate for rocks, however, they begin to perform oral sex for a single hit, sometimes for as little as 25 cents worth of crack.

The sexual exchange differs in two basic aspects—length of interaction and use of drugs. On the streets, the exchange doesn't take very long, and the use of drugs during the trade is uncommon. Such street-based interactions as car and motel tricks last between 10 and 20 minutes. For "working women" (prostitutes), time is money and they are anxious to move back onto the stroll and the next date. . . .

In the crack house, both the customer and the woman providing sex use drugs during the sexual exchange. These exchanges last from 30 minutes to an hour or longer, depending on how long the crack-house owner rents the room. And if the encounter occurs in a common area, the sex might go on even longer. . . .

PROSTITUTES WHO SMOKE CRACK AND CRACK ADDICTS WHO PROSTITUTE

. . . [A] comparison of a few of the day-to-day activities of *prostitutes who smoke crack* suggests that they are indeed different from *crack addicts who prostitute* in crack houses.

In the first place, the fact that prostitution has its monetary rewards appears throughout the literature.[9] . . .

The daily routines of street workers are not all that different than those of women working night shifts in legitimate jobs. Their crack smoking, furthermore, is often considered as no more than a means of relaxing. . . .

The schedules and daily routines of women who trade sex for crack in crack houses are driven by their addiction to the drug. Their lives are chaotic, revolving exclusively around crack-smoking and crack-seeking. There are feeble attempts to fulfill responsibilities to children and family, but these are secondary to crack use. Days and nights are spent in and out of crack houses, alternating between tricking and using, sexing and smoking. If there are customers in the crack house, then crack-addicted women will remain there. If there are none, they will leave, but only to find customers. And if they cannot find customers, then they will sell personal belongings or steal in order to keep themselves high. . . .

Not surprisingly, street prostitutes have little respect for their crack-addicted counterparts in crack houses. . . .

As a final point here, some comment seems warranted on the role of the pimp—the "street man," "street hustler," "player," or "meat salesman"—the man who is regularly in the company of prostitutes, who seems to exercise control over their activities, and who derives all or part of his livelihood from their earnings. There was a time when prostitution and pimping went hand in hand, so much so that one student of prostitution estimated in 1935 that Chicago's population of 3 million included some 8,800 prostitutes and 6,300 pimps.[10] The roles of the pimp, then and now, include staying alert for police, attempting to divert or bribe police, posting bail and obtaining an attorney when necessary, helping to steal from johns, and protecting the prostitute from beatings by tricks.

During the 1980s, the pimp/prostitute relationship was frequently used to demonstrate the patriarchal and repressive nature of prostitution.[11] Pimps have been portrayed as not only recruiting women unwillingly into prostitution, but also as keeping them in the business through violence, threats, and dependency. There is evidence, however, that the role of the pimp in the sex industry may be diminishing. Karen File noted this trend in 1976 with female addicts seeming to "depart from the male-dominated role structure."[12] Similarly, of the six prostitutes interviewed in Zausner's *The Streets,* only one had a pimp.[13]

In the Miami sex-for-crack scene, none of the women encountered used a pimp. All were "outlaws," whether they walked the streets or worked the crack houses. Repeatedly, they made the statement, "Crack is my pimp." . . .

However, women tricking or trading sex in a crack house do give a share of their earnings (or drugs) to the crack-house owner. They do not consider the owner to be a pimp, and, at least officially, he does not play the pimp's role. Nonetheless, the women are paying to use the house and, indirectly, for protection. . . .

In *Street Woman,* sociologist Eleanor Miller notes that Milwaukee women active in both street crime and drug networks rarely use the term *pimp.*[14] Rather, one hears the expression "my man" when they speak of male confederates or companions. Their "man" is usually a drug dealer, and frequently is the one who introduced these women to the fast life. Similar to the women in Milwaukee, those in Miami are typically introduced to crack by male drug-using friends, many of whom are dealers and/or crack-house owners. These same "friends" are often the gateway to crack-house prostitution. Although the women do not refer to the men as "pimps" or even as "my man," male dealers are often the conduit to drug use and prostitution. For example:

> I smoked and smoked till my money was gone. No one was left in the house except the dealer. So I told him I wanted a hit. He said you are going to have to do something for a hit. So I had oral sex with him. That's how I got started.

NOTES

1. Matthew Freund, Terri L. Leonard, and Nancy Lee, "Sexual Behavior of Resident Street Prostitutes with Their Clients in Camden, New Jersey," *Journal of Sex Research* 26 (November 1989), pp. 460–478.

2. See Michael Zausner, *The Streets* (New York: St. Martin's Press, 1986); Roberta Perkins and Garry Bennett, *Being a Prostitute* (Boston: Allen & Unwin Publishers, 1985); Eileen McLeod, *Women Working: Prostitution Now* (London: Croom Helm, 1982); Anonymous, *Streetwalker* (New York: Viking Press, 1960).

3. These observations are from the senior author's field notes compiled after his observations in crack houses.

4. Among numerous other names, fellatio is referred to as "chicken-heading" in some crack houses because the movement of the woman's head during the sex act is similar to that of a chicken. As such, women who trade sex for crack are also referred to as *chickenheads*.

5. Charles Winick and Paul M. Kinsie, *The Lively Commerce: Prostitution in the United States* (Chicago: Quadrangle Books, 1971).

6. Arlene Carmen and Howard Moody, *Working Women: The Subterranean World of Street Prostitution* (New York: Harper & Row, 1985), pp. 133–161.

7. If the john is an undercover police officer, and, depending on exactly *who* quotes the price, the outcome of the encounter might be either a legitimate arrest, or police entrapment, which is illegal. Entrapment is the *inducement* of an individual to commit a crime, undertaken for the sole purpose of instituting a criminal prosecution against the offender. In his book, *The Police Mystique: An Insider's Look at Cops, Crime, and the Criminal Justice System* (New York: Plenum Press, 1990), p. 165, former Minneapolis Police Chief Anthony V. Bouza explained it this way:

> If a cop comes up to a prostitute and engages in vague generalities or responses to her leads, this is not entrapment. The scenario might go something like this:
>
> HE: Hi.
> SHE: Hi, wanna party?
> HE: Sure. What's the tariff, and what do you do?
> SHE: Fifty dollars for a blow job.
>
> This is a perfectly legitimate vignette for a legal arrest. The twist on this exchange would be:
>
> HE: Hi.
> SHE: Hi.
> HE: I'm willing to give you $50 for a blow job. How about it?
> SHE: Sure.
>
> Because the officer initiated the action, the guilt of the target is not established. This arrest, if made, would be illegal.

8. See Zausner, *The Streets;* Lewis Diana, *The Prostitute and Her Clients* (Springfield, IL: Charles C. Thomas, 1985).

9. Lionel James, "On the Game," *New Society* 24 (May 24, 1973), pp. 426–429; Zausner, *The Streets*.

10. Ben L. Reitman, *The Second Oldest Profession* (New York: Vanguard, 1936).

11. See Kim Romenesko and Eleanor M. Miller, "The Second Step in Double Jeopardy: Appropriating the Labor of Female Street Hustlers," *Crime and Delinquency* 35 (January 1989), pp. 109–135.

12. Karen N. File, "Sex Roles and Street Roles," *International Journal of the Addictions* 11 (1976), pp. 263–268.

13. Zausner, *The Streets*.

14. Eleanor Miller, *Street Woman* (Philadelphia: Temple University Press, 1986).

PART FOUR

DEVIANT IDENTITY

When a person asks "Who am I?" there are private answers as well as public ones. The private answers—how a person views him/herself—form one's *personal* identity. The public answers—the image others have of the person—provide one's *social* identity. There is sometimes little consistency between the two. Con men, for example, may studiously present social identities that diverge widely from their true, personal identities. Thus they assume social identities that their personal identities, if known, would discredit. This is true for covert deviants generally. When in the company of heterosexuals, for example, the secret homosexual may ridicule or condemn homosexuality, or pretend to be interested in the opposite sex, in order to achieve a heterosexual social identity. The task of harmonizing one's personal and social identities is hard enough for conventional people. For certain kinds of deviants, particularly secret deviants, it is even more complex.

A deviant social identity may lead to a deviant personal identity when a person finds it prudent to accept a publicly attributed deviant status. This passive style of bringing personal and social identities together probably produces relatively little identity conflict. When a person identified as a deviant refuses to take on a deviant personal identity, however, greater identity problems are likely to result.

Social identities may be devised by the person or by others. Spies, for example, consciously devise and enact their own deceptive social identities. Public relations people, gossips, and agents of social control, on the other hand, often cast other people into social identities that may or may not conform to their personal identities.

In a complex, urban society where many people relate to a wide assortment of new, previously unknown people, the opportunity for taking on a new social identity comes up all the time. Similarly, the chance of being cast by someone else into a new social identity is also more likely. In addition, the possibility of having multiple social identities, with different identities for different audiences, also arises. In such a society, then, people often find it difficult to develop a single, coherent social identity; they may also find it difficult to harmonize their personal and social identities. In fact, attempts to manage this problem may produce the very deceitfulness that is presumed to be characteristic of so many deviants.

Because a social identity as a conforming person is usually preferred to a deviant social identity, most deviants need to practice some duplicity. The steady practice of duplicity may enable the deviant to avert conflict between his or her various positions and roles. On the other hand, duplicity may cause such a strain that the deviant gives it up. For example, Edwin Lemert found that with regard to the systematic check forger the need to assume many legitimate social roles and social identities produces a heavy strain;[1] constant impersonations are not easy to maintain. Hence, paradoxically, discovery and arrest actually solve an identity problem for the forger. In prison the forger at least has an authentic social identity. The strains confronting the systematic check forger typify the kinds of identity problems that many deviants must come to terms with in one way or another.

In this part of the book we examine the issue of deviant identity more specifically. First we consider the process of acquiring a deviant identity. Then we look at the ways a person sustains a particular identity. Finally, we consider the conditions under which a person is most likely to change a deviant identity.

ACQUIRING A DEVIANT IDENTITY

People acquire deviant identities in what is often a long drawn-out interactive process. For example, a person performs a deviant act for the very first time and then others respond to the act, usually with some form of social punishment. If the deviant act is repeated, the chances are that the social penalties will be repeated and may even increase. These social penalties, in turn, can alienate the alleged deviant; if the deviant act is repeated again, it may now be done with a degree of defiance. In time, then, a vicious circle tends to evolve. This cycle continues until others have come to expect a pattern of systematic deviant behavior from the "deviant"; in effect they have assigned that person to a deviant role. Reciprocally, the person who is now expected to perform a deviant role comes to see himself or herself in the same terms and may begin to devise ways of continuing the deviant line of action without getting caught. Thus, we see how the interactive process works: the alleged deviant *act* produces the negative *social response* which in time elicits the deviant *social role*, which in turn after a while culminates in the person's adopting a deviant *identity*. The initial deviance, as proposed by Edwin Lemert, is referred to as *primary deviance*, and the deviant role and identity that develop as a result of people's reactions to the initial deviance, *secondary deviance*.[2]

Acquiring a deviant identity follows no consistent pattern, since a reduction in either the frequency of the deviant acts or the severity of the responses of others can diminish the chances of adopting a deviant identity. Reductions in either or both may prevent assignment to a deviant role and the reciprocal deviant self-definition. Increases in either or both, on the other hand, can increase the chances of the social acquisition of a deviant identity.

Several social and cultural conditions affect the process by which people assume deviant identities. These include factors that influence the performance of deviant acts, responses of others, and the definitions of various deviant roles. For example, social responses to initial deviant acts can be extremely effective in discouraging a future career in deviance. Social responses have this effect when they call attention to the marked discrepancy between the deviant act and the kind of person most likely to perform the role, on the one hand, and the identity of the person on the other hand. Thus, middle-class housewives caught in the act of shoplifting see themselves as being treated as if they were thieves. Being caught awakens them for the first time to the way their families and friends would regard their actions if they knew of them. This awakening usually is sufficient to discourage them from future thievery because they do not see themselves as "thieves."

Usually, when a person embarks on a deviant activity such as shoplifting for the very first time, he or she does not think too much about getting caught. At the same time, the person may justify the act in one way or another. Some justifications before the fact hamper a self-definition as deviant. People who embezzle money, for example, may not define their actions as stealing. Instead, they often tell themselves that they are only borrowing the money and will repay it at the earliest opportunity. Seeing themselves as borrowers, not thieves, embezzlers can justify taking the money.

On the other hand, occasionally a person acquires a deviant identity *before* taking on a deviant role. For example, male adolescents who are aware of a sexual interest in men and who grow up in an environment which defines homosexuality negatively may come to regard themselves as "sick." In their case, though they have a personal and secret deviant identity, they may refrain from engaging in any form of homosexual behavior. Hence, they cannot be said to have assumed a homosexual role, though they do have a personal identity as homosexual. We might speculate that the greater the stigma, the more likely it is that a deviant identity can exist without either deviant acts or a deviant role to support it.

People may also engage in a deviant act and expect a severely negative social reaction, only to find that this reaction does not occur. Without a negative social reaction, there is much less chance of being officially labeled as deviant. As a result, although the act has occurred, there is no significant social response to thrust the person into the role of deviant and thereby evoke the reciprocal deviant identity that goes with such a role-assignment.

Thus, the responses of others are crucial when it comes to acquiring a deviant identity. Frequently these others are family or friends. Or they can be agents of social control, such as police officers, teachers, social workers, doctors, or priests. Sometimes, they can be fellow deviants. For instance, a person might experiment with heroin. In an initial act of experimenting with drugs in the company of others, the novice may see himself or herself as merely satisfying a curiosity about the effects of the drug. But later on, drug-using friends may tell the novice that the way to cure withdrawal distress is to take more heroin. The novice may now be on his way or her way to becoming a drug addict, along with its correlative deviant identity, acts, and roles. In this last instance, the responses of deviant others redefine the novice's situation for him/her.

MANAGING DEVIANT IDENTITY

In order to sustain a deviant social identity and membership in a deviant group, new members have to incorporate the group's signs and symbols into their own personal styles and to behave according to deviant norms even when they may not especially want to. The novice's deviant identity may then be confirmed by the group. A deviant who fails to learn the appropriate ways probably will not be truly accepted as a member of the group.

Attempts at being a deviant can fail if the audience refuses to confirm the person's deviant social identity. Then there is no effective audience to reward the person's deviant actions or to confirm his/her self-typing. A jack-of-all-trades offender, for instance, may be considered too inept or "unprofessional" to be accepted into more skillful criminal circles. An audience—conformist or deviant—will not confirm the social identity desired by a person who has obviously miscast him/herself, who does not look the part.

Some deviant statuses imply more than one audience, and the various audiences may demand different, sometimes contradictory, roles on the part of the deviant. Deviants with multiple audiences will have problems of identity unless they can clearly understand which audience they are confronting and which role is required at a particular time. It is often the case, for example, that "front ward" patients in mental hospitals are expected by fellow inmates to act "normal," while they are expected by outsiders to act "sick" and in need of treatment.

It should be noted that deviants can often choose among deviant identities, and this is often one facet of managing a deviant identity. This means that there can be "imposters" who sustain deviant identities as well as "imposters" who sustain conventional identities. Some epileptics, for example, try to pass as alcoholics because they see alcoholism as less stigmatized than epilepsy. As long as these pseudoalcoholics have only limited contact with genuine alcoholics, their secret is probably safe.

To sustain a deviant identity and membership in a deviant group, then, it is necessary to act like other members of the group. Some social conditions are more conducive to this than others. For example, becoming more involved with other deviants and avoiding contact with nondeviants facilitates developing the deviant identity and maintaining the deviant role. It also makes it easier to cast off conventional traits and loyalties. Thus a deviant identity is easier to sustain under these optimum conditions.

Persons who wish to conceal their deviant identity also confront both role and self-problems. As Erving Goffman has pointed out, they can seek to control information about their identity or, if already known about, try to control the tension possible in their face-to-face contacts with others.[3] Stutterers, for instance, may solve these role problems by hiding the fact that they stutter, revealing it on their own terms, or refusing to acknowledge the fact that they are stuttering. And, similarly, when control agents seek to assign a deviant identity, the person at risk of being so designated may try to neutralize the deviant identity. As Gresham Sykes and David Matza have pointed out with regard to delinquency, juveniles may deny responsibility for the behavior, any injury or harm to anyone, or the existence of any victim who really matters. In addition, the delinquent may cite an appeal to higher loyalties (e.g., that his behavior showed loyalty to his friends), or he may condemn the person's condemning him (e.g., as being hypocrites).[4]

THE TRANSFORMATION OF DEVIANT IDENTITY

As suggested above, some deviants have trouble managing a deviant identity. Fitting social positions, roles, and self-concepts together is too hard or undesirable. Thus the deviant may face an identity crisis that can become the turning point in his or her deviant career. Nonetheless, it is not necessarily true that most deviants are unhappy and wish to renounce their deviance. Conventional stereotypes of deviants suggest as much, but the facts are otherwise. If people can successfully conceal their deviance, for example, they can continue to enjoy their deviance without "paying the price."

A profound identity crisis usually becomes one of the conditions for transforming a deviant identity back to a more conventional one. Discovery, or recurrent feelings of remorse, can produce the crisis, impelling the person to contemplate making some radical changes in his/her life. In such a crisis the mechanisms that successfully sustain a deviant identity usually show signs of breaking down, which in turn intensifies the crisis.

As already noted, assuming and maintaining a deviant identity is not an easy matter. Renouncing one is even more difficult. Even if a deviant experiences an extreme identity crisis, that person may not succeed in transforming his/her deviant identity to a more conventional one. Three factors imperil successful transformation: lack of practice in conventional roles, continued distrust by conventional people, and pressure from fellow deviates to return to their group. Time spent in deviance is time spent away from the conventional world. Legitimate skills may fall into disuse; for example, the alcoholic toolmaker who returns to his craft after years of heavy drinking and unemployment may find that he cannot pick up where he left off. The exconvict's difficulty in finding work may exemplify the continued suspicion and disapproval that deviants arouse in the larger society. Finally, fellow deviants may press one to continue former deviations; thus the drug addict, on release from a hospital, may be quickly surrounded by former friends who are eager to supply a free fix.

Deviants who want to return to a more conventional way of life ordinarily have the best chance of success if they join a primary group with similar intentions. The best-known example of such a primary group is Alcoholics Anonymous. The group members reward the ex-drinker for making changes toward conventionality, and they confirm his/her new social identity as a nondrinker. These conditions encourage the deviant to return to conventional life. Such social and cultural supports are not available, however, to many deviants who might want to return to conformity.

NOTES

1. Edwin M. Lemert, *Human Deviance, Social Problems, and Social Control,* second edition, Englewood Cliffs, N.J.: Prentice-Hall, 1972, pp. 162–182.
2. Edwin M. Lemert, *Social Pathology,* New York: McGraw-Hill, 1951, p. 76.
3. Erving Goffman, *Stigma,* Englewood Cliffs, N.J.: Prentice-Hall, 1963.
4. Gresham M. Sykes and David Matza, "Techniques of Neutralization: A Theory of Delinquency," *American Sociological Review,* 22 (December, 1957), pp. 667–670.

CHAPTER 13

ACQUIRING A DEVIANT IDENTITY

One important factor in the development of a deviant identity is how other people respond to an alleged deviant act. These other people may be deviants, or they may be conventional friends or family. They may also be official social control agents. In all cases their responses to the would-be deviant have considerable influence on whether the person goes on to a bona fide deviant role and adopts the deviant identity that goes with it.

In the first reading Martin Weinberg, Colin Williams, and Douglas Pryor describe the process people move through in taking on a bisexual identity. Next Clinton Sanders describes the stages involved in getting a tattoo and how it affects a person's identity. Finally, Mary Owen Cameron describes how amateur shoplifters, when they are caught, generally quit shoplifting because neither they nor the people close to them think of them as being "the thieving type."

Becoming Bisexual

MARTIN S. WEINBERG, COLIN J. WILLIAMS, and DOUGLAS W. PRYOR

Becoming bisexual involves the rejection of not one but two recognized categories of sexual identity: heterosexual and homosexual. Most people settle into the status of heterosexual without any struggle over the identity. There is not much concern with explaining how this occurs; that people are heterosexual is simply taken for granted. For those who find heterosexuality unfulfilling, however, developing a sexual identity is more difficult.

How is it then that some people come to identify themselves as "bisexual"? As a point of departure we take the process through which people come to identify themselves as "homosexual." A number of models have been formulated that chart the development of a homosexual identity through a series of stages.[1] While each model involves a different number of stages, the models all share three elements. The process begins with the person in a state of identity confusion—feeling different from others, struggling with the acknowledgment of same-sex attractions. Then there is a period of thinking about possibly being homosexual—involving associating with self-identified homosexuals, sexual experimentation, forays into the homosexual subculture. Last is the attempt to integrate one's self-concept and social identity as homosexual—acceptance of the label, disclosure about being homosexual, acculturation to a homosexual way of life, and the development of love relationships. Not every person follows through each stage. Some remain locked in at a certain point. Others move back and forth between stages.

From: *Dual Attraction: Understanding Bisexuality* by Martin S. Weinberg, Colin J. Williams, and Douglas W. Pryor. Copyright © 1994 by Oxford University Press, Inc. Reprinted by permission.

To our knowledge, no previous model of *bisexual* identity formation exists.... [W]e present such a model based on the following questions: To what extent is there overlap with the process involved in becoming homosexual? How far is the label "bisexual" clearly recognized, understood, and available to people as an identity? Does the absence of a bisexual subculture in most locales affect the information and support needed for sustaining a commitment to the identity? For our subjects, then, what are the problems in finding the "bisexual" label, understanding what the label means, dealing with social disapproval from two directions, and continuing to use the label once it is adopted? From our fieldwork and interviews, we found that four stages captured our respondents' most common experiences when dealing with questions of identity: initial confusion, finding and applying the label, settling into the identity, and continued uncertainty.

THE STAGES

INITIAL CONFUSION

Many of the people interviewed said that they had experienced a period of considerable confusion, doubt, and struggle regarding their sexual identity before defining themselves as bisexual. This was ordinarily the first step in the process of becoming bisexual.

They described a number of major sources of early confusion about their sexual identity. For some, it was the experience of having strong sexual feelings for both sexes that was unsettling, disorienting, and sometimes frightening. Often these were sexual feelings that they said they did not know how to easily handle or resolve.

In the past, I couldn't reconcile different desires I had. I didn't understand them. I didn't know what I was. And I ended up feeling really mixed up, unsure, and kind of frightened. (F)

I thought I was gay, and yet I was having these intense fantasies and feelings about fucking women. I went through a long period of confusion. (M)

Others were confused because they thought strong sexual feelings for, or sexual behavior with, the same sex meant an end to their long-standing heterosexuality.

I was afraid of my sexual feelings for men and ... that if I acted on them, that would negate my sexual feelings for women. I knew absolutely no one else who had ... sexual feelings for both men and women, and didn't realize that was an option. (M)

When I first had sexual feelings for females, I had the sense I should give up my feelings for men. I think it would have been easier to give up men. (F)

A third source of confusion in this initial stage stemmed from attempts by respondents trying to categorize their feelings for, and/or behaviors with, both sexes, yet not being able to do so. Unaware of the term "bisexual," some tried to organize their sexuality by using the readily available labels of "heterosexual" or "homosexual"—but these did not seem to fit. No sense of sexual identity jelled; an aspect of themselves remained unclassifiable.

When I was young, I didn't know what I was. I knew there were people like Mom and Dad—heterosexual and married—and that there were "queens." I knew I wasn't like either one. (M)

I thought I had to be either gay or straight. That was the big lie. It was confusing. ... That all began to change in the late 60s. It was a long and slow process. ... (F)

Finally, others suggested they experienced a great deal of confusion because of their "homophobia"—their difficulty in facing up to the same-sex component of their sexuality. The con-

sequence was often long-term denial. This was more common among the men than the women, but not exclusively so.

At age seventeen, I became close to a woman who was gay. She had sexual feelings for me. I had some ... for her but I didn't respond. Between the ages of seventeen and twenty-six I met another gay woman. She also had sexual feelings towards me. I had the same for her but I didn't act on ... or acknowledge them. ... I was scared. ... I was also attracted to men at the same time. ... I denied that I was sexually attracted to women. I was afraid that if they knew the feelings were mutual they would act on them ... and put pressure on me. (F)

I thought I might be able to get rid of my homosexual tendencies through religious means—prayer, belief, counseling—before I came to accept it as part of me. (M)

The intensity of the confusion and the extent to which it existed in the lives of the people we met at the Bisexual Center, whatever its particular source, was summed up by two men who spoke with us informally. As paraphrased in our field notes:

The identity issue for him was a very confusing one. At one point, he almost had a nervous breakdown, and when he finally entered college, he sought psychiatric help.

Bill said he thinks this sort of thing happens a lot at the Bi Center. People come in "very confused" and experience some really painful stress.

FINDING AND APPLYING THE LABEL

Following this initial period of confusion, which often spanned years, was the experience of finding and applying the label. We asked the people we interviewed for specific factors or events in their lives that led them to define themselves as bisexual. There were a number of common experiences.

For many who were unfamiliar with the term bisexual, the discovery that the category in fact existed was a turning point. This happened by simply hearing the word, reading about it somewhere, or learning of a place called the Bisexual Center. The discovery provided a means of making sense of long-standing feelings for both sexes.

Early on I thought I was just gay, because I was not aware there was another category, bisexual. I always knew I was interested in men and women. But I did not realize there was a name for these feelings and behaviors until I took Psychology 101 and read about it, heard about it there. That was in college. (F)

The first time I heard the word, which was not until I was twenty-six, I realized that was what fit for me. What it fit was that I had sexual feelings for both men and women. Up until that point, the only way that I could define my sexual feelings was that I was either a latent homosexual or a confused heterosexual. (M)

Going to a party at someone's house, and finding out there that the party was to benefit the Bisexual Center. I guess at that point I began to define myself as bisexual. I never knew there was such a word. If I had heard the word earlier on, for example as a kid, I might have been bisexual then. My feelings had always been bisexual. I just did not know how to define them. (F)

Reading The Bisexual Option...*I realized then that bisexuality really existed and that's what I was. (M)*

In the case of others the turning point was their first homosexual or heterosexual experience coupled with the recognition that sex was pleasurable with both sexes. These were people who already seemed to have knowledge of the label "bisexual," yet without experiences with both men and women, could not label themselves accordingly.

The first time I had actual intercourse, an orgasm with a woman, it led me to realize I was bisexual, because I enjoyed it as much as I did with a man, although the former occurred much later on in my sexual experiences.... I didn't have an orgasm with a woman until twenty-two, while with males,

that had been going on since the age of thirteen. (M)

Having homosexual fantasies and acting those out.... I would not identify as bi if I only had fantasies and they were mild. But since my fantasies were intensely erotic, and I acted them out, these two things led me to believe I was really bisexual.... (M)

After my first involved sexual affair with a woman, I also had feelings for a man, and I knew I did not fit the category dyke. I was also dating gay-identified males. So I began looking at gay/lesbian and heterosexual labels as not fitting my situation. (F)

Still others reported not so much a specific experience as a turning point, but emphasized the recognition that their sexual feelings for both sexes were simply too strong to deny. They eventually came to the conclusion that it was unnecessary to choose between them.

I found myself with men but couldn't completely ignore my feelings for women. When involved with a man I always had a close female relationship. When one or the other didn't exist at any given time, I felt I was really lacking something. I seem to like both. (F)

The last factor that was instrumental in leading people to initially adopt the label bisexual was the encouragement and support of others. Encouragement sometimes came from a partner who already defined himself or herself as bisexual.

Encouragement from a man I was in a relationship with. We had been together two or three years at the time—he began to define as bisexual.... [He] encouraged me to do so as well. He engineered a couple of threesomes with another woman. Seeing one other person who had bisexuality as an identity that fit them seemed to be a real encouragement. (F)

Encouragement from a partner seemed to matter more for women. Occasionally the "encouragement" bordered on coercion as the men in their lives wanted to engage in a *ménage à trois* or group sex.

I had a male lover for a year and a half who was familiar with bisexuality and pushed me towards it. My relationship with him brought it up in me. He wanted me to be bisexual because he wanted to be in a threesome. He was also insanely jealous of my attractions to men, and did everything in his power to suppress my opposite-sex attractions. He showed me a lot of pictures of naked women and played on my reactions. He could tell that I was aroused by pictures of women and would talk about my attractions while we were having sex.... He was twenty years older than me. He was very manipulative in a way. My feelings for females were there and [he was] almost forcing me to act on my attractions.... (F)

Encouragement also came from sex-positive organizations, primarily the Bisexual Center, but also places like San Francisco Sex Information (SFSI),[2] the Pacific Center, and the Institute for Advanced Study of Human Sexuality....

At the gay pride parade I had seen the brochures for the Bisexual Center. Two years later I went to a Tuesday night meeting. I immediately felt that I belonged and that if I had to define myself that this was what I would use. (M)

Through SFSI and the Bi Center, I found a community of people...[who] were more comfortable for me than were the exclusive gay or heterosexual communities.... [It was] beneficial for myself to be...in a sex-positive community. I got more strokes and came to understand myself better.... I felt it was necessary to express my feelings for males and females without having to censor them, which is what the gay and straight communities pressured me to do. (F)

Thus our respondents became familiar with and came to the point of adopting the label bisexual in a variety of ways: through reading about it on their own, being in therapy, talking to friends, having experiences with sex partners, learning about the Bi Center, visiting SFSI or the Pacific Center, and coming to accept their sexual feelings.

SETTLING INTO THE IDENTITY

Usually it took years from the time of first sexual attractions to, or behaviors with, both sexes before people came to think of themselves as bisexual. The next stage then was one of settling into the identity, which was characterized by a more complete transition in self-labeling.

Most reported that this settling-in stage was the consequence of becoming more self-accepting. They became less concerned with the negative attitudes of others about their sexual preference.

I realized that the problem of bisexuality isn't mine. It's society's. They are having problems dealing with my bisexuality. So I was then thinking if they had a problem dealing with it, so should I. But I don't. (F)

I learned to accept the fact that there are a lot of people out there who aren't accepting. They can be intolerant, selfish, shortsighted and so on. Finally, in growing up, I learned to say "So what, I don't care what others think." (M)

I just decided I was bi. I trusted my own sense of self. I stopped listening to others tell me what I could or couldn't be. (F)

The increase in self-acceptance was often attributed to the continuing support from friends, counselors, and the Bi Center, through reading, and just being in San Francisco.

Fred Klein's The Bisexual Option *book and meeting more and more bisexual people...helped me feel more normal.... There were other human beings who felt like I did on a consistent basis. (M)*

I think going to the Bi Center really helped a lot. I think going to the gay baths and realizing there were a lot of men who sought the same outlet I did really helped. Talking about it with friends has been helpful and being validated by female lovers that approve of my bisexuality. Also the reaction of people who I've told, many of whom weren't even surprised. (M)

The most important thing was counseling. Having the support of a bisexual counselor. Someone who acted as somewhat of a mentor. [He] validated my frustration..., helped me do problem solving, and guide[d] me to other supportive experiences like SFSI. Just engaging myself in a supportive social community. (M)

The majority of the people we came to know through the interviews seemed settled in their sexual identity. We tapped this through a variety of questions.... Ninety percent said that they did not think they were currently in transition from being homosexual to being heterosexual or from being heterosexual to being homosexual. However, when we probed further by asking this group "Is it possible, though, that someday you could define yourself as either lesbian/gay or heterosexual?" about 40 percent answered yes. About two-thirds of these indicated that the change could be in either direction, though almost 70 percent said that such a change was not probable.

We asked those who thought a change was possible what it might take to bring it about. The most common response referred to becoming involved in a meaningful relationship that was monogamous or very intense. Often the sex of the hypothetical partner was not specified, underscoring that the overall quality of the relationship was what really mattered.

Love. I think if I feel insanely in love with some person, it could possibly happen. (M)

If I should meet a woman and want to get married, and if she was not open to my relating to men, I might become heterosexual again. (M)

Getting involved in a long-term relationship like marriage where I wouldn't need a sexual involvement with anyone else. The sex of the ... partner wouldn't matter. It would have to be someone who I could commit my whole life to exclusively, a lifelong relationship. (F)

A few mentioned the breaking up of a relationship and how this would incline them to look toward the other sex.

Steve is one of the few men I feel completely comfortable with. If anything happened to him, I don't know if I'd want to try and build up a similar relationship with another man. I'd be more inclined to look towards women for support. (F)

Changes in sexual behavior seemed more likely for the people we interviewed ... than changes in how they defined themselves. We asked "Is it possible that someday you could behave either exclusively homosexual or exclusively heterosexual?" Over 80 percent answered yes. This is over twice as many as those who saw a possible change in how they defined themselves, again showing that a wide range of behaviors can be subsumed under the same label. Of this particular group, the majority (almost 60 percent) felt that there was nothing inevitable about how they might change, indicating that it could be in either a homosexual or a heterosexual direction. Around a quarter, though, said the change would be to exclusive heterosexual behavior and 15 percent to exclusive homosexual behavior. (Twice as many women noted the homosexual direction, while many more men than women said the heterosexual direction.) Just over 40 percent responded that a change to exclusive heterosexuality or homosexuality was not very probable, about a third somewhat probable, and about a quarter very probable.

Again, we asked what it would take to bring about such a change in behavior. Once more the answers centered on achieving a long-term monogamous and involved relationship, often with no reference to a specific sex.

For me to behave exclusively heterosexual or homosexual would require that I find a lifetime commitment from another person with a damn good argument of why I should not go to bed with somebody else. (F)

I am a romantic. If I fell in love with a man, and our relationship was developing that way, I might become strictly homosexual. The same possibility exists with a woman. (M)

Thus "settling into the identity" must be seen in relative terms. Some of the people we interviewed did seem to accept the identity completely. When we compared our subjects' experiences with those characteristic of homosexuals, however, we were struck by the absence of closure that characterized our bisexual respondents—even those who appeared most committed to the identity. This led us to posit a final stage in the formation of sexual identity, one that seems unique to bisexuals.

CONTINUED UNCERTAINTY

The belief that bisexuals are confused about their sexual identity is quite common. This conception has been promoted especially by those lesbians and gays who see bisexuality as being in and of itself a pathological state. From their point of view, "confusion" is literally a built-in feature of "being" bisexual. As expressed in one study:

> While appearing to encompass a wider choice of love objects...[the bisexual] actually becomes a product of abject confusion; his self-image is that of an overgrown young adolescent whose ability to differentiate one form of sexuality from another has never developed. He lacks above all a sense of identity...[He] cannot answer the question: What am I?[3]

One evening a facilitator at a Bisexual Center rap group put this belief in a slightly different and more contemporary form:

> One of the myths about bisexuality is that you can't be bisexual without somehow being "schizoid." The lesbian and gay communities do not see being bisexual as a crystallized or complete sexual identity. The homosexual community believes there is no such thing as bisexuality. They think that bisexuals are people who are in transition [to becoming homosexual] or that they are people afraid of being stigmatized [as homosexual] by the heterosexual majority.

We addressed the issue directly in the interviews with two questions: "Do you *presently* feel confused about your bisexuality?" and "Have you *ever* felt confused...?"...For the men, a quarter and 84 percent answered "yes," respectively. For the women, it was about a quarter and 56 percent.

When asked to provide details about this uncertainty, the primary response was that *even after having discovered and applied the label "bisexual" to themselves, and having come to the point of apparent self-acceptance, they still experienced continued intermittent periods of doubt and uncertainty regarding their sexual identity.* One reason was the lack of social validation and support that came with being a self-identified bisexual.

The social reaction people received made it difficult to sustain the identity over the long haul.

While the heterosexual world was said to be completely intolerant of any degree of homosexuality, the reaction of the homosexual world mattered more. Many bisexuals referred to the persistent pressures they experienced to relabel themselves as "gay" or "lesbian" and to engage in sexual activity exclusively with the same sex. It was asserted that no one was *really* bisexual, and that calling oneself "bisexual" was a politically incorrect and inauthentic identity. Given that our respondents were living in San Francisco (which has such a large homosexual population) and that they frequently moved in and out of the homosexual world (to whom they often looked for support) this could be particularly distressing.

> Sometimes the repeated denial the gay community directs at us. Their negation of the concept and the term bisexual has sometimes made me wonder whether I was just imagining the whole thing. (M)

> My involvement with the gay community. There was extreme political pressure. The lesbians said bisexuals didn't exist. To them, I had to make up my mind and identify as lesbian.... I was really questioning my identity, that is, about defining myself as bisexual.... (F)

For the women, the invalidation carried over to their feminist identity (which most had). They sometimes felt that being with men meant they were selling out the world of women.

> I was involved with a woman for several years. She was straight when I met her but became a lesbian. She tried to "win me back" to lesbianism. She tried to tell me that if I really loved her, I would leave Bill. I did love her, but I could not deny how I felt about him either. So she left me and that hurt. I wondered if I was selling out my woman identity and if it [being bisexual] was worth it. (F)

A few wondered whether they were lying to themselves about their heterosexual side. One woman questioned whether her heterosexual desires were a result of 'acculturation" rather than being her own choice. Another woman suggested a similar social dimension to her homosexual component:

> There was one period when I was trying to be gay because of the political thing of being totally woman-identified rather than being with men. The Women's Culture Center in college had a women's studies minor, so I was totally immersed in women's culture.... (F)

Lack of support also came from the absence of bisexual role models, no real bisexual community aside from the Bisexual Center, and nothing in the way of public recognition of bisexuality, which bred uncertainty and confusion.

> I went through a period of dissociation, of being very alone and isolated. That was due to my bisexuality. People would ask, well, what was I? I wasn't gay and I wasn't straight. So I didn't fit. (F)

> I don't feel like I belong in a lot of situations because society is so polarized as heterosexual or homosexual. There are not enough bi organizations or public places to go to like bars, restaurants, clubs.... (F)

For some, continuing uncertainty about their sexual identity was related to their inability to translate their sexual feelings into sexual behaviors. (Some of the women had *never* engaged in homosexual sex.)

> Should I try to have a sexual relationship with a woman?...Should I just back off and keep my distance, just try to maintain a friendship? I question whether I am really bisexual because I don't know if I will ever act on my physical attractions for females. (F)

> I know I have strong sexual feelings towards men, but then I don't know how to get close to or be sexual with a man. I guess that what happens is I start wondering how genuine my feelings are.... (M)

For the men, confusion stemmed more from the practical concerns of implementing and managing multiple partners or from questions about how to find an involved homosexual relationship

and what that might mean on a social and personal level.

> I felt very confused about how I was going to manage my life in terms of developing relationships with both men and women. I still see it as a difficult lifestyle to create for myself because it involves a lot of hard work and understanding on my part and that of the men and women I'm involved with. (M)

> I've thought about trying to have an actual relationship with a man. Some of my confusion revolves around how to find a satisfactory sexual relationship. I do not particularly like gay bars. I have stopped having anonymous sex.... (M)

Many men and women felt doubts about their bisexual identity because of being in an exclusive sexual relationship. After being exclusively involved with an opposite-sex partner for a period of time, some of the respondents questioned the homosexual side of their sexuality. Conversely, after being exclusively involved with a partner of the same sex, other respondents called into question the heterosexual component of their sexuality.

> When I'm with a man or a woman sexually for a period of time, then I begin to wonder how attracted I really am to the other sex. (M)

> In the last relationship I had with a woman, my heterosexual feelings were very diminished. Being involved in a lesbian lifestyle put stress on my self-identification as a bisexual. It seems confusing to me because I am monogamous for the most part, monogamy determines my lifestyle to the extremes of being heterosexual or homosexual. (F)

Others made reference to a lack of sexual activity with weaker sexual feelings and affections for one sex. Such learning did not fit with the perception that bisexuals should have "balanced" desires and behaviors. The consequence was doubt about "really" being bisexual.

> On the level of sexual arousal and deep romantic feelings, I feel them much more strongly for women than for men. I've gone so far as questioning myself when this is involved. (M)

I definitely am attracted to and it is much easier to deal with males. Also, guilt for my attraction to females has led me to wonder if I am just really toying with the idea. Is the sexual attraction I have for females something I constructed to pass time or what? (F)

Just as "settling into the identity" is a relative phenomenon, so too is "continued uncertainty," which can involve a lack of closure as part and parcel of what it means to be bisexual.

We do not wish to claim too much for our model of bisexual identity formation. There are limits to its general application. The people we interviewed were unique in that not only did *all* the respondents define themselves as bisexual (a consequence of our selection criteria), but they were also all members of a bisexual social organization in a city that perhaps more than any other in the United States could be said to provide a bisexual subculture of some sort. Bisexuals in places other than San Francisco surely must move through the early phases of the identity process with a great deal more difficulty. Many probably never reach the later stages.

Finally, the phases of the model we present are very broad and somewhat simplified. While the particular problems we detail within different phases may be restricted to the type of bisexuals in this study, the broader phases can form the basis for the development of more sophisticated models of bisexual identity formation.

Still, not all bisexuals will follow these patterns. Indeed, given the relative weakness of the bisexual subculture compared with the social pressures toward conformity exhibited in the gay subculture, there may be more varied ways of acquiring a bisexual identity. Also, the involvement of bisexuals in the heterosexual world means that various changes in heterosexual lifestyles (e.g., a decrease in open marriages or swinging) will be a continuing, and as yet unexplored, influence on bisexual identity. Finally, wider societal changes, notably the existence of AIDS, may make for changes in the overall identity process. Being used to choice and being open to both sexes can give bisexuals a range of adaptations in their sexual life that are not available to others.

NOTES

1. Vivien C. Cass, "Homosexual Identity Formation: Testing a Theoretical Model." *Journal of Sex Research* 20 (1984), pp. 143–167; Eli Coleman, "Developmental Stages of the Coming Out Process." *Journal of Homosexuality* 7 (1981/2), pp. 31–43; Barbara Ponse, *Identities in the Lesbian World: The Social Construction of Self* (Westport, CT: Greenwood Press, 1978).
2. Martin S. Weinberg, Colin J. Williams, and Douglas Pryor, "Telling the Facts of Life: A Study of a Sex Information Switchboard." *Journal of Contemporary Ethnography* 17 (1988), pp. 131–163.
3. Donald Webster Cory and John P. Leroy, *The Homosexual and His Society* (New York: The Citadel Press, 1963), p. 61.

Getting a Tattoo

CLINTON R. SANDERS

Becoming tattooed is a highly social act. The decision to acquire a tattoo . . . is motivated by how the recipient defines him or herself. The tattoo becomes an item in the tattooee's personal iden-

From Clinton R. Sanders, *Customizing the Body: The Art and Culture of Tattooing,* Philadelphia: Temple University Press, 1989, pp. 41–61. © 1989 by Temple University. Reprinted by permission of Temple University Press.

tity-kit (Goffman, 1961:14–21) and, in turn, it is used by those with whom the individual interacts to place him or her into a particular, interaction-shaping social category (cf. Solomon, 1983; Csikszentmihalyi and Rochberg-Halton, 1981).

When asked to describe how they decided to get a tattoo, the vast majority of respondents made reference to another person or group. Family members, friends, business associates, and other people with whom they regularly interacted were described as being tattooed. Statements such as, "Everyone I knew was really into tattoos," "It was a peer decision," "Everyone had one so I wanted one," and "My father got one when he was in the war and I always wanted one, too," were typical. Entrance into the actual tattooing "event," however, has all of the characteristics of an impulse purchase. It typically is based on very little information or previous experience (58 percent of the questionnaire respondents reported never having been in a studio prior to the time they received their first tattoo). While tattooees commonly reported having "thought about getting (a tattoo) for a long time," they usually drifted into the actual experience when they "didn't have anything better to do," had sufficient money to devote to a nonessential purchase and were, most importantly, in the general vicinity of a tattoo establishment. The following accounts were fairly typical.

We were up in Maine and a bunch of us were just talking about getting tattoos—me and my friends and my cousins. One time my cousin came back from the service with one and I liked it.... The only place I knew about was S——'s down in Providence. We were going right by there on our way back home so we stopped and all got them.

My friends were goin' down there to get some work, you know. That was the only place I knew about anyway. My friends said there was a tattoo parlor down by the beach. Let's go! I checked it out and seen something I liked. I had some money on me so I said, "I'll get this little thing and check it out and see how it sticks," I thought if I got a tatty it might fade, you know. You never know what's goin' to happen. I don't want anything on my body that is goin' to look fucked up.

The act of getting the tattoo itself is usually, as seen in these quotes, a social event experienced with close associates. Sixty-nine percent of the interviewees (11 of 16) and 64 percent of the questionnaire sample reported having received their first tattoo in the company of family members or friends. These close associates act as "purchase

pals" (Bell, 1967). They provide social support for the decision, help to pass anxiety-filled waiting time, offer opinions regarding the design and body location, and commiserate with or humorously ridicule the recipient during the tattoo experience (see Becker and Clark, 1979).

The tattoo event frequently involves a ritual commemoration of a significant transition in the life of the recipient (cf. Van Gennep, 1960; Ebin, 1979:39–56; Brain, 1979:174–184). The tattooee conceives of the mark as symbolizing change—especially, achieving maturity and symbolically separating the self from individuals or groups (parents, husbands, wives, employers, and so on) who have been exercising control over the individual's personal choices. A tattoo artist related his understanding of his clients' motivations in this way:

I do see that many people get tattooed to find out again...to say, "Who was I before I got into this lost position?" It's almost like a tattoo pulls you back to a certain kind of reality about who you are as an individual. Either that or it transfers you to the next step in you life, the next plateau. A woman will come in and say, "Well, I just went through a really ugly divorce. My husband had control of my fucking body and now I have it again. I want a tattoo. I want a tattoo that says that I have the courage to get this, that I have the courage to take on the rest of my life. I'm going to do what I want to do and do what I have to do to survive as a person." That's a motivation that comes through the door a lot.

One interviewee expressed her initial reason for acquiring her first tattoo in almost exactly these terms:

[My friend and I] both talked semi-seriously about getting (a tattoo). I mentioned it to my husband and he was adamantly opposed—only certain seedy types get tattoos. He didn't want someone else touching my body intimately, which is what a tattoo would involve...even if it was just my arm. He was against it, which made me even more for it...I finally really decided sometime last year when my marriage was coming apart. It started to be a symbol of taking my body back. I was thinking

that about the time I got divorced would be a good time to do it.

LOCATING A TATTOOIST

Like the initial decision to get a tattoo, the tattooist one decides to patronize commonly is chosen through information provided by members of the individual's personal network. Fifty-eight percent of the questionnaire respondents located the shop in which they received their first tattoo through a recommendation provided by a friend or family member. Since, in most areas, establishments that dispense tattoos are not especially numerous, many first-time tattooees choose a studio on a very practical basis—it is the only one they know about or it is the studio that is closest to where they live (20 percent of the questionnaire sample chose the shop on the basis of location, 28 percent because it was the only one they knew about).[1]

Most first-time tattooees enter the tattoo setting with little information about the process or even about the relative skill of the artist. Rarely do recipients spend as much time and effort acquiring information about a process which is going to indelibly mark their bodies as they would were they preparing to purchase a TV set or other far less significant consumer item.

Consequently, tattooees usually enter the tattoo setting ill-informed and experiencing a considerable degree of anxiety. Their fears center around the anticipated pain of the process and the permanence of the tattoo. Here, for example, is an interaction (quoted from fieldnotes) that took place while a young man received his first tattoo.

RECIPIENT: Is this going to fade out much? There's this guy at work that has these tattoos all up and down his arms and he goes back to the guy that did them every couple of months and gets them recolored because they fade out. (General laughter)

SANDERS: Does this guy work in a shop or out of his house?

R: He just does it on the side.

TATTOOIST: He doesn't know what the fuck he's doing.

R: This friend of mine told me that getting a tattoo really hurts. He said there would be guys in here hollering and bleeding all over the place.

S: Does he have any tattoos?

R: No, but he says he wants to get some.... Hey, this really doesn't hurt that much. It doesn't go in very deep, does it? It's like picking a splinter out of your skin. I was going to get either a unicorn or a pegasus. I had my sister draw one up because I thought they just drew the picture on you or something. I didn't know they did it this way (with an acetate stencil). I guess this makes a lot more sense.

S: You ever been in a tattoo shop before this?

R: No, this is my first time. Another guy was going to come in with me, but he chickened out.

... [T]attooists, for the most part, are quite patient about answering the questions clients ask with numbing regularity (pain, price, and permanence). This helps to put the recipient more at ease, smooths the service delivery interaction, and increases the chances that a satisfied customer—who will recommend the shop to his or her friends and perhaps return again for additional work—will leave the establishment (see Govenar, 1977; Becker and Clark, 1979; St. Clair and Govenar, 1981).

CHOOSING A DESIGN AND BODY LOCATION

Tattooees commonly described the basic reasons for deciding to become tattooed in very general terms. Wearing a tattoo connected the person to significant others who were similarly marked, made one unique by separating him or her from those who were too convention-bound to so alter their bodies, symbolized freedom or self-control, and satisfied an aesthetic desire to decorate the physical self.[2]

The image one chooses, on the other hand, is usually selected for a specific reason. Typically, design choice is related to the person's connection to other people, his or her definition of self or, especially in the case of women, the desire to enhance and beautify the body.

One of the most common responses to my question, "How did you go about deciding on this particular tattoo?" was a reference to a personal associate with whom they had a close emotional relationship. Some chose a particular tattoo because it was like that worn by a close friend or a member of their family. Others chose a design that incorporated the name of their boy friend, girl friend, spouse, or child or a design associated with that person (for example, zodiac signs).

> I had this homemade cross and skull here and I needed a coverup. [The tattooist] couldn't just do anything so I thought to myself, "My daughter was born in May and that's the Bull." I'm leaving the rest of this arm clean because it is just for my daughter. If I ever get married I'll put something here [on the other arm]. I'll get a rose or something for my wife.

> This tattoo is a symbol of friendship. Me and my best friend—I've known him since I could walk—came in together and we both got bluebirds to have a symbol that when we do part we will remember each other by it.

The ongoing popularity of "vow tattoos" such as the traditional heart with "MOM" or flowers with a ribbon on which the loved one's name is written attests to the importance of tattooing as a way of symbolically expressing love and commitment (Hardy, 1982a).

Similarly, tattoos are used to demonstrate connection and commitment to a group. For example, military personnel pick tattoos that relate to their particular service, motorcycle gang members choose club insignia, and members of sports teams enter a shop en masse and all receive the same design.

Tattoos are also employed as symbolic representations of how one conceives of the self, or interests and activities that are key features of self-definition. Tattooees commonly choose their birth sign or have their name or nickname inscribed on their bodies. Others choose more abstract symbols of the self.

> I put a lot of thought into this tattoo. I'm an English lit major and I thought that the medieval castle had a lot of significance. I'm an idealist and I thought that that was well expressed by a castle with clouds. Plus, I'm blond and I wanted something blue.

> [Quote from fieldnotes] Two guys in their twenties come in and look at the flash. After looking around for a while one of the guys come over to me and asks if we have any bees. I tell him to look through the book (of small designs) because I have seen some bees in there. I ask, "Why do you want a bee? I don't think I have ever seen anyone come in here for one." He replies, "I'm allergic to bees. If I get stung by one again I'm going to die. So I thought I'd come in here and have a big, mean-looking bee put on. I want one that has this long stinger and these long teeth and is coming in to land. With that, any bee would think twice about messing with me."

Tattooees commonly represent the self by choosing designs that symbolize important personal involvements, hobbies, occupational activities, and so forth. In most street shops, the winged insignia of Harley-Davidson motorcycles and variants on that theme are the most frequently requested images. During one particularly busy week in the major shop in which I was observing, a rabbit breeder acquired a rabbit tattoo, a young man requested a cartoon frog because the Little League team he coached was named the "frogs," a fireman received a fire fighter's cross insignia surrounded by flame, and an optician chose a flaming eye.

No matter what the associational or self-definitional meaning of the chosen tattoo, the recipient commonly is aware of the decorative/aesthetic function of the design. When I asked tattooees to explain how they went about choosing a particular design, they routinely made reference to aesthetic criteria—they "like the colors" or they "thought it was pretty."

[I didn't get this tattoo] because of being bad or cool or anything like that. It's like a picture. You see a picture you like and you put it in your room or your house or something like that. It's just a piece of work that you like. I like the art work they do here. I like the color (on my tattoo). It really brings out—the orange and the green. I like that—the colors.[3]

A number of factors shape the tattooee's decision about where on the body the tattoo will be located. The vast majority of male tattooees choose to have their work placed on the arm. In his study of the tattoos carried by 2000 members of the Royal Navy, Scutt found that 98 percent had received their tattoo(s) on the arm (Scutt and Gotch, 1974:96). In my own research, 55 percent of the questionnaire respondents received their first tattoo on the arm or hand (71 percent of the males and 19 percent of the females). The sixteen interviewees had, all together, thirty-five tattoos, twenty-seven of which were carried by the ten males. Eighty-one percent (twenty-two) of the mens' tattoos were on their arms (of the remainder two were on hips, one was on the back, one on the face, and one on the recipient's chest). The six women interviewees possessed eight tattoos—three on the back or the shoulder area, three on the breast, one on an arm, and one on the lower back. Thirty-five percent of female questionnaire respondents received their first tattoo on the breast, 13 percent on the back or shoulder, and 10 percent on the hip (see Figure 1).

Clearly, there is a definite convention affecting the decision to place the tattoo on a particular part of the body—men, for the most part, choose the arm while women choose the breast, hip, lower abdomen, back, or shoulder. To some degree the tendency for male tattooees to have the tattoo placed on the arm is determined by technical features of the tattoo process. Tattooing is a two-handed operation. The tattooist must stretch the skin with one hand while inscribing the design with the other. This operation is most easily accomplished when the tattoo is being applied to an

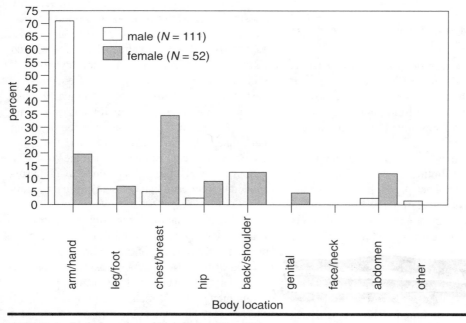

FIGURE 1   Body Location of First Tattoo (*N* = 163)

extremity. Tattooing the torso is more difficult and, commonly, tattooists have an assistant who stretches the client's skin when work is being done on that area of the body. Technical difficulty, in turn, affects price. Most tattooists charge 10 to 25 percent more for tattoos placed on body parts other than the arm or leg. The additional cost factor probably has some effect on the client's choice of body location.

Pain is another factor shaping the tattooee's decision. The tattoo machine contains needle groups that superficially pierce the skin at high speed, leaving small amounts of pigment in the tiny punctures. Obviously, this process will cause more or less pain depending on the sensitivity of the area being tattooed. In general, tattooing arms or legs generates less pain than marking body areas with a higher concentration of nerve endings or parts of the body where the bones are not cushioned with muscle tissue.[4]

The sex-based conventions regarding choice of body site are largely determined by the different symbolic functions of the tattoo for men and women. Women tend to regard the tattoo (commonly a small, delicate design) as a permanent body decoration primarily intended for personal pleasure and the enjoyment of those with whom they are most intimate. The chosen tattoos are, therefore, placed on parts of the body most commonly seen by those with whom women have primary relationships. Since tattoos on women are especially stigmatizing, placement on private parts of the body allows women to retain unsullied identities when in contact with casual associates or strangers (see Goffman, 1963a:53–55, 73–91). Here, for example, is a portion of a brief conversation with a young woman who carried an unconventional design (a snake coiled around a large rose) on what is, for women, an unconventional body location (her right bicep).

SANDERS: How did you decide on that particular design?

WOMAN: I wanted something really different and I'd never seen a tattoo like this on a woman

before. I really like it, but sometimes I look at it and wish I didn't have it.

S: That's interesting. When do you wish you didn't have it?

W: When I'm getting real dressed up in a sleeveless dress and I want to look ... uh, prissy and feminine. People look at a tattoo and think you're real bad ... a loose person. But I'm not.

Another interviewee described the decision-making process she had gone through in choosing to acquire a small rose design on her shoulder, emphasizing aesthetic issues and stigma control.

The only other place that I knew of that women got tattoos was on the breast. I didn't want it on the front of my chest because I figured if I was at work and had an open blouse or a scoop neck, then half would show and half wouldn't. I wanted to be able to control when I wanted it to show and when I didn't. If I go for a job interview I don't want a tattoo on my breast. I didn't want it, like, on my thigh or on the lower part of my stomach. I didn't like how they look there. I just thought it would look pretty on my shoulder. ... The main reason is that I can cover it up if I want to.

Men, on the other hand, typically are less inclined than women to define the tattoo primarily as a decorative and intimate addition to the body. Instead, the male tattoo is an identity symbol—a more public display of interests, associations, separation from the normative constraints of conventional society, and, most generally, masculinity. The designs chosen by men are usually larger than those favored by women and, rather than employing the gentle imagery of nature and mythology (flowers, birds, butterflies, unicorns, and so forth), they frequently symbolize more violent impulses. Snakes, bloody daggers, skulls, dragons, grim reapers, black panthers, and birds of prey are dominant images in the conventional repertoire of tattoo designs chosen by men. Placement of the image on the arm allows both casual public display and, should the male tattooee anticipate a critical judgment from someone whose negative reaction could have untoward consequences (most commonly, an employer), easy concealment with clothing. One male interviewee spoke about the public meaning of tattoos and expressed his understanding of the difference between male and female tattoos as follows:

> *You fit into a style. People recognize you by your hair-style or by your tattoo. People look at you in public and say. "Hey, they got a tattoo. They must be a particular kind of person," or, "He's got his hair cropped short (so) he must be a different kind of person." The person with a tattoo is telling people that he is free enough to do what he wants to do. He says, "I don't care who you think I am. I'm doing what I want to do." (The tattoo) symbolizes freedom. It says something about your personality. If a girl has a skull on her arm—it's not feminine at all—that would symbolize vengeance. If a woman gets a woman's tattoo, that's normal. If she gets a man's tattoo symbolizing vengeance or whatever, I feel that is too far over the boards. A woman should act like a woman and keep her tattoos feminine. Those vengeance designs say, "Look out." People see danger in them.*

IMPACT ON SELF-DEFINITION

As indicated in the foregoing presentation of the initial motives that prompt the decision to acquire a tattoo, tattooees consistently conceive of the tattoo as having impact on their definition of self and demonstrating to others information about their unique interests and social connections. Interviewees commonly expressed liking their tattoos because they made him or her "different" or "special" (see Goffman, 1963a:56–62).

> *Having a tattoo changes how you see yourself. It is a way of choosing to change your body. I enjoy that. I enjoy having a tattoo because it makes me different from other people. There is no one in the whole world who has a right arm that looks anything like mine. I've always valued being different from other people. Tattooing is a way of expressing that difference. It is a way of saying, "I am unique."*

In describing his own understanding of his clients' motives, one tattoo artist employed the analogy of the customized car.

> *Tattooing is really just a form of personal adornment. Why does someone get a new car and get all of the paint stripped off of it and paint it candy-apple red? Why spend $10,000 on a car and then spend another $20,000 to make it look different from the car you bought? I associate it with ownership. Your body is one of the things you indisputably own. There is a tendency to adorn things that you own to make them especially yours.*

Interviewees also spoke of the pleasure they got from the tattoo as related to having gone through the mysterious and moderately painful process of being tattooed. The tattoo demonstrated courage to the self ("for some people it means that they lived through it and weren't afraid"). One woman, when asked whether she intended to acquire other tattoos in the future, spoke of the excitement of the experience as the potential motivator of additional work.

> *[Do you think you will have more work done after you add something to the one you have now?] Oh God! I don't know why, but my initial reaction is, "I hope I don't, but I think I'm going to." I think getting a tattoo is so exciting and I've always been kind of addicted to excitement. It's fun. While it hurt and stuff it was a new experience and it wasn't that horrible for me. It was new and different.*

In a poignant statement, another woman spoke similarly of the tattoo as memorializing significant aspects of her past experience. "In the future when I'm sitting around and bored with my life and I wonder if I was ever young once and did exciting things, I can look at the tattoo and remember."

INTERACTIONAL CONSEQUENCES

In general, tattooees' observations concerning the effect on their self-definitions of having a tattoo and the process of being tattooed were rather basic and off-hand. In contrast, all interviewees spoke at some length about their social experiences with others and how the tattoo affected their identities and interactions. *Some stressed the affiliational consequences of being tattooed—the mark identified them as belonging to a special group.*

I got tattooed because I had an interest in it. My husband is a chef and our friends tend to be bikers, so it gets me accepted more into that community. They all think of me as "the college girl" and I'm really not. So this (tattoo) kind of brings the door open more.... The typical biker would tell you that you almost have to have tattoos to be part of the group. [Emphasis added.]

Most took pleasure in the way the tattoo enhanced their identities by demonstrating their affiliation with a somewhat more diverse group—tattooed people. [Italics added.]

Having a tattoo is like belonging to a club. I love seeing tattoos on other people. I go up and talk with other people with tattoos. It gives me an excuse because I'm not just going up to talk with them. I can say, "I have one, too." I think maybe subconsciously I got (the tattoo) to be part of that special club.

Having tattoos in some ways does affect me positively because people will stop me on the street and say, "Those are really nice tattoos," and show me theirs. We kind of... it is a way of having positive contact with strangers. We have something very much in common. We can talk about where we got them and the process of getting them and that sort of thing.

Given the symbolic meaning carried by tattoos in conventional social circles, all tattooees have the experience of being the focus of attention because of the mark they carry. The positive responses of others are, of course, the source of the most direct pleasure.

People seem to notice you more when you walk around with technicolor arms. I don't think that everyone who gets tattooed is basically an exhibitionist, someone that walks down the street and says, "Hey, look at me," you know. But it does draw attention to yourself. (How do people respond when they see your tattoos?) Well, yesterday we were sitting in a bar and the lady brings a beer over and she says, "That's gorgeous," and she's looking at the wizard and she's touching them and picking up my shirt. Everyone in the bar was looking and it didn't bother me a bit.

Not all casual encounters are as positive as this one. Revelation of the tattoo is also the source of negative attention when defined by others as a stigmatizing mark.

Sometimes at these parties the conversation will turn to tattoos and I'll mention that I have some. A lot of people don't believe it, but if I'm feeling loose enough I'll roll up my sleeve and show my work. What really aggravates me is that there will almost always be someone who reacts with a show of disgust. "How could you do that to yourself?" No wonder I usually feel more relaxed and at home with bikers and other tattooed people.

I think tattoos look sharp. I walk down the beach and people look at my tattoos. Usually they don't say anything. (When they do) I wish they would say it to my face...like, "Tattoos are ugly." But, when they say something behind my back.... "Isn't that gross." Hey, keep your comments to yourself! If you don't like it, you don't like it. I went to the beach with my father and I said, "Hey, let's walk down the beach," and he said. "No, I don't feel like it." What are you, embarrassed to walk with me?

Given the negative responses that tattooees encounter with some frequency when casual associates or strangers become aware of their body decorations, most are selective about to whom they reveal their tattoos. This is particularly the case when the "other" is in a position to exercise control over the tattooee.

Usually I'm fairly careful about who I show my tattoos to. I don't show them to people at work unless they are really close friends of mine and I know I won't get any kind of hassle because of them. I routinely hide my tattoos...I generally hide them from people who wouldn't understand or people who could potentially cause me trouble. I hide them from my boss and from a lot of the people I work with because there is no reason for them to know.

Tattooees commonly use the reactions of casual associates or relative strangers as a means of categorizing them. A positive reaction to the tattoo indicates social and cultural compatibility, while a negatively judgmental response is seen as signifying a narrow and convention-bound perspective.

I get more positive reactions than I do negative reactions. The negative reactions come from people who aren't like me—who have never done anything astray. It is the straight-laced, conservative person who really doesn't believe that this is acceptable in their set of norms. It seems as though I can actually tell how I'm going to get along with people, and vice-versa, by the way they react to my tattoo. It's more or less expressive of the unconventional side of my character right up front. Most of the people who seem to like me really dig the tattoo too (quoted in Hill, 1972:249).

While it is fairly easy to selectively reveal the tattoo in public settings when interacting with strangers or casual associates, hiding the fact that one is tattooed, thereby avoiding negative social response, is difficult when the "other" is a person with whom the tattooee is intimately associated. The majority of those interviewed recounted incidents in which parents, friends, and, especially for the women, lovers and spouses reacted badly when they initially became aware of the tattoo.

[What did your husband say when he saw your tattoo?] He said he almost threw up. It grossed him out. I had asked him years ago, "What would you think if...," and he didn't like the idea. So, I decided not to tell him. It seemed a smart thing to do. He just looked rather grossed out by the whole thing; didn't like it. Now it is accepted, but I don't think he would go for another one.

Another woman interviewee recounted a similar post-tattoo experience with her parents and boyfriend.

My family was devastated. I didn't tell them for a long time. My mother and I were on a train to New York City and I said to her, "Mom, I want to tell you something but I don't want you to get upset." She said, "You're pregnant!" I said, "No." She says, "You're getting married!" I said, "God, no!" It was downhill from there. When I said, "I got a tattoo," it was like, "Thank God! That's all it is." It wasn't that horrible. My father's reaction was

just one of disgust because women who get tattoos to him are...I don't know...they just aren't nice girls. They aren't the type of girl he wants his daughter to be. He let me know that. He let me have it right between the eyes. He said, "Do you know what kind of girls get tattoos?" and just walked out of the room. That was enough. He thought tramps get tattoos or girls that ride on the back seats of motorcycles, you know. I got a strange reaction from my boyfriend. We had a family outing to go to and there was going to be swimming and tennis and all this stuff and I was real excited about going. He said, "Are you going to go swimming?" I said, "Yeah." I was psyched because I love to swim. He looked at me and said, "You know, your tattoo is going to show if you go swimming." Probably. He didn't want me to go swimming because he didn't want his parents to know that I had a tattoo. Lucky for him it was cloudy that day and nobody swam. I told him, "I'm sorry but I know your parents can handle this kind of news." To boot, he's got a shamrock on his butt! So he has a tattoo—a real double standard there. He didn't say anything for a while after I first got it. It was subtle. He let me know he didn't like it but that, because it was on me, he could excuse it. He's got adjusted to it though. He just let me know that he's never dated a girl who's got a tattoo before. He would prefer that I didn't have it, but there isn't much he can do about that now.

Given the negative social reaction often precipitated by tattoos, it would be reasonable to expect that tattooees who regretted their decision would have emphasized the unpleasant interactional consequences of the tattoo. Interviewees and questionnaire respondents rarely expressed any doubts about their decision to acquire a tattoo. Those that did indicate regret, however, usually did not focus on the stigmatizing effect of the tattoo. Instead, regretful tattooees most commonly were dissatisfied with the technical quality of the tattoo they purchased (see Figure 2).[5]

CONCLUSION: TATTOOING, STIGMA, SELF, AND IDENTITY

When potential tattooees begin to think about altering their bodies in this manner, they devise an

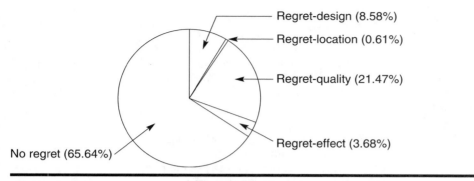

FIGURE 2   Extent and Source of Tattooee Regret (*N* = 163)

understanding of what the tattoo will signify to themselves and others through contact with tattooed associates or by attending media presentations of tattooing and tattooed people (cf. Cohen, 1973; Matza, 1969). In general, they define that tattoo as a mark of affiliation—demonstrating connection to significant groups, primary associates, or those who share specific interests—or as an isolative symbol of unconventionality, or unique personal decoration. Having come to conceive of themselves as tattooed, potential recipients locate a tattoo establishment and acquire the mark.

When revealed to others, the newly acquired corporeal embellishment affects interactions and relationships. Positive responses from co-interactants tend to reinforce social connections, certify tattooees' positive evaluations of self and the tattoo acquisition decision, and increase the likelihood that tattooees will expend the universe of situations in which they choose to reveal their unconventional body decorations.

If being tattooed leads to negative social and self-definitional consequences, regretful tattooees are faced with various alternatives. When met with disapproval tattooees may negatively evaluate the disapproving other and subsequently become more selective in disclosing the fact that they bear a tattoo (see Goffman, 1963a:11). If regretful tattooees focus the responsibility for the negative consequences of having acquired the tattoo upon themselves, they can deny responsibility for the decision or take steps to obliterate the tat-

too. Since negative evaluations of the tattoo decision are most commonly due to the perceived inferior quality of the work, regretful tattooees often have the offending mark covered or reworked by another, more skilled (one hopes), tattooist (see Figure 3).

The central factor shaping this process—from initial stages of interest through dealing with the consequences of being a tattooed person—is that the tattoo is conventionally regarded as a stigma symbol (Goffman, 1963a:43). The decision to acquire a tattoo is not only a decision to alter one's physical appearance; it is a choice to change how the person experiences his or her self and, in turn, how he or she will be defined and treated by others.

Definitions of tattoos and tattooees, held by both the general culture and the "scientific community," are predominantly negative. Tattoos are defined as being symptomatic of the psychological or social deviance of the bearer. Conventional repulsion imbues tattooing with significant power and appeal. For some tattooees the act of acquiring a tattoo marks them as being involved in an exotic social world centered around the pleasurable flaunting of authority and convention (cf. Lofland, 1969:106).

[Why do you think you initially wanted to put the tattoo someplace that is well hidden?] I guess I thought that someone would think it was creepy. It would have connotations of loose women or being foolish. Like kids don't think through the conse-

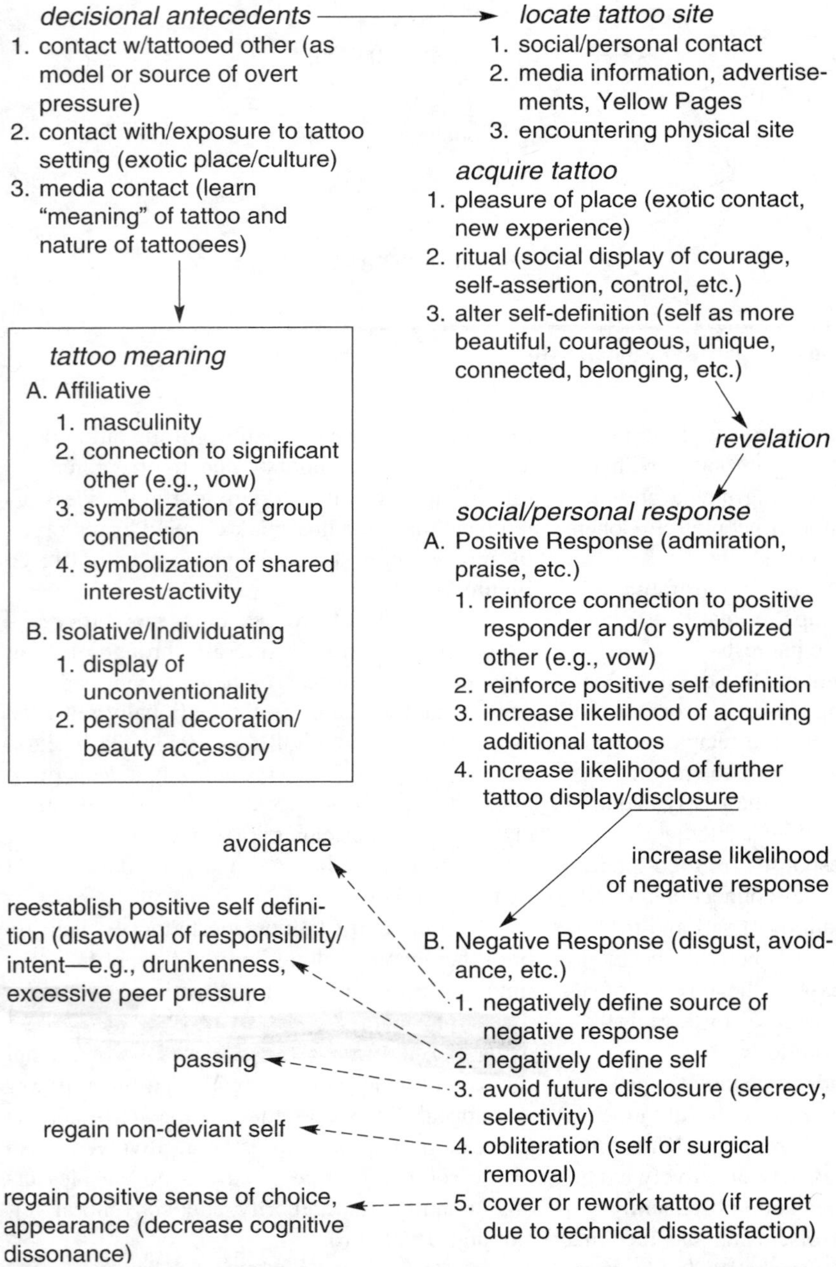

decisional antecedents ⎯⎯⎯⎯⎯⎯→ *locate tattoo site*

1. contact w/tattooed other (as model or source of overt pressure)
2. contact with/exposure to tattoo setting (exotic place/culture)
3. media contact (learn "meaning" of tattoo and nature of tattooees)

locate tattoo site

1. social/personal contact
2. media information, advertisements, Yellow Pages
3. encountering physical site

acquire tattoo

1. pleasure of place (exotic contact, new experience)
2. ritual (social display of courage, self-assertion, control, etc.)
3. alter self-definition (self as more beautiful, courageous, unique, connected, belonging, etc.)

tattoo meaning

A. Affiliative
1. masculinity
2. connection to significant other (e.g., vow)
3. symbolization of group connection
4. symbolization of shared interest/activity

B. Isolative/Individuating
1. display of unconventionality
2. personal decoration/beauty accessory

revelation

social/personal response

A. Positive Response (admiration, praise, etc.)
1. reinforce connection to positive responder and/or symbolized other (e.g., vow)
2. reinforce positive self definition
3. increase likelihood of acquiring additional tattoos
4. increase likelihood of further tattoo display/disclosure

avoidance

reestablish positive self definition (disavowal of responsibility/intent—e.g., drunkenness, excessive peer pressure

increase likelihood of negative response

B. Negative Response (disgust, avoidance, etc.)
1. negatively define source of negative response
2. negatively define self

passing

3. avoid future disclosure (secrecy, selectivity)

regain non-deviant self

4. obliteration (self or surgical removal)

regain positive sense of choice, appearance (decrease cognitive dissonance)

5. cover or rework tattoo (if regret due to technical dissatisfaction)

FIGURE 3 The Tattoo as Social Symbol: Acquisitional Process and Self-Definitional/Identity Consequences

quences of stuff. They do things impetuously. I thought that people might think I just ran down there in a fit of glee. (Actually) a tattoo is not serious. I think that is part of the pleasure of it. When I was first thinking about it it was, "Oh boy, let's do this!" It was sort of a gleeful thing. It is like being a little bit bad.

I can't think of one nice compact reason (I got a tattoo). They are pretty. But most of all they are a poke in the eye to people who don't have them— people who are straights or whatever.

The tattoo acts as more than simply a "mark of disaffiliation" (Goffman, 1963a:143–147). It may also demonstrate connection to unconventional social groups. In some cases, it symbolizes membership in subcultures (for example, outlaw motorcyclists, youth gangs) centered around socially disvalued or law-violating interests and activities.[6]

The stigmatized social definition of tattooing and the negative response tattooees commonly experience when "normals" are aware of their stigma may also precipitate identification with a subculture in which the tattoo is of primary significance. Within the informal "tattoo community" consisting of those tattooees who positively define their unconventional mark, the tattoo acts as a source of "mutual openness" (Goffman, 1963b:131–139), providing opportunities for spontaneous appreciative interaction with others who are also tattooed (Pfuhl, 1986:168–188; Goffman, 1963a:23–25).[7]

As is commonly the case with subcultural groups bound together by the problems associated with possession of a physical stigma, the tattoo world has developed an organized core. More-or-less formal groups such as the National Tattoo Association hold regular meetings and provide practitioners with technical information, legal assistance, access to the latest equipment and supplies, and other essential occupational resources. Serious tattoo "enthusiasts" and collectors are also active in this organized world. Tattoo conventions provide them with an opportunity to display their work, enlarge their collections, and associate with other tattooees in situations in which they are normal. Understandably, a major focus of organizational activity is the public redefinition of tattooing as a legitimate form of artistic production.

Contemporary commercial culture provides a variety of products (t-shirts, bumper stickers, buttons, and so forth) by which people may announce their perspectives, personal interests, and social attachments. Clothing, jewelry, hair style, and other aspects of personal decoration are used to demonstrate aesthetic taste. These modes of self-symbolization are, however, relatively safe and transitory expressions. For some, these conventional mechanisms are inadequate. Typically impelled by personal association with others who have chosen a more drastic and symbolically powerful approach, tattooees purchase what is, as yet, a "tarnished" cultural product (Shover, 1975). In so doing, tattooed people voluntarily shape their social identities and enhance their definitions of self. Drawn by both the affiliational and individuating consequences of their choice and despite the potential for disrupted interactions, tattooees choose to mark their bodies with indelible symbols of what they see themselves to be.

NOTES

1. The central importance of personal recommendation as the source of tattoo clients is well known to tattooists. All tattooists have business cards that they hand out quite freely (one maintained that he had dispensed over 50,000 cards in the past two years). Listing one's services in the Yellow Pages is the other major means employed to draw customers since it provides location information to those who, for a variety of reasons, do not have interpersonal sources....

2. Questionnaire respondents were given an open-ended question that asked them to speculate as to why people get tattooed. Of the 163 respondents, 135 provided some sort of reply to this item. Forty-four percent of those responding emphasized that becoming tattooed was moti-

vated by a desire for self-expression (for example, "vanity," "it's a personal preference," "a statement of who you are"), 21 percent emphasized tattooing as a mechanism for asserting uniqueness and individuality (for example, "people like to be different," "personal originality," "it makes you special"), and 28 percent made some form of aesthetic statement (for example, "because it is beautiful," "a form of art that lasts forever," "body jewelry"). On their part, tattooists tend to recognize the aesthetic importance of their work as seen by their clients....

3. Of the thirty-five tattoos worn by the sixteen interviewees, 14 percent (five) represented a bird, 6 percent (two) represented a mammal, 14 percent (five) represented a mythical animal, 9 percent (three) represented an insect, 3 percent (one) represented a human female, 17 percent (six) represented a human male, 14 percent (five) were noncommercial symbols (hearts, crosses, military insignia, and so on), 14 percent (five) were floral, 3 percent (one) were names or vow tattoos, and 6 percent (two) were some other image.

Questionnaire respondents were asked to indicate the design of their first tattoo. They were: 14 percent (twenty-three) bird, 11 percent (eighteen) mammal, 12 percent (nineteen) mythical animal, 10 percent (seventeen) insect, 1 percent (two) human female, 6 percent (ten) human male, 4 percent (six) commercial symbols, 8 percent (thirteen) noncommercial symbols, 21 percent (thirty-four) floral/arboreal, 4 percent (seven) name/vow, and 9 percent (fourteen) other.

4. The painfulness of the tattoo process is the most unpleasant element of the tattoo event. Only 33 percent (fifty-four) of the questionnaire respondents maintained that there was something about the tattoo experience that they disliked. One third of these (eighteen) said that the pain was what they found most unpleasant. Fourteen of the sixteen interviewees mentioned pain as a troublesome factor. Numerous observations of groups of young men discussing pain or expressing stoic disregard for the pain as they received tattoos demonstrated the importance of the tattoo event as a form of initiation ritual. In some cases the tattoo process provides a situation in which the male tattooee can demonstrate his manliness to his peers.... The cross-cultural literature on body alteration indicates that the pain of the process is an important factor. See Ebin, 1979:88–89; Brain, 1979:183–184; Ross and McKay, 1979:44–49, 67–69; Becker and Clark, 1979:10, 19; St. Clair and Govenar, 1981:100–135.

5. Other than simply accepting the regretted mark, there are few avenues of resolution open to dissatisfied tattooees. In the most extreme cases, the tattooee may try to obliterate the offending mark with acid or attempt to cut it off. A somewhat more reasoned (and considerably less painful) approach entails seeking the aid of a dermatologist or plastic surgeon who will medically remove the tattoo. The most common alternative, however, is to have the technically inferior piece redone or covered with another tattoo created by a more skilled practitioner. Tattooists estimate that 40 to 50 percent of their work entails reworking or applying cover-ups to poor quality tattoos. See Goldstein et al., 1979, and Hardy, 1983.

6. One traditional use of tattooing has been to mark indelibly social outcasts and defined deviants so that they can be easily identified and/or avoided by officials and "normals." In sixth-century Japan, for example, criminals and social outcasts were tattooed on the face or arms as a form of negative public identification and punishment (Richie and Buruma, 1980:12–13). Similarly, in the nineteenth century, inmates of the Massachusetts prison system had "Mass S. P." and the date of their release tattooed on their left arms (Ebensten, 1953:20). More recently, the Nazis tattooed identification numbers on the arms of concentration camp inmates. In April of 1986 conservative columnist William Buckley suggested that victims of AIDS (Acquired Immune Deficiency Syndrome) be tattooed on the buttocks in order to limit the spread of the disease among homosexuals (*Hartford Courant,* April 19, 1986, p. C6).

7. The literature directed at the fan world surrounding tattooing consistently makes reference to the "tattoo community."...

REFERENCES

Becker, Nickie, and Robert E. Clark. 1979. "Born to Raise Hell: An Ethnography of Tattoo Parlors." Paper presented at the meetings of Southwestern Sociological Association, March 28–31, Fort Worth, Texas.

Bell, Gerald. 1967. "Self-Confidence, Persuasibility and Cognitive Dissonance Among Automobile Buyers." In *Risk-Taking and Information Handling in Consumer Behavior,* ed. Donald Cox, 442–468. Boston: Harvard University Graduate School of Business Administration.

Brachfield, Ted. 1982. "Tattoos and the Collector." *Tattootime* 1 (Fall):24–25.

Brain, Dennis. 1979. *The Decorated Body.* New York: Harper and Row.

Cohen, Sidney. 1973. "Mods and Rockers: The Inventory as Manufactured News." In *The Manufacture of News: A Reader,* ed. S. Cohen and J. Young, 226–241. Beverly Hills, CA: Sage.

Csikszentmihalyi, Mihaly, and Eugene Rochberg-Halton. 1981. *The Meaning of Things: Domestic Symbols and the Self.* Cambridge: Cambridge University Press.

Ebensten, Hans. 1953. *Pierced Hearts and True Love.* London: Derek Verschoyle.

Ebin, Victoria. 1979. *The Body Decorated.* London: Thames and Hudson.

Goffman, Erving. 1961. *Asylums.* Garden City, NY: Doubleday.

———. 1963a. *Stigma.* Englewood Cliffs, NJ: Prentice-Hall.

———. 1963b. *Behavior in Public Places.* New York: Free Press.

Goldstein, Norman, James Penoff, Norman Price, Roger Ceilley, Leon Goldman, Victor Hay-Roe, and Timothy Miller. 1979. "Techniques and Removal of Tattoos." *Journal of Dermatologic Surgery and Oncology* 5:901–910.

Govenar, Alan. 1977. "The Acquisition of Tattooing Competence: An Introduction." *Folklore Annual of the University Folklore Association* 7 & 8:43–53.

Hardy, D. E. 1982. "The Name Game." *Tattootime* 1 (Fall):50–54.

———. 1983. "Inventive Cover Work." *Tattootime* 2:12–17.

Hill, Amie. 1972. "Tattoo Renaissance." In *Side-Saddle on the Golden Calf,* ed. G. Lewis, 245–249. Pacific Palisades, CA: Goodyear.

Lofland, John. 1969. *Deviance and Identity.* Englewood Cliffs, NJ: Prentice-Hall.

Matza, David. 1969. *Becoming Deviant.* Englewood Cliffs, NJ: Prentice-Hall.

Pfuhl, Edward. 1986. *The Deviance Process,* 2d ed. Belmont, CA: Wadsworth.

Richie, Donald, and Ian Baruma. 1980. *The Japanese Tattoo.* New York: Weatherhill.

Ross, Robert, and Hugh McKay. 1979. *Self-Mutilation.* Lexington, MA: Heath.

Scutt, R. W. B., and C. Gotch. 1974. *Art, Sex, and the Symbol: The Mystery of Tattooing.* New York: A. S. Barnes.

Shover, Neal. 1975. "Tarnished Goods and Services in the Market Place." *Urban Life and Culture* 3:471–488.

Solomon, Michael. 1983. "The Role of Products as Social Stimuli: A Symbolic Interactionist Perspective." *Journal of Consumer Research* 10:319–329.

St. Clair, Leonard, and Alan Govenar. 1981. *Stoney Knows How: Life as a Tattoo Artist.* Lexington: University of Kentucky Press.

Van Gennep, Arnold. 1960. *The Rites of Passage.* Chicago: University of Chicago Press.

Identity and the Shoplifter

MARY OWEN CAMERON

It seems probable that most adult pilferers start their careers as children or adolescents in groups where the techniques of successful pilfering are learned from other more experienced children.

Later as group activity is abandoned some of the group members continue the practices they learned as adolescents. The lavish displays of merchandise which department stores exhibit to encourage "impulse buying" are, for the experienced pilferer, there for the taking.

Adult women pilferers, generally belonging to families of rather modest income, enter department stores with a strong sense of the limitations of their household budgets. They do not steal merchandise which they can rationalize purchasing: household supplies, husband's clothes, children's wear. But beautiful and luxury goods for their personal use can be purchased legitimately only if some other member of the family is deprived. Although pilferers often have guilt feelings about their thefts, it still seems to them less wrong to steal from a rich store than to take from the family budget. Pilferers seem to be, thus, narcissistic individuals in that they steal for their own personal use, but, on the other hand, they do not use the limited family income for their own luxury goods.

Pilferers differ in one outstanding respect, at least, from other thieves: They generally do not think of themselves as thieves. In fact, even when arrested, they resist strongly being pushed to admit their behavior is theft. This became very clear as I observed a number of interrogations of shoplifters by the store detective staff, and it was supported in conversations with the detectives who drew on their own wider experience. It is quite often difficult for the store staff to convince the arrested person that he has actually been arrested, even when the detectives show their licenses and badges. Again and again store police explain to pilferers that they are under arrest as thieves, that they will, in the normal course of events, be taken in a police van to jail, held in jail until bond is raised, and tried in a court before a judge and sentenced. Much of the interview time of store detectives is devoted to establishing this point; in making the pilferer understand that what happens to him from the time of his arrest is a legal question, but it is still a question for decision, first of all, by the store staff.

Store detectives use the naivete of pilferers as an assistance in arrest procedures while the pilferer is in the presence of legitimate customers on the floor of the store. The most tactful approach possible is used. The store detective will say, for example, "I represent the store office, and I'm afraid the office will have to see what's in your shopping bag. Would you care to come with me,

please?" If the pilferer protests, the detective adds, "You wouldn't want to be embarrassed in front of all these people, would you? In the office we can talk things over in private."

Edwards states that the method of making an arrest is important in preventing excitement and even disorder.

> *A gentle approach will usually disarm any shoplifter, amateur or professional, while a rough seizure or loud accusation may immediately put him on the defensive. At other times it may result in a nervous or hysterical condition accompanied by an involuntary discharge which may be embarrassing to both the arrestor and the arrested.[1]*

Inbau adds the thought that the gentle approach is helpful too in forestalling suits for false arrest.

> *The finesse with which defendant accosts plaintiff is a definite factor also affecting the temper with which the court approaches a case. The defendant acting in good faith with probable cause, whose attitude is quiet, nonthreatening, and deferential to the plaintiff's feelings can weather an honest mistake much more cheaply than otherwise. At the most it may induce a court to find there was no imprisonment at all. At the least, it will relieve the defendant of punitive damages and reduce the amount of actual damages.[2]*

The "deference" of the arresting detective combined with the already existing rationalizations of the pilferer sustain in him the belief that whereas his behavior might be reprehensible, the objects taken were, after all, not of great value, he would be glad to pay for them and be on his way. "Yes, I took the dress," one woman sobbed as she was being closely interrogated, "but that doesn't mean I'm a thief."

Arrest forces the pilferer to think of himself as a thief. The interrogation procedure of the store is specifically and consciously aimed at breaking down any illusions the shoplifter may have that his behavior is regarded as merely "naughty" or "bad." The breakdown of illusions is, to the store detective staff, both a goal in itself and a means of establishing the fact that each innocent-appearing pilferer is not, in fact, a professional thief "putting on an act." In the interrogation the shoplifter is searched for other stolen merchandise and for identification papers. Pockets and pocketbooks are thoroughly examined. All papers, letters, tickets, bills, etc., are read in detail in spite of considerable protest from the arrested person. Each person is made to explain everything he has with him. If suspect items such as public locker keys, pawn tickets, etc., are found, he will have to explain very thoroughly indeed and agree to have the locker examined and the pawned merchandise seen to avoid formal charge. In any event, once name, address, and occupation have been established (and for women, the maiden name and names in other marriages), the file of names and identifying material of all persons who have, in the past years, been arrested in any of the State Street department stores is consulted. The shoplifter is questioned at length if similarities of names or other identifying data are encountered.

While identification and prior record are being checked, store detectives, persons in charge of refunds, and even experienced sales clerks may be summoned to look at the arrested person to determine if he has been previously suspected of stealing merchandise or has been noted as behaving suspiciously.

In the course of all this investigation, it becomes increasingly clear to the pilferer that he is considered a thief and is in imminent danger of being hauled into court and publicly exhibited as such. This realization is often accompanied by a dramatic change in attitudes and by severe emotional disturbance. Occasionally even hysterical semi-attempts at suicide result.

The professional shoplifter who has been arrested and knows he is recognized, on the other hand, behaves quite differently. He does, of course, make every effort possible to talk his way out of the situation. But once he finds that this is impossible, he accepts jail and its inconveniences as a normal hazard of his trade.

"This is a nightmare," said one woman pilferer who had been formally charged with stealing an expensive handbag. "It can't be happening to me! Why, oh why can't I wake up and find that it isn't so," she cried later as she waited at a store exit, accompanied by a city and a store policeman, for the city police van to arrive. "Whatever will I do? Please make it go away," she pleaded with the officer. "I'll be disgraced forever. I can never look anyone in the face again."

Pilferers expect no "in-group" support for their behavior. As they become aware of the possible serious consequences of their arrest (trial, jail, etc.), pilferers obviously feel isolated from all supporting relationships. Store detectives report that the most frequent question women ask is, "Will my husband have to know about this?" Men, they say, express immediate fear that their employers will be informed of their arrest when questions about employment are raised. Children are apprehensive of parental reaction. Edwards says,

> *The composure of juveniles being detained has never ceased to amaze me, that is, until notified that they must tell a parent of their misdemeanor. Then the tears flow and pleadings begin. The interviewer must be firm in his denial that notification will "kill" the parent, and he must sell the child on the idea that any deviation from accepted practice must be discussed with the person most interested in his welfare.[3]*

Pilferers feel that if their family or friends learn about their arrest they will be thoroughly disgraced. The fear, shame, and remorse expressed by arrested pilferers could not be other than genuine and a reflection of their appraisal of the attitudes they believe others will take toward them. One woman was observed who, thoroughly shaken as the realization of her predicament began to appear to her, interrupted her protestations of innocence from time to time, overwhelmed at the thought of how some particular person in her "in-group" would react to her arrest. Her conversation with the interrogator ran somewhat as follows: "I didn't intend to take the dress. I just wanted to see it in daylight. [She had stuffed it into a shopping bag and carried it out of the store.]

Oh, what will my husband do? I *did* intend to pay for it. It's all a mistake. Oh, my God, what will my mother say! I'll be glad to pay for it. See, I've got the money with me. Oh, my children! They can't find out I've been *arrested!* I'd never be able to face them again."

Pilferers not only expect no in-group support, but they feel that they have literally *no* one to turn to. The problem of being embroiled in a wholly unfamiliar legal situation is obviously not only frightening but unexpected. Apparently they had anticipated being reprimanded; they had not anticipated being searched by a licensed detective, identified, etc., and on the whole, placed in a position in which the burden of argument for keeping out of jail is theirs.

The contrast in behavior between the pilferer and the recognized and self-admitted thief is striking. The experienced thief either already knows what to do or knows precisely where and how to find out. His emotional reactions may involve anger directed at himself or at features in the situation around him, but he is not at a loss for reactions. He follows the prescribed modes of behavior, and knows, either because of prior experience or through the vicarious experiences of acquaintances, what arrest involves by way of obligations and rights. He has some familiarity with bonding practice and either already has or knows how to find a lawyer who will act for him.

Because the adult pilferer does not think of himself, prior to his arrest, as a thief and can conceive of no in-group support for himself in that role, his arrest forces him to reject the role (at least insofar as department store shoplifting is concerned). The arrest procedure, even though not followed by prosecution, is in itself sufficient to cause him to redefine his situation. He is, of course, informed that subsequent arrest by any store will be followed by immediate prosecution and probably by a considerable jail sentence. But since this does not act as a deterrent to the self-admitted thief nor could this kind of admonition deter the compulsive neurotic, neither the fear of punishment nor the objective severity of the punishment in itself is the crucial point in relation to the change from criminal to law-abiding behavior. Rather the threat to the person's system of values and prestige relationships is involved. Social scientists who have investigated criminal activities which have subcultural support are unanimous in pointing out the persistence of criminal activity, the high rate of recidivism and the resistance to reform shown by law violators. Pilfering seems to be the other side of the coin. Not having the support of a criminal subculture, pilferers are very "reformable" individuals. If the findings of this study are substantiated by studies of other offenses in which the offenders are similarly without support of a criminal subculture, there would be a strong argument in favor of keeping pilferers out of jail lest they receive there the kinds of knowledge and emotional support they need to become "successful" commercial thieves. Crime prevention would seem best achieved by helping the law violators retain their self-image of respectability while making it clear to them that a second offense will really mean disgrace.

NOTES

1. Loren Edwards, *Shoplifting and Shrinkage Protection for Stores* (Springfield, Ill.: Charles C Thomas, 1958), p. 134.

2. Inbau, Fred E., "Protection and Recapture of Merchandise from Shoplifters," *Illinois Law Review.* Vol. 46, No. 6, 1952.

3. Edwards, *op. cit.,* pp. 135–136.

CHAPTER 14

MANAGING DEVIANT IDENTITY

Once a deviant identity has been acquired, problems can arise in managing it. Deviants must decide how much to integrate their social identities with their personal identities in various social situations. With other deviants it is often wise to be open about one's deviance; with nondeviants it is seldom so. How deviants manage their deviant identities affects how they fare in their deviant careers—how long these careers last, how successful they are, and whether and how the deviants can ever terminate them.

In the first reading Michael Petrunik and Clifford Shearing describe how stutterers cope with their disability by concealing, revealing, or disavowing stuttering. Next Diana Scully and Joseph Marolla explain how convicted rapists use a variety of excuses and justifications to disavow their social identities as rapists. Then Albert Reiss describes how teenage youths can engage in homosexual activity without assuming a homosexual identity. Finally, Naomi Gerstel shows some ways in which divorced people cope with stigma.

Stutterers' Practices

MICHAEL PETRUNIK and CLIFFORD D. SHEARING

...Stuttering is a puzzling disorder of human communication which has defied explanation and cure for thousands of years (Van Riper, 1971:2). According to survey estimates in Europe and North America, stutterers constitute about 1 percent of the school-age population, regardless of language or dialect (Bloodstein, 1981:79; Van Riper, 1971:39). Although systematic data are not available—there are only impressionistic accounts from anthropologists—stuttering appears to be less common in non-western, non-industrial societies.[1] Stuttering typically appears between two and nine years of age. There is some evidence that stuttering has a genetic basis; it tends to appear in successive generations of the same family and frequently in identical twins (Bloodstein, 1981:94). Stuttering is more common among males than females, by a ratio of three or four to one (Bloodstein, 1981:86). Only about one fifth of those who stutter in early childhood continue to stutter into adulthood (Bloodstein, 1981:86; Van Riper, 1971:45).

Stuttering, as visible behavior, refers to interruptions in speech involving the prolongation or repetition of sounds or words, pauses between words or syllables, and "blocking" on words, sometimes accompanied by extraneous sounds such as grunts, facial grimaces, body movements, and postural freezing as the person struggles to "get the word out." These speech difficulties can range from a split second to, in the worst cases, about a minute (Bloodstein, 1981:3).

Like other perceived impairments, stuttering interferes with "the etiquette and mechanisms of communication" (Goffman, 1963:103) and disrupts the "feedback mechanics of spoken interaction" (1963:49). Depending on the social context,

the culture, and the health and social status of the speakers (Petrunik, 1977:37), persons who unintentionally and chronically deviate from fluency standards are likely to be defined as stutterers and subjected to various penalizing social reactions, including pity, condescension, embarrassment, amusement, ridicule, and impatience (Johnson, 1959:239; Lemert, 1967:135).

The extent and frequency of stuttering varies. No one stutters all the time. Indeed, there are some situations in which virtually all stutterers are fluent, for example, when singing, speaking in unison with others (including other stutterers), and speaking to themselves, animals, and infants. In addition, stutterers are often more fluent when speaking with a drawl, accent, or different pitch (Petrunik, 1977:34, 71). Some individuals stutter on some words or sounds but not others. ("I can never say 'g's." "I always stutter on the word 'coffee'.") Setting is also important. Many stutter more during telephone conversations than they do in face-to-face conversation; others find speaking to strangers particularly difficult; still others are more fluent in formal than informal situations, or vice versa. Stutterers have good periods and bad periods. ("Some days I wake up and I'm fine, other days I'm in for hell all day.") There are even some actors and entertainers who stutter but who are fluent when playing a role or facing an audience.

Studying the ways stutterers cope with their stuttering offers valuable insights into how people manage perceived disabilities (Freidson, 1965) and the potential stigma associated with them by highlighting processes that are usually taken for granted, and thus obscured (Davis, 1961). This strategy of using the specific to identify the general has recently been employed by Kitsuse (1980) who has used the "coming out of the closet" metaphor to examine the processes which establish new and legitimate identities. Schneider and Conrad (1980) have developed Kitsuse's analysis by

Reprinted from "Fragile Facades: Stuttering and the Strategic Manipulation of Awareness," *Social Problems*, Vol. 31, No. 2 (December 1983), pp. 125–138, by permission of the Society for the Study of Social Problems and the authors.

using epilepsy to examine how persons manage discreditable information where there is "no clear identity to move to or from" (1980:32) and where "no 'new' readily available supportive... subculture exists" (1980:33).

Both Kitsuse, and Schneider and Conrad, focus on identity rather than interactional order, and on calculated and planned management rather than moment-to-moment strategies. We broaden this analysis by examining: (1) how people coordinate the requirements of creating acceptable identities *and* orderly interaction; (2) how they integrate management strategies thought out in advance with those selected on a moment-to-moment basis; and (3) how the subjective experience of disability, together with the reactions of others, shape the management process (Higgins, 1980; Petrunik, 1983). Stuttering has three features which facilitate an examination of these issues. First, stuttering is a potentially stigmatizing disability that disrupts interaction. Second, because stutterers experience speech as a function over which they exercise partial but precarious control, their management of speech is both spontaneous and premeditated. Third, the experience of stuttering is critical for how stutterers, and others, define and manage stuttering.... We examine the central importance of stuttering as a reality experienced by the stutterer. We then examine a variety of strategies which stutterers use to manipulate awareness of their stuttering and present the fragile facade of normal speech. Although we refer throughout to Goffman's (1963) analysis of stigma management as a benchmark in demonstrating how an understanding of stuttering contributes to a more general understanding of stigma, we go beyond Goffman and those who have extended his work, such as Conrad and Schneider, in emphasizing the importance of the experiential domain for sociological analysis....

THE EXPERIENCE OF STUTTERING

I suppose that the hope of every stutterer is to awaken some morning and find that his disability has vanished. There is just enough promise of this in his experience to make it seem possible. There are days when, for some reason, the entangled web of words trips him only occasionally. In such periods of relief, he may peer back into his other condition and puzzle over the nature of the oppressive "presence"...[hoping that it] is a transitory aberration which might fade and vanish.... One feels that only an added will-power, some accretion of psychic rather than physical strength, should be necessary for its conquest. Yet, try as I might, I could not take the final step. I had come up against some invisible power which no strength of will seemed to surmount (Gustavson, 1944:466).

Like normal speakers, stutterers believe speech is something that should be intentionally controlled. Yet, somehow their words are mysteriously blocked or interrupted. Stutterers experience stuttering as the work of an alien inner force (often referred to in the third person as "it") which takes control of their speech mechanism. Stuttering is something which stutterers feel happens *to* them, not something they do: "somebody else is in charge of my mouth and I can't do anything about it" (Van Riper, 1971:158).

In coping with this subjective reality, stutterers use three general strategies: concealment, openness, and disavowal. Concealment strategies involve three principal tactics: avoidance, circumvention, and camouflage. These tactics allow most stutterers to avoid being seen as stutterers part of the time and a few to become secret stutterers. Openness tactics include: treating stuttering as unproblematic, struggle with the "it," and voluntary disclosure. Disavowal—which often calls for the tacit co-operation of others—involves the pretense that stuttering is not occurring when it is obvious that it is. We discuss in turn each of these strategies and their tactics.

CONCEALMENT

AVOIDANCE

The simplest way to conceal stuttering is to avoid speaking. Many stutterers select occupations they think will minimize speaking. Others avoid situations in which they fear stuttering will embarrass them.

> I never went to the dances at school because I was afraid of stuttering and looking silly. Because I didn't go, I didn't learn to dance or mix socially. I always felt bad when people would ask me if I was going to a dance or party. I would make up some excuse or say that I didn't want to go. I felt that people thought I was some sort of creep because I didn't go. Each time I wouldn't go because of my fears, I felt even weirder.

Stutterers avoid specific types of encounters. Instead of using the telephone they will write a letter, "drop in on someone," or go to a store to see if it has the item they want. Stutterers avoid particular words, substituting "easy" words for "hard" ones. Word substitution sometimes results in convoluted phrasing in which nothing seems to be addressed directly.

> If I didn't dodge and duck, I wouldn't be able to carry on a conversation. If I didn't circumlocute, I wouldn't be able to get certain words out at all. Unless I'm coming in through the back door and taking a run at it, I'd never get it out.

Where this tactic proves difficult or impossible, stutterers may structure conversations so others say the troublesome words for them. One way of doing this is by feigning forgetfulness:

> You know what I mean, what was it we were talking about this morning, you know, John has one, it's ah, this is annoying, it's right on the tip of my tongue....

Another tactic is to structure the situation so that someone else will be called upon to do the talking. For example, most stutterers fear they will stutter on their name (Petrunik, 1982:306). To avoid introducing themselves when they meet strangers, stutterers sometimes arrange their entry so that someone who knows them will proceed them into the situation. They then rely on the social conventions governing introductions to compel the other person to introduce them. Similarly,

stutterers often fear placing orders in restaurants because here, too, word substitution is difficult. To cope with this situation, stutterers may encourage others to order before them; as soon as an item they would like—or at least find acceptable—is mentioned, they can use words they feel more confident with to duplicate the other person's order: "me too" or "same here." With close associates such cooperation may take on the character of finely tuned team work.

> When we were visiting friends of ours and I was having blocks, my wife would sometimes get what seemed to be a slightly anxious look and would quietly supply the word. She did this in a way that seemed so natural to me that I wondered if the others noticed it.

While the willing cooperation of others, especially intimates, has been well documented (Goffman, 1963:55, 97) a study of stuttering draws attention to how others may unknowingly be coopted to conceal a potential stigma.

CIRCUMVENTION AND CAMOUFLAGE

Stutterers sometimes use tactics based on timing and rhythm to outsmart the "it." Using these tactics requires a knowledge of both the etiquette of conversation and the patterns of one's own stuttering. Some speak quickly, for example, "building up" momentum to get "past" or "over" "difficult words." Others rhythmically pace their speech with the aid of coordinated hand and/or leg movements. Some arrange their sentences so that "easy" words precede "hard" ones, to establish a "flow" which carries them uneventfully over "trouble spots." Others arrange their speech so that "difficult" sounds are said on falling (or rising) pitches. Still others find that changing their tone of voice, or speaking in dialect or with an accent, is helpful.

A similar tactic involves delaying saying a troublesome word until the stutterer feels "it" no longer threatens to control speech and the word is ready to "come out." One way of doing this is to introduce starters and fillers (well, like, er, ah, um) into speech, to postpone troublesome words until the moment when they can be said. One stutterer, for example, was walking along a street when a stranger asked him for directions: "Where is the Borden Building?" A sudden panic gripped the stutterer. He knew exactly where the building was but, to permit him to wait for a moment when "it" could be caught off guard, he responded: "Well, let me see [pause with quizzical expression] oh, ah, near…let me see…near, I think Spadina and, ah, College." A variant of this tactic involves rearranging words. The late British humorist and stutterer, Patrick Campbell, gave an example of this in a television interview. While travelling on a London bus, he feared he would not be able to say, "May I have a ticket to Marble Arch?" without stuttering. So, when the conductor approached, he said instead, "May I have a ticket to that arch which is of marble made?"—which he executed fluently.

Where stutterers fail to outwit the "it" they may attempt to camouflage their problem by, for example, visually isolating others from evidence of their stuttering. A teacher who stutters accomplished this by writing on the blackboard just as he was about to stutter, thereby disguising a "block" as a pause to write.

SECRET STUTTERERS

Most stutterers avoid detection only part of the time. However, some stutterers manage to maintain the identity of a "normal speaker" virtually all the time. They define themselves as stutterers not because they stutter in secret, like Becker's (1963:11) "secret deviants," but because they confront and respond to an inner propensity to stutter. Some stutterers report going for years without overtly stuttering. This fact—that a deviant identity can exist in the absence of visible deviant behavior—adds weight to Jack Katz's (1972) critique of those conceptions of labeling which focus exclusively on deviance as behavior and ignore deviance as an inner essence imputed to individuals. Goffman's (1963:56) refusal to recognize that stigmatized people may define themselves in terms of an inner essence and "that what distinguishes an individual from others is the core of his being" has limited his ability to comprehend how both stigmatizer and "normal" people perceive their differences and the consequences of this for defining their "real" or "natural" groupings (1963:112). Some speech pathologists, on the other hand, have long recognized that stigmatized people define themselves on the basis of their subjective experience. They refer to secret stutterers as interiorized, indicating that stuttering can be an internal experience as well as an external appearance (Douglass and Quarrington, 1952:378).

Interiorized stutterers place great importance on preserving a social identity and will go to extraordinary lengths to preserve it. For example, a self-employed businessman in his early forties concealed his stuttering from his first wife. He confided in his second wife, but continued to conceal his stuttering from his children. At work, he had his secretary handle potentially troublesome situations. He would, for example, have her make certain phone calls for him. He claimed he would lose business if his stuttering became known. At one time he fired a secretary who had been working with him for a number of years because he thought her facial expressions showed that she had noticed him stuttering. He took great care not to drink too much or become fatigued so that he would not lose control over his speech. He preferred to entertain at home rather than to go out because he felt he could better regulate his drinking at home.

Successful interiorized stutterers develop a particular sensitivity to the intricacies of syntax. They "become 'situation conscious' [and display] special aliveness to the contingencies of acceptance and disclosure, contingencies to which normals will be less alive" (Goffman, 1963:111).

Avoiding stuttering has many costs. Some tactics exclude the stutterer from fully participating in social life as a "normal person," infringing on the very status the stutterer wishes to preserve. The interactional costs may be relatively trivial (not eating what one really wants in a restaurant, or saying something quite different from what one intended), or far more consequential (depriving oneself of a social life or not pursuing a desired occupation).

> Because I wasn't normal I thought I couldn't do normal things like get married. I avoided going to parties, because I didn't want to feel bad, and then I felt bad because I didn't go and wasn't meeting people and having a good social life.

Similarly, the consequences for social identity may be relatively benign (being defined as "quiet" or "shy") or even somewhat flattering (being a "good listener" or a "strong silent type"). On the other hand, avoiding interaction may result in derogatory characterizations ("nervous," "odd," "rude," "affected," "silly," "strange," or "retarded").[2] A border crossing incident illustrates how avoidance can be interpreted as evidence of impropriety:

> The border guard asked me where I was born. Because I was afraid I would stutter on "Nova Scotia," I hesitated and started to "ah" and "um" to him. "Let me see now...it's the...uh, Maritimes...uh..." and so on. The outcome of all this evasion was that they made a thorough search of my car and even threatened to slit my seat covers.

The importance which stutterers give to the costs of concealment determines the tactics they use. Some people will do almost anything to avoid stuttering; others prefer to stutter in some situations rather than face the consequences of concealment.

> On the first day [of the Kerr course] we were gathering at the motel and going through the ritual of introductions. One man put his hand out to me and said, "My name is...uh...actually...my name is Jim." Afterwards one of the other men in the group who had a highly noticeable stutter shook his head and said, in an aside to me, "What a fool! I'd rather stammer my head off than avoid like that. It looks ridiculous. People must think he's crazy!"

OPENNESS

UNPROBLEMATIC STUTTERING

Unlike interiorized stutterers, those with visible and audible speech disruptions find that some audiences become so familiar with their stuttering that they no longer have anything to conceal. ("All my friends know I stutter. I can't hide my stuttering long enough.") These stutterers simply go ahead and speak without thinking about the consequences. As a result, particularly when speaking with persons who know their problem, they can be barely conscious of their stuttering.

> With Evelyn, if you asked me, I never stutter. If there was a tape recorder going it might show that I was stuttering. But I don't notice it and it doesn't bother me. I don't have any trouble talking to her on the phone unless others are there.

At the same time those who know stutterers well seem less conscious of their stuttering. Spouses and friends remarked:

> You know, since I've got to know you well, I hardly ever notice your stuttering.

> You know, sometimes I forget he stutters.

> I notice his stuttering only when others are present. I'm more conscious of it. At other times, I don't care.

Goffman (1963:81) argues that friends are less aware of a stigmatized person's problem because they are more familiar with the stigma. In the case of stuttering, however, what is critical is its obtrusiveness—"how much it interferes with the flow of interaction" (Goffman, 1963:49)— rather than mere visibility. When stutterers are with friends they feel less constrained to meet the exacting requirements which talk requires in other circumstances, because both parties develop idiosyncratic rules which enable them to become less dependent on such things as precise timing. For example, in telephone conversations between stutterers and their friends silences can cease to be interpreted as cues indicating the end of a speaking turn or a break in the telephone connection.

Once such understandings are developed stutterers feel less pressure to account for their problems or to work at concealing and controlling the "it"; thus, the sense of stuttering as a subjective presence wanes. For stutterers who learn to speak fluently by meticulously learning a new set of speech behaviors (Webster, 1975), the experience of stuttering as an "it" may fade away because with their speech under control there is no longer any need to account for stuttering.[3]

STRUGGLING WITH THE "IT"

Stutterers who find it difficult to conceal their stuttering face the additional problem of how to converse with people who take interruptions in the speech of stutterers as a signal to resume talking themselves. Stutterers attempt to avoid this by making two claims: first, that they are competent persons who understand the conventions of talk; and second, that they have not relinquished their speaking turn—even though they are lapsing into unusually long silences—and should be permitted to continue speaking uninterrupted. These claims are important to the stutterer because together they provide the basis for participation in conversation and for maintaining an acceptable identity. One way stutterers make these claims is by confronting a block "head on" and trying to force out the word or sound: a typical pattern is a deep breath followed by muscle tension and visible strain as the stutterer attempts to "break through" the interruption and regain control of speech. The late Japanese novelist Yukio Mishima (1959:5) vividly described this phenomenon: "When a stutterer is struggling desperately to utter his first sound he is like a little bird that is trying to extricate itself from thick lime."

By making visible the "I/it" conflict through struggle, stutterers demonstrate to those they are conversing with that they have not given up their speaking turn and are doing their utmost to limit the interruption in their speech. This process of ex-

ternalizing stuttering enables stutterers to share with others their experience of stuttering as a mysterious intrusive force. By demonstrating that their deviation from the conventions of speech is not intentional (Blum and McHugh, 1971; Goffman, 1963:128, 143; Mills, 1940) they hope to persuade others to bear with them and not to regard them as outsiders who reject, or do not understand, the norms others adhere to. The struggle that stutterers engage in is the "stigma symbol" (Goffman, 1963:46) that others recognize as stuttering. Struggle feeds into the troubles stutterers are trying to remedy in a classic vicious circle: stuttering is in part a product of attachment to the very social conventions that stutterers struggle to avoid breaking.

This analysis is supported by evidence that some members of the British upper classes view stuttering (or stammering as it is referred to in Britain) as a mark of distinction (Kazin, 1978:124; Shenker, 1970:112). They openly cultivate stuttering as a display of their superior social status and expect others to wait at their convenience. These persons make no apology for their stuttering and accordingly do not struggle with it to demonstrate its involuntary character. Consequently, their stuttering typically takes the form of a "slight stammer" characterized by relaxed repetitions and hesitations without any of the facial distortions associated with struggle.

VOLUNTARY DISCLOSURE

Like concealment, struggle also involves costs. Stuttering presents the listener with the problem of knowing how to sustain an interaction punctuated with silences, prolongations, and facial contortions. As one observer noted:

What am I supposed to do when a stutterer is struggling to say something? Should I help him by saying the word—because I usually know what he is trying to say—or am I supposed to wait? Then if you wait, what do you do? Am I supposed to watch him struggling? It can be awful. And then there is just no knowing what to do with the time. It can be a long wait. It's embarrassing.

One way stutterers deal with this, and with the fear of exposure in the case of concealment, is by voluntarily disclosing their stuttering (Van Riper, 1971:211) in much the same manner as epileptics (Schneider and Conrad, 1980).

> *The person who has an unapparent, negatively valued attribute often finds it expedient to begin an encounter with an unobtrusive admission of his own failing, especially with persons who are uninformed about him (Goffman, 1967:29).*

Stutterers who make public speeches may begin by referring to their problem so their audiences won't be unduly shocked. One university professor started off each term by talking about his stuttering and inviting students to ask questions about it. Another began his courses by deliberately stuttering, so that he would not create expectations of fluency that he might later fail to meet.

Stutterers sometimes indicate the involuntary nature of their disability by apologizing or by noting that their present stuttering is worse than usual. Through such tactics they, in effect, argue that the stigmatized and normal categories represent poles of a continuum, and that they are much further toward the normal end of this continuum than their present behavior would suggest. In doing so, stutterers typically take advantage of the fact that while struggling with some sound or word they can often make fluent asides which display their relative normality.

> *We went to the shh—shh—(s's always give me trouble)shh—show last night.*

> *I was talking to K—K—en (Wow! I had a hard time on that one) and he was saying....*

Other stutterers put listeners at ease with retrospective accounts such as, "Boy, I'm having a hard time today. I must be really tired."

Sometimes humor is used to anticipate and defuse confusion or embarrassment. One stutterer told people at informal gatherings to "go ahead and talk amongst yourselves if I take too long about saying anything." A teacher attempted to put his students at ease by inviting them to "take advantage of my stuttering to catch up on your note-taking."

Other stutterers use humor to claim more desirable identities for themselves.

> *I use humor a lot now. If I'm having a problem, I'll make a comment like, "Boy, it's a problem having a big mouth like mine and not being able to use it." When I'm having a hard time getting out a word in a store I'll say something like, "Three tries for a quarter." Once a waitress started guessing when I blocked giving my order and kept on guessing and guessing wrong. Every so often, I would smile and say, "You just keep guessing." Everyone was laughing but they were laughing at her, not me.*

Stutterers may also take a more aggressive stance. By pitting themselves against the listener, they indicate that they refuse to allow others to use their stuttering to belittle them. One of our respondents referred to this as the "fuck you, Mac" approach.

> *I challenge the listener. I can make a game out of it. I look them straight in the eye and in my mind tell them to "fuck off." I might stutter like hell, but so what. It doesn't make them any better than me.*

In using this strategy stutterers attempt to disavow the implications that they suspect others will draw about their lack of control over speech by displaying "cool." This strategy draws its impetus from the fear that many stutterers have that they will be seen as nervous and easily ruffled persons when they perceive themselves as normal persons in every respect other than their inability to control speech.

Another non-apologetic, but less aggressive, strategy that is occasionally used is one in which the stutterer systematically attempts to redefine stuttering as a "new and proud identity" (Schneider and Conrad, 1980:32) and to use this new identity as a means of getting stuttering "out of the closet" (M. Katz, 1968; Lambidakis, 1972). Some of our respondents reported that talking about their problem to new acquaintances proved to be a good way of gaining rapport. Revealing one's weakness to another can be a way of appearing honest, frank, and "more human." Others claimed that their efforts to overcome their "handicap" had strengthened their character. A few (e.g. Van Riper, Sheehan, and Douglass) have even used their personal experience of stuttering professionally, in therapy and research, to gain knowledge and rapport with patients and/or subjects. Even in occupations such as sales or journalism, where stuttering might ordinarily be seen to be a great handicap, some stutterers have used stuttering to their advantage. A Canadian journalist was said to have "disarmed" those he interviewed with his stuttering so that they were sympathetic toward him and unusually frank. A salesman had his business cards printed: "B-B-Bob G-G-Goldman the stuttering Toyota salesman."

Public figures sometimes use their stuttering as a trademark and a means to success. Some examples are the comedian "Stuttering Joe" Frisco, the humorist Patrick Campbell, and the country and western singer Mel Tillis. In his autobiography, Campbell (1967:212) reports how his stuttering on British television made him famous:

> While making the ginger ale commercials I looked upon my stammer as a nuisance that would have to be played down as much as possible if we weren't to have endless takes.... Although I didn't care to think about this aspect of it too much I did realize that my stammer fitted rather neatly into their campaign, the essence of which was never to mention the word 'Schweppes', but merely to mention the first syllable 'sch—', and that was quite enough for me in every way.
>
> It wasn't until nearly a year later [when asked to advertise butter] that I realized my mistake. [Again Campbell tried to control his stuttering. The producer called him aside and said] "I don't know quite how to put this—but could we have a little more of your trademark on the word 'butter'?"...I'd been trying to suppress the very thing it seemed that everyone wanted.

Reflecting on his "asset," Campbell claimed that while he tried to put the best possible light on it,

he never really became proud of his identity as a stutterer. The frequent and fleeting gains did not offset the losses that recurred day after day.

> If I was offered by some miraculous overnight cure the opportunity never to stammer again, I'd accept it without hesitation, even though it meant the end for me of television (1967:213).

DISAVOWAL

While stutterers sometimes try to put listeners at their ease by drawing attention to themselves, there are often circumstances in which they prefer to define their stuttering out of existence. To do this successfully, they need the tacit cooperation of their listeners. Both parties must share the assumption that the embarrassment and awkwardness associated with stuttering and attempts to control it are best dealt with by acting as if the stuttering were not happening. This provides a "phantom normalcy" (Goffman, 1963:122). By overlooking stuttering, both parties act as if "nothing unusual is happening" (Emerson, 1970) rather than acknowledge something which would require a response for which no shared guidelines exist. This tactic leaves intact the stutterer's status as a normal and competent person and the other's as a decent and tactful person who avoids needlessly embarrassing others. Tactful overlooking, as Safilios-Rothschild (1970:129) has suggested, is normatively prescribed:

> Regardless of any degree of aversion felt toward the disabled, the non-disabled are normatively not permitted to show these negative feelings in any way and their fear of making a verbal or a nonverbal "slip" indicating their emotions renders the interaction quite formal and rigid.

The importance of tacit disavowal of stuttering is indicated by the anxiety some stutterers feel when they enter a situation where they know it cannot, or will not, be ignored. Conversations with little children are one example.

> Children give me the hardest time. They know something is wrong and they don't hide it. My little

nephew embarrassed me terribly in front of the family. He said, "Your mouth moves funny." I tried to explain to him that I had something wrong with my mouth just like other people had something wrong with their ears or their eyes.

Another example is where stutterers are forced to watch and listen to themselves or others stuttering. Just as many fat people avoid scales and mirrors (Himelfarb and Evans, 1974:222), many stutterers shun mirrors and audio and video tape recorders. Similarly, stutterers are often uncomfortable watching others stutter. We witnessed stutterers in the speech clinic cover their faces with their hands or even walk out of the room rather than witness another person stutter. These attempts to distance themselves from stuttering appeared in some cases to be experienced as a disassociation of the body and the self through a loss or blurring of self-awareness. Stutterers talked of "slipping out of the situation" at the moment of stuttering and not being aware of what they or others were doing when they "returned." During these periods, stutterers experience a "time out" (Goffman, 1967:30; Scott and Lyman, 1968) from the situation. Time appears to stop so that when speech resumes it is as if the block did not occur. This sense of time having stopped, and of stuttering occurring outside the situation, is symbolized by the frozen poses stutterers sometimes adopt at the moment of stuttering: gestures are stopped, only to be resumed once speech continues. For example, one stutterer regularly "blocked" on a word just as he was about to tap the ash off his cigarette with his finger. During the few seconds he was "caught" in his block, his finger remained poised, frozen an inch or so above his cigarette. When he released the sound, the finger would simultaneously tap the ash into the ashtray.

Stutterers and their listeners manage time outs cooperatively by severing eye contact. Normally, people who are conversing indicate their attentiveness by facial expressions and eye contact, thereby reaffirming that they are listening and involved in the interaction. By breaking eye contact at the moment of stuttering, stutterers and their listeners jointly disengage from the conversation and exclude stuttering from the interaction. The moment fluent speech returns engagement is reestablished through a renewal of eye contact; the participants confirm their mutual subterfuge by acting as if nothing had happened. During time outs listeners may also confirm their disengagement by doing something unrelated, such as assuming an air of nonchalance, shuffling papers, glancing through a magazine or a book, fiddling with an object, or surveying the immediate surroundings. These signals indicate that the participants are not "in" the conversation.

While struggling to "get a word out" stutterers may avert their faces or hide their mouths with their hands. This phenomenon reveals an apparent difference in the social significance of sight and hearing. During this obscuring of the sight of stuttering, as with the time out, both parties are presumably aware that stuttering is taking place, and indeed that the stutterer is doing her or his best to "get past the block" and resume the conversation. Yet, at the same time, stuttering is denied. It is as if through the "thin disguises" (Goffman, 1963:81) which contradictory appearances provide it is possible to establish opposing social claims and thus "have one's cake and eat it too."

Time out, besides resolving the interactional problem of how to respond to stuttering, protects or hides one's vulnerability; it's much like the common response of averting your eyes when you accidentally see someone naked. Stutterers are, in a sense, "naked" at the moment of stuttering; they are without a mask, their front is crumbling and their "raw self" exposed (Goffman, 1963:16). Averting their eyes is a cue to the other to look away from the stutterer's "nakedness," thus saving both from embarrassment. The stutterers we interviewed expressed this sense of "nakedness" or vulnerability with descriptions such as "weak," "helpless," "like a little kid," and "with my shell removed." Some even said that at the point of stuttering they felt transparent. This can be related to the saying that the eyes are the mirror of the soul, which stems from the belief that the eyes reflect one's true feelings even though the rest of one's face may camouflage them.

Loss of eye contact gives stutterers time to recover their composure, manage the "unsatisfactory" image that has emerged, and, if possible, project a new image. Listeners have their own self to consider. Because they too may be held partly responsible for the stutterer's embarrassment, they can use loss of eye contact to indicate that they did not intend the embarrassment to happen and, above all, that they are not amused or uncomfortable.

While the tactic of mutual disavowal is usually a situational one the comment of one stutterer we interviewed indicates that in some cases it can be much more pervasive:

> Ever since I was a young child I can't remember my parents ever directly mentioning stuttering. It seemed obvious that they saw me stuttering, and they knew I stuttered, but they never said anything. The only incident I can remember is my father singing "K-K-Katy" a couple of times. I felt badly about that. Nothing direct was ever said, even by my brothers. My younger brother always gave me a lot of trouble. But he never mentioned stuttering once. I wondered if my parents told them not to say anything. My parents did make lots of references to me as nervous, sensitive, or different, and were always saying they were going to take me to the doctor for my nerves. But except for brief references on very few occasions, they never mentioned anything about stuttering.

In such cases, the disavowal of stigma is extended across entire situations. This requires others to tacitly agree to ignore the stigma in all encounters with the stigmatized person.

DISCUSSION

Our study of stuttering provides a vehicle to elaborate upon and extend the work of Davis, Goffman, Schneider and Conrad, and others on the strategic manipulation of awareness to manage potential stigma. The implications of our analysis also extend beyond stigma management to a consideration of the importance of the experiential dimension for the construction of social order. Because the stutterer finds problematic what others take for granted, the stutterer's social world is the world of everyman writ large.

In our consideration of stuttering we have developed three major lines of argument. First, our analysis shows the importance of considering subjective experience as well as behavior when studying the management of identity and the construction of interactional order. Stutterers engage in the ongoing creation of a subjective reality which at once shapes, and is shaped by, the management strategies they employ to regulate awareness of their disability and claim or disown identities. This consideration of the subjective experience of stuttering supports Jack Katz's (1972) argument that deviance theory should recognize that people sometimes perceive deviance as an inner essence independent of behavior. In addition, our analysis extends rather than simply elaborates upon Goffman's work, for though he writes of "ego" or "felt" identity, which he defines as "the subjective sense of [the stigmatized person's] own situation" (1963:105), he does not develop this concept.

Second, we have shown that the management of potential stigma can involve strategies conceived of, and executed, on a moment-to-moment basis, in addition to the premeditated strategies that have attracted most sociologists' attention. Advance planning was usually necessary where stutterers tried to conceal their problem through role avoidance. In speaking situations, management became more spontaneous: stutterers selected strategies in the light of opportunities and difficulties which arose in the course of interaction. In both cases, concealment strategies were marked by a high level of self-consciousness. When stutterers used openness or disavowal, however, only voluntary disclosure was consciously employed. Both struggling to overcome the "it" and time outs were non-calculated, though, especially in the latter case, stutterers were quick to recognize these tactics as coping and "restorative measures" (Goffman, 1963:128) once they were brought to their attention.

Finally, we have called attention to the fact that stutterers, like other stigmatized persons, seek to manage two interrelated, yet analytically distinguishable, problems. They are concerned both with preserving an acceptable identity and with preserving orderly interaction so that they can get on with the business of living. In exploring this issue we have shown how stutterers sometimes find themselves in situations in which it is not possible to simultaneously achieve both these objectives and thus are required to choose between them. The repertoire of tactics stutterers develop, and by implication the limits they place on their involvement in social life, depend on the importance they attach to these objectives.

NOTES

1. A good summary is provided in Bloodstein (1981:103). Some observers have reported an absence of stuttering among certain North American Midwest Indian tribes such as the Utes, the Shoshone, and the Bannock (Johnson, 1944, 1944b; Snidecor, 1947). Other studies (Clifford, 1965; Lemert, 1967:135; Sapir, 1915; Stewart, 1959; Van Riper, 1946) have noted that this is by no means true for all North American Indian tribes. Both Lemert and Stewart found that tribes (particularly those on the Pacific Northwest coast of Canada) which encouraged competition and stricter child-rearing practices, and which placed more emphasis on self-control, reported more instances of stuttering. Lemert (1967:146) also offered a similar explanation for a higher incidence of stuttering among Japanese than Polynesians.
2. See Goffman (1963:94) for a parallel between stutterers and the hard of hearing.
3. While fluency can be achieved and the sense of stuttering as an "it" can disappear, the continued maintenance of fluency is quite another matter. Time and again those who have achieved fluency—through whatever means—find themselves relapsing, even years later (Perkins, 1979; Sheehan, 1979, 1983).

REFERENCES

Becker, Howard S. 1963. *Outsiders: Studies in the Sociology of Deviance.* New York: The Free Press.

Bloodstein, Oliver. 1981. *A Handbook on Stuttering.* Chicago: National Easter Seal Society.

Blum, Alan and Peter McHugh. 1971. "The Social Ascription of Motives." *American Sociological Review,* 36 (February):98–109.

Campbell, Patrick. 1967. *My Life and Easy Times.* London: Anthony Blond.

Clifford, S. 1965. "Stuttering in South Dakota Indians." *Central States Speech Association Journal,* 26 (February):59–60.

Davis, Fred. 1961. "Deviance Disavowal: The Management of Strained Interaction by the Visibly Handicapped." *Social Problems,* 9 (Fall):120–132.

Douglass, Ernest, and Bruce Quarrington. 1952. "Differentiation of Interiorized and Exteriorized Secondary Stuttering." *Journal of Speech and Hearing Disorders,* 17 (December):377–385.

Emerson, Joan. 1970. "Nothing Unusual is Happening." In Thomas Shibutani (ed.), *Human Nature and Collective Behavior.* Englewood Cliffs, N.J.: Prentice-Hall, pp. 208–223.

Freidson, Eliot. 1965. "Disability as Social Deviance." In Marvin Sussman (ed.), *Sociology and Rehabilitation.* Washington, D.C.: American Sociological Association, pp. 71–99.

Goffman, Erving. 1963. *Stigma.* Englewood Cliffs, N.J.: Prentice-Hall.

———. 1967. *Interaction Ritual.* Garden City, N.Y.: Doubleday-Anchor.

Gustavson, Carl. 1944. "A Talisman and a Convalescence." *Quarterly Journal of Speech,* 30(1):465–471.

Higgins, Paul C. 1980. "Social Reaction and the Physically Disabled: Bringing the Impairment Back In." *Symbolic Interaction,* 3 (Spring):139–156.

Himelfarb, Alex and John Evans. 1974. "Deviance Disavowal and Stigma Management: A Study of Obesity." In Jack Haas and Bill Shaffir (eds.), *Decency and Deviance*. Toronto: McClelland and Stewart, pp. 221–232.

Johnson, Wendell. 1944a. "The Indian Has No Word for It: Part 1, Stuttering in Children." *Quarterly Journal of Speech*, 30 (October):330–337.

———. 1944b. "The Indian Has No Word for It: Part 2, Stuttering in Adults." *Quarterly Journal of Speech*, 30 (December):456–465.

———. 1959. *The Onset of Stuttering*. Minneapolis: University of Minneapolis Press.

Katz, Jack. 1972. "Deviance, Charisma, and Rule-defined Behavior." *Social Problems*, 20(2):186–202.

Katz, Murray. 1968. "Stuttering Power." *Journal of the Council of Adult Stutterers* (January):5.

Kazin, Alfred. 1978. *New York Jew*. New York: Random House.

Kitsuse, John I. 1980. "Coming Out All Over: Deviants and the Politics of Social Problems." *Social Problems*, 28 (October):1–13.

Lambidakis, Elenore. 1972. "Stutterers' Lib." *Journal of the Council of Adult Stutterers* (Winter):4–6.

Lemert, Edwin. 1967. *Human Deviance, Social Problems and Social Control*. Englewood Cliffs, N.J.: Prentice-Hall.

Mills, C. Wright. 1940. "Situated Action and Vocabularies of Motives." *American Sociological Review*, 5 (December):904–913.

Mishima, Yukio. 1959. *The Temple of the Golden Pavilion*. New York: A.A. Knopf.

Perkins, William. 1979. "From Psychoanalysis to Discoordination." In Hugo Gregory (ed.), *Controversies About Stuttering Therapy*. Baltimore: University Park Press, pp. 97–129.

Petrunik, Michael. 1974. "The Quest for Fluency: Fluency Variations and the Identity Problems and Management Strategies of Stutterers." In Jack Haas and Bill Shaffir (eds.), *Decency and Deviance*. Toronto: McClelland and Stewart, pp. 201–220.

———. 1977. "The Quest for Fluency: A Study of the Identity Problems and Management Strategies of Adult Stutterers and Some Suggestions for an Approach to Deviance Management." Unpublished Ph.D. dissertation, University of Toronto.

———. 1980. "Stutterers' Adaptations to Nonavoidance Therapy: Primary/Secondary Deviance Theory as a Professional Treatment Ideology." Paper presented at the annual meetings of the Society for the Study of Social Problems, New York, August.

———. 1982. "Telephone Troubles: Interactional Breakdown and Its Management by Stutterers and Their Listeners." *Symbolic Interaction*, 5 (Fall):299–310.

———. 1983. "Being Deviant: A Critique of the Neglect of the Experiential Dimension in Sociological Constructions of Deviance." Paper presented at the annual meetings of the Society for the Study of Social Problems, Detroit, August.

Safilios-Rothschild, Constantina. 1970. *The Sociology and Social Psychology of Disability and Rehabilitation*. New York: Random House.

Sapir, Edward. 1915. *Abnormal Types of Speech in Nootka*. Canadian Geological Survey, Memoir 62, Anthropological Series No. 5. Ottawa: Government Printing Bureau.

Schneider, Joseph W. and Peter Conrad. 1980. "In the Closet with Illness: Epilepsy, Stigma Potential, and Information Control." *Social Problems*, 28 (October):32–44.

Scott, Marvin B. and Stanford Lyman. 1968. "Accounts." *American Sociological Review*, 33 (February):44–62.

Sheehan, Joseph. 1979. "Current Issues on Stuttering Recovery." In Hugo Gregory (ed.), *Controversies About Stuttering Therapy*. Baltimore: University Park Press, pp. 175–209.

———. 1983. "Invitation to Relapse." *The Journal*, National Council on Stuttering (Summer):16–20.

Shenker, Israel. 1970. "Stammer Becomes Fashionable." *Globe and Mail* (Toronto), November 12:12.

Snidecor, John. 1947. "Why the Indian Does Not Stutter." *Quarterly Journal of Speech*, 33 (December):493–495.

Stewart, Joseph. 1959. "The Problem of Stuttering in Certain North American Societies." *Journal of Speech and Hearing Disorders* (Monograph Supplement 6):1–87.

Van Riper, Charles. 1946. "Speech Defects among the Kalabash." *Marquette County Historical Society*, 8 (December):308–322.

———. 1971. *The Nature of Stuttering*. Englewood Cliffs, N.J.: Prentice-Hall.

Webster, Ronald. 1975. *The Precision Fluency Shaping Program: Speech Reconstruction for Stutterers*. Roanoke, Virginia: Communication Development Corporation.

Rapists' Vocabulary of Motives

DIANA SCULLY and JOSEPH MAROLLA

Psychiatry has dominated the literature on rapists since "irresistible impulse" (Glueck, 1925:323) and "disease of the mind" (Glueck, 1925:243) were introduced as the causes of rape. Research has been based on small samples of men, frequently the clinicians' own patient population. Not surprisingly, the medical model has predominated: rape is viewed as an individualistic, idiosyncratic symptom of a disordered personality. That is, rape is assumed to be a psychopathologic problem and individual rapists are assumed to be "sick." However, advocates of this model have been unable to isolate a typical or even predictable pattern of symptoms that are causally linked to rape. Additionally, research has demonstrated that fewer than 5 percent of rapists were psychotic at the time of their rape (Abel *et al.*, 1980).

We view rape as behavior learned socially through interaction with others; convicted rapists have learned the attitudes and actions consistent with sexual aggression against women. Learning also includes the acquisition of culturally derived vocabularies of motive, which can be used to diminish responsibility and to negotiate a non-deviant identity.

Sociologists have long noted that people can, and do, commit acts they define as wrong and, having done so, engage various techniques to disavow deviance and present themselves as normal. Through the concept of "vocabulary of motive," Mills (1940:904) was among the first to shed light on this seemingly perplexing contradiction.

Excerpt from "Convicted Rapists' Vocabulary of Motive: Excuses and Justifications," *Social Problems,* Vol. 31, No. 5 (June 1984), pp. 530–544, by permission of the Society for the Study of Social Problems and the authors.

This research was supported by a grant (R01 MH33013) from the National Center For the Prevention and Control of Rape, National Institute of Mental Health. The authors thank the Virginia Department of Corrections for their cooperation and assistance in this research.

Wrong-doers attempt to reinterpret their actions through the use of a linguistic device by which norm-breaking conduct is socially interpreted. That is, anticipating the negative consequences of their behavior, wrong-doers attempt to present the act in terms that are both culturally appropriate and acceptable.

Following Mills, a number of sociologists have focused on the types of techniques employed by actors in problematic situations (Hall and Hewitt, 1970; Hewitt and Hall, 1973; Hewitt and Stokes, 1975; Sykes and Matza, 1957). Scott and Lyman (1968) describe excuses and justifications, linguistic "accounts" that explain and remove culpability for an untoward act after it has been committed. *Excuses* admit the act was bad or inappropriate but deny full responsibility, often through appeals to accident, or biological drive, or through scapegoating. In contrast, *justifications* accept responsibility for the act but deny that it was wrong—that is, they show in this situation the act was appropriate. *Accounts* are socially approved vocabularies that neutralize an act or its consequences and are always a manifestation of an underlying negotiation of identity.

Stokes and Hewitt (1976:837) use the term "aligning actions" to refer to those tactics and techniques used by actors when some feature of a situation is problematic. Stated simply, the concept refers to an actor's attempt, through various means, to bring his or her conduct into alignment with culture. Culture in this sense is conceptualized as a "set of cognitive constraints—objects—to which people must relate as they form lines of conduct" (1976:837), and includes physical constraints, expectations and definitions of others, and personal biography. Carrying out aligning actions implies both awareness of those elements of normative culture that are applicable to the deviant act and, in addition, an actual effort to bring the act into line with this awareness. The result is that deviant behavior is legitimized.

This paper presents an analysis of interviews we conducted with a sample of 114 convicted, incarcerated rapists. We use the concept of accounts (Scott and Lyman, 1968) as a tool to organize and analyze the vocabularies of motive which this group of rapists used to explain themselves and their actions. An analysis of their accounts demonstrates how it was possible for 83 percent (n = 114)[1] of these convicted rapists to view themselves as non-rapists.

When rapists' accounts are examined, a typology emerges that consists of admitters and deniers. Admitters (n = 47) acknowledged that they had forced sexual acts on their victims and defined the behavior as rape. In contrast, deniers[2] either eschewed sexual contact or all association with the victim (n = 35),[3] or admitted to sexual acts but did not define their behavior as rape (n = 32).

The remainder of this paper is divided into two sections. In the first, we discuss the accounts which the rapists used to justify their behavior. In the second, we discuss those accounts which attempted to excuse the rape. By and large, the deniers used justifications while the admitters used excuses. In some cases, both groups relied on the same themes, stereotypes, and images: some admitters, like most deniers, claimed that women enjoyed being raped. Some deniers excused their behavior by referring to alcohol or drug use, although they did so quite differently than admitters. Through these narrative accounts, we explore convicted rapists' own perceptions of their crimes.

METHODS AND VALIDITY

From September, 1980, through September, 1981, we interviewed 114 male convicted rapists who were incarcerated in seven maximum or medium security prisons in the Commonwealth of Virginia. All of the rapists had been convicted of the rape or attempted rape (n = 8) of an adult woman, although a few had teenage victims as well. Men convicted of incest, statutory rape, or sodomy of a male were omitted from the sample.

Twelve percent of the rapists had been convicted of more than one rape or attempted rape, 39 percent also had convictions for burglary or robbery, 29 percent for abduction, 25 percent for sodomy, and 11 percent for first or second degree murder. Eighty-two percent had a previous criminal history but only 23 percent had records for previous sex offenses. Their sentences for rape and accompanying crimes ranged from 10 years to an accumulation by one man of seven life sentences plus 380 years; 43 percent of the rapists were serving from 10 to 30 years and 22 percent were serving at least one life term. Forty-six percent of the rapists were white and 54 percent were black. Their ages ranged from 18 to 60 years; 88 percent were between 18 and 35 years. Forty-two percent were either married or cohabiting at the time of their offense. Only 20 percent had a high school education or better, and 85 percent came from working-class backgrounds. Despite the popular belief that rape is due to a personality disorder, only 26 percent of these rapists had any history of emotional problems. When the rapists in this study were compared to a statistical profile of felons in all Virginia prisons, prepared by the Virginia Department of Corrections, rapists who volunteered for this research were disproportionately white, somewhat better educated, and younger than the average inmate.

All participants in this study were volunteers. We sent a letter to every inmate (n = 3500) at each of the seven prisons. The letters introduced us as professors at a local university, described our research as a study of men's attitudes toward sexual behavior and women, outlined our procedures for ensuring confidentiality, and solicited volunteers from all criminal categories. Using one follow-up letter, approximately 25 percent of all inmates, including rapists, indicated their willingness to be interviewed by mailing an information sheet to us at the university. From this pool of volunteers, we constructed a sample of rapists based on age, education, race, severity of current offenses, and previous criminal records. Obviously, the sample was not random and thus may not be representative of all rapists.

Each of the authors—one woman and one man—interviewed half of the rapists. Both authors were able to establish rapport and obtain information. However, the rapists volunteered more about their feelings and emotions to the female author and her interviews lasted longer.

All rapists were given an 89-page interview, which included a general background, psychological, criminal, and sexual history, attitude scales, and 30 pages of open-ended questions intended to explore their perceptions of their crimes, their victims, and themselves. Because a voice print is an absolute source of identification, we did not use tape recorders. All interviews were hand recorded. With some practice, we found it was possible to record much of the interview verbatim. While hand recording inevitably resulted in some lost data, it did have the advantage of eliciting more confidence and candor in the men.

Interviews with the rapists lasted from three hours to seven hours; the average was about four-and-one-half hours. Most of the rapists were reluctant to end the interview. Once rapport had been established, the men wanted to talk, even though it sometimes meant, for example, missing a meal.

Because of the reputation prison inmates have for 'conning,' validity was a special concern in our research. Although the purpose of the research was to obtain the men's own perceptions of their acts, it was also necessary to establish the extent to which these perceptions deviated from other descriptions of their crimes. To establish validity, we used the same technique others have used in prison research: comparing factual information, including details of the crime, obtained in the interview with pre-sentence reports on file at the prisons (Athens, 1977; Luckenbill, 1977; Queen's Bench Foundation, 1976). Pre-sentence reports, written by a court worker at the time of conviction, usually include general background

information, a psychological evaluation, the offender's version of the details of the crime, and the victim's or police's version of the details of the crime. Using these records allowed us to clarify two important issues: first, the amount of change that had occurred in rapists' accounts from pre-sentencing to the time when we interviewed them; and, second, the amount of discrepancy between rapists' accounts, as told to us, and the victims' and/or police versions of the crime, contained in the pre-sentence reports.

The time between pre-sentence reports and our interviews (in effect, the amount of time rapists had spent in prison before we interviewed them) ranged from less than one year to 20 years; the average was three years. Yet despite this time lapse, there were no significant changes in the way rapists explained their crimes, with the exception of 18 men who had denied their crimes at their trials but admitted them to us. There were no cases of men who admitted their crime at their trial but denied them when talking to us.

However, there were major differences between the accounts we heard of the crimes from rapists and the police's and victim's versions. Admitters (including deniers turned admitters) told us essentially the same story as the police and victim versions. However, the admitters subtly understated the force they had used and, though they used words such as *violent* to describe their acts, they also omitted reference to the more brutal aspects of their crime.

In contrast, deniers' interview accounts differed significantly from victim and police versions. According to the pre-sentence reports, 11 of the 32 deniers had been acquainted with their victim. But an additional four deniers told us they had been acquainted with their victims. In the pre-sentence reports, police or victim versions of the crime described seven rapes in which the victim had been hitchhiking or was picked up in a bar; but deniers told us this was true of 20 victims. Weapons were present in 21 of the 32 rapes according to the pre-sentence reports, yet only nine men acknowledged the presence of a weapon and only two of the nine admitted they had used it to threaten or intimidate their victim. Finally, in at least seven of the rapes, the victim had been seriously injured,[4] but only three men admitted injury. In two of the three cases, the victim had been murdered; in these cases the men denied the rape but not the murder. Indeed, deniers constructed accounts for us which, by implicating the victim, made their own conduct appear to have been more appropriate. They never used words such as *violent,* choosing instead to emphasize the sexual component of their behavior.

It should be noted that we investigated the possibility that deniers claimed their behavior was not criminal because, in contrast to admitters, their crimes resembled what research has found the public define as a controversial rape, that is, victim an acquaintance, no injury or weapon, victim picked up hitchhiking or in a bar (Burt, 1980; Burt and Albin, 1981; Williams, 1979).... [T]he crimes committed by deniers were only slightly more likely to involve these elements.

This contrast between pre-sentence reports and interviews suggests several significant factors related to interview content validity. First, when asked to explain their behavior, our sample of convicted rapists (except deniers turned admitters) responded with accounts that had changed surprisingly little since their trials. Second, admitters' interview accounts were basically the same as others' versions of their crimes, while deniers systematically put more blame on the victims.

JUSTIFYING RAPE

Deniers attempted to justify their behavior by presenting the victim in a light that made her appear culpable, regardless of their own actions. Five themes run through attempts to justify their rapes: (1) women as seductresses; (2) women mean "yes" when they say "no"; (3) most women eventually relax and enjoy it; (4) nice girls don't get raped; and (5) guilty of a minor wrongdoing.

WOMEN AS SEDUCTRESSES

Men who rape need not search far for cultural language which supports the premise that women provoke or are responsible for rape. In addition to common cultural stereotypes, the fields of psychiatry and criminology (particularly the subfield of victimology) have traditionally provided justifications for rape, often by portraying raped women as the victims of their own seduction (Albin, 1977; Marolla and Scully, 1979). For example, Hollander (1924:130) argues:

> Considering the amount of illicit intercourse, rape of women is very rare indeed. Flirtation and provocative conduct, i.e. tacit (if not actual) consent is generally the prelude to intercourse.

Since women are supposed to be coy about their sexual availability, refusal to comply with a man's sexual demands lacks meaning and rape appears normal. The fact that violence and, often, a weapon are used to accomplish the rape is not considered. As an example, Abrahamsen (1960:61) writes:

> The conscious or unconscious biological or psychological attraction between man and woman does not exist only on the part of the offender toward the woman but, also, on her part toward him, which in many instances may, to some extent, be the impetus for his sexual attack. Often a women [sic] unconsciously wishes to be taken by force— consider the theft of the bride in Peer Gynt.

Like Peer Gynt, the deniers we interviewed tried to demonstrate that their victims were willing and, in some cases, enthusiastic participants. In these accounts, the rape became more dependent upon the victim's behavior than upon their own actions.

Thirty-one percent (n = 10) of the deniers presented an extreme view of the victim. Not only willing, she was the aggressor, a seductress who lured them, unsuspecting, into sexual action. Typical was a denier convicted of his first rape and accompanying crimes of burglary, sodomy, and abduction. According to the pre-sentence reports, he had broken into the victim's house and raped her at knife point. While he admitted to the breaking and entry, which he claimed was for altruistic purposes ("to pay for the prenatal care of a friend's girlfriend"), he also argued that when the victim discovered him, he had tried to leave but she had asked him to stay. Telling him that she cheated on her husband, she had voluntarily removed her clothes and seduced him. She was, according to him, an exemplary sex partner who "enjoyed it very much and asked for oral sex.[5] Can I have it now?" he reported her as saying. He claimed they had spent hours in bed, after which the victim had told him he was good looking and asked to see him again. "Who would believe I'd meet a fellow like this?" he reported her as saying.

In addition to this extreme group, 25 percent (n = 8) of the deniers said the victim was willing and had made some sexual advances. An additional 9 percent (n = 3) said the victim was willing to have sex for money or drugs. In two of these three cases, the victim had been either an acquaintance or picked up, which the rapists said led them to expect sex.

WOMEN MEAN "YES" WHEN THEY SAY "NO"

Thirty-four percent (n = 11) of the deniers described their victim as unwilling, at least initially, indicating either that she had resisted or that she had said no. Despite this, and even though (according to pre-sentence reports) a weapon had been present in 64 percent (n = 7) of these 11 cases, the rapists justified their behavior by arguing that either the victim had not resisted enough or that her "no" had really meant "yes." For example, one denier who was serving time for a previous rape was subsequently convicted of attempting to rape a prison hospital nurse. He insisted he had actually completed the second rape, and said of his victim: "She semi-struggled but deep down inside I think she felt it was a fantasy come true." The nurse, according to him, had asked a question about his conviction for rape, which he interpreted as teasing. "It was like she

was saying, 'rape me'." Further, he stated that she had helped him along with oral sex and "from her actions, she was enjoying it." In another case, a 34-year-old man convicted of abducting and raping a 15-year-old teenager at knife point as she walked on the beach, claimed it was a pickup. This rapist said women like to be overpowered before sex, but to dominate after it begins.

> A man's body is like a coke bottle, shake it up, put your thumb over the opening and feel the tension. When you take a woman out, woo her, then she says "no, I'm a nice girl," you have to use force. All men do this. She said "no" but it was a societal no, she wanted to be coaxed. All women say "no" when they mean "yes" but its a societal no, so they won't have to feel responsible later.

Claims that the victim didn't resist or, if she did, didn't resist enough, were also used by 24 percent (n = 11) of admitters to explain why, during the incident, they believed the victim was willing and that they were not raping. These rapists didn't redefine their acts until some time after the crime. For example, an admitter who used a bayonet to threaten his victim, an employee of the store he had been robbing, stated:

> At the time I didn't think it was rape. I just asked her nicely and she didn't resist. I never considered prison. I just felt like I had met a friend. It took about five years of reading and going to school to change my mind about whether it was rape. I became familiar with the subtlety of violence. But at the time, I believed that as long as I didn't hurt anyone it wasn't wrong. At the time, I didn't think I would go to prison, I thought I would beat it.

Another typical case involved a gang rape in which the victim was abducted at knife point as she walked home about midnight. According to two of the rapists, both of whom were interviewed, at the time they had thought the victim had willingly accepted a ride from the third rapist (who was not interviewed). They claimed the victim didn't resist and one reported her as saying she would do anything if they would take her home. In this rapist's view, "She acted like she enjoyed it, but maybe she was just acting. She wasn't crying, she was engaging in it." He reported that she had been friendly to the rapist who abducted her and, claiming not to have a home phone, she gave him her office number—a tactic eventually used to catch the three. In retrospect, this young man had decided, "She was scared and just relaxed and enjoyed it to avoid getting hurt." Note, however, that while he had redefined the act as rape, he continued to believe she enjoyed it.

Men who claimed to have been unaware that they were raping viewed sexual aggression as a man's prerogative at the time of the rape. Thus they regarded their act as little more than a minor wrongdoing even though most possessed or used a weapon. As long as the victim survived without major physical injury, from their perspective, a rape had not taken place. Indeed, even U.S. courts have often taken the position that physical injury is a necessary ingredient for a rape conviction.

MOST WOMEN EVENTUALLY RELAX AND ENJOY IT

Many of the rapists expected us to accept the image, drawn from cultural stereotype, that once the rape began, the victim relaxed and enjoyed it.[6] Indeed, 69 percent (n = 22) of deniers justified their behavior by claiming not only that the victim was willing, but also that she enjoyed herself, in some cases to an immense degree. Several men suggested that they had fulfilled their victims' dreams. Additionally, while most admitters used adjectives such as "dirty," "humiliated," and "disgusted," to describe how they thought rape made women feel, 20 percent (n = 9) believed that their victim enjoyed herself. For example, one denier had posed as a salesman to gain entry to his victim's house. But he claimed he had had a previous sexual relationship with the victim, that she agreed to have sex for drugs, and that the opportunity to have sex with him produced "a glow, because she was really into oral stuff and fascinated by the idea of sex with a black man. She felt satisfied, fulfilled, wanted me to stay, but I didn't want her." In another case, a denier who had broken into his victim's house but who insisted the victim was his lover and let him in voluntarily, declared "She felt good, kept kissing me and wanted me to stay the night. She felt proud after sex with me." And another denier, who had hid in his victim's closet and later attacked her while she slept, argued that while she was scared at first, "once we got into it, she was ok." He continued to believe he hadn't committed rape because "she enjoyed it and it was like she consented."

NICE GIRLS DON'T GET RAPED

The belief that "nice girls don't get raped" affects perception of fault. The victim's reputation, as well as characteristics or behavior which violate normative sex role expectations, are perceived as contributing to the commission of the crime. For example, Nelson and Amir (1975) defined hitch-hike rape as a victim-precipitated offense.

In our study, 69 percent (n = 22) of deniers and 22 percent (n = 10) of admitters referred to their victims' sexual reputation, thereby evoking the stereotype that "nice girls don't get raped." They claimed that the victim was known to have been a prostitute, or a "loose" woman, or to have had a lot of affairs, or to have given birth to a child out of wedlock. For example, a denier who claimed he had picked up his victim while she was hitchhiking stated, "To be honest, we [his family] knew she was a damn whore and whether she screwed one or 50 guys didn't matter." According to pre-sentence reports this victim didn't know her attacker and he abducted her at knife point from the street. In another case, a denier who claimed to have known his victim by reputation stated:

> If you wanted drugs or a quick piece of ass, she would do it. In court she said she was a virgin, but I could tell during sex [rape] that she was very experienced.

When other types of discrediting biographical information were added to these sexual slurs, a total of 78 percent (n = 25) of the deniers used the victim's reputation to substantiate their accounts. Most frequently, they referred to the victim's emotional state or drug use. For example, one denier claimed his victim had been known to be loose and, additionally, had turned state's evidence against her husband to put him in prison and save herself from a burglary conviction. Further, he asserted that she had met her current boyfriend, who was himself in and out of prison, in a drug rehabilitation center where they were both clients.

Evoking the stereotype that women provoke rape by the way they dress, a description of the victim as seductively attired appeared in the accounts of 22 percent (n = 7) of deniers and 17 percent (n = 8) of admitters. Typically, these descriptions were used to substantiate their claims about the victim's reputation. Some men went to extremes to paint a tarnished picture of the victim, describing her as dressed in tight black clothes and without a bra; in one case, the victim was portrayed as sexually provocative in dress and carriage. Not only did she wear short skirts, but she was observed to "spread her legs while getting out of cars." Not all of the men attempted to assassinate their victim's reputation with equal vengeance. Numerous times they made subtle and offhand remarks like, "She was a waitress and you know how they are."

The intent of these discrediting statements is clear. Deniers argued that the woman was a "legitimate" victim who got what she deserved. For example, one denier stated that all of his victims had been prostitutes; pre-sentence reports indicated they were not. Several times during his interview, he referred to them as "dirty sluts," and argued "anything I did to them was justified." Deniers also claimed their victim had wrongly accused them and was the type of woman who would perjure herself in court.

ONLY A MINOR WRONGDOING

The majority of deniers did not claim to be completely innocent and they also accepted some accountability for their actions. Only 16 percent (n = 5) of deniers argued that they were totally free of blame. Instead, the majority of deniers pleaded guilty to a lesser charge. That is, they obfuscated the rape by pleading guilty to a less serious, more acceptable charge. They accepted being over-sexed, accused of poor judgment or trickery, even some violence, or guilty of adultery or contributing to the delinquency of a minor, charges that are hardly the equivalent of rape.

Typical of this reasoning is a denier who met his victim in a bar when the bartender asked him if he would try to repair her stalled car. After attempting unsuccessfully, he claimed the victim drank with him and later accepted a ride. Out riding, he pulled into a deserted area "to see how my luck would go." When the victim resisted his advances, he beat her and he stated:

> I did something stupid. I pulled a knife on her and I hit her as hard as I would hit a man. But I shouldn't be in prison for what I did. I shouldn't have all this time [sentence] for going to bed with a broad.

This rapist continued to believe that while the knife was wrong, his sexual behavior was justified.

In another case, the denier claimed he picked up his under-age victim at a party and that she voluntarily went with him to a motel. According to pre-sentence reports, the victim had been abducted at knife point from a party. He explained:

> After I paid for a motel, she would have to have sex but I wouldn't use a weapon. I would have explained. I spent money and, if she still said no, I would have forced her. If it had happened that way, it would have been rape to some people but not to my way of thinking. I've done that kind of thing before. I'm guilty of sex and contributing to the delinquency of a minor, but not rape.

In sum, deniers argued that, while their behavior may not have been completely proper, it should not have been considered rape. To accomplish this, they attempted to discredit and blame the victim while presenting their own actions as justified in the context. Not surprisingly, none of the deniers thought of himself as a rapist. A minority of the admitters attempted to lessen the impact of their crime by claiming the victim enjoyed being raped. But despite this similarity, the nature and tone of admitters' and deniers' accounts were essentially different.

EXCUSING RAPE

In stark contrast to deniers, admitters regarded their behavior as morally wrong and beyond justification. They blamed themselves rather than the victim, although some continued to cling to the belief that the victim had contributed to the crime somewhat, for example, by not resisting enough.

Several of the admitters expressed the view that rape was an act of such moral outrage that it was unforgivable. Several admitters broke into tears at intervals during their interviews. A typical sentiment was,

> I equate rape with someone throwing you up against a wall and tearing your liver and guts out of you.... Rape is worse than murder...and I'm disgusting.

Another young admitter frequently referred to himself as repulsive and confided:

> I'm in here for rape and in my own mind, it's the most disgusting crime, sickening. When people see me and know, I get sick.

Admitters tried to explain their crime in a way that allowed them to retain a semblance of moral integrity. Thus, in contrast to deniers' justifications, admitters used excuses to explain how they were compelled to rape. These excuses appealed to the existence of forces outside of the rapists' control. Through the use of excuses, they attempted to demonstrate that either intent was absent or responsibility was diminished. This allowed them to admit rape while reducing the threat to their identity as a moral person. Excuses also permitted them to view their behavior as idiosyncratic rather than typical and, thus, to believe they were not "re-

ally" rapists. Three themes run through these accounts: (1) the use of alcohol and drugs; (2) emotional problems; and (3) nice guy image.

THE USE OF ALCOHOL AND DRUGS

A number of studies have noted a high incidence of alcohol and drug consumption by convicted rapists prior to their crime (Groth, 1979; Queen's Bench Foundation, 1976). However, more recent research has tentatively concluded that the connection between substance use and crime is not as direct as previously thought (Ladouceur, 1983). Another facet of alcohol and drug use mentioned in the literature is its utility in disavowing deviance. McCaghy (1968) found that child molesters used alcohol as a technique for neutralizing their deviant identity. Marolla and Scully (1979), in a review of psychiatric literature, demonstrated how alcohol consumption is applied differently as a vocabulary of motive. Rapists can use alcohol both as an excuse for their behavior and to discredit the victim and make her more responsible. We found the former common among admitters and the latter common among deniers.

Alcohol and/or drugs were mentioned in the accounts of 77 percent (n = 30) of admitters and 84 percent (n = 21) of deniers and both groups were equally likely to have acknowledged consuming a substance—admitters, 77 percent (n = 30); deniers, 72 percent (n = 18). However, admitters said they had been affected by the substance; if not the cause of their behavior, it was at least a contributing factor. For example, an admitter who estimated his consumption to have been eight beers and four "hits of acid" reported:

> Straight, I don't have the guts to rape. I could fight a man but not that. To say, "I'm going to do it to a woman," knowing it will scare and hurt her, takes guts or you have to be sick.

Another admitter believed that his alcohol and drug use,

> ...brought out what was already there but in such intensity it was uncontrollable. Feelings of being

dominant, powerful, using someone for my own gratification, all rose to the surface.

In contrast, deniers' justifications required that they not be substantially impaired. To say that they had been drunk or high would cast doubt on their ability to control themself or to remember events as they actually happened. Consistent with this, when we asked if the alcohol and/or drugs had had an effect on their behavior, 69 percent (n = 27) of admitters, but only 40 percent (n = 10) of deniers, said they had been affected.

Even more interesting were references to the victim's alcohol and/or drug use. Since admitters had already relieved themselves of responsibility through claims of being drunk or high, they had nothing to gain from the assertion that the victim had used or been affected by alcohol and/or drugs. On the other hand, it was very much in the interest of deniers to declare that their victim had been intoxicated or high: that fact lessened her credibility and made her more responsible for the act. Reflecting these observations, 72 percent (n = 18) of deniers and 26 percent (n = 10) of admitters maintained that alcohol or drugs had been consumed by the victim. Further, while 56 percent (n = 14) of deniers declared she had been affected by this use, only 15 percent (n = 6) of admitters made a similar claim. Typically, deniers argued that the alcohol and drugs had sexually aroused their victim or rendered her out of control. For example, one denier insisted that his victim had become hysterical from drugs, not from being raped, and it was because of the drugs that she had reported him to the police. In addition, 40 percent (n = 10) of deniers argued that while the victim had been drunk or high, they themselves either hadn't ingested or weren't affected by alcohol and/or drugs. None of the admitters made this claim. In fact, in all of the 15 percent (n = 6) of cases where an admitter said the victim was drunk or high, he also admitted to being similarly affected.

These data strongly suggest that whatever role alcohol and drugs play in sexual and other types of violent crime, rapists have learned the ad-vantage to be gained from using alcohol and drugs as an account. Our sample were aware that their victim would be discredited and their own behavior excused or justified by referring to alcohol and/or drugs.

EMOTIONAL PROBLEMS

Admitters frequently attributed their acts to emotional problems. Forty percent (n = 19) of admitters said they believed an emotional problem had been at the root of their rape behavior, and 33 percent (n = 15) specifically related the problem to an unhappy, unstable childhood or a marital-domestic situation. Still others claimed to have been in a general state of unease. For example, one admitter said that at the time of the rape he had been depressed, feeling he couldn't do anything right, and that something had been missing from his life. But he also added, "being a rapist is not part of my personality." Even admitters who could locate no source for an emotional problem evoked the popular image of rapists as the product of disordered personalities to argue they also must have problems:

The fact that I'm a rapist makes me different. Rapists aren't all there. They have problems. It was wrong so there must be a reason why I did it. I must have a problem.

Our data do indicate that a precipitating event, involving an upsetting problem of everyday living, appeared in the accounts of 80 percent (n = 38) of admitters and 25 percent (n = 8) of deniers. Of those experiencing a precipitating event, including deniers, 76 percent (n = 35) involved a wife or girlfriend. Over and over, these men described themselves as having been in a rage because of an incident involving a woman with whom they believed they were in love.

Frequently, the upsetting event was related to a rigid and unrealistic double standard for sexual conduct and virtue which they applied to "their" woman but which they didn't expect from men, didn't apply to themselves, and, obviously, didn't honor in other women. To discover that the "pedestal" didn't apply to their wife or girlfriend sent them into a fury. One especially articulate and typical admitter described his feeling as follows. After serving a short prison term for auto theft, he married his "childhood sweetheart" and secured a well-paying job. Between his job and the volunteer work he was doing with an ex-offender group, he was spending long hours away from home, a situation that had bothered his wife. In response to her request, he gave up his volunteer work, though it was clearly meaningful to him. Then, one day, he discovered his wife with her former boyfriend "and my life fell apart." During the next several days, he said his anger had made him withdraw into himself and, after three days of drinking in a motel room, he abducted and raped a stranger. He stated:

> My parents have been married for many years and I had high expectations about marriage. I put my wife on a pedestal. When I walked in on her, I felt like my life had been destroyed, it was such a shock. I was bitter and angry about the fact that I hadn't done anything to my wife for cheating. I didn't want to hurt her [victim], only to scare and degrade her.

It is clear that many admitters, and a minority of deniers, were under stress at the time of their rapes. However, their problems were ordinary—the types of upsetting events that everyone experiences at some point in life. The overwhelming majority of the men were not clinically defined as mentally ill in court-ordered psychiatric examinations prior to their trials. Indeed, our sample is consistent with Abel *et al.* (1980) who found fewer than 5 percent of rapists were psychotic at the time of their offense.

As with alcohol and drug intoxication, a claim of emotional problems works differently depending upon whether the behavior in question is being justified or excused. It would have been counter-productive for deniers to have claimed to have had emotional problems at the time of the rape. Admitters used psychological explanations

to portray themselves as having been temporarily "sick" at the time of the rape. Sick people are usually blamed for neither the cause of their illness nor for acts committed while in that state of diminished capacity. Thus, adopting the sick role removed responsibility by excusing the behavior as having been beyond the ability of the individual to control. Since the rapists were not "themselves," the rape was idiosyncratic rather than typical behavior. Admitters asserted a non-deviant identity despite their self-proclaimed disgust with what they had done. Although admitters were willing to assume the sick role, they did not view their problem as a chronic condition, nor did they believe themselves to be insane or permanently impaired. Said one admitter, who believed that he needed psychological counseling: "I have a mental disorder, but I'm not crazy." Instead, admitters viewed their "problem" as mild, transient, and curable. Indeed, part of the appeal of this excuse was that not only did it relieve responsibility, but, as with alcohol and drug addiction, it allowed the rapist to "recover." Thus, at the time of their interviews, only 31 percent (n = 14) of admitters indicated that "being a rapist" was part of their self-concept. Twenty-eight percent (n = 13) of admitters stated they had never thought of themselves as rapists, 8 percent (n = 4) said they were unsure, and 33 percent (n = 16) asserted they had been a rapist at one time but now were recovered. A multiple "exrapist," who believed his "problem" was due to "something buried in my subconscious" that was triggered when his girlfriend broke up with him, expressed a typical opinion:

> I was a rapist, but not now. I've grown up, had to live with it. I've hit the bottom of the well and it can't get worse. I feel born again to deal with my problems.

NICE GUY IMAGE

Admitters attempted to further neutralize their crime and negotiate a non-rapist identity by painting an image of themselves as a "nice guy." Admitters projected the image of someone who had made a serious mistake but, in every other respect, was a decent person. Fifty-seven percent (n = 27) expressed regret and sorrow for their victim, indicating that they wished there were a way to apologize for or amend their behavior. For example, a participant in a rape-murder, who insisted his partner did the murder, confided, "I wish there was something I could do besides saying 'I'm sorry, I'm sorry.' I live with it 24 hours a day and, sometimes, I wake up crying in the middle of the night because of it."

Schlenker and Darby (1981) explain the significance of apologies beyond the obvious expression of regret. An apology allows a person to admit guilt while at the same time seeking a pardon by signalling that the event should not be considered a fair representation of what the person is really like. An apology separates the bad self from the good self, and promises more acceptable behavior in the future. When apologizing, an individual is attempting to say: "I have repented and should be forgiven," thus making it appear that no further rehabilitation is required.

The "nice guy" statements of the admitters reflected an attempt to communicate a message consistent with Schlenker's and Darby's analysis of apologies. It was an attempt to convey that rape was not a representation of their "true" self. For example,

It's different from anything else I've ever done. I feel more guilt about this. It's not consistent with me. When I talk about it, it's like being assaulted myself. I don't know why I did it, but once I started, I got into it. Armed robbery was a way of life for me, but not rape. I feel like I wasn't being myself.

Admitters also used "nice guy" statements to register their moral opposition to violence and harming women, even though, in some cases, they had seriously injured their victims. Such was the case of an admitter convicted of a gang rape:

I'm against hurting women. She should have resisted. None of us were the type of person that would use force on a woman. I never positioned myself on a woman unless she showed an interest

in me. They would play to me, not me to them. My weakness is to follow. I never would have stopped, let alone pick her up without the others. I never would have let anyone beat her. I never bothered women who didn't want sex; never had a problem with sex or getting it. I loved her—like all women.

Finally, a number of admitters attempted to improve their self-image by demonstrating that, while they had raped, it could have been worse if they had not been a "nice guy." For example, one admitter professed to being especially gentle with his victim after she told him she had just had a baby. Others claimed to have given the victim money to get home or make a phone call, or to have made sure the victim's children were not in the room. A multiple rapist, whose pattern was to break in and attack sleeping victims in their homes, stated:

I never beat any of my victims and I told them I wouldn't hurt them if they cooperated. I'm a professional thief. But I never robbed the women I raped because I felt so bad about what I had already done to them.

Even a young man, who raped his five victims at gun point and then stabbed them to death, attempted to improve his image by stating:

Physically they enjoyed the sex [rape]. Once they got involved, it would be difficult to resist. I was always gentle and kind until I started to kill them. And the killing was always sudden, so they wouldn't know it was coming.

SUMMARY AND CONCLUSIONS

Convicted rapists' accounts of their crimes include both excuses and justifications. Those who deny what they did was rape justify their actions; those who admit it was rape attempt to excuse it or themselves. This study does not address why some men admit while others deny, but future research might address this question. This paper does provide insight on how men who are sexually aggressive or violent construct reality, describing the different strategies of admitters and deniers.

Admitters expressed the belief that rape was morally reprehensible. But they explained themselves and their acts by appealing to forces beyond their control, forces which reduced their capacity to act rationally and thus compelled them to rape. Two types of excuses predominated: alcohol/drug intoxication and emotional problems. Admitters used these excuses to negotiate a moral identity for themselves by viewing rape as idiosyncratic rather than typical behavior. This allowed them to reconceptualize themselves as recovered or "exrapists," someone who had made a serious mistake which did not represent their "true" self.

In contrast, deniers' accounts indicate that these men raped because their value system provided no compelling reason not to do so. When sex is viewed as a male entitlement, rape is no longer seen as criminal. However, the deniers had been convicted of rape, and like the admitters, they attempted to negotiate an identity. Through justifications, they constructed a "controversial" rape and attempted to demonstrate how their behavior, even if not quite right, was appropriate in the situation. Their denials, drawn from common cultural rape stereotypes, took two forms, both of which ultimately denied the existence of a victim.

The first form of denial was buttressed by the cultural view of men as sexually masterful and women as coy but seductive. Injury was denied by portraying the victim as willing, even enthusiastic, or as politely resistant at first but eventually yielding to "relax and enjoy it." In these accounts, force appeared merely as a seductive technique. Rape was disclaimed: rather than harm the woman, the rapist had fulfilled her dreams. In the second form of denial, the victim was portrayed as the type of woman who "got what she deserved." Through attacks on the victim's sexual reputation and, to a lesser degree, her emotional state, deniers attempted to demonstrate that since the victim wasn't a "nice girl," they were not rapists. Consistent with both forms of denial was the self-interested use of alcohol and drugs as a justification. Thus, in contrast to admitters, who accentuated their own use as an excuse, deniers emphasized the victim's consumption in an effort to both discredit her and make her appear more responsible for the rape. It is important to remember that deniers did not invent these justifications. Rather, they reflect a belief system which has historically victimized women by promulgating the myth that women both enjoy and are responsible for their own rape.

While admitters and deniers present an essentially contrasting view of men who rape, there were some shared characteristics. Justifications particularly, but also excuses, are buttressed by the cultural view of women as sexual commodities, dehumanized and devoid of autonomy and dignity. In this sense, the sexual objectification of women must be understood as an important factor contributing to an environment that trivializes, neutralizes, and, perhaps, facilitates rape.

Finally, we must comment on the consequences of allowing one perspective to dominate thought on a social problem. Rape, like any complex continuum of behavior, has multiple causes and is influenced by a number of social factors. Yet, dominated by psychiatry and the medical model, the underlying assumption that rapists are "sick" has pervaded research. Although methodologically unsound, conclusions have been based almost exclusively on small clinical populations of rapists—that extreme group of rapists who seek counseling in prison and are the most likely to exhibit psychopathology. From this small, atypical group of men, psychiatric findings have been generalized to all men who rape. Our research, however, based on volunteers from the entire prison population, indicates that some rapists, like deniers, viewed and understood their behavior from a popular cultural perspective. This strongly suggests that cultural perspectives, and not an idiosyncratic illness, motivated their behavior. Indeed, we can argue that the psychiatric perspective has contributed to the vocabulary of motive that rapists use to excuse and justify their behavior (Scully and Marolla, 1984).

Efforts to arrive at a general explanation for rape have been retarded by the narrow focus of the medical model and the preoccupation with clinical populations. The continued reduction of such complex behavior to a singular cause hinders, rather than enhances, our understanding of rape.

NOTES

1. These numbers include pretest interviews. When the analysis involves either questions that were not asked in the pretest or that were changed, they are excluded and thus the number changes.

2. There is, of course, the possibility that some of these men really were innocent of rape. However, while the U.S. criminal justice system is not without flaw, we assume that it is highly unlikely that this many men could have been unjustly convicted of rape, especially since rape is a crime with traditionally low conviction rates. Instead, for purposes of this research, we assume that these men were guilty as charged and that their attempt to maintain an image of non-rapist springs from some psychologically or sociologically interpretable mechanism.

3. Because of their outright denial, interviews with this group of rapists did not contain the data being analyzed here and, consequently, they are not included in this paper.

4. It was sometimes difficult to determine the full extent of victim injury from the pre-sentence reports. Consequently, it is doubtful that this number accurately reflects the degree of injuries sustained by victims.

5. It is worth noting that a number of deniers specifically mentioned the victim's alleged interest in oral sex. Since our interview questions about sexual history indicated that the rapists themselves found oral sex marginally acceptable, the frequent mention is probably another attempt to discredit the victim. However, since a tape recorder could not be used for the interviews and the importance of these claims didn't emerge until the data was being coded and analyzed, it is possible that it was mentioned even more frequently but not recorded.

6. Research shows clearly that women do not enjoy rape. Holmstrom and Burgess (1978) asked 93 adult rape victims, "How did it feel sexually?" Not one said they enjoyed it. Further, the trauma of rape is so great that it disrupts sexual functioning (both frequency and satisfaction) for the overwhelming majority of victims, at least during the period immediately following the rape and, in fewer cases, for an extended period of time (Burgess and Holmstrom, 1979; Feldman-Summers et al., 1979). In addition, a number of studies have shown that rape victims experience adverse consequences prompting some to move, change jobs, or drop out of school (Burgess and Holmstrom, 1974; Kilpatrick et al., 1979; Ruch et al., 1980; Shore, 1979).

REFERENCES

Abel, Gene, Judith Becker, and Linda Skinner. 1980. "Aggressive Behavior and Sex." *Psychiatric Clinics of North America,* 3(2):133–151.

Abrahamsen, David. 1960. *The Psychology of Crime.* New York: Wiley.

Albin, Rochelle. 1977. "Psychological Studies of Rape." *Signs,* 3(2):423–435.

Athens, Lonnie. 1977. "Violent Crimes: A Symbolic Interactionist Study." *Symbolic Interaction,* 1(1):56–71.

Burgess, Ann Wolbert and Lynda Lytle Holmstrom. 1974. *Rape: Victims of Crisis.* Bowie: Robert J. Brady.

———. 1979. "Rape: Sexual Disruption and Recovery." *American Journal of Orthopsychiatry,* 49(4):648–657.

Burt, Martha. 1980. "Cultural Myths and Supports for Rape." *Journal of Personality and Social Psychology,* 38(2):217–230.

Burt, Martha and Rochelle Albin. 1981. "Rape Myths, Rape Definitions, and Probability of Conviction." *Journal of Applied Psychology,* 11(3):212–230.

Feldman-Summers, Shirley, Patricia E. Gordon, and Jeanette R. Meagher. 1979. "The Impact of Rape on Sexual Satisfaction." *Journal of Abnormal Psychology,* 88(1):101–105.

Glueck, Sheldon. 1925. *Mental Disorders and the Criminal Law.* New York: Little Brown.

Groth, Nicholas A. 1979. *Men Who Rape.* New York: Plenum Press.

Hall, Peter M. and John P. Hewitt. 1970. "The Quasi-theory of Communication and the Management of Dissent." *Social Problems,* 18(1):17–27.

Hewitt, John P. and Peter M. Hall. 1973. "Social Problems, Problematic Situations, and Quasi-theories." *American Sociological Review,* 38(3):367–374.

Hewitt, John P. and Randall Stokes. 1975. "Disclaimers." *American Sociological Review,* 40(1):1–11.

Hollander, Bernard. 1924. *The Psychology of Misconduct, Vice, and Crime.* New York: Macmillan

Holmstrom, Lynda Lytle and Ann Wolbert Burgess. 1978. "Sexual Behavior of Assailant and Victim During Rape." Paper presented at the annual meetings of the American Sociological Association, San Francisco, September 2–8.

Kilpatrick, Dean G., Lois Veronen, and Patricia A. Resnick. 1979. "The Aftermath of Rape: Recent Empirical Findings." *American Journal of Orthopsychiatry,* 49(4):658–669.

Ladouceur, Patricia. 1983. "The Relative Impact of Drugs and Alcohol on Serious Felons." Paper presented at the annual meetings of the American Society of Criminology, Denver, November 9–12.

Luckenbill, David. 1977. "Criminal Homicide as a Situated Transaction." *Social Problems,* 25(2):176–187,

McCaghy, Charles. 1968. "Drinking and Deviance Disavowal: The Case of Child Molesters." *Social Problems,* 16(1):43–49.

Marolla, Joseph, and Diana Scully. 1979. "Rape and Psychiatric Vocabularies of Motive." In Edith S. Gomberg and Violet Franks (eds.), *Gender and Disordered Behavior: Sex Differences in Psychopathology.* New York: Brunner/Mazel, pp. 301–318.

Mills, C. Wright. 1940. "Situated Actions and Vocabularies of Motive." *American Sociological Review,* 5(6):904–913.

Nelson, Steve and Menachem Amir. 1975. "The Hitchhike Victim of Rape: A Research Report." In Israel Drapkin and Emilio Viano (eds.), *Victimology: A New Focus.* Lexington, KY: Lexington Books, pp. 47–65.

Queen's Bench Foundation. 1976. *Rape: Prevention and Resistance.* San Francisco: Queen's Bench Foundation.

Ruch, Libby O., Susan Meyers Chandler, and Richard A. Harter. 1980. "Life Change and Rape Impact." *Journal of Health and Social Behavior,* 21(3):248–260.

Scott, Marvin and Stanford Lyman. 1968. "Accounts." *American Sociological Review,* 33(1):46–62.

Schlenker, Barry R. and Bruce W. Darby. 1981. "The Use of Apologies in Social Predicaments." *Social Psychology Quarterly,* 44(3):271–278.

Scully, Diana and Joseph Marolla. 1984. "Rape and Psychiatric Vocabularies of Motive: Alternative Perspectives." In Ann Wolbert Burgess (ed.), *Handbook on Rape and Sexual Assault.* New York: Garland Publishing. Forthcoming.

Shore, Barbara K. 1979. *An Examination of Critical Process and Outcome Factors in Rape.* Rockville, MD: National Institute of Mental Health.

Stokes, Randall and John P. Hewitt. 1976. "Aligning Actions." *American Sociological Review,* 41(5):837–849.

Sykes, Gresham M. and David Matza. 1957. "Techniques of Neutralization." *American Sociological Review,* 22(6):664–670.

Williams, Joyce. 1979. "Sex Role Stereotypes, Women's Liberation, and Rape: A Cross-cultural Analysis of Attitude." *Sociological Symposium,* 25 (Winter):61–97.

The Social Integration of Queers and Peers

ALBERT J. REISS, JR.

... An attempt is made in this paper to describe the sexual relations between "delinquent peers" and "adult queers" and to account for its social organization. This transaction is one form of homosexual prostitution between a young male and an adult male fellator. The adult male client pays a delinquent boy prostitute a sum of money in order to be allowed to act as a fellator. The transaction is limited to fellation and is one in which the boy develops no self-conception as a homosexual person or sexual deviator, although he perceives adult male clients as sexual deviators, "queers" or "gay boys." ...

Reprinted from *Social Problems,* Vol. 9, No. 2 (Fall, 1961), pp. 102, 104, 106–109, 112–119, by permission of the Society for the Study of Social Problems and the author.

THE DATA

Information on the sexual transaction and its social organization was gathered mostly by interviews, partly by social observation of their meeting places. Though there are limitations to inferring social organization from interview data (particularly when the organization arises through behavior that is negatively sanctioned in the larger society), they provide a convenient basis for exploration.

Sex histories were gathered from 18.6 per cent of the 1008 boys between the ages of 12 and 17 who were interviewed in the Nashville, Tennessee, SMA for an investigation of adolescent conforming and deviating behavior. These represent all of the interviews of one of the interviewers during a two-month period, together with interviews with all Nashville boys incarcerated at the Tennessee State Training School for Boys. . . .

HOW PEERS AND QUEERS MEET

Meetings between adult male fellators and delinquent boys are easily made, because both know how and where to meet within the community space. Those within the common culture know that contact can be established within a relatively short period of time, if it is wished. The fact that meetings between peers and queers can be made easily is muted evidence of the organized understandings which prevail between the two populations.

There are a large number of places where the boys meet their clients, the fellators. Many of these points are known to all boys regardless of where they reside in the metropolitan area. This is particularly true of the central city locations where the largest number of contact points are found within a small territorial area. Each community area of the city, and certain fringe areas, inhabited by substantial numbers of lower-class persons, also have their meeting places, generally known only to the boys residing in the area.

Queers and peers typically establish contact in public or quasi-public places. Major points of contact include street corners, public parks, men's toilets in public or quasi-public places such as those in transportation depots, parks or hotels, and "second" and "third-run" movie houses (open around the clock and permitting sitting through shows). Bars are seldom points of contact, perhaps largely because they are plied by older male hustlers who lie outside the peer culture and groups, and because bar proprietors will not risk the presence of under-age boys.

There are a number of prescribed modes for establishing contact in these situations. They permit the boys and fellators to communicate intent to one another privately despite the public character of the situation. The major form of establishing contact is the "cruise," with the fellator passing "queer-corners" or locations until his effort is recognized by one of the boys. A boy can then signal—usually by nodding his head, a hand gesticulation signifying OK, following, or responding to commonly understood introductions such as "You got the time?"—that he is prepared to undertake the transaction. Entrepreneur and client then move to a place where the sexual activity is consummated, usually a place affording privacy, protection and hasty exit. "Dolly," a three-time loser at the State Training School, describes one of these prescribed forms for making contact:

> Well, like at the bus station, you go to the bathroom and stand there pretendin' like . . . and they're standin' there pretendin' like . . . and then they motions their head and walks out and you follow them, and you go some place. Either they's got a car, or you go to one of them hotels near the depot or some place like that . . . most any place.

Frequently contact between boys and fellators is established when the boy is hitchhiking. This is particularly true for boys' first contacts of this nature. Since lower-class boys are more likely than middle-class ones to hitch rides within a city, particularly at night when such contacts are most frequently made, they perhaps are most often solicited in this manner.

The experienced boy who knows a "lot of queers," may phone known fellators directly from a public phone, and some fellators try to establish continued contact with boys by giving them their phone numbers. However, the boys seldom use this means of contact for reasons inherent in their orientation toward the transaction, as we shall see below.

We shall now examine how the transaction is facilitated by these types of situations and the prescribed modes of contact and communication. One of the characteristics of all these contact situations is that they provide a *rationale* for the presence of *both* peers and queers in the *same* situation or place. This rationale is necessary for both parties, for were there high visibility to the presence of either and no ready explanation for it, contact and communication would be far more difficult. Public and quasi-public facilities provide situations which account for the presence of most persons since there is relatively little social control over the establishment of contacts. There is, of course, some risk to the boys and the fellators in making contact in these situations since they are generally known to the police. The Morals Squad may have "stake-outs," but this is one of the calculated risks and the communication network carries information about their tactics.

A most important element in furnishing a rationale is that these meeting places must account for the presence of delinquent boys of essentially lower-class dress and appearance who make contact with fellators of almost any class level. This is true despite the fact that the social settings which fellators ordinarily choose to establish contact generally vary according to the class level of the fellators. Fellators of high social class generally make contact by "cruising" past streetcorners, in parks, or the men's rooms in "better" hotels, while those from the lower class are likely to select the public bath or transportation depot. There apparently is some general equation of the class position

of boys and fellators in the peer-queer transaction. The large majority of fellators in the delinquent peer-queer transaction probably are from the lower class ("apes"). But it is difficult to be certain about the class position of the fellator clients since no study was made of this population.

The absence of data from the fellator population poses difficulties in interpreting the contact relationship. Many fellators involved with delinquent boys do not appear to participate in any overt or covert homosexual groups, such as the organized homosexual community of the "gay world."[1] The "gay world" is the most visible form of organized homosexuality since it is an organized community, but it probably encompasses only a small proportion of all homosexual contact. Even among those in the organized homosexual community, evidence suggests that the homosexual members seek sexual gratification outside their group with persons who are essentially anonymous to them. Excluding homosexual married couples, Leznoff and Westley maintain that there is "... a prohibition against sexual relationships within the group.... "[2] Ross indicates that young male prostitutes are chosen, among other reasons, for the fact that they protect the identity of the client.[3] Both of these factors tend to coerce many male fellators to choose an anonymous contact situation.

It is clear that these contact situations not only provide a rationale for the presence of the parties to the transaction but a guarantee of anonymity. The guarantee does not necessarily restrict social visibility as both the boys and the fellators may recognize cues (including, but not necessarily, those of gesture and dress) which lead to mutual role identification.[4] But anonymity is guaranteed in at least two senses; anonymity of presence is assured in the situation and their personal identity in the community is protected unless disclosed by choice.

There presumably are a variety of reasons for the requirement of anonymity. For many, a homosexual relationship must remain a secret since their other relationships in the community—families, business relationships, etc.—must be protected. Leznoff and Westley refer to these men as the "secret" as contrasted with the "overt" homosexuals,[5] and in the organized "gay world," they are known as "closet fags." For some, there is also a necessity for protecting identity to avoid blackmail.[6] Although none of the peer hustlers reported resorting to blackmail, the adult male fellator may nonetheless hold such an expectation, particularly if he is older or of high social class. Lower-class ones, by contrast, are more likely to face the threat of violence from adolescent boys since they more often frequent situations where they are likely to contact "rough trade."[7] The kind of situation in which the delinquent peer-queer contact is made and the sexual relationship consummated tends to minimize the possibility of violence.

Not all male fellators protect their anonymity; some will let a boy have their phone number and a few "keep a boy." Still, most fellators want to meet boys where they are least likely to be victimized, although boys sometimes roll queers by selecting a meeting place where by prearrangement, their friends can meet them and help roll the queer, steal his car, or commit other acts of violence. Boys generally know that fellators are vulnerable in that they can't report their victimization. Parenthetically, it might be mentioned that these boys are not usually aware of their own institutional invulnerability to arrest. An adolescent boy is peculiarly invulnerable to arrest even when found with a fellator since the mores define the boy as exploited.[8]

Situations of personal contact between adolescent boys and adult male fellators also provide important ways to *communicate intent* or to carry out the transaction *without* making the contact particularly visible to others. The wall writings in many of these places are not without their primitive communication value, e.g., "show it hard," and places such as a public restroom provide a modus operandi. The entrepreneur and his customer in fact can meet with little more than an exchange of non-verbal gestures, transact their business with a minimum of verbal communication and part without a knowledge of one another's identity. In most cases, boys report "almost nothing" was said. The sexual transaction may occur with the only formal transaction being payment to the boy....

NORMS GOVERNING THE TRANSACTION

Does the peer society have any norms about personal relations with fellators? Or, does it simply induct a boy into a relationship by teaching him how to effect the transaction? The answer is that there appear to be several clear-cut norms about the relations between peers and queers, even though there is some deviation from them.

The first major norm is that *a boy must undertake the relationship with a queer solely as a way of making money; sexual gratification cannot be actively sought as a goal in the relationship.* This norm does not preclude a boy from sexual gratification by the act; he simply must not seek this as a goal. Put another way, a boy cannot admit that he failed to get money from the transaction unless he used violence toward the fellator and he cannot admit that he sought it as a means of sexual gratification.

The importance of making money in motivating a boy to the peer-queer transaction is succinctly stated by Dewey H.:

> *This guy in the Rex Theatre came over and sat down next to me when I was 11 or 12, and he started to fool with me. I got over and sat down another place and he came over and asked me, didn't I want to and he'd pay me five bucks. I figured it was easy money so I went with him ... I didn't do it before that. That wasn't too long after I'd moved to South Nashville. I was a pretty good boy before that ... not real good, but I never ran with a crowd that got into trouble before that. But, I met a lot of 'em there. (Why do you run with queers?) It's easy money ... like I could go out and break into a place when I'm broke and get money that way ... but that's harder and you take a bigger risk ... with a queer it's easy money.*

Dewey's comments reveal two important motivating factors in getting money from queers, both suggested by the expression, "easy money." First, the money is easy in that it can be made quickly. Some boys reported that when they needed money for a date or a night out, they obtained it within an hour through the sexual transaction with a queer. All the boy has to do is go to a place where he will be contacted, wait around, get picked up, carried to a place where the sexual transaction occurs, and in a relatively short period of time he obtains the money for his service.

It is easy money in another and more important sense for many of these boys. Boys who undertake the peer-queer transaction are generally members of career-oriented delinquent groups. Rejecting the limited opportunities for making money by legitimate means or finding them inaccessible, their opportunities to make money by illegitimate means may also be limited or the risk may be great. Theft is an available means, but it is more difficult and involves greater risk than the peer-queer transaction. Delinquent boys are not unaware of the risks they take. Under most circumstances, delinquents may calculate an act of stealing as "worth the risk." There are occasions, however, when the risk is calculated as too great. These occasions occur when the "heat" is on the boy or when he can least afford to run the risk of being picked up by the police, as is the case following a pickup by the police, being put on probation or parole, or being warned that incarceration will follow the next violation. At such times, boys particularly calculate whether they can afford to take the risk. Gerald L., describing a continuing relationship with a fellator who gave him his phone number, reflects Dewey's attitude toward minimizing risk in the peer-queer transaction: "So twic'd after that when I was gettin' real low and couldn't risk stealin' and gettin' caught, I called him and he took me out and blowed me." Here is a profit with no investment of capital and a minimum of risk in social, if not in psychological, terms.

The element of risk coupled with the wish for "easy money" enters into our understanding of the peer-queer relationship in another way. From a sociological point of view, the peer-queer sexual transaction occurs between two major types of deviators—"delinquents" and "queers." Both types of deviators risk negative sanctions for their deviant acts. The more often one has been arrested or incarcerated, the more punitive the sanctions from the larger social system for both types of deviators. At some point, therefore, both calculate risks and seek to minimize them, at least in the very short-run. Each then becomes a means for the other to minimize risk.

When the delinquent boy is confronted with a situation in which he wants money and risks little in getting it, how is he to get it without working? Illegitimate activities frequently provide the "best" opportunity for easy money. These activities often are restricted in kind and number for adolescents and the risk of negative sanctions is high. Under such circumstances, the service offered a queer is a chance to make easy money with a minimum of risk.

Opportunities for sexual gratification are limited for the adult male fellator, particularly if he wishes to minimize the risk of detection in locating patrons, to avoid personal involvement and to get his gratification when he wishes it. The choice of a lower-class male, precisely because of his class position somewhat reduces the risk. If the lower-class male also is a delinquent, the risk is minimized to an even greater degree.

This is not to say that the parties take equal risks in the situation. Of the two, the fellator perhaps is less able to minimize his risk since he still risks violence from his patron, but much less so if a set of expectations arise which control the use of violence as well. The boy is most able to minimize his risk since he is likely to be defined as "exploited" in the situation if caught.

Under special circumstances, boys may substitute other gratifications for the goal of money, provided that these gratifications do not include sexual gratification as a major goal. These special circumstances are the case where an entire gang will "make a night (or time) of it" with one or more adult male fellators. Under these circumstances, everyone is exempted from the subcultural expectations about making money from the fellator because everyone participates and there is no reason for everyone (or anyone) to make money. For the group to substitute being given a "good time" by a "queer" for the prescribed financial transaction is, of course, the exception which proves the rule.

Several examples of group exemption from the prescribed norm of a financial gain were discovered. Danny S., leader of the Black Aces, tells of his gang's group experiences with queers: "There's this one guy takes us to the Colonial Motel out on Dickerson Pike ... usually it's a bunch of us boys and we all get drunk and get blowed by this queer ... we don't get any money then ... it's more a drinking party." The Black Aces are a fighting gang and place great stress on physical prowess, particularly boxing. All of its members have done time more than once at the State Training School. During one of these periods, the school employed a boxing instructor whom the boys identified as "a queer," but the boys had great respect for him since he taught them how to box and was a game fighter. Danny refers to him in accepting terms: "He's a real good guy. He's fought with us once or twice and we drink with him when we run into him. . . . He's taken us up to Miter Dam a coupla times, he's got a cabin up there on the creek and he blows us. . . . But mostly we just drink and have a real good time." These examples illustrate the instrumental orientation of the gang members. If the expense of the gang members getting drunk and having a good time are borne by a "queer," each member is released from the obligation to receive cash. The relationship in this case represents an exchange of services rather than that of money for a service.

The second major norm operating in the relationship is that *the sexual transaction must be limited to mouth-genital fellation. No other sexual acts are generally tolerated.*[9] The adult male fellator must deport himself in such a way as to reenforce the instrumental aspects of the role rela-

tionship and to insure affective neutrality.[10] For the adult male fellator to violate the boy's expectation of "getting blowed," as the boys refer to the act, is to risk violence and loss of service. Whether or not the boys actually use violent means as often as they say they do when expectations are violated, there is no way of knowing with precision. Nevertheless, whenever boys reported they used violent means, they always reported some violation of the subcultural expectations. Likewise, they never reported a violation of the subcultural expectations which was not followed by the use of violent means, unless it was clearly held up as an exception. Bobby A. expresses the boys' point of view on the use of violent means in the following exchange: "How much did you usually get?" "Around five dollars; if they didn't give that much, I'd beat their head in." "Did they ever want you to do anything besides blow you?" "Yeh, sometimes ... like they want me to blow them, but I'd tell them to go to hell and maybe beat them up."

Boys are very averse to being thought of in a queer role or engaging in acts of fellation. The act of fellation is defined as a "queer" act. Most boys were asked whether they would engage in such behavior. All but those who had the status of "punks" denied they had engaged in behavior associated with the queer role. Asking a boy whether he is a fellator meets with strong denial and often with open hostility. This could be interpreted as defensive behavior against latent homosexuality. Whether or not this is the case, strong denial could be expected because the question goes counter to the subcultural definitions of the peer role in the transaction.

A few boys on occasion apparently permit the fellator to perform other sexual acts. These boys, it is guessed, are quite infrequent in a delinquent peer population. Were their acts known to the members of the group, they would soon be defined as outside the delinquent peer society. Despite the limitation of the peer-queer sexual transaction to mouth-genital fellation, there are other sexual transactions which the peer group permits members to perform under special circumstances. They are, for example, permitted to perform the *male* roles in "crimes against nature," such as in pederasty ("cornholing" to the boys), bestiality (sometimes referred to as buggery) and carnal copulation with a man involving no orifice (referred to as "slick-legging" among the boys) provided that the partner is roughly of the same age and not a member of the group and provided also that the boys are confined to the single-sex society of incarcerated delinquent boys. Under no circumstances, however, is the female role in carnal copulation acceptable in any form. It is taboo. Boys who accept the female role in sexual transactions occupy the lowest status position among delinquents. They are "punks."

The third major norm operating on the relationship is that *both peers and queers, as participants, should remain affectively neutral during the transaction.* Boys within the peer society define the ideal form of the role with the fellator as one in which the boy is the entrepreneur and the queer is viewed as purchasing a service. The service is a business deal where a sexual transaction is purchased for an agreed upon amount of money. In the typical case, the boy is neither expected to enjoy or be repulsed by the sexual transaction; mouth-genital fellation is accepted as a service offered in exchange for a fee. It should be kept in mind that self-gratification is permitted in the sexual act. Only the motivation to sexual gratification in the transaction is tabooed. But self-gratification must occur without displaying either positive or negative affect toward the queer. In the prescribed form of the role relationship, the boy sells a service for profit and the queer is to accept it without show of emotion.

The case of Thurman L., one of three brothers who are usually in trouble with the law, illustrates some aspects of the expected pattern of affective neutrality. Thurman has had a continuing relationship with a queer, a type of relationship in which it would be anticipated that affective neutrality would be difficult to maintain. This relationship continued, in fact, with a 21-year-old "gay" until the man was "sent to the pen." When queried about his relationship with this man and why he went with him, Thurman replied:

> Don't know...money and stuff like that I guess. (What do you mean?...stuff like that?) Oh, clothes.... (He ever bought you any clothes?) Sure, by this one gay.... (You mind being blowed?) No. (You like it?) Don't care one way or the other. I don't like, and I don't not like it. (You like this one gay?) Nope, can't say that I liked anythin' about him. (How come you do it then?) Well, the money for one thing.... I need that. (You enjoy it some?) Can't say I do or don't.

More typical than Thurman's expression of affective neutrality is the boy who accepts it as "OK" or, "It's all right; I don't mind it." Most frequent of all is some variant of the statement: "It's OK, but I like the money best of all." The definition of affective neutrality fundamentally requires only that there be no positive emotional commitment to the queer *as a person.* The relationship must be essentially an impersonal one, even though the pure form of the business relationship may seldom be attained. Thus, it is possible for a boy to admit self-gratification without admitting any emotional commitment to the homosexual partner.

Although the peer group prescribes affective neutrality toward the queer in the peer-queer transaction, queers must be regarded as low prestige persons, held in low esteem, and the queer role is taboo. The queer is most commonly regarded as "crazy, I guess." Some boys take a more rationalistic view "They're just like that, I guess" or, "They're just born that way." While there are circumstances under which one is permitted to like a particular fellator, as in the case of all prejudices attached to devalued status, the person who is liked must be the exception which states the rule. Though in many cases both the boy and the fellator are of very low class origins, and in many cases both are altogether repulsive in appearance, cleanliness and dress by middle-class standards, these are not the standards of comparison used by the boys. The deviation of the queers from the boy's norms of masculine behavior places the fellator in the lowest possible status, even "beneath contempt." If the fellator violates the expected affective relationship in the transaction, he may be treated not only with violence but with contempt as well. The seller of the service ultimately reserves the right to set the conditions for his patrons.

Some boys find it difficult to be emotionally neutral toward the queer role and its occupants; they are either personally offended or affronted by the behavior of queers. JDC is an instance of a boy who is personally offended by their behavior; yet he is unable to use violence even when expectations governing the transaction are violated. He does not rely very much on the peer-queer relationship as a source of income. JDC expresses his view: "I don't really go for that like some guys; I just do it when I go along with the crowd.... You know.... That, and when I do it for money.... And I go along.... But...I hate queers. They embarrass me." "How?" "Well, like you'll be in the lobby at the theatre, and they'll come up and pat your ass or your prick right in front of everybody. I just can't go for that—not me." Most of the boys wouldn't either, but they would have resorted to violent means in this situation.

Two principal types of boys maintain a continuing relationship with a known queer. A few boys develop such relationships to insure a steady income. While this is permitted within peer society for a short period of time, boys who undertake it for extended periods of time do so with some risk, since in the words of the boys, "queers can be got too easy." The boy who is affectively involved with a queer or his role is downgraded in status to a position, "Ain't no better'n a queer." There are also a few boys affectively committed to a continuing relationship with an adult male homosexual. Such boys usually form a strong dependency relationship with him and are kept much as the cabin boys of old. This type of boy is clearly outside the peer society of delinquents and is isolated from participation in gang activity. The sociomet-

ric pattern for such boys is one of choice into more than one gang, none of which is reciprocated.

Street-hustlers are also downgraded within the peer society, generally having reputations as "punk kids." The street-hustler pretty much "goes it alone." Only a few street-hustlers were interviewed for this study. None of them was a member of an organized delinquent group. The sociometric pattern for each, together with his history of delinquent activity, placed them in the classification of nonconforming isolates.

A fourth major norm operating on the peer-queer relationship serves as a primary factor in stabilizing the system. This norm holds that *violence must not be used so long as the relationship conforms to the shared set of expectations between queers and peers*. So long as the fellator conforms to the norms governing the transaction in the peer-queer society, he runs little risk of violence from the boys.

The main reason, perhaps, for this norm is that uncontrolled violence is potentially disruptive of any organized system. All organized social systems must control violence. If the fellator clients were repeatedly the objects of violence, the system as it has been described could not exist. Most boys who share the common expectations of the peer-queer relationship do not use violent means unless the expectations are violated. To use violence, of course, is to become affectively involved and therefore another prescription of the relation is violated.

It is not known whether adult male fellators who are the clients of delinquent entrepreneurs share the boys' definition of the norm regarding the use of violence. They may, therefore, violate expectations of the peer society through ignorance of the system rather than from any attempt to go beyond the set of shared expectations.

There are several ways the fellator can violate the expectations of boys. The first concerns money: refusal to pay or paying too little may bring violence from most boys. Fellators may also violate peer expectations by attempting to go beyond the mouth-genital sexual act. If such an attempt is made, he is usually made an object of aggression as in the following excerpt from Dolly's sex history:

> *(You like it?) It's OK. I don't mind it. It feels OK. (They ever try anything else on you?) They usually just blow and that's all. (Any ever try anything else on you?) Oh sure, but we really fix 'em. I just hit 'em on the head or roll 'em...throw 'em out of the car.... Once a guy tried that and we rolled him and threw him out of the car. Then we took the car and stripped it (laughs with glee).*

Another way the fellator violates a boy's expectations is to introduce considerable affect into the relationship. It appears that affect is least acceptable in two forms, both of which could be seen as "attacks on his masculinity." In one form, the queer violates the affective neutrality requirement by treating the adolescent boy as if he were a girl or in a girl's role during the sexual transaction, as for example, by speaking to him in affectionate terms such as "sweetie." There are many reasons why the feminine sex role is unacceptable to these lower-class boys, including the fact that such boys place considerable emphasis on being "tough" and masculine. Walter Miller, for example, observes that:

> *...The almost compulsive lower class concern with "masculinity" derives from a type of compulsive reaction-formation. A concern over homosexuality runs like a persistent thread through lower class culture—manifested by the institutionalized practice of "baiting queers," often accompanied by violent physical attacks, an expressed contempt for "softness" or frills, and the use of the local term for "homosexual" as a general pejorative epithet (e.g., higher class individuals or upwardly mobile peers are frequently characterized as "fags" or "queers").[11]*

Miller sees violence as part of a reaction-formation against the matriarchal lower-class household where the father often is absent. For this reason, he suggests, many lower-class boys find it difficult to identify with a male role, and the "collective" reaction-formation is a cultural emphasis on

masculinity. Violence toward queers is seen as a consequence of this conflict. Data from our interviews suggest that among career-oriented delinquents, violation of the affective neutrality requirement in the peer-queer relationship is at least as important in precipitating violence toward "queers." There are, of course, gangs which were not studied in this investigation which "queer-bait" for the express purposes of "rolling the queer."

The other form in which the fellator may violate the affective neutrality requirement is to approach the boy and make suggestive advances to him when he is with his age-mates, either with girls or with his peer group when he is not located for "business." In either case, the sexual advances suggest that the boy is not engaged in a business relationship within the normative expectations of the system, but that he has sexual motivation as well. The delinquent boy is expected to control the relationship with his customers. He is the entrepreneur "looking" for easy money or at the very least he must appear as being merely receptive to business; this means that he is receptive only in certain situations and under certain circumstances. He is not in business when he is with girls and he is not a businessman when he is cast in a female role. To be cast in a female role before peers is highly unacceptable, as the following account suggests:

> *This gay comes up to me in the lobby of the Empress when we was standin' around and starts feelin' me up and callin' me Sweetie and like that...and, I just couldn't take none of that there...what was he makin' out like I was a queer or somethin'...so I jumps him right then and there and we like to of knocked his teeth out.*

The sexual advance is even less acceptable when a girl is involved:

> *I was walkin' down the street with my steady girl when this gay drives by that I'd been with once before and he whistles at me and calls, "Hi Sweetie."...And, was I mad...so I went down to where the boys was and we laid for him and beat*

*on him 'til he like to a never come to . . . ain't gonna
take nothin' like that off 'n a queer.*

In both of these instances, not only is the boys'
masculinity under attack, but the affective neutrality requirement of the business transaction is violated. The queer's behavior is particularly
unacceptable, however, because it occurs in a peer
setting where the crucial condition is the maintenance of the boy's status within the group. A
lower-class boy cannot afford to be cast in less
than a highly masculine role before lower-class
girls nor risk definition as a queer before peers.
His role within his peer group is under threat even
if he suffers *no* anxiety about masculinity. Not
only the boy himself but his peers perceive such
behavior as violating role expectations and join
him in violent acts toward the fellator to protect
the group's integrity and status.

If violence generally occurs only when one of
the major peer norms has been violated, it would
also seem to follow that *violence is a means of en-
forcing the peer entrepreneurial norms of the system.* Violence or the threat of violence is thus used
to keep adult male fellators in line with the boys'
expectations in his customer role. It represents social control, a punishment meted out to a fellator
who violates the cultural expectation. Only so
long as the fellator seeks gratification from lower-
class boys in a casual pick-up or continuing relationship where he pays money for a "blow-job" is
he reasonably free from acts of violence.

There is another, and perhaps more important reason for the use of violence when the peer
defined norms of the peer-queer relationship are
violated. The formally prescribed roles for peers
and queers are basically the roles involved in all
institutionalized forms of prostitution, the prostitute and the client. But in most forms of prostitution, whether male or female, the hustlers
perceive of themselves in hustler roles, and furthermore the male hustlers also develop a conception of themselves as homosexual whereas *the
peer hustler in the peer-queer relationship develops no conception of himself either as prostitute
or as homosexual.*

The fellator risks violence, therefore, if he
threatens the boy's self-conception by suggesting
that the boy may be homosexual and treats him as
if he were.

Violence seems to function, then, in two basic
ways for the peers. On the one hand, it integrates
their norms and expectations by controlling and
combatting behavior which violates them. On the
other hand, it protects the boy's self-identity as
nonhomosexual and reinforces his self-conception
as "masculine."

The other norms of the peer society governing the peer-queer transaction also function to prevent boys in the peer-queer society from defining
themselves as homosexual. The prescriptions that
the goal is money, that sexual gratification is not
to be sought as an end in the relationship, that affective neutrality be maintained toward the fellator and that only mouth-genital fellation is
permitted, all tend to insulate the boy from a homosexual self-definition. So long as he conforms
to these expectations, *his "significant others" will
not define him as homosexual;* and this is perhaps
the most crucial factor in his own self-definition.
The peers define one as homosexual not on the
basis of homosexual *behavior* as such, but on the
basis of participation in the homosexual *role,* the
"queer" role. The reactions of the larger society, in
defining the *behavior* as homosexual is unimportant in their own self-definition. What is important
to them is the reactions of their peers to violation
of peer group norms which define roles in the
peer-queer transaction.

NOTES

1. See, for example, Maurice Leznoff and William A.
Westley, "The Homosexual Community," *Social Problems,* 4 (April, 1956), pp. 257–263.
2. *Ibid.,* p. 258.
3. H. Laurence Ross, "The 'Hustler' in Chicago," *The
Journal of Student Research,* 1 (September, 1959), p. 15.
4. The cues which lead to the queer-peer transaction can
be subtle ones. The literature on adult male homosexuality makes it clear that adult males who participate in ho-

mosexual behavior are not generally socially visible to the public by manner and dress. Cf., Jess Stearn, *The Sixth Man,* New York: Macfadden Publications, 1962, Chapters 1 and 3.

5. *Op. cit.,* pp. 260–261.

6. Ross notes that, failing in the con-man role, some hustlers resort to extortion and blackmail since they provide higher income. See Ross, *op. cit.,* p. 16. Sutherland discusses extortion and blackmail of homosexuals as part of the practice of professional thieves. The "muzzle" or "mouse" is part of the role of the professional thief. See Edwin Sutherland, *The Professional Thief,* Chicago: University of Chicago Press, 1937, pp. 78–81. See also the chapter on "Blackmail" in Jess Stearn, *op. cit.,* Chapter 16.

7. Jess Stearn, *op. cit.,* p. 47.

8. Albert J. Reiss, Jr., "Sex Offenses: The Marginal Status of the Adolescent," *Law and Contemporary Problems,* 25 (Spring, 1960), pp. 322–324 and 326–327.

9. It is not altogether clear why mouth-genital fellation is the only sexual act which is tolerated in the peer-queer transaction. The act seems to conform to the more "masculine" aspects of the role than do most, but not all possible alternatives. Ross has suggested to me that it also involves less bodily contact and therefore may be less threatening to the peers' self-definitions. One possible explanation therefore for the exclusiveness of the relationship to this act is that it is the most masculine alternative involving the least threat to peers' self-definition as nonhustler and nonhomosexual.

10. Talcott Parsons in *The Social System* (New York: The Free Press, 1951, Chapter III) discusses this kind of role as "...the segregation of specific instrumental performances, both from expressive orientations other than the specifically appropriate rewards and from other components of the instrumental complex." (p. 87).

11. Walter Miller, "Lower-Class Culture as a Generating Milieu of Gang Delinquency," *The Journal of Social Issues,* 14, No. 3 (1958), p. 9.

Divorce and Stigma

NAOMI GERSTEL

By most accounts, tolerance of variation in family life has increased dramatically in the United States. Public opinion polls over the last two decades reveal declining disapproval of extended singlehood (Veroff et al., 1981), premarital sex and pregnancy (Gerstel, 1982), employment of mothers with young children (Cherlin, 1981), and voluntary childlessness (Huber and Spitze, 1983).

Reprinted from "Divorce and Stigma," *Social Problems,* Vol. 34, No. 2 (April, 1987), pp. 172–186, by permission of the Society for the Study of Social Problems and the author.

An earlier version of this paper was presented at the annual meeting of the American Sociological Association, August, 1986. For helpful comments and criticisms, I would like to thank Robert Zussman, Toby Ditz, Allan Horwitz, Mary Claire Lennon, Jack Pressman, and Sarah Rosenfield. In addition, I would like to express appreciation to three anonymous reviewers for providing valuable suggestions. I would also like to thank Catherine Kohler Riessman with whom I collaborated on this study.

Divorce resembles these other situations; in fact public tolerance of divorce appears to have increased especially dramatically over the last few decades (Veroff et al., 1981).

In the mid-1950's, Goode (1956:10) could still observe: "We know that in our own society, divorce has been a possible, but disapproved, solution for marital conflict." However, comparing attitudes in 1958 and 1971, McRae (1978) found an increasing proportion of adults believing that divorce was only "sometimes wrong" while a decreasing proportion felt that it was "always wrong." These data, he claimed, indicated attitudes toward divorce had shifted "from moral absolutism to situational ethics" (1978:228). In an analysis of panel data collected between 1960 and 1980, Thornton (1985) found that changes in attitudes toward divorce were not only large but pervasive: all subgroups—whether defined by age, class, or even religion—showed substantial declines in disapproval of marital separation.

What are the implications of declining disapproval of divorce? In historical perspective, it is clear that the divorced are no longer subject to the moral outrage they encountered centuries, or even decades, ago. Certainly, divorce is no longer treated as a sin calling for repressive punishment, as it was in theological doctrine and practice (be it Catholic or Protestant) until the beginning of the twentieth century (Halem, 1980; O'Neil, 1967). In electing a divorced president and many divorced senators and governors, U.S. citizens seem to have repudiated the idea that divorce is grounds for exclusion from public life. With the recent passage of no-fault divorce laws in every state, U.S. courts no longer insist on attributing wrongdoing to one party to a divorce (Weitzman, 1985).

Most recent commentators on a divorce even argue that it is no longer stigmatized. For example, Spanier and Thompson (1984:15) claim that "the social stigma associated with divorce has disappeared" and Weitzman (1981:146) suggests that "the decline in the social stigma traditionally attached to divorce is one of the most striking changes in the social climate surrounding divorce."

However, I argue in this paper that the stigma attached to divorce has disappeared in only two very limited senses. First, although other studies have shown a clear decline in disapproval of divorce as a general category, disapproval of divorced individuals persists contingent on the specific conditions of their divorce. Thus, as I show below, some divorced people experience disapproval and at least one party to a divorce often feels blamed.

Second, while many of the formal, institutional controls on divorce—imposed in the public realm of church or state—have weakened, the individual who divorces suffers informal, relational sanctions. These are the interpersonal controls that emerge more or less spontaneously in social life. I will present evidence indicating that the divorced believe the married often exclude them

and that the divorced themselves frequently pull toward, yet devalue, others who divorce.

In these two senses, I argue that the divorced are still subject to the same social processes and evaluations associated with stigmatization more generally. As in Goffman's (1963:3) classic formulation—which stresses both the conditional and relational aspects of stigma—my findings suggest that the divorced come to be seen (and to see themselves) as "of a less desired kind ...reduced in our minds from a whole and usual person to a tainted, discounted one."

METHODS

My data come from interviews with 104 separated and divorced respondents: 52 women and 52 men. Based on a conception of marital dissolution as a process rather than a static life event, the research team sampled respondents in different stages of divorce: one-third of the respondents were separated less than one year; one-third separated one to two years; one-third separated two or more years. To obtain respondents, we could not rely on court records alone, for most couples who have filed for a divorce have already been living apart for at least a year. Thus, 61 percent of the respondents were selected from probate court records in two counties in the Northeast; the others came from referrals.[1] Comparisons between the court cases and referred respondents show no statistically significant differences on demographic characteristics.

A team of three interviewers conducted household interviews, using a schedule composed of both open- and closed-ended items. Each interview, lasting from two to seven hours (an average of three hours), was taped and transcribed in full. My analysis is based primarily on the extensive information collected on social ties. Using measures adapted from Fischer (1982), interviewers asked each respondent to name all those individuals with whom, in the last month, they had a series of common exchanges: engaged in social activities, discussed personal worries, received advice in decisions, etc. Respondents were also asked to name those individuals with whom interaction had become difficult since the separation. To complete the network list, the interviewer compiled a list of those named, gave it to the respondent, and asked: "Is there anyone important to you who doesn't show up on this list?" Any new names were then added to the network list. Respondents (both women and men) named a mean of 18 people (with a minimum of 8 and a maximum of 35). Using the list, the interviewer asked the respondents a series of questions about each person named including, for example, the person's marital status, how long they had known the person, and whether or not he or she disapproved of the divorce. Respondents were also asked to expand on these close-ended items, to answer a number of open-ended questions about how their relationships had changed since the divorce, and to discuss their participation in organized groups (including sports, cultural, religious, and service groups as well as those "singles groups" set up by and for the divorced—e.g., Parents Without Partners). In addition, two measures of mental health status were included: the Center for Epidemiological Studies Depression Scale (CES-D) and a generalized emotional distress or demoralization scale (PERI).[2]

SAMPLE CHARACTERISTICS

In contrast to the samples in most previous research on separation and divorce, the respondents are a heterogeneous group. They include people in the working class as well as in the middle class whose household incomes ranged from under $4,000 to over $50,000, with a median of $18,000 (with women's significantly lower than men's).[3] Levels of education varied widely: about one-fourth had less than a high school degree, and slightly less than one-fourth had four or more years of college. The sample also includes significant numbers whose primary source of income came from public assistance and from manual, clerical, and professional jobs. Only 11 percent were not currently employed while another 9 percent were working part-time. The median age

of the respondents was 33 years, and the mean number of years married was nine. Finally, 30 percent of the sample had no children, 19 percent had one child, and 51 percent had more than one child.

FINDINGS

DISAPPROVAL OF DIVORCE

When asked whether people they knew disapproved of their divorce, 34 percent of the respondents named no one and another 21 percent named only one person (out of a total of eight to thirty-five people in their networks), although the number named as disapproving did range from zero to nine. If we consider just respondents' perceptions of friends (or non-kin), only 18 percent (of the total) said more than one friend disapproved while fully 60 percent said no friend disapproved. The respondents were somewhat more likely to suggest that relatives disapproved. However, only 23 percent named more than one relative who disapproved while just over half (51 percent) named none. Moreover, although the respondents perceived more criticism from relatives than friends—perhaps because one of the privileges accorded kin in our society is to remark on things friends might think better left unsaid—the divorced nonetheless often dismissed their few critical relatives as "outdated," "old farts," or "living in the past."

Of course, these data are based only on the perceptions by the divorced of others' reactions to them. It is possible the divorced misperceive the true feelings of friends and relatives. But, as noted earlier, large scale surveys find that relatively few Americans say they disapprove of divorce. More importantly, a person's perceptions of the disapproval of others is central to the production of a lessened sense of self-worth (e.g., see Rosenberg, 1979). Conversely, the very belief that people do not disapprove of one's divorce may diminish the negative consequences of any disapproval that might exist. As one indicator of this, I found that the higher the proportion of those, especially non-kin, in their network whom the divorced believed disapproved, the greater the depression they experienced: the correlation of the CES-D scale and proportion of non-kin who disapproved is .23 (significant at .05 level).[4]

However, other evidence suggests that a mere count of those who disapprove gives an incomplete view of the stigma attached to divorce. As Table 1 shows, the respondents' experience of disapproval varied to some extent with the circumstances surrounding divorce.[5] For example, men—though not women—who had begun affairs during marriage that continued after separation were more likely than other men to say they encountered disapproval of the divorce. In particular, men who had such affairs were significantly more likely to experience the disapproval of non-kin. For women, what mattered most was children. Women with children believed a larger proportion of their kin network disapproved than did women without children. Such disapproval mounted when women's children were young. In contrast, the presence—or age—of children did not significantly affect the amount of disapproval men believed they encountered.

In sum, the circumstances of divorce, rather than the mere fact, are now the subject of disapproval. The conditions associated with the experience of disapproval vary for women and men, reflecting a gender-based ideology of divorce— and marriage. If a "bad" man is a cavalier homewrecker, a "bad" woman is one who does not (or cannot) sacrifice for her children. While McRae's (1978) longitudinal data suggest divorce has been removed from the realm of absolute moral condemnation or categorical blame, these findings indicate that the specific conditions of the divorce may nonetheless generate disapproval.

THE EXPERIENCE OF BLAME

Even though categorical disapproval of divorce has declined, individuals may still feel they are held accountable and blamed for their divorce. Evidence for this can be seen in the "splitting of friends." Numerous studies show that ex-spouses often split friends they shared while married (e.g., see Spanier and Thompson, 1984; Weiss, 1975). Among those interviewed in this study, over half of the men (55 percent) and close to half (43 per-

TABLE 1   Correlations Between Percentage of Kin or Non-Kin Who Disapprove of Divorce and Other Variables by Sex of Respondent

| | MALE RESPONDENTS | | FEMALE RESPONDENTS | |
| | DISAPPROVAL | | DISAPPROVAL | |
Variable	Kin	Non-Kin	Kin	Non-Kin
Education	.14	.13	−.05	.04
Income	.23	.07	.07	−.02
Age	.17	−.04	.05	.12
Affair[a]	.16	.38**	.10	−.18
Child[b]	.15	.11	.36**	.07
Yngch[c]	.02	.10	.41***	.18

Notes:
[a]Respondent had an affair before marriage ended: no=0; yes=1.
[b]Respondent has any children: no=0; yes=1.
[c]Respondent has any children less than 12 years old: no=0; yes=1.
*p < .05
**p < .01
***p < .001

cent) of the women spoke spontaneously[6] and sadly of dividing friends—e.g., finding "our friends polarized" (C007, male), "our social group split down the middle" (C035, female). Many divorced people lose friends who feel loyal to their ex-spouse and, *consequently,* are estranged from them as well.

To be sure, the respondents reported that this process of splitting friends is complicated: one spouse keeps particular friends because she or he brought those friends to the marriage—from childhood, from work, or from independent leisure activities. That spouse then "owns" those friends and receives them almost as if they were property when the marriage ends. But this pattern of splitting also indicates ways the divorced individual comes to experience social devaluation. In the splitting of friends, we discover processes that provoke others to at least act as if they blame one party to a divorce.

Feeling hurt or angry, the divorced themselves may put pressure on friends to take sides. One woman said it quite emphatically:

> I am furious at Ted [her ex-spouse]. I can't stand him being with my friends. I don't want him to have anything (N004, female).

To be supportive to one ex-spouse, a friend may have to agree to attribute blame (or at least act as if they do) to the other. As one young mother of two put it:

> Things have become difficult with friends. He [her ex-husband] has tried to put friends in the middle (N013, female).

When asked, "What do you mean?" she replied:

> He tries to get them to choose sides or to, I think, feel sorry for him. To turn them against me.

Her response suggests that friends and kin are pushed to define one ex-spouse as "guilty," the other as "innocent." They may feel pressured to blame at least one spouse in order to justify their detachment from that one and attachment to the other. One 37-year-old nurse felt she had been unfairly assessed:

> I find that some of our friends avoid me, they're not as friendly. It's the old double standard, I think. It's funny; I was saying to my father last night, that it doesn't make any difference that he was the one who left, that some people will just feel that it's the woman's fault (N010, female).

Like many others, she feels that most of the divorced split friends and that the split implies "fault," the assumption that somebody acted badly. But she incorrectly assumes her entire experience is typical, or that when other ex-spouses split friends, they become the husband's. In fact, friends were reported to be somewhat more likely to "leave" husbands than wives. One 35-year-old CPA, feeling he had been unfairly blamed, put it this way:

> I guess I wasn't very happy or thrilled with the people that put blame on one person or another. Obviously those were the people who thought my wife was correct (C005, male).

Such responses suggest that blame is attached to the individual rather than the institution: while both ex-spouses got a divorce, wrongdoing is attached to only one.

To forestall such blame, many of the respondents "told the story" of their divorce to those they had known when married. Some dreaded that telling:

> Telling other people, that is the greatest difficulty. I'd just rather people didn't know. I would almost go out of my way to avoid them rather than face them and tell them (C023, male).

When asked what the greatest difficulty with separation was, one man even replied:

> Facing your friends. I thought I was doing something wrong all the time. It was all my fault. I started thinking what if, what if this or what if that. That is a hard thing to do. Telling my friends was the hardest. It tore me up to tell my friends. Eventually I had to tell them (C011, male).

Many worried, in particular, about acquaintances: if they "knew" (N019, female) "will I have to tell them, will they find out?" (N014, female) or whether "I could just keep it to myself for a while" (N024, female). The divorced, then, come to believe they have a potentially discreditable attribute. As Goffman (1963:42) suggests, the issue becomes not simply "managing tension generated during social contacts" but "managing information" about their "failing."

But "managing information" also may mean giving it out: some of the divorced clearly also wanted to get their side across—"to win people over" (C041, male)—because they anticipated friends' "side-choosing" (C027, male). One woman spoke of "gathering her colleagues to announce" her divorce because she "wanted to rally the troops around" (C008, female). To give their own story or "account" would, they hoped, ease and legitimate their divorce.

Many divorced individuals want to provide such accounts and, as Weiss (1975) found, people often call upon the divorced to explain why their relationships did not work out. So, too, we have recent public declarations—novels written and stories told—which seek to provide "accounts."[7] For example, in her recent book *Heartburn,* Nora Ephron makes one such plea with the public not just to accept but to understand who (not what) went wrong. Such accounts allocate blame in divorce.

In his study of the divorced, Weiss (1975:15) argues that "developing the story" or the "account" of the divorce is a "device of major psychological importance not only because it settles the issue of who was responsible but because . . . it organizes the events into a conceptual, manageable unity." I would argue that the development of accounts is not simply a psychological mechanism but a social device. As Scott and Lyman (1968:46) observe, "accounts" are "statements made by a social actor to explain unanticipated or untoward behavior."[8] The development of accounts is a means by which the divorced justify their actions not only to themselves but to others as well. That the divorced feel the need to develop such accounts suggests that divorce is neither experienced nor greeted neutrally. Rather, it is an aspect of biography that must be managed and negotiated socially. In the splitting of friends, then, others often are pressured to "blame" one ex-spouse. And, by offering "accounts" for their actions, the divorced not only share but sustain the notion that blame should and will be allocated.

SOCIAL EXCLUSION: REJECTION BY THE MARRIED

Partners to a divorce not only split friends; they are often excluded from social interaction with the married more generally.[9] Many ex-husbands and ex-wives found they could not maintain friendships with married couples: about one-half of both men (43 percent) and women (58 percent) agreed with the statement: "Married couples don't want to see me now." Moreover, less than one-fourth (23 percent) of the women and men agreed: "I am as close to my married friends as when I was married."[10] By getting a divorce, then, they became marginal to at least part of the community on which they had previously relied.

One man summed up the views of many when he spoke of the "normal life" of the married.

One of the things I recognized not long after I was separated is that this is a couple's world. People do things in couples, normally (C043, male).

Remembering his own marriage, he now recognized its impact:

We mostly went out with couples. I now have little or no contact with them.

Discovering "they don't invite me anymore" or "they never call," many of the divorced felt rejected:

The couples we shared our life with, uh, I'm an outsider now. They stay away. Not being invited to a lot of parties that we was always invited to. It's with males and females. It sucks (C030, male).

The divorced developed explanations for their exclusion. Finding themselves outsiders, some simply thought that their very presence destabilized the social life of couples: "I guess I threaten the balance" (N004, female). They found themselves social misfits in that world, using terms like "a third wheel" (N010, female; N027, male) and "odd person out" (N006, male) to describe their newly precarious relationship with the married.

Some went further, suggesting that those still in couples felt threatened by the divorce or were afraid it would harm their own marriages. "They say, 'My God, it's happening all over.' It scares them" (N019, male). Men and women expressed this form of rejection in terms of "contagion" (C027, male) and "a fear it's going to rub off on them" (N010, female).[11] Because the difficulties of marriage are often concealed, others found their divorce came as a surprise to married friends. That surprise reinforced the idea "it can happen to anyone" and "so they tend to stay away" (C027, male).

A few turned the explanation around, suspecting that married couples rejected them out of jealousy rather than fear. One woman, speaking of a friend who no longer called, explained: "It was like me living out her fantasies" (N008, female). A salesman in his mid 40s who had an affair before getting a divorce, believed:

I get a kick out of it because . . . I am the envy of both men and women because, some of it is courage, others look upon it as freedom. Both words have been used a number of times. People become very envious, and a spouse of the envious person will feel extremely threatened (N043, male).

These few could turn an unpleasant experience into an enviable one. For a small minority, then, the experience of exclusion did not produce a sense of devaluation.

But more of the divorced, men as well as women, were troubled by the thought that old friends now defined them in terms of their sexual availability and, as a result, avoided them. One woman, a teacher's aide with a very young daughter and son at home, felt insulted that friends misconstrued her situation:

Well, I now have no married friends. It's as if I all of a sudden became single and I'm going to chase after their husbands (N011, female).

And a plumbing contractor, unusual because he had custody of his five children, was particularly hurt by the image of sexual availability because he had resisted any sexual entanglements. Describing one woman who "couldn't understand why I didn't want to hop into bed with her," he noted "she told me there must be something wrong with me" (C047, male). He went on:

I would say couples in general, there seems to be a, well, they are nice to me, but distant. I think the men don't want a single man around their wives.

And when asked, "Can you tell me about that?," he associated his seeming sexual availability with a threat to the cohesion of the community:

[They] don't really want to involve me in things that are going on . . . neighborhood picnics . . . couples' things. . . . I have had men say that they figure that I'm out casing women all over. So I'm considered somewhat of an unstable person.

He added that he was not the only person who had reached this conclusion:

And this is quite common with divorced people. In group discussions, everyone seems to experience the same thing.

As his final comment indicates, the divorced talk to each other about this experience and generate a shared explanation for it—that they are viewed as somewhat "unstable." Thus, some divorced people come to believe that married acquaintances saw them as "misfits"—unstable individuals who could not maintain a stable marriage, a threat to the routines of a community made of the "normal" married.[12]

The exclusion of the divorced from the social life they had enjoyed while married constitutes a negative sanction on divorce. This is not simply a functional process of friendship formation based on homogamy (cf. Lazarsfeld and Merton, 1964): it involves conflict, producing a sense of devaluation on the part of one group (the divorced) who feel rejected by another group still considered normal (the married).[13]

The divorced try to come to terms with their experience by talking to others who share it. Together they develop a shared understanding similar to what Goffman (1963:5) calls a "stigma theory": the married feel uncomfortable, even threatened by them, and act as if divorce, as a "social disease," is contagious. Or divorce poses a threat because of the desired freedom and sexuality it (perhaps falsely) represents. Finally, divorced people mutually develop a broader explanation for the modern response to them: they are avoided because the dissolution of marriage is so common, so possible, that it becomes a real threat both to any given couple and to the social world built on, and routinized by, groups consisting of couples.

COLLEAGUES AND DEMORALIZATION

The separation of the divorced from the married is even more clearly apparent in the social life developed by the divorced themselves. The divorced pull away from the married and into the lives of others like them. Goffman (1963:18) argues that the stigmatized turn to others like them in anticipation that "mixed social contact will make for anxious, unanchored interaction." Accordingly, many of the divorced said they felt "uncomfortable" (C042, female), "strained" (C003, male; N014 and C029, females), "strange" (C034, female), and "awkward" (C019, male) in a world composed of couples. And some abandoned the married: "I've been pulling way from my coupled friends" (C026, female).

Drawing together with other divorced, they can develop as well as share their "sad tales" (Goffman, 1963:19) and learn how to behave. In fact, over half of the people with whom these divorced men (52 percent) and women (62 percent) socialized were other divorced individuals, a far higher proportion than is found in the general population (U.S. Bureau of the Census, 1983). The divorced used many well-worn phrases to talk about others who shared their marital status: "birds of a feather flock together" (N021, male) and "likes attract likes" (N025, female).

Many discovered their interests and concerns, at least for a time, were based on their new found marital status. When asked to respond to the statement, "I have more in common with singles now," over half of the men (55 percent) and women (58 percent) agreed. One 28-year-old working-class man sought out divorced people for the same reason many respondents avoided the married. He said of others who shared his marital status:

> We have something in common. We have almost right off the bat something to talk about. It makes it easier to talk because you have gone through it (C018, male).

Equally important, respondents often felt they could turn to other divorced people as experienced "veterans" (Caplan, 1974) and "colleagues" (Best and Luckenbill, 1980) for their new-found marital state. These others served as role models, showing them ways to cope as spouseless adults and, in doing so, bolstered their new identities. A man referred to other divorced as providing an "experience bank" and elaborated by saying:

> I solicited assistance, guidance from people who had gone through or who were going through similar experiences. So I might get a better understanding of how they reacted to it (C043, male).

So, too, other divorced people could help them do what Hochschild (1983:254) has called "feeling work" or "the shaping, modulating, or inducing of feelings." That is, colleagues encouraged them to manage and change their feelings, and to realize how their marriage (or many marriages) were not as good as they had thought. That helped them disengage from their ex-spouses.

But these colleagues could do something more. They showed them that the life of a divorced adult was not all anguish and pain. One 30-year-old middle-class woman found she felt closest to her old friends who had been through divorce because:

> I could talk to them and they helped me to talk about my problems. What went wrong. I felt they could understand. And it was interesting to hear

what they had been through, you know (C016, female).

Importantly, she added:

I wanted to hear what it was like. It sorta helped me to think that they had made a go of their life again. They were happy afterwards.

The divorced needed reassurance that divorce did not imply a serious character flaw. They needed to find those who, after getting a divorce, had made a successful transition. A 32-year-old man, who in the first month "isolated" himself "for fear that people might think I'm doing something wrong," found a few months later that:

It's nice to hear people who have gone through the same experience, talking to me about it. It's nice to hear a lot of these things because you realize: "Hey, I'm not so bad. I'm not the only one this happens to." And looking at the person and seeing that they made it okay. And that I will, too (N009, male).

What Goffman (1963:20) wrote more generally about the stigmatized, then, characterizes the modern divorced: "They can provide instruction for tricks of the trade and a circle of lament to which he can withdraw for moral support and comfort of feeling at home, at ease, accepted as a person who is really like any normal person." The divorced turn to others like themselves to get reassurance, advice, and encouragement, and to make sense of their often dislocated lives. Telling their story to those like themselves is therapeutic (Conrad and Schneider, 1980).

Yet, there are also pitfalls in this attraction to others like them. As time passes, the divorced may find themselves bored by constant discussion of divorce, that "the whole matter of focusing on atrocity tales . . . on the 'problem' is one of the largest penalties for having one" (Goffman, 1962:21). As a man divorced close to two years put it:

You see, I've been locked in too much with divorced people. You're relating to them relative to the separation. And what happened to you, when you did it, you know (N019, male).

The divorced, especially those who had been separated more than a year, spoke of how they were getting tired of "problems dominating the conversation" (C042, female, divorced three years) as they felt "dissipated" (C009, male, divorced two years) and "wanted to talk to people about something different" (N016, female, divorced a year-and-a-half) because "the less you talk about the problems, the less you think about them, and the less you feel about them" (N028, female, divorced a year-and-a-half). One man described how, in the first months of divorce, he had "learned a lot about divorce" from others who had the same experience because "they understood me." But then he went on to complain about the problems with this association: "You feel up and then someone drags you down with their problems" (C021, male).

In fact, additional quantitative evidence indicates that association with others who are divorced becomes, over time, demoralizing. Among those separated less than one year, demoralization (PERI) is negatively correlated with the proportion of divorced in their networks ($r = -.27$, $p < .05$). In contrast, for those separated one to two years, the correlation between demoralization and proportion of divorced in networks becomes positive ($r = .26$, $p < .05$). And, for those separated more than two years, this positive correlation becomes even stronger ($r = .37$, $p < .01$).[14] Thus, while the divorced may initially seek out others like them, association with others who are divorced eventually may come to produce a lowered sense of self-esteem.[15]

THE DEVALUATION OF SELF

Perhaps the most striking evidence that the divorced devalue their own condition is found in their assessment of organizations established for the divorced. Only 10 percent of the respondents were in such groups.[16] In fact, most of the divorced—male as well as female—explicitly rejected such formal mechanisms of integration set up by and for others like them.

For the relatively small number of people who did join, such groups provided both a source of entertainment for their children as well as an opportunity to meet other adults. However, in explaining why they joined, the divorced typically stressed child care. Thus, children were not simply a reason for joining; they provided legitimation for membership. By explaining membership in instrumental rather than expressive terms, and in terms of children rather than themselves, the divorced distanced themselves from the potentially damaging implications of membership for their own identity. In this sense, children provide a "face saving device," much like those inventoried by Berk (1977) among people who attended single dances.

The notion that groups for the divorced—and therefore those who join them—are stigmatized is substantiated still further by the comments of those who did not join. They gave a number of reasons for their reluctance. Some attributed their lack of participation to a lack of knowledge. Others simply felt they did not have the time or energy. When asked why she had not joined any divorce group, one 25-year-old saleswoman said:

> I've thought about it, but I have just never done anything about it. I know it is not getting me anywhere by not doing anything. Basically I am a lazy person (C024, female).

But while she first blamed herself for non-participation in these groups, she then went on to add a more critical note: "I think I would feel funny walking into a place like that." Her second thought reiterated a common theme—an attitude toward divorce and membership in organizations for them—which came through with compelling force. Many imagined that people who joined such groups were unacceptable in a variety of ways, or even that to join them was somehow a sign of weakness. For example:

> These people really don't have somebody to turn to. I guess that's the main reason for them belonging and I do have someone to turn to, matter of fact, more than one. They're really not sure of themselves, they're insecure (N013, female).

Such comments reveal that respondents saw divorce as a discredit, at least insofar as it became the axis of one's social life. Consequently, to join such groups was to reinforce the very devaluation they hoped to avoid. One welfare mother with a young child had been told by her social worker that joining a singles' group might alleviate the enormous loneliness she experienced. But she resisted:

> It's kind of degrading to me or something. Not that I'm putting these other people down. I could join something but I couldn't join something that was actually called a single's group (N016, female).

Others reiterated the same theme. To them, groups of the divorced were "rejects looking, you know, going after rejects. They need a crutch" (N011, female). Or they asked rhetorically, "Is that for the very, very lonely?" (C016, female). These to them were "people with as many, if not worse, problems than I have" (C040, male) or "weirdos" (N029, female). As these comments show, the divorced were quick to put a pejorative label on groups consisting of other divorced.

Or, the divorced we spoke to felt that such groups were unacceptable because they were sexual marketplaces. In the words of a 28-year-old plant supervisor, who (like most others) had never actually been to any organization for the divorced:

> I refuse to go to a place where I'm looked at as a side of beef and women are looked at as sides of beef. It disgusts me (C040, male).

Association with such groups would reinforce the very view that so many of the divorced work so hard to dispel. While their rejection of such groups is a way to separate themselves from a stigmatized status (Berk, 1977:542), the very character and strength of the rejection confirms that the status is stigmatized. Thus, in distancing themselves, the divorced reveal that they share the belief that individuals who divorce, especially if they use that divorce to organize their social worlds, continue to be somehow tainted.

Despite their negative reaction to divorce groups, respondents did not reject all organized routes to friendship formation. The majority (82 percent) were members of at least one group—including, for example, sports, cultural, religious and service groups. Women participated in a median of 2.24 groups; men, a median of 3.56. In fact, many spoke of joining these other groups as a way to "make friends" and to cope with the loneliness they felt. Such groups may provide access to others who are divorced, but only coincidentally. These organizational memberships—and the relationships they allow—are legitimized by their *dissociation* from marital status. It is in this context that respondents' resistance to joining divorce groups becomes especially compelling as evidence for their devaluation of the status of divorce.

CONCLUSION

To argue that the divorced are no longer stigmatized is to misunderstand their experience. To be sure, divorce is now less deviant in a statistical sense than it was a decade ago. As a group, the divorced are not categorized as sinful, criminal, or even wrong. Moreover, even though the divorced lose married friends and have smaller networks than the married, they do not become completely ghettoized into subcultures of the divorced (Gerstel et al., 1985; Weiss, 1979). Finally, as I have shown here, the divorced themselves do not think that most of their kin and friends disapprove.

However, a decrease in statistical deviance, a relaxation of institutional controls by church or state, or a decline in categorical disapproval is not the same as an absence of stigmatization. Although a majority of Americans claim they are indifferent in principle to those who make a "personal decision" to leave a "bad" marriage, this indifference does not carry over into the social construction of private lives. The divorced believe they are the targets of informal relational sanctions—exclusion, blame, and devaluation. If we understand stigma as referring not simply to the realm of public sanctions but rather see it as emerging out of everyday experience, then we can see that the divorced continue to be stigmatized.

I have shown that divorced individuals believe they are subject to censure for what others see as their misdeeds. Such disapproval is, however, not categorical; it is contingent on the particular conditions of the divorce. The experience of devaluation attaches to the cause or circumstances surrounding the divorce rather than to divorce *per se*.

The conditional response to divorce, and the blame attached to one party, is still embodied in the law. Critics of the fault grounds in divorce law argued they were too restrictive and invaded privacy (Krause, 1986). But most states have *added* no-fault bases to laws concerning marital dissolution; they have not completely replaced the traditional (or modernized) set of fault grounds. As legal scholar Harry Krause (1986:337) explains:

> *Many legislators remained persuaded that fault grounds should continue to provide immediate relief in severe cases. And, at least in the popular mind, there* does *remain a 'right' and 'wrong' in marriage and divorce.*

Thus, as I have argued, the decline of categorical disapproval of the institution of divorce is not the same thing as the absence of notions of wrongdoing concerning individuals who divorce. And we should not be surprised that the divorced still think of themselves as "failures" even when they live in an era of "no-fault divorce."

Moreover, we might expect that the very disjunction between public tolerance and private, interpersonal sanctions would itself chagrin and distress the divorced. Feeling shame or guilt, they carefully manage information about their divorce. As one strategy of information control, they engage in "preventive disclosure"—a kind of "instrumental telling" used by the stigmatized to "influence others' actions and ideas toward the self" (Schneider and Conrad, 1980:40). Thus, the divorced create "accounts" to pressure old friends to take sides. While it may remove blame from the self, such preventive disclosure attaches blame to the ex-spouse. In fact, it is intended to do so. Here, we see that much of the censure they experience is created out of the interaction between the divorced and those in the networks surrounding them. The assumption, then, still lingers (or is socially reaffirmed) that divorce is linked to or results from defects in at least one partner.

The divorced also seek out others "like them" from whom they can learn how to behave and present themselves. With these other divorced, their "sad tales" have a different purpose: they are meant to be "therapeutic" (Schneider and Conrad, 1980:40). However, the cathartic effects of such disclosures are temporary; over time, interaction with other divorced men and women produces demoralization. Thus, either type of information management—preventive disclosure or therapeutic telling—may reinforce the very stigmatization it is intended to dispel.

The divorced are not merely victims. In both their talk and action, the divorced sustain the idea that to be married is to be "normal." Similar to other "outsiders," they "subscribe to the very rules they have broken" (Becker, 1963:3). In so doing, the divorced reinforce rather than criticize the social order. Rather than attacking marriage, they uphold it. Given these processes, it is not surprising that most of the divorced hope to and do remarry rather quickly (Furstenberg, 1982).

My findings suggest a methodological weakness of previous research. Studies of the divorced, and the stigmatized more generally, often look only at those who join self-help groups. However, as I have shown, many do not join. More importantly, they label those who do as somehow tainted. While many self-help groups have developed to counter the view of the disabled as pathetic or as victims (Zola, 1983), the need for such groups implies—rather than denies—that these groups experience stigma. In particular, the very development of singles' groups is further evidence that the divorced (like other disabled) are stigmatized and that such groups are "stigmatic situations" (Berk, 1977). Only by comparing those who join with those who do not can we establish whether participation in such groups promotes the favorable sense of self many claim for it (see Best and Luckenbill, 1980).

Future research might fruitfully look at the issues explored here—conditional disapproval and relational sanctions—from the perspective of those who compose the networks of the divorced. A full understanding of the processes of stigmatization must include an analysis of the interaction between self-labeling and the actual response of the "normals."

Finally, my findings may be generalizable beyond the divorced. Those discussed at the beginning of this paper—the unwed mother, the childless adult, and even the employed mother with an infant—may encounter some of the same relational sanctions and conditional disapproval as do the divorced. Thus, for example, Miall (1986) found that involuntarily childless women view their infertility as discreditable and experience isolation and conflict. But she also found conditions under which childlessness is less personally stigmatizing: if involuntary rather than voluntary, the "fault" of the husband rather than the wife. While some observers suggest that we can transform deviance to diversity by relabeling these arrangements as "alternative lifestyles," the consequent decline in public disapproval towards them may be as limited, and conditional, as is the case with divorce.

NOTES

1. A small number of these referrals were located through a "snowball" strategy: various people who heard about our study told us about individuals who had just separated. But the majority of referrals were located through respondents. At the end of each interview, we asked for the names of other people who had been separated less than a year and interviewed a maximum of one person named by each respondent.

2. A shortened 27-item version of PERI was chosen because of its reliability and validity as a measure of nonspecific emotional distress or demoralization. The shortened version was chosen in consultation with Bruce Dohrenwend, the creator of the scale. The self report CES-D scale was included to measure the more specific items of depression experienced during the week previous to the interview. Developed for studies of the general

population, the CES-D scale consists of 20 items selected from previously existing scales which represent the major factors in the clinical syndrome of depression. Items measure depressed mood, including feelings of guilt, worthlessness, helplessness, and hopelessness as well as psychophysiological manifestations such as psychomotor retardation, loss of appetite, and sleep disturbance.

3. Women's mean household income was $14,000 while the men's mean income was $22,000.

4. Controlling for income and the presence of children (two characteristics often found to be associated with depression e.g., Gove and Geerkin, 1977; Kessler, 1982), I found the correlation between the CES-D scale and disapproval of non-kin was .21 (still significant at the .05 level). Depression was not significantly associated with proportion of kin who disapproved. Of course, the causal order of the relationship between depression and disapproval is difficult to determine: those who are more depressed may, as a result of their depression, believe more people disapprove of them. Alternatively, those who believe they encounter more disapproval may, as a result, become more depressed. These two explanations are not necessarily mutually exclusive but instead probably interact in complex ways.

5. In Table 1, I have presented correlations between *percent* of kin and non-kin who disapproved and other variables. I do not present the data on correlations between *number* of kin and non-kin who disapproved and other variables because of the range in number of network members named. However, it should be noted that the correlations for *number* are almost identical with those for *percent*.

6. We did not directly ask a question about the splitting of friends; these figures are based on the number of people who brought up the topic spontaneously in the open-ended questions. Thus, these figures are probably conservative.

7. For further discussion of the "accounts" of the divorced, see Riessman and Gerstel (1986).

8. Given the social import of accounts for divorce, it is likely that they have varied historically—as have the legal rationales for divorce. The work of Kitson and Sussman (1982) provides some support for this expectation. They compared the reasons respondents offered for separation to those Goode (1956) received several decades earlier. The more recent explanations emphasized affectional and sexual incompatibilities as opposed to the instrumental ones offered in earlier decades. While such listings of complaints to an interviewer are clearly differ-

ent from the accounts of which I write, they do reinforce my argument that accounts offered to interviewers and probably others will vary over time.

9. Using a variety of methods and samples, a number of other studies also find that the divorced lose married friends (e.g., Spanier and Thompson, 1984; Wallerstein and Kelly, 1980; Weiss, 1979).

10. In contrast to my finding that divorced men and women were equally likely to experience a certain distance from the married, Hetherington et al. (1976:422) found "dissociation from married friends was greater for women than for men." However, they studied only divorced parents of children in nursery school. Fischer's (1982) findings would lead us to believe that, of any group, mothers—married or divorced—of young children are most isolated. In fact, my data suggest that the gender differences may well characterize only this very special group. Among male respondents, the presence of children is not significantly associated with their belief that "married couples don't want to see them" or their feeling they "are not as close to those couples." In contrast, for women, the presence of any children, especially young children, increases disassociation from the married. Among female respondents, the correlation between "married couples don't want to see me now" and the presence of any children is .25 (p < .05) and with having children less than 12-years-old is .39 (p < .01). This difference between women and men may well be a result of the fact that women obtain custody of the children far more often than do men. While Hetherington's findings are often cited as evidence for general gender differences in the social life of the divorced, this implication probably should be limited to this special group—the parents of young children.

11. This belief that others see their "condition" as "contagious" is similar to the experience of others who are stigmatized, like the mentally ill. See Foucault (1967) for a discussion of the development of the belief that "unreason" is contagious, that anyone could "catch it," and the consequent movement to isolate the insane.

12. Wallerstein and Kelly (1980:33) hypothesize that still another factor may explain why the married move away from the divorced: the married "feel uncomfortable and inadequate in providing solace." While this is certainly a possible (and generous) explanation, the divorced nonetheless experience the loss of friendship as rejection and exclusion.

13. To be sure, research on "single individuals"—be they widows (Lopata, 1979), never married (Stein, 1981), or

divorced—suggests there is a general pattern of friendship based on homogeneity of marital status. Indeed, as Simmel (1950) points out in his classic work, the triad is a more unstable group than the dyad. Hence, a "third party" is likely to be excluded. Here, I am suggesting that such third parties, especially the divorced, are likely to interpret the separation of marital groups as exclusion and hence as devaluation.

14. This relationship—a different effect of proportion of divorced in networks on depression across stages of the divorce process—is maintained after controls for income and presence of children are introduced in a multiple regression procedure: the interaction term of length of time separated and proportion divorced is significantly significant at the .05 level.

15. Of course, the direction of causation between homogeneity and depression is unclear: I am suggesting that association with other divorced produces depression over time. However, it is possible that in the later stages of divorce, those who are especially demoralized are more likely to seek out other divorced while in the earlier stages those less demoralized are most likely to seek out other divorced.

16. These findings suggest, of course, that those studies which draw entirely on members of singles' groups are seriously flawed: they represent a small and atypical population of the divorced.

REFERENCES

Becker, Howard S. 1963. *Outsiders: Studies in the Sociology of Deviance.* New York: Free Press.

Berk, Bernard. 1977. "Facet saving at the singles dance." *Social Problems* 24:530–44.

Best, Joel, and David Luckenbill. 1980. "The social organization of deviants." *Social Problems* 28:14–31.

Caplan, Gerald. 1974. *Social Supports and Community Mental Health.* New York: Behavioral Publications.

Cherlin, Andrew. 1981. *Marriage, Divorce and Remarriage.* Cambridge, MA: Harvard University Press.

Conrad, Peter, and Joseph W. Schneider. 1980. *Deviance and Medicalization: From Badness to Sickness.* St. Louis: C. V. Mosby.

Ephron, Nora. 1983. *Heartburn.* New York: Pocket Books.

Fischer, Claude. 1982. *To Dwell Among Friends.* Chicago: University of Chicago Press.

Foucault, Michel. 1967. *Madness and Civilization.* London: Tavistock.

Furstenberg, Frank P. 1982. "Conjugal succession: reentering marriage after divorce." Pp. 107–46 in Paul B. Bates and Orville G. Brim (eds.), *Life-Span Development and Behavior.* Volume 4, New York: Academic Press.

Gerstel, Naomi. 1982. "The new right and the family." Pp. 6–20 in Barbara Haber (ed.), *The Woman's Annual.* New York: G. K. Hall.

Gerstel, Naomi, Catherine Kohler Riessman, and Sarah Rosenfield. 1985. "Explaining the symptomatology of separated and divorced women and men: the role of material resources and social networks." *Social Forces* 64:84–101.

Goffman, Erving. 1963. *Stigma.* Englewood Cliffs, NJ: Prentice-Hall.

Goode, William. 1956. *Women in Divorce.* New York: Free Press.

Gove, Walter R., and Michael Geerkin. 1977. "The effect of children and employment on the mental health of married men and women." *Social Forces* 56:66–76.

Halem, Lynne Carol. 1980. *Divorce Reform.* New York: Free Press.

Hetherington, E. M., M. Cox, and R. Cox. 1976. "Divorced fathers." *The Family Coordinator* 25:417–28.

Hochschild, Arlie Russell. 1983. "Attending to, codifying and managing feelings: sex differences in love." Pp. 250–62 in Laurel Richardson and Verta Taylor (eds.), *Feminist Frontiers.* Reading, MA: Addison-Wesley.

Huber, Joan, and Glenna Spitze. 1983. *Stratification: Children, Housework, and Jobs.* New York: Academic Press.

Kessler, Ronald D. 1982. "A disaggregation of the relationship between socioeconomic status and psychological distress." *American Sociological Review* 47:752–64.

Kitson, Gay, and Marvin Sussman. 1982. "Marital complaints, demographic characteristics and symptoms of mental distress in marriage." *Journal of Marriage and the Family* 44:87–101.

Krause, Harry D. 1986. *Family Law.* Second Edition. St. Paul, MN: West.

Lazarsfeld, Paul, and Robert K. Merton. 1964. "Friendship as a social process: a substantive and methodological analysis." Pp. 18–66 in Monroe Berger, Theodore Abel and Charles Page (eds.), *Freedom and Control in Modern Society.* New York: Van Norstrand.

Lopata, Helena. 1979. *Women as Widows*. New York: Elsevier.

McRae, James A. 1978. "The secularization of divorce." Pp. 227–42 in Beverly Duncan and Otis Dudley Duncan (eds.), *Sex Typing and Sex Roles*. New York: Academic Press.

Miall, Charlene E. 1986. "The stigma of involuntary childlessness." *Social Problems* 33:282–88.

O'Neil, William L. 1967. *Divorce in the Progressive Era*. New Haven: Yale University Press.

Riessman, Catherine, and Naomi Gerstel. 1986. "It's a long story: women and men account for marital failure." Paper presented at the World Congress of Sociologists, New Delhi, India.

Rosenberg, Morris. 1979. *Conceiving the Self*. New York: Basic Books.

Schneider, Joseph W., and Peter Conrad. 1980. "In the closet with illness: epilepsy, stigma potential and information control." *Social Problems* 28:32–44.

Scott, Marvin B., and Stanford M. Lyman. 1968. "Accounts." *American Sociological Review* 33:46–62.

Simmel, Georg. 1950. *The Sociology of Georg Simmel*. Kurt H. Wolff, Translator. New York: Free Press.

Spanier, Graham, and Linda Thompson. 1984. *Parting*. Beverley Hills, CA: Sage.

Stein, Peter (ed.). 1981. *Single Life*. Englewood Cliffs, NJ: Prentice-Hall.

Thornton, Arland. 1985. "Changing attitudes toward separation and divorce: causes and consequences." *American Journal of Sociology* 90:856–72.

U.S. Bureau of Census. 1983. "Marital status and living arrangements: March, 1983." *Current Population Reports,* Series P-20, #389. Washington, DC: U.S. Government Printing Office.

Veroff, Joseph, Elizabeth Douvan, and Richard A. Kulka. 1981. *The Inner American: A Self-Portrait from 1957–1976*. New York: Basic Books.

Wallerstein, Judith S., and Joan B. Kelly. 1980. *Surviving the Breakup*. New York: Basic Books.

Weiss, Robert. 1975. *Marital Separation*. New York: Basic Books.

———. 1979. *Going It Alone*. New York: Basic Books.

Weitzman, Lenore. 1981. *The Marriage Contract*. New York: Free Press.

———. 1985. *The Divorce Revolution: The Unexpected Social and Economic Consequences for Women and Children in America*. New York: Free Press.

Zola, Irving. 1983. *Sociomedical Inquiries: Recollections, Reflections and Reconsiderations*. Philadelphia, PA: Temple University Press.

CHAPTER 15

TRANSFORMING DEVIANT IDENTITY

Over the course of time deviance sometimes proves to be more punishing than rewarding. People whose deviance is self-destructive (e.g., alcoholics, drug addicts) are especially apt to try to relinquish their deviant ways and identity. But terminating a deviant career is no easy matter. The conditions for successfully transforming a deviant identity are narrow and exacting. They include the development of a conventional lifestyle and identity, support from deviants and nondeviants alike, and opportunities to adopt conventional ways. Without these conditions, a transformation of identity is unlikely.

In the first reading Harrison Trice and Paul Michael Roman analyze the factors involved in the success of Alcoholics Anonymous. David Brown then shows how some substance abusers draw on the capital of their deviant experiences by becoming substance abuse counselors and describes the stages involved in this process. Finally, Neal Shover analyzes some of the temporal as well as interpersonal contingencies that combine to help ordinary property offenders renounce their criminal careers.

Delabeling, Relabeling, and Alcoholics Anonymous

HARRISON M. TRICE and PAUL MICHAEL ROMAN

An increasing amount of research emphasis in social psychiatry in recent years has been placed upon the rehabilitation and return of former mental patients to "normal" community roles (Sussman, 1966). The concomitant rapid growth of community psychiatry as a psychiatric paradigm parallels this interest, with community psychiatry having as a primary concern the maintenance of the patient's statuses within the family and community throughout the treatment process so as to minimize problems of rehabilitation and "return" (Pasamanick *et al.*, 1967; Susser, 1968). Despite these emphases, successful "delabeling" or destigmatization of mental patients subsequent to treatment appears rare (Miller, 1965; Freeman and Simmons, 1963). It is the purpose of this paper to explore an apparent negative instance of this phenomenon, namely a type of social processing which results in *successful* delabeling, wherein the stigmatized label is replaced with one that is socially acceptable.

The so-called labeling paradigm which has assumed prominence within the sociology of deviant behavior offers a valuable conceptualization of the development of deviant careers, many of which are apparently permanent (Scheff, 1966). In essence, labeling theory focuses upon the processes whereby a "primary deviant" becomes a "secondary deviant" (Lemert, 1951:75–76). Primary deviance may arise from myriad sources. The extent and nature of the social reaction to this behavior is a function of the deviant's reaction to his own behavior (Roman and Trice, 1969), the behavior's visibility, the power vested in the statuses of the deviant actor, and the normative parameters of tolerance for deviance that exist within the

Reprinted from *Social Problems,* Vol. 17, No. 4 (Spring 1970), pp. 538–546, by permission of the Society for the Study of Social Problems and the authors.

community. Primary deviance that is visible and exceeds the tolerance level of the community may bring the actor to the attention of mandated labelers such as psychiatrists, clinical psychologists, and social workers.

If these labelers see fit "officially" to classify the actor as a type of deviant, a labeling process occurs which eventuates in (1) self concept changes on the part of the actor and (2) changes in the definitions of him held by his immediate significant others, as well as the larger community. Behavior which occurs as a consequence of these new definitions is called secondary deviance. This behavior is substantively similar to the original primary deviance but has as its source the actor's revised self concept, as well as the revised social definition of him held in the community.

Previous research and theoretical literature appear to indicate that this process is irreversible, particularly in the cases of mental illness or so-called residual deviance (Miller, 1965; Myers and Bean, 1968). No systematic effort has been made to specify the social mechanisms which might operate to "return" the stigmatized secondary deviant to a "normal" and acceptable role in the community. In other words, delabeling and relabeling have received little attention as a consequence of the assumption that deviant careers are typically permanent.

Conceptually, there appear to be at least three ways whereby delabeling could successfully occur. First, organizations of deviants may develop which have the primary goal of changing the norms of the community or society, such that their originally offending behavior becomes acceptable (Sagarin, 1967). For example, organized groups of homosexuals have strongly urged that children be educated in the dual existence of homosexuality and heterosexuality as equally acceptable forms of behavior.

Secondly, it is possible that the mandated professionals and organizations who initially label deviant behavior and process the deviant through "treatment" may create highly visible and explicit "delabeling" or "status-return" ceremonies which constitute legitimized public pronouncements that the offending deviance has ceased and the actor is eligible for re-entry into the community. Such ceremonies could presumably be the reverse of "status degradation" rituals (Garfinkel, 1956).

A third possible means is through the development of mutual aid organizations which encourage a return to strict conformity to the norms of the community as well as creating a stereotype which is socially acceptable. Exemplary of this strategy is Alcoholics Anonymous. Comprised of 14,150 local groups in the United States in 1967, this organization provides opportunities for alcoholics to join together in an effort to cease disruptive and deviant drinking behavior in order to set the stage for the resumption of normal occupational, marital, and community roles (Gellman, 1964).

The focus of this paper is the apparent success in delabeling that has occurred through the social processing of alcoholics through Alcoholics Anonymous and through alcoholics' participation in the A.A. subculture. The formulation is based chiefly on participant observation over the past 15 years in Alcoholics Anonymous and data from various of our studies of the social aspects of alcoholism and deviant drinking. These observations are supplemented by considerable contact with other "self-help" organizations. These experiences are recognized as inadequate substitutes for "hard" data; and the following points are best considered as exploratory hypotheses for further research.

THE "ALLERGY" CONCEPT

The chronic problem affecting the reacceptance into the community of former mental patients and other types of deviants is the attribution of such persons with taints of permanent "strangeness," "immorality," or "evil." A logical method for neutralizing such stigma is the promulgation of ideas or evidence that the undesirable behavior of these deviants stems from factors beyond their span of control and responsibility. In accord with Parsons' (1951) cogent analysis of the socially neutralizing effects of the "sick role," it appears that permanent stigmatization may be avoided if stereotypes of behavior disorders as forms of "illness" can be successfully diffused in the community.

Alcoholics Anonymous has since its inception attempted to serve as such a catalyst for the "delabeling" of its members through promulgating the "allergy concept" of alcohol addiction. Although not part of official A.A. literature, the allergy concept plays a prominent part in A.A. presentations to non-alcoholics as well as in the A.A. "line" that is used in "carrying the message" to non-member deviant drinkers. The substance of the allergy concept is that those who become alcoholics possess a physiological allergy to alcohol such that their addiction is pre-determined even before they take their first drink. Stemming from the allergy concept is the label of "arrested alcoholic" which A.A. members place on themselves.

The significance of this concept is that it serves to diminish, both in the perceptions of the A.A. members and their immediate significant others, the alcoholic's responsibility for developing the behavior disorder. Furthermore, it serves to diminish the impression that a form of mental illness underlies alcohol abuse. In this vein, A.A. members are noted for their explicit denial of any association between alcoholism and psychopathology. As a basis for a "sick role" for alcoholics, the allergy concept effectively reduces blame upon one's *self* for the development of alcoholism.

Associated with this is a very visible attempt on the part of A.A. to associate itself with the medical profession. Numerous publications of the organization have dealt with physicians and A.A. and with physicians who are members of A.A. (*Grapevine*, 1968). Part of this may be related to the fact that one of the co-founders was a physician; and a current long time leader is also a physician. In any event, the strong attempts to associate A.A. with the medical profession stand in contrast to the lack of such efforts to become associated with such professions as law, education, or the clergy.

Despite A.A.'s emphasis upon the allergy concept, it appears clear that a significant portion of the American public does not fully accept the notion that alcoholism and disruptive deviant drinking are the result of an "allergy" or other organic aberration. Many agencies associated with the treatment of alcohol-related problems have attempted to make "alcoholism is an illness" a major theme of mass educational efforts (Plaut, 1967). Yet in a study of 1,213 respondents, Mulford and Miller (1964) found that only 24 percent of the sample "accepted the illness concept without qualification." Sixty-five percent of the respondents regarded the alcoholic as "sick," but most qualified this judgment by adding that he was also "morally weak" or "weak-willed."

The motivation behind public agencies' efforts at promulgating the "illness" concept of behavior disorders to reduce the probability of temporary or permanent stigmatization was essentially upstaged by A.A. Nonetheless, the data indicate that acceptance of the "illness" notion by the general public is relatively low in the case of alcoholism and probably lower in the cases of other behavior disorders (cf. Nunnally, 1961). But the effort has not been totally without success. Thus it appears that A.A.'s allergy concept does set the stage for reacceptance of the alcoholic by part of the population. A more basic function may involve the operation of the A.A. program itself; acceptance of the allergy concept by A.A. members reduces the felt need for "personality change" and may serve to raise diminished self-esteem.

Other than outright acceptance of the allergy or illness notion, there appear to be several characteristics of deviant drinking behavior which reduce the ambiguity of the decision to re-accept the deviant into the community after his deviance has ceased.

Unlike the ambiguous public definitions of the causes of other behavior disorders (Nunnally, 1961), the behaviors associated with alcohol addiction are viewed by the community as a direct consequence of the inappropriate use of alcohol. With the cessation of drinking behavior, the accompanying deviance is assumed to disappear. Thus, what is basically wrong with an alcoholic is that he drinks. In the case of other psychiatric disorders the issue of "what is wrong" is much less clear. This lack of clarity underlies Scheff's (1966) notion of psychiatric disorders as comprising "residual" or relatively unclassifiable forms of deviance. Thus the mentally ill, once labeled, acquire such vague but threatening stereotypes as "strange," "different," and "dangerous" (Nunnally, 1961). Since the signs of the disorder are vague in terms of cultural stereotypes, it is most difficult for the "recovered" mental patient to convince others that he is "cured."

It appears that one of the popular stereotypes of former psychiatric patients is that their apparent normality is a "coverup" for their continuing underlying symptoms. Thus, where the alcoholic is able to remove the cause of his deviance by ceasing drinking, such a convincing removal may be impossible in the case of the other addictions and "mental" disorders. Narcotic addiction represents an interesting middle ground between these two extremes, for the cultural stereotype of a person under the influence of drugs is relatively unclear, such that it may be relatively difficult for the former addict to convince others that he has truly removed the cause of his deviance. This points up the fact that deviant drinking and alcoholism are continuous with behavior engaged in by the majority of the adult population, namely "normal" drinking (Mulford, 1964). The fact that the deviant drinker and alcohol addict are simply carrying out a common and normative behavior to excess reduces the "mystery" of the alcoholic experience and creates relative confidence in the average citizen regarding his abilities to identify a truly "dry" alcoholic. Thus the relative clarity of the cultural stereotype regarding the causes of deviance accompanying alcohol abuse provides much better means for the alcoholic to claim he is no longer a deviant.

To summarize, A.A. promulgates the allergy concept both publicly and privately, but data clearly indicate that this factor alone does not account for the observed success at "re-entry" achieved by A.A. members. Despite ambiguity in public definitions of the etiology of alcoholism, its continuity with "normal" drinking behavior results in greater public confidence in the ability to judge the results of a therapeutic program. An understanding of A.A.'s success becomes clearer when this phenomenon is coupled with the availability of the "repentant" role.

THE REPENTANT ROLE

A relatively well-structured status of the "repentant" is clearly extant in American cultural tradition. Upward mobility from poverty and the "log cabin" comprises a social type where the individual "makes good" for his background and the apparent lack of conformity to economic norms of his ancestors. Redemptive religion, emergent largely in American society, emphasizes that one can correct a moral lapse even of long duration by public admission of guilt and repentance (cf. Lang and Lang, 1960).

The A.A. member can assume this repentant role; and it may become a social vehicle whereby, through contrite and remorseful public expressions, substantiated by visibly reformed behavior in conformity to the norms of the community, a former deviant can enter a new role which is quite acceptable to society. The re-acceptance may not be entirely complete, however, since the label of alcoholic is replaced with that of "arrested alcoholic"; as Gusfield (1967) has stated, the role comprises a social type of a "repentant deviant." The acceptance of the allergy concept by his significant others may well hasten his re-acceptance, but the more important factor seems to be the relative clarity by which significant others can judge the deviant's claim to "normality." Ideally the re-

pentant role is also available to the former mental patient; but as mentioned above, his inability to indicate clearly the removal of the symptoms of his former deviance typically blocks such an entry.

If alcohol is viewed in its historical context in American society, the repentant role has not been uniquely available to A.A. members. As an object of deep moral concern no single category of behavior (with the possible exception of sexual behavior) has been laden with such emotional intensity in American society. Organized social movements previous to A.A. institutionalized means by which repentants could control their use of alcohol. These were the Washingtonians, Catch-My-Pal, and Father Matthews movements in the late 1800's and early 1900's, which failed to gain widespread social acceptance. Thus not only is the repentant role uniquely available to the alcoholic at the present time, but Alcoholics Anonymous has been built on a previous tradition.

SKID ROW IMAGE AND SOCIAL MOBILITY

The major facet of Alcoholics Anonymous' construction of a repentant role is found in the "Skid Row image" and its basis for upward social mobility. A central theme in the "stories" of many A.A. members is that of downward mobility into Skid Row or near Skid Row situations. Research evidence suggests that members tend to come from the middle and lower middle classes (Trice, 1962; Straus and Bacon, 1951). Consequently a "story" of downward mobility illustrates the extent to which present members had drastically fallen from esteem on account of their drinking. A.A. stories about "hitting bottom" and the many degradation ceremonies that they experienced in entering this fallen state act to legitimize their claims to downward mobility. Observation and limited evidence suggests that many of these stories are exaggerated to some degree and that a large proportion of A.A. members maintained at least partially stable status-sets throughout the addiction process. However, by the emphasis on downward mobility due to drinking, the social mobility "distance" traveled by the A.A. member is maximized in the stories. This clearly sets the stage for impressive "comeback accomplishments."

Moral values also play a role in this process. The stories latently emphasize the "hedonistic underworld" to which the A.A. member "traveled." His current status illustrates to others that he has rejected this hedonism and has clearly resubmitted himself to the normative controls and values of the dominant society, exemplified by his A.A. membership. The attempt to promulgate the "length of the mobility trip" is particularly marked in the numerous anonymous appearances that A.A. members make to tell their stories before school groups, college classes, church groups, and service clubs. The importance of these emphases may be indirectly supported by the finding that lower-class persons typically fail in their attempts to successfully affiliate with A.A., i.e., their social circumstances minimize the distance of the downward mobility trip (Trice and Roman, 1970; Trice, 1959).

A.A. AND AMERICAN VALUES

The "return" of the A.A. member to normal role performance through the culturally provided role of the repentant and through the implied social mobility which develops out of an emphasis upon the length of the mobility trip is given its meaning through tapping directly into certain major American value orientations.

Most importantly, members of Alcoholics Anonymous have regained self control and have employed that self control in bringing about their rehabilitation. Self control, particularly that which involves the avoidance of pleasure, is a valued mode of behavior deeply embedded in the American ethos (Williams, 1960). A.A. members have, in a sense, achieved success in their battle with alcohol and may be thought of in that way as being "self-made" in a society permeated by "a systematic moral orientation by which conduct is judged" (Williams, 1960:424). This illustration of

self control lends itself to positive sanction by the community.

A.A. also exemplifies three other value orientations as they have been delineated by Williams: humanitarianism, emphases upon practicality, and suspicion of established authority (Williams, 1960:397–470). A definite tendency exists in this society to identify with the helpless, particularly those who are not responsible for their own afflictions.

A.A. taps into the value of efficiency and practicality through its pragmatism and forthright determination to "take action" about a problem. The organization pays little heed to theories about alcoholism and casts all of its literature in extremely practical language. Much emphasis is placed upon the simplicity of its tenets and the straightforward manner in which its processes proceed.

Its organizational pattern is highly congruous with the value, suspicion of vested authority. There is no national or international hierarchy of officers, and local groups maintain maximum autonomy. Within the local group, there are no established patterns of leadership, such that the organization proceeds on a basis which sometimes approaches anarchy. In any event, the informality and equalitarianism are marked features of the organization, which also tend to underline the self control possessed by individual members.

A.A.'s mode of delabeling and relabeling thus appears in a small degree to depend upon promulgation of an allergy concept of alcoholism which is accepted by some members of the general population. Of greater importance in this process is the effective contrivance of a repentant role. Emphasis upon the degradation and downward mobility experienced during the development of alcoholism provides for the ascription of considerable self control to middle-class members, which in turn may enhance their prestige and "shore up" their return to "normality." The repentance process is grounded in and reinforced by the manner in which the A.A. program taps into several basic American value orientations.

A.A.'S LIMITATIONS

As mentioned above, A.A. affiliation by members of the lower social classes is frequently unsuccessful. This seems to stem from the middleclass orientation of most of the A.A. programs, from the fact that it requires certain forms of public confessions and intense interpersonal interaction which may run contrary to the images of masculinity held in the lower classes, as well as interpersonal competence.

Perhaps an equally significant limitation is a psychological selectivity in the affiliation process. A recent followup study of 378 hospitalized alcoholics, all of whom had been intensely exposed to A.A. during their treatment, revealed that those who successfully affiliated with A.A. upon their re-entry into the community had personality features significantly different from those who did not affiliate (Trice and Roman, 1970). The successful affiliates were more guilt prone, sensitive to responsibility, more serious, and introspective. This appears to indicate a definite "readiness" for the adoption of the repentant role among successful affiliates. To a somewhat lesser extent, the affiliates possessed a greater degree of measured ego strength, affiliative needs, and group dependency, indicating a "fit" between the peculiar demands for intense interaction required for successful affiliation and the personalities of the successful affiliates. Earlier research also revealed a relatively high need for affiliation among A.A. affiliates as compared to those who were unsuccessful in the affiliation process (Trice, 1959).

These social class and personality factors definitely indicate the A.A. program is not effective for all alcoholics. Convincing entry into the repentant role, as well as successful interactional participation in the program, appear to require middle-class background and certain personality predispositions.

SUMMARY

In summary, we shall contrast the success of A.A. in its delabeling with that experienced by other self help groups designed for former drug addicts and mental patients (Wechsler, 1960; Landy and Singer, 1961). As pointed out above, the statuses of mental patients and narcotic addicts lack the causal clarity accompanying the role of alcoholic. It is most difficult for narcotic addicts and former mental patients to remove the stigma since there is little social clarity about the cessation of the primary deviant behavior. Just as there is no parallel in this respect, there is no parallel in other self-help organizations with the Skid Row image and the status-enhancing "mobility trip" that is afforded by this image. The primary deviant behaviors which lead to the label of drug addict or which eventuate in mental hospitalization are too far removed from ordinary social experience for easy acceptance of the former deviant to occur. These behaviors are a part of an underworld from which return is most difficult. On the other hand, Alcoholics Anonymous possesses, as a consequence of the nature of the disorder of alcoholism, its uniqueness as an organization, and the existence of certain value orientations within American society, a pattern of social processing whereby a labeled deviant can become "delabeled" as a stigmatized deviant and relabeled as a former and repentant deviant.

REFERENCES

Anonymous. 1968. "Doctors, Alcohol and A.A." *Alcoholics Anonymous Grapevine* (October).

Freeman, H. and O. Simmons. 1963. *The Mental Patient Comes Home.* New York: Wiley.

Garfinkel, H. 1956. "Conditions of Successful Degradation Ceremonies." *American Journal of Sociology,* 61 (March):420–424.

Gellman, I. 1964. *The Sober Alcoholic.* New Haven: College and University Press.

Gusfield, J. 1967. "Moral Passage: The Symbolic Process in Public Designations of Deviance." *Social Problems,* 15 (Winter):175–188.

Landy, D. and S. Singer. 1961. "The Social Organization and Culture of a Club for Former Mental Patients." *Human Relations,* 14 (January):31–40.

Lang, K. and G. Lang. 1960. "Decisions for Christ: Billy Graham in New York City." In M. Stein *et al.* (eds.),

Identity and Anxiety. New York: The Free Press, pp. 415–427.

Lemert, E. 1951. *Social Pathology.* New York: McGraw-Hill.

Miller, D. 1965. *Worlds That Fail.* Sacramento, California: California Department of Mental Hygiene.

Mulford, H. 1964. "Drinking and Deviant Drinking, U. S.A, 1963." *Quarterly Journal of Studies on Alcohol,* 25 (December):634–650.

Mulford, H. and D. Miller. 1964. "Measuring Public Acceptance of the Alcoholic as a Sick Person." *Quarterly Journal of Studies on Alcohol,* 25 (June):314–323.

Myers, J. and L. Bean. 1968. *A Decade Later.* New York: Wiley.

Nunnally, J. 1961. *Popular Conceptions of Mental Health.* New York: Holt, Rinehart and Winston.

Parsons, T. 1951. *The Social System.* Glencoe, Ill.: The Free Press.

Pasamanick, B. *et al.* 1967. *Schizophrenics in the Community.* New York: Appleton, Century, Crofts.

Plaut, T. 1967. *Alcohol Problems: A Report to the Nation.* New York: Oxford University Press.

Roman, P. and H. Trice (1969). "The Self Reaction: A Neglected Dimension of Labeling Theory." Presented at American Sociological Association Meetings, San Francisco.

Sagarin, E. 1967. "Voluntary Associations among Social Deviants." *Criminologica* 5 (January):8–22.

Scheff, T. 1966. *Being Mentally Ill.* Chicago: Aldine.

Susser, M. 1968. *Community Psychiatry.* New York: Random House.

Sussman, M. (ed.) 1966. *Sociology and Rehabilitation.* Washington: American Sociological Association.

Straus, R. and S. Bacon. 1951. "Alcoholism and Social Stability." *Quarterly Journal of Studies on Alcohol,* 12 (June):231–260.

Trice, H. 1959. "The Affiliation Motive and Readiness to Join Alcoholics Anonymous." *Quarterly Journal of Studies on Alcohol,* 20 (September):313–320.

———. 1962. "The Job Behavior of Problem Drinkers." In D. Pittman and C. Snyder (eds.), *Society, Culture and Drinking Patterns.* New York: Wiley, pp. 493–510.

Trice, H. and P. Roman. 1970. "Sociopsychological Predictors of Successful Affiliation with Alcoholics Anonymous." *Social Psychiatry,* 5 (Winter):51–59.

Wechsler, H. 1960. "The Self-help Organization in the Mental Health Field: Recovery, Inc." *Journal of Nervous and Mental Disease,* 130 (April):297–314.

Williams, R. 1960. *American Society.* New York: A. A. Knopf.

The Professional Ex-: An Alternative for Exiting the Deviant Career

J. DAVID BROWN

This study explores the careers of professional ex-s, persons who have exited their deviant careers by replacing them with occupations in professional counseling. During their transformation professional ex-s utilize vestiges of their deviant identity to legitimate their past deviance and generate new careers as counselors.

Reprinted from *The Sociological Quarterly,* Volume 32, Number 2, pages 219–230, by permission of the publisher and the author.

Author's Note: An earlier version of this article received the Mary Rue Bucher Award of the Midwest Sociological Society for best graduate student paper in 1990. Special thanks to Peter Adler, Paul Colomy, Patricia Adler, George J. McCall, and the anonymous reviewers for their support, insights, and constructive suggestions on earlier drafts of this article.

Recent surveys document that approximately 72% of the professional counselors working in the over 10,000 U. S. substance abuse treatment centers are former substance abusers (NAADAC 1986; Sobbel and Sobbel 1987). This attests to the significance of the professional ex- phenomenon. Though not all ex-deviants become professional ex-s, such data clearly suggest that the majority of substance abuse counselors are professional ex-s.[1]

Since the inception of the notion of deviant career by Goffman (1961) and Becker (1963), research has identified, differentiated, and explicated the characteristics of specific deviant career stages (e.g., Adler and Adler 1983; Luckenbill and Best 1981; Meisenhelder 1977; Miller 1986; Shover 1983). The literature devoted to exiting deviance primarily addresses the process whereby individuals abandon their deviant behaviors, ideologies, and identities and replace them with more conventional lifestyles and identities (Irwin 1970; Lofland 1969; Meisenhelder 1977; Shover 1983). While some studies emphasize the role of authorities or associations of ex-deviants in this change (e.g., Livingston 1974; Lofland 1969; Volkman and Cressey 1963), others suggest that exiting deviance is a natural process contingent upon age-related, structural, and social psychological variables (Frazier 1976; Inciardi 1975; Irwin 1970; Meisenhelder 1977; Petersilia 1980; Shover 1983).

Although exiting deviance has been variously conceptualized, to date no one has considered that it might include adoption of a legitimate career premised upon an identity that embraces one's deviant history. Professional ex-s exemplify this mode of exiting deviance.

Ebaugh's (1988) model of role exit provides an initial framework for examining this alternative mode of exiting the deviant career. Her model suggests that former roles are never abandoned but, instead, carry over into new roles. I elaborate her position and contend that one's deviant identity is not an obstacle that must be abandoned prior to exiting or adopting a more conventional lifestyle. To the contrary, one's lingering deviant identity facilitates rather than inhibits the exiting process.

How I gathered data pertinent to exiting, my relationship to these data, and how my personal experiences with exiting deviance organize this article, follow. I then present a four stage model that outlines the basic contours of the professional ex- phenomenon. Finally I suggest how the pro-

fessional ex- phenomenon represents an alternative interpretation of exiting deviance that generalizes to other forms of deviance....

Qualitative data were collected over a six month period of intensive interviews with 35 counselor ex-s employed in a variety of community, state, and private institutions that treat individuals with drug, alcohol, and/or eating disorder problems.[2]

These professional ex-s worked in diverse occupations prior to becoming substance abuse counselors. A partial list includes employment as accountants, managers, salespersons, nurses, educators, and business owners. Although they claimed to enter the counseling profession within two years of discharge from therapy, their decision to become counselors usually came within one year. On the average they had been counselors for four and one half years. Except one professional ex- who previously counseled learning disabled children, all claimed they had not seriously considered a counseling career before entering therapy.

THE EXIT PROCESS

Ebaugh (1988) contends that the experience of being an "ex" of one kind or another is common to most people in modern society. Emphasizing the sociological and psychological continuity of the ex phenomenon she states, "[I]t implies that interaction is based not only on current role definitions but, more important, past identities that somehow linger on and define how people see and present themselves in their present identities" (p. xiii). Ebaugh defines role exit as the "process of disengagement from a role that is central to one's self-identity and the reestablishment of an identity in a new role that takes into account one's ex-role" (p. 1).

Becoming a professional ex- is the outcome of a four stage process through which ex-s capitalize on the experience and vestiges of their deviant career in order to establish a new identity and role in a respectable organization. This process comprises emulation of one's therapist, the call to a

counseling career, status-set realignment, and cre-
dentialization.

STAGE ONE: EMULATION OF ONE'S THERAPIST

The emotional and symbolic identification of
these ex-s with their therapists during treatment,
combined with the deep personal meanings they
imputed to these relationships, was a compelling
factor in their decisions to become counselors.
Denzin (1987, pp. 61–62) identifies the therapeutic relationship's significance thus: "Through a
process of identification and surrender (which
may be altruistic), the alcoholic may merge her
ego and her self in the experiences and the identity of the counselor. The group leader... is the
group ego ideal, for he or she is a successful recovering alcoholic.... An emotional bond is thus
formed with the group counselor...."

Professional ex-s not only developed this
emotional bond but additionally aspired to have
the emotions and meanings once projected toward
their therapists ascribed to them. An eating disorders counselor discussed her relationship with her
therapist and her desire to be viewed in a similar
way with these words:

> My counselor taught me the ability to care about
> myself and other people. Before I met her I was lit-
> erally insane. She was the one who showed me
> that I wasn't crazy. Now, I want to be the person
> who says, "No, you're not crazy!" I am the one,
> now, who is helping them to get free from the igno-
> rance that has shrouded eating disorders.

Counselors enacted a powerfully charismatic
role in professional ex-s' therapeutic transformation. Their "laying on of verbal hands" provided
initial comfort and relief from the ravaging symptoms of disease. They came to represent what ex-s
must do both spiritually and professionally for
themselves. Substance abuse therapy symbolized
the "sacred" quest for divine grace rather than the
mere pursuit of mundane, worldly, or "profane"
outcomes like abstinence or modification of substance use/abuse behaviors; counselors embodied
the sacred outcome.

Professional ex-s claimed that their therapists
were the most significant change agent in their
transformation. "I am here today because there
was one very influential counselor in my life who
helped me to get sober. I owe it all to God and to
him," one alcoholism counselor expressed. A heroin addiction counselor stated, "The best thing
that ever happened in my life was meeting Sally
[her counselor]. She literally saved my life. If it
wasn't for her I'd still probably be out there shoo-
tin' up or else be in prison or, dead."

Subjects' recognition and identification of a
leader's charismatic authority, as Weber (1968)
notes, is decisive in validating that charisma and
developing absolute trust and devotion. The special virtues and powers professional ex-s perceived in their counselors subsequently shaped
their loyalty and devotion to the career.

Within the therapeutic relationship, professional ex-s perform a priestly function through
which a cultural tradition passes from one generation to the next. While knowledge and wisdom
pass downward (from professional ex- to patient),
careers build upward (from patient to professional
ex-). As the bearers of the cultural legacy of therapy, professional ex-s teach patients definitions of
the situation they learned as patients. Indeed, part
of the professional ex- mystique resides in once
having been a patient (Bissell 1982). In this regard,

> My counselor established her legitimacy with me
> the moment she disclosed the fact that she, too,
> was an alcoholic. She wasn't just telling me what
> to do, she was living her own advice. By the exam-
> ple she set, I felt hopeful that I could recover. As I
> reflect upon those experiences I cannot think of
> one patient ever asking me about where I received
> my professional training. At the same time, I can-
> not begin to count the numerous times that my pa-
> tients have asked me if I was "recovering."

Similar to religious converts' salvation
through a profoundly redemptive religious experience, professional ex-s' deep career commitment
derives from a transforming therapeutic resocialization. As the previous examples suggest, salva-

tion not only relates to a changed universe of discourse; it is also identified "with one's personal therapist."[3]

At this stage, professional ex-s trust in and devote themselves to their counselors' proselytizations as a promissory note for the future. The promise is redemption and salvation from the ever-present potential for self-destruction or relapse that looms in their mental horizon. An eating disorders counselor shared her insights in this way:

> I wouldn't have gotten so involved in eating disorders counseling if I had felt certain that my eating disorder was taken care of. I see myself in constant recovery. If I was so self assured that I would never have the problem again there would probably be less of an emphasis on being involved in the field but I have found that helping others, as I was once helped, really helps me.

The substance abuse treatment center transforms from a mere "clinic" occupied by secularly credentialed professionals into a moral community of single believers. As Durkheim (1915) suggests, however, beliefs require rites and practices in order to sustain adherents' mental and emotional states.

STAGE TWO: THE CALL TO A COUNSELING CAREER

At this juncture, professional ex-s begin to turn the moral corner on their deviance. Behaviors previously declared morally reprehensible are increasingly understood within a new universe of discourse as symptoms of a much larger disease complex. This recognition represents one preliminary step toward grace. In order to emulate their therapist, however, professional ex-s realize they must dedicate themselves to an identity and lifestyle that ensure their own symptoms' permanent remission. One alcoholism counselor illustrated this point by stating:

> I can't have my life, my health, my family, my job, my friends, or anything, unless I take daily necessary steps to ensure my continued recovery. My

> program of recovery has to come first. Before I can go out there and help my patients I need to always make sure that my own house is in order.

As this suggests, a new world-view premised upon accepting the contingencies of one's illness while maintaining a constant vigilance over potentially recurring symptoms replaces deviant moral and social meanings. Professional ex-s' recognition of the need for constant vigilance is internalized as their moral mission from which their spiritual duty (a counseling career) follows as a natural next step.

Although professional ex-s no longer engage in substance abuse behaviors, they do not totally abandon deviant beliefs or identity. "Lest we become complacent and forget from whence we came," as one alcoholism counselor indicated the significance of remembering and embracing the past.

Professional ex-s' identification with their deviant past undergirds their professional, experiential, and moral differentiation from other professional colleagues. A heroin addiction counselor recounted how he still identified himself as an addict and deviant:

> My perspective and my affinity to my clients, particularly the harder core criminals, is far better than the professors and other doctors that I deal with here in my job. We're different and we really don't see things the same way at all. Our acceptance and understanding of these people's diseases, if you will, is much different. They haven't experienced it. They don't know these people at all. It takes more than knowing about something to be effective. I've been there and, in many respects, I will always be there.

In this way, other counselors' medical, psychiatric, or therapeutic skills are construed as part of the ordinary mundane world. As the quotation indicates, professional ex-s intentionally use their experiential past and therapeutic transformations to legitimate their entrance into and authority in counseling careers.

Professional ex-s embrace their deviant history and identity as an invaluable, therapeutic resource and feel compelled to continually reaffirm its validity in an institutional environmnent. Certainly, participating in "12 Step Programs"[4] without becoming counselors could help others but professional ex-s' call requires greater immersion than they provide. An alcoholism counselor reflected upon this need thus:

> For me, it was no longer sufficient to only participate "anonymously" in A. A. I wanted to surround myself with other spiritual and professional pilgrims devoted to receiving and imparting wisdom.

Towards patients, professional ex-s project a saintly aura and exemplify an "ideal recovery." Internalization of self-images previously ascribed to their therapist and now reaffirmed through an emotional and moral commitment to the counseling profession facilitate this ideation. Invariably, professional ex-s' counseling careers are in institutions professing treatment ideologies identical to what they were taught as patients. Becoming a professional ex- symbolizes a value elevated to a directing goal, whose pursuit predisposes them to interpret all ensuing experience in terms of relevance to it.

STAGE THREE: STATUS-SET REALIGNMENT

Professional ex-s' deep personal identification with their therapist provides an ego ideal to be emulated with regard to both recovery and career. They immerse themselves in what literally constitutes a "professional recovery career" that provides an institutional location to reciprocate their counselors' gift, immerse themselves in a new universe of discourse, and effectively lead novitiates to salvation. "I wouldn't be here today if it wasn't for all of the help I received in therapy. This is my way of paying some of those people back by helping those still in need," one alcoholism counselor related this.

Professional ex-s' identities assume a "master status" (Hughes 1945) that differs in one fundamental respect from others' experiencing therapeutic resocialization. Specifically, their transformed identities not only become the

"most salient" in their "role identity hierarchy" (Stryker and Serpe 1982), but affect all other roles in their "status-sets" (Merton 1938). One alcoholism counselor reflected upon it this way:

> Maintaining a continued program of recovery is the most important thing in my life. Everything else is secondary. I've stopped socializing with my old friends who drink and have developed new recovering friends. I interact differently with my family. I used to work a lot of overtime but I told my old boss that overtime jeopardized my program. I finally began to realize that the job just didn't have anything to do with what I was really about. I felt alienated. Although I had been thinking about becoming a counselor ever since I went through treatment, I finally decided to pursue it.

Role realignment is facilitated by an alternative identity that redefines obligations associated with other, less significant, role identities. In the previous example, the strains of expectations associated with a former occupation fostered a role realignment consistent with a new self-image. This phenomenon closely resembles what Snow and Machalek 1983, p. 276) refer to as "embracement of a master role" that "is not merely a mask that is taken off or put on according to the situation.... Rather, it is central to nearly all situations...." An eating disorders counselor stated the need to align her career with her self-image, "I hid in my former profession, interacting little with people. As a counselor, I am personally maturing and taking responsibility rather than letting a company take care of me. I have a sense of purpose in this job that I never had before."

Financial remuneration is not a major consideration in the decision to become a professional ex-. The pure type of call, Weber (1968, p. 52) notes, "disdains and repudiates economic exploitation of the gifts of grace as a source of income...." Most professional ex-s earned more money in their previous jobs. For instance, one heroin addiction counselor stated:

> When I first got out of treatment, my wife and I started an accounting business. In our first year we cleared nearly sixty thousand dollars. The

money was great and the business showed promise but something was missing. I missed being around other addicts and I knew I wanted to do more with my life along the lines of helping out people like me.

An additional factor contributing to professional ex-s' abandonment of their previous occupation is their recognition that a counseling career could resolve lingering self-doubts about their ability to remain abstinent. In this respect becoming a professional ex- allows "staying current" with their own recovery needs while continually reaffirming the severity of their illness. An eating disorders counselor explained:

I'm constantly in the process of repeating insights that I've had to my patients. I hear myself saying, to them, what I need to believe for myself. Being a therapist helps me to keep current with my own recovery. I feel that I am much less vulnerable to my disease in this environment. It's a way that I can keep myself honest. Always being around others with similar issues prevents me from ignoring my own addiction clues.

This example illustrates professional ex-s' use of their profession to secure self-compliance during times of self-doubt. While parroting the virtues of the program facilitates recognition that they, too, suffer from a disease, the professional ex- role, unlike their previous occupations, enables them to continue therapy indirectly.

Finally, the status the broader community ascribes to the professional ex- role encourages professional ex-s' abandonment of previous roles. Association with an institutional environment and an occupational role gives the professional ex- a new sense of place in the surrounding community, within which form new self-concepts and self-esteem, both in the immediate situation and in a broader temporal framework.

The internal validation of professional ex-s' new identity resides in their ability to successfully anticipate the behaviors and actions of relevant alters. Additionally, they secure validation by other members of the professional ex- community in a manner atypical for other recovering individuals.

Affirmation by this reference community symbolizes validation by one's personal therapist and the therapeutic institution, as a heroin addiction counselor succinctly stated:

Becoming a counselor was a way to demonstrate my loyalty and devotion to helping others and myself. My successes in recovery, including being a counselor, would be seen by patients and those who helped me get sober. It was a return to treatment, for sure, but the major difference was that this time I returned victorious rather than defeated.

External validation, on the other hand, comes when others outside the therapeutic community accord legitimacy to the professional ex- role. In this regard, a heroin addiction counselor said:

I remember talking to this guy while I was standing in line for a movie. He asked me what I did for a living and I told him that I was a drug abuse counselor. He started asking me all these questions about the drug problem and what I thought the answers were. When we finally got up to the door of the theater he patted me on the back and said, "You're doing a wonderful job. Keep up the good work. I really admire you for what you're trying to do." It really felt good to have a stranger praise me.

Professional ex-s' counseling role informs the performance of all other roles, compelling them to abandon previous work they increasingly view as mundane and polluting. The next section demonstrates how this master role organizes the meanings associated with their professional counselor training.

STAGE FOUR: CREDENTIALIZATION

One characteristic typically distinguishing the professions from other occupations is specialized knowledge acquired at institutions of higher learning (Larson 1977; Parsons 1959; Ritzer and Walczak 1986, 1988). Although mastering esoteric knowledge and professional responsibilities in a therapeutic relationship serve as gatekeepers for entering the counseling profession, the moral and emotional essence of being a professional ex- involves much more.

Professional ex-s see themselves as their patients' champions. "Knowing what it's like" and the subsequent education and skills acquired in training legitimate claims to the "entitlements of their stigma" (Gusfield 1982), including professional status. Their monopoly of an abstruse body of knowledge and skill is realized through their emotionally lived history of shame and guilt as well as the hope and redemption secured through therapeutic transformation. Professional ex-s associate higher learning with their experiential history of deviance and the emotional context of therapy. Higher learning symbolizes rediscovery of a moral sense of worth and sacredness rather than credential acquisition. This distinction was clarified by an alcoholism counselor:

> Anymore, you need to have a degree before anybody will hire you. I entered counseling with a bachelors but I eventually received my MSW about two years ago. I think the greatest benefit in having the formal training is that I have been able to more effectively utilize my personal alcoholism experiences with my patients. I feel that I have a gift to offer my patients which doesn't come from the classroom. It comes from being an alcoholic myself.

These entitlements allow professional ex-s to capitalize on their deviant identity in two ways: the existential and phenomenological dimensions of their lived experience of "having made their way from the darkness into the light" provide their experiential and professional *legitimacy* among patients, the community, and other professionals, as well as occupational *income*. "Where else could I go and put bulimic and alcoholic on my resume and get hired?" one counselor put it.

Professional ex-s generally eschew meta-perspective interpretations of the system in which they work. They desire a counseling method congruent with their fundamental universe of discourse and seek, primarily, to perpetuate this system (Peele 1989; Room 1972, 1976). The

words of one educator at a local counselor training institute are germane:

> These people [professional ex-s]...are very fragile when they get here. Usually, they have only been in recovery for about a year. Anyone who challenges what they learned in therapy, or in their program of recovery [i.e., A.A., Narcotics Anonymous, Overeaters Anonymous]...is viewed as a threat. Although we try to change some of that while they're here with us, I still see my role here as one of an extended therapist rather than an educator.

Information challenging their beliefs about how they, and their patients, should enact the rites associated with recovery is condemned (Davies 1963; Pattison 1987; Roizen 1977). They view intellectual challenges to the disease concept as attacks on their personal program of recovery. In a Durkheimian sense, such challenges "profane" that which they hold "sacred."

Within the walls of these monasteries professional ex-s emulate their predecessors as one generation of healers passes on to the next an age old message of salvation. Although each new generation presents the path to enlightenment in somewhat different, contemporary terms, it is already well lit for those "becoming a professional ex-."

DISCUSSION

Focusing on their lived experiences and accounts, this study sketches the central contours of professional ex-s' distinctive exit process. More generally, it also endeavors to contribute to the existing literature on deviant careers.

An identity that embraces their deviant history and identity undergirds professional ex-s' careers. This exiting mode is the outcome of a four stage process enabling professional ex-s to capitalize on their deviant history. They do not "put it all behind them" in exchange for conventional lifestyles, values, beliefs, and identities. Rather, they use vestiges of their deviant biography as an explicit occupational strategy.

My research augments Ebaugh's (1988) outline of principles underlying role exit in three ways. First, her discussion suggests that people are unaware of these guiding principles. While this holds for many, professional ex-s' intentional rather than unintentional embracement of their deviant identity is the step by which they adopt a new role in the counseling profession. Second, Ebaugh states that significant others' negative reactions inhibit or interrupt exit. Among professional ex-s, however, such reactions are a crucial precursor to their exit mode. Finally, Ebaugh sees role exit as a voluntary, individually initiated process, enhanced by "seeking alternatives" through which to explore other roles. Professional ex-s, by contrast, are compelled into therapy. They do not look for this particular role. Rather, their alternatives are prescribed through their resocialization into a new identity.

Organizations in American society increasingly utilize professional ex-s in their social control efforts. For example, the state of Colorado uses prisoners to counsel delinquent youth. A preliminary, two year, follow-up study suggests that these prisoner-counselors show only 13% recidivism (Shiller 1988) and a substantial number want to return to college or enter careers as guidance counselors, probation officers, youth educators, or law enforcement consultants. Similarly, a local effort directed toward curbing gang violence, the Open Door Youth Gang Program, was developed by a professional ex- and uses former gang members as counselors, educators, and community relations personnel.

Further examination of the modes through which charismatic, albeit licensed and certified, groups generate professional ex- statuses is warranted. Although the examples just described differ from the professional ex-s examined earlier in this research in terms of therapeutic or "medicalized" resocialization, their similarities are even more striking. Central to them all is that a redemptive community provides a reference group whose moral and social standards are internalized. Professional ex- statuses are generated as individuals intentionally integrate and embrace rather than abandon their deviant biographies as a specific occupational strategy.

NOTES

1. Most individuals in substance abuse therapy do not become professional ex-s. Rather, they traverse a variety of paths not articulated here including (1) dropping out of treatment, (2) completing treatment but returning to substance use and/or abuse, and (3) remaining abstinent after treatment but feeling no compulsion to enter the counseling profession. Future research will explore the differences among persons by mode of exit. Here, however, analysis and description focus exclusively on individuals committed to the professional ex- role.

2. I conducted most interviews at the subject's work environment, face-to-face. One interview was with a focus group of 10 professional ex-s (Morgan 1988). Two interviews were in my office, one at my home, and one at a subject's home. I interviewed each individual one time for approximately one hour. Interviews were semi-structured, with open-end questions designed to elicit responses related to feelings, thoughts, perceptions, reflections, and meanings concerning subjects' past deviance, factors facilitating their exit from deviance, and their counseling career.

3. I contend that significantly more professional ex-s pursue their careers due to therapeutic resocialization than to achieving sobriety/recovery exclusively through the 12 Step Program (e.g., A.A.). It is too early, however, to preclude that some may enter substance abuse counseling careers lacking any personal therapy. My experiences and my interviews with other professional ex-s suggest that very few professional ex-s enter the profession directly through their contacts with the 12 Step Program. The program's moral precepts—that "sobriety is a gift from God" that must be "given freely to others in order to assure that one may keep the gift"—would appear to discourage rather than encourage substance abuse counseling careers. Financial remuneration for assisting fellow substance abusers directly violates these precepts. Further, professional ex-s are commonly disparaged in A.A. circles as "two hatters" (cf. Denzin 1987). They are, therefore, not a positive reference group for individuals recovering exclusively through the 12 Step Program. Sober 12 Step members are more inclined to emulate their "sponsors" than pursue careers with no experiential referents or direct relevance to their recovery. Further data collection and analysis will examine these differences.

Extant data, however, strongly indicate that therapeutic resocialization and a professional role model provide the crucial link between deviant and substance abuse counseling careers.

4. "12 Step Program" refers to a variety of self-help groups (e.g., A.A., Narcotics Anonymous, Overeaters Anonymous) patterning their recovery model upon the original 12 Steps and 12 Traditions of A.A.

REFERENCES

Adler, Patricia, and Peter Adler. 1983. "Shifts and Oscillations in Deviant Careers: The Case of Upper-Level Drug Dealers and Smugglers." *Social Problems* 31:195–207.

Becker, Howard. 1963. *Outsiders: Studies in the Sociology of Deviance.* New York: Free Press.

Best, Joel, and David F. Luckenbill. 1962. *Organizing Deviance.* Englewood Cliffs, NJ: Prentice-Hall.

Bissell, LeClair. 1982. "Recovered Alcoholism Counselors." Pp. 810–817 in *Encyclopedic Handbook of Alcoholism,* edited by E. Mansell Pattison and Edward Kaufman. New York: Gardner.

Davies, D. L. 1963. "Normal Drinking in Recovered Alcoholic Addicts" (comments by various correspondents). *Quarterly Journal of Studies on Alcohol* 24:109–121, 321–332.

Denzin, Norman. 1987. *The Recovering Alcoholic.* Beverly Hills: Sage.

Durkheim, Emile. 1915. *The Elementary Forms of the Religious Life.* New York: Free Press.

Ebaugh, Helen Rose Fuchs. 1988. *Becoming an Ex: The Process of Role Exit.* Chicago: University of Chicago Press.

Frazier, Charles. 1976. *Theoretical Approaches to Deviance.* Columbus: Charles Merrill.

Glassner, Barry, Margret Ksander, Bruce Berg, and Bruce D. Johnson. 1983. "A Note on the Deterrent Effect of Juvenile vs. Adult Jurisdiction." *Social Problems* 31:219–221.

Goffman, Erving. 1961. *Asylums.* Garden City, NY: Anchor.

Gusfield, Joseph. 1982. "Deviance in the Welfare State: The Alcoholism Profession and the Entitlements of Stigma." *Research in Social Problems and Public Policy* 2:1–20.

Hughes, Everett. 1945. "Dilemmas and Contradictions of Status." *American Journal of Sociology* L:353–359.

Inciardi, James. 1975. *Careers in Crime.* Chicago: Rand McNally.

Irwin, John. 1970. *The Felon.* Englewood Cliffs: Prentice-Hall.

Larson, Magali. 1977. *The Rise of Professionalism.* Berkeley: University of California Press.

Livingston, Jay. 1974. *Compulsive Gamblers.* New York: Harper and Row.

Lofland, John. 1969. *Deviance and Identity.* Englewood Cliffs: Prentice-Hall.

Luckenbill, David F., and Joel Best. 1981. "Careers in Deviance and Respectability: The Analogy's Limitations." *Social Problems* 29:197–206.

Meisenhelder, Thomas. 1977. "An Exploratory Study of Exiting from Criminal Careers." *Criminology* 15: 319–334.

Merton, Robert. 1938. *Social Theory and Social Structure.* Glencoe: Free Press.

Miller, Gale. 1986. "Conflict in Deviant Occupations." Pp. 373–401 in *Working: Conflict and Change,* 3rd ed., edited by George Ritzer and David Walczak. Englewood Cliffs: Prentice-Hall.

Morgan, David L. 1988. *Focus Groups as Qualitative Research.* Beverly Hills: Sage.

NAADAC. 1986. *Development of Model Professional Standards for Counselor Credentialing.* National Association of Alcoholism and Drug Abuse Counselors. Dubuque: Kendall-Hunt.

Parsons, Talcott. 1959. "Some Problems Confronting Sociology as a Profession." *American Sociological Review* 24:547–559.

Pattison, E. Mansell. 1987. "Whither Goals in the Treatment of Alcoholism." *Drugs and Society* 2/3:153–171.

Peele, Stanton. 1989. *The Diseasing of America: Addiction Treatment Out of Control.* Toronto: Lexington.

Petersilia, Joan. 1980. "Criminal Career Research: A Review of Recent Evidence." Pp. 321–379 in *Crime and Justice: An Annual Review of Research,* vol. 2, edited by Norval Morris and Michael Tonry. Chicago: University of Chicago Press.

Ritzer, George, and David Walczak. 1986. *Working: Conflict and Change.* 3rd ed. Englewood Cliffs: Prentice-Hall.

———. 1988. "Rationalization and the Deprofessionalization of Physicians." *Social Forces* 67:1–22.

Roizen, Ron. 1977. "Comment on the Rand Report." *Quarterly Journal of Studies on Alcohol* 38:170–178.

Room, Robin. 1972. "Drinking and Disease: Comment on the Alcohologist's Addiction." *Quarterly Journal of Studies on Alcohol* 33:1049–1059.

———. 1976. "Drunkenness and the Law: Comment on the Uniform Alcoholism Intoxication Treatment Act." *Quarterly Journal of Studies on Alcohol* 37:113–144.

Shiller, Gene. 1988. "A Preliminary Report on SHAPE-UP." Paper presented to the Colorado District Attorneys Council, Denver.

Shover, Neil. 1983. "The Later Stages of Ordinary Property Offenders' Careers." *Social Problems* 31:208–218.

Snow, David, and Richard Machalek. 1983. "The Convert as a Social Type." Pp. 259–289, in *Sociological Theory 1983,* edited by Randall Collins. San Francisco: Jossey-Bass.

Sobell, Mark B., and Linda C. Sobell. 1987. "Conceptual Issues Regarding Goals in the Treatment of Alcohol Problems." *Drugs and Alcohol* 2/3:1–37.

Stryker, Sheldon, and Richard Serpe. 1982. "Commitment, Identity Salience, and Role Behavior: Theory and Research Example." Pp. 199–218 in *Personality, Roles, and Social Behavior,* edited by William Ickes and Eric S. Knowles. New York: Springer-Verlag.

Volkman, Rita, and Donald Cressey. 1963. "Differential Association and the Rehabilitation of Drug Addicts." *American Journal of Sociology* 69:129–142.

Weber, Max. 1968. *On Charisma and Institution Building.* Edited by S. N. Eisenstadt. Chicago: University of Chicago Press.

The Later Stages of Property Offender Careers

NEAL SHOVER

Most sociological research on deviant and criminal careers has focused on their initial stages. We know little about their later stages, and the pathways out of deviance (Frazier, 1976; Luckenbill and Best, 1981). This is unfortunate for scholars and policy makers alike, because evidence suggests that most serious youthful miscreants eventually alter or terminate their criminal behavior (Cline, 1980).

The concept of career refers to common experiences among individuals who have encountered, grappled with, and resolved similar problems. Careers have two related, though ana-

Excerpt from "The Later Stages of Ordinary Property Offender Careers," *Social Problems,* Vol. 31, No. 2 (December 1983), pp. 208–218 by permission of the Society for the Study of Social Problems and the author.

This study was supported by a grant from the National Institute of Justice (80-IJ-CX-0047) during the author's tenure as a visiting fellow. Points of view or opinions expressed in this paper are the author's, and do not necessarily reflect the official position or policies of the Department of Justice. The author thanks Edward Bunker, Daniel Glaser, John Irwin, Patrick Langan, David Luckenbill, John Lynxwiler, Stephen Norland, and a *Social Problems* reviewer for their comments.

lytically distinct, sides—the objective and the subjective (Stebbins, 1970). The objective career is open to public view, and includes changes in life style and official position. The subjective career is less visible: it includes changes in identity, self-concept, and the framework employed to judge oneself and others. Changes in both the objective and the subjective careers often occur together. Thus, to understand careers adequately, not only must we examine each of the two sides, but also how they fit together,

Career contingencies are significant events, common to members of a social category, which produce movement along, or transformations of, career lines (Goffman, 1961:133). Just as we can speak of objective and subjective careers, so too can we distinguish between objective and subjective career contingencies. The former are "objective facts of social structure" while the latter designates "changes in the perspectives, motivations, and desires" of individuals (Becker, 1963:24).

This paper explores the later stages of the criminal careers of a group of ordinary property offenders. I begin with a review of previous research on the topic.... Then I discuss the major contingencies which led to a modification of the subjects' criminal behavior. I conclude with a discussion of the similarities between my findings and previous research, a theoretical interpretation of the findings, and some comments on the study's relevance for contemporary crime control programs.

LITERATURE

For years, social scientists have known of the inverse relationship among adults between age and the probability of arrest (Glueck and Glueck, 1937; Hirschi and Gottfredson, in press; Moberg, 1953; Rowe and Tittle, 1977; Sellin, 1958). When referring to former offenders, this relationship has been known, albeit imprecisely, as the "maturation effect."

Bull (1972), Irwin (1970), and Meisenhelder (1975; 1977) have examined some aspects of the process of exiting from crime. Bull examined the merits of Kierkegaard's philosophy of the stages of personal and spiritual growth in the human life cycle. He found that as the 15 ex-convicts he interviewed aged, feelings of despair motivated them to modify their lives and so reduce their criminal behavior. The modifications represented a shift, in Kierkegaard's terms, from the aesthetic stage of life to an ethical one.

Irwin interviewed 15 ex-convicts who had remained out of prison for many years. Those who had modified or terminated their criminal involvement did so for several reasons: (1) fear of further imprisonment; (2) "exhaustion from years of a desperate criminal life and a deprived prison life" (1970:196); (3) a reduction in sexual and financial expectations; (4) "an adequate and satisfying relationship with a woman" (1970:203); and (5) involvement in "extravocational, extradomestic activities" such as sports or hobbies (1970:203).

Meisenhelder interviewed 20 incarcerated, nonprofessional property offenders about earlier periods of their lives when they temporarily had terminated their criminal behavior. Their motivation to discontinue crime was (1) "fear of 'doing more time' in prison" (1977:322); and (2) a "subjective wish to lead a more normal life" (1977:324). Successful exit from crime resulted from (1) establishment of a "meaningful bond to the conventional social order" (1977:325); and (2) symbolic certification by a noncriminal that the offender had changed and was "to be considered essentially noncriminal" (1977:329)[1]...

TEMPORAL CONTINGENCIES

AN IDENTITY SHIFT

During their late 30s to early 40s, most of the men began to take stock of their lives and their accomplishments. In the process, most confronted for the first time the realization that (1) their criminality had been an unproductive enterprise; and (2) this situation was unlikely to change. In short, they realized that ordinary property crime was a dead end. They developed a critical, detached perspective toward an earlier portion of their lives and the personal identity which they believed it exemplified. Just as many aging non-offenders develop a wistful, detached perspective toward their youth, the aging men gradually viewed their youthful self as "foolish" or "dumb." They decided that their earlier identity and behavior were of limited value for constructing the future. This new perspective symbolized a watershed in their lives.

A 54-year-old man said he learned how to serve time when he was young.

> I can handle it, if I have to serve time. But now I know how stupid I have been. And for me now to do something as stupid as I have done, and go back to serving time, it would drive me crazy.

Q: Why would it drive you crazy?

A: Because now I, like I told you, I see these things. I see myself. And see how my path has been so wrong when I thought I was bein' smart, or thought that I was bein' hep, or thought that I was this or that. And it's a dream.

As this suggests, the aging process of most ordinary property offenders includes a redefinition of their youthful criminal identity as self-defeating, foolish, or even dangerous.

INCOMMODIOUS TIME

While taking stock of their lives, most of the men became acutely aware of time as a diminishing, exhaustible resource. They began constructing plans for how to use the remainder of their lives. As this new perspective developed, the future became increasingly valuable, and the possibility of spending additional time in prison especially threatening. Not only would another prison sentence subject them to the usual deprivations, but it would expropriate their few remaining, potentially productive years. They feared losing their last remaining opportunity to accomplish something and to prepare financially for old age. A 45-year-old parolee said he did not want to serve any more time in prison. Asked if he was "afraid of doing time now," he replied:

No, I'm not really afraid of it. I don't know, I just don't want to do it.... It's just knocking time out of my life.

Q: Are you trying to say that the years you have left are more precious to you?

A: True. And they're a lot more precious to me than when I was 25 or 30.... I guess you get to the point where you think, well,... you're getting old, you're getting ready to die and you've never really lived, or something. You don't want to spend it in the joint, treading water.

The men dreaded receiving a long sentence, but believed that because of their previous convictions, any prison terms they received would be lengthy.

Hey, I'm 47, you know. And if I get one of them big numbers [long sentences] now, hey, I'm through

bookin', you know. I'm through bookin'.... One of them big numbers, man, would do me in, you know. And I could not stand it.

This growing awareness of time as a limited resource intensified subjects' fears of dying inside prison.

ASPIRATIONS AND GOALS

Many men no longer felt they wanted or needed to strive for the same level of material fulfillment and recognition which they had sought when younger. As an ex-offender has written:

I've got to a point where things that were important to me twelve, fifteen years ago aren't important now. I used to have a lot of ambitions, like everybody else has—different business ventures, stuff like that. But today, why, with what I have to buck up against, why, I could be just as happy and just as satisfied with a job that I'm getting by on, where I knew I wasn't going to run into trouble or anything (Martin, 1952:277).

Just as important, the men revised their aspirations, assigning higher priority to goals which formerly were less important. Like the middle-aged non-offender, an interest in such things as "contentment" and "peace" became important to them. Referring to his earlier activities, a 56-year-old man said:

I don't want to live that kind of life no more. I want peace. I want joy and harmony. I want to be with my children and my grandchildren, I got a bunch of grandkids, and I want to be with them. I want to be with my mother. And when she passes on—I was in prison when my daddy died, I got to come home for five hours in handcuffs to see him—and when my mother passes on, I want to be there with her.

This man's newly kindled interest in family members is not unique. Several other men revealed similar sentiments which, they acknowledged, developed only as they approached or attained middle age.

Many subjects realized that they could achieve their revised aspirations on a modest income, as long as it was consistent and predictable. Those who continued their criminal activities often were content with committing less hazardous offenses, even if this meant accepting smaller economic rewards. Those who turned to legitimate work began to appreciate the advantages of a job with secure benefits such as sick leave or a pension. A 56-year-old man said:

> I'm satisfied now, you know. There ain't nobody can get me to do nothin' [commit a crime]. Not now. Not the way I'm goin' now.... Every year I go away on vacation. I got three weeks now. Next year I get four weeks. Yeah. So I'm happy, you know, right now.

TIREDNESS

The men began to see the entire criminal justice system as an apparatus which clumsily but relentlessly swallows offenders and wears them down. They began to experience the prison as an imposing accumulation of aggravations and deprivations. They grew tired of the problems and consequences of criminal involvement. Asked why he had abandoned crime, a 53-year-old man answered succinctly:

> Being tired, you know. Just collapsing, that's all. I'd say age made me weak, made me tired, you know. That's all.

The men gave different reasons why they gradually tired of their former experiences. For example:

Q: Do the main problems of doing time change as you age?
A: They *intensify,* you know. The rhetoric, the environment itself, you know. I mean, who wants to walk around talkin' about fuckin' somebody all day long, or somebody gettin' fucked in the ass and shit?... I mean, this kind of shit, you, when you get older you can't relate to that kind of shit.

Still, for some ex-offenders the specific origins of this perspective are obscure and difficult to articulate. One has written:

> I really don't know why I went straight. I just decided that after I got out. It wasn't fear of the law, it isn't fear of the penitentiary, 'cause I've sat down and thought it out very seriously, but I just had enough of it, that's all (King, 1972:158).

A 53-year-old man explained that he never committed and would never again attempt the "big score," the one highly lucrative crime which would permit him to retire in comfort. Asked why he had given up this dream of many thieves, he said: "Because I know how the system is.... The system is bigger than me."

INTERPERSONAL CONTINGENCY

Of the 30 ordinary offenders not in prison, 27 reported experiencing one or more of the four temporal contingencies. Typically, for those men who altered their criminal behavior, these changes produced a disenchantment with the activities and lifestyles of their youth, and an interest in and a readiness for fundamental change in their lives. A 47-year-old man said that after two terms of imprisonment,

> I had already been convinced that I couldn't beat the system anyway, you know. What I was doin' wasn't gettin' nowhere, you know. It was just a dream.

Disenchanted with themselves and their unsuccessful attempts at crime, the aging men wanted to "give something else a try." They frequently developed an interest in supportive and satisfying social relationships; actually building such a relationship represented an interpersonal contingency in their lives. More specifically, I use this concept to refer to the establishment of a personally meaningful tie to either another person, especially a woman, or an activity, especially a job. The social relationships resulting from this interpersonal contingency assumed a special importance for the men. It provided them with commitment or "side bets" which they realized would be jeopardized by involvement in crime—or at least high-risk crimes (Becker, 1962).

TIES TO ANOTHER PERSON

The establishment of a mutually satisfying relationship with a woman was a common pattern. Of the 30 respondents not in prison, seven mentioned this, either alone or together with other contingencies, as an important factor in the transformation of their career line.[2] Although many subjects maintained involvements with women when younger, they said these were not important influences on their behavior. With age, the meaning of such relationships changed and they assumed more importance.

> When I reached the age of 35 it just seemed like my life wanted to change. I needed a change in life, and I was tired of going to jail. And I wanted to change my life and stay out here. And by meeting the woman that I met, it just turned my life completely around.... When I met her it just seemed like something in my life had been fulfilled.

Another man, who still engaged occasionally in property crimes, said he had once stopped committing crimes entirely while living with a woman for several years.

> I started living with this woman, you know, and my life suddenly changed.... I was contented, you know, bein' with her.... I cared about her, you know. I wanted to be with her, you know. That was it.... And, hey, I just found enjoyment there.

A 56-year-old man, separated from his wife at the time of the interview, talked about her influence on him during earlier periods of unemployment:

> I loved my wife—I love her still—and she talked to me a lot.... And if it wouldn't been for her, no tellin' where I'd be at, 'cause I'd most likely had a gun in my hand and robbed a bank or something. Or took something from somebody to get some food, you know.... She helped me along.

TIES TO A JOB

Five of the 30 men indicated that having a satisfying job, either alone or combined with other experiences, was an important influence on their career. Several men acknowledged that they had held potentially satisfying jobs earlier in their lives but had not seen or appreciated them at the time. One man told of securing a job as a youth in the U. S. Government Printing Office, where an older employee wanted to teach him how to mix and use inks.

> I said to myself I didn't even want to be there. As much as possible I went into the men's restroom and went to sleep. And I was glad to get out of there when it was time to get off, and I wound up resigning the job.

As the subjects' perspectives changed with age, legitimate employment assumed more importance. For example, a 56-year-old man remembered when, as a younger man, he was interviewed for a job with a beauty and barber supply company:

> The guy liked me from the jump. And that's when I hooked up with him. And I went straight a long time without the intentions of going straight.... That was one turning point in the later part of my life.

A 48-year-old man recalled his experiences 17 years earlier:

> When I got out [the second time].... I sold a suit for 10 dollars and I bought [some tools], just the bare necessities of what I needed, and I met a guy who carried me on the job.... So, at that time I could make $160 a week.... And so, with this earning power I didn't have—I didn't have to steal ... so this was right down my alley.

Successful participation in either a personal relationship or a job provided personal rewards and reinforced a noncriminal identity. For many, development of commitment to someone or some line of action gradually generated a pattern of routine activities—a daily agenda—which conflicted with, and left little time for, the daily activities associated with crime.

In addition to ties to another person and a job, two men said that religious experiences and the close social relationships they were involved in influenced their criminal careers.

CONTINGENCIES: TEMPORAL ORDER AND INTERDEPENDENCE

The five contingencies discussed above did not occur in a fixed sequence. They varied in the age at which they occurred and their interdependence.

1. In some cases, the precise point of occurrence of the separate temporal contingencies could not be easily isolated. Rather, one or more occurred simultaneously. A 55-year-old man reported:

> I think I had been up [at the state reformatory]. I just said to myself, "Well, shit, this isn't getting me nowhere."... So I come out and I did get a good job...and they treated me good, and they trusted me, you know.... And I figured, well, these people are good enough to trust me, I'm good enough to play it straight with them.... Then I got married and that more or less helped too.

Q: How so?

A: Well, I married a good woman, I guess.

2. While the temporal and interpersonal contingencies operated both independently and jointly, each produced modifications in the nature, or reductions in the frequency, of criminal behavior.[3] In several cases, the two types of contingencies interacted with or followed one another as part of a dynamic process, with one type preceding and increasing the probability of occurrence for the other(s). Imposition of a rigid temporal and causal order on this process would violate its dynamic nature and, given our present state of knowledge, would be arbitrary and premature.

3. Although the temporal contingencies typically set the stage for the interpersonal one, occasionally the latter occurred independently. It then produced a set of subjective career contingencies which strengthened the man's sense of commitment and his resolve to avoid crime—or at least high-risk crime. Meisenhelder (1977) refers to

these secondary subjective contingencies as the "pull of normality." They were of some importance in my subjects' retrospective accounts, especially the feeling of relief over no longer having to fear the police. Several men spontaneously mentioned this as one of the advantages of the "square" life.

> I can go to bed, hey man, I don't have to worry about [the police] kickin' my door down, you know, comin' and gettin' me. Because I'm not doin' nothin'. And man, I can remember one time, every time I see the police, hey man, I know they was comin' to my house. And sometimes I wasn't wrong.... But I don't worry about that now.

4. While any combination of the five contingencies usually led to changes in criminal behavior, the nature of these changes varied. In general, the most abrupt and complete changes seemed to result when all five contingencies occurred.

Various combinations of the foregoing contingencies modified the subjects' attitude toward and willingness to engage in crime. First, men who experienced the interpersonal contingency were increasingly reluctant to risk losing their new-found social ties. They began to include factors which had previously been absent from their deliberations over potential criminal activities. A 45-year-old former addict said:

> If I go out there and commit a crime—now, I got to think about this: Hey, man, I ain't got to get away. See what I'm sayin'? I have—man, it would be just my luck that I would get busted. Now I done fucked up everything I done tried to work hard for, man, you know, to get my little family together.

Second, they began to see ordinary property crime as a poor risk. Not only was there little chance of reaping a large reward, but they believed there was a good chance they would receive a long prison sentence if convicted. In sum, the perceived odds narrowed; the perceived risks became greater; and the offenders decided to avoid the high-visibility crimes they had engaged in when younger. One man said he could no longer imagine committing an armed robbery because "I would be so nervous, and my hand would be shakin' so bad."

When the men did commit crimes, they planned them more carefully than they had in their youth. And they often endeavored to minimize the frequency of their criminal acts. As one man said: "It's what they call 'exposure time,' you know. You don't want to get 'exposed' too much." This does not mean that they ceased entirely *thinking* about crime, only that they developed an extended and modified set of rationales for self restraint.

NEGATIVE CASES

Clearly, not all cases fit the pattern I have described. The most troubling and perplexing cases were men who, despite their failure at crime and the fact that they experienced one or more of the temporal contingencies, reacted alternately with resignation or desperation to the belief that it was "too late" for them to accomplish anything in life. The years they had spent in prison made it difficult for them to achieve some objectives. For example, a 50-year-old man said:

> I wants to have a good life, you know, but certain things will always be out of my reach because it's been so long, you know. I've been incarcerated so long.

While most of the men revised their aspirations and grudgingly accepted this fact, others did not. Animated in part by a sense of "nothing to lose," some sustained a pattern of petty hustles or long-term drunkenness.[4] Searching for a magic solution of their problems, others resorted to desperate, high risk crimes, with apparent disregard for the potential consequences (Camp, 1968; Parker, 1963). For example, after several years of freedom, a divorced 56-year-old man experienced severe strains in his family relationships. Making little effort to conceal his identity, he robbed a bank. Apprehended several hours later, he insisted on pleading guilty at arraignment. He told the judge that his only friends were police and correctional officials, and that prison was the only place in which he felt accepted and comfortable. He was pleased when he received a 20-year sentence.

Four men not in prison spontaneously mentioned the care older persons receive in nursing homes and similar establishments. Arguing that convicts are treated better than nursing home residents, they said they would opt to spend their final years in prison if they had a choice.

> If I got to a point where it's either go to an old folks' home or an old soldier's home—[I'd] figure, hell, if I robbed a bank ... if I got away I'd get enough money to last me the rest of my life, if I got caught I'd go to prison and they'd give me better treatment there. . . . They got the best doctors there, and they got the best medical care. . . . What would a fella have to lose, even if he went in and pretended to hold up ... if he had nothing to lose on the outside? . . . You got somebody [in prison] checkin' on you all the time. And in an old soldier's home, if you call a nurse, you're lucky to get anybody.[5]

While viewing the prison as a tolerable residence in old age was rare among those I interviewed, an imprisoned 62-year-old said:

> In a way, I'm looking forward to getting out, and another way it don't much matter to me. . . . I know everybody here. . . . I do almost like I want. I go to early chow. [Earlier today] I went down to the law library and used their copying machine. I can do fairly well what I want to do without anybody bugging me about it 'cause all the officials know me.

CONCLUSIONS

My findings support Glaser's (1980) theory of differential expectation. Focusing on the interpretive process which precedes decisions to forego or to engage in criminal acts, the theory asserts that a person refrains from or commits crime because of the expected consequences. Obviously, it assumes that individuals, based on personal experiences, may alter their expectations of potential outcomes of criminal behavior. I have shown that there are distinct, age-related changes in the expectations of likely criminal success held by ordinary property offenders. Insights and propositions based on this theory can be developed at both the individual and aggregate levels of analysis. In either case, empirical testing and theoretical reformulation would be enhanced substantially by an improved understanding of typical changes over the life cycle in the calculus of alternative types of criminal behaviors.

With two exceptions, my findings are compatible with those of both Irwin (1970) and Meisenhelder (1977). Contrary to Irwin, my analysis did not find "extravocational" and "extradomestic activities" especially important in the eventual termination of criminality. Similarly, unlike Meisenhelder I did not find that "certification" was a necessary or even an important component of the process of exiting from crime.

My study clearly shows age-related social psychological changes in the subjects' later criminal careers. On the one hand, some of these changes result from their unique experiences at the hands of the criminal justice apparatus. After one man described some age-related changes he experienced, I suggested these might be similar to those experienced by non-offenders as well. He replied: "Similar, yeah, yeah. Really. But I would say doing time has [affected me] too, because I didn't want to go back to the penitentiary." On the other hand, some other contingencies described here, such as changes in aspirations and goals, are not unique to men who have been involved in crime. Rather, they seem common to the broader, socially comparable segment of the non-criminal population (Kuhlen, 1968; Neugarten, 1968). Scholars and policy makers who sometimes are tempted to view offenders as a different species of human beings should take special note of this fact.

More importantly, my findings challenge the argument, used by proponents of the death penalty, mandatory and determinate sentences, and similar repressive crime-control measures that such "reforms" are justified by the existence of intractable offenders. The findings clearly show that even offenders who committed serious crimes while young are capable of, and do, change as they get older.

NOTES

1. There is also a body of work on the process of "natural recovery" from heroin addiction (Brill, 1972; Jorquez, 1980; Waldorf, 1983; Waldorf and Biernacki, 1979; 1981; Winick, 1962).
2. In one case, a long-term homosexual relationship produced similar effects.
3. In a sense, the latter provide negative incentives to change, while the former provide positive incentives.
4. Others commit suicide (King, 1972).
5. Responding to a question, the man subsequently stipulated that his comments applied only to "federal joints." It had been 20 years since his last state confinement and, he acknowledged, "I don't know much about these state places."

REFERENCES

Becker, Howard S. 1962. "Notes on the Concept of Commitment." *American Journal of Sociology,* 66 (July):32–40.

———. 1963. *Outsiders: Studies in the Sociology of Deviance.* New York: The Free Press.

Brill, Leon. 1972. *The De-Addiction Process.* Springfield, Ill.: Charles Thomas.

Bull, James L. 1972. "Coming Alive: The Dynamics of Personal Recovery." Unpublished Ph.D. dissertation, University of California, Santa Barbara.

Camp, George M. 1968. "Nothing to Lose: A Study of Bank Robbery in America." Unpublished Ph.D. dissertation, Yale University.

Cline, Hugh F. 1980. "Criminal Behavior over the Life Span." In Orville G. Brim Jr. and Jerome Kagan (eds.), *Constancy and Change in Human Development.* Cambridge, Mass.: Harvard University Press, pp. 641–674.

Frazier, Charles F. 1976. *Theoretical Approaches to Deviance.* Columbus, Ohio: Charles Merrill.

Glaser, Daniel. 1980. "The Interplay of Theory, Issues, Policy, and Data." In Malcolm W. Klein and Katherine S. Teilmann (eds.), *Handbook of Crimi-*

nal Justice Evaluation. Beverly Hills, Cal.: Sage Publications, pp. 123–142.

Glueck, Sheldon and Eleanor Glueck. 1937. *Later Criminal Careers.* New York: The Commonwealth Fund.

Goffman, Erving. 1961. *Asylums.* Garden City, N. Y.: Anchor Books.

Hirschi, Travis and Michael Gottfredson. In press. "Age and the Explanation of Crime." *American Journal of Sociology.*

Irwin, John. 1970. *The Felon.* Englewood Cliffs, N. J.: Prentice-Hall.

Jorquez, James S. 1980. "The Retirement Phase of Heroin-using Careers." Unpublished Ph.D. dissertation, University of California, Los Angeles.

King, Harry. 1972. *Box Man* (as told to and edited by Bill Chambliss). New York: Harper Torchbooks.

Kuhlen, Raymond G. 1968. "Developmental Changes in Motivation During the Adult Years." In Bernice L. Neugarten (ed.), *Middle Age and Aging: A Reader in Social Psychology.* Chicago: University of Chicago Press, pp. 115–136.

Luckenbill, David and Joel Best. 1981. "Careers in Deviance and Respectability: The Analogy's Limitations." *Social Problems,* 29 (December):197–206.

Martin, John Bartlow. 1952. *My Life in Crime.* New York: Harper & Row.

Meisenhelder, Thomas N. 1975. "The Nonprofessional Property Offender: A Study in Phenomenological Sociology." Unpublished Ph.D. dissertation, University of Florida.

———. 1977. "An Exploratory Study of Exiting from Criminal Careers." *Criminology,* 15 (November):319–334.

Moberg, David O. 1953. "Old Age and Crime." *Journal of Criminal Law, Criminology and Police Science,* 43 (March-April):764–776.

Neugarten, Bernice L. 1968. "Adult Personality: Toward a Psychology of the Life Cycle. In Bernice L. Neugarten (ed.), *Middle Age and Aging: A Reader in Social Psychology.* Chicago: University of Chicago Press, pp. 134–147.

Parker, Tony. 1963. *The Unknown Citizen.* London: Hutchinson.

Rowe, Alan R. and Charles R. Tittle. 1977. "Life Cycle Changes and Criminal Propensity." *The Sociological Quarterly,* 18 (Spring):223–236.

Sellin, Thorsten. 1958. "Recidivism and Maturation." *National Probation and Parole Association Journal,* 4 (July):241–250.

Stebbins, Robert A. 1970. "Career: The Subjective Approach." *The Sociological Quarterly,* 11 (Winter):32–50.

Waldorf, Dan. 1983. "Natural Recovery from Opiate Addiction: Some Social Psychological Processes of Untreated Recovery." *Journal of Drug Issues.* In press.

Waldorf, Dan and Patrick Biernacki. 1979. "Natural Recovery from Heroin Addiction: A Review of the Incidence Literature." *Journal of Drug Issues,* 9 (Spring):281–289.

———. 1981. "The Natural Recovery from Opiate Addiction: Some Preliminary Findings." *Journal of Drug Issues,* 11 (Winter):61–74.

Winick, Charles. 1962. "Maturing out of Narcotic Addiction." *Bulletin on Narcotics,* 14 (January–March):1–7.